Maui

Lana'i & Moloka'i p249

West Maui p99

Lahaina p79

'Iao Valley & Central Maui p127

The Road to Hana p215

North Shore & Upcountry p175

Kihei & South Maui p151

Haleakalā National Park p199

Hana & East Maui p231

Amy C Balfour, Jade Bremner

PLAN YOUR TRIP

ON THE ROAD

MATT MUNRO / LONELY PLANET ©

ONO ORGANIC FARMS, KIPAHULU P246

ED FREEMAN / GETTY IMAGES ©

KEONEHE'EHE'E (SLIDING SANDS) TRAIL P202

Contents

SURFING P52

UNDERSTAND

SURVIVAL GUIDE

COVID-19

We have re-checked every business in this book before publication to ensure that it is still open after 2020's COVID-19 outbreak. However, the economic and social impacts of COVID-19 will continue to be felt long after the outbreak has been contained, and many businesses, services and events referenced in this guide may experience ongoing restrictions. Some businesses may be temporarily closed, have changed their opening hours and services, or require bookings; some unfortunately could have closed permanently. We suggest you check with venues before visiting for the latest information.

SPECIAL FEATURES

Right: Wailua Falls (p246), near Hana

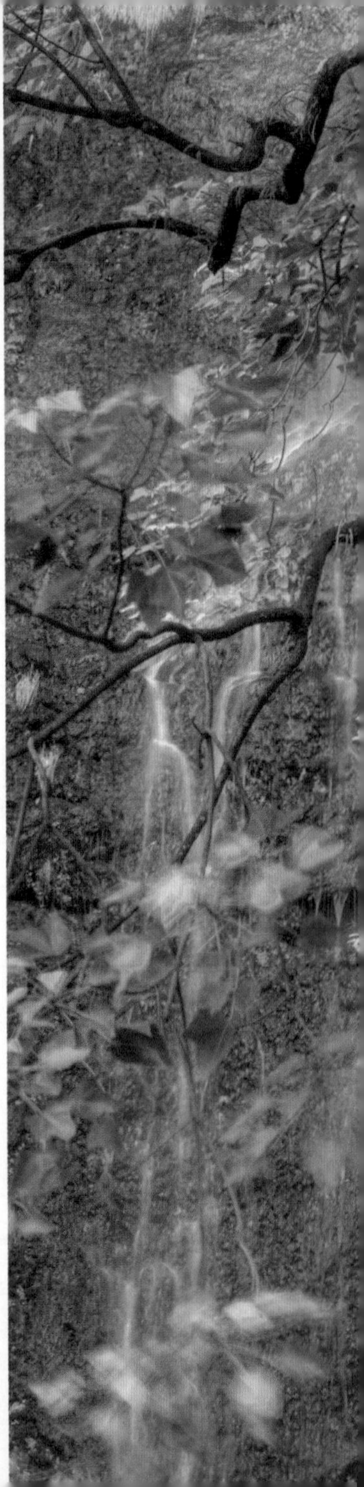

DARRELL GULIN / GETTY IMAGES ©

WELCOME TO

Maui

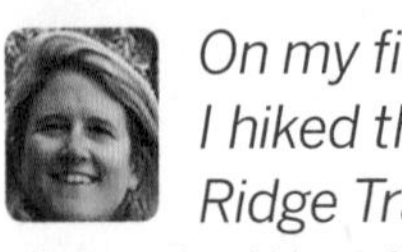

On my first visit to Maui I hiked the Waihe'e Ridge Trail and ziplined down the West Maui mountains. Thanks to those adventures, I'm hooked on the island's outdoor charms. Since then I've kayaked Makena Bay and bundled up for a Haleakalā sunrise. It's the mix of beautiful scenery and easy-to-access adventures that pulls me back. That and the genuine alohas from the residents, who have invited me to gatherings at their homes, met me for drinks and shared their favorite island spots. Aloha and mahalo!

By Amy C Balfour, Writer

amycbalfour

For more about our writers, see p320

Maui

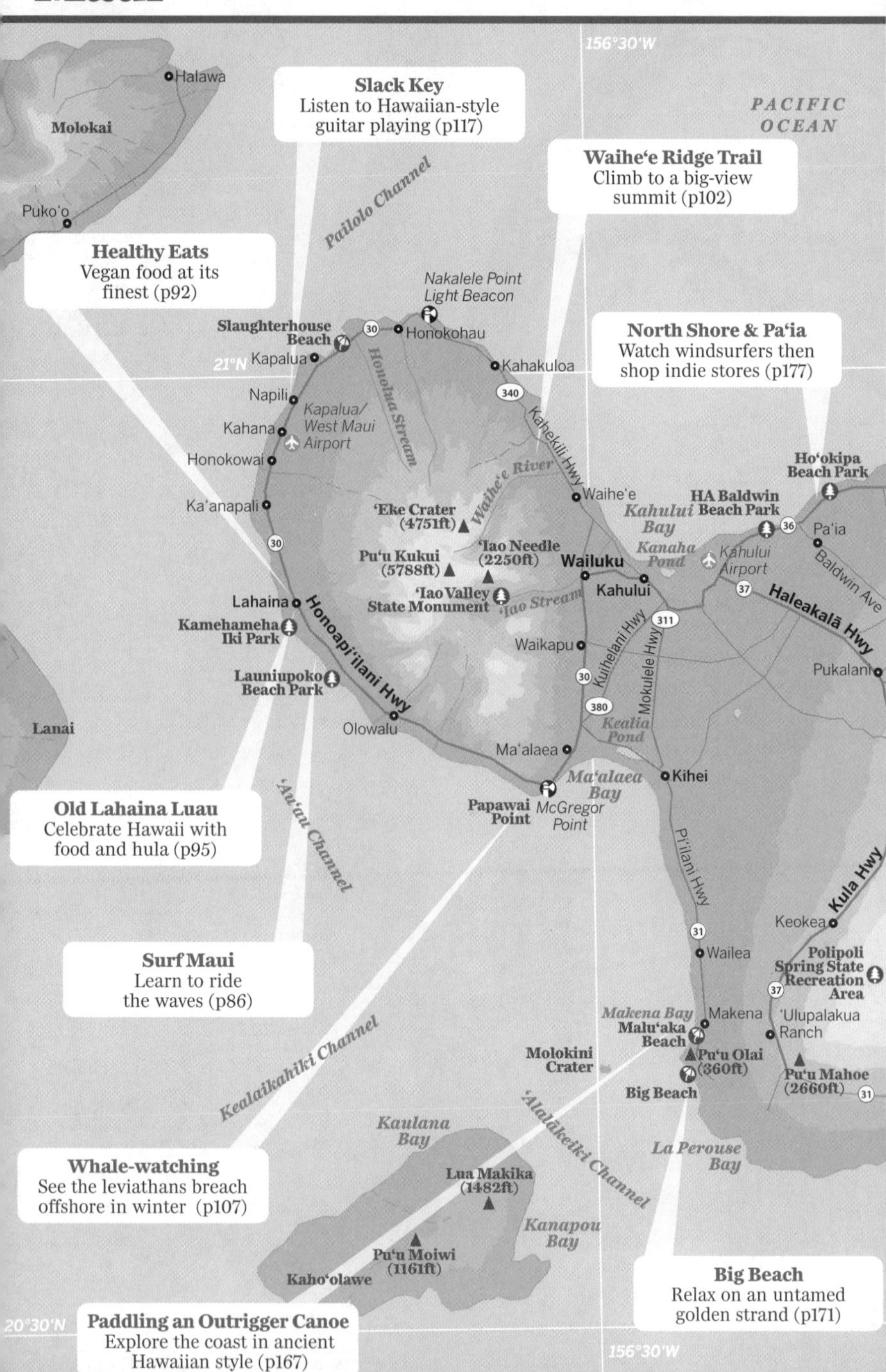

Slack Key
Listen to Hawaiian-style guitar playing (p117)
Waihe'e Ridge Trail
Climb to a big-view summit (p102)
Healthy Eats
Vegan food at its finest (p92)
North Shore & Pa'ia
Watch windsurfers then shop indie stores (p177)
Old Lahaina Luau
Celebrate Hawaii with food and hula (p95)
Surf Maui
Learn to ride the waves (p86)
Whale-watching
See the leviathans breach offshore in winter (p107)
Big Beach
Relax on an untamed golden strand (p171)
Paddling an Outrigger Canoe
Explore the coast in ancient Hawaiian style (p167)
PACIFIC OCEAN
Molokai
Halawa
Puko'o
Pailolo Channel
Nakalele Point Light Beacon
Slaughterhouse Beach
Honokohau
Kapalua
Kahakuloa
Napili
Kapalua/West Maui Airport
Kahana
Honokowai
Honolua Stream
Kahekili Hwy
Waihe'e River
Waihe'e
Ka'anapali
'Eke Crater (4751ft)
Pu'u Kukui (5788ft)
'Iao Needle (2250ft)
'Iao Valley State Monument
'Iao Stream
Wailuku
Kahului
Kahului Bay
Kanaha Pond
Kahului Airport
Ho'okipa Beach Park
HA Baldwin Beach Park
Pa'ia
Baldwin Ave
Haleakalā Hwy
Pukalani
Lahaina
Kamehameha Iki Park
Honoapi'ilani Hwy
Waikapu
Kuihelani Hwy
Mokulele Hwy
Launiupoko Beach Park
Olowalu
Kealia Pond
Ma'alaea
Lanai
Ma'alaea Bay
Kihei
Papawai Point
McGregor Point
'Au'au Channel
Pi'ilani Hwy
Kula Hwy
Keokea
Wailea
Polipoli Spring State Recreation Area
Makena Bay
Makena
'Ulupalakua Ranch
Malu'aka Beach
Molokini Crater
Pu'u Olai (360ft)
Big Beach
Pu'u Mahoe (2660ft)
Kealaikahiki Channel
'Alalākeiki Channel
Kaulana Bay
La Perouse Bay
Lua Makika (1482ft)
Kanapou Bay
Pu'u Moiwi (1161ft)
Kaho'olawe
156°30'W
21°N
20°30'N

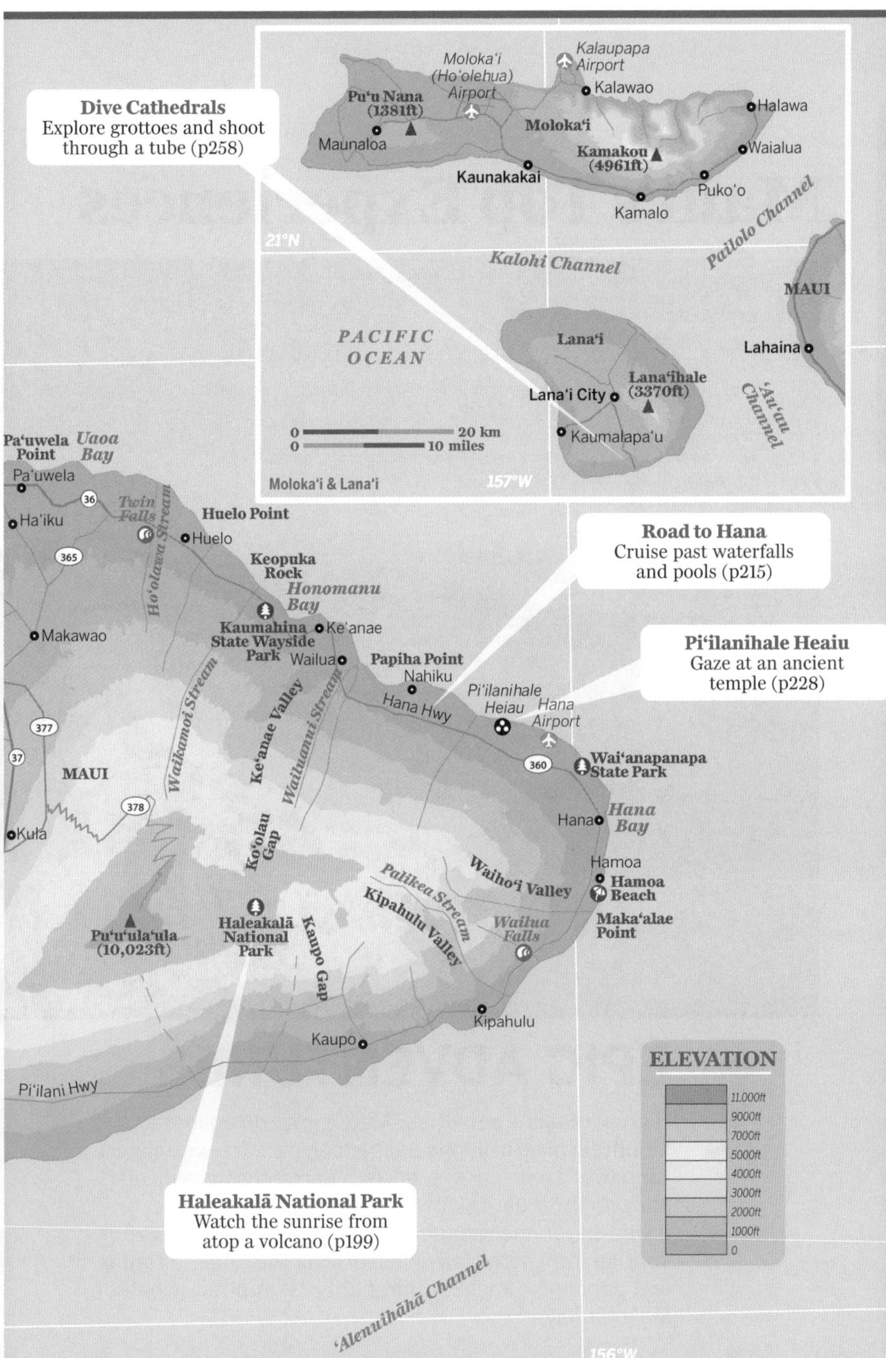

0 20 km
0 10 miles
Dive Cathedrals
Explore grottoes and shoot through a tube (p258)
Moloka'i (Ho'olehua) Airport
Kalaupapa Airport
Kalawao
Pu'u Nana (1381ft)
Maunaloa
Moloka'i
Halawa
Waialua
Kamakou (4961ft)
Kaunakakai
Puko'o
Kamalo
21°N
Kalohi Channel
Pailolo Channel
MAUI
PACIFIC OCEAN
Lana'i
Lahaina
Lana'i City
Lana'ihale (3370ft)
'Au'au Channel
Kaumalapa'u
Moloka'i & Lana'i
157°W
Pa'uwela Point
Uaoa Bay
Pa'uwela
Ha'iku
Twin Falls
Huelo Point
Huelo
Ho'olawa Stream
Keopuka Rock
Honomanu Bay
Road to Hana
Cruise past waterfalls and pools (p215)
Kaumahina State Wayside Park
Ke'anae
Makawao
Wailua
Papiha Point
Nahiku
Pi'ilanihale Heiau
Gaze at an ancient temple (p228)
Hana Hwy
Pi'ilanihale Heiau
Hana Airport
Waikamoi Stream
Ke'anae Valley
Wailuanui Stream
MAUI
Wai'anapanapa State Park
Hana
Hana Bay
Kula
Ko'olau Gap
Hamoa
Hamoa Beach
Waiho'i Valley
Palikea Stream
Kipahulu Valley
Wailua Falls
Maka'alae Point
Pu'u'ula'ula (10,023ft)
Haleakalā National Park
Kaupo Gap
Kipahulu
Kaupo
Pi'ilani Hwy
ELEVATION
11,000ft
9000ft
7000ft
5000ft
4000ft
3000ft
2000ft
1000ft
0
Haleakalā National Park
Watch the sunrise from atop a volcano (p199)
'Alenuihāhā Channel
156°W

Maui's Top Experiences

SAMURAIGIRL/SHUTTERSTOCK ©

1 EPIC ADVENTURES

High adrenaline activities? Maui's got you covered. Mountain bikers plunge past eucalyptus trees, zipliners whip over green valleys, surfers barrel through waves and windboarders skim across whitecaps. And we haven't even mentioned the most iconic: watching the sunrise from atop Haleakalā; driving the Road to Hana; and paddling a kayak within sight of humpback whales in Makena Bay.

Left: Mountain biking, Skyline Trail (p204)

Right: Sunrise, Haleakalā National Park (p198); bottom left: Road to Hana (p214); bottom right: outrigger canoes (p43)

PIERRE LECLERC/SHUTTERSTOCK ©

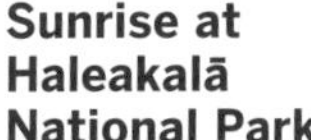

Sunrise at Haleakalā National Park

A soft, orange glow pierces the darkness. Cottony clouds appear. Rich tones of amber and ocher blaze on the crater floor below. To quote Mark Twain, sunrise at Haleakalā was 'the sublimest spectacle I ever witnessed.' p201

ARKANTO / SHUTTERSTOCK ©

Driving the Road to Hana

The Road to Hana winds through jungly valleys and up towering cliffs, curling around more than 600 twists and turns. Some 54 bridges cross nearly as many waterfalls – some are breathtaking torrents and others so gentle they beg a dip. p215

KARL WEATHERLY / GETTY IMAGES ©

Paddling an Outrigger Canoe

Continuing in the wake of Hawaii's first settlers and their loaded canoes, outrigger-canoe clubs paddle their graceful vessels across the surf offshore. To test your skills, try an outrigger paddling trip with an outfitter such as Hawaiian Paddle Sports. p172

Below left: Guitar recital, Napili (p115); top right: Old Lahaina Luau (p95); bottom right: lei (p294)

2 CULTURAL IMMERSION

Hawaiian culture today is about much more than melodic place names and simple luau shows. Traditional arts and healing arts are experiencing a revival, ancient heiau (temples) and fishponds are being restored, native forests replaced and endangered birds bred and released. Resorts and outdoor outfitters across the island are more thoughtfully discussing and sharing long-held traditions, customs and activities.

Feel the Music

Slack key tuning, with its simultaneous playing of bass and melody, practically defines Hawaiian music. The host of this Wednesday night show in Napili, Grammy Award–winner George Kahumoku Jr, interweaves music with banter on growing up Hawaiian-style. p117

PETE RYAN / GETTY IMAGES ©

Old Lahaina Luau

Maui's most authentic luau focuses on Hawaiian history, culture and culinary prowess. Highlights include the unearthing of the *imu*-cooked pig, the the *hula kahiko* (traditional hula) dancing and the savoring of the feast. p95

Arts & Crafts

Thanks to an ongoing cultural renaissance, traditional crafts are flourishing. Visitors can take Hawaiian quilting and lei-making classes, while crafts can be purchased at the Celebration of the Arts festival in April. p121

EQROY / SHUTTERSTOCK ©

Below: Big Beach (Oneloa; p171)

3 NATURAL BEAUTY

MEREDITH NARROWE / GETTY IMAGES ©

GREG ELMS / LONELY PLANET ©

From the golden sands of Keawakapu Beach to the green flanks of Haleakalā, Maui's gorgeous sights have drawn admirers for generations. There's inspiration in every direction. But just when you think you have a handle on the island's sublime scenery, an unexpected view catches you by surprise. It's these unplanned glimpses of beauty that linger in your memory.

Big Beach (Oneloa)

Wild, vast and in a completely natural state – the way Maui used to be. Big Beach is an expanse of gleaming sands, and unbelievably blue wate, with no development in sight. p171

Waterfalls

Streams tumble down the lush slopes of the West Maui mountains and Haleakalā. Catch the best photo ops on the Road to Hana. p220

Sunsets

Where has all the romance gone? It's gone to the west and southern shores of Maui, where the golden orb drops spectacularly below the horizon. The view from Keawakapu Beach is especially nice. p153

Top left: Lahaina (p78); bottom left: Pi'ilanihale Heiau (p228); right: 'Iao Valley State Monument (p144)

4 HISTORIC HOTSPOTS

Maui is dotted with portals to the past, where natural formations and historic structures are direct links to history. And the 100-year-old Komoda Store & Bakery? The past still makes tasty cream puffs.

EQROY / SHUTTERSTOCK ©

GREG ELMS / LONELY PLANET ©

SHANE MYERS PHOTOGRAPHY / SHUTTERSTOCK ©

Lahaina

Downtown Lahaina, with its old wooden storefronts and rowdy pubs, channels the whaling era. You'd hardly blink if Edward Bailey, an 1800s missionary, stepped from the entry of the Bailey House. p79

'Iao Valley State Monument

Snuggled in rainforest-covered mountains, 'Iao and its green pinnacle are such sumptuous sights that it's hard to imagine that a violent interisland battle raged here in the 18th century. p144

Pi'ilanihale Heiau

Archaeologists believe construction began on Hawaii's largest temple as early as 1200 CE and continued in phases. You can imagine the high priest walking up the terraced stone steps to offer sacrifices. p228

Bottom: Mama's Fish House (p186)

5 TASTING THE LOCAL CUISINE

LIVIA DE JESUS WIPPICH / SHUTTERSTOCK ©

RICK BEAUREGARD / SHUTTERSTOCK ©

Healthy Eats

Several vegetarian and vegan restaurants have quickly earned a passionate following for delicious and artfully presented produce, typically sourced locally. The talented folks at Moku Roots follow a no-waste policy. p92

Seafood

Fresh and locally caught fish is a highlight across the island, and you'll find it served up at food trucks, beach-town shacks and special-occasion seaside digs like Mama's Fish House. p186

Farm Tours

Farm fare may be as varied as the landscapes, but the tours similarly reveal their owners' love for the land. Learn about tropical produce, coffee beans and goat cheese. p193

From food trucks to white-linen dining rooms, eateries are embracing locally sourced food, including Upcountry vegetables and grass-fed beef from Maui ranches. The new vegan places skip the beef, but the pack-a-punch flavors of their produce are equally addictive. And the local dishes? Their names may be unfamiliar – *loco moco*, shave ice, *kalua* pork – but the flavors are rich and delicious, and the portions typically hearty.

6 WHALE-WATCHING

Humpback whales keep things frisky off Maui's western coast each winter, when thousands arrive to court, mate and calve. It's prime time for whale-watching. If you're in Maui at the same time – typically December through April – treat yourself to a whale-watching cruise. Snorkelers and divers who stick their heads underwater at the right time can even hear them singing: love songs, we presume!

Top right: Whale-watching, Papawai Point (p106); bottom right: Humpback whales (p107)

Sunset Cruise

Sunsets and humpback whales are two of Maui's most prized accessories. Enjoy both on a late afternoon sail that departs the Ka'anapali coast. The folks at Teralani Sailing serve cocktails on a catamaran. p109

Coastal Viewing

Whales are readily spotted from cliffside lookouts such as Papawai Point, from west-facing beaches and from oceanfront condos and trails overlooking the ocean, like the ridgetop Lahaina Pali Trail. p130

Get an Education

Maui Ocean Center offers the immersive Humpbacks of Hawaii Exhibit & Sphere, while the Hawaiian Islands Humpback Whale National Marine Sanctuary Headquarters has whale talks and a viewing deck. p158

Left: surfing, Kihei(p153); Top right: snorkeling, Molokini Crater (p51); bottom right: kayaking (p43)

7 WATER SPORTS FOR ALL

You don't have to be an experienced surfer, diver or kayaker to get out on the water in Maui. Heck, you can see a rainbow's array of tropical fish just by kicking off-shore with $7 snorkel gear. Adventure outfitters and rental shops line the main drags in all the major towns and most resorts rent gear to the general public from the beach.

Surfing

Surfers of all abilities flock to Maui's coasts, but beginners will be just fine. Newbies should head to Lahaina, West Maui and Kihei, where the waves are more accessible. Beginners can easily join a class. p53

MUDSKIPPERANNE / GETTY IMAGES ©

JOE BENNING / SHUTTERSTOCK ©

Snorkeling & Diving

Snorkelers can kick off from shore at Malu'aka Beach and other spots along the west coast. Molokini Crater is reached by boat. Divers head to the Cathedrals in Lana'i. p46

Kayaking

Kayakers with snorkel gear paddle across Makena Bay every morning – all in search of tropical fish and a whale sighting. Guides with Aloha Kayaks teach paddlers about the environment. p172

Below: Keonehe'ehe'e (Sliding Sands) Trail (p202), Haleakalā National Park

8 HITTING THE TRAIL

Hikers are spoiled for choice on the Valley Isle, where tropical jungles, a volcanic crater and ancient lava-stone highways drop visitors into unfamiliar worlds. Most trails can be accessed by a short drive from town and many can be hiked – or at least partially explored – by day-trippers of all skill levels. Waterfalls, blowholes, ancient ruins and eucalyptus trees await.

Waihe'e Ridge Trail

The Waihe'e Ridge Trail climbs the rugged green slopes of the West Maui Mountains, sharing bird's-eye views of cloud-topped peaks and overgrown valleys along the way. p102

Keonehe'ehe'e (Sliding Sands) Trail

With lava cones in the distance and a stark and barren landscape unfurling straight ahead, the vibe becomes distinctly lunar as the trail drops into Haleakalā's famous volcanic crater. p202

Hoapili Trail

Instead of dirt beneath your feet, you'll find chunky lava rocks, which underlie the ancient road known as the King's Highway. The road once encircled the island. p154

Need to Know

For more information, see Survival Guide (p301)

Currency
US Dollar ($)

Language
English, Hawaiian

Visas
Generally not required for stays of up to 90 days for citizens of Visa Waiver Program countries.

Money
ATMs common. Credit cards widely accepted; often required for car and hotel reservations.

Cell Phones
International travelers need GSM multiband phones. Buy prepaid SIM cards locally. Coverage can be spotty outside developed areas.

Time
Hawaii-Aleutian Standard Time (HAST) is GMT minus 10 hours. Hawaii does not observe daylight-saving time. It has about 11 hours of daylight in midwinter and almost 13½ hours in midsummer.

When to Go

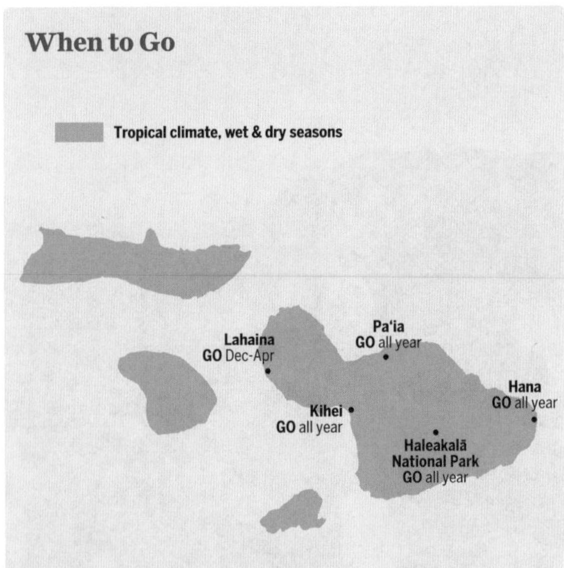

High Season (mid-Dec–Mar; Jun-Aug)

➡ Lodging prices are at their highest.

➡ Coincides with Christmas, New Year and summer breaks.

➡ Whale-watching is a top activity in winter (but it's rainier); many festivals in June and July.

Shoulder Season (Apr; Sep)

➡ Prices for accommodations drop as demand slows, but Easter and the US spring break draw crowds.

➡ Temperatures mild, with mostly sunny, cloudless days.

➡ Book rental car early; fleets may be reduced.

Low Season (May; Oct-Nov)

➡ Lodging prices are at their lowest.

➡ Crowds – and prices – may jump for Halloween and Thanksgiving.

➡ Quiet time to visit, and the Road to Hana may be less crowded.

Useful Websites

Hawaii Visitors and Convention Bureau (www.gohawaii.com/islands/maui) Official tourism site; comprehensive events calendar and multilingual planning guides.

The Maui News (www.mauinews.com) Latest headlines.

Maui Time (http://mauitime.com) Weekly newspaper with in-depth local news features and entertainment listings.

Lonely Planet (www.lonelyplanet.com/usa/hawaii/maui) Destination information, hotel bookings, traveler forum and more.

Important Numbers

Emergency	☎ 911
Country code	☎ 1
Area code	☎ 808
International access code	☎ 011

Exchange Rates

Australia	A$1	$0.67
Canada	C$1	$0.75
Europe	€1	$1.08
Japan	¥100	$0.91
New Zealand	NZ$1	$0.64
UK	£1	$1.30

For current exchange rates see www.xe.com

Daily Costs

Budget: Less than $200

➡ Hostel dorm: $39–59

➡ Semi-private hostel room, guesthouse or budget B&B: $84–119

➡ Groceries or fast food: $7–15

➡ Walking tour or beach days: free

➡ Maui Bus one-way fare: $2

Midrange: $200–350

➡ B&Bs, hotel rooms or condos: $150–199

➡ Dinner at midrange restaurant: $20–35

➡ Hiking, snorkeling, aquarium: free–$35

➡ Small rental car: per day/week from $51/323

Top End: More than $350

➡ Beach-resort room: from $298

➡ Three-course meal at top restaurant: from $100

➡ Guided outdoor adventure tour: from $99

➡ Spacious rental car: per day/week from $62/357

Opening Hours

Opening hours may vary slightly throughout the year. High-season opening hours are provided in listings; hours generally decrease in shoulder and low seasons.

Banks 8:30am–4pm Monday to Friday; some to 6pm Friday and 9am–noon or 1pm Saturday

Bars and clubs Noon–midnight daily; some to 2am Thursday to Saturday

Businesses 8:30am–4:30pm Monday to Friday

Post offices 8:30am–4:30pm Monday to Friday; some also 9am–noon Saturday

Shops 9am–5pm Monday to Saturday, some also noon–5pm Sunday; major shopping areas and malls keep extended hours

Arriving in Maui

Kahului International Airport Most people rent a car when they arrive. Bus service is limited. Roberts Hawaii, with a booking counter in baggage claim, offers frequent service to most tourist points. Book ahead for the shuttle vans of Hawaii Executive Transportation and Speedi Shuttle. The latter carries surfboards.

Kapalua Airport Taxis to West Maui resorts cost $20 or less.

Top Tips

➡ Never turn your back on the ocean when swimming or wading. Powerful waves can take you by surprise.

➡ Tackle the sunrise at Haleakalā and other early morning adventures at the start of your trip, before you've adjusted to the time change.

➡ When snorkeling, take care not to step on the coral. It's fragile.

➡ Don't touch the green turtles or get too close on land or sea.

➡ Don't feed fish or animals.

➡ Stay aware of your surroundings while exploring the outdoors and slow down on slippery trails.

➡ Watch for clouds and surging water while wading in pools and streams, which are susceptible to flash floods.

➡ Fill your gas tank before driving the Road to Hana. The only gas station on the route is in Hana.

➡ Keep valuables in your hotel room, not in your car.

➡ Slow down, enjoy conversations and embrace living on island time.

For much more on **getting around**, see p309

What's New

On the foodie front, the new vegan cafes are the talk of the island, while Sheldon Simeon of *Top Chef* fame opened Lineage, which spotlights Korean favorites. Several resorts and a PGA golf course are aglow after megabuck renovations. Also buzzworthy? Booming tourism in recent years. Brush fires. Mermaids. And 'Iao Valley State Monument – looking fresh!

Culture & Conservation

From outdoor outfitters to big resorts to the state government, everyone with a stake in Maui's future is making an effort to educate travelers about Native Hawaiian customs, with a particular emphasis on Hawaii's culture of *aloha 'aina,* or love for the land. Whether it's a cultural tour, a new water filling station or fresh signage about reef-safe sunscreen, reminders about thoughtful travel are becoming the norm. Ka'anapali's new Hawaiian Wildlife Discovery Center at Whalers Village will spotlight Hawaiian marine life and local conservation issues.

Resort Renovations

Several resorts are looking oh-so-fresh in Ka'anapali after multimillion-dollar upgrades. Improvements have run the gamut, from sleek new rooms and reimagined lobbies to cool new lawns with imaginative beachside distractions.

Kapalua Plantation Course

The beloved Plantation Course (p119) in Kapalua, home of the PGA's annual kickoff golf tournament in January, is sporting faster new greens and brand-new tee boxes after a nine-month closure for improvements. The clubhouse, home of the popular Plantation House restaurant, also has a fresh look.

Sheldon Simeon

Former *Top Chef* contender Sheldon Simeon successfully opened Lineage (p168) restaurant in the posh Shops at Wailea, with a focus on Hawaiian comfort fare. He stepped back in 2020 to let a new chef de

LOCAL KNOWLEDGE

WHAT'S HAPPENING IN MAUI

Amy C Balfour, Lonely Planet writer

Prior to the Covid-19 pandemic, travelers were flocking to Maui in record numbers, with mixed results for the island. In 2019 the island welcomed more than three million visitors, a jump of 5.4% from the previous year. These visitors injected more than $5 billion into the local economy. For resorts, this is good news, and occupancy rates now remain high year-round. For travelers, this means you've got to book early and prepare to open your wallet – wide! Booming tourism has also put added stress on the island's fragile natural ecosystems. Efforts to control the crowds and their ill effects have popped up island-wide, from a permit requirement for viewing the sunrise at Haleakalā National Park to coral-safety signage at 'Ahihi-Kina'u Natural Area Reserve. Large brush fires are an increasing problem, exacerbated by dry conditions and trade winds. The Central-South Maui fire in the summer of 2019 burned 9000 acres, leading to a large-scale evacuation and forcing the temporary closure of major roads and the Kahului International Airport.

cuisine, MiJin Kang Toride, take the reins. The menu now reflects her Korean heritage. Also serves amazing cocktails at the welcoming front bar.

'Iao Valley State Monument

This lush state park has reopened after suffering extensive damage during the severe storms and flooding in September of 2016. The soaring 'Iao Needle (p144) is just as green and eye-catching as ever.

Vegan Eats

New plant-powered restaurants are garnering rave reviews island-wide and drawing appreciative crowds with amazing food. Put Moku Roots (p90) in Lahaina and A'a Roots (p116) in Napili on your list.

Food Truck Parks

With the opening of new food truck parks in Kihei (p162), Honokowai (p115) and Kahului (p137), quick and cheap dining just got easier, with loads of choices too. Bring cash.

Camp Olowalu

Long known as a rough-and-tumble campground packed tight among gnarled trees beside the Olowalu coast, Camp Olowalu (p106) has cleaned up its tent area. It has also introduced canvas glamping tents, which are set across a manicured lawn. Hot water and a sink are just steps from your cot. More family friendly too.

Pickleball

Enthusiasts of this increasingly popular outdoor paddle game, which combines elements of tennis, badminton and table tennis, can now play the game at tennis complexes in Ka'anapali (p109), Kapalua (p120) and Wailea (p166).

LISTEN, WATCH & FOLLOW

For inspiration and up-to-date news, visit www.lonelyplanet.com/usa/hawaii/maui/articles

Insta @mauivisit Inspirational photos from the Maui Visitors Bureau.

Maui Time (www.mauitime.com) Get the story behind the story from the website of Maui's weekly newspaper.

Aloha 360 (www.thealoha360.com) Podcast from local couple John and Leslie Cobble that shares helpful travel information about Maui.

Twitter @mauiNOW Up-to-the-minute news about the island.

FAST FACTS

Food trend Vegan restaurants

Miles of coastline 120

Official languages English and Hawaiian

Pop 167,207

population per sq mile

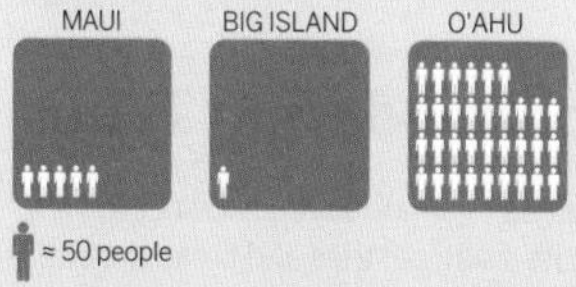

Mermaids & Mermen

Whether you are a kid or an adult, you can slip on a fin and swim like a mermaid these days in Maui. The ecofriendly Hawaii Mermaid Adventure (p172) will let you take your pick of ocean or pool for your lesson.

Accommodations

Find more accommodations reviews throughout the On the Road chapters (from p77)

PRICE RANGES

The following price ranges refer to a West Maui double room with bathroom in high season (mid-December to mid-April). Unless otherwise stated, breakfast isn't included in the price. Tax is not included in the prices.

$ less than $200

$$ $200–$350

$$$ more than $350

Accommodation Types

B&Bs Homes or small lodgings. Owner usually lives on-site. Fruit, pastries and bread are typically served for breakfast.

Camping Maui's national, state and county parks offer campgrounds; book permits in advance.

Condominiums Individually owned units grouped in one complex. Typically include a full kitchen. Cleaning fees are typically added per stay, as are administrative costs.

Guesthouses Similar to B&Bs in their room setup, but interaction with the owner is minimal or nonexistent. Rooms are often accessed by typing in a code on a keypad. May have a communal area.

Hostels Simple places in older buildings that provide a cheap place to crash. Usually offer both dorms and private rooms.

Hotels Price is usually based on room size and view, with top rates for bigger rooms and full ocean views.

Resorts Sprawling and expensive complexes that are typically on the coast. Many have several pools and restaurants and offer lots of on-site activities. Look for children's programs too.

Best Places to Stay

Best Sleeping

Maui's seaside resorts are some of the best in the world, offering gorgeous beach views, plush decor and an array of on-site distractions. Top B&Bs and condos provide beach gear and instructions to maximize your fun. From hostels to high end, what sets the best apart? The warm alohas of the staff.

- **Four Seasons Maui at Wailea** (p167), **Wailea**
- **Hale Napili** (p116), **Napili**
- **Hamoa Bay House & Bungalow** (p241), **Hana**
- **Aloha Surf Hostel** (p183), **Pa'ia**
- **Camp Olowalu** (p106), **Olowalu**

Best on a Budget

Budget lodging is extremely hard to find on Maui, especially in the resort- and condo-heavy enclaves of South and West Maui. Great hostels and guesthouses dot the island, but only a handful are near the coast. Budget hotels are almost nonexistent. Camping is best in Haleakalā National Park or at Camp Olowalu.

- **Aloha Surf Hostel** (p183), **Pa'ia**
- **Northshore Hostel** (p142), **Wailuku**
- **Haleakalā Wilderness Cabins** (p210), **Haleakalā National Park**
- **Camp Olowalu** (p106), **Oluwalu**

Best for Families

Most resorts have organized children's programs and several have outdoor pools with slides and fun water features. Condos are another good option, with pools and beach gear typically on offer, plus kitchens

EQROY / SHUTTERSTOCK ©

Grand Wailea Resort Hotel & Spa (p168)

– but some skew toward an older crowd. Honokowai, Kahana and Napili have some of the best condo selections.

➡ **Hyatt Regency Maui Resort & Spa** (p110), **Ka'anapali**

➡ **Grand Wailea Resort Hotel & Spa** (p168), **Wailea**

➡ **Honua Kai Resort & Spa** (p110), **Ka'anapali**

➡ **Ka'anapali Beach Hotel** (p110), **Ka'anapali**

➡ **Napili Kai Beach Resort** (p116), **Napili**

Best for Solo Travelers

With dorms, communal kitchens and planned activities, hostels are great places to meet other travelers. For solo travelers who prefer more privacy, consider a studio-style condominium. Condo complexes, particularly in West Maui, often have a weekly mai-tai party where guests can mingle. Resorts can be a bit much with their honeymooners and families, but small hotels and guesthouses can be a great option for introverts. Hermits should head to Hana.

➡ **Aloha Surf Hostel** (p183), **Pa'ia**

➡ **Hale Napili** (p116), **Napili**

➡ **Ka'anapali Beach Hotel** (p110), Ka'anapali

➡ **Camp Olowalu** (p106), **Olowalu**

Booking

Expect high prices in peak season, which is mid-December though mid-April. Prices are also high June through August. Holiday periods, especially between Christmas and New Year, command premium prices and often book up far in advance. It's wise to reserve at least several months in advance almost any time of the year to lock in a good deal. Many hotels and condos offer year-round internet specials well below the advertised 'rack rates.'

Lonely Planet (lonelyplanet.com/hotels) Find independent reviews, as well as recommendations on the best places to stay – and then book them online.

Airbnb (www.airbnb.com) Quality and price vary among condo and vacation rentals. Helpful reviews.

BedandBreakfast.com Somewhat comprehensive national website covering B&Bs and inns across Maui.

HomeAway (www.homeaway.com) Search for condos, cottages and houses.

Getting Around Maui

For more information, see Transportation (p309)

Traveling by Car

To reach both cities and off-the-beaten-path sights, you will need your own car. Bus service is limited to major roads linking the main towns such as Lahaina, Kihei and Kahului. Much of the island is not suitable for bicycle.

Car Hire

Eight national rental car firms have offices at Kahului International Airport. Most of these rental companies also have branches in Ka'anapali and will pick you up at the nearby Kapalua Airport. For a green option, consider Bio-Beetle (p310) in Kahului. For cheaper rentals – of older cars – check out efficient but friendly Kihei Rent A Car (p310).

Look for any road restrictions on your vehicle rental contract. Some car rental agencies, for instance, may prohibit driving on dirt roads, which you'll find across the island and sometimes even along sections of paved highways, such as in the Kaupo district of the Pi'ilani Hwy.

Driving Conditions

Most main roads on Maui are called highways, whether they're busy four-lane thoroughfares or just quiet country roads. Indeed, there are roads in remote corners of the island that are barely one lane but nonetheless are designated highways.

➡ Islanders refer to highways by name, and rarely by number. If you stop to ask someone how to find Hwy 36, chances are you'll get a blank stare – ask for the Hana Hwy instead.

RESOURCES

American Automobile Association (www.aaa.com) Along with maps and trip planning information, AAA members receive discounts on car rentals, hotels and attractions, plus roadside emergency service and towing.

Hawaii Department of Transportation (http://hidot.hawaii.gov/highways/roadwork) Shares details about lane closures and highway work.

Maui County (www.mauicounty.gov) Check here for information about bus routes and schedules.

➡ Most Maui roads are paved. Some, like the Hana Hwy, are extremely curvaceous. The notorious Pi'ilani Hwy (p234) in southeast Maui is only part-paved but is usually passable for cars. Check the conditions of these roads after rains.

➡ Cell-phone use without a hands-free device is prohibited.

Road Trip

For a driving adventure, tackle the narrow Pi'ilani Hwy, which links Kipahulu and 'Ulupalakua in East Maui. It twists alongside the coast, passing lush foliage, vast pastures, and historic sites.

No Car?

Bus

Operated by Maui County and Roberts Hawaii, Maui Bus (p310) runs buses between the major towns, but not to out-of-the-way places, such as Haleakalā National Park or Hana. Buses come with front-load bike racks.

The main routes run every hour daily, roughly 7am to 8pm. Kahului is a hub. The Upcountry Islander and Haiku Islander routes stop at Kahului International Airport.

Costs Fares are $2 per ride, regardless of distance. There are no transfers; you have to pay the fare each time you board a bus. A day pass costs $4.

Carry-on All buses allow you to carry on only what fits under your seat or on your lap, so forget the surfboard. There are bike racks, however, for cyclists.

Resort Shuttle Many of the Ka'anapali and Wailea resorts operate shuttles for guests that serve the resort areas..

Ka'anapali Trolley Open to the public, this free shuttle loops past the Ka'anapali resorts, Whalers Village and the golf courses every 20 to 30 minutes between 10am and 10pm.

Train

There is no train service on Maui.

Bicycle

Narrow roads, frequent hills and mountains, and strong winds can make cycling very challenging on Maui. Although this might be daunting for casual riders thinking of cycling between towns, Maui's gorgeous landscape is catnip for hard-core cyclists. Getting around by bicycle within a small area is also feasible for the average rider.

Boat

There is no boat service on Maui, but you can take the Expeditions Ferry (p309) from Lahaina Harbor to Manele Bay Harbor on Lana'i (one hour) five times daily between 6:45am and 5:45pm. The ferry returns to Lahaina five times between 8am and 6:45pm. The Moloka'i ferry no longer runs.

DRIVING FAST FACTS

➡ Drive on the right.

➡ Minimum age for a full license is 18 years. The minimum age to rent a car varies by rental agency.

➡ Maximum speed limit is 55mph.

➡ Adults cannot use a handheld mobile device while driving.

➡ Maximum blood alcohol concentration is .08%. For drivers under 21 years, it's .02%.

➡ All vehicle occupants must wear a seatbelt.

ROAD DISTANCES (MILES)

	Lahaina	Kihei	Kapalua	Kahului
Kihei	22			
Kapalua	10	32		
Kahului	24	10	33	
Hana	72	58	82	51

Month by Month

TOP EVENTS

➡ **World Whale Day**, February

➡ **East Maui Taro Festival**, April

➡ **Maui Film Festival**, June

➡ **Ki Hoʻalu Slack Key Guitar Festival**, June

➡ **Halloween in Lahaina**, October

January

Regular events include the Friday Town Parties, which rotate weekly between Wailuki, Lahaina and Kihei, and feature live music, food trucks and arts and crafts. There's a fantastic slack key guitar show every Wednesday night in Napili.

PGA Tournament of Champions

The season opener for the PGA tour tees off in Kapalua in early January, when the previous year's golf champions compete for a multi-million-dollar purse. (p121)

Chinese New Year Festival

Fireworks and lion dancers welcome the New Year in January or February at various locations, including Lahaina's Wo Hing Museum. (p82)

February

Between December and April, about 10,000 humpback whales return to Hawaii to breed and give birth in the shallow waters. View them along the West Maui coast. February is the best month for spotting them.

World Whale Day

A huge bash, Kihei's mid-February beachside parade and celebration honors the North Pacific humpback whale. (p161)

March

Lahaina Whale & Ocean Arts Festival

Hawaiian music, hula and games in Banyan Tree Park mark the return of migrating humpback whales. (p89)

April

April is shoulder season, a nice time to rejuvenate between winter's whale-watching crowds and the arrival of summer's families. Quirky festivals keep the scene entertaining.

Celebration of the Arts

The Ritz-Carlon Kapalua hosts traditional artisans from across the Hawaiian islands, with craft-making demonstrations, live entertainment and a focus on Native customs and beliefs. (p121)

Banyan Tree Birthday Party

Celebrate Maui's most renowned tree with a birthday party under its sprawling branches. Lahaina's beloved banyan is more than 140 years old. The event occurs the weekend closest to April 24. (p89)

East Maui Taro Festival

Hana, Maui's most Hawaiian town, throws the island's most Hawaiian party in late April, with everything from hula dances and a top-notch Hawaiian music festival to a taro-pancake breakfast. (p240)

May

Maui Brewers Festival

Head to Kahului's Maui Arts & Cultural Center in mid-May to sip microbrews from more than 40 local and national craft breweries and cideries (http://mauiarts.org/brew_fest). There's also live music and local food.

June

June and July have a busy festival schedule. You'll find at least one big summer celebration in almost every region.

Upcountry Ag & Farm Fair

Farm and ranch life are the focus of this Makawao fair (http://mauiagfest.org) with a farm-goods tent, horseback rides, a pie-eating contest and a livestock auction. Plus live music. Held in late May to mid-June.

King Kamehameha Day Parade & Celebration

In early June, head to Front St in Lahaina to honor the birthday of King Kamehameha I with food, live music and a bright floral parade. Also known as Kamehameha the Great, this warrior chieftain eventually united the islands of Hawaii. (p89)

Kapalua Wine & Food Festival

Hawaii's hottest chefs vie for attention in this culinary extravaganza of cooking demonstrations and wine tasting for four days in mid-June. (p121)

Maui Film Festival

In mid-June, movie lovers gather in Wailea, where the golf course is transformed into the 'Celestial Theater' and Hollywood stars show up for added bling. (p167)

Ki Ho'alu Slack Key Guitar Festival

Slack key guitar music doesn't get any better than this. The one-day event in late June brings in all the big-name players from throughout the state. Held at the Maui Arts & Cultural Center in Kahului. (p135)

July

Lahaina throws the biggest Fourth of July party on Maui. Head to Banyan Tree Park and Front St for live music, strolling entertainment, arts and fireworks.

Makawao Paniolo Parade

A colorful downtown parade showcases the Upcountry's *paniolo* (Hawaiian cowboy) past, held on the weekend closest to Independence Day. (p191)

Pineapple Festival

Pineapples, the symbol of hospitality, are feted on the island of Lana'i on or near the weekend of July 4 with live music, food and fireworks. (p254)

October

Maui County Fair

Maui is a garden, so it's no surprise that its old-fashioned agricultural fair is a bountiful event with orchids, luscious produce and lots of good food. Late September or early October in Wailuku. (p140)

Halloween in Lahaina

Lahaina hosts Maui's biggest street festival on Halloween night, attracting more than 20,000 revelers. Fun for families early in the night; later things get a bit more wild. (p89)

November

Hula O Nā Keiki

Talented *na keiki* (children) are the headliners of this annual hula competition at the Ka'anapali Beach Hotel in early to mid-November. (p110)

Nā Mele O Maui

Children's choral groups sing Native Hawaiian music at this late-November event at the Maui Arts & Cultural Center in Kahului. (p135)

December

Holiday Lighting of the Banyan Tree

On the first weekend of December, Lahaina illuminates America's oldest banyan tree with thousands of lights. Even Santa stops by for this one. (p89)

Itineraries

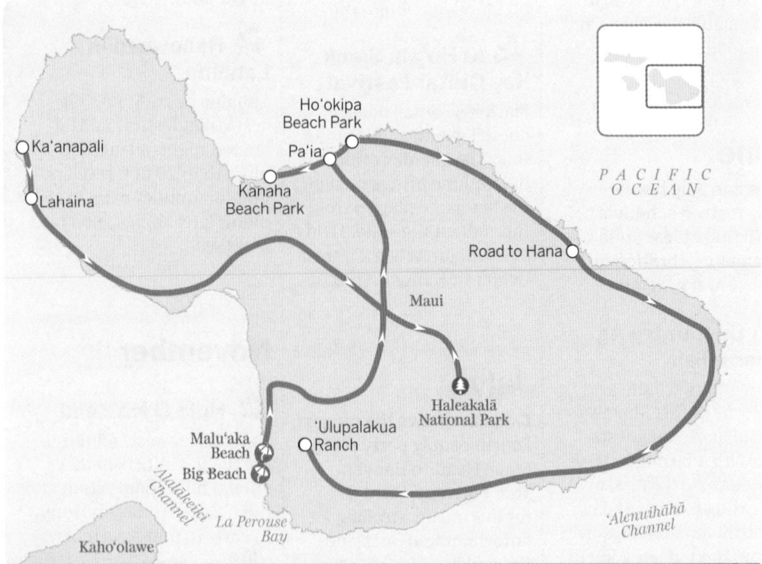

Island Tour

To embrace the magic that is Maui, remember: quality over quantity. Yes, the ziplines are fun, the restaurants excellent and the resorts posh, but spending time in small towns and remote parks will connect you with the land and its people. This trip covers many stops; allow yourself to reschedule if a place's mana (spiritual essence) is strong.

Splash into the scene with an ocean dip in coastal **Ka'anapali**, followed by a sunset cruise. Next, stroll the historic whaling town of **Lahaina,** then treat yourself to the Old Lahaina Luau. Still got jet lag? Drive to **Haleakalā National Park** to catch a breathtaking sunrise and hike into the crater.

The next few days are all about those gorgeous beaches. Begin by snorkeling with turtles at **Malu'aka Beach**, followed by a picnic at magnificent **Big Beach**. For adventure, check out **Kanaha Beach Park** for the sailboarding scene.

Head to **Pa'ia** for Maui's hippest cafes and check out the surf action at **Ho'okipa Beach Park**. Wrap up with waterfalls galore on the most legendary drive in Hawaii, the wildly beautiful **Road to Hana**. On your last day, look out for leviathans on a whale-watching cruise or savor a fine dinner on the western coast.

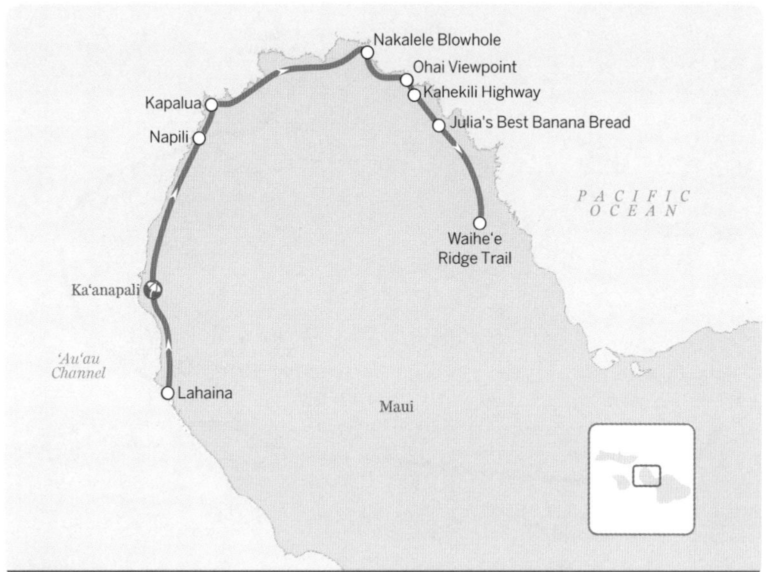

Lahaina to Waiheʻe Ridge Trail

History buffs, hikers and those with a sense of adventure will most enjoy this multiday excursion in West Maui. The trip starts with urban exploring and ends with a wild drive along a remote and rugged coastline. There's a bit of snorkeling and Hawaiian dining in the middle.

In **Lahaina** the exhibits at the Lahaina Heritage Museum set the tone for adventure, with tales of warring ancient Hawaiians, hardy whalers and determined missionaries. From here, relax under the USA's largest banyan tree then stroll around Maui's captivating old whaling town, which is packed tight with historic buildings, art galleries, great restaurants and indie shops. In the evening, feast your stomach and your eyes at the Old Lahaina **Luau**, where the Hawaiian buffet and the storytelling – through hula – are highlights.

The next morning, plunge into Maui with a dip in the sea at **Kaʻanapali Beach**. Snorkel out to Puʻu Kekaʻa (Black Rock) to check out Maui's dazzling underwater scenery, then pop into Whalers Village for a breezy lunch and fine local shopping. Enjoy the sunset on a sailboat cruise or on shore at Kaʻanapali's Hula Grill & Barefoot Bar.

Start day three early – and we mean early – at the Gazebo restaurant in **Napili** for chocolate macnut pancakes. Swimmers should then head to **Kapalua Bay**, bodysurfers to DT Fleming Beach and snorkelers to Honolua Bay. Kapalua's menu of adventures also includes hiking and ziplining, while golfers probably already know about Kapalua's courses from the tournament coverage. Catch the sunset at Merriman's Kapalua. In the morning, stroll lovely beaches on the Coastal Trail.

On your last day, drive around the wild northern tip of Maui. Follow the Kahekili Hwy to **Nakalele Blowhole**, and don't miss **Ohai Viewpoint**. Other than fruit stands, dining options are few, but **Julia's Best Banana Bread** should see you through.

In the early afternoon, lace up your hiking boots. Lofty mountain views and waterfalls are just starters on the fun **Waiheʻe Ridge Trail** in the West Maui Mountains. Return to Lahaina or continue to Paʻia.

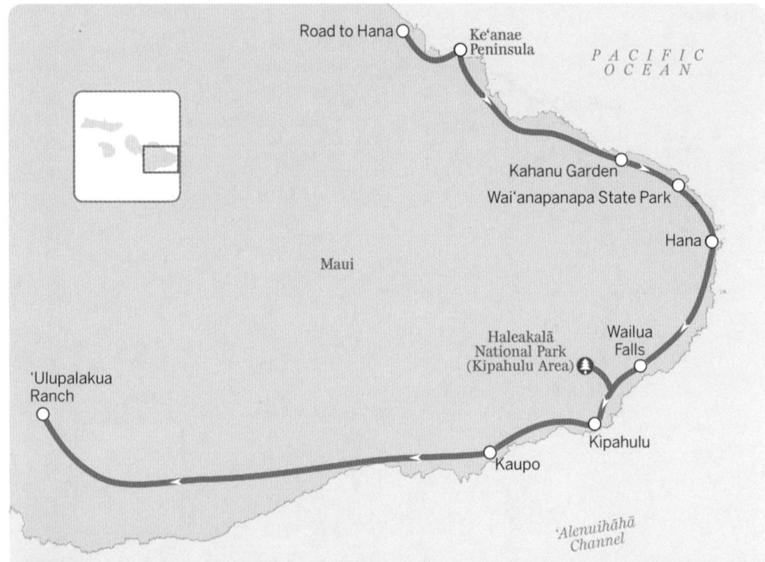

The Road to Hana to 'Ulupalakua Ranch

This magical drive along the remote east Maui coast is lined with waterfalls and lush scenery. If you want to escape the resort scene while digging into local culture and exploring untamed nature at a leisurely pace, this is your trip.

The trip begins on the Hana Hwy, dubbed the **Road to Hana**. The roadway begins as Hwy 36 then flips to Hwy 360 at mile marker 16. Waterfalls, pools and thick forests line the route. About halfway to Hana, swing down to **Ke'anae Peninsula** for windswept views of the rough lava coast, pounded by surf. You'll be humbled by Hawaii's largest temple at **Kahanu Garden**. Views of the striking black-lava coast and the unusual black-sand beach at **Wai'anapanapa State Park** are also memorable.

The old Hawaiian community of **Hana** is well worth a poke around and a two-night stay. Enjoy Thai food for lunch, visit Hana's museum and the Hasegawa General Store, and the marvelous beaches. Hike to the top of **Pu'u o Kahaula Hill** for a broad view of the town and Hana Beach.

It's time for more local exploring in the morning. First stop? **Wailua Falls**. This roadside cascade is a top contender for Maui's most gorgeous waterfall. The road rolls on through the Kipahulu district of **Haleakalā National Park**, home to 'Ohe'o Gulch and its 24 pools, each backed by its own little waterfall. Make time to hike to the 200ft plunge of Makahiku Falls on the **Pipiwai Trail**.

In jungle-tangled **Kipahulu**, visit the grave of aviator Charles Lindbergh, before returning to Hana for drinks and live music at posh but hospitable **Travaasa Hana**. In the morning you'll follow the lonely Pi'ilani Hwy for an occasionally hair-raising drive with memorable hairpin turns, which eventually straighten out in the cowboy region of **Kaupo**.

Conclude with a taste of Maui Splash, a refreshing pineapple wine, at the tasting room at **Maui Wine** on the **'Ulupalakua Ranch**. Spend the night in the Upcountry, home to several inviting B&Bs and inns.

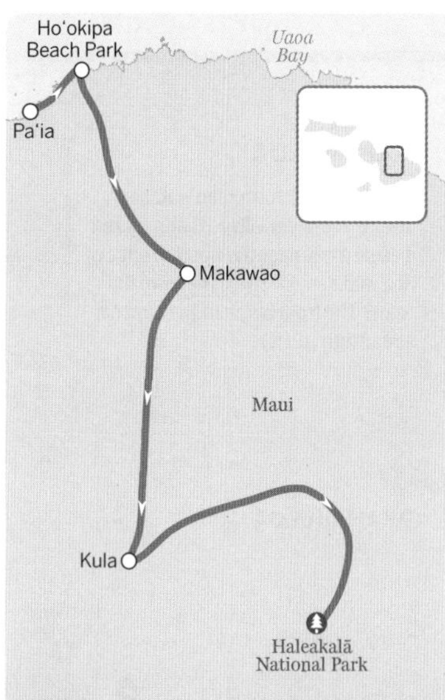

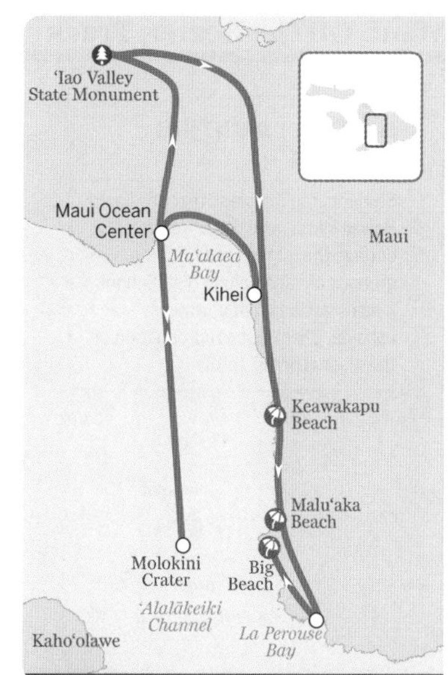

3 DAYS Pa'ia to Haleakalā National Park

Low-key charms are the draw on this trip, which includes several small towns on the flanks of Haleakalā, all with distinct personalities, from the surf-and-granola vibe of Pa'ia to the artsy cool of Makawao. It ends with a scenic bang in lofty Haleakalā National Park.

On day one, explore downtown **Pa'ia** to find the right breakfast joint then wander the boutiques or hit the beach. At **Ho'okipa Beach Park**, watch the windsurfers from the overlook. Splurge for dinner at the renowned Mama's Fish House.

It's *paniolo*-meets-Picasso in downtown **Makawao**, a gallery-filled cowboy town. Here, enjoy a cream puff from **Komoda Store & Bakery** or explore the trails at **Makawao Forest Reserve**.

For Upcountry's sweetest green scene, visit Ali'i Kula Lavender in **Kula** and nibble lavender scones while soaking up rainbow-lit coastal views from the farm.

The next morning, grab a coat and picnic lunch, and leave early to catch the sunrise atop **Haleakalā** volcano in its namesake national park. Follow with a hike into the otherworldly crater.

Kihei to Big Beach

Adventures are sprinkled with history and science on this short trip, which heads out to sea then dives into the wild landscapes of Central and South Maui.

The doors open early at **Kihei Caffe**, a good place to fuel up before a morning of snorkeling. For offshore fish-gazing, journey to **Molokini Crater**, a sunken volcanic crater rim with brilliant fish and coral.

Where the Molokini boat docks you'll find the **Maui Ocean Center**, an inviting tropical aquarium. In the afternoon, drive to **'Iao Valley State Monument**, known for its cool streams, misty mountains and Maui's emerald jewel, the 'Iao Needle.

The star of Kihei's beaches, **Keawakapu Beach** is tops for sunset. The next morning, snorkel and swim to the coral gardens at **Malu'aka Beach**, also known as Turtle Beach. Here, green sea turtles abound.

Continue south to **La Perouse Bay**, a stunning volcanic landscape at road's end. Wander past historic structures and ponder the twisted black lava flows.

On your way back to Kihei, stop at **Big Beach** for another fine sunset.

Maui: Off the Beaten Track

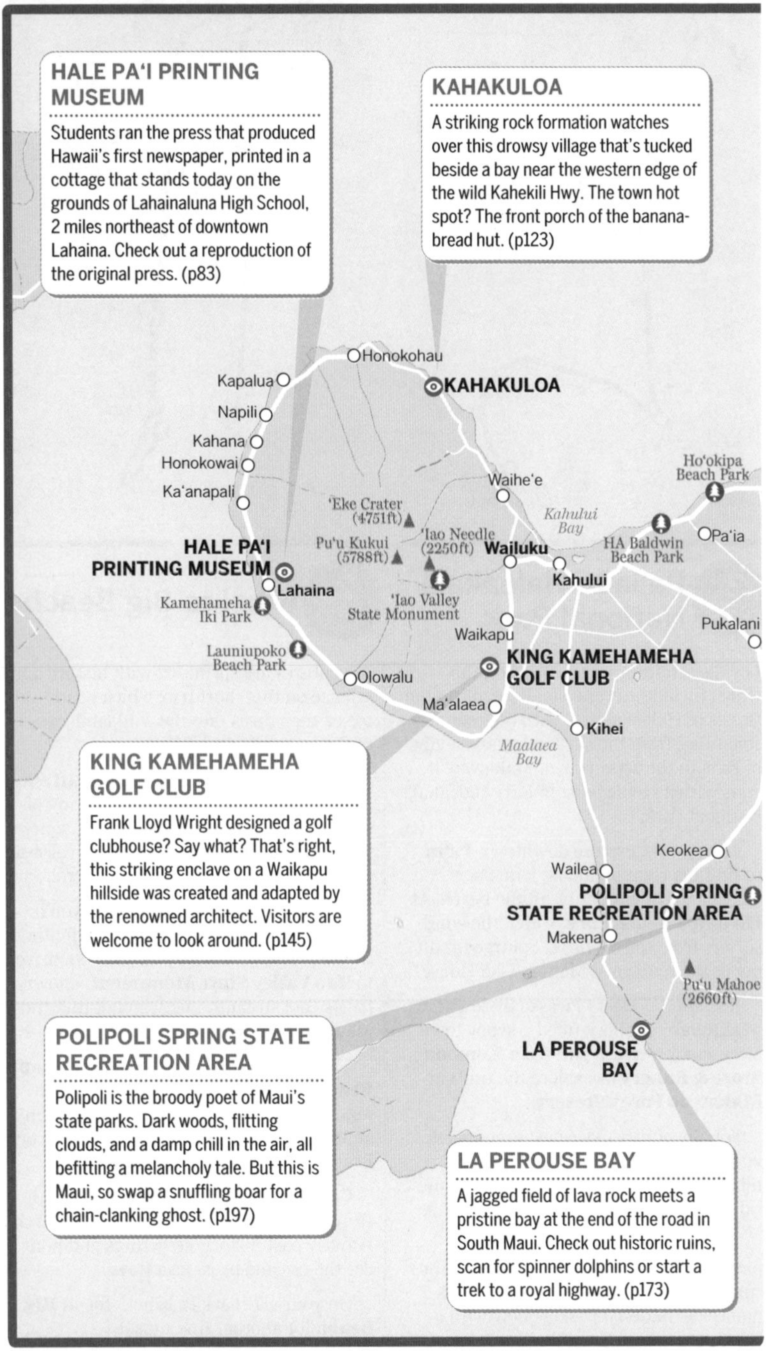

HALE PA'I PRINTING MUSEUM

Students ran the press that produced Hawaii's first newspaper, printed in a cottage that stands today on the grounds of Lahainaluna High School, 2 miles northeast of downtown Lahaina. Check out a reproduction of the original press. (p83)

KAHAKULOA

A striking rock formation watches over this drowsy village that's tucked beside a bay near the western edge of the wild Kahekili Hwy. The town hot spot? The front porch of the banana-bread hut. (p123)

KING KAMEHAMEHA GOLF CLUB

Frank Lloyd Wright designed a golf clubhouse? Say what? That's right, this striking enclave on a Waikapu hillside was created and adapted by the renowned architect. Visitors are welcome to look around. (p145)

POLIPOLI SPRING STATE RECREATION AREA

Polipoli is the broody poet of Maui's state parks. Dark woods, flitting clouds, and a damp chill in the air, all befitting a melancholy tale. But this is Maui, so swap a snuffling boar for a chain-clanking ghost. (p197)

LA PEROUSE BAY

A jagged field of lava rock meets a pristine bay at the end of the road in South Maui. Check out historic ruins, scan for spinner dolphins or start a trek to a royal highway. (p173)

ʻULAʻINO ROAD

Waterfalls on the Hana Hwy may blur in your memory. But the mysterious temple and the dark lava tube on ʻUlaʻino Rd? They'll likely stay sharp in your thoughts for years to come. Make time for these unique destinations. (p227)

KIPAHULU AREA

Unbeknownst to many, Haleakalā National Park holds two separate and distinct units. The lesser known is Kipahulu, a lush oceanfront wonderland of waterfalls, pools and one awesome bamboo grove. (p213)

PIʻILANI HIGHWAY

Rewards are earned on the challenging back road to Hana, where landscapes are lonely but dramatic: tropical flora, volcanic slopes, crumbly cliffs and vast ranchlands. (p234)

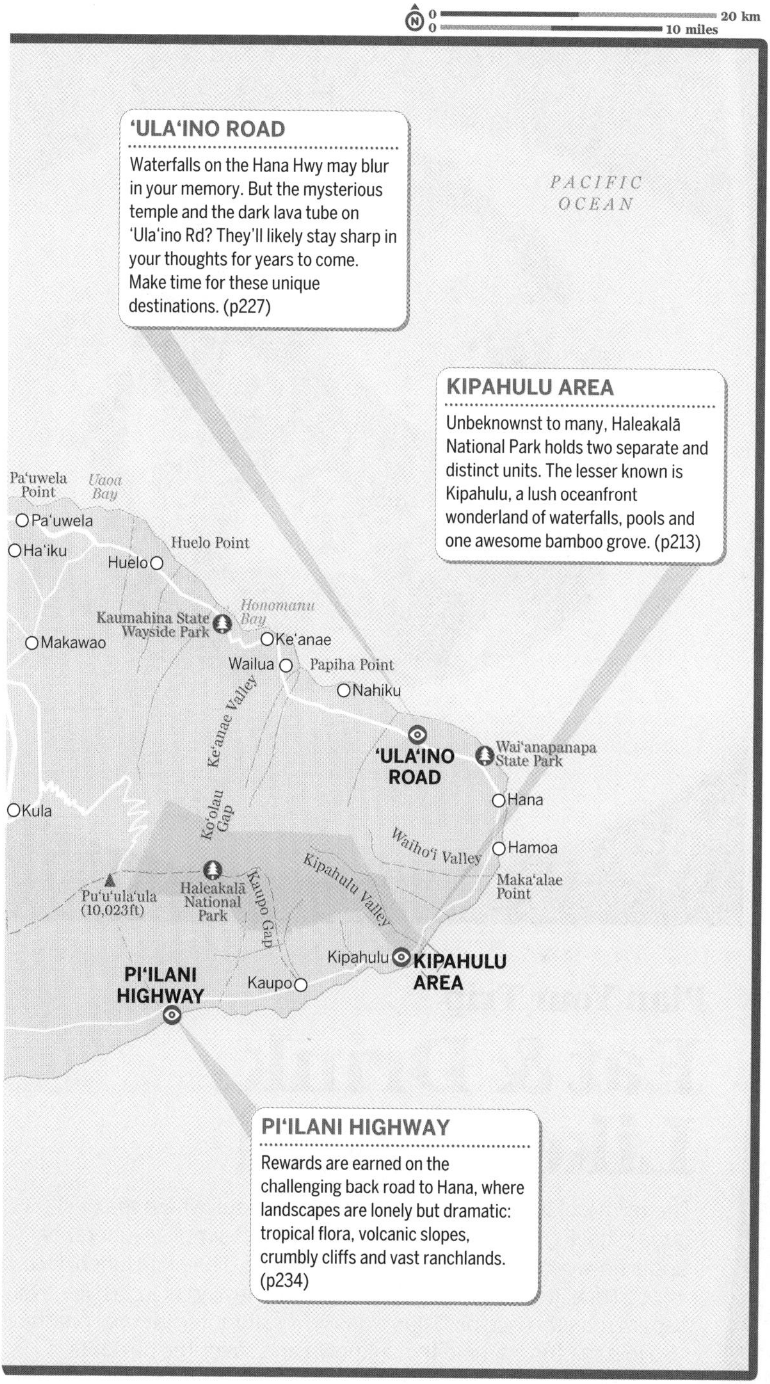

Loco moco

Plan Your Trip

Eat & Drink Like a Local

The term 'cuisine' sounds pretentious for Maui, where the best *pupu* (snacks) and entrees share a tasty and simple exuberance and a no-worries embrace of foreign flavors. The plate lunch, *loco moco* (rice, fried egg and hamburger with gravy) is a classic– even Spam *musubi* (rice ball) has a sassy, if salty, international charm. So join the fun, sample the unknown and savor the next bite.

The Year in Food

Year-round

It's always a good time to dig into produce grown in Maui's Upcountry. Due to the island's consistently warm tropical climate, most fruits and vegetables are harvested year-round.

Spring (April)

Head to Hana to celebrate taro, a unique and revered Hawaiian plant with a starchy potato-like quality. It's used in burgers, chips and mashed into a paste-like pudding called poi.

Fall (October)

To check out the range of produce grown on the island, wander the aisles at the Maui County Fair in early October in Kahului. As Halloween approaches, take the family to the pumpkin patch at Kula Country Farms, where there's also a corn maze.

Food Experiences

Meals of a Lifetime

➡ **Lahaina Grill** (p93) Savor seafood and steaks in artsy digs in downtown Lahaina.

➡ **Restaurant at Hotel Wailea** (p168) At the only Relais & Chateaux restaurant in Hawaii, seafood and sunsets impress.

➡ **Mama's Fish House** (p186) Celebrate a special occasion with exquisite fish, impeccable service and a prime beach view.

➡ **Monkeypod Kitchen** (p168) It's your favorite neighborhood restaurant, done Hawaiian style.

➡ **Geste Shrimp Truck** (p135) These hot bundles of spicy goodness demand a stack of napkins.

➡ **Mana Foods** (p187) What? An organic grocery? Well, have you tried the deli buffet? Feel the mana at this locals' joint.

➡ **Hana Farms Grill** (p243) *The* local choice for lunch, serving fresh seafood plates, grass-fed Maui beef burgers and more.

Best Breakfasts

➡ **Gazebo** (p116) Dig into macadamia-nut pancakes beside the Napili coast.

➡ **Plantation House** (p122) Did somebody says crab-cakes Benedict? Oh yes, they did.

➡ **Kihei Caffe** (p162) Quick and hearty is the name of the game at this Kihei hotspot.

➡ **808 Grindz Cafe** (p90) Arrive early for the satisfying local-style breakfast that costs only $8.08.

➡ **Leoda's Kitchen & Pie Shop** (p106) Locally sourced, and served with friendly style in Olowalu.

Dare to Try

Spam musubi A rice ball with a slice of fried Spam on top, or in the middle, wrapped with a strip of sushi nori (dried seaweed). It's commonly seen at grocers and convenience stores.

Local Specialties

Hawaiian food can be divided into three general categories: local food, Native Hawaiian and Hawaii Regional Cuisine.

Local Food

Day-to-day eats reflect the state's multicultural heritage, with Asian, Portuguese and Native Hawaiian influences the most immediately evident. Cheap, fattening and tasty, local food is also the stuff of cravings and comfort. Can be found across the island.

➡ **Plate lunch** The classic example of local food is the ubiquitous plate lunch. Picture this: chunky layers of tender *kalua* pork (cooked in an underground pit), a dollop of smooth, creamy macaroni and two hearty scoops of white rice. Yum, right? The pork can be swapped for other proteins, such as fried mahimahi (fish) or teriyaki chicken. Dished up almost like street food, the plate lunch is often served on disposable plates and eaten using chopsticks. A favorite breakfast combo includes fried egg and spicy Portuguese sausage (or bacon, ham, Spam etc) and, always, two scoops of rice.

➡ **Pupu** The local term used for all kinds of munchies or 'grazing' foods is *pupu*. Much more than just cheese and crackers, *pupu* represent the ethnic diversity of the islands and might include boiled peanuts in the shell, edamame (boiled fresh soybeans in the pod) and universal items such as fried shrimp.

➡ **Poke** Raw fish marinated in *shōyu* (soy sauce), oil, chili peppers, green onions and seaweed, *poke* comes in many varieties. Sesame ahi (yellowfin tuna) is particularly delicious and goes well with beer.

➡ **Shave ice** Ignore those joyless cynics who'll tell you that shave ice is nothing more than a snow cone. Shave ice is not just a snow cone. It's a tropical 21-gun salute – the most spectacular snow cone on earth. The specifics? The ice is shaved as fine as powdery snow, packed into a paper cone and drenched with sweet fruit-flavored syrups in dazzling hues. For added decadence, add Kaua'i cream, azuki beans and ice cream.

Native Hawaiian

Across Maui you'll find preparation methods and dishes that trace back to the island's first settlers.

➡ **Kalua pig and poi** These are the 'meat and potatoes' of Native Hawaiian food. *Kalua* pork is traditionally baked in an underground oven. Poi is served as the main side dish with every Hawaiian-style meal. The purple paste is pounded from cooked taro roots, with water added to make it pudding-like. It's nutritious and easily digested, but for many nonlocals it is also an acquired taste, largely because of its pasty consistency.

➡ **Laulau** This common main dish is a bundle of pork or chicken and salted butterfish wrapped in a taro leaf that's steamed until it has a soft spinach-like texture.

➡ **Baked 'ulu** Breadfruit that has a texture similar to a potato.

➡ **Haupia** This delicious pudding is made of coconut cream thickened with cornstarch or arrowroot. *Haupia* ice cream made on Maui offers a nice cross between traditional and modern cuisine.

Shave ice

Hawaii Regional Cuisine

Thirty years ago Hawaii was a culinary backwater. Sure, you could slum it on local *grinds* (food) and get by on the slew of midrange Asian eateries, but fine dining was typically a European-style meal that ignored locally grown fare and the islands' unique flavors.

Then, in the 1990s, a handful of island chefs smashed this tired mold and created a new cuisine, borrowing liberally from Hawaii's various ethnic influences. They partnered with local farmers, ranchers and fishers to highlight fresh local fare and transform their childhood favorites into grown-up, gourmet masterpieces. The movement was dubbed 'Hawaii Regional Cuisine' and the pioneering chefs became celebrities. A trio with Maui connections is Roy Yamaguchi of Roy's Ka'anapali (p113), Beverly Gannon of Hali'imaile General Store (p189) and Mark Ellman of Frida's Mexican Beach House (p93), Mala Ocean Tavern (p93) and Honu Seafood & Pizza (p93) in Lahaina.

The real catchwords for Hawaii Regional Cuisine are fresh, organic and locally

Gazebo restaurant (p116), Napili

grown. Think Upcountry greens, Maui chèvre (goat cheese), Kula onions, free-range Hana beef and locally caught fish. The spread of the movement has been a boon to small-scale farmers, who are contributing to a greening of Maui's gardens and menus.

How to Eat & Drink

When to Eat

Maui locals eat meals early and on the dot. Restaurants are packed around the habitual mealtimes, but they clear out an hour or two later, as locals are not lingerers. If you dine at 8:30pm, you might not have to wait at all. But bear in mind that restaurants also close early and night owls must hunt for places to eat.

➡ **Breakfast** Typically 6am for the day's first meal.

➡ **Lunch** Noon.

➡ **Dinner** Locals eat at 6pm.

Where to Eat

For top-end restaurants in Maui, book a week in advance, and earlier during the winter holiday season.

➡ **Plate-lunch eateries** Great choices for quick takeout. They pack things tidily so you can carry your meal to a nearby beach for an impromptu picnic lunch. One tip: at lunchtime, decide what you want before reaching the register. Lines typically move quickly and the indecisive can muck up the system.

➡ **Food trucks** Known as *kaukau* (food) wagons, food trucks have become common on Maui. They typically park near the beach or shopping centers. Bring cash.

➡ **Cafes** The best places to relax over a good lunch in an engaging setting at a fair price. If the setting isn't important, there are plenty of diner-style Asian restaurants with Formica tables and vinyl chairs, no view and no decor. They generally offer quick service and often have surprisingly good food at decent prices.

➡ **Top-end restaurants** These are outright impressive and include some of the most highly rated chef-driven places in Hawaii. These establishments are typically found on prime oceanfront perches as well as in resorts

FOOD GLOSSARY

Hawaii's cuisine is multiethnic and so is the lingo.

adobo – Filipino chicken or pork cooked in vinegar, *shōyu,* garlic and spices

'awa – kava, a Polynesian plant used to make a mildly intoxicating drink

bentō – Japanese-style box lunch

broke da mout – delicious; literally 'broke the mouth'

char siu – Cantonese barbecued pork

chirashizushi – assorted sashimi served over rice

crack seed – Chinese-style preserved fruit; a salty, sweet and/or sour snack

donburi – Japanese-style large bowl of rice topped with a protein (eg pork *katsu*)

furikake – catch-all Japanese seasoning or condiment, usually dry and sprinkled atop rice; in Hawaii, sometimes mixed into *poke*

grind – to eat

grinds – food (usually local)

guava – fruit with green or yellow rind, moist pink flesh and lots of edible seeds

haupia – coconut-cream custard, often thickened with arrowroot or cornstarch

hulihuli chicken – rotisserie-cooked chicken with island-style barbecue sauce

imu – underground earthen oven used to cook *kalua* pig and other luau food

'inamona – roasted, ground *kukui* (candlenut), used as a condiment (eg mixed into *poke*)

izakaya – Japanese pub serving tapas-style dishes

kalbi – Korean-style grilled meats, typically marinated short ribs

kalo – Hawaiian word for taro, often pounded into poi

kalua – Hawaiian method of cooking pork or other luau food, traditionally in an *imu*

kare-kare – Filipino oxtail stew

katsu – Japanese deep-fried cutlets, usually pork or chicken

kaukau – food

laulau – bundle of pork or chicken and salted butterfish, wrapped in taro and *ti* leaves and steamed

li hing mui – sweet-salty preserved plum, a type of crack seed; also refers to the flavor powder

liliko'i – passion fruit

loco moco – hearty dish of rice, fried egg and hamburger patty topped with gravy or other condiments

lomilomi salmon – minced, salted salmon with diced tomato and green onion

luau – Hawaiian feast

mai tai – tiki-bar drink typically containing rum and tropical fruit juices

malasada – sugar-coated, fried Portuguese doughnut (no hole), often filled with flavored custard

manapua – Chinese *bao* (baked or steamed buns) with *char siu* or other fillings

manjū – Japanese steamed or baked cake, often filled with sweet bean paste

and golf-course clubhouses. Most forgo the pompous fastidiousness common to upscale urban restaurants on the US mainland. Meals start at $30 per person. To sample top cuisine at a good price, visit during happy hour, when prices of appetizers are often reduced.

mochi – Japanese pounded-rice cake, sticky and sweet

musubi – Japanese *onigiri* (rice ball or triangle) wrapped in *nori*

noni – type of mulberry with strong-smelling yellow fruit, used medicinally by Hawaiians

nori – Japanese seaweed, usually dried

ogo – crunchy seaweed, sometimes added to *poke; limu* in Hawaiian

okazu-ya – Japanese takeout delicatessen, often specializing in home-style Hawaiian and local dishes

'ono – delicious

'ono kine grinds – good food

pau hana – happy hour (literally 'stop work')

pipikaula – Hawaiian beef jerky

poha – cape gooseberry

poi – staple Hawaiian starch made of steamed, mashed taro *(kalo)*

poke – cubed, marinated raw fish

ponzu – Japanese citrus sauce

pupu – snacks or appetizers

saimin – local-style noodle soup

shave ice – cup of finely shaved ice doused with sweet syrups

shōyu – soy sauce

star fruit – translucent green-yellow fruit with five ribs like the points of a star, and sweet, juicy pulp

taro – plant with edible corm used to make poi and with edible leaves to wrap around *laulau; kalo* in Hawaiian

uni – sea urchin

Hawaii's Fish

ahi – yellowfin or bigeye tuna; red flesh, excellent rare or raw

aku – skipjack tuna; red flesh, strong flavor; *katsu* in Japanese

'ama'ama – striped mullet; delicate white flesh

awa – milkfish; tender white flesh

mahimahi – dolphinfish or dorado; firm pink flesh

moi – Pacific threadfish; flaky white flesh, rich flavor; reserved for royalty in ancient times

nairagi – striped marlin; firm flesh, colored pink to deep red-orange; *a'u* in Hawaiian

onaga – long-tail red snapper; soft and moist

ono – wahoo; white-fleshed and flaky

opah – moonfish; firm and rich flesh; colored pink,orange, white or dark red

'opakapaka – pink snapper; delicate flavor; firm flesh

tako – octopus; chewy texture; *h'e* in Hawaiian

➡ **Groceries** Chains and locally owned markets can be found across the island. You'll find local specialties such as *poke* bowls and Spam *musubi* at most of them.

EQROY / SHUTTERSTOCK ©

ROCKSTERWHO / GETTY IMAGES ©

Top: Fresh fruit at farmers market

Bottom: Spam *musubi*

➡ **Farmers markets and produce stands** Local farms and food purveyors share their fare at kiosk-lined farmers markets in West Maui, Central Maui, South Maui and the Upcountry. Most farmers markets occur once per week. Fruit and farm stands are common along the Road to Hana, in Hana and in Kula, but it's estimated that about 85% of Hawaii's food supply is imported. If absolute freshness matters to you, choose locally raised beef, island-caught fish and Maui-grown produce.

Habits & Customs

➡ **Food portions** Locals tend to consider quantity as important as quality – and the portion sizes are telling, especially at plate-lunch places. If you're a light eater, feel free to split a meal or take home the leftovers.

➡ **Potluck meals** Home entertainment for local folks always revolves around food, which is usually served 'potluck style' with all the guests adding to the anything-goes smorgasbord. Locals rarely serve dinner in one-at-a-time courses. Rather, meals are served 'family style,' where diners help themselves. Throwaway paper plates and wooden chopsticks make for an easy clean-up, and the rule is 'all you can eat' (and they definitely mean it!).

➡ **Dinner guest** If you're invited to someone's home, show up on time and bring a dish – preferably homemade, but a bakery cake or *manjū* (Japanese cakes filled with sweet bean paste) from Sam Sato's (p142) in Wailuku are always a certain hit. Remove your shoes at the door. And don't be surprised if you're forced to take home a plate of leftovers.

Menu Decoder

You'll find a few staples in just about every Hawaiian meal. One word of caution: Maui's attempts at nonlocal classics such as pizza, bagels, croissants and southern BBQ can be disappointing. Stick with local-local food.

➡ **Sticky white rice** More than just a side dish in Hawaii, sticky white rice is a culinary building block, an integral partner in everyday meals. Without rice, Spam *musubi* would be a slice of canned meat. *Loco moco* would be nothing more than an egg-covered hamburger. And without two-scoop rice, the plate lunch would be a ho-hum conversation between meat and macaroni, rather than a multicultural party. And by the way, sticky white rice means sticky white rice. While you might find couscous or mashed potatoes at fancy restaurants, day-to-day meals are served with sticky white rice. Not flaky rice. Not wild rice. Not flavored rice. And definitely not Uncle Ben's. Locals can devour mounds of the stuff and it typically comes as two scoops. The top condiment is soy sauce, known by its Japanese name *shōyu,* which combines well with sharp Asian flavors such as ginger, green onion and garlic.

➡ **Protein** Meat, chicken or fish are often key components of a meal, too. For quick, cheap eating, locals devour anything tasty, from Portuguese sausage to hamburger steak to corned beef. But the dinner-table highlight is always seafood, especially freshly caught fish.

SPAM A LOT

Spam arrived in Hawaii during WWII, when fresh meat imports were replaced by this standard GI ration. By war's end, Hawaiians had developed a taste for the fatty canned stuff. Today, Hawaiians consume about eight million cans of Spam annually!

Spam looks and tastes different in Hawaii. It's eaten cooked (typically sautéed to a light crispiness in sweetened *shōyu*), not straight from the can, and served as a tasty meat dish.

Kitesurfing, Kanaha Beach Park (p129)

Plan Your Trip

On the Water

The Pacific Ocean is Maui's ultimate playground. And take note: when renting ocean gear, you'll pay premium prices at resort beach shacks. Stop by a surf or snorkel shop in town for the best rates. Buy coral-safe sunscreen before hitting the water.

Best Beaches for Water Sports

Honolua Bay

Drop in for surfing (p120) in winter, snorkeling in summer.

Ka'anapali Beach

Stroll the beach walk at this happening beach (p107) for your pick of activities.

Keawakapu Beach

Take a sunset swim at Keawakapu (p153).

Malu'aka Beach

The best place to snorkel with turtles (p170).

Kapalua Beach

Enjoy scenic and low-key paddleboarding at Kapalua (p117), followed by a bit of snorkeling.

DT Fleming Beach Park

The backdrop here is South Pacific scenery (p119), with waves that are best for experienced surfers and bodysurfers.

Bodysurfing & Bodyboarding

If you want to catch your waves lying down, bodysurfing and bodyboarding are suitable water activities for anybody.

There are good beginner to intermediate shorebreaks at the Kama'ole Beach Parks and Charley Young Beach in Kihei, and at Ulua Beach and Wailea Beach in Wailea. Experienced bodysurfers should head to DT Fleming Beach Park and Slaughterhouse Beach in Kapalua, Big Beach in Makena, and HA Baldwin Beach Park near Pa'ia.

Special bodysurfing flippers, which are smaller than snorkel fins, will help you paddle out. Bodyboard rentals range from $8 to $20 per day.

Kayaking

There's a lot to see underwater just off Maui's coast, so most outfitters offer snorkel-kayak combos. The top spot is Makena, an area rich with marine life, including sea turtles, dolphins and wintering humpback whales. In the calmer summer months, another excellent destination is Honolua–Mokule'ia Bay Marine Life Conservation District at Honolua Bay and Mokule'ia Bay north of Kapalua, where there are turtles aplenty and dolphin sightings. Water conditions on Maui are usually clearest and calmest early in the morning, so that's an ideal time to go.

For tours in South Maui try Aloha Kayaks (p172), Hawaiian Paddle Sports (p172) and South Pacific Kayaks & Outfitters (p172), which also provides kayaks for rent.

Kitesurfing

Kitesurfing is a bit like strapping on a snowboard, grabbing a huge kite and riding with the wind across the water. It looks damn hard and certainly takes stamina, but if you already know how to ride a board, there's a good chance you'll master it quickly. According to surf legend Robby Naish, who pioneered kitesurfing, it's the most accessible of all extreme sports.

There's no better place to learn than on Maui's Kite Beach, at the western end of Kanaha Beach Park. Visiting kitesurfers need to check with locals to clarify the no-fly zones. Get the lowdown from the Maui Kiteboarding Association (www.mauikiteboardingassociation.com) and Maui Kitesurfing Community (www.mauikitesurf.org).

Outrigger Canoeing

Polynesians were Hawaii's first settlers, paddling outrigger canoes across 2000 miles of open ocean – so you could say canoeing was Hawaii's earliest sport. The first Europeans to arrive were awestruck at the skill Hawaiians displayed, timing launches and landings perfectly and paddling among the waves like dolphins.

Today, canoe clubs keep the outrigger tradition alive. Hawaiian Sailing Canoe Adventures (p167) in Wailea and Hawaiian Paddle Sports (p172) in Makena offer guided outrigger canoe tours, sharing cultural insights as you paddle along the coast. Some resorts, including Andaz Maui (p167), offer tours that are open to nonguests.

Stand-Up Paddleboarding

The stand-up paddle surf invasion is complete. For proof, drive from Pāpalaua State Wayside Park (p147) northwest to Lahaina and look seaward. Platoons of paddle-wielding surfers, standing on 9ft to 11ft boards, are plying the waves just off the coast at seemingly every beachside park.

Abbreviated to SUP, and known in Hawaii as *ku hoe he'e nalu,* the sport is great for less limber adventurers, as you don't need to pop up into a stance. It takes coordination, but it's no harder than regular surfing – although you should be a strong swimmer. Consider a class with paddle surf champ Maria Souza (p159) in Kihei, or with the instructors at Maui Wave Riders (p86) in Lahaina. Beachside rentals run $30 to $55 per hour.

Stand-up paddleboarding

PARKS & BEACHES

Details about county parks and beaches in Maui, including contact information and lifeguard availability, can be found on the Maui County government website (www.mauicounty.gov).

Whale-Watching

With their tail slaps, head lunges and spy hops, humpback whales know how to impress a crowd. Each winter, about 10,000 of these graceful leviathans – two thirds of the entire North Pacific humpback whale population – come to the shallow coastal waters off the Hawaiian Islands to breed and give birth. And like other discerning visitors to Hawaii, these intelligent creatures favor Maui. The western coastline of the island is their chief birthing and nursing ground. Luckily for whale-watchers, humpbacks are coast-huggers, preferring shallow waters to protect their newborn calves.

Much of Hawaii's ocean waters are protected as the Hawaiian Islands Humpback Whale National Marine Sanctuary (p158), whose Kihei headquarters is abuzz with cool whale happenings. Along the coast there's great whale-watching at many places, including Papawai Point (p106), and along beach walks in Kihei and Wailea.

To get within splashing distance of 40-ton leviathans acrobatically jumping out of the water, take a whale-watching cruise. No one does them better than Lahaina's Pacific Whale Foundation (p86), a conservation group that takes pride in its green, naturalist-led trips. Maui's peak whale-watching season is from January

Windsurfing

through March, although whales are usually around for a month or so on either side of those dates.

Windsurfing

This sport reaches its peak on Maui. Ho'okipa Beach, near Pa'ia, hosts top international windsurfing competitions. The wind and waves combine at Ho'okipa in a way that makes gravity seem arbitrary, but this beach is for experts only, as hazards include razor-sharp coral and dangerous shorebreaks. For kick-ass wind without risking life and limb, the place to launch is Kanaha Beach in Kahului, but avoid the busy weekends when the water becomes a sea of sails.

Overall, Maui is known for its consistent winds. Windsurfers can find action in any month, but, as a general rule, the best wind is from June to September and the flattest spells are from December to February.

At Ma'alaea, where the winds are usually strong and blow offshore toward Kaho'olawe, conditions are ripe for advanced speed sailing. In winter, on those rare occasions when kona (leeward) winds blow, the Ma'alaea–Kihei area can be the only place windy enough to sail.

Most windsurfing shops are based in Kahului and handle rentals, lessons and gear sales.

Plan Your Trip

Diving & Snorkeling Maui

The underwater scenery around Maui is just as impressive as what you'll see on land. Dive companies run frequent trips to hotspots such as Molokini. Many of the best snorkeling areas are only a few kicks from shore.

Diving & Snorkeling Outfitters

Lahaina Divers

Boat dives and snorkeling trips departing from Lahaina (p83).

Maui Dive Shop

Boat dives and snorkeling out of Ma'alaea (p159).

Maui Dreams Dive Co

Friendly outfit (p158) leading shore dives and boat dives from Ma'alaea.

Pacific Whale Foundation

Informative snorkeling trips (p148) departing from Ma'alaea and Lahaina.

Aloha Kayaks

Paddle (p172) from Makena Landing and West Maui.

Hawaiian Paddle Sports

Kayak-snorkeling trips (p172) departing Makena Landing and West Maui.

South Pacific Kayaks & Outfitters

Kayak and snorkel (p172) off Makena Landing.

Diving

Excellent visibility, warm water temperatures, hundreds of rare fish species – Maui is a diving hub for a reason. Here you can often see spinner dolphins, green sea turtles, manta rays and moray eels. With luck, you might even hear humpback whales singing underwater – you'll never forget it.

Most dive operations on Maui offer a full range of dives as well as refresher and advanced certification courses. Introductory dives for beginners get you beneath the surface in just a couple of hours. Experienced divers needn't bring anything other than a swimsuit and certification card. Don't monkey around with activity desks – book directly with the dive operators.

On Maui, the granddaddy of dives is crescent-shaped Molokini. The other prime destination is the untouched Cathedrals on the south side of Lana'i, which takes its name from the amazing underwater caverns, arches and connecting passages.

For a basic but helpful map of dive and snorkel spots around Maui, pick up Maui Dive Shop's free pull-out map at its Kihei store (www.mauidiveshop.com).

Responsible Diving

The popularity of diving is placing immense pressure on many sites. Consider the following tips to help preserve the ecology and beauty of reefs while on Maui:

- Avoid touching living marine organisms with your body or dragging equipment across the reef. Polyps can be damaged by even the gentlest contact. Never stand on coral. If you must hold on to the reef, touch only exposed rock or dead coral.
- Be conscious of your fins. Even without contact, the surge from heavy fin strokes near the reef can damage delicate organisms. When treading water in shallow reef areas, take care not to kick up clouds of sand. Settling sand can easily smother the delicate organisms of the reef.
- Protect fragile reefs by wearing a coral-safe sunscreen.
- Don't use reef anchors and take care not to ground boats on coral.
- Minimize your disturbance of marine animals. It is illegal to approach endangered marine species too closely; these include whales, dolphins, sea turtles and the Hawaiian monk seal. In particular, don't ride on the backs of turtles!
- Practice and maintain proper buoyancy control. Major damage can be done by divers descending too fast and colliding with the reef. Make sure you are correctly weighted and that your weight belt is positioned so that you stay horizontal.
- Resist the temptation to feed marine animals. You might disturb their normal eating habits, encourage aggressive behavior or feed them food that is detrimental to their health.
- Spend as little time in underwater caves as possible, as your air bubbles may be caught within the roof and leave previously submerged organisms high and dry.
- Don't leave any rubbish, and remove any litter you find. Plastics in particular are a serious threat to marine life. Turtles can mistake plastic for jellyfish and eat it.
- Don't collect (or buy) coral or shells. Aside from the ecological damage, taking home marine souvenirs depletes the beauty of a site and spoils the enjoyment of others.
- **Divers Alert Network** (DAN; ☎800-446-2671, emergency 919-684-9111; www.diversalertnetwork.org; membership per year from $35) gives advice on diving emergencies, insurance, decompression services, illness and injury.

SNORKELING SAFETY

The leading cause of death for tourists in Hawaii is not shark attacks or car accidents. Nope, it's drowning while snorkeling, which seems surprising when you compare snorkeling to more adrenaline-charged activities such as ziplining and kiteboarding. But the numbers bear it out – on average there are 21 fatal drownings per year in Hawaii, and the numbers are spiking upward, with 31 deaths in 2018. More than 90% of the victims are visitors. Increased tourism probably plays into the spiking numbers, but another culprit may be full-face snorkel masks, which may have a stressful effect on a snorkeler's ability to breathe, particularly for novice snorkelers. Victims also tend to be men in their 50s and 60s, and 40% of them have heart conditions. To reduce your risk of drowning, swim in pairs, watch currents and know your physical abilities. A fair number of drownings have occurred at Ka'anapali Beach around Pu'u Keka'a (Black Rock).

Snorkeling

The waters around Maui are a kaleidoscope of coral, colorful fish and super-big sea turtles. Best of all, you don't need special skills to view them. If you can float, you can snorkel – it's a cinch to learn. If you're a newbie, fess up at the dive shop or beach hut where you rent your snorkel gear – mask, snorkel and fins – and they'll show you everything you need to know. And it's cheap: most snorkel sets rent for $12 or less per day.

Snorkelers should get an early start. Not only does the first half of the morning offer the calmest water, but at some of the popular places crowds begin to show by 10am.

The hottest spots for snorkeling cruises are the largely submerged volcanic crater of Molokini, off Maui's southwest coast, and Lana'i's Hulopo'e Beach. Both brim with untouched coral and an amazing variety of sea life.

Remember to wear reef-safe sunscreen lotion before kicking off. Many modern

Maui: Diving & Snorkeling

HONOLUA BAY

A short walk through tropical flora ends at this pristine bay, a conservation district loaded with tropical fish. Reefs and coral hug the edge of the bay. (p120)

PU'U KEKA'A (BLACK ROCK)

The legendary lava promontory is an easy snorkel spot if you're staying in Ka'anapali. Look for tropical fish, coral and the occasional green sea turtle. Strong swimmers may find more fish in the cove at the tip of the rock. (p108)

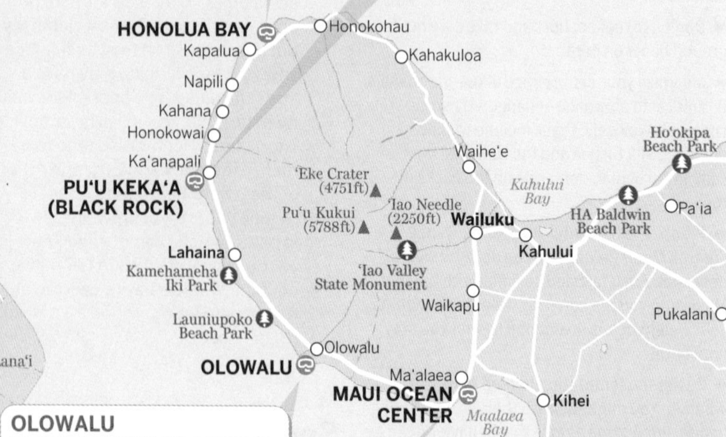

OLOWALU

Check out the shallow coral reef here if you're driving toward Lahaina from the airport and just can't wait to look for fish. (p105)

MAUI OCEAN CENTER

Drop into the 750,000-gallon ocean tank at this oceanside aquarium for an inside dive with reef sharks and hammerheads. (p147)

MOLOKINI CRATER

Hop aboard a boat for a snorkel or dive trip to this crescent-shaped volcanic rim, a marine conservation district. Boats fill the inner rim in the morning, when visibility is best. Experienced divers also like to explore the back wall. (p51)

MAKENA BAY

Paddle out into the bay in a kayak then hop overboard to snorkel past colorful fish and green sea turtles. There's even an underwater arch to marvel at. Scan for whales in winter. Also a popular spot for shore dives. (p170)

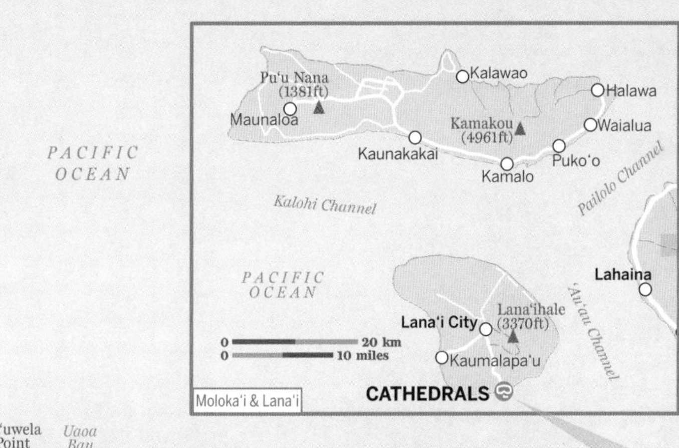

CATHEDRALS

Ride a boat to the south shores of Lana'i for fantastic diving. Kick through grottoes and swoosh through a short tube. Look for sharks, turtles and tropical fish. (p258)

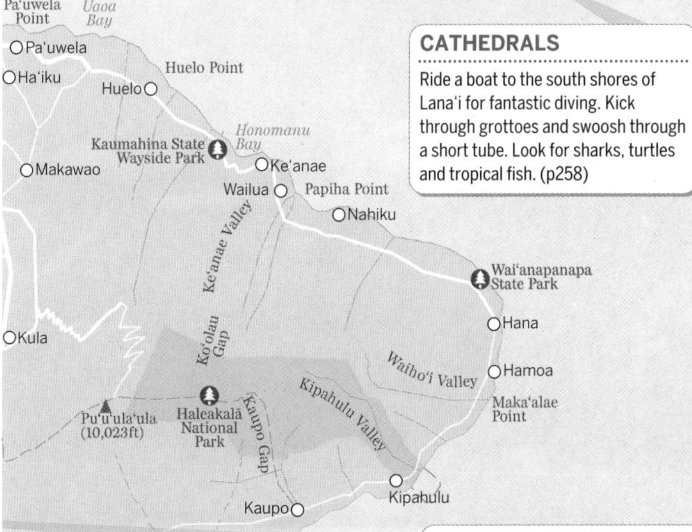

MALU'AKA BEACH

Dubbed Turtle Town, this is the place to come if you'd like to glide beside *honu*, Maui's beloved green sea turtles. Remember, look but don't touch. Fantastic coral is about 100 yards out – head south. (p170)

'AHIHI-KINA'U NATURAL AREA RESERVE

Fishing is prohibited in this natural reserve near the edge of an old lava flow, so there are fish aplenty. The secret is out, however, and this remote spot can now see 500 snorkelers per day. Arrive early and enter the water at the fish sign. It's a good spot to look for rainbow parrot fish. (p173)

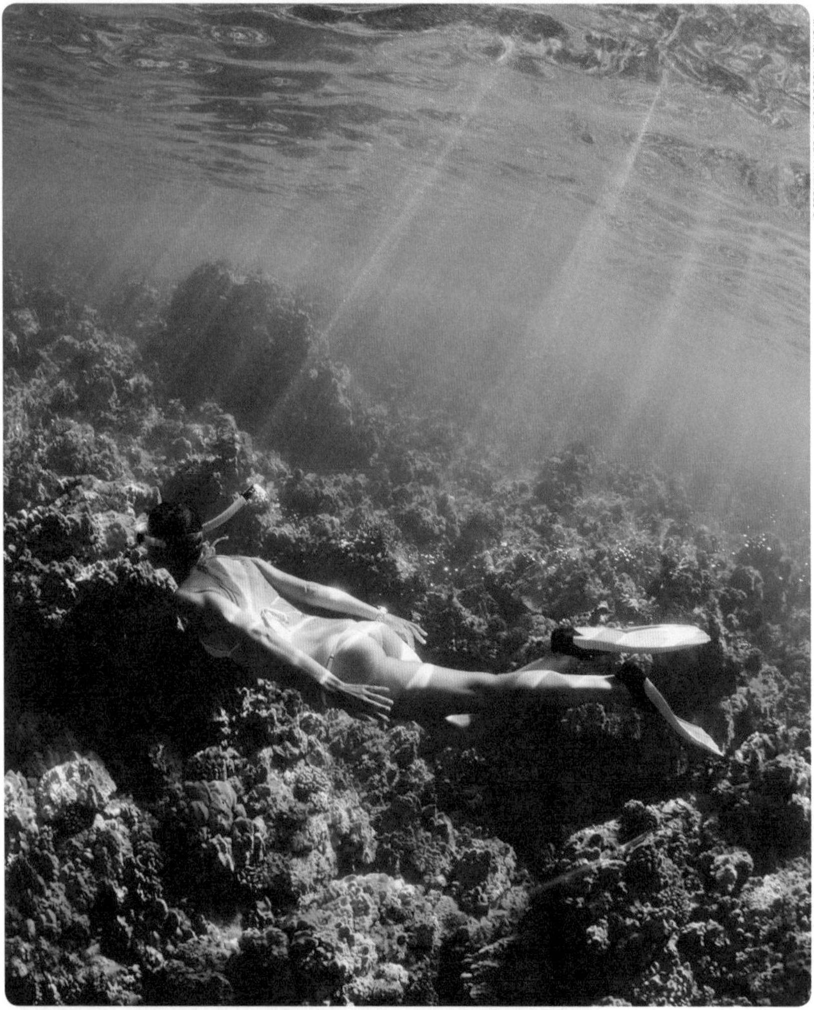

M SWIET PRODUCTIONS / GETTY IMAGES ©

BEAT J KORNER / SHUTTERSTOCK ©

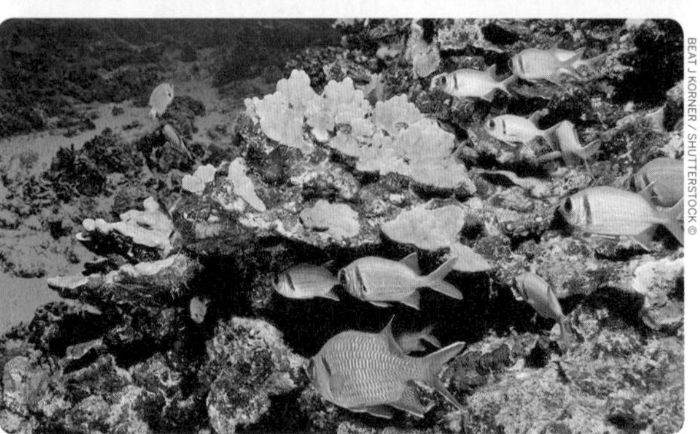

Top: Snorkeling, Wailea (p165)

Bottom: Coral, Molokini Crater

MOLOKINI CRATER

This fascinating volcanic crater lies midway between the islands of Maui and Kaho'olawe. Molokini is extremely popular with travelers, and according to one study, this underwater site may see 1000 visitors in a day. Half of the crater rim has eroded, leaving a crescent-moon shape that rises 160ft above the ocean surface, with a mere 18 acres of rocky land high and dry. But it's what's beneath the surface that draws the crowds. Snorkelers and divers will be thrilled by steep walls, ledges, white-tipped reef sharks, manta rays, turtles and abundant fish.

The legends about Molokini are myriad. One says Molokini was a beautiful woman who was turned to stone by jealous Pele, goddess of fire and volcanoes. Another claims one of Pele's lovers angered her by secretly marrying a *mo'o* (shape-shifting water lizard). Pele chopped the sacred lizard in half, leaving Molokini as its tail and Pu'u Ola'i in Makena as its head. Yet another tale alleges that Molokini, which means 'many ties' in Hawaiian, is the umbilical cord left over from the birth of Kaho'olawe.

The coral reef that extends outward from Molokini is awesome, though it's lost some of its variety over the years. Most of the black coral, once prolific in Molokini's deeper waters, made its way into Lahaina jewelry stores before the island was declared a marine conservation district in 1977. During WWII the US Navy shelled Molokini for target practice, and live bombs are still occasionally spotted on the crater floor. In 2006 a tour boat with an inexperienced captain sank at Molokini. No one was injured, but after an inept salvage job, 1200 coral colonies had been destroyed. The company incurred a $396,000 state-imposed fine.

In early 2019, Hawaii's Department of Land & Natural Resources (DLNR) proposed a limit on the number of commercial boats allowed at the site per day – possibly to only a dozen. The DLNR argued that the massive number of annual visitors to Molokini – more than 360,000 – may be driving away predator fish, which are an important factor in maintaining the overall health of the reef. The state legislature passed a very watered down version of the proposal – one supported by commercial vessel owners – which capped the daily vessels at Molokini to half the number of available commercial use permits, which could be as high as 40. The bill was vetoed by Governor Ige, who said it did not address the overcrowding concerns of the DNLR.

There are a few things to consider when planning a Molokini excursion. The water is calmest and clearest in the morning, so don't fall for discounted afternoon tours – go out early for the smoothest sailing and best conditions. For snorkelers, there's simply not much to see when the water's choppy. The main departure points for Molokini trips are Ma'alaea and Lahaina Harbors. You'll get out there quicker if you hop on a boat from Ma'alaea, which is closer to Molokini. Going from Lahaina adds on more sail time, but in winter it'll also increase the possibilities for spotting whales along the way, so it's sometimes worth an extra hour out of your day.

lotions are reef killers. Safe ingredients are titanium dioxide and zinc oxide. Avoid sunscreens with oxybenzone and other chemical UV-radiation filters.

Best Snorkeling Spots

➡ **Honolua Bay** (p120) Fish-filled reefs and loads of coral in West Maui.

➡ **'Ahihi-Kina'u Natural Area Reserve** (p173) Enter the water beside the 'fish' signs in this marine conservation area.

➡ **Molokini Crater** See colorful tropical fish inside a volcanic rim.

➡ **Malu'aka Beach** (p170) Come to Turtle Beach to ogle graceful green sea turtles.

➡ **Ulua Beach** (p165) For easy-access snorkeling in Wailea, grab a parking spot at this beach near the Andaz Maui resort.

Surfing, Honolua Bay (p120)

Plan Your Trip

Surfing Maui

Maui lies smack in the path of all the major swells that race across the Pacific, creating legendary peaks for surfing. The north shore sees the biggest waves, which roll in from November to March, though some places, including famed Hoʻokipa Beach, have good wave action year-round.

Helpful Resources

Knowing the when and size of the next swell is essential. This is where streaming webcams, surf reports and forecasts come in. For Maui, the following sources are very useful; and don't forget common sense – if conditions look intimidating, stay on shore.

Surf News Network

Provides comprehensive island weather-and-wave reports (www.surfnewsnetwork.com).

Live Surf Cam Hawaii

An index to scores of live surf cams on Maui and across the state (http://livesurfcamhawaii.com).

Omaui

Get surf and weather reports here (http://omaui.com).

Surfline

Great omnibus site with massive amounts of information (www.surfline.com).

Swellwatch

Has surf reports and forecasts (https://forecast.surfer.com).

Maui Surf Beaches & Breaks

For action sports, head to Maui's beaches. On the north shore, near the town of Ha'iku, is the infamous big-wave spot known as Pe'ahi, or Jaws (p184). Determined pro surfers, such as Laird Hamilton, Dave Kalama and Derrick Doerner, helped put the planet's largest, most perfect wave on the international map. Jaws' waves are so high that surfers must be towed into them by wave runners. At Ho'okipa Beach (p177) near Pa'ia, surfers have their pick of four different breaks, which can churn out large waves in winter.

Not into risking your life? No worries, there are plenty of other waves to ride. Maui's west side, especially around Lahaina, offers a wider variety of surf. The fun reef breaks at Lahaina Breakwall (p86) and Harbor cater to both beginner and intermediate surfers. To the south is Ma'alaea Pipeline (p147), a fickle right-hand reef break that is often considered one of the fastest waves in the world. On the island's northwest corner is majestic Honolua Bay (p120). Its right point break works best on winter swells and is considered one of the premier points not just in Hawaii, but around the world.

Gentler shorebreaks good for bodysurfing can be found around Pa'ia, Kapalua and the beaches between Kihei and Makena.

Beginners

Newbies should head directly to Lahaina, which has beginner-friendly waves and instructors who can get you up on a board in just one lesson. You won't be tearing across mammoth curls, but riding a board is easier than it looks and there's no better place to get started. Two primo owner-operated surf schools with the perfect blend of patience and persistence are Goofy Foot Surf School (p86) and Maui Surf Clinics (p86). In South Maui, head to The Cove (p159) for good beginner waves. For lessons try Maui Wave Riders (p159), just up the street.

Surfing Etiquette

Just as Hawaiian royalty had certain breaks reserved just for them, so goes it on Hawaii's surf breaks. Respect locals and local customs or you might ruffle feathers (and end up with a bad reputation). Tourists are welcome, but deference to local riders is always recommended.

In the water, basic surf etiquette is vital. The person closest to the peak of the wave has the right of way. When somebody is already up and riding, don't take off on the wave in front of them. Don't paddle straight through the lineup. Rather, head out through the channel where the waves aren't breaking and then find your way into the lineup. When you wipe out – and

Maui: Surfing

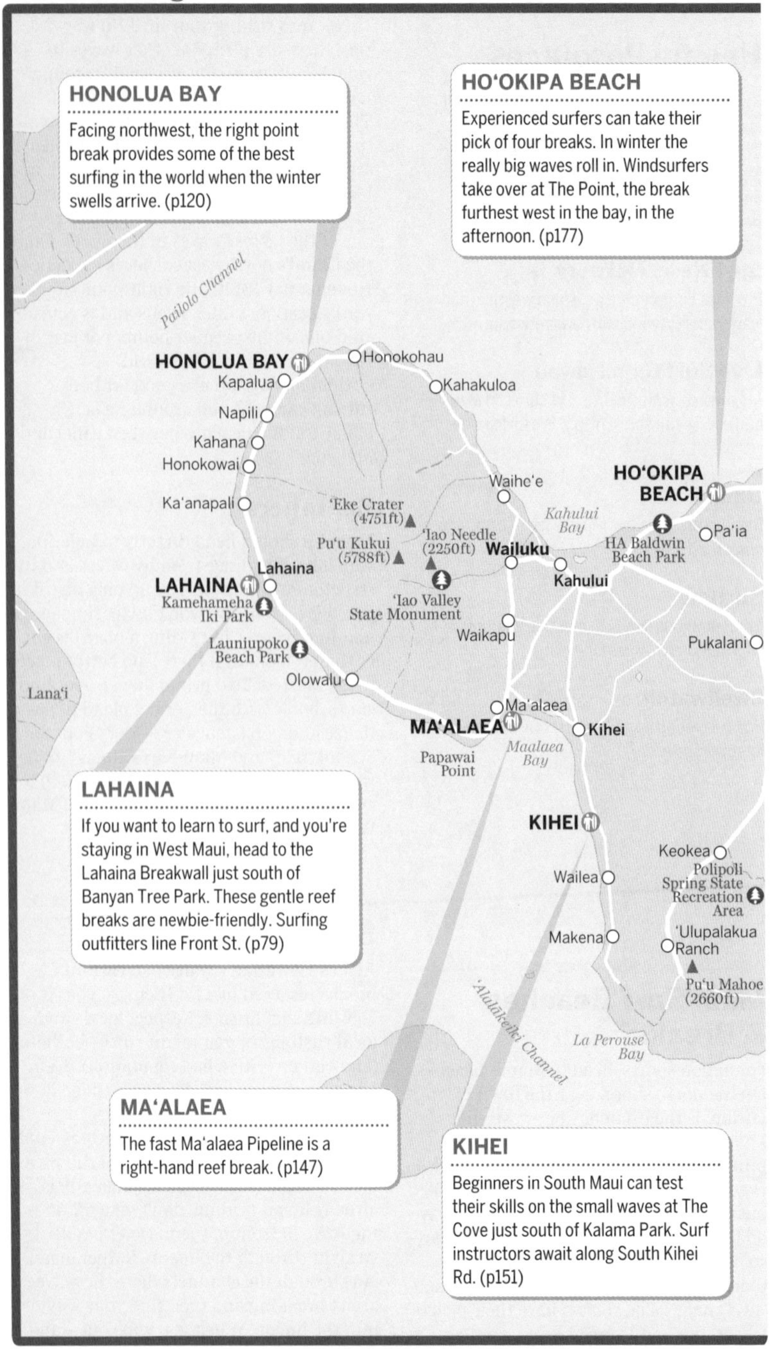

HONOLUA BAY

Facing northwest, the right point break provides some of the best surfing in the world when the winter swells arrive. (p120)

HO'OKIPA BEACH

Experienced surfers can take their pick of four breaks. In winter the really big waves roll in. Windsurfers take over at The Point, the break furthest west in the bay, in the afternoon. (p177)

Pailolo Channel
HONOLUA BAY
Honokohau
Kapalua
Kahakuloa
Napili
Kahana
Honokowai
Waihe'e
HO'OKIPA BEACH
Ka'anapali
'Eke Crater (4751ft)
Kahului Bay
HA Baldwin Beach Park
Pa'ia
Pu'u Kukui (5788ft)
'Iao Needle (2250ft)
Wailuku
Kahului
Lahaina
LAHAINA
Kamehameha Iki Park
'Iao Valley State Monument
Waikapu
Pukalani
Launiupoko Beach Park
Lana'i
Olowalu
Ma'alaea
MA'ALAEA
Kihei
Papawai Point
Maalaea Bay
KIHEI
Keokea
Polipoli Spring State Recreation Area
Wailea
Makena
'Ulupalakua Ranch
Pu'u Mahoe (2660ft)
'Alalakeiki Channel
La Perouse Bay

LAHAINA

If you want to learn to surf, and you're staying in West Maui, head to the Lahaina Breakwall just south of Banyan Tree Park. These gentle reef breaks are newbie-friendly. Surfing outfitters line Front St. (p79)

MA'ALAEA

The fast Ma'alaea Pipeline is a right-hand reef break. (p147)

KIHEI

Beginners in South Maui can test their skills on the small waves at The Cove just south of Kalama Park. Surf instructors await along South Kihei Rd. (p151)

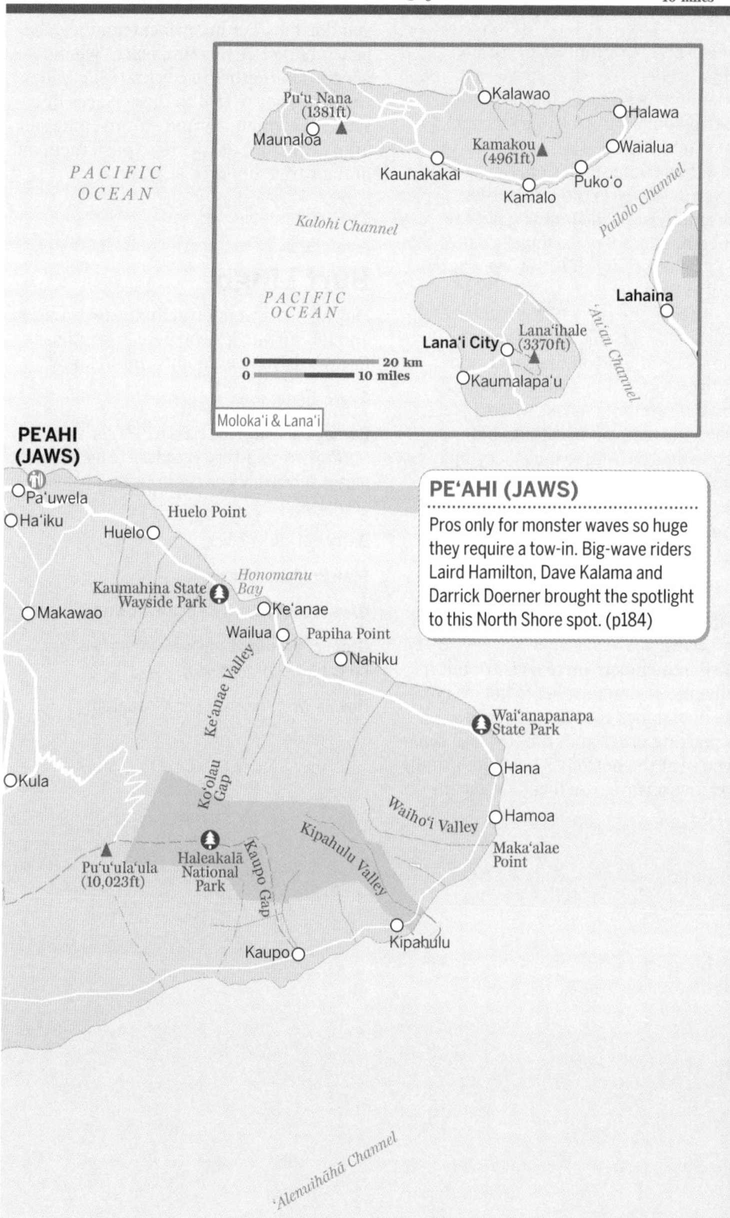

PE'AHI (JAWS)

Pros only for monster waves so huge they require a tow-in. Big-wave riders Laird Hamilton, Dave Kalama and Darrick Doerner brought the spotlight to this North Shore spot. (p184)

THE ORIGINAL BOARDRIDERS

Hawaii is the birthplace of surfing. Researchers have traced chants mentioning *he'e nalu* (surfing) and petroglyphs depicting surfers back to at least 1500 CE.

When the first missionaries arrived in Hawaii in the 1820s, they promptly started stamping out the 'hedonistic' act of surfing and, save a few holdouts, by 1890 surfing was all but extinct.

Then in the early 1900s modern surfing's first icon, Duke Kahanamoku, stepped off the beach and into history. Kahanamoku grew up on the sands of Waikiki, where he rode the reefs on traditional *olo*-style boards. After winning Olympic gold in swimming at Stockholm in 1912, Duke began to travel the world demonstrating the Hawaiian 'Sport of Kings.'

you'll do this plenty – try to keep track of your board.

Also, remember you're a visitor out in the lineup, so don't expect to get every wave that comes your way. There's a definite pecking order and, frankly, as a tourist you're at the bottom. That said, usually if you give a wave, you'll get a wave in return.

As a tourist in Hawaii, there are some places you go and there are some places you don't go. For many local families, the beach parks are meeting places where generations gather to celebrate life under the sun. They're tied to these places by a sense of community and culture, and they aren't eager for outsiders to push them out of their time-honored surf spots.

Surf Lingo

Hawaii has a wonderful linguistic tradition, and the surfing lexicon here is fabulous. A few words you definitely want to know:

Aggro Aggressive.

Barney Defined in the classic 1987 surf movie *North Shore* as a 'kook in and out of the water,' it means somebody who doesn't know what they are doing.

Betty Hot surfer chick.

Brah Brother or friend.

Green room The inside of a wave's tube.

Grom or grommet Younger surfers (who are probably better than you).

Howlie White person or non-Hawaiian.

Horseback riding (p58)

Plan Your Trip

On the Land

Epic adventures aren't limited to the sea; there is a plethora of fun activities on land. Maui's hiking and horse trails traverse some of the most unique ecosystems on earth. And if knocking around a little white ball is your thing, would-be pros can stalk the very greens where the professionals play.

ANCIENT HAWAII'S EXTREME SPORTS

Never let it be said that ancient Hawaiians didn't know how to play. Every male ruler had to prove his prowess in sports – to demonstrate mana (spiritual essence) – and the greater the danger, the better. No contest topped the *holua* – an ancient sled just a little wider than a book, on which Hawaiians raced down mountains at speeds of up to 50mph. Not every sport was potentially deadly, though many involved gambling – like foot and canoe racing, wrestling and *'ulu maika* (stone bowling). Annual makahiki harvest celebrations featured four months of feasting, hula dancing, religious ceremonies and sports competitions.

Golf

Surrounded by scenic ocean vistas and emerald mountain slopes, golfing just doesn't get much better. The most prestigious of Maui's courses is the Plantation course (p119) in Kapalua, which kicks off the year for the PGA tour. It's fresh off a nine-month, tee-to-greens renovation in 2020, with faster fairways. Only slightly less elite are the championship greens at Wailea (p166) and Ka'anapali (p109).

At the other end of the spectrum, you can enjoy a fun round at the friendly Waiehu Municipal Golf Course (p125) and at lesser-known country clubs elsewhere around the island.

A good resource, with course reviews, is Maui Golf (www.golf-maui.com).

Helicopter Tours

Helicopters buzz into amazing places that you otherwise might not experience. When you book, ask about seat guarantees, and let it be known you want a seat by a window, not a middle seat. On Maui, winds pick up by midday and carry clouds up the mountains with them. For the clearest skies and calmest ride, book a morning flight. There are four main tours:

West Maui tour (30 minutes) Takes in tropical rainforest, remote waterfalls and 'Iao Valley – this is Maui's prettiest face.

East Maui tour (45 minutes) Spotlights Hana, Haleakalā Crater and 'Ohe'o Gulch. Keep in mind this is the rainiest side of Maui. The good news: waterfalls galore stream down the mountainsides if you hit clear weather after a rainstorm. The bad news: it can be socked in with clouds.

Circle Island tour (one hour) Combines the West and East Maui tours.

West Maui & Moloka'i tour (one hour) Includes the drama of West Maui as well as a zip along the spectacular coastal cliffs of Moloka'i. Definitely the Big Kahuna of knockout photo ops!

All operate out of the **Kahului Heliport** at the southeast side of Kahului International Airport. Discounts on the list prices are common; ask when you book, or look for coupons online or in the free tourist magazines.

Horseback Riding

With its abundant ranchland and vibrant cowboy culture, Maui offers some of Hawaii's best riding experiences. Choose a ride based on the landscape you'd like to see, since all are friendly, reputable outfitters. Most rides last a few hours and often include lunch or a snack. Many outfitters also offer sunset rides.

Makena Stables (p173) takes riders along the volcanic slopes that overlook pristine La Perouse Bay, while Mendes Ranch (p125) offers rides along the cliffs of the Kahekili Hwy. Families will like the easy trips at Thompson Ranch (p196) in Keokea. Families with older kids and riders with a sense of adventure can explore lava fields in the volcanic Ka'naio region, with longer rides leading to a remote beach. You won't see many other people! The folks at long-running Pi'iholo Ranch Stables (p191) offer a Cowboy for a Day experience, allowing guests to help round up cattle. Traditional horseback rides across its Upcountry ranch, with mountain and valley views, are also offered. In West Maui, saddle up with Ironwood Ranch Horseback Riding (p116) for a ride in the foothills and valleys of the West Maui Mountains.

Spas

Hawaiian spa treatments may sound whimsical, but they're based on herbal traditions. Popular body wraps and 'cocoons' use seaweed to nourish; ginger, papaya and healing plants are applied as moisturizers. Other tropical treatments sound good enough to eat: coconut-milk baths and coffee-chocolate scrubs...mmm.

Most spas are in the large resort hotels, such as the Travaasa Hana (p239), Grand Wailea Resort Hotel & Spa (p168) and the spa at Montage Kapalua Bay (p120). You can enjoy a massage in an oceanfront *hale* – a thatched hut – at the Four Seasons Maui at Wailea (p167) spa. But if you prefer a more traditional setting away from the resorts, consider the Luana Spa (p240), which offers treatments under a thatched hut in Hana.

Tennis

Singles? Doubles? Or perhaps a lesson? Take your pick at the world-class facilities of Wailea Tennis Club (p166), Royal Lahaina Tennis Ranch (p109) in Ka'anapali and Kapalua Tennis Garden (p120). At Kapalua, they'll match you with another player if you need an opponent. If you just want to knock a ball around, many hotels have tennis courts for their guests and the county maintains free tennis courts at many public parks.

Pickleball courts are now open for play at all three of the aforementioned tennis facilities.

Ziplining

Click in. Grab tight. Thumbs up. And whoooosh...you're off. Maui's ziplines let you soar freestyle on a series of cables over gulches, woods and waterfalls while strapped into a harness. The hardest part is stepping off the platform for the first zip – the rest is pure exhilaration!

Flyin Hawaiian Zipline (p145)

The 3600ft-long line at the Flyin Hawaiian Zipline (p145) is impressing riders, while the Pi'iholo Ranch Zipline (p191) in Makawao is winning rave reviews with its 2800ft final line. It also offers side-by-side ziplines, allowing you to swoop the course alongside up to three of your friends. First on the Maui scene was Skyline Eco-Adventures' (p195) Haleakalā tour, which often books out months in advance. The company has a second zipline in the hills above the Ka'anapali Resort; this one is pricier but easier to book. In Kapalua, the Kapalua Ziplines (p120) course offers side-by-side zipping on dual lines as well as moonlight rides. If you have younger kids or are wary about ziplining, try the low-key Maui Zipline (p146) in Waikapu.

Waihe'e Ridge Trail (p102)

Plan Your Trip

Hiking & Biking Maui

The diversity is what makes hiking and cycling on Maui so cool. Trails hug lofty ridges, twist through green jungles, swing past waterfalls and meander across rough lava fields. You'll also find trails for every level of skill, from easy paths with big coastal views to thrilling mountainside routes that climb and plunge with abandon.

Maui's National, State & County Parks

The commanding Haleakalā National Park (p199), with its steep slopes and cloud-capped volcanic peaks, gives rise to East Maui. The park has two distinct faces. The main section encompasses Haleakalā's summit with its breathtaking crater-rim lookouts and lunar hiking trails. In the park's rainforested Kipahulu section, you're in the midst of dramatic waterfalls, swimming holes and ancient Hawaiian archaeological sites.

Top among Maui's state parks is 'Iao Valley State Monument (p144), whose towering emerald pinnacle rises picture-perfect from the valley floor. For the ultimate stretch of unspoiled beach, head to Makena State Park (p170). On the east side of Maui, Wai'anapanapa State Park (p228) sits on a distinctive black-sand beach.

Maui's county parks center on beaches and include the windsurfing hubs of Kanaha Beach Park (p129) and Ho'okipa Beach Park (p177). Details about county parks and beaches, including contact information and lifeguard availability, can be found on the Maui County government website: www.mauicounty.gov..

Where to Hike

The most extraordinary trails are in Haleakalā National Park (p201), where hikes range from half-day walks to quad-busting multiday treks meandering across the moonscape of Haleakalā Crater. In the Kipahulu ('Ohe'o Gulch) section of the park, linked trails climb past terraced pools and onto the towering waterfalls that feed them.

In Maui's Upcountry, Polipoli Spring State Recreation Area (p197) has an extensive trail system in cloud forest, including the breathtaking Skyline Trail that connects with Haleakalā summit. For a walk through a fantasy-novel forest, spend an hour or two among the tall trees on the Kahakapao Loop Trail in the Makawao Forest Reserve (p190).

North of Wailuku is the lofty **Waihe'e Ridge Trail**. This wonderful footpath penetrates deep into the misty West Maui Mountains, offering sweeping views of green valleys and the rugged northern coast. Near Ma'alaea Bay, the Lahaina Pali Trail (p130) follows an old footpath on the drier western slope of the same mountain mass.

The Kapalua Resort offers several trails with a range of scenery. The Coastal Trail (p117) links Kapalua Beach and DT Fleming Beach, while the **Village Walking Trails** wander through an overgrown golf course. Unfortunately, the resort is no longer running complimentary shuttles to the trailhead for the lofty and flora-filled **Maunalei Arboretum Trail**, which begins in the mountainous foothills above the resort. The road to the trailhead is privately owned and off limits to the general public, so access involves a lengthy full-day round-trip hike, which maxes out at more than 20 miles if you hike out and back. The Maunalei Arboretum Trail links to the jungle-like **Honolua Ridge Trail**. From the latter, the diverse **Mahana Ridge Trail** drops through lush slopes to the shimmering coast at DT Fleming Beach or the Kapalua Village center. For basic maps and brief trail summaries, visit www.kapalua.com/activities/hiking-trails.

Several pull-offs along the Road to Hana offer short nature walks that lead to hidden waterfalls and unspoiled coastal views, including the **Waikamoi Nature Trail** (https://hawaiitrails.org; Hana Hwy). A longer coastal trail between Wai'anapanapa State Park and Hana Bay follows an ancient Hawaiian footpath past several historic sights, as does the Hoapili Trail (p154) from La Perouse Bay on the other side of the island.

Short nature walks that combine bird- and whale-watching include the Kealia Coastal Boardwalk (p149) in Ma'alaea and the **Kihei Coastal Trail** (Map p158). For an easy but unshaded walk that's a short drive from the coastal crowds, try the Honokohau Ditch Trail (p105) in West Maui, which offers lofty views of the coast.

Maui: Hiking

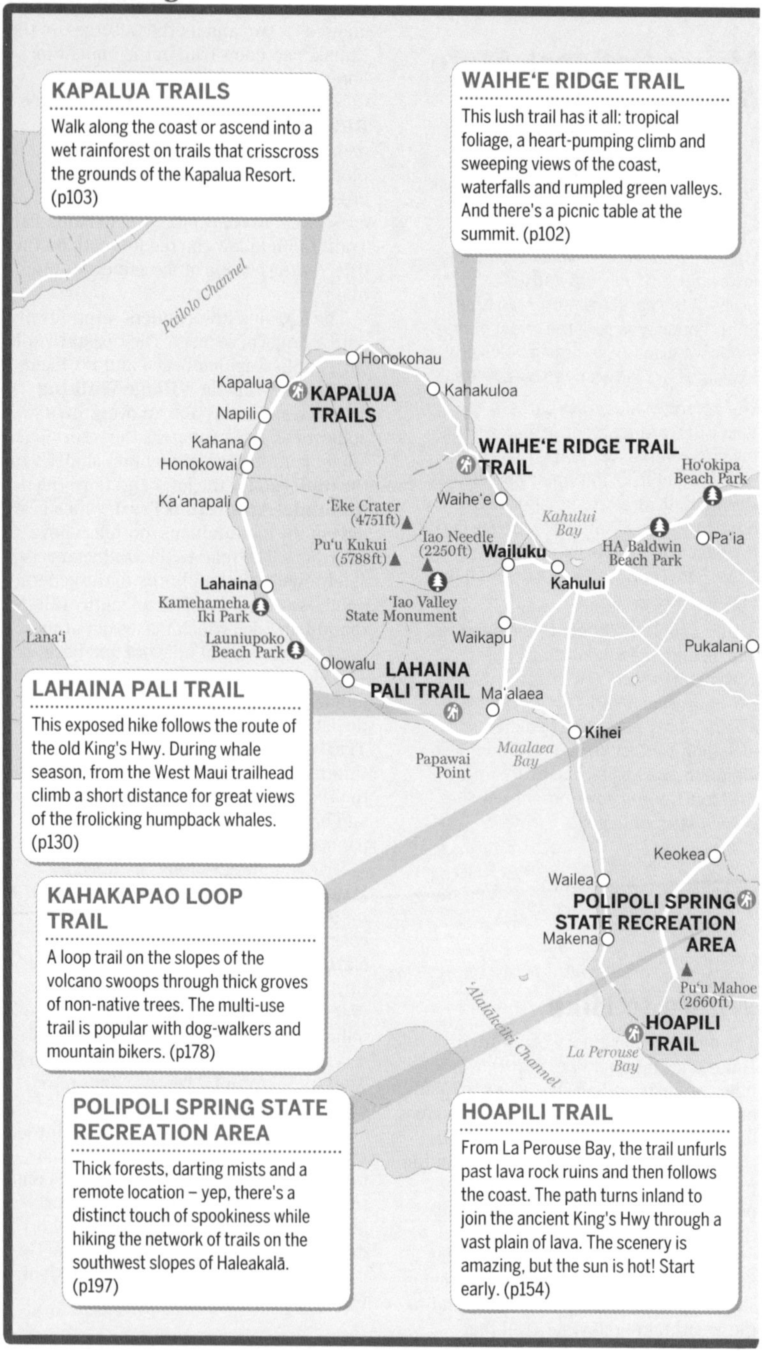

KAPALUA TRAILS

Walk along the coast or ascend into a wet rainforest on trails that crisscross the grounds of the Kapalua Resort. (p103)

WAIHE'E RIDGE TRAIL

This lush trail has it all: tropical foliage, a heart-pumping climb and sweeping views of the coast, waterfalls and rumpled green valleys. And there's a picnic table at the summit. (p102)

LAHAINA PALI TRAIL

This exposed hike follows the route of the old King's Hwy. During whale season, from the West Maui trailhead climb a short distance for great views of the frolicking humpback whales. (p130)

KAHAKAPAO LOOP TRAIL

A loop trail on the slopes of the volcano swoops through thick groves of non-native trees. The multi-use trail is popular with dog-walkers and mountain bikers. (p178)

POLIPOLI SPRING STATE RECREATION AREA

Thick forests, darting mists and a remote location – yep, there's a distinct touch of spookiness while hiking the network of trails on the southwest slopes of Haleakalā. (p197)

HOAPILI TRAIL

From La Perouse Bay, the trail unfurls past lava rock ruins and then follows the coast. The path turns inland to join the ancient King's Hwy through a vast plain of lava. The scenery is amazing, but the sun is hot! Start early. (p154)

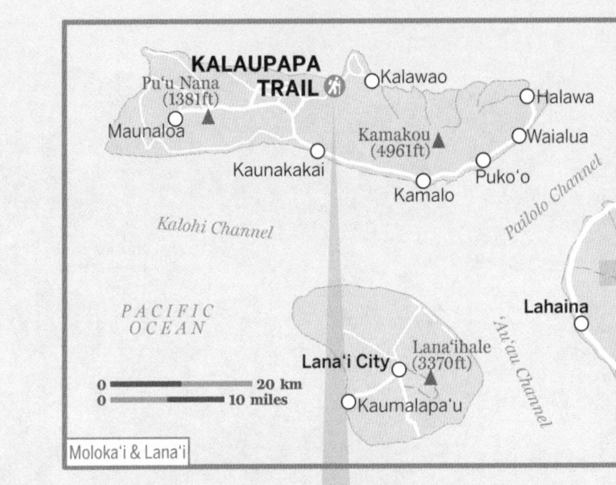

PACIFIC OCEAN

Pa'uwela Point
Uaoa Bay
Pa'uwela
Ha'iku
Huelo Point
Huelo
Honomanu Bay
Kaumahina State Wayside Park
Makawao
Ke'anae
KAHAKAPAO LOOP TRAIL
Wailua
Papiha Point
Nahiku
Ke'anae Valley
Wai'anapanapa State Park
Hana
Kula
HALEAKALĀ NATIONAL PARK (SUMMIT)
Waiho'i Valley
Hamoa
Kipahulu Valley
Maka'alae Point
Kaupo Gap
Pu'u'ula'ula (10,023ft)
HALEAKALĀ NATIONAL PARK (KIPAHULU)
Kipahulu
Kaupo

KALAUPAPA TRAIL

You'll tackle 26 switchbacks on this steep cliffside path that ends at a beach near a former Hansen's disease (leprosy) settlement. Mules carrying visitors also use this 3-mile trail. (p271)

HALEAKALĀ NATIONAL PARK (SUMMIT)

Hike into the lunar-like crater of the volcano to see cinder cones and silverswords. On the slopes, explore a non-native forest. (p202)

HALEAKALĀ NATIONAL PARK (KIPAHULU)

Trails climb past waterfalls and terraced pools, with a swing through a towering bamboo forest. (p205)

MONICA AND MICHAEL SWEET / GETTY IMAGES ©

ISHOOTPHOTOS, LLC / GETTY IMAGES ©

Top: Haleakalā National Park (p201)

Bottom: Cycling the Downhill from Haleakalā to Pa'ia route (p180)

One of Maui's top environmental shakers, the **Sierra Club** (www.mauisierraclub.org), sponsors guided hikes, often educational, to various places around the island. Everyone is welcome; nonmembers are asked to pay a $5 donation. Not only will you be sharing the trails with other eco-minded hikers, but the Sierra Club sometimes hikes into fascinating places that are otherwise closed to the public.

Hiking Considerations

- Maui has no snakes, no poison ivy and few wild animals that will fuss with hikers. There's only the slimmest chance of encountering a large boar in the backwoods, but they're unlikely to be a problem unless cornered.
- Be careful on the edge of steep cliffs, as cliffside rock in Maui tends to be crumbly.
- Flash floods are a potential threat in many of the steep, narrow valleys on Maui that require stream crossings. Warning signs include a distant rumbling, the smell of fresh earth and a sudden increase in the stream's current. If the water begins to rise, get to higher ground immediately.
- A walking stick is good for bracing yourself on slippery approaches, gaining leverage and testing the depth of streams.
- Darkness falls fast once the sun sets, and ridgetop trails are no place to be caught unprepared in the dark. Always carry a flashlight. Wear long pants for protection from overgrown parts of the trail, and sturdy footwear with good traction. Pack 2 quarts (2L) of water per person for a day hike, carry a whistle to alert rescue workers if necessary, wear sunscreen and start early.

BEST EASY WALKS

- **Kapalua Coastal Trail** (p103)
- **Wailea Beach Walk** (p166)
- **Kihei Coastal Trail** (p61)
- **Ka'anapali Beach Walk** (p111)
- **North Ka'anapali Beach Walk** (p111)
- **Kealia Coastal Boardwalk** (p149)
- **Honokohau Ditch Trail** (p105)

Biking

Mountain Biking

To explore the wilderness on a mountain bike, head to the Upcountry. Experienced downhill riders will find adrenaline-stoked thrills on the Skyline Trail (p207), which follows the mountain's spine from Haleakalā National Park into Polipoli Spring State Recreation Area. Closer in, you'll find single-track trails at the Makawao Forest Reserve (p190). There, several short trails intersect with the 5.75-mile Kahakapao Trail Loop, giving riders a variety of options. The reserve also has pump tracks and skills courses. For mountain bike rentals, try Island Biker (p134) in Kahului. The website for West Maui Cycles (p85) provides a basic map showing the mountain-biking trails in the reserve.

Road Cycling

Road cyclists on Maui face a number of challenges: narrow roads, heavy traffic, an abundance of hills and mountains, and the same persistent winds that so delight windsurfers. Many roads, however, including the Pi'ilani Hwy in South Maui, do have bike lanes. Reliable shops include West Maui Cycles (p85) in Lahaina, South Maui Bicycles (p160) in Kihei and Island Biker (p134) in Kahului.

The full-color *Maui County Bicycle Map* is no longer being published, but you can peruse it online on the websites for West Maui Cycles and South Maui Bicycles. The map is outdated, but it shows all the roads on Maui that have been suitable for cycling and gives other nitty-gritty details. It's worth a look if you intend to explore by pedal power.

Ali'i Kula Lavender (p194)

Plan Your Trip

Green Maui

For Hawaiians, respect and love for the land is of utmost importance, and many traditions reflect their feelings of responsibility for its care. Islanders of all backgrounds are activists, from Native Hawaiians volunteering to restore an ancient fishpond to scientists fighting invasive plants. As a traveler, understanding and respecting this concept of care will help protect this delicate place – and likely enrich your experience.

Sites for Agritourism

Ali'i Kula Lavender

On the slopes of Haleakalā with views of the isthmus and central coasts, this vast farm (p194) is a pleasant place to wander and to shop for lavender-based products. Walking tours also offered.

Surfing Goat Dairy

Famous for its fresh chèvre, which comes in numerous flavors, Surfing Goat (p193) is open for dairy tours. Children and adults can join the 'Evening Chores and Milking Tours' or check out the playful young goats. Free samples.

O'o Farm

The lunch tour at this organic farm (p195) offers glimpses of its produce fields as well as its coffee trees. Enjoy a meal as part of your tour, as well as coffee samples.

Maui Wine

In the far reaches of the Upcountry, Maui's only winery (p197) offers tastings as well as tours at its historic property, a longtime ranch and a favorite spot of King David Kalakaua.

Ono Organic Farms

Tropical fruit is a highlight at this farm (p246), which is tucked in the lush foliage of East Maui. Tours offered on Tuesday afternoons. You can also stop by their fruit stand in Hana.

Responsible Travel

Hawaiians embrace the concept of *kuelana*. At its simplest, *kuelana* is defined as active and mutual responsibility. It can be a responsibility to the land, a person, the community, or an object – and all of them reciprocate in their own way. It is an ingrained tradition of mutual care that is both spiritual and practical.

There is also a long cultural history of loving and protecting the land. This love for the land – encapsulated by the Hawaiian phrase *aloha 'aina* – is a deeply felt part of life here, and it's expressed through the active responsibility of *kuelana*.

The effects of overtourism, however, threaten these efforts. More than 2.9 million people visited Maui in 2018, a jump of 6.2% from the previous year. This means that Maui is facing an unusual tourism problem: success. Yes, visitors spent more than $5 billion in 2018, which is an economic boon, but all this love is arguably beginning to harm the very places and traditions that make the island special.

To reduce the ill effects of mass tourism, and enrich your experience in the process, consider practicing the concept of active responsibility.

Sacred Sites

Obey all signage at sacred spots, from Makaluapuna Point and the Honokahua burial grounds beside the Ritz-Carlton in Kapalua to the the lava-rocks ruins at the start of the Hoapili Trail at La Perouse Bay. Some signs may say that entry is discouraged, while others may say entry is prohibited. Err on the side of 'visiting' from afar, which can be challenging when others are traipsing all over the site. But will staying back really negatively affect your experience?

Private Property

Maui's resorts can't restrict access to the gorgeous beaches fronting their hotels. At the popular resort-front beaches in Wailea and West Maui, look for the beach access signs. There you'll find a path to the coast and free public parking lots. On the other hand, don't follow trails across private property to check out a waterfall or natural pool. This can be tricky along the Road to Hana when you see clusters of cars parked seemingly at random. Respect the 'Kapu – No Trespassing' signs. Waterfalls and trails in this guide are on public land and trails, or those that have allowed access. When in doubt, skip it or ask the landowner for permission.

National, State & County Parks

Obey signage and be aware of your surroundings at the island's many parks. At Haleakalā National Park, be sure to park in paved lots. Parking outside designated areas can damage the delicate and unique flora found here, particularly at the summit. For the same reason, stay on established trails and avoid short-cutting the switchbacks. While driving, keep an eye out near the summit for the slow-moving nene, the threatened state bird that is a cousin of the Canadian goose.

Maui Goes Green

Maui and its residents are leaders in eco-activism. Maui was the first island in Hawaii to approve a ban on single-use plastic bags. Businesses and restaurants that violate the ordinance, which came into effect in 2011, incur a $500 daily fine. A powerful incentive!

Parks, forest reserves and watersheds cover nearly half of the island. The crowning glory is Haleakalā National Park, which, thanks to the collaborative work of environmental groups, now extends from its original perch in the center of Maui clear down to the south coast. On the first and third Saturday of every month, volunteers (p308) can visit the park to remove invasive plants and work on other projects that help preserve the Haleakalā ecosystem.

Maui is home to three major wind farms, which provided more than 23% of the island's energy requirements in 2018. Maui Electric, one of three electricity companies serving the islands, generates 37% of its power from a variety of renewable sources, including wind farms.

Sustainable Maui

As you plan your trip, consider your impact on the island. There are numerous ways to lighten your tourist footprint.

Sustainable Icon

It seems like everyone's going 'green' these days, but how can you know which Maui businesses are genuinely ecofriendly and which are simply jumping on the sustainability bandwagon? In Lonely Planet listings, the Sustainable icon indicates businesses that we are highlighting because they demonstrate an active sustainable-tourism policy. Some are involved in conservation

Organic farm, Haiku

or environmental education, while others maintain and preserve Hawaiian identity and culture. Many are owned and operated by local and indigenous operators.

Transportation

On a short trip to Maui, consider ditching the car. The Maui Bus (p310) loops past convenient stops in Lahaina, Ka'anapali, Kihei, Kahului and Wailuku. It also runs several 'islander' routes between major towns and resorts. In Ka'anapali, a free resort shuttle swings past major hotels and beaches.

For longer stays, rent a smaller, less gas-guzzling vehicle. Not only will that be gentler on Maui's environment, but the island's narrow roads will be easier to negotiate. Consider renting a Bio-Beetle (p310), which runs on recycled cooking oil.

Treading Lightly

Before arriving on Maui, clean your shoes and wipe off your luggage so you don't inadvertently bring seeds or insects from elsewhere, introducing yet another invasive species. This advice especially applies

PHOTO IMAGE / SHUTTERSTOCK ©

Wind turbines

if you're arriving on Maui from the Big Island, where Rapid 'Ohi'a Death (p300) fungal disease has recently killed millions of *'ohi'a lehua,* a native tree and a key part of the ecosystem across Hawaii's islands.

When hiking, stay on trails; when snorkeling, stay off the coral.

Eating & Drinking Locally & Responsibly

Every food product not grown or raised on Maui is shipped to the island by boat or plane. Considering the great distances and the amount of fuel used, that makes the 'locavore' or 'eat local' movement particularly relevant. One delicious standout is Moku Roots (p92) in Lahaina. This new vegan restaurant has a zero-waste policy, evident to diners in the cloth napkins and sustainable to-go containers. Leftover food is used as compost in their garden. Frequenting farmers markets is also an eco-minded option.

Tap water on Maui is perfectly fine for drinking, so resist those California spring-water imports. At the very least, refill your plastic bottle once it's emptied.

On the Ground & in the Sea

Environmentally friendly organizations across Maui offer ways to be active and adventurous with lower environmental impact.

Instead of a boat dive, try a shore dive (no diesel fuel, no dropped anchors) with a company that specializes in them, such as Maui Dreams Dive Co (p158) in Kihei. Opt for a sailboat cruise over a motorboat cruise. Riding with the wind is more eco-friendly, plus sailboats get closer to whales and dolphins, which are repelled by motorboat noise. Consider companies such as Trilogy Excursions (p86) that fly a green flag, indicating that the boat adheres to strict environmental practices and doesn't discharge waste into the ocean.

To really go local, take an outrigger-canoe trip with Hawaiian Paddle Sports (p172) or Hawaiian Sailing Canoe Adventures (p167).

Local farms sell fruits and vegetables at farmers markets in the Upcountry, Kihei

GREEN BEER

OK, so the beer at Maui Brewing Co (p164) isn't *green,* but the folks who brew it are committed to eco-minded business practices. For example, spent grain is given to local ranchers for composting, and the brewery's retail beers are sold in recyclable cans. Cans over glass? Yep, cans aren't breakable, so they're less of a threat on the beach. Cans are also lighter than glass, meaning you can move more product in one trip, saving fuel and ultimately leaving a smaller environmental footprint. Today, 100% of the company's power at its 85,000-sq-ft Kihei facility comes from self-sustainable and off-the-grid sources – much of that from the building's solar panels and Tesla Powerpack battery storage units. For a sudsy and sustainable toast, stop by one of its two Maui locations. Cheers for green beers!

and Honokowai, and at the Maui Swap Meet in Kahului. More and more eateries are showcasing locally caught seafood as well as Maui-raised beef and Maui-grown produce. The range of restaurants is wide, from the deli at Mana Foods (p187) in Pa'ia to the gourmet pub grub at Monkeypod Kitchen (p168) in Wailea to the new vegan restaurant Moku Roots (p92) in Lahaina. One buy-local restaurant, Flatbread Company (p186) in Pa'ia, gives a cut of the night's profits to local environmental groups who show up to rap with customers every Tuesday night.

Buying Maui-made products supports the local economy and often helps sustain the environment as well. Ali'i Kula Lavender (p194) in Kula produces organic lavender blossoms, which are used by two dozen home-based businesses to make the lavender jams, vinegars and salad dressings sold at the farm. For picnics, buy cheese from Surfing Goat Dairy (p193) and wine from Maui Wine (p197).

Family Travel

Children are welcome everywhere on Maui. Hawaiians love kids – large families are common and *na keiki* (children) are an integral part of the scenery. Maui has everything for a child on vacation: sandy beaches, fun hotel pools, tasty food and outdoor activities galore. The island also offers cool cross-cultural opportunities, from hula lessons to outrigger-canoe rides.

Children Will Love...

Water Adventures

➡ **Surf lessons, Lahaina and Kihei** Gentle waves! Surf schools line the streets. For the very young, try Maui Surf Clinics (p86) in Lahaina.

➡ **Snorkeling, Honolua Bay** (p120) Fantastic underwater sights are a few kicks from shore. Careful on the slippery entry!

➡ **Whale-watching, Lahaina and Ma'alaea** From mid-December to April, hop on a boat to glimpse these mighty beasts. Kids are a focus at the Pacific Whale Foundation (p148).

➡ **Outrigger-canoe tour, Hawaiian Paddle Sports** (p172) Join a family-friendly trip to look for green sea turtles in a traditional Hawaiian canoe.

Plants & Animals

➡ **Maui Ocean Center** (p147), **Ma'alaea** A 54ft clear tunnel funnels families through a fish-filled 750,000-gallon tank.

➡ **Surfing Goat Dairy** (p193), **Pukalani** Hang with the kids – of the goat variety.

➡ **Ono Organic Farms** (p246), **Kipahulu** Sample exotic fruit as you explore a 300-acre farm in the Upcountry.

➡ **Maui Tropical Plantation** (p145), **Waikapu** Enjoy two ziplines, a touch of history and exotic fruit at the Coconut Station.

Keeping Costs Down

Accommodations

Maui's sprawling resorts may have kids' programs and fun pools, but they are the island's most expensive lodging option. Your best bet is a condominium, where the rates are often lower. You can also save money by cooking meals in your condo's kitchen. Many units provide snorkeling and beach gear, so you can save on rentals too.

Sights & Activities

Beaches are free, and snorkeling gear can be rented cheaply at snorkel shops off the beach. Avoid the pricey beach shacks. Coastal and mountain trails are also free of charge, as is the banyan tree in Lahaina – although no climbing is allowed. The heritage museum next door is no cost. First Friday celebrations have free entertainment.

Eating

Some of Maui's most popular restaurants have short but solid kids' menus, with offerings typically under $10. Food truck parks offer lots of lower-cost options in one spot, from burgers to tacos, with picnic tables nearby. Most beach parks also have grills and picnic tables, so pack low-cost food from the supermarket for a picnic.

Easy Exploring

➡ **Banyan Tree Park** (p81), **Lahaina** With its sprawling canopy and thick trunks, Lahaina's favorite tree would make the Swiss Family Robinson feel at home.

➡ **Kealia Coastal Boardwalk** (p149), **Kealia Pond National Wildlife Refuge** Burn off energy on this elevated boardwalk through coastal wetlands.

➡ **Kalakupua Playground** (p188), **Ha'iku** This jungle gym at the Fourth Marine Division Memorial Park looks like a sprawling castle.

➡ **Kula Country Farms** (p195), **Kula** In October, bring the kids to the pumpkin patch.

Older Kids & Teens

➡ **Haleakalā National Park** (p201) Hike into the crater to see cinder cones and silverswords.

➡ **Makena Bay** (p170), **Makena** Paddle from shore to see green sea turtles, tropical fish and maybe a breaching whale.

➡ **Hana Lava Tube** (p228), **Hana** At Ka'eleku Caverns, wander through a long underground tunnel formed by lava.

➡ **Makena Stables** (p173), **La Perouse Bay** Ride through coastal lava fields on horseback.

➡ **Molokini Crater** (p51) Snorkel among tropical fish inside the rim of an underwater volcano.

Region by Region

Lahaina

A decent spot for family travel, but be aware that the beach scene is limited. First stop? Banyan Tree Park (p81) to play beneath those wonderful banyan tree branches. Kids will find lots of water attractions at the adjacent harbor, from a submarine ride to surfing lessons.

West Maui

Families can't help but have fun in West Maui, particularly in happening Ka'anapali. You'll find water sports galore, especially for older kids – think swimming, snorkeling, bodyboarding, catamaran sails, whale-watching, kayaking and stand up paddleboarding. On land, kids can hike and zipline. Younger kids will enjoy the playground at Whalers Village (p113).

South Maui

Another great place for kids, teens and adults to hit the water, with surf lessons in Kihei and kayaking in Makena Bay. Many beaches have lifeguard stands as well as grassy areas for picnics. Try an outrigger-canoe trip, available at many resorts.

Haleakalā National Park

Kid of all ages love playing astronaut on a crunchy walk into the wildly lunar crater or taking in a ranger talk. Younger travelers can complete the requirements to become a Junior Ranger. In Kipahulu, adventurous kids will enjoy the diverse Pipiwai Trail (p205), which winds through a cool bamboo grove.

Central Maui

Lacking good beaches, Kahului and Wailuku aren't great destinations for overnight stays for families. In Ma'alaea, however, both kids and adults can ogle cool sea creatures at the Maui Ocean Center (p147). Ma'alaea is also the launch point for snorkel trips to Molokini and for seasonal whale-watching excursions with Pacific Whale Foundation (p148). Search for wildlife on the Kealia Coastal Boardwalk (p149). You'll find a low-stress zipline and other family distractions at the Maui Tropical Plantation (p145).

North Shore & Upcountry

The Upcountry is not particularly family friendly, but younger kids may enjoy watching the goats at Surfing Goat Dairy (p193) in Pukalani. The children's garden at Kula Country Farms (p195) is a nice distraction, and you can pull over for the fun pumpkin patch here in October. Older kids can zipline in Kula and Makawao.

Road to Hana

For splashing around beneath a waterfall, try Pua'a Ka'a State Wayside Park (p225). The Hana Lava Tube (p228) is spooky and easy to explore.

Hana

Hana is not particularly family focused, but snorkeling and kayaking in Hana Bay are a possibility. Kids who are nine and older can horseback ride with Travaasa

Hana Stables (p240). Adventurous teens can take a sailplane ride with Skyview Soaring (p239).

Lana'i & Moloka'i

Take the kids snorkeling in Lana'i and hiking in Moloka'i.

Good to Know

Look out for the icon for family-friendly suggestions throughout this guide.

- Children are welcome at hotels throughout Maui. Those under 17 typically stay free when sharing a room with their parents and using existing bedding. Request cots and cribs in advance when booking a room.
- Many sights and activities offer discounted children's rates, sometimes as cheap as half price.
- Car-rental companies on Maui lease child-safety seats, but they don't always have enough, so don't book your car at the last minute.
- If you're traveling with infants and forget to pack some of your gear, visit www.mauibabyequipment.com to rent cribs, playpens, pushchairs and other baby items.
- Grocers and convenience stores sell nappies and diapers.
- For an evening out alone, the easiest and most reliable way to find a babysitter is through the hotel concierge.
- Maui is an open-minded place, and although public breast-feeding is not commonplace, it's unlikely to elicit unwanted attention. Changing facilities are found in shopping malls and resorts.

Useful Resources

Lonely Planet Kids (www.lonelyplanetkids.com) Loads of activities and great family travel blog content.

Go Hawaii (www.gohawaii.com) The state's official tourism website lists family-friendly activities, special events and more – easily search the site using terms such as 'kid' or 'family.'

Maui Family Magazine (www.mauifamilymagazine.com) Geared to locals, but the website has a weekend guide for families.

Kids' Corner

Say What?

Hello.	*Aloha.*
Goodbye.	*Aloha.*
Thank you.	*Mahalo.*
Welcome, come in	*E komo mai...*

Did You Know?

- Adult humpback whales break the surface of the water to breathe every seven to 10 minutes.

Have You Tried?

Loco Moco
Fried egg and a burger with gravy

Regions at a Glance

Ready for an adventure? Whether you're seeking outdoor fun, great food, engaging history, cultural distractions or natural beauty, Maui offers a top-notch experience. The weather's darn nice, too. Each region has its own specialties though. Lahaina lures 'em in with history and great restaurants. West Maui entertains honeymooners and families with bustling resorts and a lively beach scene. Ancient history and modern hustle collide in Central Maui. Kihei is the quintessential beach town, while Wailea feels like a tropical country club with its posh resorts and golf courses. The Road to Hana offers waterfalls and Hana shares history and old Hawaiian charm. The landscapes and the sunrise bring the masses to Haleakalā National Park, but you can get away from the crowds on the islands of Lana'i and Moloka'i.

Lahaina

Food
History
Shopping

Sheer Diversity

From food trucks and shave-ice stands to oceanfront lunch spots and white-linen romantic restaurants, Lahaina's range of dining establishments is broad. Food options include seafood, burgers and various ethnic cuisines.

Whalers & Missionaries

Two forces collided in mid-1800s Lahaina. Strict Christian missionaries spread God's word while rowdy whalers sought a good time. Museums and homes spotlight their lifestyles.

Galleries & Outlet Stores

Art galleries and shopping discounters don't usually frequent the same neighborhoods, except here in Lahaina. Along Front St you'll find both local art and brand-name outlet stores.

p79

West Maui

Beaches
Water Sports
Resorts

Sunbathing Heaven

From Ka'anapali to Kapalua, the beaches are wide, golden crescents with gorgeous views of the coast and nearby islands. Catch a tan, enjoy a beach read and show off your bikinis and board shorts.

Snorkeling & Paddleboarding

West Maui's beach coves are ready-made for low-key water sports. Kick off from shore to snorkel the reefs, or hop aboard a stand up paddleboard for an hour of paddling.

Resorts & Condos

Two types of lodging flank the west coast's gorgeous beaches: resorts catering to your every need and do-it-yourself condominium complexes. Both are typically upscale.

p99

'Iao Valley & Central Maui

History
Offshore Adventures
Nature

Chieftains & Church Life

Steeped in ancient Hawaiian legend, the 'Iao Valley was also the site of a terrible battle between Kamehameha the Great and Maui warriors. The nearby Bailey House was home to missionaries.

Kanaha Beach Park

Winds blast through the flat Maui isthmus, providing sustained power for the windsurfers and kiteboarders skimming across the ocean off this mile-long beach.

Kealia Pond National Wildlife Refuge

Look for endangered Hawaiian seabirds in the pond and the marshy waters buffering it from the sea on the coastal boardwalk.

p127

Kihei & South Maui

Beaches
Food
Happy Hours

Family Fun

The three Kama'ole Beach parks feature picnic tables, showers, restrooms and lifeguards, making them great spots for birthday parties and long days at the beach with the kids.

Local Food

Loco moco, shave ice and lunch plates are easy to find in Kihei – just drive down Kihei Rd, which is lined with eateries. From breakfast through dinner, all meals are local-style in Da Kitchen Express.

5 Palms

Overlooking Keawakapu Beach, this buzzy place does happy hour right, with great food and drink deals, welcoming bartenders and a darn fine sunset.

p151

North Shore & Upcountry

Food & Drink
Outdoors
Shopping

Nature's Bounty

Blessed with fertile volcanic soils, the Upcountry is the island's fruit basket, providing the produce, cheese and beef found on Maui restaurant menus.

Land & Sea

Surfers and windsurfers enjoy world-class waves and winds on the rugged north shore. Hikers and mountain bikers tackle the leafy trails of the Makawao Forest Reserve. With great restaurants and stores, Pai'a and Haiku are adventure base camps.

Local Goods

Cool boutiques and beloved mom-and-pop businesses line the main roads in Pai'a and Makawao. Roadside fruit stands and bountiful farmers markets draw chefs and cooks in search of the freshest fare.

p175

Haleakalā National Park

Landscape
Hiking
Flora & Fauna

Craters & Cascades

In the Summit District, cinder cones dot the lunar floor of the crater atop the park's namesake volcano. In Kipahulu, waterfalls drop from lofty heights and splash into terraced pools.

Summit Trails

The crater is the park's marquee attraction, with a handful of trails crisscrossing the vast depression. The trails pass cinder cones, big views and peaks shrouded in fog.

Rare Species

Silver-spiked leaves adorn the *'ahinahina* (silversword) flowers, which dot the summit. The threatened nene, a native goose, can sometimes be seen near the Park Headquarters Visitor Center.

p199

The Road to Hana

Natural Beauty
Flora & Fauna
History

Waterfalls

They say every time you cross a bridge on the Road to Hana you also pass a waterfall – and that sounds about right. Waterfalls are the star attraction on this lush drive along the windward coast.

Tropical Gardens

Stretch your legs on a walk through the well-manicured plants at the Garden of Eden, then gaze at an ancient temple bordered by Kahanu Garden, a lovely 294-acre ethnobotanical garden beside the sea.

King's Trail

Follow the ancient King's Trail in Wai'anapanapa State Park. You can still see ancient stepping stones along this striking coastal path.

p215

Hana & East Maui

Beaches
Slow Travel
Landscape

Hamoa Beach

Lined with thick tropical greenery and flanked by black lava reefs, this golden crescent is your Maui postcard. Dr Beach dubbed it one of the country's best in 2015.

Old Hawaii

Daily rhythms are slow on the backside of Haleakalā, where conversation is key, homegrown-food trucks dominate the dining scene and the Hasegawa General Store stocks everything from hardware to liquor.

From Lush to Lava

The Pi'ilani Hwy twists along the lonely eastern coastline, linking the green tropical flora of Kipahulu and its environs with the black-lava fields covering Haleakalā's southern slopes.

p231

Lana'i & Moloka'i

Remoteness
History
Water Sports

Ferries & Planes

Getting to Lana'i or Moloka'i takes a bit of planning. To access either island, hop aboard a ferry in Lahaina or catch an interisland flight.

Kalaupapa National Historical Park

Hike, or ride a mule, down a steep cliffside trail to the Kalaupapa Peninsula, the site of a long-running settlement for people with Hansen's disease (leprosy). Obligatory tours include stories about life here in the past.

Diving

Shhh…divers may not want to share the existence of the Cathedrals, a fantastic dive site near Manele Bay in Lana'i, with lava-made caverns, ledges, walls and the exciting 'Shotgun' lava tube.

p249

On the Road

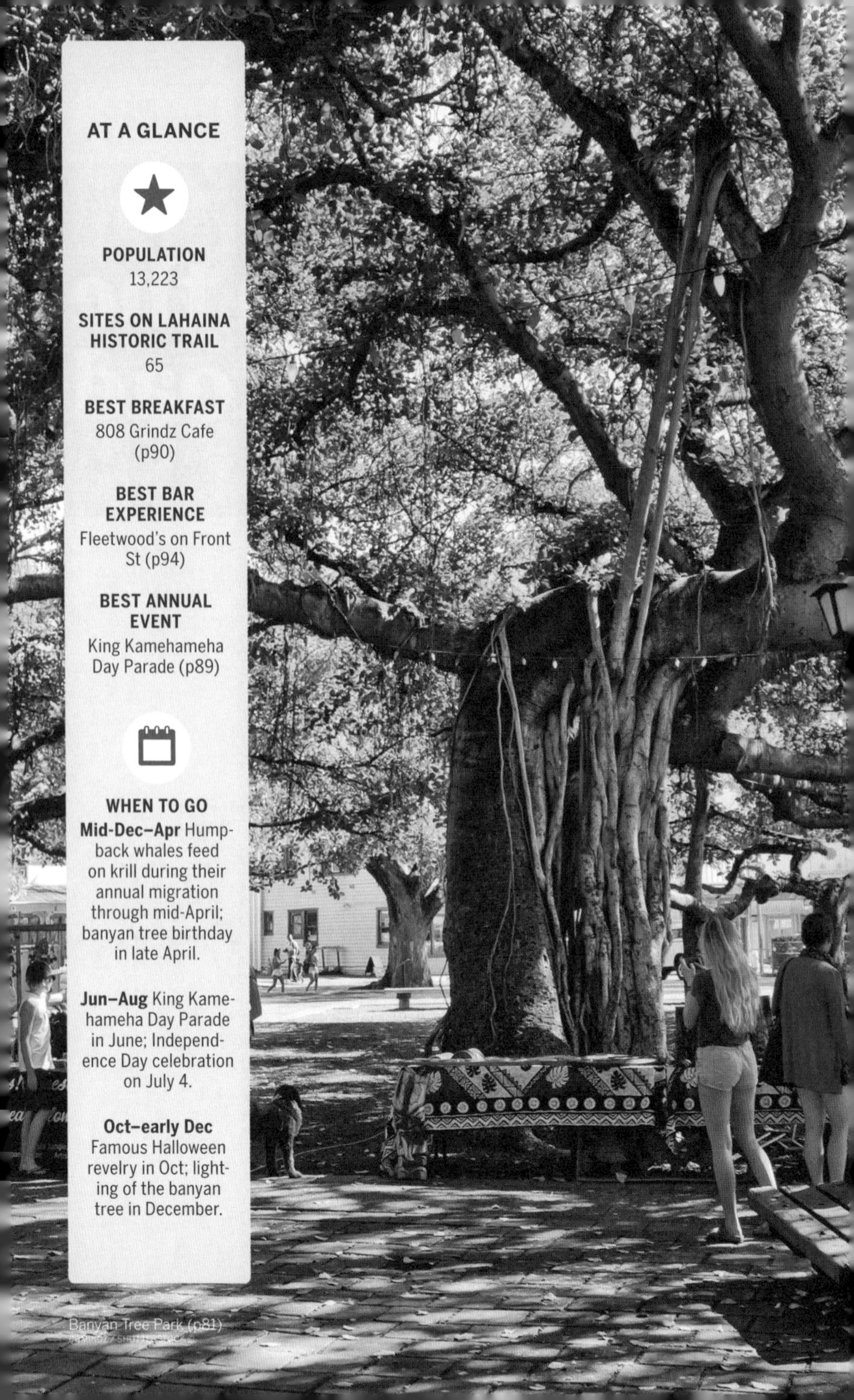

AT A GLANCE

POPULATION
13,223

SITES ON LAHAINA HISTORIC TRAIL
65

BEST BREAKFAST
808 Grindz Cafe (p90)

BEST BAR EXPERIENCE
Fleetwood's on Front St (p94)

BEST ANNUAL EVENT
King Kamehameha Day Parade (p89)

WHEN TO GO

Mid-Dec–Apr Humpback whales feed on krill during their annual migration through mid-April; banyan tree birthday in late April.

Jun–Aug King Kamehameha Day Parade in June; Independence Day celebration on July 4.

Oct–early Dec Famous Halloween revelry in Oct; lighting of the banyan tree in December.

Banyan Tree Park (p81)

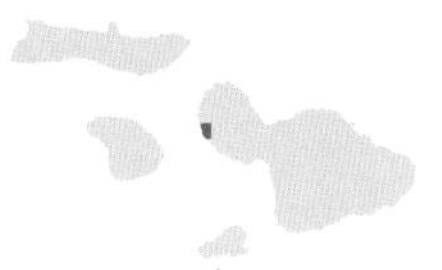

Lahaina

Tucked between the West Maui Mountains and a tranquil sea, Lahaina has long been a popular convergence point. Ancient Hawaiian royals were the first to gather here, followed by missionaries, whalers and sugar plantation workers. Today it's a base for creative chefs, passionate artists and dedicated surf instructors.

Near the harbor, storefronts that once housed whaling-era saloons, dance halls and brothels now teem with art galleries, souvenir shops and, well, still plenty of watering holes. As for the whalers, they've been replaced by a new kind of leviathan hunter: whale-watchers scanning for photographic prey. Between January and March, they don't have to look hard.

INCLUDES

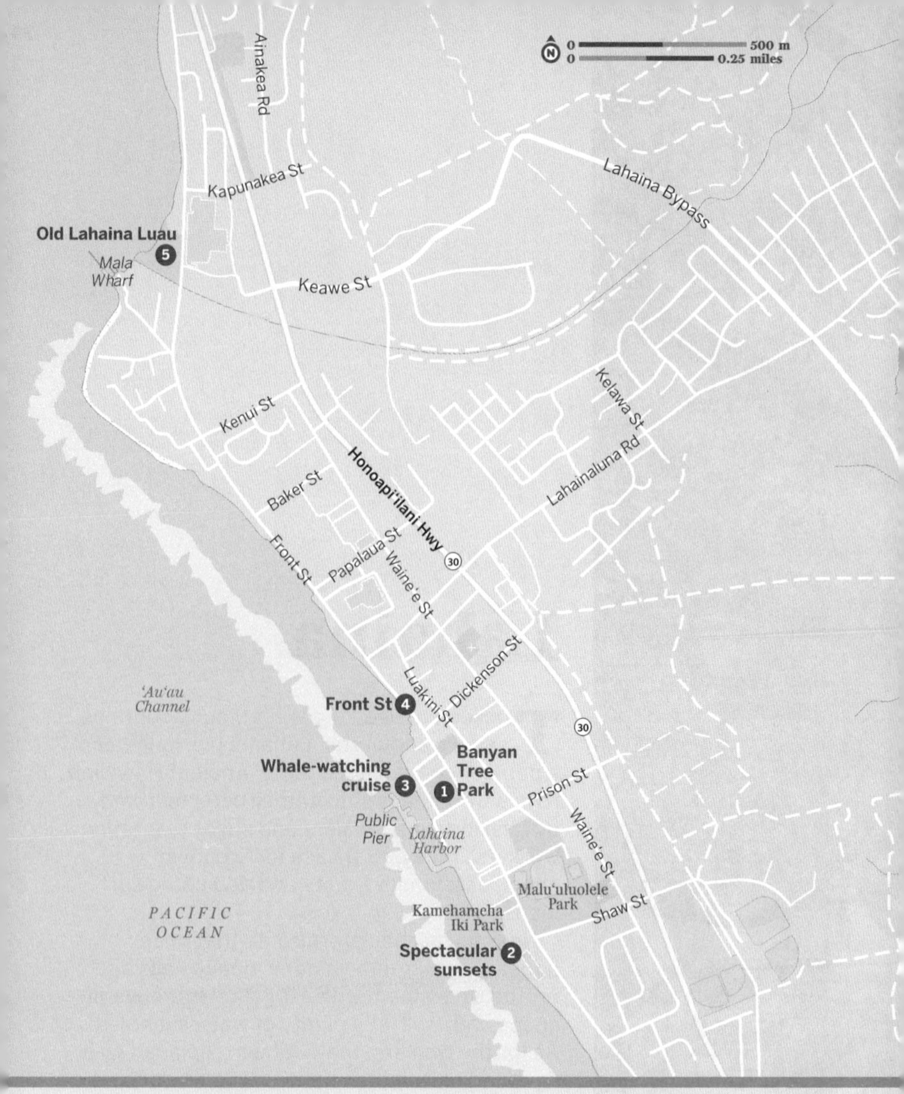

Lahaina Highlights

❶ **Banyan Tree Park** (p81) Reveling in the beauty of Lahaina's central landmark, including the Old Lahaina Courthouse.

❷ **Spectacular Sunsets** (p93) Thrilling to the spectacle over the Pacific from the terrace of a restaurant along Front St, like Pacific'O.

❸ **Whale-watching Cruise** (p86) Enjoying good odds that you'll see a whale in winter, especially when you're in the skilled hands of an operator such as Pacific Whale Foundation.

❹ **Front St** (p95) Strolling while viewing dawdling sailboats and a languid Lana'i, and browsing galleries such as Peter Lik.

❺ **Old Lahaina Luau** (p95) Celebrating Hawaiian culture with traditional hula, tropical cocktails and food a few cuts above the average luau experience.

History

In ancient times Lahaina – then known as Lele – housed a royal court for high chiefs and was the breadbasket (or, more accurately, the breadfruit basket) of West Maui. After Kamehameha the Great unified the islands, he chose the area as his base. The capital remained here until 1845, centered on **Moku'ula Island & Mokuhinia Pond Site** (Map p84; cnr Front & Shaw Sts). The first Christian missionaries arrived in the 1820s and, within a decade, Hawaii's first stone church, missionary school and printing press were in place.

Lahaina became the dominant port for whalers, not only in Hawaii but in the entire Pacific. The whaling era reached its peak in the 1840s, with hundreds of ships pulling into port each year. When the whaling industry fizzled in the 1860s, Lahaina became all but a ghost town. In the 1870s sugarcane came to Lahaina, and it remained the backbone of the economy until tourism took over in the 1960s.

Sights

Lahaina's top sights cluster around the harbor, with other sights either on Front St or within a few blocks of it. This makes Lahaina an ideal town to explore on foot. The top free sight? The sunset view from Front St, at its intersection with Lahainaluna Rd.

During our research period, the harbor front was in the midst of a multiphase improvement project. The city and local media are now referring to Banyan Tree Park and the improved strip of land beside the harbor as **Keawaiki Park**.

★Old Lahaina Courthouse — MUSEUM

(Map p84; visitor center 808-667-9193; http://lahainarestoration.org/old-lahaina-courthouse; 648 Wharf St, Banyan Tree Park; 9am-5pm) FREE Tucked in the shadows of the iconic banyan tree, Lahaina's 1859 courthouse is a repository of history and art. Its location beside the harbor is no coincidence: smuggling was so rampant during the whaling era that officials deemed this the ideal spot for customs operations, the courthouse and the jail – all neatly wrapped into a single building. It also held the governor's office. On August 12, 1898, the US annexation of Hawaii was formally concluded here.

The excellent Lahaina Visitor Center (p96) is on the building's 1st floor. On the 2nd floor, there is the Lahaina Heritage Museum (p81).

There are also two art galleries operated by the Lahaina Arts Society (p95), one in the old jail in the basement (entrance outside).

The building was given the Greek Revival style you see today in 1925 and the courthouse and other government offices here were used until the 1970s.

Lahaina Heritage Museum — MUSEUM

(Map p84; www.lahainarestoration.org; 648 Wharf St, Banyan Tree Park; 9am-5pm) FREE This small museum on the 2nd floor of the Old Lahaina Courthouse celebrates Lahaina's prominent role in Maui's history. Exhibits spotlight ancient Hawaiian culture, missionary days, 19th-century whaling, and local plantations and mills. Check out the lemon-shaped sling stones. Made from volcanic rock, they were deadly projectiles used in early Hawaiian warfare. The 1898 Kingdom of Hawaii flag that once flew above the courthouse hangs above the stairwell.

Free guided tours are offered on Tuesday and Wednesday at 10am, 11am and noon. Meet on the ocean-side steps.

★Banyan Tree Park — PARK

(Map p84; cnr Front & Hotel Sts) A leafy landmark (the largest tree in Hawaii) stands in the center of Lahaina. Remarkably, it sprawls across the entire square. Planted as a seedling on April 24, 1873, to commemorate the 50th anniversary of missionaries in Lahaina, the tree has become a virtual forest unto itself, with 16 major trunks and scores of horizontal branches reaching across the better part of an acre. The square was recently given a major restoration, which fixed the paving tiles and teak benches.

The songs of thousands of mynah birds keep things lively at night. Most weekends artists and craftsmen set up booths beneath the tree's shady canopy.

Fort Ruins — RUINS

(Map p84; cnr Wharf & Canal Sts) This imposing stack of coral stone blocks standing at attention is a reconstruction of a section of an 1832 fort, originally built to keep rowdy whalers in line. Each day at dusk, a Hawaiian sentinel would beat a drum to alert sailors to return to their ships. Stragglers who didn't make it in time were imprisoned here.

At the height of its use, the fort had some 47 cannons, most salvaged from foreign ships that sank in Lahaina's tricky waters.

When the fort was dismantled in the 1850s, its stone blocks were used to build Hale Pa'ahao prison.

Baldwin House MUSEUM

(Map p84; ☎808-661-3262; www.lahainarestoration.org/baldwin-home-museum; 120 Dickenson St; adult/child incl admission to Wo Hing Museum $7/free; ⏲10am-4pm, candlelit tours dusk-8:30pm Fri) Built in 1834–35, the Baldwin House is the oldest surviving Western-style building in Lahaina. It served as the home of Reverend Dwight Baldwin, a missionary doctor, and as the community's first medical clinic. The coral-and-rock walls are a hefty 24in thick, which keeps the house cool year-round. The exterior walls have been plastered over, but you can get a sense of how they originally appeared through a glass panel in the study.

It took the Baldwins 161 days to get here from their native Connecticut, sailing around Cape Horn at the southern tip of South America. Dr Baldwin's passport and representative period furniture are on display. A doctor's 'scale of fees' states that $50 was the price for treating a 'very great sickness,' while a 'very small sickness' cost $10. It's only a cold, Doc, I swear.

Hale Pa'ahao Prison MUSEUM

(Stuck-in-Irons House; Map p84; www.lahainarestoration.org/hale-paahao-prison; 187 Prison St; ⏲10am-4pm) FREE A remnant of the whaling era, this shady coral-stone jail was built in 1852 and looks much as it did 150 years ago thanks to a 1988 restoration. One of the tiny reconstructed cells displays a list of arrests in 1855. The top three offenses were drunkenness (330 arrests), 'furious riding' (89) and lascivious conduct (20). Other transgressions of the day included profanity, aiding deserting sailors and drinking *'awa* (kava; native plant used to make an intoxicating drink).

Wo Hing Museum MUSEUM

(Map p84; ☎808-661-5553; www.lahainarestoration.org/wo-hing-museum; 858 Front St; adult/child incl admission to Baldwin House $7/free; ⏲10am-4pm) This three-story temple, built in 1912 as a meeting hall for the benevolent Chee Kung Tong society, gave Chinese immigrants a place to preserve their cultural identity, celebrate festivities and socialize in their native tongue. After WWII, Lahaina's ethnic Chinese population spread far and wide and the temple fell into decline. Now restored and turned into a cultural museum, it houses an intricately carved 11-panel screen from the 1850s, jade Fu dog statues weighing 300lb each and early-1900s artifacts.

The tin-roof **cookhouse** out back holds a tiny theater showing films of Hawaii shot by Thomas Edison in 1898 and 1906, soon after he invented the motion-picture camera. These grainy black-and-white shots are surprisingly entertaining, capturing poignant images of old Hawaii, including *paniolos* (cowboys) herding cattle, cane workers in the fields and everyday street scenes.

Pioneer Mill Smokestack MUSEUM

(Map p84; www.lahainarestoration.org; 275 Lahainaluna Rd; ⏲sunrise-sunset) FREE The hard-to-miss Pioneer Mill smokestack is a local icon. Outdoor exhibits spotlight equipment and vehicles used on the company's sugar plantation, in operation from 1860 until 1999. There are two restored late-1800s steam locomotives, formerly used by Pioneer Mill, and excellent informational signs explaining the history of sugarcane plantations in Lahaina.

Lahaina Jodo Mission BUDDHIST TEMPLE

(Map p87; ☎808-661-4304; 12 Ala Moana St; ⏲sunrise-sunset) A 12ft-high bronze Buddha sits serenely in the courtyard at this Buddhist mission, looking across the Pacific toward its Japanese homeland. Cast in Kyoto, the Buddha is the largest of its kind outside Japan and was installed here in 1968 to celebrate the centennial of Japanese immigration to Hawaii. The grounds also hold a 90ft pagoda and a whopping 3.5-ton temple bell, which is rung 11 times each evening at 8pm. Inside the temple are priceless Buddhist paintings by Haijin Iwasaki.

Hauola Stone HISTORIC SITE

(Map p84; off Market St) Well, that doesn't look entirely comfortable. At the northern shoreline of the small plaza behind the Lahaina Public Library, look beneath the water's surface for the middle of three lava stones. In the 14th and 15th centuries, royal women gave birth to the next generation of chiefs and royalty here.

Lahaina Public Library Grounds PARK

(Map p84; 680 Wharf St) The gardens here were once a royal taro field, where Kamehameha II toiled in the mud to instill in his subjects the dignity of labor. Today they

OFF THE BEATEN TRACK

HALE PA'I PRINTING MUSEUM

A small white cottage on the grounds of Lahainaluna High School, what is now **Hale Pa'i Printing Museum** (808-662-0560; http://lahainarestoration.org/hale-pai-museum; 980 Lahainaluna Rd; 10am-4pm Mon-Wed) housed Hawaii's first printing press. Although its primary mission was making the Bible available to Hawaiians, the press also produced, in 1834, Hawaii's first newspaper. Named *Ka Lama* (The Torch), it held the distinction of being the first newspaper west of the Rockies. Call in advance; Hale Pa'i is staffed by volunteers so hours can vary. To get there, follow Lahainaluna Rd uphill for 2 miles northeast from downtown.

The adjacent school was founded in 1831, and students operated the press. Typography tools and a replica of the original Rampage Press are on display. The original press was so heavily used that it wore out in the 1850s. Displays discuss various items and publications printed on the press. There's also an exhibit explaining the history of Hawaii's 12-letter alphabet and a reprint of an amusing 'Temperance Map,' drawn by an early missionary to illustrate the perils of drunkenness. Don't be alarmed if an ear-splitting siren breaks your 1850s reverie; it's just the high school's 'bell' for changing classes. Boarding students, about 10% of the student body, have traditionally worked in neighboring fields – so the bell has to be loud.

offer a bit of a green respite near the historic waterfront.

Brick Palace HISTORIC SITE

(Map p84; off Market St) The first Western-style building in Hawaii, the Brick Palace was erected by Kamehameha I around 1800 to keep watch on arriving ships. Despite the name, this 'palace' was a simple two-story structure built by a pair of ex-convicts from Botany Bay. All that remains is a vague representation of the excavated foundation. It's behind the Lahaina Public Library.

Lahaina Lighthouse LIGHTHOUSE

(Map p84; Wharf St) Directly in front of the Pioneer Inn (p94) is the site of the first lighthouse in the Pacific. It was commissioned in 1840 to aid whaling ships pulling into the harbor. The current concrete structure dates from 1916.

Beaches

Launiupoko Beach Park BEACH

(Map p104; Honoapi'ilani Hwy; P) Beginner and intermediate surfers head to this beach park, a popular wayside 3 miles south of Lahaina. The park is an ideal spot for families; *na keiki* (children) have a blast wading in the large rock-enclosed shoreline pool and good picnic facilities invite you to linger. Launiupoko is at the traffic light at the 18-mile marker on Honoapi'ilani Hwy, at its intersection with Kai Hele Ku St. There are restrooms and outdoor showers but no lifeguards.

Wahikuli Wayside Park PARK

(808-661-4685; Honoapi'ilani Hwy; P) Just 2 miles north of the heart of Lahaina and right on the road to Ka'anapali, this multi-section county park follows the shore and is great for walking and cycling. There are dozens of shady picnic tables, reef-protected beaches and fine views of Lana'i. It's a short bike ride or nice stroll from central Lahaina.

Activities

Lahaina is not known for its beaches, which are generally shallow and rocky, though you can find good ones at parks just north and south of the center. It is a good place to take a surfing lesson.

For a sunset cruise, a whale-watching tour or other maritime adventures, head to Lahaina Harbor, which is lined with kiosks and boats ready to set you up for a maritime adventure.

Dive boats leave from Lahaina Harbor, offering dives suitable for all levels.

★ **Lahaina Divers** DIVING

(Map p84; 808-667-7496; www.lahainadivers.com; 143 Dickenson St; 2-tank dives from $149; 9am-6pm) Offers a full range of dives, from a wreck dive to 'discover scuba' dives for newbies.

The latter go to a reef thick with green sea turtles – a great intro to diving. There are also lessons and a huge range of packages, as well as scuba gear rentals.

Lahaina Downtown

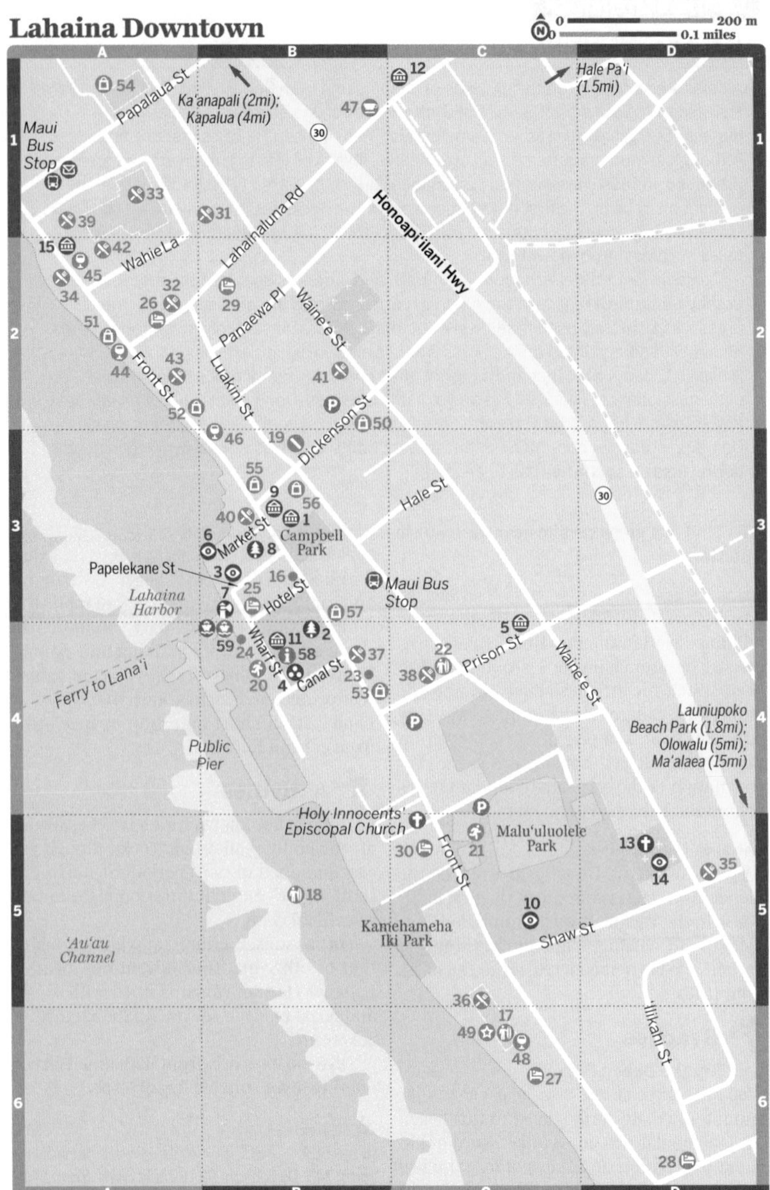

★ Snorkel Bob's SNORKELING

(Map p87; ☎808-661-4421; www.snorkelbob.com; 1217 Front St; snorkel gear package per week from $30; ⊙8am-5pm) With 12 shops on four islands, Snorkel Bob's is famous for cheap snorkel-set rentals, offering a huge range of equipment and deals by the day or week. You can even pick up your gear in Lahaina and return it on another island. The store is on Front St north of downtown. The bare-bones Budget Crunch Special is $9 per week.

Lahaina Downtown

Sights

1 Baldwin House B3
2 Banyan Tree Park B4
3 Brick Palace B3
4 Fort Ruins B4
5 Hale Pa'ahao Prison C4
6 Hauola Stone B3
Lahaina Heritage Museum .... (see 11)
7 Lahaina Lighthouse B3
8 Lahaina Public Library Grounds B3
9 Masters' Reading Room B3
10 Moku'ula Island & Mokuhinia Pond Site C5
11 Old Lahaina Courthouse B4
12 Pioneer Mill Smokestack C1
13 Waiola (Waine'e) Church D5
14 Waiola Cemetery D5
15 Wo Hing Museum A2

Activities, Courses & Tours

16 Atlantis Submarine B3
17 Goofy Foot Surf School C6
Hawaii Ocean Project .... (see 7)
18 Lahaina Breakwall B5
19 Lahaina Divers B3
20 Makai Adventures B4
21 Malu'uluolele Park Tennis Courts C5
Maui Ocean Sports .... (see 17)
Maui Surf Clinics .... (see 49)
22 Maui Wave Riders C4
23 Pacific Whale Foundation B4
24 Scotch Mist II B4
Trilogy Excursions .... (see 59)

Sleeping

25 Best Western Pioneer Inn B3
26 Lahaina Inn A2
27 Lahaina Shores C6
28 Old Lahaina House D6
29 Plantation Inn B2
30 Tiki Beach Hostel C5

Eating

31 808 Grindz Cafe B1
32 Cafe Cafe A2
Cool Cat Cafe .... (see 57)
33 Foodland A1
Gerard's .... (see 29)
34 Kimo's A2
Lahaina Grill .... (see 26)
35 Maka'i Malasadas D5
Ono Gelato Co .... (see 51)
36 Pacific'O C5
37 Paia Fishmarket B4
Pho Saigon 808 .... (see 57)
38 Prison Street Pizza C4
39 Sale Pepe A1
40 Sunrise Cafe B3
41 TaquerEATa B2
42 Thai Chef A2
43 Ululani's Hawaiian Shave Ice A2

Drinking & Nightlife

44 Cheeseburger In Paradise A2
45 Dirty Monkey A2
Down the Hatch .... (see 57)
46 Fleetwood's on Front St B3
47 MauiGrown Coffee B1
Pioneer Inn Bar .... (see 25)
48 Spanky's Riptide C6

Entertainment

49 Feast at Lele C6

Shopping

50 Hale Zen Home Decor & More B2
51 HI, i like you A2
Lahaina Arts Society .... (see 11)
52 Lahaina Printsellers A2
53 Maui Hands B4
54 Outlets of Maui A1
55 Peter Lik Gallery B3
56 Village Galleries B3
Village Gifts & Fine Arts .... (see 9)
57 Wharf Cinema Center B3

Information

58 Lahaina Visitor Center B4

Transport

59 Expeditions Ferry B4

West Maui Cycles CYCLING

(Map p87; ☎808-661-9005; www.westmauicycles.com; 1087 Limahana Pl; per day $15-100; ⏰9am-5pm Mon-Sat, to 4pm Sun) Quality road and hybrid bikes for rent, as well as cheaper cruisers for kicking around town.

Check the website for route maps and trail locations. Rental includes helmet, lock and tire repair kit. No mountain bikes. The office is a hub for cyclists.

Maui Ocean Sports KAYAKING

(Map p84; ☎808-214-3491; www.mauioceansports.com; 505 Front St; guided tour adult/child from $59/49; ⏰trips from 7am) Offers guided kayaking and kayak-snorkel tours along the western coast of Maui. The Lahaina Paddle trip doubles as a whale-watching excursion in season. Kayak rentals are also available (per two hours/day $49/65).

This outfit formerly operated as Maui Kayaks.

Malu'uluolele Park Tennis Courts TENNIS
(Map p84; Front St, Malu'uluolele Park) These popular public tennis courts have lights to enable night playing.

Surfing

Lahaina is a great place to learn to surf, with first-class instructors, gentle waves and ideal conditions for beginners. The section of shoreline known as **Lahaina Breakwall** (Map p84), north of Kamehameha Iki Park, is a favorite spot for novices. Surfers also take to the waters just offshore from Launiupoko Beach Park.

Several companies in Lahaina offer surfing lessons, most based on or near Front St.

★**Maui Surf Clinics** SURFING
(Map p84; ☎808-244-7873; www.mauisurfclinics.com; 505 Front St, Suite 201; 2hr lesson from $85, surfboard rentals per day $25-30, SUP rentals per day $40;) This welcoming school offers a huge range of group and private lessons. Highlights include classes geared to children (from $135), and instructors will work with youngsters as young as four if they can swim. Also has courses for intermediate surfers looking to improve their form, as well as SUP lessons, an eco-cultural SUP tour, and surfboard and SUP rentals.

Goofy Foot Surf School SURFING
(Map p84; ☎808-244-9283; www.goofyfootsurfschool.com; 505 Front St, Suite 123; 2hr lesson from $80; lessons 7am, 8:30am, 10am, 11:30am, 1pm Mon-Sat;) This top surf school combines fundamentals with fun. In addition to surf and SUP lessons, it runs day-long surf camps. Pick up a free beginner surf map with safety guidelines at the shop. It also rents surfboards and SUP boards to experienced surfers and paddlers – if you've taken a lesson or been on a board, you should be good.

Maui Wave Riders SURFING
(Map p84; ☎808-661-0003; www.mauiwaveriders.com; 133 Prison St; 2hr class from $70; group lessons 7:30am, 10am & 12:30pm Mon-Fri, 7:30am & 10am Sat) Offers surfing classes for all ages, as well as SUP lessons. Also has gear rentals, with a huge range of boards.

Tours

Catamarans and other vessels in Lahaina Harbor cater to tourists, and outfitters staff booths along the harbor's edge. Most companies offer discounts or combo deals on their websites. Check with the company for the specifics about where to meet pre-trip.

During whale season from mid-December to mid-April, snorkeling trips and cocktail cruises often double as whale-watching excursions.

★**Trilogy Excursions** BOATING
(Map p84; ☎808-874-5649; www.sailtrilogy.com; 675 Wharf St, Lahaina Harbor; 4hr snorkel trip adult/child from $125/70) Offering snorkeling tours in Maui for more than 40 years, this family-run operation specializes in catamaran tours. There's a variety of trips, including ones to the reef at Olowalu and the much-loved islet of Molokini, plus dinner and sunset sails. Day trips to Lana'i are also popular. In season look for whale-watching excursions. Trips launching from Lahaina meet at Lahaina Harbor.

★**Pacific Whale Foundation** WILDLIFE
(PacWhale Eco-Adventures; Map p84; ☎808-650-7223; www.pacwhale.com; 612 Front St; whale-watching adult/child from $38/25; store 6:30am-8pm;) The whale-watching cruises, which depart several times a day in winter, are immensely popular. In the unlikely event that you don't spot whales, your next trip is free. Well-versed naturalists add context to the trips. Snorkel and dolphin-watching cruises (adult/child $105/65) are popular year-round. The outfit also offers other snorkeling trips as well as various sunset and dinner cruises.

Most trips leave from Lahaina Harbor, but some depart from Ma'alaea Harbor to the south.

Makai Adventures WHALE WATCHING
(Map p84; ☎808-495-1001; www.makaiadventures.com; 675 Wharf St, Slip 16, Lahaina Harbor; 2hr whale-watching trips adult/child $51/37; sales booth 7am-7pm, whale-watching trips Dec–mid-Apr) Runs well-regarded whale-watching trips several times a day during the humpback-whale season. The small boat carries a maximum of 20 people.

Scotch Mist II CRUISE
(Map p84; ☎808-661-0386; www.scotchmistsailingcharters.com; 675 Wharf St, Slip 2, Lahaina Harbor; adult/child from $59/35) The *Scotch Mist II*, a beautiful 50ft sailing yacht, serves champagne, wine and chocolate-covered macadamia nuts on its sunset cruise. Book in advance, as the boat carries just 22 passengers per sail, and scan for whales in

North Lahaina

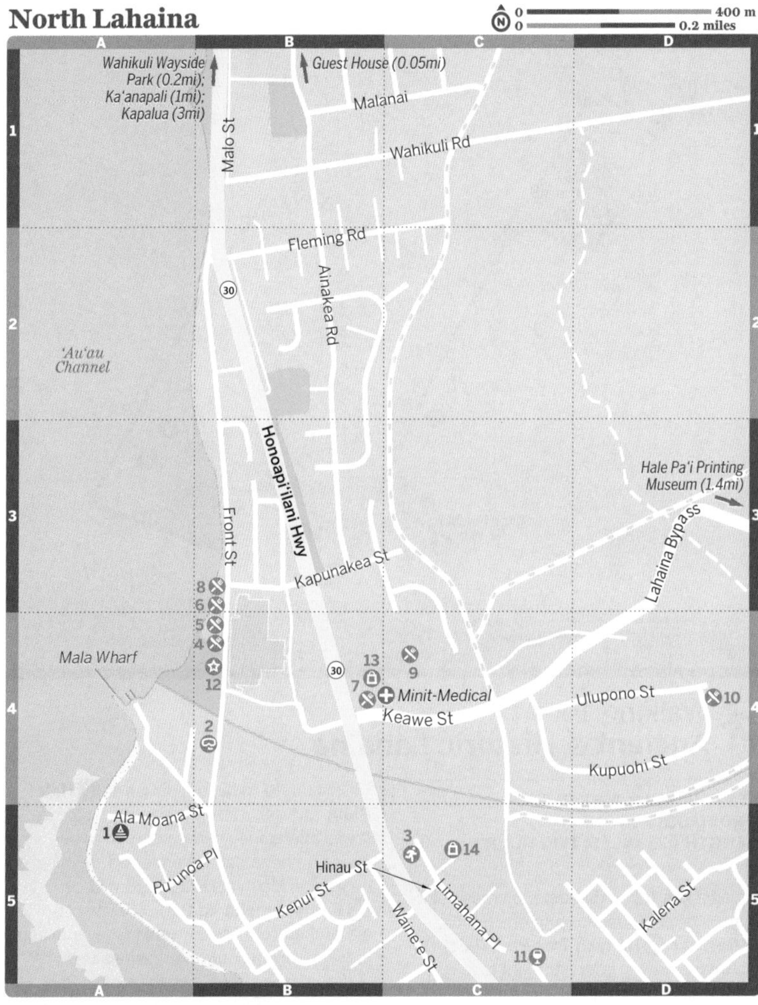

North Lahaina

Sights

1 Lahaina Jodo Mission A5

Activities, Courses & Tours

2 Snorkel Bob's B4
3 West Maui Cycles C5

Eating

4 Aloha Mixed Plate B4
Choice Health Bar .... (see 3)
5 Frida's Mexican Beach House B4
6 Honu Seafood & Pizza B3
7 Island Cream Co B4
8 Mala Ocean Tavern B3
9 Moku Roots C4
10 Star Noodle D4

Drinking & Nightlife

11 Koholā Brewery C5

Entertainment

12 Old Lahaina Luau B4

Shopping

13 Lahaina Gateway B4
14 Ole Surfboards C5

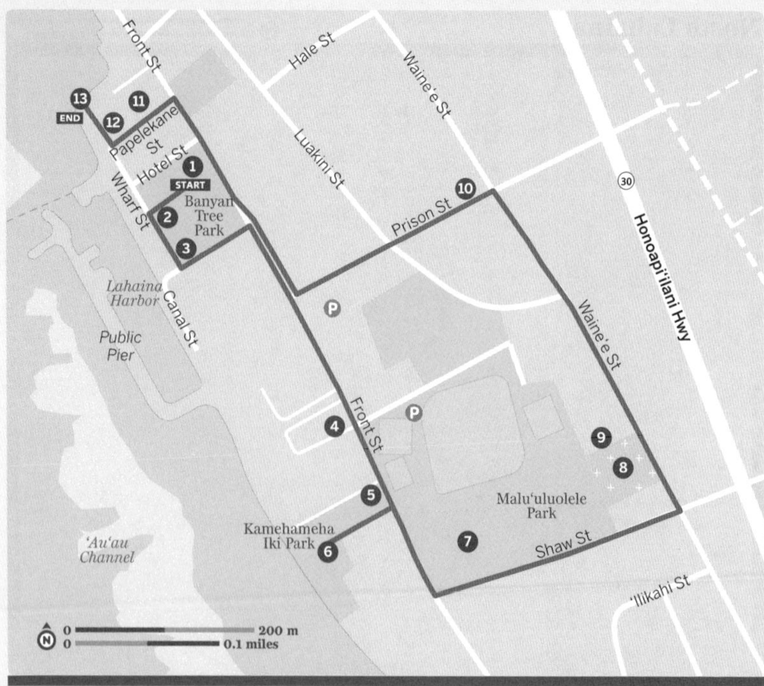

Walking Tour
Ancient & Historic Lahaina

START BANYAN TREE PARK
END HAUOLA STONE
LENGTH 1.25 MILES; TWO HOURS

Lahaina has sights that date to times before the arrival of Europeans and Americans.

Begin at 1 **Banyan Tree Park** (p81). Its landmark banyan is a testament to extraordinary natural architecture.

The adjacent 2 **Old Lahaina Courthouse** (p81) symbolizes the start of the modern era of the United States in Lahaina. Inside, stop by the Lahaina Visitor Center for the excellent brochure ($2.50) describing Lahaina's historic sites, many of which are fronted by interpretative markers.

Just south, the 3 **Fort Ruins** (p81) recall efforts to control whalers in the 1830s.

Turn right onto Front St to reach 4 **Holy Innocents' Episcopal Church** (Map p84; 808-661-4202; www.holyimaui.org; open dawn-dusk, services 7:30am & 9am Sun), which has a colorful interior depicting a Hawaiian Madonna. The site was once a summer home of Hawaii's last monarch, Queen Lili'uokalani.

Just south is the foundation of 5 **Hale Piula**, Lahaina's attempt at a royal palace. It was abandoned mid-construction because Kamehameha III preferred sleeping nearby on Moku'ula Island. Fronted by 6 **Kamehameha Iki Park**, the site now has a thatched-roof pavilion used for events and carvers building outrigger canoes.

Across the street in Malu'uluolele Park, ponder the 7 **Moku'ula Island & Mokuhinia Pond Site**. This freshwater pond and sacred island were used as a home by generations of Hawaiian royalty.

Pivotal figures in 19th-century Maui are buried in 8 **Waiola Cemetery** (Map p84; Waine'e St). Just north is the 9 **Waine'e Church** (Map p84; 535 Waine'e St) – rebuilt several times. At the corner of Prison and Waine'e Sts, 10 **Hale Pa'ahao Prison** (p82) held drunken whalers serving time.

Near the harbor behind the 11 **Lahaina Public Library Grounds** (p82), look for the scant legacy of the 12 **Brick Palace** (p83). Finish at the ancient 13 **Hauola Stone** (p82) while gazing out to the ocean.

season (December to April). Snorkel cruises and group charters are also available.

Hawaii Ocean Project CRUISE

(Map p84; ☎808-667-6165; www.hawaiiocean-project.com; 675 Wharf St, Lahaina Harbor; dinner cruise adult/child $100/60; ⏰office 7am-7pm) This flotilla of boats includes the 70ft-long *Kaulana*, the largest catamaran in the harbor. It's used for snorkeling tours along with the 65ft-long *Lahaina Princess* (from adult/child $120/70). The sunset dinner cruise on the 120ft-long *Maui Princess* includes open-air table service and live music.

Atlantis Submarine BOATING

(Map p84; ☎808-667-2494; www.atlantisadventures.com; 658 Wharf St, Best Western Pioneer Inn; adult/child $124/48; ⏰tours hourly 9am-2pm, office 7:30am-6pm; 👪) To see Maui's undersea wonders without getting wet, consider a trip on the *Atlantis*. The price is steep, but this 65-footer is a real sub, and it dives to a depth of more than 100ft. Sights include coral, tropical fish and the sunken *Carthaginian:* a sailing brig that played a leading role in the 1965 movie *Hawaii*.

Festivals & Events

Lahaina's top festivals draw huge crowds, with Front St closed to traffic during many of these events. Check http://visitlahaina.com/events for the latest schedule.

★**King Kamehameha Day Parade** PARADE

(http://visitlahaina.com; ⏰mid-Jun) Traditionally dressed Hawaiian riders on horseback, marching bands and floral floats take to Front St to honor Kamehameha the Great on this public holiday in mid-June. An awards ceremony and arts festival follow at Banyan Tree Park.

★**Whale & Ocean Arts Festival** CULTURAL

(http://visitlahaina.com; ⏰early Mar) Celebrate the annual humpback whale migration during this weekend-long celebration with Hawaiian music, hula and games. Naturalists are on hand to share their knowledge about whales. Also features marine-themed art. Held at Kamehameha III Elementary School on Front St.

Holiday Lighting of the Banyan Tree CHRISTMAS

(http://visitlahaina.com; ⏰Dec) Lahaina illuminates Hawaii's biggest tree on the first weekend in December with thousands of colorful lights, accompanied by hula performances, carolers, cookie decorating and a craft show. And, of course, Santa shows up for the *na keiki*.

Friday Town Party CARNIVAL

(www.mauifridays.com; ⏰5-8:30pm) This outdoor festival features music and food vendors. It's held the second Friday of the month at Campbell Park, which is across from the Pioneer Inn on Front St.

Halloween in Lahaina CARNIVAL

(http://visitlahaina.com; ⏰Oct 31) Front St morphs into a costumed street festival on Halloween night. The party is fun for families in the late afternoon, with a *na keiki* costume parade, but things gets a bit wilder as the night goes on – although a strong police presence keeps rowdiness in check. Forget parking; take a shuttle or taxi.

Banyan Tree Birthday STREET CARNIVAL

(http://visitlahaina.com; ⏰Apr) Lahaina's favorite tree gets a two-day birthday party, complete with a birthday cake, music and art, a cake decorating contest and activities for *na keiki*. It's held on the weekend closest to April 24. The tree celebrates its 150th birthday in 2023.

Fourth of July FIREWORKS

(⏰Jul 4) Enjoy live music along Front St in the late afternoon then watch fireworks light up the sky over the harbor at 8pm.

Sleeping

Despite the throngs of tourists filling its streets, Lahaina has limited places to stay. West Maui's resort hotels are to the north, where the beaches are better. On the other hand, Lahaina's accommodations put you right in the heart of one of Hawaii's most compelling places. A handful of hostels and guesthouses are clustered along Front St just north of Kamehameha Iki Park.

Tiki Beach Hostel HOSTEL $

(Map p84; ☎808-280-1166; www.tikibeachmaui.com; 545 Front St; dm/tent $59/45; ⏰reception 8am-8pm; 📶) Folks are packed in tight – with a few guests sleeping in tents outside – at this busy but friendly hostel, set in lush gardens near both the water and Lahaina's center. There are mixed and female-only dorms, with free linens and towels for rent. OK for a night or two and may suit younger travelers best.

Formerly known as the Tiki Hale.

Lahaina Inn INN $

(Map p84; ☎808-661-0577; www.lahainainn.com; 127 Lahainaluna Rd; r from $189, suite $249; ⏰reception 9am-5pm; P❄📶) Small and spare but sporting a hint of style from a recent refresh, the rooms at the Lahaina Inn are a fine choice if budget and a central location are your primary goals. Rooms have a lanai for taking in the downtown action, but all are on the 2nd floor with no elevator.

The inn is perched above the recommended Lahaina Grill (p93) and enjoys guest privileges with it sister property, the Royal Lahaina resort in Ka'anapali.

Old Lahaina House GUESTHOUSE $

(Map p84; ☎808-667-4663; www.oldlahaina.com; 407 Ilikahi St; r $110-200; P❄📶🏊) Set around a small pool in a compact garden, the four comfortable rooms in this two-story modern house have amenities including fridges, coffee pots and access to an outdoor kitchen with grill. Bed choices include two twins, or a queen or king. The center of town is under a 10-minute walk away, and it's an easy walk to a small and low-key beach.

★**Plantation Inn** B&B $$

(Map p84; ☎808-667-9225, reservations 800-433-6815; www.kbhmaui.com/plantation-inn; 174 Lahainaluna Rd; r/ste incl breakfast from $206/354; P❄📶🏊) Alohas are warm at this genteel oasis, which is set back from the hustle and bustle of Lahaina's waterfront. Modern amenities blend seamlessly with plantation-era decor inside the stylish rooms. Victorian-style standard rooms come with four-poster beds. The highlight? Complimentary breakfast from in-house **Gerard's** (Map p84; ☎808-661-8939; www.gerardsmaui.com; 174 Lahainaluna Rd; mains from $42, 8-course prix fixe per person $105; ⏰seatings 6-8pm) served by the pool – the savory eggs Florentine are delicious. Most rooms have a lanai (porch, balcony or veranda).

Lahaina Shores CONDO $$

(Map p84; ☎808-661-4835; www.destinationhotels.com/lahaina-shores; 475 Front St; r from $295, 3-night minimum; P❄📶🏊) This seven-story property, central Lahaina's only oceanfront condo complex, operates hotel-style with a front desk and full services. All the units are roomy, and even the studios have a full kitchen and lanai. Premier rooms shine with a breezy island style, which is much better than the lackluster architectural style. Check the website as well as www.vrbo.com for availability.

Best Western Pioneer Inn HOTEL $$

(Map p84; ☎808-661-3636; www.bestwestern.com; 658 Wharf St; r from $251; P❄@📶🏊) Built in 1901 and perfectly located, the historic Pioneer Inn may look salty and sea-worn at first glance, but step inside for a pleasant surprise. The 34 rooms are modern and many have direct access to the wide 2nd-floor terrace. The accommodating staff keep the sailing smooth. Ship figureheads and the saloon's swinging doors give a nod to Lahaina's whaling past.

Eating

Lahaina has the finest dining scene on Maui and a huge range of choices. But remember, fine food draws hungry hordes. Many folks staying in Ka'anapali pour into Lahaina at dinnertime and traffic jams up. Allow extra time and book popular places in advance.

★**808 Grindz Cafe** BREAKFAST $

(Map p84; ☎808-868-4147; www.808grindzcafe.com; 843 Waine'e St, Foodland Shopping Center; mains $7-15; ⏰7am-2pm) This is the Maui we love. *Ono kine grinds* (good food), budget-friendly prices and down-home aloha. This reincarnation of the beloved North Shore Cafe in Haiku, which closed a few years back, offers an $8.08 menu that is one of the best deals around for a hearty breakfast. The eggs Benedict cost a bit more, but options include crab cakes and salmon.

The secret is out, so put your name on the list and enjoy a chat with the locals and tourists waiting with you. Also, if you're wondering, 808 is a nod to Maui's area code.

Ululani's Hawaiian Shave Ice SWEETS $

(Map p84; www.ululanishawaiianshaveice.com; 790 Front St; regular ice $6; ⏰10:30am-9pm) For over-the-top (literally) shave ice, amble up to the counter at the second location of Ululani's Hawaiian Shave Ice and take your pick of tropical flavors.

Choice Health Bar HEALTH FOOD $

(Map p87; ☎808-661-7711; www.choicehealthbar.com; 1087 Limahana Pl; mains $10-15; ⏰8am-5pm Mon-Sat, 9am-2pm Sun; 🌱) This breezy box of healthy deliciousness whips up addictive organic fare. The fruit-stuffed acai bowls – loaded with berries, greens and

WORSHIPPERS & WHALE HUNTERS

Two diametrically opposed groups of New Englanders clashed in Lahaina in the 1820s – missionaries and whalers.

In 1823 William Richards, Lahaina's first missionary, converted Maui's native governor, Hoapili, to Christianity and persuaded him to pass laws against 'drunkenness and debauchery.' However, after months at sea, sailors weren't looking for a prayer service when they pulled into port – to them there was 'no God west of the Horn.' Missionaries and whalers almost came to battle in 1827, when Governor Hoapili arrested a whaler captain for allowing women to board his ship. The crew retaliated by shooting cannonballs at Richards' house. The captain was released, but laws forbidding liaisons between seamen and Hawaiian women remained in force. This actually proved popular with many ship captains, as their crews were less likely to become incapacitated while docked in Lahaina as opposed to Honolulu, which was something of a den of iniquity.

It wasn't until Governor Hoapili's death in 1840 that laws prohibiting liquor and prostitution were no longer enforced and whalers began to frolic in Lahaina. Among the sailors who roamed Lahaina's streets was Herman Melville in 1843; he later penned *Moby Dick*.

granola – are invigorating. Smoothies, juices and health shots are perfect for travelers on the go. Menu items and ingredients reflect what's in season.

TaquerEATa MEXICAN $

(Map p84; ☎808-866-7078; 741 Waine'e St; mains $5-15; ⊙8am-4pm) Breakfast and lunch tacos can be customized in myriad ways at this silver-hued food truck, part of a pod of trucks. The lines form early for the super fresh and tasty fare. Choose from an array of housemade salsas that sparkle with fresh flavors.

Cafe Cafe CAFE $

(Map p84; ☎808-661-0006; http://cafecafemaui.com; 129 Lahainaluna Rd, Old Lahaina Center; pastries $3-4, mains $8-13; ⊙7am-3pm) A great place for coffee coffee. This laid-back, island-casual joint serves extraordinary coffee drinks and teas, with a collection of ragtag tables out front. Enjoy a bevy of fruit and veggie smoothies, as well as bagel sandwiches and breakfast treats.

Maka'i Malasadas DESSERTS $

(Map p84; 520 Waine'e St; malasada $1.50-2.50; ⊙7:30-11am Mon, Tue, Thu & Fri) Step up to the front-yard register and prepare to be wowed by the hefty *malasadas* that arrive piping hot. You can order them plain or stuffed with everything from chocolate to pineapple. These fried balls of sugar-coated deliciousness – think donuts without holes – were originally brought to the island by Portuguese immigrants. Come early because they do sell out.

Island Cream Co ICE CREAM $

(Map p87; ☎808-298-0916; www.islandcreamco.com; 305 Keawe St, Lahaina Gateway; 1 scoop $6) This creamy homemade delight is worth the short drive from downtown. Creative flavors show off the best of Hawaii, with tubs of macadamia nut, mango and coconut poi (steamed, mashed taro) on offer. We liked the cookies and cream. In the Lahaina Gateway mall, this is a good stop after a meal in northern Lahaina or Ka'anapali.

Sunrise Cafe BREAKFAST $

(Map p84; ☎808-661-8558; 693 Front St; mains $5-16; ⊙7am-3pm) Next to the verdant gardens of the Lahaina Public Library is a great reason to get out of bed: Sunrise Cafe serves up fantastic cheap breakfasts. Choices include cinnamon rolls, lox Benedicts, breakfast burritos and good old bacon and eggs. The small dining area under a tin roof gets crowded and waits can be long. It's cash-only.

Pho Saigon 808 VIETNAMESE $

(Map p84; ☎808-661-6628; http://thewharfcinemacenter.com/pho-saigon-808; 658 Front St, Wharf Cinema Center; mains $12-17; ⊙11am-9pm) Excellent Asian fare is cooked up fast and fresh at this small restaurant buried in the recesses of the Wharf Cinema Center mall. Choose from a large number of noodle dishes, pho and curries. There's also a smattering of Thai dishes, and they deliver.

Prison Street Pizza PIZZA $

(Map p84; ☎808-662-3332; http://prisonstreetpizza.com; 133 Prison St; slice $4, mains $9-28; ⊙9:30am-10pm Mon-Sat, from 11am Sun) For a

LOCAL KNOWLEDGE

LOCAL POKE

The ahi *poke* (raw tuna) is served in an astounding number of flavors at the Foodland grocery store seafood counter. It's one of the best culinary deals on the island. Our favorite part? The free samples! If you want a meal to go, ask for a *poke* bowl ($6.99), which comes with a hefty helping of rice. The spiced ahi *poke* is outstanding.

Once you've checked it out, go for a picnic overlooking the water on Front St.

fantastic budget meal, pop in here for the Surfer's Special: two cheese slices and a soda for $6.99.

Near Banyan Tree Sq, this low-key pizza joint serves Jersey-style pizza (soft crust, loaded with ingredients and plenty of tomatoes in the base). Also offers calzones and a few sandwiches. Eat in the simple dining room, grab takeout or get delivery.

Aloha Mixed Plate HAWAIIAN **$**

(Map p87; ☎808-661-3322; www.alohamixedplate.com; 1285 Front St; mains $10-19; ⏲8am-10pm; 📶) This is the Hawaii you came to find: friendly, open-air and beside the beach (although the view is somewhat obscured).

The food's first rate, the prices reasonable. For a true experience of Hawaii, order the Ali'i Plate, packed with *laulau* (pork, chicken or butterfish wrapped in leaves and steamed), *kalua* pig, *lomilomi* salmon, poi and *haupia* (coconut pudding) – and, of course, macaroni salad and white rice.

The restaurant serves breakfast, including *loco moco* (dish of rice, fried egg and hamburger patty topped with gravy or other condiments) and *kalua* pig omelets.

Ono Gelato Co GELATO **$**

(Map p84; ☎808-495-0203; www.facebook.com/OnoGelato; 815 Front St; medium gelato $6.45; ⏲8am-10pm) Enjoy your silky gelato on the back deck overlooking the sea. There's a hard-to-resist array of smooth gelati as you enter, and a fine coffee bar.

★**Moku Roots** VEGAN **$$**

(Map p87; ☎808-214-5106; www.mokuroots.com; 335 Keawe St, Lahaina Gateway; mains $12-15; ⏲8am-8pm Mon-Sat, 10:30am-3pm Sun; 🖉) 🍃 This small but snazzy vegan restaurant is garnering kudos across Maui. With a commitment to zero waste, evidenced by cloth napkins and no single-use items, Moku Roots describes itself as farm-to-table-to-farm, with leftovers used as farm compost. Beyond sustainability, the appeal lies in the fantastic food, from the popular taro burger to the enormous vegan Cobb salad, our favorite.

★**Star Noodle** ASIAN **$$**

(Map p87; ☎808-667-5400; www.starnoodle.com; 286 Kupuohi St; shared plates $10-18, mains $10-17; ⏲10:30am-10pm) This hillside hot spot is constantly busy – and rightly so. Inside this sleek noodle shop, grazers can nibble on an eclectic array of Asian-fusion share plates. Those seeking heartier fare can dive into garlic noodles, kimchi ramen and a saimin (local-style noodle soup; Spam included). A central communal table and the chatty bar keep the vibe lively.

It's about 1.5 miles from the center of Lahaina, in an otherwise humdrum industrial park.

Paia Fishmarket SEAFOOD **$$**

(Map p84; ☎808-662-3456; http://paiafishmarket.com; 632 Front St; mains $10-22; ⏲10:30am-9:30pm) This branch of the Maui original is located in an appealing vintage building near the banyan tree. There are picnic tables on a shady terrace, while inside it's all bright and airy. Of course the reason to come here is the superb seafood. The menu changes daily depending on what's fresh.

Sale Pepe ITALIAN **$$**

(Map p84; ☎808-667-7667; www.salepepemaui.com; 878 Front St, Old Lahaina Center; mains $16-32; ⏲5-9pm Mon-Sat) Who needs the ocean? The only view at this attractive Italian restaurant trapped inside a strip mall is of fabulous pastas and pizza. The rigatoni, spaghetti, lasagna and more are made fresh daily, as are the many sauces, including the rich tomatoey one used on the superb pizzas. Most ingredients are sourced locally, except for certain essential items imported from Italy.

Thai Chef THAI **$$**

(Map p84; ☎808-667-2814; www.thaichefrestaurantmaui.com; 878 Front St, Old Lahaina Center; mains $13-24; ⏲11am-2pm Mon-Fri, 5-9pm Mon-Sat; 🖉) Hidden in the back of an aging strip mall, this place looks like a dive from the outside, but the food's incredible. Start with the fragrant ginger coconut soup and the fresh summer rolls and then move on to savory curries that explode with flavor. It's BYOB so pick up refreshments from the nearby Foodland.

Cool Cat Cafe DINER **$$**
(Map p84; ☎808-667-0908; www.facebook.com/CoolCatCafeMaui; 658 Front St, Wharf Cinema Center; mains $7-30; ⏲10:30am-10:30pm; 👪) It's a hunka-hunka burger love at this lively 2nd-floor doo-wop diner, where most of the burgers, sandwiches and salads are named for 1950s icons, honoring the likes of Marilyn Monroe, Chubby Checker and, of course, Elvis Presley. The burgers get rave reviews. The view from the large open terrace overlooking Banyan Tree Park isn't bad either.

Kimo's HAWAIIAN **$$**
(Map p84; ☎808-661-4811; www.kimosmaui.com; 845 Front St; lunch & bar menu mains $14-20, dinner mains $25-49; ⏲11am-10pm; 👪) A locally beloved standby with one of the best oceanfront patios on Front St, Hawaiian-style Kimo's keeps everyone happy with reliably good food, a superb water view and a family-friendly setting. Try one of the fresh fish dishes and the towering hula pie. At lunch, order the delicious Caesar salad. Mai tais are served in glass totems; there's a tasty happy-hour menu.

★**Lahaina Grill** HAWAIIAN **$$$**
(Map p84; ☎808-667-5117; www.lahainagrill.com; 127 Lahainaluna Rd; mains $35-99; ⏲from 5pm) The windows at the Lahaina Grill frame a simple but captivating tableau: beautiful food being enjoyed in beautiful surrounds. Once inside, expectations are confirmed by both the service and the food. The menu uses fresh local ingredients sourced from top local purveyors. The steak and seafood dishes are given innovative twists and presented with artistic style.

Frida's Mexican Beach House MEXICAN **$$$**
(Map p87; ☎808-661-1287; www.fridasmaui.com; 1287 Front St; mains $17-40; ⏲11am-9pm) Not your cheap taco joint, Frida's (with plenty of imagery from its namesake Frida Kahlo) has a superb waterfront location, featuring a large open dining area on a terrace that will have your blood pressure falling minutes after arriving. Steaks and seafood with a Latin flair feature on the upscale menu. The thick tortilla chips and kicky salsa are fantastic.

Pacific'O ASIAN **$$$**
(Map p84; ☎808-667-4341; www.pacificomaui.com; 505 Front St; lunch mains $16-23, dinner mains $30-49; ⏲11:30am-9:30pm) 🍃 Enjoy Pacific Rim cuisine prepared with contemporary flourishes at chef James McDonald's chic oceanfront restaurant. Bold and innovative seafood and beef dishes are accompanied by the best of Maui's garden bounty. Lunch is a less fancy affair, with island-inspired salads, sandwiches and tacos, but the same up-close ocean view across a small beach.

Mala Ocean Tavern FUSION **$$$**
(Map p87; ☎808-667-9394; www.malaoceantavern.com; 1307 Front St; mains brunch $10-23, dinner $13-46; ⏲9am-10pm) This inviting waterfront restaurant from local restaurateur Mark Ellman fuses Mediterranean and Pacific influences with upmarket flair. Tapas dishes include comfort foods such as flatbreads and fries ($7 to $15). For entrees, the choices are more sophisticated: anything with fish is a sure pleaser, as is the renowned grass-fed Hawaiian beef burger. At sunset, tiki torches on the waterfront lanai add a romantic touch.

Honu Seafood & Pizza SEAFOOD, PIZZA **$$$**
(Map p87; ☎808-667-9390; www.honumaui.com; 1295 Front St; mains $18-46; ⏲11am-9pm) Named for Maui's famous green sea turtles, this stylish venture from restaurateur Mark Ellman is wowing crowds with expansive ocean views and a savory array of popular wood-fired pizzas, fresh salads, and comfort foods such as burgers. The fresh seafood is seasoned with global flavors. The beer list features over 50 brews (10 on tap).

Foodland SUPERMARKET
(Map p84; ☎808-661-0975; www.foodland.com; 878 Front St, Old Lahaina Center; ⏲6am-midnight) Has everything you need for self-catering, as well as a good deli. The ahi *poke* is served fresh, cheap and in numerous varieties at the seafood counter. For discounts, you can use your phone number in place of a customer card.

Drinking & Nightlife

Front St is the center of the action. Check the entertainment listings in the free *MauiTime Weekly* (www.mauitime.com), published on Thursdays, or the *Lahaina Times* (www.lahainanews.com). Many of Lahaina's waterfront restaurants have live music at

DON'T MISS

FRIDAY NIGHT IS PARTY NIGHT

If it's Friday night, suit up for a party in the street. The **Maui Friday Town Parties** (www.mauifridays.com) celebrate local art, food and musicians. On the first Friday of the month, the party is held in downtown Wailuku. It moves to Lahaina the second Friday, followed by Makawao on the third Friday and Kihei on the fourth. The occasional fifth Friday is held on Lana'i. For exact locations, check the website. Festivities typically start at 6pm.

Local food trucks are a town party highlight – graze your way through myriad treats.

dinnertime. Happy hours with live music before 5pm and after 8pm are common.

★Koholā Brewery BREWERY
(Map p87; ☎808-868-3198; www.koholabrewery.com; 910 Honoapi'ilani Hwy, No 55; ⊙noon-9pm) Bags of barley and corrugated metals give this microbrewery an industrial vibe. But you'll hardly notice the spartan surrounds as you sample brews including American pale ale, lager, pilsner, IPAs, and many seasonal specials. The beers are some of the islands' best and the bartenders are great at offering samples of the latest creations.

Tuesday is trivia night (7pm). You can also find Koholā beers at Lahaina restaurants including Frida's, Honu Seafood & Pizza, Down the Hatch, and Fleetwood's.

★Down the Hatch BAR
(Map p84; ☎808-731-2386; www.dthmaui.com; 658 Front St, Wharf Cinema Center; ⊙8am-2am) 'Aloha y'all' is the welcoming slogan at Lahaina's best late-night bar, tucked in the lower level of the mall – the owner is from Georgia we hear. All open-air, its fountains are muffled by the raucous revelry of locals and visitors. During happy hour (3pm to 7pm), enjoy the long list of drinks at big discounts. Piña coladas and tropical drinks are excellent.

The bar food features seafood – good fish tacos! – and is served late.

★Fleetwood's on Front St BAR
(Map p84; ☎808-669-6425; www.fleetwoodsonfrontst.com; 744 Front St; ⊙11am-10pm Sun-Thu, to 11pm Fri & Sat) With its comfy pillows, cushy lounges and ornate accents, this rooftop oasis – owned by Fleetwood Mac drummer Mick Fleetwood – evokes Morocco. But views of the Pacific and the West Maui Mountains keep you firmly rooted in Hawaii. At sunset, a conch-shell blast announces a brief cultural introduction to Maui and a tiki-lighting ceremony.

Several cocktails are 50% off during happy hour (2pm to 5pm). Hungry? The top-end dinner menu features complex Med-flavored dishes. If you see the red flag flying, it means Mick is on the island. On many nights there is live music, sometimes featuring Mick: check the website for schedules.

Cheeseburger In Paradise BAR
(Map p84; ☎808-661-4855; www.cheeseburgerland.com; 811 Front St; ⊙8am-11pm) Perched above the sea at the corner of Front St and Lahainaluna Rd, this open-air spot is a lively – and iconic – place to watch the sunset. The music (no surprise) is Jimmy Buffett–style, and the setting is pure tropics, from the rattan decor to the frosty piña coladas. Live soft rock from 5:30pm to 9:30pm nightly.

Opened in 1989, this original location spawned an empire. It was recently completely reconstructed. There were eight baby strollers parked out front on our visit – not sure what this means!

Pioneer Inn Bar PUB
(Map p84; ☎808-661-3636; www.pioneerinnmaui.com; 658 Wharf St; ⊙7am-9pm) Ahoy matey! If Captain Ahab himself strolled through the swinging doors, no one would look up from their grog. With its whaling-era atmosphere and scenic harborside lanai, the captain would blend right in at this century-old landmark.

Although the food is nothing special, the drinks are well priced (happy hour 3pm to 6pm). Local musicians perform familiar standards outside at night.

Dirty Monkey BAR
(Map p84; ☎808-419-6268; www.thedirtymonkey.com; 844 Front St) From Buffalo Trace to Woodford Reserve, the bourbon menu is impressive, and we haven't even gotten to the scotch list. There's a bit of a disconnect between the breezy, open-air surroundings and the serious-business whiskey list, but mariners have always liked their grog. There's also a game room, sports on the TVs and daily live music.

Spanky's Riptide SPORTS BAR

(Map p84; ☎808-667-2337; www.spankysmaui.com; 505 Front St; ⏲11am-10pm Mon-Sat, from 8am Sun) If you want to catch the big game, Spanky's Riptide is the place. Follow the whoops and cheers, stroll right in, step around the dog, pick your brew, then look up at the wall of action-packed TV screens. Happy hour is 2pm to 4pm.

MauiGrown Coffee COFFEE

(Map p84; ☎808-661-2728; www.mauigrowncoffee.com; 277 Lahainaluna Rd; ⏲6:30am-5pm Mon-Sat) Your view from the lanai at MauiGrown's historic bungalow? The famous Pioneer Mill Smokestack (p82) and the cloud-capped West Maui Mountains. A 12oz cup of their delicious coffee is only $1.50, and a few pastries are on offer. There's a fine range of locally grown and roasted coffees in the small retail store.

☆ Entertainment

When it comes to hula and luau (Hawaiian feast), Lahaina offers several options. And if you just want music, check out the bars and lounges during happy hour and later.

★ Old Lahaina Luau LUAU

(Map p87; ☎808-667-1998; www.oldlahainaluau.com; 1251 Front St; adult/child $120/75; ⏲5:15-8:15pm Oct-Feb, 5:45-8:45pm Mar-May & Sep, 6:15-9:15pm Jun-Aug; 👪) From the warm greeting to the feast and hula dances, everything here is premium (including the drinks). No other luau on Maui comes close to matching this one for its authenticity, presentation and all-around aloha. The feast is good, with typical Hawaiian fare that includes *kalua* pork, ahi *poke,* grilled beefsteak and an array of salads and sides.

Feast at Lele LUAU

(Map p84; ☎808-667-5353; www.feastatlele.com; 505 Front St; adult/child $136/99; ⏲from 5:30pm Oct-Jan, 6pm Feb-Apr & Sep, 6:30pm May-Aug) Food takes center stage at this intimate three-hour Polynesian luau on the beach. Dance performances in Hawaiian, Maori, Tahitian and Samoan styles are each matched to a food course.

With the Hawaiian music, you're served *kalua* pork and vegetables; with the Maori, braised short ribs with a vegetable medley; and so on for five courses. Premium drinks are included.

Shopping

Classy boutiques, tacky souvenir shops and flashy art galleries run thick along Front St, with notable outlets on surrounding streets.

★ Village Galleries ARTS & CRAFTS

(Map p84; ☎808-661-4402; www.villagegalleries-maui.com; 120 Dickenson St; ⏲9am-9pm) Stop here for fine art – Hawaiian-style.

★ Lahaina Arts Society ARTS & CRAFTS

(Map p84; ☎808-661-0111; www.lahainaarts.com; 648 Wharf St, Old Lahaina Courthouse; ⏲9am-5pm) Representing more than 55 island artists, this nonprofit collective runs two galleries in the Old Lahaina Courthouse (p81). The Banyan Tree Gallery is on the 1st floor, in the former post office. The Old Jail Gallery is in the basement; the entrance to the jail is outside, on the north side of the building.

★ Maui Hands ARTS & CRAFTS

(Map p84; ☎808-667-9898; www.mauihands.com; 612 Front St; ⏲10am-7:30pm Mon-Sat, to 7pm Sun) Excellent selection of island-made crafts from 300 local artists, jewelers and craftspeople. One of four locations on the island.

Ole Surfboards SPORTS & OUTDOORS

(Map p87; ☎808-661-3459; 277 Wili Ko Pl; ⏲hours vary) Bob 'Ole' Olson has come far from South Dakota, where he was born in 1929. One of the world's foremost surfboard shapers still plies his trade in an obscure warehouse close to the center of Lahaina. Using only hand tools, he designs and shapes boards for some of the world's best surfers. For the right price, he'll outfit you as well.

Peter Lik Gallery PHOTOGRAPHY

(Map p84; ☎808-661-6623; www.lik.com/galleries/lahaina.html; 712 Front St; ⏲10am-10pm) Vibrant colors, stunning landscapes – nature is king in the stylish lair of Australian photographer Peter Lik (who has galleries worldwide).

The pillars in front of this store are remnants of a bank that was here until the tragic Lahaina fire of 1919.

HI, i like you CLOTHING

(Map p84; http://hiilikeyou.com; 819 Front St; ⏲10am-9pm) The double meaning of this shop's name (HI = Hawaii) is a fun introduction to its range of T-shirts and hats, which sport hip and upbeat slogans as well as Maui and Hawaiian themes. T-shirts are made from a mix of organic cotton, recycled water bottle and Modal, a soft, cellulose-fiber fabric.

Owner John Edellstein came up with the name after someone told him they liked him, and he's wanted to spread the positivity ever since.

Hale Zen Home Decor & More HOMEWARES

(Map p84; ☎808-661-4802; www.halezen.com; 180 Dickenson St; ⊙10am-6pm Mon-Sat, to 4pm Sun) This inviting shop embraces stylish island living with candles, lotions and gifts, as well as crafted furniture, cute children's clothes and women's apparel.

Lahaina Printsellers MAPS

(Map p84; ☎808-667-7843; www.printsellers.com; 764 Front St; ⊙10am-10pm) Hawaii's largest purveyor of antique maps, including fascinating originals dating back to the voyages of Captain Cook. It also sells affordable reproductions.

This location shares space with **Lahaina Giclee**, a gallery selling a wide range of fine-quality Hawaiian giclée (zhee-clay) digital prints.

Village Gifts & Fine Arts ARTS & CRAFTS

(Map p84; ☎808-661-5199; www.villagegalleriesmaui.com; cnr Front & Dickenson Sts; ⊙10am-6pm Sat-Thu, to 9pm Fri) This one-room shop in the historic **Masters' Reading Room** (Map p84; cnr Front & Dickenson Sts) sells prints, wooden bowls and other crafts.

For fine art, visit the shop's sister property, the Village Galleries (p95), which is located in a separate building behind the store, across the parking lot.

Wharf Cinema Center MALL

(Map p84; ☎808-661-8748; www.thewharfcinemacenter.com; 658 Front St) Lots of shops and restaurants in an open-air mall just across from Banyan Tree Park. The namesake cinema has closed.

Lahaina Gateway MALL

(Map p87; www.lahainagateway.com; 305 Keawe St; ⊙9am-10pm) This strip mall is just off Hwy 30 (Honoapi'ilani Hwy). The most interesting options here are **Mahina**, a women's clothing boutique, and the restaurants and market. It hosts a **gift and craft fair** on Sundays from 9am to 2pm.

Outlets of Maui MALL

(Map p84; ☎808-661-8277; www.theoutletsofmaui.com; 900 Front St; ⊙9:30am-10pm) Factory-store retailers at this open-air outlet mall include all the same chains you'll find at outlet malls everywhere.

ℹ Information

For urgent but not critical care, try the **Minit-Medical** (Map p87; ☎808-670-1994; www.minitmed.com; 305 Keawe St, Lahaina Gateway; ⊙8am-6pm Mon-Sat, to 4pm Sun). Otherwise call 911 for transport to the ER in Wailuku.

Post Office (Map p84; ☎808-661-0904; www.usps.com; 132 Papalaua St, Old Lahaina Center; ⊙10am-4pm Mon-Fri) Lahaina's place for mail.

Lahaina Visitor Center (Map p84; ☎808-667-9175; www.visitlahaina.com; 648 Wharf St, Old Lahaina Courthouse; ⊙9am-5pm) This excellent tourist office is located on the 1st floor of the Old Lahaina Courthouse (p81). You can get gifts, books, info and a walking-tour map ($2.50).

ℹ Getting There & Away

It takes about one hour to drive between Lahaina and the airport in Kahului.

SpeediShuttle (☎877-242-5777; www.speedishuttle.com; 1 passenger $20-86) provides van service between the airport and Lahaina, and serves most addresses in town.

A taxi between Lahaina and the airport costs about $78.

The **Maui Bus** (☎808-871-4838; www.mauicounty.gov/bus; single ride $2, day/month pass $4/45) runs the Lahaina Islander route 20 between Kahului and Lahaina (one hour), stopping at Ma'alaea Harbor, where a connection can be made to Kihei (various stops) via the Kihei Villager bus service. Another route, the Ka'anapali Islander, connects Lahaina and Ka'anapali (30 minutes), while the West Maui Islander connects Lahaina to Napili and Kapalua. All three Islander routes depart from the bus stop on Luakini St, behind the Wharf Cinema Center, hourly from 6:30am to 8:30pm. There is no direct bus service from the airport to Lahaina.

The Expeditions Ferry (p97) to Lana'i uses the **Ferry Dock** (Map p84; off Wharf St) in the harbor.

If you're driving to Lahaina from the airport, be aware that the Lahaina Bypass now automatically takes you east around downtown before dropping you back on the Honoapi'ilani Hwy via Keawe St. There are several Lahaina exits along the way. From the north, you must turn left at the light at Keawe St, or at other roads along the Honoapi'ilani Hwy, to access the bypass heading south. You can also just putter south through town, missing the bypass altogether.

Getting Around

BUS

The Maui Bus Lahaina Villager route runs hourly along Front St downtown and connects to Lahaina Cannery Mall and Lahaina Gateway. Many of the Ka'anapali resorts operate shuttles for guests, which serve the resort areas and Lahaina.

FERRY

Expeditions Ferry (Map p84; ☎808-661-3756; www.go-lanai.com; Lahaina Harbor; adult/child one way $30/20) Worth it just for the ride, this ferry links Lahaina Harbor with Manele Bay Harbor on Lana'i (one hour) several times daily. In winter there's a fair chance of seeing humpback whales; spinner dolphins are a common sight all year, especially on morning sails.

TAXI

For a taxi in Lahaina, call **Maui Pleasant Taxi** (☎808-344-4661; www.mauipleasanttaxi.com) or **West Maui Taxi** (☎808-661-1122, 888-661-4545; www.westmauitaxi.com). Expect to pay $14 to $20 one way between Lahaina and Ka'anapali. Uber and Lyft are usually cheaper.

AT A GLANCE

POPULATION
Ka'anapali: 968

GAZEBO OPENING HOURS
7:30am-2pm (p116)

BEST BEACH
Kapalua Beach (p117)

BEST BAR AT SUNSET
Merriman's Kapalua (p122)

BEST VEGAN FOOD
A'a Roots (p116)

WHEN TO GO

Jan–Apr Prime whale-watching; PGA tour kick-off in January; Celebration of the Arts festival in Kapalua in April.

Jun–Aug High season for families; Kapalua Wine & Food Festival in June.

Nov–Dec Hula O Nā Keiki hula competition at the Ka'anapali Beach Hotel in November.

Olowalu Beach (p105)
ZANE VERGARA / SHUTTERSTOCK ©

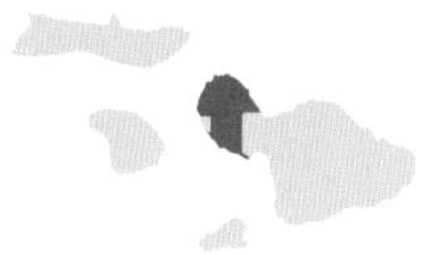

West Maui

Celebrate. Explore. Relax. Dine like royalty. Whatever your pleasure, West Maui has you covered. Active travelers have it especially good: snorkel beside lava rocks, zipline down the mountains, thwack a golf ball, hike through the jungle or sail beneath the setting sun.

Ka'anapali is West Maui's splashy center, with world-class golf courses, stylish resorts, oceanfront dining and a dazzling, mile-long beach. Further north, Hawaiian history and swanky exclusivity have formed an intriguing, sometimes uneasy alliance in Kapalua, also home to gorgeous beaches. Kahana and Napili are lovely seaside communities known for condos and budget-friendly prices. For off-the-grid excitement, buckle up for a hair-raising drive around the untamed northern coast.

INCLUDES

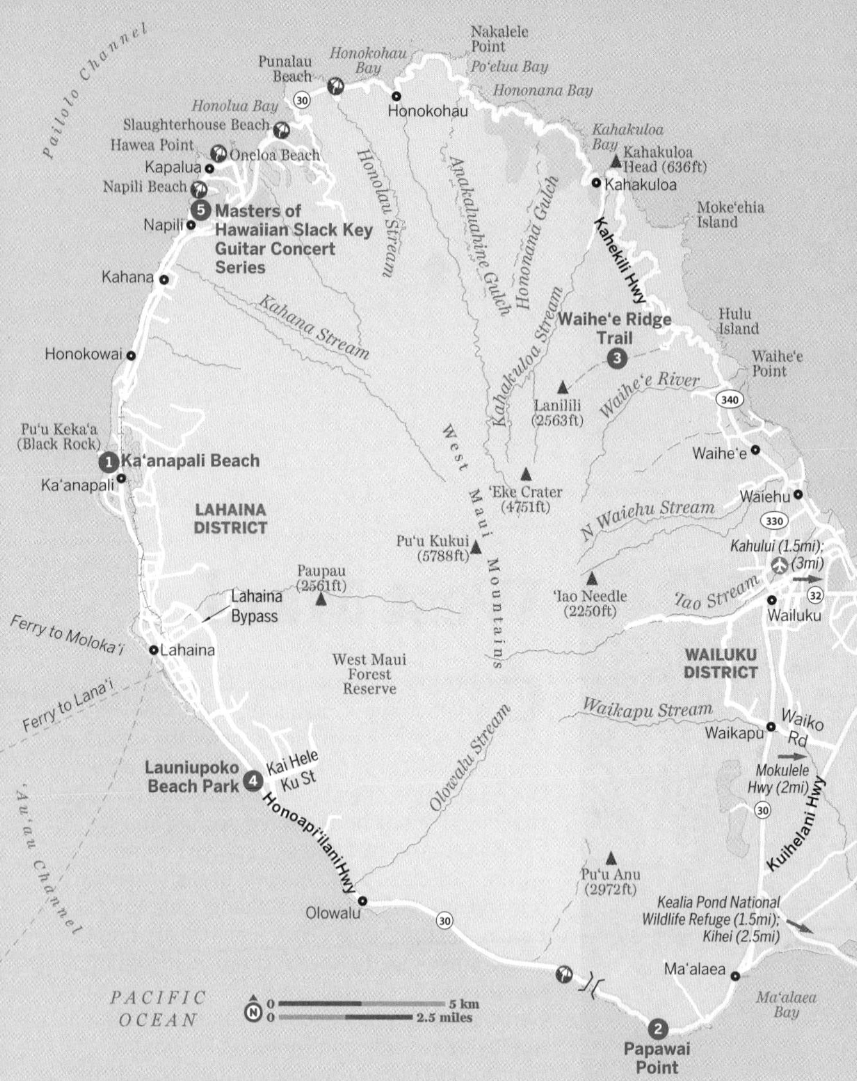

West Maui Highlights

❶ **Ka'anapali Beach** (p107) Snorkeling beside Pu'u Keka'a (Black Rock) then strutting your stuff resort-style at 'Dig-Me Beach.'

❷ **Papawai Point** (p106) Crying 'thar she blows!' at this cliffside perch, a primo whale-watching spot come winter.

❸ **Waihe'e Ridge Trail** (p102) Climbing into the clouds on this scenic 5-miler with sweeping north-coast views.

❹ **Balancing on a board** (p101) Surfing, bodyboarding and stand-up paddling: everyone's catching waves at the likes of Launiupoko Beach Park.

❺ **Masters of Hawaiian Slack Key Guitar Concert Series** (p117) Enjoying these old-style jams in Napili: cultural celebrations that make everyone feel like *'ohana* (extended family).

WEST MAUI

Getting There & Away

The best way to get around West Maui is by car. There are eight hire companies located at Kahului International Airport, including **Dollar Rent a Car** (www.dollar.com) and **Enterprise** (www.enterprise.com). However, hiring on the spot can be expensive – for the lowest rates, book in advance of your trip. US and international driving licenses are accepted, but a permit may be required for licenses from non-English-speaking countries.

Shuttle services are also available to and from the airport to Maui towns and hotels, starting at $10 one way. See **Roberts Hawaii** (808-871-6226; www.robertshawaii.com; airport-to-hotel shuttle bus from $10; airport counter 5:30am-last flight) or Speedi Shuttle (p96) for rates.

Taxis are available at the airport to West Maui locations, starting from $78. Uber and Lyft, while limited, are available, and the app services can be an inexpensive and convenient way to get around.

Buses are by far the cheapest way to get around. Routes run hourly throughout the day between various resorts and towns, costing $2 for a single journey, although there are no direct bus routes from the airport to West Maui. For up-to-date timetables, visit www.mauicounty.gov/bus.

Route Name (No.)	Between	Time
Lahaina Islander (20)	Queen Ka'ahumanu Center (Kahului), Ma'alaea Harbor, Wharf Cinema Center (Lahaina)	5:30am-9:30pm
Lahaina Villager (23)	Loop around Lahaina, from Wharf Cinema Center, along Front St, to Lahaina Gateway and Lahaina Cannery Mall	8am-11pm
Ka'anapali Islander (25)	Whalers Village (Ka'anapali), Lahaina Cannery Mall, Wharf Cinema Center	2:30pm-5:30pm
West Maui Islander (28)	Wharf Cinema Center, Whalers Village, Napili Plaza, along Lower Honoapi'ilani Rd, to Kapalua	5:30am-9:30pm

Lahaina to Ma'alaea

The drive between Lahaina and Ma'alaea bursts with staggering views of the rugged West Maui Mountains on one side and the shimmering ocean on the other. In winter, this section of Honoapi'ilani Hwy is like a ready-made whale-watching safari. Stay alert, though! Too many distracted drivers have their heads facing the shore, trying to spot humpback whales cruising just off land. Stand-up paddle boarders and surfers are also a common sight and the rolling waves will make you want to pull your car over (like the locals often do) and jump in the water for a surf.

Puamana Beach Park & Launiupoko Beach Park

Launiupoko Beach Park BEACH

(Honoapi'ilani Hwy; P) Beginner and intermediate surfers head to this beach park, a popular wayside 3 miles south of Lahaina. The park is an ideal spot for families; *na keiki* (children) have a blast wading in the large rock-enclosed shoreline pool and good picnic facilities invite you to linger. Launiupoko is at the traffic light at the 18-mile marker on Honoapi'ilani Hwy, at its intersection with Kai Hele Ku St. There are restrooms and outdoor showers but no lifeguards.

Middles SURFING

Situated at Launiupoko Beach Park, this beautiful slow wave breaks left and right and is ideal for beginners and long-boarders. As with most Maui breaks, it's better in the morning before the wind picks up. It's a mellow reef break, but beginners should wear booties as rocks can be sharp underfoot. It gets very busy, especially at weekends.

Guardrails SURFING

Peeling straight off Honoapi'ilani Hwy, between the 18- and 19-mile markers, this welcoming and uncrowded beginner/intermediate reef break has long right and left

HIKING IN WEST MAUI

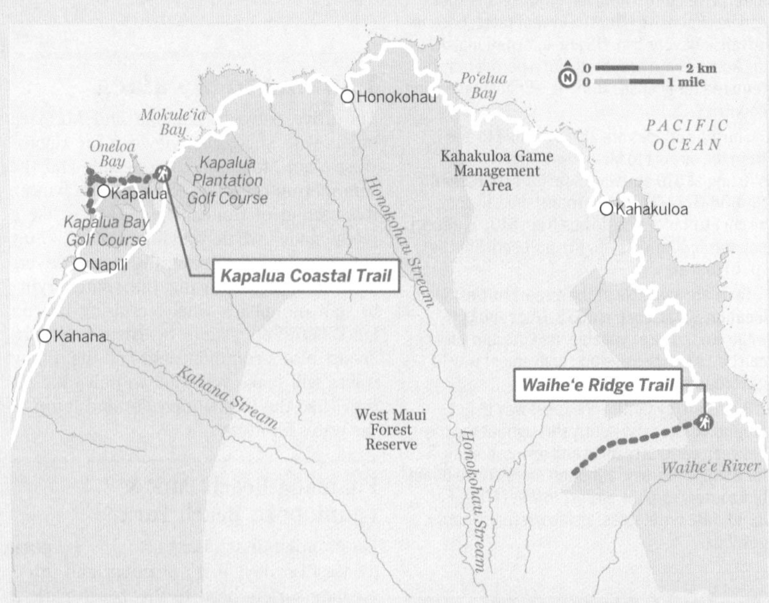

WAIHE'E RIDGE TRAIL

START WAIHE'E RIDGE TRAILHEAD
END WAIHE'E RIDGE TRAILHEAD
LENGTH ROUND TRIP 5 MILES; ROUGHLY THREE HOURS
DIFFICULTY MODERATE

For jaw-dropping views over the long, lush carpets of Waihe'e Gorge, waterfalls, tropical forests and a bird's-eye view of Wailuku and Maui's wild northern coast, it doesn't get much better than the Waihe'e Ridge Trail.

To get to the trailhead, take the one-lane paved road that starts on the inland side of the Kahekili Hwy just south of the 7-mile marker. Drive about 1 mile to find parking before the trailhead (open 7am to 7pm). Brush off your shoes at the start and end of your hikes per signage to reduce the risk of carrying invasive species. Begin your walk by climbing a sheer concrete ramp, and pass blue water tanks on the right.

Suitable for solo walkers, fit seniors and active kids, the initial path is a bit steep and can get boggy – Waihe'e means 'slippery water' in Hawaiian, but don't let this dishearten you. It's a fairly steady climb to the 2563ft summit of Lanilili Peak, but it's not a strenuous one. Be prepared to walk back down the mountain afterwards. There are intervals of flat terrain throughout the trail. It's best to bring good walking shoes to tackle mud, stones and exposed tree roots. Set off before 8am to beat the heat and the clouds, which can obscure the view later in the morning. Walking sticks or tree branches, often left behind by hikers at the gate leading onto the trail, can be helpful if you are in need of extra support.

Starting at an elevation of 1000ft, it's already possible to spy the vast blue ocean. The trail, which crosses reserve land, climbs a ridge, passing from mainly shaded humid woodland areas of ancient undergrowth to open pastures nearer the summit. Guava trees and groves of eucalyptus are prominent, and the aroma of fallen fruit may accompany you after a rainstorm. From the 0.75-mile post, panoramic views open up,

Whether you're after an easy coastal stroll or a trek through tropical flora, West Maui has a trail for you.

with a scene that sweeps clear down to the ocean along the Waihe'e Gorge and deep into pleated valleys.

Continuing, you'll enter *'ohi'a lehua* forest; look out for butterflies and native birds, such as the bright crimson *'apapane* (bright red Hawaiian honeycreeper). A clearing offers a bench with a prime view of the cascading Makamaka'ole Falls in the distance. On the ridge, views are similar to those you'd see from a helicopter – and you'll probably see a handful of them dart into the adjacent valley like gnats on a mission.

There are several natural pausing places along the trail to soak up the scenery and remarkable stillness. Birdsong, chirping insects, a rushing stream, muffled bits of hiker conversation below – these are the only interruptions. The trail ends with a series of sharp bends and a steep climb to a picnic table on the 2563ft **peak of Lanilili**. You'll be rewarded with a staggering 360-degree view, and with clear skies it's possible to see Haleakalā volcano in the distance. If it's foggy, wait 10 minutes or so; it may blow off.

The Division of Forestry and Wildlife claims 50 to 100 people hike the trail daily, so expect company. See http://dlnr.hawaii.gov/recreation/nah for more details.

KAPALUA COASTAL TRAIL

START DT FLEMING BEACH PARK
END KAPALUA BEACH PARKING LOT
LENGTH ONE WAY 1.76 MILES; 40 MINUTES TO ONE HOUR
DIFFICULTY EASY

This spectacular, easy **hike** (www.kapalua.com/activities/hiking-trails; ⏲ sunrise-sunset) is one you can do solo. Wear a good pair of walking shoes, as some coastal sections cross sharp rocks. The path crosses pristine resorts, beautiful beaches and an ancient burial ground, and runs adjacent to the jagged **Makaluapuna Point** (p119). The end of the trail next to **DT Fleming Beach Park** (p119) has lots of parking spaces.

From here, a wooden church and the entrance to the **Mahana Ridge Trail** mark the walk's beginning. Don't take the Mahana dirt path up; instead, follow the road east past the **Ritz Carlton's Burger Shack** (p121) toward the resort's immaculate, shell-lined lawns, cultivated garden beds and tennis courts. Coastal winds pick up here, cooling walkers as they stroll. At the top of the hill there's an arresting view of the ocean and, in the winter, a chance to spot whales. A hotel pool to the left jars with the **Honokahua burial site** (p119) to the right. This graveyard – dating back to 610 CE, and marked with a plaque – is off-limits to the general public. An estimated 2000 Hawaiians have been laid to rest here and it's believed that their ancestral spirits watch over these lands.

A slight detour onto the roadside sidewalk leads to **Oneloa Beach** (p117); take the alley toward the bluest of sea views, where the trail turns into a raised boardwalk adjacent to the beach. It is flanked with tropical, pink-petaled *pohuehue* (beach morning glory) and *'akia* (native Hawaiian shrub) plants, with orange fruits and tiny yellow flowers. Surfers and kiteboarders ride waves out to sea and holidaymakers occupy luxury condos to the left. Stairs down to the beach offer the chance to dip your toes in the sea. At the end of the beach, the boardwalk turns into a rocky path onto the cliffside. Follow the bridge over the channel at the eastern side of **Hawea Point** or explore the impressive razor-sharp lava formations of the point, which jut out to sea and upward to 3ft. Be careful not to get too close to the edge or disturb the signposted nesting areas of seabirds.

Rejoining the main path, continue on the paved pathway, through plush condos and the **Montage Kapalua Bay** (p121) resort on **Kapalua Beach** (p117). This calm, crescent-shaped bay is excellent for snorkeling; at the west side of the beach, it's possible to spot the former Hawaii State Fish *humuhumunukunukuapua'a* (Hawaiian triggerfish), as well as goat fish, porcupine fish, parrotfish and more (hire equipment at the water-sports shack on Kapalua Beach). The path unfurls under lime trees, and ends with a foot tunnel to restrooms and a car park with limited spaces.

West Maui

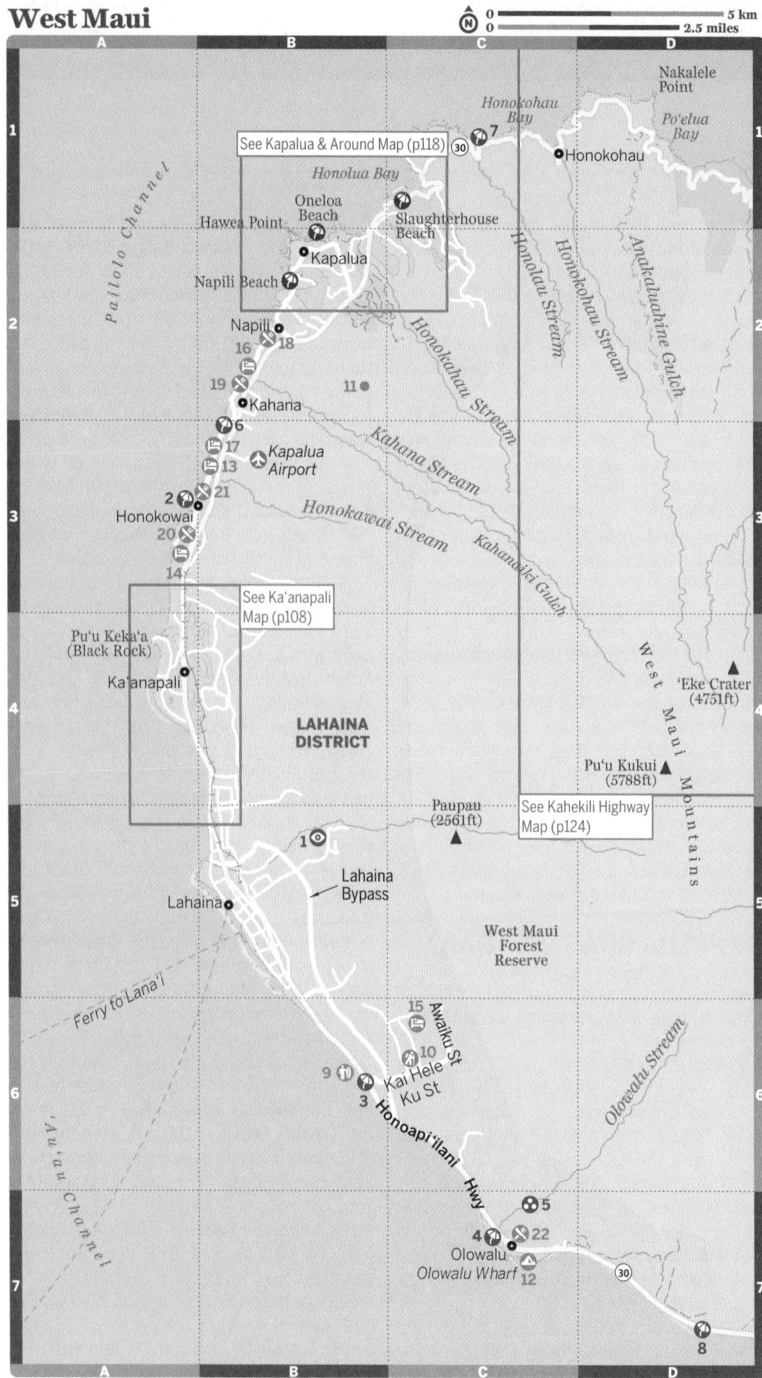
0 5 km
0 2.5 miles
See Kapalua & Around Map (p118)
See Ka'anapali Map (p108)
See Kahekili Highway Map (p124)
Nakalele Point
Honokohau Bay
Po'elua Bay
Honokohau
Honolua Bay
Pailolo Channel
Oneloa Beach
Slaughterhouse Beach
Hawea Point
Kapalua
Napili Beach
Napili
Kahana
Kapalua Airport
Honokowai
Honolau Stream
Honokohau Stream
Anakaluahine Gulch
Honokahau Stream
Kahana Stream
Honokawai Stream
Kahanaiki Gulch
Pu'u Keka'a (Black Rock)
Ka'anapali
LAHAINA DISTRICT
West Maui Mountains
'Eke Crater (4751ft)
Pu'u Kukui (5788ft)
Paupau (2561ft)
Lahaina Bypass
Lahaina
West Maui Forest Reserve
Ferry to Lana'i
Awaiku St
Kai Hele Ku St
Honoapi'ilani Hwy
Olowalu Stream
'Au'au Channel
Olowalu
Olowalu Wharf

West Maui

Sights

1 Hale Pa'i Printing Museum....................B5
2 Honokowai Beach Park.........................A3
3 Launiupoko Beach Park........................B6
4 Olowalu Beach....................................C7
5 Olowalu Petroglyphs.............................C7
6 Pohaku Park..B3
7 Punalau Beach.....................................C1
8 Ukumehame Beach Park........................D7

Activities, Courses & Tours

Boss Frog.....................................(see 13)
9 Guardrails..B6
10 Honokohau Ditch Trail.........................C6
11 Ironwood Ranch Horseback Riding......B2
Middles.......................................(see 3)
Thousand Peaks..............................(see 8)

Sleeping

12 Camp Olowalu.....................................C7
13 Hale Kai..B3
14 Honua Kai Resort & Spa.......................A3
15 Ho'oilo House.....................................C6
16 Kahana Village....................................B2
17 Noelani..B3

Eating

18 A'a Roots..B2
Farmers Market Deli......................(see 13)
19 Hawaiian Village Coffee........................B2
20 Honokowai Food Pod............................A3
21 Honokowai Okazuya.............................B3
Joey's Kitchen Napili.....................(see 18)
22 Leoda's Kitchen & Pie Shop...................C7
Maui Tacos....................................(see 18)

Drinking & Nightlife

Coffee Store in Napili......................(see 18)
Maui Brewing Co............................(see 19)

rides. Be aware, currents here can be stronger than at other spots and it's tricky getting in and out of the water, as you have to negotiate the rocks as the waves crash in.

Honokohau Ditch Trail WALKING, CYCLING
(Kai Hele Ku St; sunrise-sunset) For a morning stroll away from the crowded coastal trails, head to this paved path that begins above Launiupoko Beach Park. It follows an irrigation ditch built in 1902 for a sugar plantation. There's little shade, and it can be hot by midday, but the ocean views as you walk north are superb. About 3 miles round trip.

The trail runs beside a well-manicured residential area and is maintained by a neighborhood association, so don't stray from the path onto private property. The trail is mostly flat, making it nice for easy cycling with kids. There is signage and designated parking at the trailhead plus a shaded picnic table.

★ **Ho'oilo House** B&B $$$
(808-667-6669; www.hooilohouse.com; 138 Awaiku St; r $629; P) Up the road from Launiupoko Beach Park, this calming retreat on the slopes of the West Maui Mountains is a place for relaxation. Six Asian- and Maui-themed rooms hug an A-framed community area with a sweeping view of Lana'i. Stylish furnishings differ by room – many contain Balinese imports – but all have a private lanai (porch, balcony or veranda) and an eclectically designed outdoor shower.

Breakfast includes fresh muffins and bread, cereal, granola and fruit, which is often plucked from the 2-acre property's pesticide-free orchard. Solar panels generate 80% of the house's power, soap products are recycled in partnership with Clean the World and biodegradables are returned to the orchards as compost.

Olowalu

The West Maui Mountains provide the scenic backdrop and give Olowalu its name, which means 'many hills.' The tiny village is marked by a general store, the popular Leoda's Kitchen & Pie Shop (p106), and a juice-and-fruit stand. Behind the village sits a hidden historical site (p106), with ancient stone carvings dating back hundreds of years. Limited parking next to the general store is available for those wanting to explore. Across the Honoapi'ilani Hwy, at the 14-mile marker, is Olowalu's famed coral reef. The coast here is popular for kayaking and snorkeling.

Olowalu was the sight of a terrible massacre (p278) in 1790, when more than 100 locals were killed by Westerners.

Olowalu Beach BEACH
(Honoapi'ilani Hwy, at 14-mile marker) The coral reef of Olowalu Beach, which is popular with snorkelers, is shallow and silty. There was a reported minor shark attack near Olowalu in March 2016.

Olowalu Petroglyphs ARCHAEOLOGICAL SITE

A short walk behind Olowalu general store leads to 200–300-year-old petroglyphs (ancient Hawaiian stone carvings). Park just beyond the water tower at the back of the general store. It's a half-mile walk up a dirt road; keep the cinder cone straight ahead of you as you follow the road. Bear left at the Olowalu Cultural Reserve sign then continue to an interpretive marker on your right.

As with most of Maui's petroglyphs, these figures are carved into the vertical sides of cliffs (rather than on horizontal lava as they are on Hawai'i, the Big Island). Most of the Olowalu figures have been damaged, but you can still make out some of them. Don't climb the rocks for a better look, however, and do watch for falling rocks. There's interpretive signage at the site. You can see a few more after a short walk up the road.

If you have mobility issues, it's OK to drive to the site, instead of walking, but be careful on the bumpy dirt road and be respectful of neighboring landowners.

Camp Olowalu CAMPGROUND $

(808-661-4303; www.campolowalu.com; 800 Olowalu Village Rd; tentalows from $160, campsites per adult/child 6-12yr $24/7; P) Look at you Camp Olowalu, all fresh and fancy. A tangled grove of gnarled trees once gave this seaside campground a rugged, *Survivor*-esque vibe, but today it feels safe and welcoming, offering a tidy camping area for tents. Nearby, relatively posh canvas 'tentalows' with cots, sinks, hot water and showers line a picturesque lawn dotted with fruit trees and native plants.

Car camping is also permitted for $24 per night per adult and $7 per child.

Enter across the highway from the Olowalu general store then drive southeast beside Hwy 30 to the campground.

★ **Leoda's Kitchen & Pie Shop** BAKERY $

(808-662-3600; www.leodas.com; 820 Olowalu Village Rd, on Honoapi'ilani Hwy; breakfast $7-20, lunch & dinner $8-16, dessert pies $5-9; 7am-8pm;) Wear your stretchy pants to Leoda's. Diet-busters at this simple-but-stylish restaurant include savory pot pies, topping-laden burgers and rich sandwiches such as the 'pork, pork...mmm pork.' Save room for one of the mini dessert pies – gorgeous creations vying for attention at the front counter. It's also a great breakfast spot on your way into or out of Lahaina.

Located at the 15-mile marker on the Honoapi'ilani Hwy.

Ukumehame Beach Park & Around

Heading south from Lahaina, look for **Ukumehame Beach Park** (Honoapi'ilani Hwy, Mile 12; P). Shaded by ironwood trees, this sandy beach is OK for a quick dip, but because of the rocky conditions most locals stick with picnicking and fishing. Dive and snorkel boats anchor offshore at Coral Gardens. This reef also creates **Thousand Peaks** toward its western end, with breaks favored by long-boarders and beginner surfers.

Midway between mile markers 11 and 12 is **Pāpalaua Wayside Park**, a county park squeezed between the road and the ocean. It's lackluster but it does have BBQ grills, portable toilets and tent camping under thorny kiawe trees. For more details about obtaining a camping permit and fees, visit the Maui County website (www.mauicounty.gov). Note that the place buzzes all night with traffic noise.

The pull-off for the western end of the Lahaina Pali Trail (p130) is just south of the 11-mile marker, on the inland side of the road.

Papawai Point VIEWPOINT

(Map p132; www.pacificwhale.org/information-stations; Honoapi'ilani Hwy, btwn Mile 8 & Mile 9; naturalists 8am-1pm whale season; P) This cliffside perch overlooks Ma'alaea Bay, which is a favored nursing ground for humpback whales. Pull over in winter to watch their annual time here. Beginning December 1 and continuing through whale season (which lasts until April or May), Pacific Whale Foundation naturalists are on site daily, as staffing and weather allow, to share information about the whales (staffing times may vary year to year). Also a great spot to catch sunsets, the overlook is 3 miles west of Ma'alaea Harbor.

Grandma's SURFING

(Map p132) One of the few surf breaks you can camp right next to is at Pāpalaua Wayside Park between mile markers 11 and 12 on Honoapi'ilani Hwy. Waves on this reef break are not as well formed as Thousand Peaks (p106) next door, but are gentle, often long rides, good for beginners, and uncrowded.

Lahaina to Ka'anapali

The drive between Lahaina and Ka'anapali offers great ocean views out to the island of Lana'i, plus a couple of roadside beach parks including Hanaka'o'o Beach Park and **Wahikuli Wayside Park** (Honoapi'ilani Hwy), both good spots to get away from the crowds of Ka'anapali and Lahaina.

Hanaka'o'o Beach Park BEACH

The long, sandy Hanaka'o'o Beach Park, extending south from Hyatt Regency Maui Resort & Spa, has a sandy bottom and water conditions that are usually safe for swimming. However, southerly swells, which sometimes develop in summer, can create powerful waves and shorebreaks, while the occasional kona (leeward) storm can kick up rough water conditions in winter. Snorkelers head to the second clump of rocks on the southern side of the park, but it really doesn't compare with sites further north.

Guest House B&B $

(808-661-8085; www.mauiguesthouse.com; 1620 Ainakea Rd; s/d $179/199; P ❄ @ ≈) The welcoming Guest House, hosting travelers for more than 25 years, provides amenities that put nearby resorts to shame. Every room has its own hot tub and 42in plasma TV. Stained-glass windows reflect a tropical motif, and a rooftop deck offers ocean views. Perks include beach towels, snorkel gear, saltwater pool, community kitchen and a guest shower (good before your midnight flight).

WHALE-WATCHING

During the winter humpback whales occasionally breach as close as 100yd from the coast of West Maui: 40 tons of leviathan suddenly exploding straight up through the water can be a real showstopper!

Beach parks and pull-offs along the Honoapi'ilani Hwy offer great vantage points for watching the action. The very best spot is Papawai Point (p106), a clifftop overlook jutting into the western edge of Ma'alaea Bay, a favored humpback nursing ground. **The Pacific Whale Foundation** posts volunteers at the parking lot to share their knowledge and point out the whales (8am to 1pm; daily December 1 through whale season). Note that staffing is dependent on weather and the availability of naturalists.

Papawai Point is midway between the 8- and 9-mile markers on the highway, about 3 miles west of Ma'alaea. Note that the road sign simply reads 'scenic point,' not the full name, but there's a turning lane to the point, so slow down and you won't miss it.

Ka'anapali

Honeymoons, anniversaries, holidays – Ka'anapali is a place to celebrate. Maui's flashiest resort destination welcomes guests with 3 miles of sandy beach, a dozen oceanfront hotels, two 18-hole golf courses and an ocean full of water activities. You can sit at a beachfront bar with a tropical drink, soak up the gorgeous views of Lana'i and Moloka'i across the channel and listen to guitarists strum their wiki-wacky-woo.

The beloved Whalers Village Museum has closed, but look out for the **Hawaiian Wildlife Discovery Center**, which is scheduled to open in the museum's old spot in Whaler's Village in 2020. The discovery center will still cover the history of whaling in the region, but it will now also spotlight Hawaiian marine life and local sustainability and conservation issues.

Beaches

★ **Ka'anapali Beach** BEACH

(P) Home to West Maui's liveliest beach scene, this gorgeous stretch unfurls alongside Ka'anapali's resort hotels, linking the Hyatt Regency Maui (p110) with the Sheraton Maui 1 mile north. Dubbed 'Dig-Me Beach' for all the preening, it's a vibrant spot. Surfers, bodyboarders and parasailers rip across the water, snorkelers admire the sea life, and sailboats pull up on shore. There are no lifeguards, so check with the hotel beach huts before jumping in: water conditions vary with the season and currents are sometimes strong.

Kahekili Beach Park BEACH

(P) This idyllic golden-sand beach at Ka'anapali's less-frequented northern end is a good place to lose the look-at-me crowds strutting their stuff further south. The swimming's better, the snorkeling's good and the park has everything you'll need for a day at the beach – showers, restrooms, a covered picnic pavilion and barbecue grills. Access is easy and there's ample free parking.

Snorkelers will find plenty of coral and marine life right in front of the beach, and sea turtle sightings are common. To go a bit further afield, swim north to **Honokowai Point** and then ride the mild current, which runs north to south, all the way back.

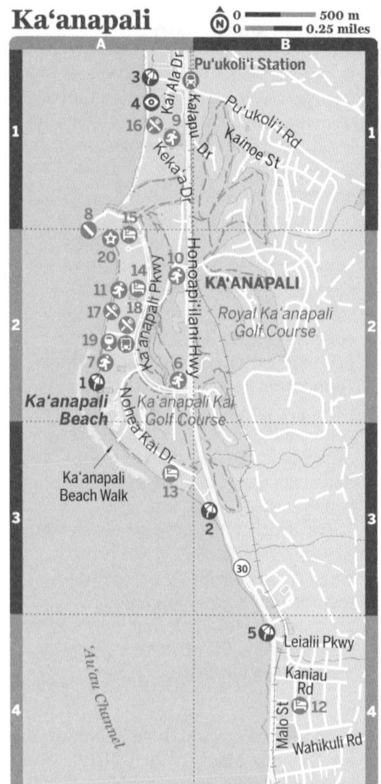

The wide beach, backed by swaying palms and flowering morning glory, is also ideal for strolling. It's a 15-minute walk south on the paved **Beach Walk** (P) to Pu'u Keka'a (aka Black Rock). Alternatively, you could walk north along the beach for about 20 minutes to Honokowai Point and have lunch at the Honokowai Food Pod (p115) or the Farmers Market Deli (p114).

To get to the beach from the Honoapi'ilani Hwy, turn *makai* (seaward) 350yd north of the 25-mile marker onto Kai Ala Dr, then bear right.

Activities

If you're traveling with younger kids, check out the new playground in the lower level courtyard at Whalers Village (p113). It has a netted climbing structure and a splash pad.

Pu'u Keka'a DIVE SITE

(Black Rock) You'll find the best underwater sights off this lava promontory, which protects the beach in front of the Sheraton (p112). First-time snorkelers will be happy with the coral and fish at the protected southern side of Pu'u Keka'a, but the highlight is the horseshoe cove cut into the tip of the rock, where there's more pristine coral, abundant tropical fish and the occasional turtle.

There's often a current to contend with off the point, which can make getting to the cove a little risky, but when it's calm you can swim right around into the horseshoe. Pu'u Keka'a is also a popular shore-dive spot. If you want to see what the horseshoe cove looks like, take the short footpath to the top of the rock, where you can peer right down into it.

Tour of the Stars STARGAZING

(☎808-667-4727; www.hyatt.com; 200 Nohea Kai Dr, Hyatt Regency Maui Resort & Spa; guest adult/child $30/20, nonguest $40/25; ⊙viewing 8pm & 9pm) Enjoy stellar stargazing in a secret observatory atop the Hyatt resort. Held on clear nights, these 50-minute viewings are limited to 14 people and use a 14in-diameter telescope. Romantic types should opt for the couples-only viewing at 10pm, which rolls out the champagne and chocolate-covered strawberries (guest/nonguest $45/50).

Skyline Eco-Adventures ADVENTURE SPORTS

(☎808-518-4189; www.zipline.com; 2580 Keka'a Dr, Fairway Shops; 3½hr outing $169; ⊙departures 8am-1:30pm) Zoom through the lush West Maui Mountains among the tree canopies, reaching speeds of around 20mph on an adrenaline-fueled zipline adventure. The Ka'anapali course takes you 2 miles up the wooded cliffsides to platforms and drops of up to 150ft. You can free-glide along eight separate lines, taking over three hours, or 11 lines (four hours) above waterfalls, stream beds and valleys.

Island Scuba & Surf DIVING

(☎808-446-4135; www.scubadivingmaui.com; 50 Nohea Kai Dr, Ka'anapali Ali'i Resort; 1-tank dive $79; ⊙8am-7pm) Formerly the Ka'anapali Dive Co, Island Scuba & Surf offers an introductory one-tank dive ($99) for novices, with equipment, starting with instruction in a pool and moving on to a guided dive from the beach. It also offers one- and two-tank beach dives for certified divers. No separate rentals. Walk up or call to make a reservation.

Ka'anapali Golf Courses GOLF

(☎808-661-3691; www.kaanapaligolfcourses.com; 2290 Ka'anapali Pkwy; greens fee nonguests $205-

Ka'anapali

Top Sights
1 Ka'anapali Beach A2

Sights
2 Hanaka'o'o Beach Park B3
3 Kahekili Beach Park A1
4 North Ka'anapali Beach Walk A1
5 Wahikuli Wayside Park B4

Activities, Courses & Tours
Island Scuba & Surf .... (see 7)
6 Ka'anapali Golf Courses A2
7 Ka'anapali Surf Club A2
8 Pu'u Keka'a A2
9 Royal Lahaina Tennis Ranch A1
10 Skyline Eco-Adventures A2
Teralani Sailing .... (see 18)
Tour of the Stars .... (see 13)
11 Trilogy Ocean Sports A2

Sleeping
12 Guest House B4
13 Hyatt Regency Maui Resort & Spa A3
14 Ka'anapali Beach Hotel A2
15 Sheraton Maui A2
Westin Maui Resort & Spa .... (see 7)

Eating
16 Castaway Cafe A1
17 Hula Grill & Barefoot Bar A2
Japengo .... (see 13)
Joey's Kitchen .... (see 18)
18 Monkeypod Kitchen A2
Roy's Ka'anapali .... (see 6)

Drinking & Nightlife
Hula Grill & Barefoot Bar .... (see 17)
19 Leilani's A2

Entertainment
Drums of the Pacific .... (see 13)
Ka'anapali Beach Hotel .... (see 14)
20 Sheraton Maui A2
Whalers Village .... (see 18)

Shopping
Malibu Shirts .... (see 18)
Martin & MacArthur .... (see 18)
Whalers Village .... (see 18)

255; hours vary seasonally, from 6:30am) Get away from the buzzing beach for a golf session at Ka'anapali's two courses. Advanced golfers prefer the Royal Ka'anapali Golf Course – the place to practice your precise putting. Meanwhile, Ka'anapali Kai Golf Course is shorter and has wonderful views of islands Lana'i and Moloka'i. Staying at Ka'anapali Resort? The guest rate will save you about $70.

Royal Lahaina Tennis Ranch TENNIS
(808-667-5200; www.royallahaina.com/activities; 2780 Keka'a Dr; per half-day per person $10, racket hire $2.50; pro shop 8am-noon & 2-6pm Mon-Fri, 2-5pm Sat & Sun) Regularly named the Facility of the Year by the United States Tennis Association, this is the largest tennis complex in West Maui, with four courts lit for night play. Private lessons and group clinics are available. Courts with floodlights are open until 9:30pm; book ahead if you'd like to use these. It now has two courts lined as pickleball courts.

Tours

Teralani Sailing BOATING
(808-661-7245; www.teralani.net; sunset outing adult/teen/child 3-12yr from $78/67/54; check-in 3:30pm winter, 4pm summer;) This friendly outfit offers a variety of sails on two custom-built catamarans that depart from the beach beside Whalers Village (p113). The easygoing sunset sail offers an inspiring introduction to the gorgeous West Maui coast. Snorkel sails and whale-watching outings are additional options, but no matter which you choose, you'll find an amiable crew, refreshing cocktails and decent food.

Trilogy Ocean Sports WATER SPORTS
(808-661-7789; www.sailtrilogy.com; Ka'anapali Beach; 5hr tour adult/teen/child $135/115/80; 6:30am-5pm) Trilogy runs snorkel trips from Ka'anapali Beach to nearby sites, including Honolua, located just north of Kapalua. Here marine life, including tropical fish and turtles, can be seen underwater and dolphins can occasionally be spied from the boat. All equipment is provided, plus cinnamon rolls and teriyaki BBQ chicken for lunch. And, the bar opens on the return sail to shore.

Ka'anapali Surf Club WATER SPORTS
(808-270-0044; www.kaanapalisurfclub.com; Ka'anapali Beach Walk; surfboard hire 1st hour $30, then per hour $15, group surfing classes from $85, kayak tours per person from $99; 7am-5pm) Pop by the desk next to the Westin resort to rent a surfboard or SUP, or join the early-morning kayak tour (7:30am check-in), which takes groups out to Black Rock at the north

of the beach, where you can jump out of the boat to snorkel (equipment provided). It's teeming with marine life here – including parrotfish, turtles and snapper.

Festivals & Events

Hula O Nā Keiki DANCE

(www.kbhmaui.com; 2525 Ka'anapali Pkwy; ⏲ Nov) Children take center stage at this hula-dance competition in early to mid-November, which features some of the best *keiki* (child) dancers in Hawaii. It's held at the Ka'anapali Beach Hotel (p113).

Sleeping

The flashiest and gaudiest resorts on the island can be found on the idyllic, sand-lined stretch of Ka'anapali. And luxury prices are to be expected. Many also tack on daily resort fees as well as parking fees. In 2020 several properties were in the midst of multimillion-dollar renovations. For something out of the ordinary, the Hyatt Regency Maui Resort & Spa (p110) features a flamingo pool and penguin pool (both with real birds).

Ka'anapali Beach Hotel RESORT **$$**

(☎808-661-0011; www.kbhmaui.com; 2525 Ka'anapali Pkwy; r $298-335, ste $360; P ❄ @ 📶 🏊) This welcoming property feels like summer camp – but in the best possible way. The hotel is a little older than its neighbors and the style is more comfy than posh, but it has its own special charms: warm staff, hula shows, an outdoor tiki bar, tidy grounds framed by palm trees, and an enviable location on a gorgeous stretch of beach.

Family-friendly cultural activities include lei-making, storytelling and playing the ukulele. For churchgoers there's a nondenominational outdoor service on Sunday mornings (8am). On your last day, bring a camera and a hankie to your farewell lei ceremony.

Self-parking is $14 per day.

Hyatt Regency Maui Resort & Spa RESORT **$$$**

(☎808-661-1234; www.maui.hyatt.com; 200 Nohea Kai Dr; r/ste from $427/769; P ❄ @ 📶 🏊) Exotic birds and extravagant artwork fill the airy lobby atrium, while gardens and swan ponds catch the eye across the grounds. Kids of all ages will thrill in the water world of meandering pools, swim-through grottoes and towering waterslides. At the time of writing, a multimillion-dollar renovation project covering all guest rooms was expected to finish in late 2020.

The new rooms are set to exude bright and sleek modern style while giving a nod to the islands. Improvements include double sinks, open closets and glass-railing balconies.

The daily resort fee of $32 includes wi-fi, but self-parking is a separate $22 per day. Valet parking is $32 per night.

Honua Kai Resort & Spa CONDO **$$$**

(☎855-718-5789; www.honuakai.com; 130 Kai Malina Pkwy; r from $382; P ❄ @ 📶) This breezy oasis in northern Ka'anapali feels less frenetic than similar properties 2 miles south along Ka'anapali Beach. From the open-air lobby with its well-placed couches to the aesthetically pleasing pools and the extra-spacious lanai adjoining the units, there's a consistent and effective blend of style, functionality and comfort. Units are individually owned so decor varies. The spa offers honeymoon massage packages.

In each unit, Bosch appliances, Maui-made coffee, and washers and dryers round out the appeal. Daily resort fee is $35. Check the website for deals and packages.

One quibble: for a family-friendly resort that touts its fun pools, there sure are a lot of posted rules!

Westin Maui Resort & Spa HOTEL **$$$**

(☎808-667-2525; www.westinmaui.com; 2365 Ka'anapali Pkwy; r/ste from $469/769; P ❄ @ 📶 🏊) Kids will likely love the waterslides and water features at this beachside hotel, which emerged from an extensive 'transformation' in 2020. Improvements also include the elevation of the Beach Tower – one of the property's two towers – into a luxury property. Guest rooms across the towers provide views of either the mountains or ocean, while palm trees dot the immaculate grounds.

The daily resort fee is $30 and parking, which is valet only, is $35 daily.

Sheraton Maui RESORT **$$$**

(☎808-661-0031; www.sheraton-maui.com; 2605 Ka'anapali Pkwy; r/ste from $479/729; P ❄ @ 📶 🏊) This sleek resort bumps against the striking Pu'u Keka'a (p108) at the northern end of the Ka'anapali Beach Walk (p111). Selling points include the sunset cliff dive (p113), whale-watching from the rooms and snorkeling beside green turtles, but the aloha spirit here can be surprisingly disappointing for the price point. It recently

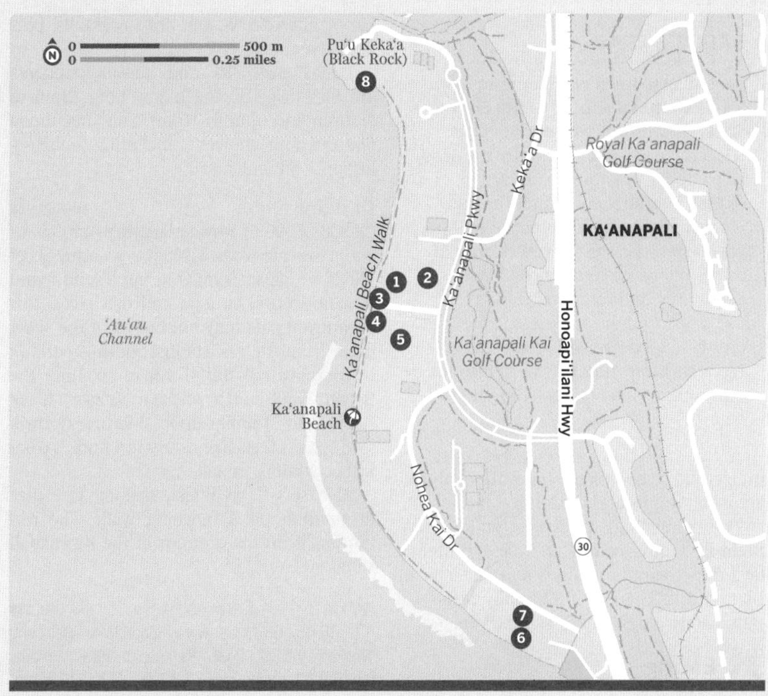

Walking Tour Ka'anapali Beach Walk

START WHALERS VILLAGE
END PU'U KEKA'A (BLACK ROCK)
LENGTH 2.3 MILES; ONE HOUR

With light crowds and gorgeous views of the sea, an early-morning stroll on the Ka'anapali Beach Walk is an inspiring way to greet the day. Later, the paved pathway, which is sandwiched between flashy hotels and white sand, buzzes with holidaymakers promenading under the fronds, snapping pictures of the beach, and catching snippets of early evening ukulele or guitar entertainment.

Start with lunch outdoors at 1 **Hula Grill & Barefoot Bar** (p112) then visit 2 **Whalers Village** (p113) mall for the Hawaiian Wildlife Discovery Center's exhibitions about the area's whaling past and the mammals that frequent these waters. Buy a local piece of art, or let the kids play in the splash pad.

Back on the promenade, sailboats and the outlines of Lana'i and Moloka'i sparkle on the horizon. Tour operators 3 **Teralani Sailing** (p109) and 4 **Trilogy Ocean Sports** (p109) operate off the beach near the shops. Adjacent resorts, such as the 5 **Westin** (p110), hum with activity, from yoga classes by the beach to people relaxing in cabanas and hammocks. Dazzling garden statuary and fairy-tale landscaping, replete with rushing waterfalls, border the sidewalk.

Heading south, vendors dot the route, selling beachwear, jewelry and tickets to the nightly 6 **Drums of the Pacific** (p113) luau, situated at the end of the walk. Detour from the pathway into the 7 **Hyatt Regency** (p110) for the resort's swan and flamingo ponds and pampered black African penguins. Trailside, *The Acrobats*, a graceful 17ft-high bronze sculpture, makes a dramatic silhouette as the sun drops.

For a cool sunset performance, return the way you came, making 8 **Pu'u Keka'a** (p108) to the north your final stop. Sheraton Maui hosts a torch-lit cliff-diving ritual daily for King Kahekili, the last chief of Maui, who demonstrated his strength by cliff diving here. By day, the cliffside water is a popular place to snorkel.

SPIRIT'S LEAP

According to traditional Hawaiian beliefs, **Pu'u Keka'a** (p108) – aka Black Rock, the westernmost point of Maui – is a place where the spirits of the dead leap into the unknown to be carried to their ancestral homeland. The rock is said to have been created during a scuffle between the demigod Maui and a commoner who questioned Maui's superiority. Maui chased the man to this point, froze his body into stone then cast his soul out to sea. Today, daring teens wait their turn to leap off the rock, making a resounding splash in the cove below.

underwent a two-phase renovation project across all rooms and the lobby.

The sprawling, 23-acre grounds have night-lit tennis courts, a fitness center, a lava-rock swimming pool and the spa at Black Rock. There is a $30 daily resort fee plus a separate $24 daily self-parking fee.

Eating

Joey's Kitchen HAWAIIAN **$**
(808-868-4474; Whalers Village, 2435 Ka'anapali Pkwy; mains breakfast $8-10, mains lunch & dinner $11-23; 8am-9pm) Chef Joey Macadangdang has lived on Maui for more than 20 years and fuses Hawaiian-island flavors with Filipino dishes at this no-frills canteen-style eatery: expect breakfast, lunch and dinner on paper plates. What it lacks in ambience, Joey's makes up for in flavor – the seafood is freshly caught and prepared as mahimahi tacos or butter garlic shrimp with veggies.

Huli-huli (rotisserie-grilled) chicken and beef short ribs are also on the menu. Ingredients are locally sourced and the marinades are homemade.

Monkeypod Kitchen PUB FOOD **$$**
(808-878-6763; www.monkeypodkitchen.com; Whalers Village, 2435 Ka'anapali Pkwy; mains lunch $16-30, mains dinner $16-50; 11am-11pm) A spin-off of popular Monkeypod Kitchen (p168) in Wailea, this latest branch of chef Peter Merriman's open-air restaurant is doing just fine in its infancy. A sun-kissed collection of stylish couples and ever-cute families crush in early for the wood-fired pizzas, succulent burgers and fresh seafood dishes. Nice accompaniments include a long list of microbrews and craft cocktails, plus daily live music.

Pizzas are $10 and most appetizers are half price during happy hour (3pm to 5:30pm and 9pm to 11pm). The kids' menu features four choices – including a cheeseburger – all under $11.

Castaway Cafe AMERICAN **$$**
(808-661-9091; www.castawaycafe.com; 45 Kai Ala Dr; mains breakfast $11-15, mains lunch & dinner $12-25; 7:30am-9pm) Offering a solid menu of sandwiches, burgers and fish tacos, this oceanfront cafe may not be worth the short drive from the resorts just south – parking is complicated! But if you're strolling the Beach Walk north of Pu'u Keka'a (Black Rock) and stumble upon this breezy trailside spot, it feels like a very fun find. A tropical cocktail is a must.

Also serves breakfast, making it a nice destination on a morning walk. The restaurant is on the grounds of the Ka'anapali Villas.

★ **Hula Grill & Barefoot Bar** HAWAIIAN **$$$**
(808-667-6636; www.hulagrillkaanapali.com; Whalers Village, 2435 Ka'anapali Pkwy; mains bar $16-23, dining room $25-46; bar 10:45am-10pm, dining room 4:45-9:30pm) Coconut-frond umbrellas, sand beneath your sandals, guy strumming guitar. The Barefoot Bar is the best spot on the beach walk to sip mai tais and nibble *pupu* (snacks) of ceviche, sashimi and coconut calamari. There are two menus, for bar and dining room. The bar menu is cheaper, but it's not a romantic experience – convivial is more like it.

Japengo SUSHI **$$$**
(808-667-4727; www.maui.hyatt.com; 200 Nohea Kai Dr, Hyatt Regency Maui Resort & Spa; sushi $9-24, mains $24-69; 5-10pm) Got the sun-kissed tan and the windswept hair? Japengo bar-restaurant at the Hyatt is the place to show off your Ka'anapali glow. At the tiki-lit patio bar, enjoy an artist's array of tropical cocktails before tucking into sushi as the sun goes down. Roasted meat and seafood dishes, such as the grilled ahi (yellowfin tuna) with Hamakua mushrooms and wasabi butter, have Pacific Rim flair.

Roy's Ka'anapali HAWAIIAN **$$$**
(808-669-6999; www.royyamaguchi.com; 2290 Ka'anapali Pkwy, Ka'anapali Resort; breakfast mains $14-18, lunch mains $15-21, dinner mains $40-69; breakfast 6-10:30am, lunch 11am-2pm, bar pupu from 2:30pm, dinner from 4:30pm) The Maui out-

post of chef Roy Yamaguchi's upscale dining empire sits inside the golf-course clubhouse at the Ka'anapali Resort (p109). Views of the greens are a pleasant backdrop for the exquisitely prepared island and regional fare. Main meals include the sashimi-like blackened ahi with Chinese mustard, and Roy's meatloaf with Maui cattle beef, onion rings and mushroom gravy.

Drinking & Nightlife

Bars in Whalers Village (p113) mall and at many Ka'anapali resorts offer live music in the evening. It's typically Jimmy Buffett–style guitar tunes, occasionally spiced up with some ukulele strumming. Luau and hula shows are also popular. Check www.mauitime.com for performers and schedules.

Hula Grill & Barefoot Bar BAR
(808-667-6636; www.hulagrillkaanapali.com; Whalers Village, 2435 Ka'anapali Pkwy; bar 10:45am-10pm) This is your Maui postcard: coconut-frond umbrellas, sunset mai tais, sand beneath your sandals and the lullaby sounds of Hawaiian slack key guitar. Live music daily (2pm to 5pm and 6pm to 9pm; from 11am on Fridays).

Leilani's BAR
(808-661-4495; www.leilanis.com; Whalers Village, 2435 Ka'anapali Pkwy; 11am-11pm) This open-air bar and restaurant beside the beach is a pleasant place to linger over a cool drink while catching a few rays. It also has a good grill and *pupu* menu. Live music daily from 3pm to 5pm.

Entertainment

Drums of the Pacific LUAU
(808-667-4727; www.drumsofthepacificmaui.com; 200 Nohea Kai Dr, Hyatt Regency Maui Resort & Spa; adult/child 6-12yr from $123/76; 5:30pm;) Ka'anapali's best luau includes an *imu* ceremony (unearthing of a roasted pig from an underground oven), an open bar, a Hawaiian-style buffet and a South Pacific dance-and-music show.

Ka'anapali Beach Hotel DANCE
(808-661-0011; www.kbhmaui.com; 2525 Ka'anapali Pkwy;) Maui's most Hawaiian hotel cheerfully entertains with a free hula show and Hawaiian music beginning at 6:30pm. Enjoy mai tais and brews at the adjacent Tiki Bar (open 10am to 10pm), with music and dancing nightly in the Tiki Courtyard.

Sheraton Maui LIVE PERFORMANCE
(808-661-0031; www.sheraton-maui.com; 2605 Ka'anapali Pkwy; sunset) Everybody swings by to watch the Sheraton-organized Pu'u Keka'a (p108) torch-lighting and cliff-diving ceremony, which takes place at sunset. Afterwards, there's live music at the Sheraton's Cliff Dive Grill (open 11am to 9pm).

Whalers Village OUTDOOR CINEMA
(808-661-4567; www.whalersvillage.com; 2435 Ka'anapali Pkwy; movies dusk Tue & Thu, hula shows 7-8pm Sat, hula lessons 3-4pm Thu;) Ka'anapali's shopping center shows free outdoor movies, with free popcorn, on Tuesday and Thursday nights in the lower-level courtyard. These family-friendly movies begin 15 minutes after the sun goes down. Hula shows and lessons are also offered weekly. Check the online calendar for occasional classes and demos, from lei-making to instruction about coconuts.

Shopping

Fresh from a $27-million renovation project, open-air **Whalers Village** (808-661-4567; www.whalersvillage.com; 2435 Ka'anapali Pkwy; 9:30am-10pm;) shopping center holds more than 70 shops and restaurants, including surf brands, local Hawaii-inspired fashion and decor, and the rare local arts and crafts at **Martin & MacArthur** (808-667-7422; www.martinandmacarthur.com 9:30am-10pm). Check out **Malibu Shirts** (808-667-2280; www.malibushirts.com; 9am-10pm) for its retro styles and its displays spotlighting surfing history.

Getting There & Away

Popular Ka'anapali is one of the easiest areas to get to on Maui. It takes roughly 50 minutes by road (Hwy 380, Hwy 30 and the Lahaina Bypass) from Kahului International Airport. It's also easy to travel from Ka'anapali to the nearby towns of Lahaina (10 minutes away heading south on Hwy 30) and Kapalua (15 minutes' drive heading north on Hwy 30).

Beach-access parking can be found at Whalers Village ($3 per half-hour, free when validated at certain shops).

Getting Around

BUS

Maui Bus (808-871-4838; www.mauicounty.gov; per trip $2; most routes 6:30am-8pm) currently departs from the bus stop at the entrance to Whalers Village (p113) shopping center in Ka'anapali for the Wharf Cinema

Center (p96) in Lahaina on the West Maui Islander route (hourly from 6:07am to 9:07pm and half-hourly between 2:30pm and 5:30pm). The West Maui Islander runs north up the coast to Kahana (15 minutes), Napili (22 minutes) and finally Kapalua (32 minutes) from 5:58am to 8:58pm.

The free **Ka'anapali Trolley** loops between the Ka'anapali hotels, Whalers Village and the golf courses every 20 to 30 minutes between 10am and 10pm (with lunch and dinner breaks for the driver). The trolley schedule is posted at the Whalers Village stop.

CAR & MOTORCYCLE

For Harley-Davidson motorcycle rentals, try **Eagle Rider** (808-667-7000; www.eaglerider.com; 30 Halawai Dr A-3; motorcycle per day incl helmet from $139; 9am-5pm), located just north of Ka'anapali off the Honoapi'ilani Hwy. The company shares space with **Aloha Motorsports** (808-667-7000; http://alohamotorsports.com; 30 Halawai Dr; 9am-5pm), which rents scooters.

TAXI

Cabs are often found outside Ka'anapali's resorts and Whalers Village (p113) on Ka'anapali Pkwy.

Honokowai

This is the best place in West Maui to spot passing whales right from your room lanai over the winter months. The main road, which bypasses the condos, is Honoapi'ilani Hwy (Hwy 30). The parallel shoreline road is Lower Honoapi'ilani Rd, which leads into Honokowai and continues north into Kahana and Napili.

Sights & Activities

Honokowai Beach Park BEACH

() The real thrills here are on land, not in the water. This family-friendly park in the center of Honokowai has playground facilities and makes a nice spot for a picnic. But forget swimming. The water is shallow and the beach is lined with a submerged rock shelf. Water conditions improve at the southern side of town, and you could continue walking along the shore down to lovely Kahekili Beach Park (p107) at the northern end of Ka'anapali.

Boss Frog SNORKELING

(808-665-1200; www.bossfrog.com; 3636 Lower Honoapi'ilani Rd; snorkel set per day from $1.50; 8am-5pm) Not super welcoming on our visit, but they do offer great prices for rental mask, snorkel and fins.

Sleeping & Eating

Hale Kai CONDO $

(808-669-6333; www.halekai.com; 3691 Lower Honoapi'ilani Rd; 1/2/3 bedroom from $155/234/450; P) 'Glad you're here' friendliness lifts this two-story condo complex from the ho-hum into something special. The property offers nice Hawaiian accents, from the room decor to the lava-rock exterior. It's perched on the water's edge: step off your lanai and onto the sand. The three-bedroom corner unit has a cool loft, wraparound ocean-view windows and all the character of a Hawaiian beach house.

Noelani CONDO $$

(808-669-8374; www.noelanicondoresort.com; 4095 Lower Honoapi'ilani Rd; studios from $200, 1/2/3 br from $270/395/455; P) Meet your neighbors at the weekly mai tai party at this compact hideaway, a small complex that's so close to the water you can sit on your lanai and watch turtles swimming in the surf. Units range from cozy studios to three-bedroom suites, all with ocean views. A pool, Jacuzzi, lei-making classes, small exercise room and concierge services are additional perks.

Not all units have A/C, so check before booking if that's important. The cleaning fee is typically $150 to $165 per stay.

Farmers Market Deli DELI $

(808-669-7004; www.farmersmarketsmaui.com; 3636 Lower Honoapi'ilani Rd; sandwiches $8-13; 7am-7pm;) This welcoming indie market is a great spot to pick up healthy and tasty takeout fare. The hot entrees bar ($10 per pound) includes organic goodies and hot veggie dishes; the smoothies are first rate; and free samples of dips are on offer. The place becomes even greener on Monday, Wednesday and Friday mornings (7am to 11am), when vendors sell locally grown produce in the parking lot.

Honokowai Food Pod FOOD TRUCK $

(Lower Honoapi'ilani Rd; from 5pm) Some 10 food trucks cluster around picnic tables in a field along Lower Honoapi'ilani Rd. Stop here for tacos, ribs, seafood, Thai, Japanese dishes, Hawaiian plates and more. Trucks in this pod seem to open later in the day, so visit after 5pm or so, and bring cash.

It's located just north of Honua Kai Resort & Spa (p110).

Honokowai Okazuya INTERNATIONAL $$
(☎808-665-0512; 3600 Lower Honoapi'ilani Rd; mains $10-19; ⏲11am-2:30pm & 4:30-8:30pm Mon-Sat) This place is tiny, not super friendly and the choices are weird (*kung pao* chicken *and* spaghetti with meatballs?). So why do we like it? First you nibble the Mongolian beef. Hmm, it's OK. Chomp, chomp. That's pretty interesting. Gulp, gulp. What is that spice? Savor, savor – until the whole meal is devoured. Here, plate lunches take a delicious gourmet turn.

Primarily takeout. Cash only.

Kahana

Trendy Kahana, a village just north of Honokowai, boasts million-dollar homes, upscale beachfront condominiums and a Maui microbrewery. This sleepy enclave is for those who like privacy and marine life – you can often see turtles swimming in the water from your hotel lanai.

The sandy **beach** fronting Kahana village offers reasonable swimming. Park at seaside **Pohaku Park** (☎808-661-4685; www.mauicounty.gov; P) and walk north to get there. Pohaku Park itself has an offshore break, **S-Turns**, which attracts intermediate surfers.

Kahana Village CONDO $$
(☎808-669-5111; www.kahanavillage.com; 4531 Lower Honoapi'ilani Rd; 2/3 bedroom from $343/651; P) A welcome sign greets guests by name at Kahana Village, where A-frame ceilings, airy lofts and oceanfront views – in the 2nd-story units – have a fun vacation vibe. The breezy appeal of the interior is well matched outside with lush tropical flora. Some condos have views of Lana'i while others face Moloka'i. Every unit has a full kitchen plus washer and dryer.

There's a weekly mai tai party on Wednesdays with live Hawaiian music.

Hawaiian Village Coffee CAFE $
(☎808-665-1114; Kahana Gateway, 4405 Honoapi'ilani Hwy; pastries $4-5, sandwiches $7-9; ⏲5am-3pm Mon, 6am-6pm Tue-Thu, Sat & Sun, 5am-11pm Fri;) Off-duty surfers shoot the breeze at this low-key coffee shop, which sells sweet pastries, cupcakes and the probiotic drink kombucha (on tap $6).

Maui Brewing Co BREWERY
(☎808-669-3474; www.mbcrestaurants.com; Kahana Gateway, 4405 Honoapi'ilani Hwy; ⏲11am-10pm) From the burgers made from local grass-fed beef to the wild-pork flatbread, bar food (mains $12 to $23) takes a Hawaiian spin at this cavernous brewpub. The company, which has been honored as one of Hawaii's top green businesses, implements sustainable practices where possible. Happy hour runs from 3:30pm to 5:30pm daily, with $1 off a selection of craft beers.

Their year-round beers include the Bikini Blonde lager, Mana Wheat, Big Swell IPA and Coconut Hiwa Porter, and they offer limited-release brews.

Maui Brewing also has a production facility, taproom and new restaurant in Kihei (p164).

Napili

Napili is a bayside oasis flanked by the posh grounds of Kapalua to the north and the hustle and bustle of Kahana and Ka'anapali to the south. For an oceanfront retreat that's a bit more affordable – and not far from the action – we highly recommend this sun-blessed center of calm.

Sights & Activities

Napili Beach BEACH
(P) The deep golden sands and gentle curves of Napili Beach offer good beachcombing at any time and excellent swimming and snorkeling when it's calm. Look for green sea turtles hanging out by the rocky southern shore. Big waves occasionally make it into the bay in winter, and when they do it's time to break out the skimboards – the steep drop at the beach provides a perfect run into the surf.

Ironwood Ranch Horseback Riding HORSEBACK RIDING
(☎808-669-4702; www.ironwoodranch.com; 22 Hui Rd A; 90min/2hr ride $110/170, 1/1½/2hr nature walk $55/68/85) These welcoming folks will guide you into the foothills and valleys of the lush West Maui Mountains, home to pineapple fields and ironwood trees. Excursions include an eco-minded history ride and a sunset trip. For hikers, guided nature walks covering West Maui history and local medicinal plants are offered too. The ranch is 1.5 miles from the Honoapi'ilani Hwy.

The road to the ranch is mostly dirt but is easily driveable.

Sleeping

Mauian HOTEL $$

(808-669-6205; www.mauian.com; 5441 Lower Honoapi'ilani Rd; studio with kitchen from $279, r from $259;) Your fellow guests feel like friendly neighbors at this compact hideaway that is simultaneously stylish and down-home. Studios at this 44-room condo-hotel hybrid feature bamboo ceilings, frond prints, crisp whites and browns, and Tempur-Pedic mattresses. There's a hearty continental breakfast available in the common room and beach chairs for guests. Enjoy the breeze from the lanai.

Units do not have TVs or phones, but both are available in the common area. Hotel rooms do not have kitchens. Good choice if you want a room in Napili for only a night or two without exorbitant cleaning fees.

Napili Sunset Beachfront Resort CONDO $$

(808-669-8083; www.napilisunset.com; 46 Hui Dr; studio $199, 1/2 br $360/550, 1 br with loft $400;) The Napili Sunset is a little worn around the edges, but it is also well loved. Staff is welcoming and repeat guests enjoy talking story, which gives the place a friendly vibe. Condos are spread across three buildings. One- and two-bedroom units are beachfront, and studios are a few steps further back. The 42 units have kitchens and lanai, and studios have A/C.

★ **Hale Napili** CONDO $$$

(808-669-6184; www.halenapili.com; 65 Hui Dr; studio $260-360, 1 bedroom $410;) A welcome throwback to an earlier era, this small and personable place will win you over with its island hospitality. Guests receive a list of occupants, making it easier to strike up conversations, and there's a central Keurig coffee machine so you can chat over morning coffee. The 18 neat-as-a-pin units have tropical decor, full kitchens and oceanfront lanai.

Napili Kai Beach Resort CONDO, HOTEL $$$

(808-669-6271; www.napilikai.com; 5900 Lower Honoapi'ilani Rd; r/studio/ste from $415/340/680;) This low-key yet sophisticated resort covers 11 acres at the northern end of Napili Bay. The units, which tastefully blend Polynesian decor with Asian touches, have private lanai, and the studios and rooms have kitchenettes. Some units have A/C. Alohas are a touch less personable here than you'd hope for the price point. The Sea House Restaurant (p117) is on site.

Eating & Drinking

★ **A'a Roots** VEGAN $

(www.aarootsmaui.com; 5059 Napilihau St, Napili Plaza; mains $9-19, acai bowls $13-15, juices & smoothies $9; 8am-4pm Wed-Mon;) There are lots of 'Hey babes' flying around between owners and regulars at this welcoming place, where bronzed and waifish surfer girls and health-minded dudes dig into a fantastic array of acai, noodle and curry bowls, plus wraps and salads. Meals look like big works of art and taste just as dreamy. Order at the counter. Juices and smoothies available too.

Gazebo CAFE $

(808-669-5621; 5315 Lower Honoapi'ilani Rd, Outrigger Napili Shores; mains $11-16; 7:30am-2pm) A wait is inevitable, and you'll need to queue by 6:45am (!) to nab a table at the 7:30am opening. But the wait is worth it for this beloved open-air restaurant – a gazebo on the beach – with a gorgeous waterfront setting. The tiny cafe is known for its breakfasts, and those with a sweet tooth love the white-chocolate–macnut pancakes.

Meal-size salads, hearty sandwiches and the *kalua* pig plate steal the scene at lunch. Those in the know order ahead to-go and pick up their meal at the window, but the line can be entertaining with its international array of visitors. The restaurant is behind **Outrigger Napili Shores** (808-669-8061; www.outriggernapilishorescondo.com; 5315 Lower Honoapi'ilani Rd; studio from $272, 1br $306;).

Maui Tacos MEXICAN $

(808-665-0222; www.mauitacos.com; Napili Plaza, 5095 Napilihau St; mains $7-15; 9am-9pm Mon-Sat, to 8pm Sun) The burritos are huge at Maui Tacos, where the Mexican fare is island-style healthy. The salsas and beans are prepared fresh daily, trans-fat-free oil replaces lard, and fresh veggies and local fish feature on the menu. It's fast-food style and good for a quick meal. This location sells beer and beachy cocktails.

★ **Joey's Kitchen Napili** FILIPINO $$

(808-214-5590; www.joeyskitchenhimaui.com; Napili Plaza, 5095 Napilihau St; mains breakfast $9-12, dinner $10-25; 11am-2pm Mon-Fri, 8:30am-2pm Sat & Sun, 4-9pm daily) If chef Joey Macadangdang is working the counter at this place close to A'a Roots, grab a seat and let him tell you what's fresh and what's good. But really, it's all good. Macadangdang was born in the Philippines, and his menu is a delicious romp across Asia and Hawaii, spotlighting noodle dishes, local plates and seafood entrees. The scrumptious shrimp *pancit* is always a good place to start.

Sea House Restaurant HAWAIIAN **$$$**
(☎808-669-1500; www.seahousemaui.com; 5900 Lower Honoapi'ilani Rd, Napili Kai Beach Resort; breakfast & lunch mains $9-20, dinner mains $26-44, happy hour appetizers under $9; ⏲7am-10pm, happy hour 2-4:30pm) The Sea House offers a solid steak and seafood menu, but the main reason you're here is the million-dollar sunset. Our advice? Sidle up to the bar at this tiki-lit favorite in the late afternoon, order a few happy hour appetizers – we like the *poke* nachos and the *kalua* pork taco – then watch the sun drop below the horizon. Bravo!

Coffee Store in Napili CAFE
(☎808-669-4170; www.napilicoffeestore.com; Napili Plaza, 5095 Napilihau St; pastries $2-7, sandwiches $8; ⏲6am-6pm; 📶) The ice-blended mocha at Napili's favorite coffee shop, which is near A'a Roots, is nothing less than aloha in a cup. Utterly delicious. Locals also line up for the pleasant service and the pastries, from banana bread to pumpkin-cranberry muffins and chocolate peanut-butter bars. Sandwiches available Monday through Saturday.

☆ Entertainment

★Masters of Hawaiian Slack Key Guitar Concert Series LIVE MUSIC
(☎808-669-3858; www.slackkeyshow.com; 5900 Lower Honoapi'ilani Rd, Napili Kai Beach Resort; $38-95; ⏲7:30pm Wed) Ledward Kaapana and other top slack key guitarists appear regularly at this exceptional concert series. George Kahumoku Jr, a slack key legend in his own right, is the weekly host. As much a jam session as a concert, this is a true Hawaiian cultural gem that's worth going out of your way to experience. Reservations recommended.

Kapalua & Northern Beaches

Kapalua has long been a sacred place for Native Hawaiians, but now it's more known for world-class golf courses, an adventure zipline company and glitzy five-star resorts. The rugged northern coast is not far from Kapalua's manicured greens, where untamed views are guaranteed to replenish your soul. The nightlife doesn't exactly sizzle here, but the beaches – all with public access – sure do.

In the 1900s this area was the site of a productive pineapple plantation, and hikes around the area will take adventurers though forests planted by DT Fleming, the tree surgeon who developed Maui's pineapple industry.

If uninterrupted sunshine is your goal in West Maui, note that Kapalua can be a bit rainier and windier than points south.

> **ⓘ BEACH PARKING IN KAPALUA & NAPILI**
>
> If the public-access parking lots for Napili Bay and its neighbor Kapalua Beach are full, and on-street parking is also maxed out, don't despair. In a pinch, you can pay $10 to park in the paved lot at the Kapalua Tennis Garden (p120). It's just a short walk through the trees from here to the public-access lots and beaches.

Beaches

★Kapalua Beach BEACH
(Ⓟ) For a long day on the beach, it's hard to beat this crescent-shaped strip at the southwestern tip of Kapalua. Snorkel in the morning, grab lunch at the Sea House (p117), try stand-up paddle surfing, then sip cocktails at Merriman's (p122) next door. Or simply sit on the sand and gaze across the channel at Moloka'i. Long rocky outcrops at both ends of the bay make Kapalua Beach the safest year-round swimming spot on this coast.

You'll find colorful snorkeling on the right side of the beach, with abundant tropical fish and orange slate-pencil sea urchins. There's a rental hut here for beach gear.

Take the drive immediately north of Napili Kai Beach Resort (p116) to get to the beach parking area, where there are restrooms and showers. A tunnel leads from the parking lot north to the beach. This is also a starting point for the Coastal Trail (p103).

Oneloa Beach BEACH
(Ⓟ) Also known as Ironwoods Beach, this white-sand jewel is fringed by low sand dunes covered in beach morning glory. It's

Kapalua & Around

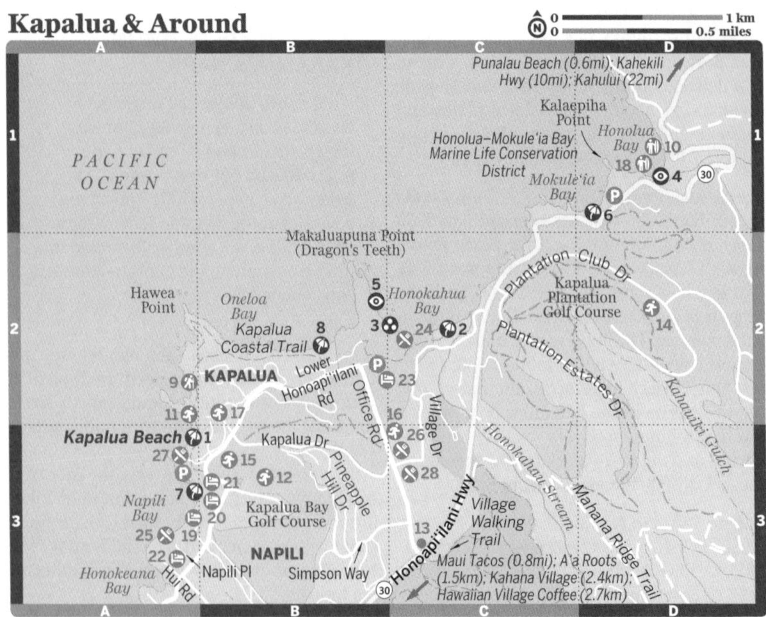

a picturesque place to soak up the rays. On calm days, swimming is good close to shore, as is snorkeling in the protected area along the rocky point at the northern side of the beach. When there's any sizable surf, strong rip currents can be present.

The half-mile strand – Oneloa means 'long sand' – sits beside the Coastal Trail (p103) and is backed by gated resort condos and restricted golf greens. Beach access requires a sharp eye. Turn onto Ironwood Lane and then left into the small parking lot opposite the Ironwoods gate. Arrive early or at lunchtime to get a parking space, freshly emptied by the people leaving.

DT Fleming Beach Park BEACH

(Honoapi'ilani Hwy; P) Surrounded by ironwood trees and backed by an old one-room schoolhouse, this sandy crescent looks like an outpost from another era. In keeping with its Hawaiian nature, the beach is the domain of wave riders. Experienced surfers and bodysurfers find good action here, especially in winter. The shorebreaks can be brutal, however, and the beach is a hot spot for injuries. The reef on the right is good for snorkeling in summer when the water is very calm.

Fleming has restrooms, showers, grills, picnic tables and a lifeguard. The access road is off Honoapi'ilani Hwy (Hwy 30), immediately north of the 31-mile marker.

The Coastal Trail (p103) and the Mahana Ridge Trail intersect here.

Sights

Makaluapuna Point NATURAL FEATURE

(Dragon's Teeth) Razor-sharp spikes crown rocky Makaluapuna Point, known informally by the nickname Dragon's Teeth. The formation does look uncannily like the mouth of an imaginary dragon. The 3ft-high spikes are the work of pounding winter waves that have ripped into the lava rock point, leaving the pointy 'teeth' behind. The point is also potentially hazardous. It is subject to powerful waves, particularly the northern winter swells, and covered by uneven, sometimes sharp rocks.

Signage states that the outcropping is sacred to Native Hawaiians. Although the public is allowed access to the ocean by law, visitors are strongly discouraged from walking onto the formation, out of respect for native customs. The adjacent Honokahua burial site (p119) is off-limits to the general public. Both sites are of cultural significance to Native Hawaiians and should not be inspected up close. Respect the signage.

For a view of Makaluapuna Point, you can stand beside the plaque detailing the burial site. The plaque sits along the Coastal Trail (p103) beside the parking area and above the 13-acre burial site. Don't enter areas marked 'Please Kokua,' which are easily visible islets of stones bordering the Ritz's manicured golf greens. Do not walk across the greens.

Get here by driving north to the very end of Lower Honoapi'ilani Rd, where you'll find parking, beside the northern edge of the Kapalua Bay Golf Course.

Honokahua Burial Site RUINS

This site is of cultural significance to Native Hawaiians and is off-limits to the general public. There are an estimated 2000 Hawaiians laid to rest here, dating back to 610 CE. The burial site is covered with well-maintained grass and flanked by a native *hau* hedge. Hawaiians believe that their ancestors' spirits continue to protect these lands; please respect the signage.

Activities

Most activity reservation offices are along Office Rd or Kapalua Rd. The dramatically scenic Kapalua Coast Trail (p103) has trailheads at Kapalua Beach and DT Fleming Beach Park.

Kapalua Golf GOLF

(808-669-8044; www.golfatkapalua.com; greens fee $169-359; tee times vary seasonally) Kapalua boasts two of the island's top championship-golf courses, both certified by Audubon International as sanctuaries for native plants and animals. The **Kapalua Bay Golf Course** (808-662-7720; 300 Kapalua Dr; twilight/standard round $169/229; pro shop 6am-7pm, 1st tee 6:40am) is the tropical ocean course, meandering across a lava peninsula. The challenging **Plantation course** (808-662-7710; 2000 Plantation Club Dr; standard round $359; pro shop 6am-7pm, 1st tee 6:40am), which sweeps over a rugged landscape of hills and deep gorges, reopened in late 2019 after a nine-month refresh. Look for harder and faster greens and new tee boxes.

Coconuts SURFING

Considered by many as one of the best surf spots in the world, Coconuts is an expert point-break on the far outside of Honolua Bay, producing big, fast right-hand rides. Winds and currents are strong. Parking is very limited off Honoapi'ilani Hwy, and car break-ins are common.

The Cave SURFING

Named after a small Honolua Bay cave, which has occasionally trapped surfers. Strong northwesterly offshore winds help produce first-rate barrels here in the bay. It's

HONOLUA–MOKULE'IA BAY MARINE LIFE CONSERVATION DISTRICT

The narrow Kalaepiha Point separates **Mokule'ia Beach**, also known as Slaughterhouse Beach, and **Honolua Bay**. Together they form the Honolua–Mokule'ia Bay Marine Life Conservation District, which is famed for its snorkeling and surfing.

Honolua Bay is a surfer's dream. It faces northwest and, when it catches the winter swells, it has some of the gnarliest surfing in the world. In summer snorkeling is excellent in both bays, thanks in part to prohibitions on fishing in the preserve. Honolua Bay is the favorite, with thriving reefs and abundant coral along its rocky edges.

Spinner dolphins sometimes hang near the mouth of the bays, swimming just beyond snorkelers. When it's calm, you can snorkel around Kalaepiha Point from one bay to the other, but forget it after heavy rains: Honolua Stream empties into its namesake Bay and the runoff clouds the water.

The land fronting Honolua Bay has long been owned by Maui Land & Pineapple. The company has allowed recreational access to the bay for no fee. A few families have the right to live on this land, but they cannot charge an access fee or restrict visiting hours. In 2014, with community support, the state of Hawaii purchased more than 240 acres beside the bay to protect them from development.

Once you reach the bay, read the signage about protecting the coral (sunscreen, for example, should be avoided) then enter via the rocky coastline. Do not enter the water via the concrete boat ramp, which is very slippery and potentially hazardous.

When the waters are calm, the bays offer superb kayaking. Mokule'ia Beach is also a top-rated bodysurfing spot during the summer. Its attractive white-sand crescent is good for sunbathing and beachcombing – look for glittering green olivine crystals in the rocks at the southern end of the beach.

Just north of the 32-mile marker, there's public parking and a concrete stairway leading down the cliffs to Mokule'ia Beach. After passing Mokule'ia Beach, look ahead for a large parking area on the left. Here you'll find a nice view of Honolua Bay below. A half-mile past the 32-mile marker, there's room for about six cars to park adjacent to the path down to Honolua Bay, or continue around a couple of bends and park beside the port-o-johns. From here, follow the gravel path through the junglelike flora to the bay.

a super-local spot for advanced surfers only. Be courteous and don't go dropping in on anyone.

Kapalua Tennis Garden TENNIS

(☎808-662-7730; http://golfatkapalua.com; 100 Kapalua Dr; per person per hour $25, racket rental $15; ⏲pro shop 8am-4pm) Maui's premier full-service tennis club has 10 Plexipave courts, with four lit for evening games, plus an array of clinics. If you're on your own, give the club a ring and they'll match you with other players for singles or doubles games. New pickleball courts are available too.

Kapalua Ziplines ADVENTURE SPORTS

(☎808-756-9147; www.kapaluaziplines.com; 500 Office Rd; 5-/6-/7-line zip $180/200/210; ⏲7am-5pm) Ready to soar across the West Maui Mountains for nearly 2 miles? On the self-proclaimed ultimate adventure tour (3¾ hours) you'll glide down seven ziplines, two of them extending a breathtaking 2000ft in length. All ziplines have a dual track, allowing you to zip beside a friend – but solos are fine too!

Spa Montage Kapalua Bay SPA

(☎808-665-8282; www.montagehotels.com; 1 Bay Dr; body therapies from $210, massages from $215; ⏲facilities 6am-7pm, treatments 9am-7pm) This soothing place has a eucalyptus steam room, cedar-wood sauna, whirlpool, bamboo rainfall showers and aesthetically pleasing treatment areas. It embraces native Hawaiian ingredients and traditions from both *mauka* (mountain) and *makai* (sea). This is the place for a couple's massage or a *lomilomi* massage ($210 for 60 minutes), which follows the rhythmic motions of the ocean.

Kapalua Bay Beach Crew WATER SPORTS

(☎808-649-8222; Kapalua Bay; ⏲8:30am-sunset) Rent a basic snorkel set for $20 per day and a SUP board for $40 per hour. A SUP lesson is $139 for an hour (you can keep the board for the rest of the day). Look for its hut at the northern end of Kapalua Beach.

Courses

Kapalua Golf Academy GOLF
(808-662-7740; www.golfatkapalua.com; 1000 Office Rd; 1hr private lesson $175, 1-day school $350; 8am-5pm) Hawaii's top golf academy is staffed by PGA pros.

Festivals & Events

PGA Tournament of Champions SPORTS
(www.pgatour.com; early Jan) Watch the world's top players tee off at the PGA Tour's season opener at the Kapalua Plantation Golf Course (p119), vying for a multimillion-dollar purse.

Celebration of the Arts CULTURAL
(www.celebrationofthearts.org; Ritz-Carlton Kapalua; Apr) This festival celebrates traditional Hawaiian culture with art, hula, music, films and cultural panels.

Kapalua Wine & Food Festival FOOD & DRINK
(www.kapaluawineandfoodfestival.com; Ritz-Carlton Kapalua; mid-Jun) A culinary extravaganza held over four days in mid-June. It features renowned winemakers and Hawaii's hottest chefs, offering cooking demonstrations and wine tastings.

Xterra World Championship SPORTS
(www.xterraplanet.com; Ritz-Carlton Kapalua; Oct) A major off-road triathlon race, boasting a $105,000 purse for the winner. It starts with a 1-mile rough water swim, followed by a 20-mile dirt-trail bike ride through a ravine and tropical landscape, and then a 6.5-mile trail run through forest and across beach.

Sleeping

★ **Montage Kapalua Bay** RESORT $$$
(808-662-6600; www.montagehotels.com; 1 Bay Dr; ste from $825; P ❄ @ 🛜 ≋) Swanky yet inviting, this 24-acre resort takes style, comfort and hospitality to an utterly pleasing level. With only 50 units, all of them suites, the property feels more intimate and less hectic than other resorts across Maui. Bright pillows add a colorful splash to the subdued but appealing in-room furnishings.

Suites come with kitchens, washer and dryers, and spacious lanai. And beyond your suite? You can relax beside the three-tiered pool, enjoy pampering at the tranquil spa (p120) or hop into the bright blue waters lapping below the 1940 Cliff House, once used by the Honolua Plantation. The resort fee is $55 per day and valet-only parking is $35 per day.

Ritz-Carlton Kapalua RESORT $$$
(808-669-6200; www.ritzcarlton.com; 1 Ritz-Carlton Dr; r/ste from $832/1419; P ❄ @ 🛜 ≋) Understated elegance attracts the exclusive golf crowd to this luxe northern outpost. On a hillside fronting the greens and the sea, the hotel has a heated multilevel swimming pool flanked by palm trees, a spa and a fitness club. Redesigned rooms feel soothing, with modern and subdued style: dark-wood floors, pops of color from modern local art, and oversize marble bathrooms.

The $35 daily resort fee covers wi-fi, plus use of the fitness center and resort shuttle. Valet-only parking is $30 per day.

Eating & Drinking

The dining scene in Kapalua is among the island's best. It's hard to get a bad meal in this area, whether you go for low-end or high-end options.

Honolua Store DELI $
(808-665-9105; http://honoluastore.com; 502 Office Rd; mains breakfast $8-14, mains lunch $5-16; store 6am-8pm, deli 6am-7pm; 🛜) This porch-wrapped bungalow opened in 1929 as the general store for the Honolua pineapple plantation. Today, the Honolua Store has been stylishly revamped, but it remains a nod to normalcy in the midst of lavish exclusiveness. The deli is known for its reasonable prices and fantastic plate lunches. Grab-and-go sandwiches and *bentō* (Japanese-style box lunch) items are available in the deli case.

Burger Shack BURGERS $$
(808-669-6200; DT Fleming Beach Park; mains $17-24; 11am-4pm;) You put the lime in the coconut, Burger Shack. This casual and fun oceanfront joint beside DT Fleming Beach sells gourmet burgers, fun shakes and inventive cocktails under the coconut trees. Creative patties include a *katsu* burger with ramen chicken breast, a smoked pork burger, and a black bean, beet and tofu burger.

Taverna ITALIAN $$
(808-667-2426; www.tavernamaui.com; 2000 Village Rd; lunch mains $7-21, dinner mains $24-42; from 11am Mon-Fri, 10am-2pm & from 5:30pm Sat & Sun) Interior design: wow! Golf course view: wow! Food...solidly OK. With all the hoopla about this addition to the Kapalua dining scene, we were ready to be blown away. But keep your expectations low to medium and you'll be just fine. We found the

pizza surprisingly disappointing. The salad was good though! Great cocktail list too.

Sansei Seafood Restaurant & Sushi Bar JAPANESE **$$$**
(☎808-669-6286; www.sanseihawaii.com; 600 Office Rd; sushi $5-36, mains $24-65; ⊙dinner 5-10pm Sat-Wed, to 1am Thu & Fri) Sansei's innovative sushi menu is the draw, but the non-sushi house specials, which often blend Japanese and Pacific Rim flavors, shouldn't be overlooked. The spicy Dungeness crab ramen with truffle broth is a noteworthy prize. Order before 5:30pm for an early-bird dinner special. No reservation? Queue up early for one of the seats at the sushi or cocktail bar.

Plantation House HAWAIIAN **$$$**
(☎808-669-6299; www.theplantationhouse.com; 2000 Plantation Club Dr, Plantation Golf Course Clubhouse; breakfast mains $14-22, lunch mains $16-24, dinner mains $28-59; ⊙8am-3pm & 6-9pm) Recently revamped, this beloved golf clubhouse eatery is looking fresh. Fortunately for both newcomers and old-timers, the menu has retained the favorites. These include the crab-cake Benedict, a fluffy, hollandaise-splashed affair that will have you kissing your plate. For dinner, fresh fish and beef dishes are prepared with global flair.

Merriman's Kapalua HAWAIIAN **$$$**
(☎808-669-6400; www.merrimanshawaii.com/kapalua; 1 Bay Club Pl; restaurant mains $31-68, happy hour menu $9-27; ⊙restaurant 4:30-9pm, bar 3pm-late) We especially like Merriman's at happy hour (3pm to 5pm). Perched on a scenic point between Kapalua Bay and Napili Bay, the tiki- and palm-dotted Point Bar is a gorgeous place to unwind after braving the Kahekili Hwy (p122). At the acclaimed restaurant, Maui-caught fish and locally sourced meats and produce are highlights. Live music daily in the dining room from 5pm to 8:30pm.

Hideaway BAR
(☎808-662-6620; www.montagehotels.com; 1 Bay Dr, Montage Kapalua Bay; ⊙4:30-10pm) Tucked in a lower-level corner of the swanky Montage resort, this breezily sophisticated cocktail bar looks like a private cub. But everyone who enters is treated like a member, and the gourmet libations – which often feature locally produced spirits and island flavors – have everyone gabbing like friends.

A nice spot to relax before the Wednesday slack key show (p117) at the nearby Napili Kai Beach Resort.

Kahekili Highway

Bring your hat, water, suncreen, your scrambling shoes and your sense of adventure on this challenging 20-to-35-mile road trip, which hugs the rugged northern tip of Maui. And a small dose of common sense will make the day more enjoyable – and safer.

Optimistically called a highway (Rte 340), the route is generally driven from east of Punalau Beach, where Honoapi'ilani Hwy/Rte 30 turns into the Kahekili Hwy. It charges around hairpin turns, careens over one-lane bridges and teeters beside treacherous cliffs. Finishing in Wailuku, it's one of Maui's most adventurous drives. The area is so ravishingly rural that it's hard to imagine trendy West Maui could hold such untouched countryside.

Not for the faint of heart, some sections slow to just 5mph as the road wraps around blind curves. A lengthy stretch around the village of Kahakuloa is just one lane with cliffs on one side and a sheer drop on the other – if you meet oncoming traffic here, you may be doing your traveling in reverse! But if you can handle that, this largely overlooked route offers all sorts of adventures, with horse and hiking trails, a mighty blowhole and delicious banana bread.

The road is paved and open to the public the entire way, but there are no services, so gas up beforehand. Give yourself a good two hours' driving time, not counting stops. If you get stuck behind a slow-moving vehicle, it could take much longer.

Property between the highway and the coast is both privately and publicly owned. Trails to the shore are often uneven, rocky and slippery, and the coast is subject to dangerous waves. If you decide to explore, take appropriate precautions, and get access permission when possible.

Punalau Beach

Manicured golf courses and ritzy enclaves drop away and the scenery gets wilder as you drive toward Maui's northernmost point. Ironwood-lined **Punalau Beach**, 0.7 miles after the 34-mile marker on Honoapi'ilani Hwy, makes a worthy stop if you're up for a solitary stroll. Swimming is a no-go though, as a rocky shelf creates unfavorable conditions for water activities. Don't attempt the drive down the rough dirt beach road unless you've got 4WD and know what you're doing. Park by the highway.

OFF THE BEATEN TRACK

KAHAKULOA

An imposing 636ft-tall volcanic dome guards the entrance to Kahakuloa Bay like a lurking, watchful dragon. This photogenic landmark, known as **Kahakuloa Head**, was believed to be a favorite cliff-diving spot of Chief Kahekili in the 18th century. Before the road drops into the valley, there's a pull-off above town providing a bird's-eye view.

The bayside village of Kahakuloa, tucked at the bottom of a lush valley and embraced by towering sea cliffs, retains a solidly Hawaiian character. Kahakuloa's isolation has protected it from the rampant development found elsewhere on Maui. Farmers tend taro patches, dogs wander across the road, and a missionary-era Protestant church marks the village center. One of Hawaii's most accomplished ukulele players, Richard Ho'opi'i, grew up here.

You won't find any stores, but villagers set up hard-to-miss roadside stands selling fruit and snacks to day-trippers. For shave ice, hit Ululani's hot-pink stand. For chilled homemade lemonade and free samples of macadamia nuts, coconut candy and *'ono* (delicious) banana bread, stop at **Julia's lime-green shack** (www.juliasbananabread.com; Kahekili Hwy, Mile 13; ⌚9am-5pm or until sold out)

Nakalele Point

The terrain turns hilly after Punalau Beach, with rocky cattle pastures punctuated by tall sisal plants. At a number of pull-offs you can stop and explore. The lush pastures are quite enticing, willing you to traipse down the cliffs and out along the rugged coastline.

At the Kahekili Hwy's 38-mile marker, a mile-long trail leads to a **light station** at the end of windswept Nakalele Point. Here you'll find a coastline of arches and other formations carved out of the rocks by the pounding surf. There are several worn paths toward the light station, but you can't really get lost – just walk toward the point, passing down and then up through a grove of trees. Bring water and wear a hat, as there's little shade.

The **Nakalele Blowhole** (Kahekili Hwy, Mile 38) roars when the surf is up but is a sleeper when the seas are calm. To check on its mood, park at the boulder-lined pull-off 0.6 miles beyond the 38-mile marker. You can glimpse the action, if there is any, a few hundred yards beyond the parking lot. It's a 15-minute scramble down a jagged moonscape of lava rocks to the blowhole, which can shoot up to 100ft. Keep a safe distance and watch your footing carefully. A tourist fell into the hole and vanished in 2011. Another died after falling from a cliff in the area in 2013. More recently, a visitor was swept out to sea by a large wave here and drowned. And it probably goes without saying, but don't sit on, or peer into, the blowhole!

Look for the **Ohai Viewpoint** 0.8 miles after the 40-mile marker, on the *makai* (seaward) side of the road. The viewpoint isn't marked but there's a sign announcing the start of the Ohai Trail, a 1.2-mile loop with interpretative signage and coastal views. For the best vistas, bear left from the trailhead and walk to the top of the point for a jaw-dropping coastal panorama that includes a glimpse of the Nakalele Blowhole. If you have kids, be careful – the crumbly cliff edge has a sudden drop of nearly 800ft!

Ocean Baths & Bellstone

After the 42-mile post on the Kahekili Hwy (coming from Lahaina), the mile markers change; the next marker is 16 and the numbers drop as you continue.

One-tenth of a mile before the 16-mile marker, look seaward for a large dirt pull-off. From here, a well-beaten path leads 15 minutes down lava cliffs to **natural ocean baths** on the water's edge. Cut out of slippery lava rock and encrusted with olivine minerals, these incredibly clear pools sit in the midst of roaring surf.

Signage states that visitors should not go beyond the sign, listing the various hazardous conditions just ahead and noting that the ocean is dangerous at all times. A new plaque near the base of the sign memorializes the death here of a visitor, who was swept out to sea and drowned in 2017. Although the baths are on public land, state officials do not recommend accessing them due to the hazardous conditions, including slippery rocks, large and powerful surf, waves crashing over ledges and strong currents.

The huge boulder with concave marks on the inland side of the road just before the pull-off is a bellstone, **Pohaku Kani** (Kahekili Hwy, Mile 16). According to local history, if you hit it with a rock on the Kahakuloa side,

Kahekili Highway

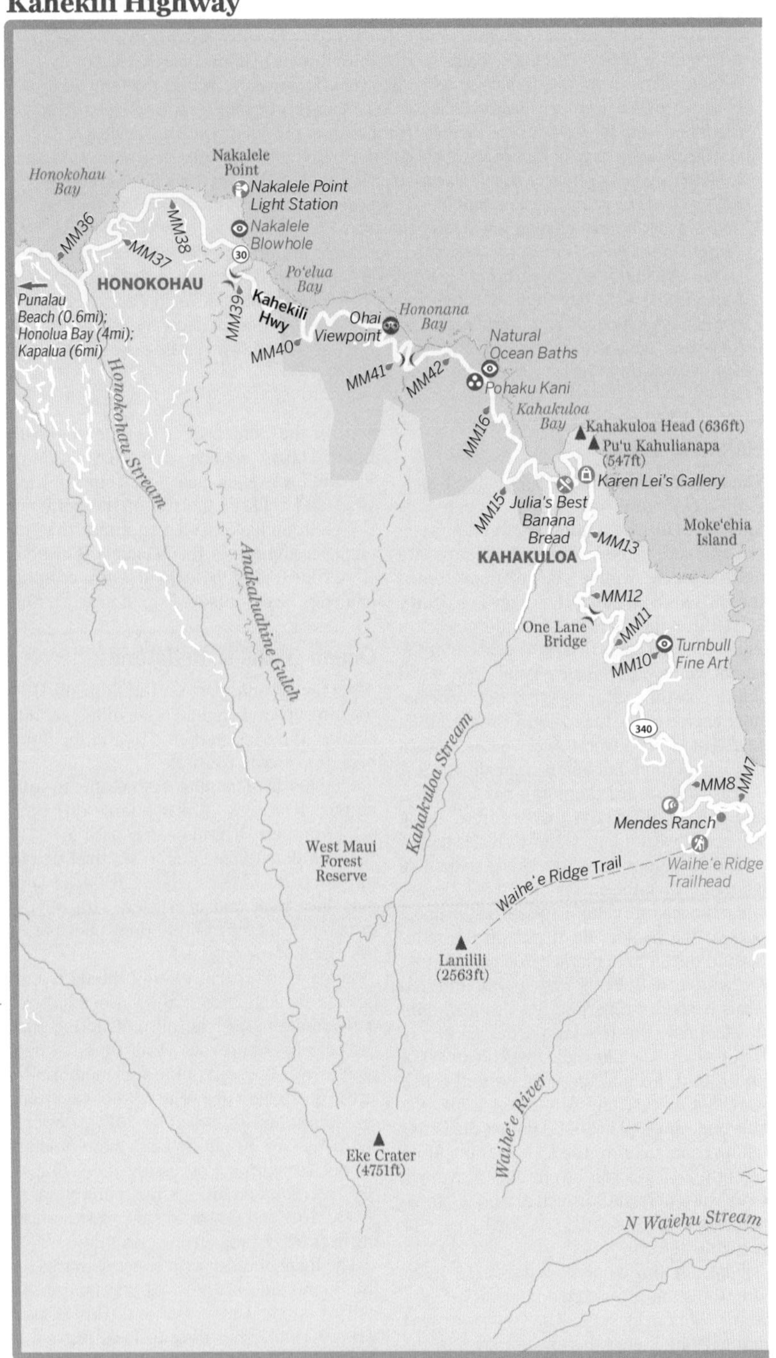

where the deepest indentations are, you might be able to get a hollow sound that's a bit resonant. However, signage asks visitors not to hit, rub or throw things at the rock, which is sacred to Native Hawaiians.

Kahakuloa to Waihe'e

On the outskirts of Kahakuloa, after a heart-stopping, narrow climb (coming from Lahaina), you'll reach the hilltop **Karen Lei's Gallery** (☎808-244-3371; http://karenleisgallery.com; Kahekili Hwy, Mile 13; ⏰9am-5pm). Filled with trinkets, local jewelry, artworks and tableware from more than 100 island artists, the shop makes a nice place to browse and buy unique gifts. A **food truck** (mains $9 to $16) on-site sells coffee, acai bowls, tacos, sandwiches, and fish and shrimp plates. The picnic tables here have great views.

East of the 10-mile marker, look for the towering giraffe statue marking the entrance to **Turnbull Fine Art** (☎808-244-0101; www.turnbullfineart.com; 5030 Kahekili Hwy; ⏰10am-5pm). Here you can view Bruce Turnbull's ambitious bronze and wood creations, and works by his nephew Steve and Steve's wife Christine, who specializes in clay. You can also peer into a working studio and wander through a small gallery selling an attractive collection of work by local artists.

Continuing around beep-as-you-go blind turns, the highway gradually levels out atop sea cliffs. Stop at the pull-off 175yd north of the 8-mile marker and look down into the ravine below, where you'll see a cascading **waterfall** framed by double pools.

For a real *paniolo* experience, saddle up at **Mendes Ranch** (☎808-871-5222; www.mendesranch.com; 3530 Kahekili Hwy; 1½hr rides $135; ⏰rides 8:45am & 12:15pm), a working cattle ranch near the 7-mile marker and the road to the spectacular Waihe'e Ridge Trail (p102). The scenery on these rides includes everything from jungle valleys to lofty sea cliffs.

Waihe'e to Wailuku

Aside from the world-class Waihe'e Ridge Trail (p102), the other activity in this sleepy part of West Maui is a round of golf. The county-run **Waiehu Municipal Golf Course** (Map p132; ☎808-270-7400; www.mauicounty.gov; 200 Halewaiu Rd; greens fee from $63, twilight rate $32, optional cart $21; ⏰6:45am-5pm Mon-Fri, from 6am Sat & Sun) offers an affordable 18 holes on the coast, plus a 24-tee driving range at which to let off some steam.

AT A GLANCE

POPULATION
Kahului: 26,337

HEIGHT OF ʻIAO NEEDLE
2250ft

BEST LOCAL SCENE
Tasty Crust (p142)

BEST HOSTEL
Northshore Hostel (p142)

BEST FOOD TRUCK
Geste Shrimp Truck (p135)

WHEN TO GO

May–Aug Maui Brewers Festival in May; Ki Hoʻalu Slack Key Guitar Festival in June; strong winds bring kiteboarders and windsurfers June through August.

Sep–Oct Good flight and accommodations deals.

Nov–Dec Nā Mele O Maui Hawaiian culture celebration in late November and early December.

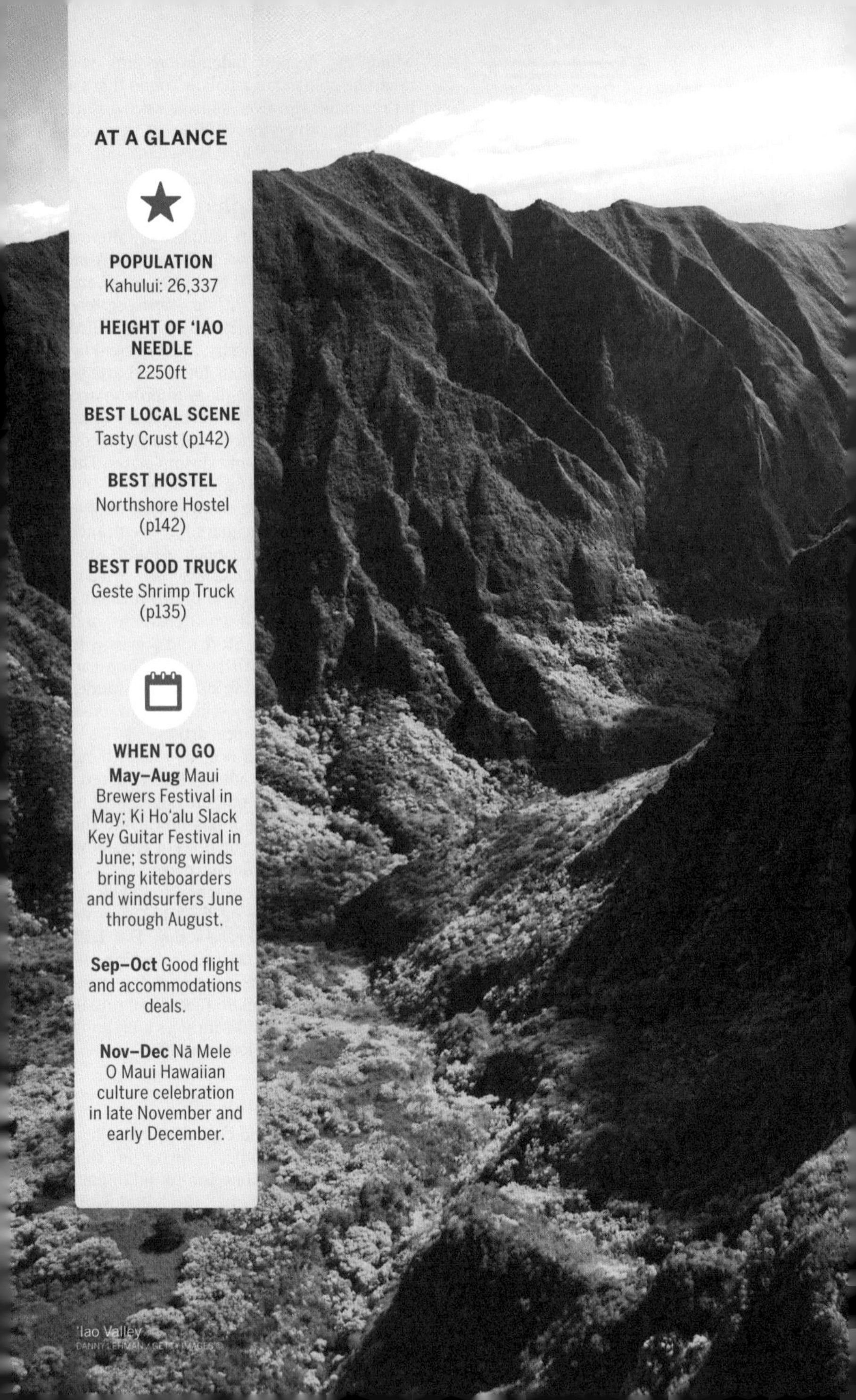

ʻIao Valley

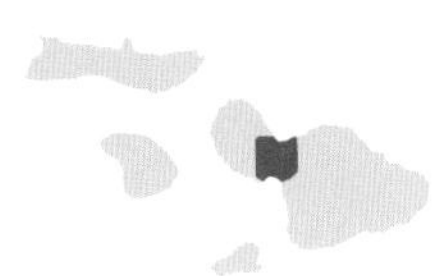

'Iao Valley & Central Maui

Welcome to the flat middle. Central Maui is the isthmus connecting the West Maui Mountains to mighty Haleakalā, giving the island its distinctive three-part shape. This odd wedge of topography, Maui's most arable piece of land, was once known for its fields of waving sugarcane. To the north, the island's commercial center, Kahului, contains a kiteboarder's paradise – the windswept Kanaha Beach. Sister city Wailuku has a welcoming local feel and is *the* place for lunch after a trip to the lush 'Iao Valley. On the southern coast, Ma'alaea is home to a fine aquarium, and its harbor is the launchpad for a snorkeling cruise to the submerged crater of Molokini.

INCLUDES

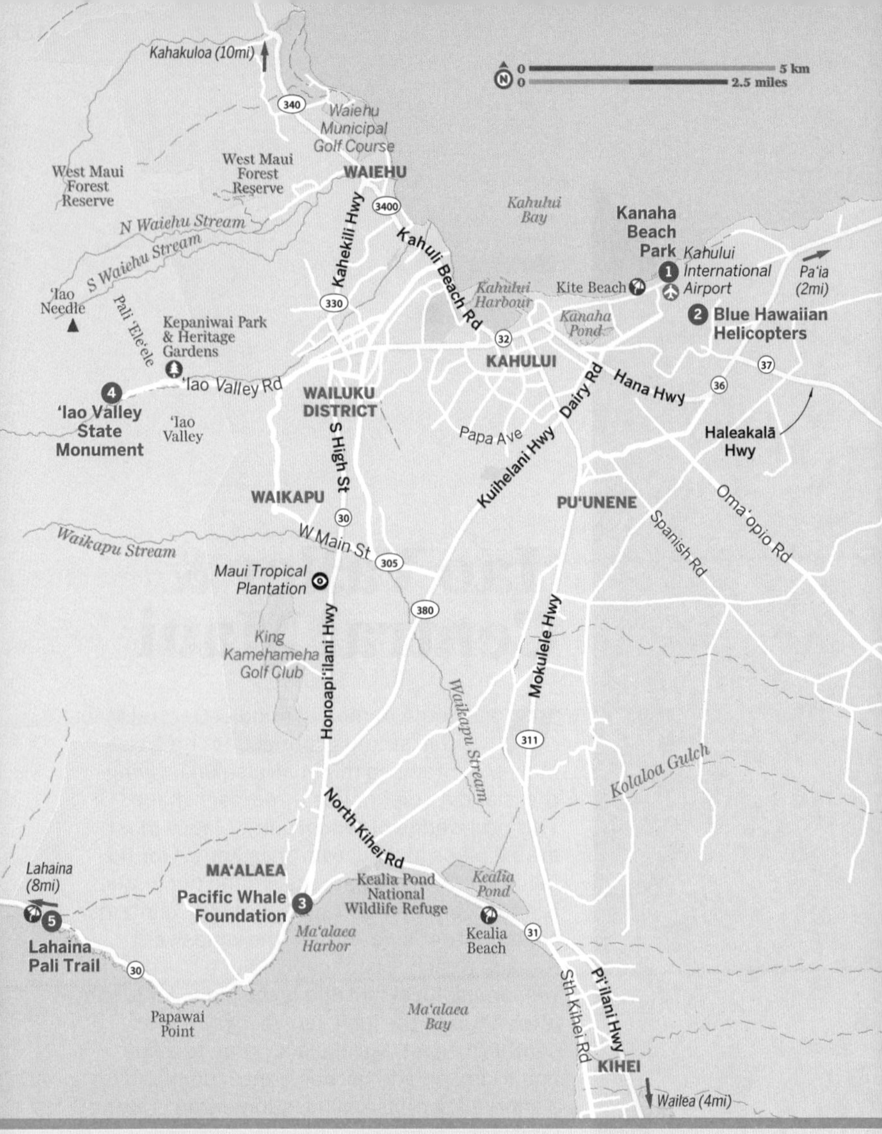

'Iao Valley & Central Maui Highlights

❶ **Kanaha Beach Park** (p129) Kite- and windsurfing at this beautifully blustery stretch.

❷ **Blue Hawaiian Helicopters** (p135) Taking an unforgettable aerial trip through the West Maui Mountains to Moloka'i.

❸ **Pacific Whale Foundation** (p148) Cruising to a submerged crater teeming with marine life off the south coast.

❹ **'Iao Valley State Monument** (p144) Exploring Maui's lush interior and soaring emerald peaks.

❺ **Lahaina Pali Trail** (p130) Walking up over Kealaoloa Ridge for belly-flipping views of Central Maui.

Kahului

Most Hawaiian Islands have a working town like Kahului, full of warehouses, strip malls, shopping centers, and that island-wide magnet: the big-box store. Like its counterparts, Kahului also contains Maui's main harbor and airport, turning it, in the eyes of many, into a transit stop. But at the same time you'll find a great swath of local life here if you linger a little longer. You can talk to the locals at the Saturday swap meet, watch a concert on the lawn of the cultural center and join the wave-riders at Kanaha Beach.

Beaches

★Kanaha Beach Park BEACH

(Map p132; Alahao St; 6:30am-8pm) Well, you can't judge a beach by its cover. Wedged between downtown Kahului and the airport, and hidden behind a strip of ironwood trees, this mile-long stretch of sand is kitesurf city, with scores of brilliant sails zipping across the waves. Kitesurfers converge at the southwest end, known as **Kite Beach**, while windsurfers head northeast. A roped-off swimming area lies in between. Facilities include restrooms, showers and shaded picnic tables.

Sights

Kanaha Pond Bird Sanctuary BIRD SANCTUARY

(Map p136; Hwy 37; sunrise-sunset) FREE You wouldn't expect a wildlife sanctuary to be so close to the main road, but a short walk leaves the traffic behind. This shallow marsh is a haven for rare Hawaiian birds, including native coots, black-crowned night herons, and the *ae'o* (Hawaiian black-necked stilt), a graceful wading bird with long orange legs that feeds along the pond's marshy edges. According to various Fish & Wildlife surveys the *ae'o* population probably hovers around 1500 statewide, but you can count on spotting some here.

Maui Nui Botanical Gardens GARDENS

(Map p136; 808-249-2798; www.mnbg.org; 150 Kanaloa Ave; Mon-Fri adult/child under 13yr $5/free, Sat free, garden tours per person $10; 8am-4pm Mon-Sat) For botanophiles interested in native Hawaiian plants, this garden on the grounds of a former zoo has a wealth of knowledge. An excellent audio tour ($5 on Saturday, free with admission Monday to Friday) brings it to life. Don't expect the exotic tropicals that dominate most Hawaiian gardens; do expect dedicated staff. Staff also lead personal guided tours by appointment.

Schaefer International Gallery MUSEUM

(Map p136; 808-242-2787; www.mauiarts.org; 1 Cameron Way; 10am-5pm Tue-Sun) FREE This art gallery at the Maui Arts & Cultural Center (p138) has a number of exhibitions per year, ranging from native Hawaiian arts to contemporary local artists working in all mediums.

Kahului Harbor HARBOR

(Map p136; 103 Ala Luina St) Kahului's large protected harbor is the island's only deep-water port, so all boat traffic, from cruise ships to cargo vessels, docks here. But it's not all business. Late afternoon you might see outrigger-canoe clubs such as Na Kai 'Ewalu (www.nakaiewalucanoeclub.org) practicing near **Ho'aloha Park** – a timeless scene.

Activities

Kanaha Beach Park (p129) is the best place to windsurf on Maui, unless you're an aspiring pro ready for Ho'okipa. Board-and-rig rentals start at $64 per day, while group introductory classes cost around $100. For more info, see www.mauiwindsurfcompany.com.

Kitesurfing (or kiteboarding) is enormously popular in Kahului. The action centers on Kite Beach, the southwest end of Kanaha Beach Park. Here you can learn the ropes from some real pros, and you're likely to see vans from various water-sports companies parked in the lot. Expect to pay about $100 for a discovery/intro lesson.

Be sure to shop around and ask about discounts on lessons and rentals.

Dunes at Maui Lani GOLF

(Map p132; 808-873-0422; www.dunesatmauilani.com; 1333 Maui Lani Pkwy; greens fee incl cart $58-99, club hire $45; 6:30am-5:30pm) Set on volcanic land, this 18-hole course will give scratch golfers playing from the tips a lot of fun. It's easy to underestimate, but it has lots of bunkers, some blind holes and the highest slope rating of any course on Maui. At the time of research the greens had recently been re-grassed.

Kanaha Kai WATER SPORTS

(Map p136; 808-877-7778; www.kanahakai.com; 96 Amala Pl; rental per day SUP $35, surfboard from $20, windsurfing rigs from $57, foil board per day $45; 9:30am-6pm Mar-Oct, to 5pm Nov-Feb) Windsurfing, SUP, kitesurfing and surfing rentals and lessons. Very competitive pricing. Look out for prebooked offers on the website.

WALKING THROUGH HISTORY

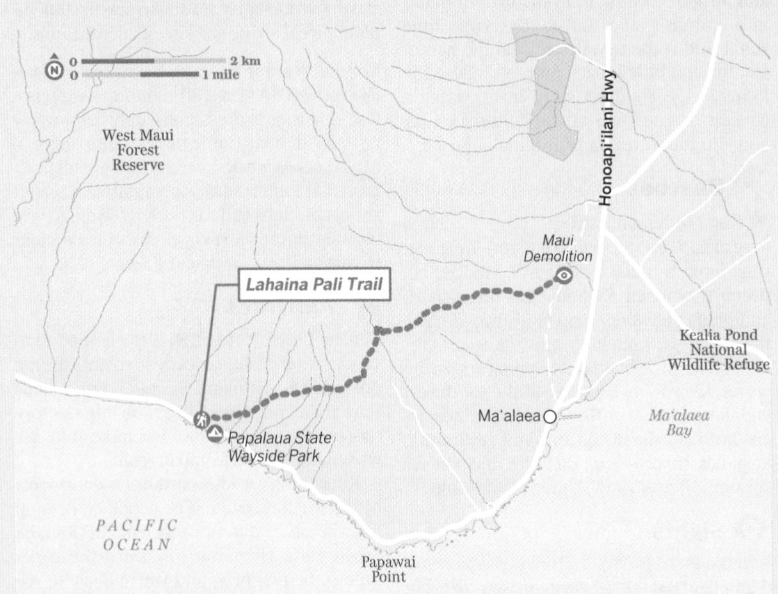

CONNECTING MAUI

King Pi'ilani ruled Maui during the 16th century, when the island was independent from the rest of Hawaii. Pi'ilani's reign was full of notable accomplishments. Although he was born and died in Lahaina, he would often stay in Wailuku and Hana, and he traveled the island's 12 *moku* (districts) collecting taxes, re-enforcing laws and ensuring that industry was thriving. These journeys were arduous, so Pi'ilani wanted to make it easier to connect all areas of Maui. He began building a basalt-lined road, wide enough for eight people to walk abreast. It would become a 138-mile route named the King's Hwy, which was the most efficient way to travel the island. The Lahaina Pali Trail is one of the most accessible and magnificent parts of this ancient route, and old stones and carvings can still be seen throughout. Only a century ago this hike was still the main route to Lahaina from North Maui. The full King's Trail (p226) is not as well marked but can still be undertaken by experienced hikers. Pi'ilani successfully united East and West Maui and, although his son completed the full pathway, he is honored with creating the only road in Hawaii that encircles an entire island.

LAHAINA PALI TRAIL

START LAHAINA TRAILHEAD ON HONOAPI HONOAPI'ILANI HWY BEFORE 12-MILE MARKER
END MA'ALAEA TRAILHEAD ON HONOAPI'ILANI HWY NEAR MAUI DEMOLITION
LENGTH 5 MILES ONE WAY; THREE OR MORE HOURS
DIFFICULTY DIFFICULT

This spectacular and challenging **route** (Map p132; https://hawaiitrails.ehawaii.gov) FREE was used more than a century ago by missionaries traveling by horse and foot from Lahaina to Wailuku. The old road is now used by able hikers on a pulse-pounding climb up and down rocky pathways, ascending 1600ft

Follow in the footsteps of missionaries on a high and scrubby trail that's a prime lookout for whale-watching in winter.

above sea level to a 36-turbine wind farm. Mesmerizing views stretch to the north and south coastlines, the central valley, Haleakalā volcano and Kealia Pond National Wildlife Refuge.

The climb is arguably easier than the higgledy-piggledy descent over boulders of all shapes and sizes, yet you'll likely see skilled hill runners hopping down at speed – sprinting down is only for experts: loose rocks can be treacherous.

Find the Lahaina trailhead on Honoapi'ilani Hwy after the Olowalu Tunnel (if heading toward Lahaina). The first part of the trail from here is shaded, although some of the trees have suffered from brushfires. The pathway quickly becomes arid and exposed. Beautiful, sweeping views appear almost immediately. Examine the blue ocean hues for whales in winter, and along the trail look for petroglyphs and stone walls, marking the resting spots of ancient travelers. The path winds up the mountain, passing cavernous, moody valleys. Lone trees provide moments of shade. Distractions from the silence include fluttering butterflies, the hum of crickets and an occasional plane on its way to Kahului airport. The blades of the windmills of the Kaheawa Wind Farm mark the breezy midpoint of the route. From this area, known as the Kaheawa Pastures, you can see Molokini islet and Kaho'olawe to the south, the West Maui mountains to the west and Haleakalā to the east on a clear day. It's all downhill from here. Phew! Choose to continue, or return the way you came.

You can reach the trailheads on either side of the route by car; there's parking on the Ukumehame side (just after the tunnel on the right, before Ukumehame Beach Park at the 12-mile marker) and on the Ma'alaea side near Maui Demolition on the Honoapi'ilani Hwy. If you plan to complete the entire trail you'll need two cars, one parked at either end. Alternatively, walk the route again or book an Uber/taxi to your parked car (check car availability before you set off). Bring sunscreen, a hat and plenty of water, and start early before the sun is overhead.

'Iao Valley & Central Maui

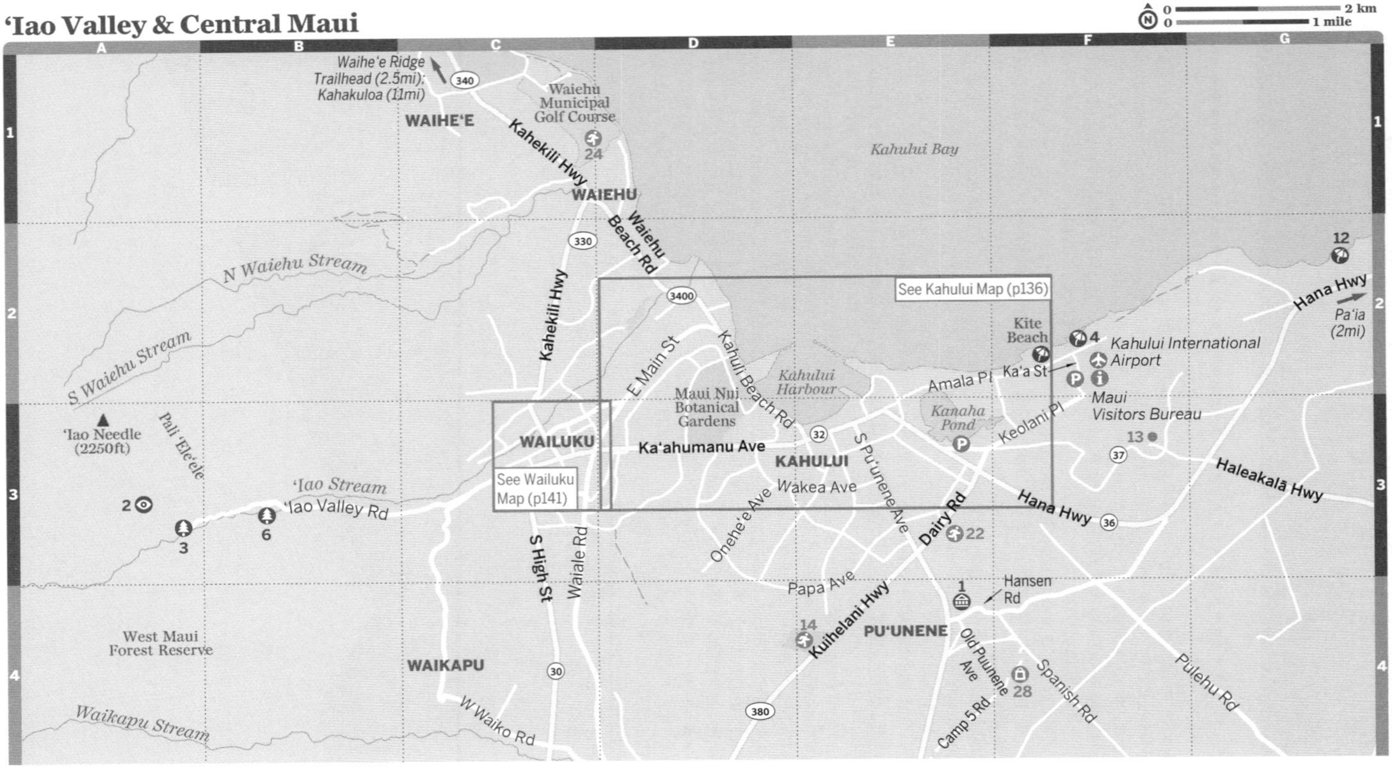

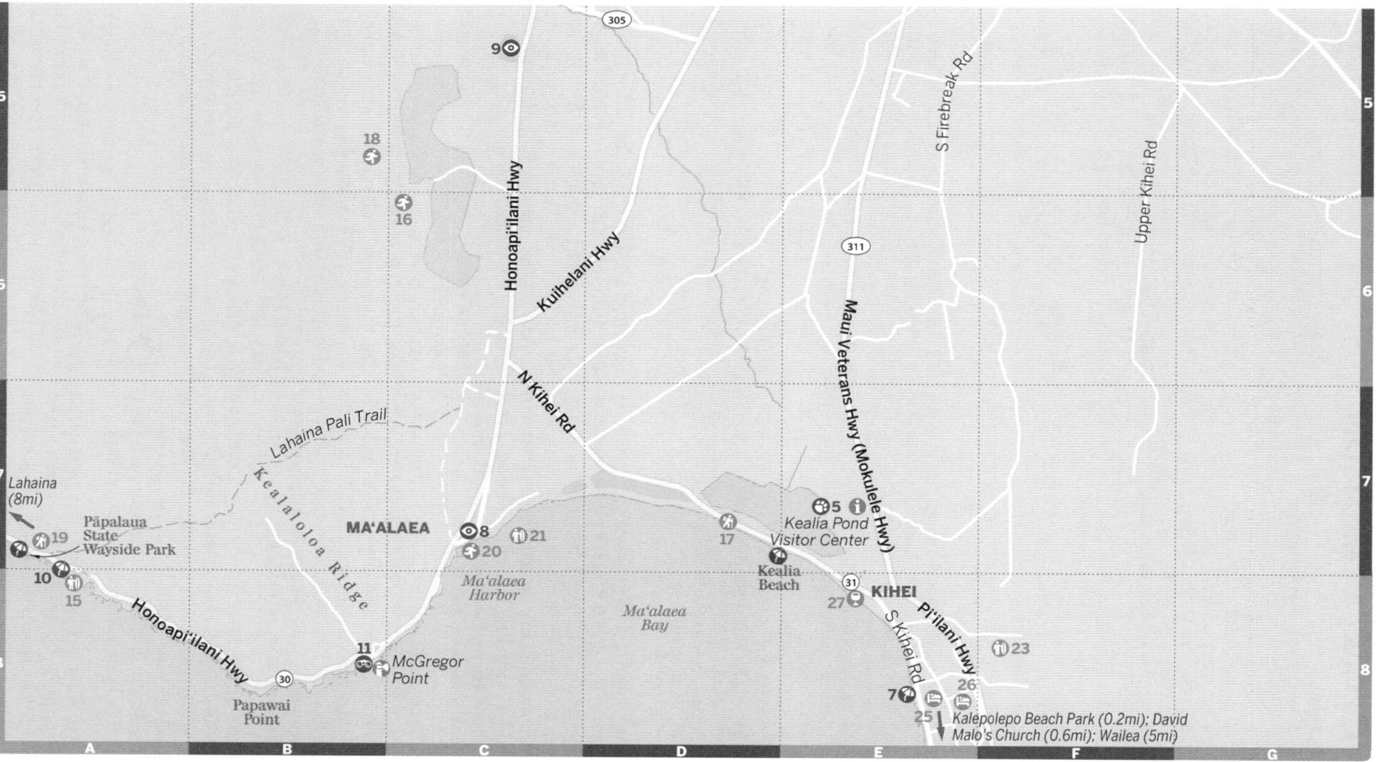
305
9
18
16
Honoapi'ilani Hwy
Kuihelani Hwy
311
S Firebreak Rd
Upper Kihei Rd
Maui Veterans Hwy (Mokulele Hwy)
N Kihei Rd
Lahaina Pali Trail
Kealaloloa Ridge
Lahaina (8mi)
Pāpalaua State Wayside Park
19
10
15
MA'ALAEA
8
20
21
Ma'alaea Harbor
17
5
Kealia Pond Visitor Center
Kealia Beach
Ma'alaea Bay
31
KIHEI
27
Pi'ilani Hwy
S Kihei Rd
23
26
7
25
Kalepolepo Beach Park (0.2mi); David Malo's Church (0.6mi); Wailea (5mi)
Honoapi'ilani Hwy
30
Papawai Point
11
McGregor Point
A
B
C
D
E
F
G
5
6
7
8

'Iao Valley & Central Maui

Sights
1 Alexander & Baldwin Sugar Museum E4
2 'Iao Needle A3
3 'Iao Valley State Monument A3
4 Kanaha Beach Park F2
5 Kealia Pond National Wildlife Refuge E7
6 Kepaniwai Park & Heritage Gardens B3
Ma'alaea Bay .... (see 17)
7 Mai Poina 'Oe Ia'u Beach Park E8
8 Maui Ocean Center C7
9 Maui Tropical Plantation C5
10 Pāpalaua State Wayside Park A8
11 Papawai Point B8
12 Spreckelsville Beach G2

Activities, Courses & Tours
Air Maui Helicopter Tours .... (see 13)
13 Blue Hawaiian Helicopters F3
Boss Frogs .... (see 8)
14 Dunes at Maui Lani E4
Flyin Hawaiian Zipline .... (see 9)
15 Grandma's A8
16 Kahili Course C6
17 Kealia Coastal Boardwalk D7
18 King Kamehameha Golf Club B5
19 Lahaina Pali Trail A7
20 Ma'alaea Harbor Activities C7
21 Ma'alaea Pipeline C7
22 Maui Motorcycle Company E3
Maui Zipline .... (see 9)
Pacific Whale Foundation .... (see 8)
Shark Dive Maui .... (see 8)
23 Stand Up Paddle Surf School F8
Sunshine Helicopters .... (see 13)
24 Waiehu Municipal Golf Course C1

Sleeping
25 Nona Lani Cottages E8
26 Ocean Breeze Hideaway E8

Eating
Beach Bums Bar & Grill .... (see 8)
Hula Cookies & Ice Cream .... (see 8)
Ma'alaea General Store & Cafe .... (see 20)
Maui Chef's Table .... (see 9)
Mill House Roasting Co .... (see 9)
Thai Paradise .... (see 8)
The Scoop .... (see 9)

Drinking & Nightlife
27 Dina's Sandwitch E8
Mile House Roasting Co. .... (see 9)

Shopping
28 Old Pu'unene Bookstore F4

Maui Motorcycle Company OUTDOORS
(Map p132; ☎808-877-1859; www.mauimotorcycleco.com; 150 Dairy Rd; Harley rentals per day from $206; ⏲9am-5pm) See the island in style with the wind in your hair by renting a motorbike, including Harley-Davidsons, at this Kahului-based store near the airport. Motorbike licence required.

Hi-Tech Surf Sports WATER SPORTS
(Map p136; ☎808-877-2111; www.surfmaui.com; 425 Koloa St; rental per day surfboard from $25, SUP from $35, windsurfing gear $60; ⏲9am-6pm) Surfboard, SUP and windsurfing rentals. Plus a good store selling all manner of water-sports gear and clothing.

Aqua Sports Maui KITESURFING
(☎808-242-8015; www.mauikiteboardinglessons.com; 1hr beach basics from $69, 3hr intro from $240, 6hr lesson $540) Specializes in one-on-one kitesurfing lessons. Lessons take place on Kite Beach, near Kanaha Beach Park.

Maui Windsurf Company WINDSURFING
(Map p136; ☎808-877-4816; www.mauiwindsurfcompany.com; 22 Hana Hwy; 2½hr lesson per person from $100, rentals SUP/surfboard/windsurf board from $29/15/64; ⏲8:30am-5:30pm) Want to get up and ride on a windsurf board? Maui Windsurf Company is friendly and all equipment is included in your lesson. Good rates on rentals on SUP, surfboard and windsurf rigs available, too.

Second Wind WATER SPORTS
(Map p136; ☎808-877-7467; www.secondwindmaui.com; 111 Hana Hwy; rentals per day surfboard from $25, SUPs from $35, windsurfing rig from $70; ⏲9am-6pm) Full range of kiteboarding, windsurfing, SUP and surfing rentals, plus a store packed with water-sports gear.

Island Biker CYCLING
(Map p136; ☎808-877-7744; www.islandbikermaui.com; 415 Dairy Rd; per day/week $75/250; ⏲9am-5pm Mon-Fri, to 2pm Sat) Rents quality mountain bikes and road bikes for island discovery.

Tours

In Hawaii the best helicopter tours operate out of Maui and Kaua'i. So if you aren't visiting the latter, this is your chance for pinch-me island views. Various tour routes are available, but the finest combines the West Maui

Mountains with the eastern end of Moloka'i, a jaw-dropping, uninhabited region of unspoiled emerald-green valleys and waterfalls.

Several tour companies operate out of Kahului Heliport, alongside the airport. Check online and in free tourist magazines for significant discounts; don't forget to ask about fuel surcharges.

Blue Hawaiian Helicopters TOURS
(Map p132; ☎808-871-8844; www.bluehawaiian.com; 1 Kahului Airport Rd, Hangar 105; tours $279-459; ⊙office 7am-7pm) One of the industry leaders, Blue Hawaiian flies the hi-tech Eco-Star, which has an enclosed tail rotor. Excellent visibility means you see everything, noise-cancelling headsets let you hear everything, and digital in-flight video brings the entire experience home. Tour prices depend on the itinerary and chopper; it also flies A-Stars, the industry workhorse. Professional staff operate like clockwork.

★**Air Maui Helicopter Tours** TOURS
(Map p132; ☎808-877-7005; www.airmaui.com; 1 Kahului Airport Rd, Hangar 110; tours $100-350; ⊙booking office 7am-9pm) A full range of tour options, including a complete island tour, a West Maui and Moloka'i tour, an oceanfront landing option and a thrilling doors-off tour. Professionally run and very good value. Solo travelers should check for single-seater deals from $100 before booking.

Sunshine Helicopters TOURS
(Map p132; ☎808-270-3999; www.sunshinehelicopters.com; 1 Kahului Airport Rd, Hangar 107; tours $225-515; ⊙booking office 6am-8pm) Well-established firm operating on four islands, with tours over Moloka'i, Hana and West Maui.

Festivals & Events

★**Ki Ho'alu Slack Key Guitar Festival** MUSIC
(www.mauiarts.org; Maui Arts & Cultural Center, 1 Cameron Way; ⊙Jun) FREE Top slack-key guitarists take the stage at this fun event, held on the lawn of the Maui Arts & Cultural Center each June.

Maui Marathon SPORTS
(www.mauimarathonhawaii.com; ⊙Sep) This road race begins in Kahului and ends 26.2 miles later at Whalers Village in Ka'anapali.

Maui Ukulele Festival MUSIC
(www.ukulelefestivalhawaii.org; Maui Arts & Cultural Center, 1 Cameron Way; ⊙Sep or Oct) FREE Held outdoors at the Maui Arts & Cultural Center usually on a Sunday in fall, this free aloha event showcases uke masters from Maui and beyond.

Nā Mele O Maui MUSIC
(www.mauiarts.org; Maui Arts & Cultural Center, 1 Cameron Way; ⊙Nov or Dec) FREE This celebration of Hawaiian culture features children's choral groups singing Native Hawaiian music. The aloha-rich event is held in late November or early December at the Maui Arts & Cultural Center.

Sleeping

Maui Seaside Hotel HOTEL $
(Map p136; ☎808-877-3311; www.mauiseasidehotel.com; 100 W Ka'ahumanu Ave; r from $174; ❄@🛜≋) If you want to stay on the beach, this retro hotel is the only decent option. It's a plain Jane with exterior decor like an aging '80s motel, but the rooms are clean. Each has a flat-screen TV, AC and a ceiling fan. There's a large pool in the grounds.

★**Courtyard Marriott Kahului Airport** HOTEL $$
(Map p136; ☎808-871-1800; www.marriott.com; 532 Keolani Pl; r from $270; P❄@🛜≋) Hands down your best option in Kahului, and just a stone's throw from the airport. The stylish modern lobby contains a breezy coffee shop, complete with media booths. Large rooms, including family suites, offer crisp white bedding and lots of light (pay up for a deluxe).

Eating

★**Geste Shrimp Truck** SEAFOOD $
(Map p136; ☎808-298-7109; www.gesteshrimp.com; Kahului Beach Rd; mains $15; ⊙11am-5:30pm Tue-Sat) Beside Kahului Harbor, this small white food truck, emblazoned with a giant shrimp, serves the tastiest shrimp on Maui – maybe even the world! A dozen cost $15 and you'll get a scoop of crab mac salad and rice to go with them. At research time the owners said the truck would move to Food Truck Park (p137) in the future.

★**Tin Roof** HAWAIIAN $
(Map p136; ☎808-868-0753; www.tinroofmaui.com; 360 Papa Pl; mains $8-14; ⊙10am-2pm Mon-Sat) This creation by celebrity chef Sheldon Simeon proves that a restaurant can be successful no matter the venue – in this case a tin-roofed outlet next to Payday Loans. Be prepared to queue for exceptional *kaukau* tins of flavorsome pork belly,

Kahului

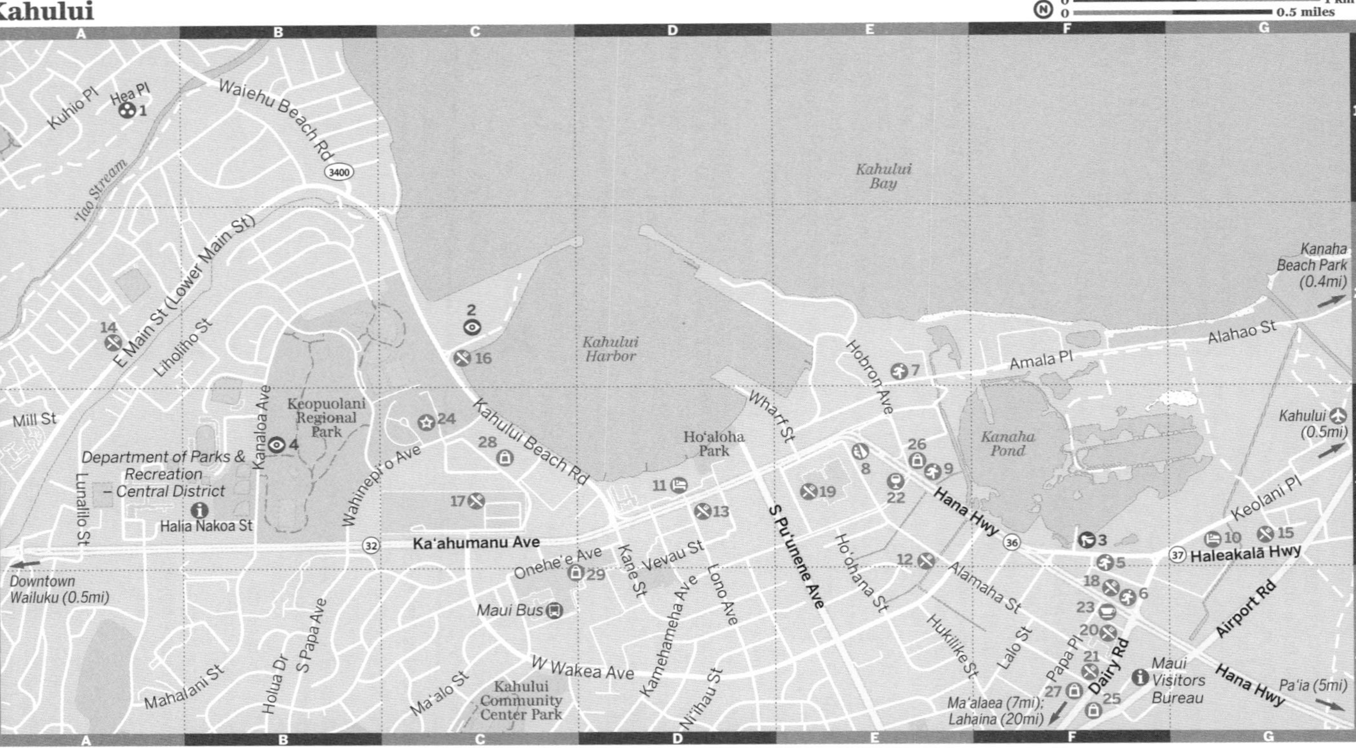

0 1 km
0 0.5 miles
Kahului Bay
Kahului Harbor
Kanaha Pond
Kanaha Beach Park (0.4mi)
Kahului (0.5mi)
Pa'ia (5mi)
Ma'alaea (7mi); Lahaina (20mi)
Downtown Wailuku (0.5mi)
Kuhio Pl
Hea Pl
'Iao Stream
Waiehu Beach Rd
3400
E Main St (Lower Main St)
Liholiho St
Mill St
Kanaloa Ave
Keopuolani Regional Park
Department of Parks & Recreation – Central District
Lunalilo St
Halia Nakoa St
Wahinepi'o Ave
Kahului Beach Rd
Ka'ahumanu Ave
32
Onehe'e Ave
Maui Bus
Kane St
Vevau St
Kamehameha Ave
Lono Ave
Ni'ihau St
W Wakea Ave
Kahului Community Center Park
Ma'alo St
Mahalani St
Holua Dr
S Papa Ave
Ho'aloha Park
Wharf St
S Pu'unene Ave
Ho'ohana St
Hobron Ave
Amala Pl
Alahao St
Hana Hwy
36
Alamaha St
Hukilike St
Lalo St
Papa Pl
Dairy Rd
Maui Visitors Bureau
Airport Rd
Keolani Pl
37
Haleakalā Hwy
1 2 3 4 5 6 7 8 9 10 11 12 13 14 15 16 17 18 19 20 21 22 23 24 25 26 27 28 29
A B C D E F G

Kahului

Sights
1 Haleki'i-Pihanakalani Heiau State Monument ... A1
2 Kahului Harbor ... C2
3 Kanaha Pond Bird Sanctuary ... F3
4 Maui Nui Botanical Gardens ... B3
Schaefer International Gallery ... (see 24)

Activities, Courses & Tours
5 Hi-Tech Surf Sports ... F3
6 Island Biker ... F4
7 Kanaha Kai ... E2
8 Maui Windsurf Company ... E3
9 Second Wind ... E3

Sleeping
10 Courtyard Marriott Kahului Airport ... G3
11 Maui Seaside Hotel ... D3

Eating
12 Acevedo's Hawaicano Cafe ... E3
13 Bistro Casanova ... D3
Da Kitchen ... (see 5)
14 Donut Dynamite! ... A2
15 Food Truck Park ... G3
16 Geste Shrimp Truck ... C2
17 Leis Family Class Act ... C3
18 Poi by the Pound ... F4
19 Tasaka Guri-Guri ... E3
Thailand Cuisine II ... (see 19)
20 Tin Roof ... F4
21 Wow-Wee Maui's Kava Bar & Grill ... F4

Drinking & Nightlife
22 Kahului Ale House ... E3
23 Maui Coffee Roasters ... F4

Entertainment
24 Maui Arts & Cultural Center ... C3

Shopping
25 Barnes & Noble ... F4
26 Bounty Music ... E3
27 Down to Earth ... F4
28 Maui Swap Meet ... C3
29 Queen Ka'ahumanu Center ... C4
Whole Foods ... (see 19)

rice and salsa, or *mochiko* (batter-fried) chicken marinated in ginger-sake *shōyu*, topped with su-miso sauce, *gochujang* aioli, and mochi crunch.

Wow-Wee Maui's Kava Bar & Grill GRILL $
(Map p136; ☎808-871-1414; 333 Dairy Rd; mains $12-17; ⏰10:30am-9pm) The grill dominates the kava at this buzzing local joint, but it's still your best chance to try *piper methysticum,* a ceremonial drink made from the kava plant (grown on the slopes of Haleakalā volcano) with an earthy taste that numbs your mouth. Also offers sushi, good burgers, wraps and mains including Hawaiian barbecue pork, grilled salmon and baby back ribs.

Tasaka Guri-Guri ICE CREAM $
(Map p136; ☎808-871-4513; Maui Mall, 70 E Ka'ahumanu Ave; 2 scoops/quart $1.40/6.50; ⏰9am-6pm Mon-Sat, to 4pm Sun) For the coolest treat in town, queue up at this hole-in-the-wall shop dishing up homemade pineapple sherbet. The *guri-guri,* as it's called, is so popular that locals take it to friends on neighboring islands. Cash only.

Food Truck Park INTERNATIONAL $
(Map p136; 591 Haleakalā Hwy; items $9-20; ⏰10:30am-8pm) Around a dozen entrepreneurial and yummy food trucks have congregated in this parking lot, around a canopy-shaded setup of picnic tables. Choose between Thai Mee Up (serving lemongrass chicken, garlic shrimp, and green curry), Ono Teppanyaki and Seafood (for grilled steak or lobster plates) and Kalei's Lunch Box, serving Hawaiian food (local breakfasts, fish and rice plates and the like).

This is also set to be the new home of the famous Geste Shrimp Truck (p135).

Acevedo's Hawaicano Cafe MEXICAN $
(Map p136; ☎808-871-7766; https://acevedoshawaicanocafe.com; 90 Alamaha St; mains $8-14; ⏰11am-6pm Mon-Fri, to 3pm Sat) The place to get your Mexican fix with a Hawaiian spin. This counter joint serves up classics done well, such as carne asada, chicken ranchero, packed burritos and tangy ceviche (using fish from the local area). Top off your meal with some housemade salsa.

Poi by the Pound HAWAIIAN $$
(Map p136; ☎808-283-9381; www.poibythepound.com; 430 Kele St; $8.50-24.99; ⏰10am-10pm Mon, to 11pm Thu-Sat, to 9pm Sun) You can't beat the value at this casual local spot serving tasty Hawaiian eats. Don't come for the setting (brown furniture under fluorescent lights); come for the tasty plate dinners: *kalua* (pit-oven-cooked) pork, local-style ramen, fried mahimahi, and poke and rice bowls. Finish with a slice of Kona mud pie or a taro sundae.

Thailand Cuisine II THAI $$

(Map p136; ☎808-873-0225; www.thailandcuisinemaui.net; Maui Mall, 70 E Ka'ahumanu Ave; mains $14-23; ⏰11am-3:30pm & 5-9:30pm Mon-Thu, to 10pm Fri-Sun;) Welcoming family-run eatery with Thai favorites, plus fun variations (such as the Thai Evil Prince with chicken, beef or pork sautéed in hot spices with coconut milk and sweet basil). You can't go wrong with the shrimp summer rolls to start, then the aromatic green curries or ginger-grilled mahimahi.

★ **Bistro Casanova** MEDITERRANEAN $$$

(Map p136; ☎808-873-3650; www.casanovamaui.com; 33 Lono Ave; mains $14-42; ⏰11am-9:30pm Mon-Sat) An offshoot of the popular Casanova in Makawao (p192), this is Kahului's classiest dining option. Seafood and steaks are great quality and come with plenty of Kula veggies. The setting is upscale and urban, and attracts an older clientele. Reservations are recommended at dinner, when the bistro can fill with a pre-theater crowd en route to the Maui Arts & Cultural Center (p138).

Signature cocktails include lychee martinis, ocean cosmos and Aperol spritzes ($12 each); draft beer includes Maui Brewing IPA and Kona Longboard ($6).

Leis Family Class Act INTERNATIONAL $$$

(Map p136; ☎808-984-3280; www.facebook.com/leisfamilyclassact; Maui College, 310 W Ka'ahumanu Ave; prix fixe per person $30-42; ⏰11am-12:30pm Wed & Fri) Maui Culinary Academy's fine-dining restaurant connects an ocean view with the opportunity to watch up-and-coming chefs create a four-course locavore meal. The menu rotates with different cuisines. Reserve online via https://www.opentable.com.

Drinking & Nightlife

Maui Coffee Roasters CAFE

(Map p136; ☎800-645-2877; www.mauicoffeeroasters.com/cafe; 444 Hana Hwy; ⏰7am-6pm Mon-Sat, 8am-4pm Sun, kitchen 7am-5pm Mon-Sat, 8am-2:30pm Sun;) Enjoy good vibes and good java at this bright, upbeat cafe where locals sip lattes and nibble wraps while surfing the free wi-fi. Pastries cost $4 to $9, sandwiches and wraps $8 to $10.

Kahului Ale House SPORTS BAR

(Map p136; ☎808-877-0001; http://kahuluialehouse.com; 355 E Kamehameha Ave; ⏰11am-11pm Mon-Fri, 7am-11pm Sat & Sun) With 35 flat-screen TVs, Maui's top sports bar won't let you miss a single play. Pub grub includes burgers, sandwiches and pizzas. There's live music from 5pm to 8pm or so daily. The kitchen's open late. Happy hours with discounts on selected drinks run 3pm to 6pm.

Entertainment

Maui Arts & Cultural Center CONCERT VENUE

(MACC; Map p136; ☎808-242-7469; www.mauiarts.org; 1 Cameron Way; ⏰box office 10am-6pm Tue-Sat) This snazzy performance complex opened in 1994 and boasts two indoor theaters and an outdoor amphitheater. As Maui's main venue for music, theater and dance, the MACC hosts everything from ukulele jams to touring rock bands. Look out for the Ki Ho'alu Slack Key Guitar Festival (p135), usually in June, and the Maui Ukulele Festival, held in September or October.

Shopping

Kahului hosts Maui's household-name shops and big-box discount chains of the Costco variety, as well as shopping complexes **Queen Ka'ahumanu Center** (Map p136; ☎808-877-3369; www.queenkaahumanucenter.com; 275 W Ka'ahumanu Ave; ⏰9:30am-9pm Mon-Sat, 10am-5pm Sun;) and Maui Mall.

Down to Earth FOOD & DRINKS

(Map p136; ☎808-877-2661; www.downtoearth.org; 305 Dairy Rd; ⏰6am-10pm Mon-Sat, 7am-9pm Sun, deli 7am-9pm;) Open since the '70s, Down to Earth was one of Hawaii's pioneers of organic and vegetarian produce. It feels like an independent Whole Foods, with plenty of baked goods and premade foods to take out or eat in. There's a full deli serving veggie dogs and earth burgers. Buy a range of local beauty products here, from sunscreen to balms.

Take out or eat in the small seating area upstairs.

★ **Maui Swap Meet** MARKET

(Map p136; ☎808-244-3100; Maui College, 310 Ka'ahumanu Ave; adult/child 12yr & under 50¢/free; ⏰7am-1pm Sat) Don't be misled by 'swap meet.' This outdoor market is neither garage sale nor farmers market but an arts-and-crafts show of the highest order. Scores of white tents, set up behind Maui College, are chock-full of fascinating, quality merchandise, most of it locally made, including jewelry, sculpture, clothing and Hawaii memorabilia. Come here for a meaningful souvenir.

Whole Foods FOOD & DRINKS

(Map p136; ☎808-872-3310; www.wholefoodsmarket.com; Maui Mall, 70 E Ka'ahumanu

ISLAND INSIGHTS: THE GREAT EUROPEAN DISCOVERY ENIGMA

While most historians credit Captain Cook with the European discovery of Hawaii, there is evidence that the Spanish may have preceded him. From South America to the Philippines, the vast Pacific was once part of Spain's overseas empire. For more than two centuries galleons made the trip from Mexico to Manila and back at the mercy of the winds. Is it possible that they discovered Hawaii? Conversely, is it possible that in hundreds of round trips they did *not*? Spanish tradition contains references to the Islas del Rey, Islas de los Jardines, Islas de las Tables and Islas de las Mesas, any one of which could be Hawaii. Top candidates for European discoverer include Juan Gaytan, based on his rudimentary account of a trip outbound from New Spain in 1555, and Francisco Gauli, whose 1582 expedition strayed from the normal galleon route.

Ave; 7am-9pm) Whole Foods carries island-grown produce, fish and beef. Massive salad bar and deli, plus small eating area.

Bounty Music MUSIC
(Map p136; 808-214-1591; www.bountymusicmaui.com; 111 Hana Hwy; 9am-6pm Mon-Sat, 10am-4pm Sun) Hawaiian-music lovers should step inside for all sorts of ukuleles, from inexpensive imported models to handcrafted masterpieces. Rentals, too. And if you're lucky you might catch some impromptu live music.

Barnes & Noble BOOKS
(Map p136; 808-214-6807; www.barnesandnoble.com; 270 Dairy Rd; 9am-9pm Mon-Sat, 10am-7pm Sun) Good selection of travel and local info books on Maui and Hawaii.

Information

Bank of Hawaii (www.boh.com; 11 E Kamehameha Ave; 8:30am-4pm Mon-Thu, to 6pm Fri, 9am-1pm Sat) ATM available here.

Department of Parks & Recreation – Central District (Map p136; 808-270-7389; www.mauicounty.gov; War Memorial Gymnasium, 700 Hali'a Nakoa St; 8am-4pm Mon, Tue, Thu & Fri, 10am-4pm Wed) An office to apply for camping permits. Also useful for updates on national parks.

Longs Drugs (808-877-0068; Maui Mall, 70 E Ka'ahumanu Ave; 24hr, pharmacy 8am-9pm) More than just a pharmacy – a gift shop with everything from flip-flops to souvenirs.

Maui Memorial Medical Center (808-244-9056; www.mauimemorialmedical.org; 221 Mahalani St; 24hr) The island's main hospital. For extreme emergencies, flying to Queen's Medical Center in Honolulu may be recommended.

Maui Visitors Bureau (Map p132; 808-872-3893; www.gohawaii.com/maui; Kahului International Airport; 5am-10pm) This staffed booth in the airport's arrivals area has tons of tourist brochures and useful info.

Getting There & Away

Most people fly into **Kahului International Airport** (OGG; Map p132; 808-872-3830; www.airports.hawaii.gov/ogg; 1 Kahului Airport Rd), Maui's main airport, which is located at the eastern side of town, just a short taxi or bus ride from the restaurants and shops of the city. Direct flights arrive here from the US mainland and Canada.

The majority of the car-hire companies on the island operate from the airport. Local **Bio-Beetle** (808-873-6121; https://mauicarrentals.us; 55 Amala Pl; per day/week from $40/240) rents a spread of ecofriendly vehicles, including biodiesel VW bugs, gas and electric Chevy Volts, and the purely electric Nissan Leaf. Airport pickup and drop-off available.

Getting Around

Maui Bus (www.co.maui.hi.us) connects Kahului airport with downtown Kahului via the Haiku Islander (route 35) and the Upcountry Islander (route 40), both of which run every hour and a half throughout the day. Maui Bus routes also connect with Wailuku, Paia and Haiku (change at Queen Ka'ahumanu Center if traveling from Kahului airport). Each route costs $2. Infants under two years old travel for free.

Shuttle services from the airport, including Roberts Hawaii (p101), run to various destinations in Maui. Fares start at $10 one way; taxi fare from the airport to central Kahului starts at $14.

Wailuku

Four streams feed the lush landscape surrounding Wailuku, which made the area an important food source and landholding for Maui chieftains. Missionaries took up residence here in the 1800s. Today, while offering more sights on the National Register of Historic Places than any other town on Maui, Wailuku sees few tourists. And that is its appeal. An earthy mishmash of curio shops, galleries and mom-and-pop stores surrounds the quaint center of the county capital, all begging to be browsed. If you're here at lunchtime you're in luck: thanks to a combination of low rent and hungry government employees, Wailuku dishes up tasty eats at prices that put the more touristy towns to shame.

Sights & Activities

A cluster of historic buildings anchors the small downtown area. Hawaii's best-known architect, Maui-born CW Dickey, left his mark here before moving on to fame in Honolulu. The c 1928 **Wailuku Public Library** (808-243-5766; www.librarieshawaii.org; 251 High St; 9am-5pm Mon-Wed & Fri, 1-8pm Thu) is a classic example of his distinctive regional design, while the Ka'ahumanu Church (p140) is a handsome Gothic New England–style missionary church, built in 1875.

★Hale Hō'ike'ike at the Bailey House MUSEUM
(808-244-3326; www.mauimuseum.org; 2375a Main St; adult/child 7-12yr $7/2; 10am-4pm Mon-Sat) This small but historically evocative museum occupies the 1833 home of Wailuku's first Christian missionary, Edward Bailey. He was the second missionary to occupy the house and lived here nearly 50 years. The home gives you a sense of what it was like to live in missionary times while also containing a collection of interesting artifacts, including a shark-tooth dagger and a notable collection of native-wood bowls, stone adzes, feather lei and tapa cloth.

Ka'ahumanu Church CHURCH
(808-244-5189; www.kaahumanuchurch.org; 103 S High St; services 9am Sun) This handsome missionary church, in Gothic New England style, was built in 1875 by missionary Edward Bailey and named for Queen Ka'ahumanu, who cast aside the old Hawaiian gods and allowed Christianity to flourish. The clock in the steeple, brought around the Horn in the 19th century, still keeps accurate time. The church is usually locked, but hymns still ring out in Hawaiian at Sunday services.

Haleki'i-Pihanakalani Heiau State Monument RUINS
(Map p136; Hea Pl; 7am-7pm;) Haleki'i-Pihana Heiau is the hilltop ruins of two of Maui's most important heiau (ancient stone temples). The site was the royal court of Kahekili, Maui's last ruling chief, and the birthplace of Keopuolani, wife of Kamehameha the Great. After his victory at the battle of 'Iao in 1790, Kamehameha marched to this site to worship his war god Ku, offering the last human sacrifice on Maui.

Mystery Maui Escape Room LIVE CHALLENGE
(808-249-2062; www.mysterymaui.com; 81 N Market St; adult/child 7-12yr $35/20; 1-9pm Tue-Thu, 1-10:30pm Fri, 10:30am-10:30pm Sat, 10:30am-9pm Sun) The escape-room craze has finally made it to Maui. Admittedly, this isn't the best puzzle-solving mystery out there, but it makes for a fun way to spend a rainy afternoon in Wailuku. Choose from one-hour-scenario games including the Ramen Shop, in which your team has to find out what happened to Chef Masato, who is reported missing.

Meanwhile, in the Stella Superstar game you get invited to a personal show at Stella's house, but people keep disappearing. Your team has to solve the mystery before the time runs out. The entrance is off the main parking lot for Market St.

Festivals & Events

★Wailuku First Friday CARNIVAL
(www.mauifridays.com; N Market St; 6-9pm 1st Fri of month) On the first Friday of every month Market St turns into a pedestrian zone and laid-back street party, with several bands, lots of tasty food options, and special events such as vintage-car exhibitions and even a beer garden. This is Wailuku at its finest, so don't miss it if you're nearby.

Maui County Fair FAIR
(www.mauifair.com; War Memorial Stadium Complex, 700 Hali'a Nakoa St; Sep or Oct) Get a feel for Maui's agricultural roots at this venerable fair, held in late September or early October, with farm exhibits, entertainment, tasty island *grinds* (local food), activities and competitions (in 2019 there was a baby-of-the-year contest!).

Sleeping

Wailuku Guesthouse GUESTHOUSE $
(808-986-8270; www.wailukuhouse.com; 210 S Market St; 1 bedroom $119-149, 2 bedroom $179-249;) This affordable, friendly, family-run guesthouse has simple, clean, midsize en suite rooms, each with its own private entrance and a refrigerator. Rooms are tasteful, with a tropical twist, and the grounds have an aviary with resident macaws. All rooms except the Hibiscus Room have air-con. Complimentary use of chairs, towels and coolers for the beach.

Wailuku

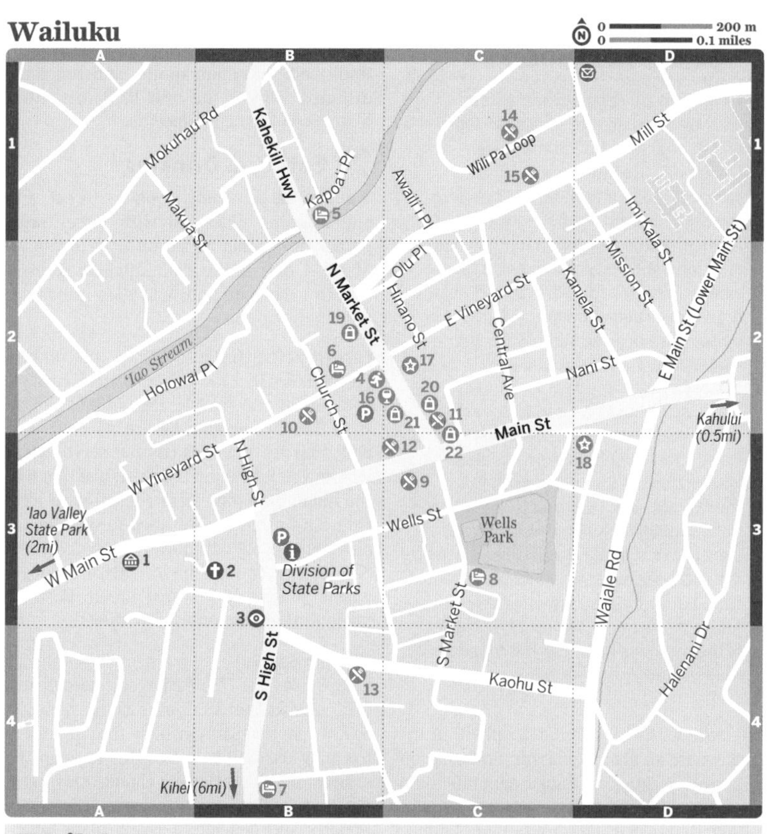

Wailuku

Sights
1 Hale Hō'ike'ike at the Bailey House......A3
2 Ka'ahumanu Church......B3
3 Wailuku Public Library......B3

Activities, Courses & Tours
4 Mystery Maui Escape Room......B2

Sleeping
5 Banana Bungalow......B1
6 Northshore Hostel......B2
7 Old Wailuku Inn......B4
8 Wailuku Guesthouse......C3

Eating
9 808 on Main......C3
10 Empanada Lady......B2
11 Farmacy Health Bar......C2
12 Food Court......C3
Giannotto's Pizza......(see 12)
13 Ichiban Okazuya......B4
14 Sam Sato's......C1
15 Tasty Crust......C1
Wailuku Coffee Co......(see 11)

Drinking & Nightlife
16 Wai Bar......C2

Entertainment
17 'Iao Theater......C2
18 Maui Coffee Attic......D3

Shopping
19 Antique Freak......B2
20 Brown-Kobayashi......C2
21 Cut Market......C2
22 Native Intelligence......C3
Request Music......(see 11)

Banana Bungalow HOSTEL $
(808-846-7835; www.mauihostel.com; 310 N Market St; dm $48, s/d $106/119; @ 📶) A free keg party every Friday night? If you're young, or young at heart, few hostels can

WORTH A TRIP

WORTH A TRIP: MOLOKINI

Molokini is a volcanic crater sitting midway between the islands of Maui and Kaho'olawe. Half of the crater has eroded, leaving a pretty 18-acre crescent moon that rises 160ft above the sea. But what lies beneath is the main attraction. Although tourism has affected the quality of the reef in recent years, white-tipped reef sharks, manta rays, turtles and abundant fish can still be spied among the steep walls and ledges. There are some 1000 visitors per day, most armed with a snorkel and mask, so it's important to wear reef-safe sunscreen and not touch the reef. Basic snorkeling trips from Ma'alaea Harbor start at $90 per person from the **Ma'alaea Harbor Activities** (Map p132; ☎808-280-8073; www.maalaeaharboractivities.com; Ma'alaea Harbor; lobster dinner cruise per person from $90; ⊙9am-8pm) hut. Avoid discounted afternoon tours: the water is calmest and clearest in the morning, but it can get rough and murky later.

compare with the party atmosphere of this one, where an always-changing international crowd of 20-somethings generates constant fun. Ideal for those looking to socialize rather than sleep. Free tours daily (subject to availability), plus free airport transfers, pancakes and coffee every morning.

★**Northshore Hostel** HOSTEL $
(☎808-354-0435, 808-986-8095; www.northshorehostel.com; 2080 W Vineyard St; dm $39, r with shared bath $84-120; ⊙reception 8am-2pm & 5-11pm; ❄@📶) This quiet and traditional hostel attracts all ages. Located in an old building with a fresh coat of paint, it has separate male and female dorms as well as private rooms, a full kitchen, rental beach gear ($5), laundry, and valuable freebies, including an airport shuttle, a free 'Iao Valley and beach shuttle and a pancake breakfast.

★**Old Wailuku Inn** B&B $$
(☎808-244-5897; www.mauiinn.com; 2199 Kaho'okele St; r from $195; ❄📶) Hawaiian hospitality is a highlight at this elegant period home. With its classic veranda and lightly vintage style, it transports you back to the breezy 1920s, while discreetly adding modern amenities. Each room has its own personality, but all are large and comfy, with traditional Hawaiian quilts. Full breakfast included. This is the best B&B in Central Maui. See website for specials.

Eating & Drinking

Wailuku has a variety of places to eat, and one drinking place, all with better price points than other more resort-y towns on Maui. A hole-in-the-wall Japanese joint, a superb salad bar and a low-key diner are among the options.

Farmacy Health Bar HEALTH FOOD $
(☎808-866-4312; www.thefarmacymaui.com; 12 N Market St; smoothies $9, mains $8-15; ⊙8am-7pm) The acai creations are so cold they chill your teeth at this counter-serve eatery where you'll feel invigorated just reading the menu. Smoothies are packed with local fruit, and a handful of good-for-you salads and soups come with locally grown veggies. Sandwiches can be made with sourdough, wheat, pita or gluten-free bread. Best for takeout: there are only a few stools.

★**Sam Sato's** JAPANESE $
(☎808-244-7124; 1750 Wili Pa Loop; noodles from $7.50, omelets from $8.25, plate lunches from $10; ⊙7am-2pm Mon-Sat) On busy days, Sam Sato's may use 350lb of noodles to keep the crowds sated. A Hawaii classic, this retro diner packs them in with steaming bowls of noodles and delicious teriyaki plate lunches. You'll find yourself waiting for a table at lunchtime, but there's often room at the counter. The dry mein is the signature dish. American breakfast also available.

Ichiban Okazuya JAPANESE $
(☎808-244-7276; 2133 Kaohu St; mains $11-16; ⊙10am-8pm Mon-Fri) Little more than a tin-roofed shed, this place tucked behind the government buildings has been dishing out tasty Japanese-style plate lunches to office workers for half a century, so you'd better believe it has the recipes down pat. Order up steaming *katsu*, tempura and *nabeyaki* (hot) udon.

Tasty Crust DINER $
(☎808-244-0845; 1770 Mill St; breakfast $6-17, lunch & dinner $7-21; ⊙6am-3pm Mon, to 10pm Sun & Tue-Thu, to 11pm Fri & Sat) The old-school American diner gets a Hawaiian twist at this low-frills locals' joint. Breakfast standbys such as Denver omelets and banana pancakes jostle for attention with *loco moco*, Spam, and fried rice with egg and mahimahi plates. Settle in

among the families and breakfast-steak-eating businesspeople for a solid budget meal before visiting the 'Iao Valley. Healthy eaters, get the fresh papaya!

Wailuku Coffee Co CAFE $
(808-495-0259; www.wailukucoffeeco.com; 26 N Market St; coffee from $2.75, menu items $4.50-13; 7am-5pm Mon-Sat, 8am-3pm Sun;) Located in the bays of a 1920s gas station, this is (as a sign proclaims) 'where the hip come to sip.' In Wailuku this means surfing the web in your T-shirt while downing a toddy (iced coffee). All brews are made from Maui-grown beans. Enjoy the smoothies, sandwiches, salads and brekkie options indoors or on outdoor curbside tables.

Donut Dynamite! BREAKFAST $
(Map p136; 808-280-6442; www.donutdynamite.com; 1246 Lower Main St; per donut $5; 6am-1pm Mon-Sat) This counter joint does the best donuts on Maui. The handcrafted brioche delights are made using local ingredients. Flavors rotate, but expect to find creations such as mango poi, maple bacon, *lilikoi* (passion fruit) and honey–goat cheese–walnut. It also does occasional savory buns in flavors such as egg and asparagus. Takeout only.

Empanada Lady CARIBBEAN $
(808-868-4544; 2119 W Vineyard St; meals $9-16; 11am-6pm Mon-Fri) Enjoy delicious home-cooked Caribbean fare in a lovely, casual indoor courtyard-garden setting. Along with empanadas (puff pastry stuffed with fillings), order flavorful plate lunches with coconut–black bean rice, gandule rice or white rice. Try everything from Dominican Republic–style *pernil* (roast pork) and Puerto Rican *pasteles guisados* stew to Jamaican coconut-chicken curry and Cuban *ropa vieja* (braised beef).

808 on Main HAWAIIAN $
(808-242-1111; www.808onmain.com; 2051 Main St; mains $9.50-18; 10am-8pm Mon-Fri, 11am-3pm Sat) Serving hearty salads, sandwiches and burgers, this restaurant has simple, airy decor and fairy lights inside. The *pupu* (snacks) menu includes dishes such as buffalo brussels sprouts with hot sauce and blue cheese, and lamb lettuce wraps. *Pupu,* beer and wine are discounted during the daily happy-hour deal from 3pm to 6pm.

Food Court FAST FOOD $
(2050 Main St; mains from $7; usually 10:30am-2:30pm) For quick bites, this handy food court has four takeout restaurants offering ramen and plate lunches, but the real reason to visit is the excellent, fragrant Fijian-Indian curry from Jiji's. Chef Sarojini Harris will let you sample before you buy. There are street-side picnic tables, too. Hours vary at each restaurant in the food court.

Giannotto's Pizza ITALIAN $$
(808-244-8282; www.giannottospizza.com; 2050 Main St; pizza slices $2-4, whole pies $17-27; 11am-9pm Mon-Sat) Brando, Sinatra and the Sopranos look down in approval from the cluttered walls of Giannotto's, a family-run pizza joint known for its home recipes.

Wai Bar BAR
(808-214-9829; www.waibarmaui.com; 45 N Market St; noon-11pm Mon-Thu, to 2am Fri, 5pm-2am Sat) Central Wailuku's only proper bar is the place to come after hours. The small, simple space holds only a few tables. There are special nights during the week: karaoke on Monday (8:30pm to 11pm), trivia on Tuesday (7pm to 10pm) and DJs on Saturday, plus ad-hoc live music. It attracts a young crowd.

☆ Entertainment

Maui Coffee Attic LIVE MUSIC
(808-250-9555; https://mauicoffeeattic.com; 59 Kanoa St; coffee from $3, ticketed events $10; 6am-6pm later during concerts) The polar opposite of a corporate coffee-shop chain, Maui Coffee Attic has a living room–style lounge of mismatched furniture, overflowing bookshelves, and guitars and ukuleles on the walls that patrons can pick up and play. Downstairs is a stage where open-mic sessions and small concerts are held. It serves Maui coffee, sandwiches, wraps and breakfast bagels (from $5).

Check the website for upcoming live shows.

'Iao Theater THEATER
(808-242-6969; www.mauionstage.com; 68 N Market St; box office 10am-2pm Mon-Fri) Nicely restored after years of neglect, this 1928 art-deco theater, which once hosted big names such as Frank Sinatra, is now *the* venue for community theater productions.

Shopping

Cut Market CLOTHING
(808-868-0666; https://cut-market.business.site; 45 N Market St; 10:30am-4:30pm Mon-Fri, 10am-2pm Sat) Pre-loved-clothing boutique, for hip, eco-conscious, upcycled one-of-a-kind creations made in-house. Sometimes has live music for Wailuku First Friday (p140) events.

Native Intelligence GIFTS & SOUVENIRS
(☎808-249-2421; www.native-intel.com; 1980 Main St; ⊙10am-5pm Mon-Fri, to 4pm Sat) Superb gift stop for hula instruments, koa bowls and fine handcrafted items.

Antique Freak ANTIQUES
(☎808-870-8598; www.facebook.com/pg/antiquefreak808/posts; 139 N Market St; ⊙10am-5pm Mon-Fri, 11am-4pm Sat) Aladdin's cave of curios and collector's items in various rooms around a converted house. Items are displayed in cabinets, stacked and hanging everywhere. Peruse old tapestries and books, drums, vintage Hawaiian shirts, reggae vinyl, furniture, and retro figurines of Obama holding a surfboard for your dashboard. It's a magical place to wander and purchase a unique gift.

Request Music MUSIC
(http://requestmusichawaii.com; 10 N Market St; ⊙10am-6pm Mon-Sat) Pick up some vintage Hawaiiana at this independent record shop selling new and old CDs, DVDs and vinyl, plus posters.

Information

First Hawaiian Bank (www.fhb.com; 27 N Market St; ⊙8:30am-4pm Mon-Thu, to 6pm Fri) ATM available here.

Maui Visitors Bureau (Map p136; ☎800-525-6284, 808-244-3530; www.gohawaii.com/maui; 427 Ala Makani St, Room 101; ⊙8am-4:30pm Mon-Fri) For local information, pop into the Maui Visitors Bureau or visit its website to download or order a Maui visitors guide. Also represents Lana'i and Moloka'i.

Post Office (☎808-244-1653; www.usps.com; 250 Imi Kala St; ⊙9am-4pm Mon-Fri, to noon Sat)

Wailuku to 'Iao Valley State Monument

It's hard to believe today, but the route from Wailuku to 'Iao Valley was the site of Maui's bloodiest battle. In 1790 Kamehameha the Great invaded Kahului by sea and drove the defending Maui warriors up 'Iao Stream. As the valley walls closed in, those unable to escape over the mountains were slaughtered. The waters of 'Iao Stream were so choked with bodies that the area was named Kepaniwai (Dammed Waters).

Kepaniwai Park & Heritage Gardens PARK
(Map p132; www.mauicounty.gov; 870 'Iao Valley Rd; ⊙7am-5:30pm) This unique and pretty park celebrates the various ethnic groups of Hawaii by displaying a building for each one. There's a traditional Hawaiian *hale* (house), a New England–style missionary home, a Filipino farmer's hut, Japanese gardens and a Chinese pavilion, all of which can be seen on a 15-minute walk. Note that at the time of research the park was open, but many of the pavilions and gardens were being renovated.

Enlivened by 'Iao Stream, this is a perfect picnic spot and barbecue area, and a refreshing monument to social harmony.

'Iao Valley State Monument

As you drive out of Wailuku, 'Iao Valley's emerald lushness envelops you, concluding with an explosion of riparian and mountain greenery at 'Iao Valley State Monument, deep in the bosom of the West Maui Mountains. The scenery is dramatic, with sheer peaks soaring in all directions, most notably 'Iao Needle. Rising above the lush rainforest, and caressed by passing mist, this rock pinnacle stands as a monument to your journey, while marking the entrance to the mysterious, uninhabited valley beyond. Most will never go beyond the viewpoint, but the park extends clear up to Pu'u Kukui (5788ft), Maui's highest and wettest place.

Sights & Activities

★ **'Iao Valley State Monument** PARK
(Map p132; ☎808-587-0400; http://dlnr.hawaii.gov/dsp; per car $5; ⊙7am-6pm) If you've seen just one photograph of Maui's lush interior, odds are it was of the iconic 2250ft **'Iao Needle** (Kūka'emoko; Map p132; parking $5; ⊙7am-6pm), the green pinnacle that provides the focal point for 'Iao Valley State Monument. During periods of warfare, the needle was used as a lookout to spot invaders.

Visitors can climb the 133 steps to a viewing platform with stunning views of the valley and Wailuku. The walk takes 30 minutes round trip. On the way up, take the left fork for a quick detour to a paved loop through a tropical garden.

Most people shoot their mandatory photos of the needle from the bridge near the parking lot. A better idea, though, is to take the walkway just before the bridge that loops downhill by 'Iao Stream. This leads to the nicest angle, one that captures the stream, the bridge and the 'Iao Needle together.

OFF THE BEATEN TRACK

A FRANK LLOYD WRIGHT MASTERPIECE

The **clubhouse** at the King Kamehameha Golf Club is Maui's great anomaly: a building that should be known worldwide is hardly mentioned on the island, or visited by anyone save its members.

The spectacular rose building looks like a set from *Star Wars*, and is beautifully sited in the Waikapu Valley, at the foot of the West Maui Mountains. A whopping 74,000 sq ft in area, it can be seen from the slopes of Haleakalā. Originally designed as a much smaller home by famed American architect Frank Lloyd Wright, it contains many artistic flourishes, including art glass, etched designs and an elegant Hawaiian art collection.

Wright adapted the design for three successive clients, including Marilyn Monroe, but never broke ground. In 1988, three decades after his death, Japanese investors purchased the plans, intent on building a clubhouse in Maui. They poured $35 million into the project, including further adaptation by one of Wright's apprentices. Then the Japanese economy collapsed in 1999, the club closed, and the greens turned brown. In 2004 another Japanese investor bought the property, and spent $40 million more. Today the club is working to fill its roster, but this is no reflection on the course, or the magnificent building that crowns it.

The public is welcome to visit the building, and to enjoy the restaurant. A brochure about the building and the art collection is available at the entrance. Note that the clubhouse is a short drive up the hill beyond the pro shop.

The Hawaiian garden also provides a good vantage point to snap a picture of the needle. Then you'll reach the bridge crossing the stream – you may see locals jumping from it, but don't even try: it's dangerous. Those looking for a paddle can continue to another left-hand loop, where the river rushes slower and pools provide a good opportunity to cool off. Check the conditions before you dip, as these waters are subject to flash floods.

At the end of the marked pathway there's a petroglyph of a stick man at the base of a big boulder (usually with offerings wrapped in leaves at the bottom of it). Look out for other petroglyphs along the way. Hundreds of years ago waters in this area helped create the largest irrigated agricultural system in Maui.

The park is 3 miles west of central Wailuku.

Waikapu

Located in the foothills of the West Maui Mountains, Waikapu was once a taro-farming area but is now a large tract of land with thousands of residents. For visitors, highlights include a tropical plantation, a top-notch golf course and a thrilling zipline.

Sights & Activities

★Maui Tropical Plantation FARM

(Map p132; ☎808-244-7643; www.mauitropicalplantation.com; 1670 Honoapi'ilani Hwy; admission free, tram tour adult/child 3-12yr $24/12; 9am-9pm, tram tours hourly 10am-4pm; P) This long-standing tourist attraction is a cross between a farm, a dining destination and a botanic garden. The large gift shop stocks art, aloha wear, chocolate and gift food. There's also a lovely short walk through the gardens, plus ziplining and the Kumu Farms store – a superb choice for organic goods. Meanwhile, a restaurant and coffee shop serves up excellent local produce.

★Flyin Hawaiian Zipline ADVENTURE SPORTS

(Map p132; ☎808-463-5786; www.flyinhawaiianzipline.com; Maui Tropical Plantation, 1670 Honoapi'ilani Hwy; per person $185) Wheeeee! Adrenaline junkies will revel in this new ziplining addition. Located high in the crumpled folds of the West Maui Mountains, the course spans nine valleys with eight lines, including one 3600ft monster, achieving speeds of more than 50mph. Allow four to five hours. Minimum age 10 years; permissible weight range 75lb to 250lb.

King Kamehameha Golf Club GOLF

(Map p132; ☎808-249-0033; www.kamehamehagolf.com; 2500 Honoapi'ilani Hwy; morning round $249; 6:30am-6:30pm) The only 18-hole private club on Maui, and the island's most challenging course, is surprisingly friendly to the public. Visitors can play before 8am or after 11am. The extraordinary bicoastal vistas are matched only by the spectacular 74,000-sq-ft Frank Lloyd Wright clubhouse (p145), considered by *Golf Digest* to be possibly the best in the country.

Kahili Course GOLF

(Map p132; ☎808-242-4653; www.kahiligolf.com; 2500 Honoapi'ilani Hwy; greens fees $39-175; ⏲6am-6:30pm) Nestled at the base of the West Maui Mountains, just down the street from its private sister, King Kamehameha Golf Club (p145), this beautiful public course is in outstanding condition and offers great value. The topography is very hilly, but the course is only moderately difficult. Fees vary depending on tee times and whether a cart is included (midday is cheapest).

Maui Zipline ADVENTURE SPORTS

(Map p132; ☎808-633-2464; www.mauizipline.com; Maui Tropical Plantation, 1670 Honoapi'ilani Hwy; per person $110; ⏲9am-3pm) Located on the grounds of Maui Tropical Plantation (p145), this is an extremely tame five-line course designed for families, with a low 50lb limit and dual lines. The zip over a pond adds some spice. However, families pay a lot for this two-hour experience: there's no discount for kids.

Eating & Drinking

The Scoop ICE CREAM $

(Map p132; https://mauitropicalplantation.com/the-scoop; Maui Tropical Plantation, 1670 Honoapi'ilani Hwy; per scoop $5, smoothies from $6, ice pops $4; ⏲10am-5pm) Wow, this ice cream is seriously good. Made from ingredients from local farms, such as Maui gold pineapples, Kula strawberries and Sunrise papayas, these delicious creamy creations are contenders for best on the island. A fave is the Sandy Beach, with peanut-butter gelato, graham cracker, coconut and lava salt. Serves smoothies and excellent Shaka Pops (p243), too.

Mill House FUSION $$$

(Map p132; ☎808-270-0333; www.millhousemaui.com; Maui Tropical Plantation, 1670 Honoapi'ilani Hwy; mains $14-55; ⏲11am-9pm) With an emphasis on local farm-fresh food and set in an upmarket farmhouse, the Mill House restaurant is impress-your-friends-dining without being stuffy. Exceptional dishes include Kaua'i prawn and fish coconut curry with seasonal veggies, and *paniolo* (Hawaiian cowboy) rib eye with a coffee glaze and smoked potato puree. Some ingredients are handpicked from the beautiful setting: the surrounding 900-acre plantation fields.

★ **Maui Chef's Table** AMERICAN $$$

(Map p132; ☎808-270-0333; www.mauichefstable.com; Maui Tropical Plantation, 1670 Honoapi'ilani Hwy; per person $190; ⏲6-9pm Sat) In one of the priciest but most memorable dining experiences you're likely to have on Maui, gourmet fare is whipped up by the top chefs of the Mill House restaurant. Watch the culinary artists prepare an outstanding multicourse meal using super-fresh seasonal local ingredients while telling stories about cooking and the surrounding farms. Tables are outside and communal. Menus change nightly.

There are typically six small-plate courses. Guests receive a complimentary glass of

THE STORY OF KAHO'OLAWE

The sacred but uninhabited island of Kaho'olawe lies 7 miles southwest of Maui. It has long been central to the Hawaiian rights movement, and many consider the island a living spiritual entity, a *pu'uhonua* (refuge) and *wahi pana* (sacred place).

Yet for nearly 50 years, from WWII to 1990, the US military used Kaho'olawe as a bombing range. Beginning in the 1970s, liberating the island from the military became a rallying point for a larger resurgence of Native Hawaiian pride. Today, the bombing has stopped, the navy is gone and healing the island is considered both a symbolic act and a concrete expression of Native Hawaiian sovereignty. For a more detailed historic timeline for the island, visit www.kahoolawe.hawaii.gov.

The island (11 miles long and 6 miles wide) and its surrounding waters are now a reserve that is off limits to the general public because of unexploded ordnance. However, **Protect Kaho'olawe 'Ohana** (PKO; www.protectkahoolaweohana.org) conducts monthly visits to pull weeds, plant native foliage, clean up historic sites and honor the land. It welcomes respectful volunteers who are ready to work (not just sightsee). Visits are scheduled during or near the full moon; the volunteer fee covers food and transportation. You'll need your own sleeping bag, tent and personal supplies. For more details, see the 'Huaka'i' section on the PKO website. Note: these trips book up at least two years ahead, so pre-planning is essential.

sparkling wine during the first course (and can pay for extra wine or beer), plus a coffee during dessert. Live music is usually performed during the meal. Children must be over 11 years. Book weeks in advance of your trip.

Mill House Roasting Co. COFFEE
(Map p132; 808-270-0319; www.millhouseroasting.com; Maui Tropical Plantation, 1670 Honoapi'ilani Hwy; coffee from $2.50; 8am-5pm) Serving 100% Hawaii-grown coffee, Mill House Roasting makes a fine pit stop for a craft cup o' joe. Beans include those sourced from mokka, yellow caturra, red catuai, and typica varieties. Red catuai is the variety grown in the surrounding grounds of Maui Tropical Plantation. Find it housed in a red corrugated-iron outhouse.

Pastries and gifts are on sale, too.

Ma'alaea

Ma'alaea is the jumping-off point for exploring Maui's coastline by boat. Many tour companies work out of this cute little harbor. The biggest draw is the whale-watching and snorkeling trips that run from here to Molokini – a submerged volcanic crater offshore with excellent visibility. Ma'alaea Bay is home to a surf-spot pipeline, which can produce fast barrels. It's no coincidence that Maui's first windmill farm marches up the slopes here. By midday the winds pick up and you might need to hold onto your hat.

Beaches

Ma'alaea Bay BEACH
(Map p132; N Kihei Rd) Ma'alaea Bay is fronted by a 3-mile stretch of sand running from Ma'alaea Harbor south to Kihei. Access is from several places along N Kihei Rd, including **Kealia Beach**, which parallels the Kealia Coastal Boardwalk (p149). Parking is limited, but the beach is mostly deserted.

Pāpalaua State Wayside Park BEACH
(Map p132; 808-661-4685; www.mauicounty.gov; Honoapi'ilani Hwy, btwn Miles 11 & 12; camping adult/child incl permit Mon & Thu $10/6, Fri-Sun $20/12; sunrise-sunset) This beachside county park isn't as stunning as its neighbors, but you will find picnic tables, barbecue grills and portable toilets here. It also has a killer south-sea view and gorgeous sunsets over Lana'i island. Tent **camping** under the kiawe trees is permitted nightly, except on Tuesday and Wednesday. Note that the park is beside the loud and busy Honoapi'ilani Hwy. Maximum stay four consecutive nights.

Sights

Maui Ocean Center AQUARIUM
(Map p132; 808-270-7000; www.mauioceancenter.com; 192 Ma'alaea Rd; adult/child 3-12yr $35/25, behind-the-scenes tour per person additional $15; 9am-5pm) This midsize aquarium showcases Hawaii's dazzling marine life, including species found nowhere else. The floor plan takes you on an ocean journey, beginning with nearshore reefs teeming with colorful tropical fish and ending with deep-ocean life. The grand finale is a 54ft acrylic tunnel that leads you through a large tank as sharks and rays glide by. Behind-the-scenes tours available Monday, Wednesday, Thursday and Friday. Audioguides $3.

Activities

Wicked winds from the north shoot straight out toward Kaho'olawe, creating excellent windsurfing conditions that, unlike elsewhere, persist throughout the winter. The bay also has a couple of hot surfing spots. The **Ma'alaea Pipeline** (Map p132), east of the harbor, freight-trains right and is the fastest surf break in all Hawaii. Summer's southerly swells produce huge tubes here.

Shark Dive Maui DIVING
(Map p132; 808-270-7000; https://mauioceancenter.com/product/shark-dive-maui; Maui Ocean Center, 192 Ma'alaea Rd; shark dives from $200; 3pm Mon, Wed & Fri) Shark Dive Maui takes intrepid divers on a daredevil's plunge into the 750,000-gallon deep-ocean tank at Maui Ocean Center (p147) to swim with around 20 sharks, including five species, among them the black-tip reef shark, the sandbar shark and, gasp, the tiger shark. Also in the water are stingrays and tropical fish. Aquarium admission included in price.

Boss Frogs WATER SPORTS
(Map p132; 808-242-0088; https://bossfrog.com; 300 Ma'alaea Rd; rentals per day snorkel set/bodyboard/beach chair/surfboard/cooler $12/8/7/25/3; 6am-5pm) Competitively priced beach rentals, from underwater digital cameras and snorkel gear to bodyboards, surfboards, coolers and beach chairs. Discounts on weekly rentals.

Tours

The tour operators at Ma'alaea Harbor have consolidated reservations at the Ma'alaea Harbor Activities (p142) hut, facing Slip 47. Here you can book fishing trips, snorkeling excursions, dinner, cocktail and sunset cruises, and seasonal whale-watching trips. It's great for comparison shopping.

Pacific Whale Foundation BOATING
(Map p132; 808-249-8811; www.pacificwhale.org; Ma'alaea Harbor Shops, 300 Ma'alaea Rd; cruises adult/child over 12yr from $120/106; most tours depart 7-8am;) Led by naturalists, these boat tours do it right, offering snorkeling lessons and wildlife talks. Breakfast and a barbecue lunch are provided, and kids under 12 travel free (one per paying adult). Half-day tours concentrate on the spectacular ocean crater of Molokini. Full-day tours add Lana'i. There's great variety, including whale-watching, catamaran sailing trips and Molokini crater snorkeling.

Eating

★ **Ma'alaea General Store & Cafe** CAFE $
(Map p132; 808-242-8900; www.maalaeastore.com; 132 Ma'alaea Rd; mains $8-13; 6am-7pm Mon-Thu, to 6pm Fri-Sun;) Located in the only building left from the days when Ma'alaea was a small Japanese fishing village, this friendly general store and cafe offers locally sourced deli eats, fresh-baked bread, and a rare focus on veggie and gluten-free solutions. Plus great cakes and fresh fish plates. The porch is a great place to watch the world go by.

The grilled fresh catch ($14) is great value; it comes with a blackened fillet, two scoops of rice and salad.

Thai Paradise THAI $
(Map p132; 808-793-3714; 300 Ma'alaea Rd; mains $12-18; 11am-3pm & 5-9pm) Good fix for a Thai-food craving, with tangy papaya salads and fresh local garlic shrimp. Classics such as green, red and massaman curry, plus pad Thai noodles are done well. Try the mango with sticky rice and coconut for dessert.

Hula Cookies & Ice Cream DESSERTS $
(Map p132; 808-243-2271; www.hulacookies.com; Ma'alaea; Harbor Shops, 300 Ma'alaea Rd; ice cream from $5, shave ice from $5.50; 10am-7:30pm) Serving shave ice, fresh-baked cookies and Maui-made ice cream chock-full of macadamia nuts, pineapple and coconut, Hula Cookies & Ice Cream is a good place to take the kids after visiting the nearby aquarium.

Beach Bums Bar & Grill BARBECUE $$
(Map p132; 808-243-2286; www.beachbumshawaii.com; Ma'alaea Harbor Shops, 300 Ma'alaea Rd; breakfast items $2.50-16, lunch & dinner mains $9-24; 8am-9pm) For harbor views and barbecue, settle in at this lively eatery. Beach Bums uses a wood-burning rotisserie smoker to grill up everything from burgers and ribs to turkey and Spam. Come from 3pm to 6pm for drafts from $2.50, or from 5pm to 8pm Monday to Friday (except Wednesday) to enjoy live local music. Hearty breakfasts served 8am to 11am.

Getting There & Away

Ma'alaea has good connections to the rest of Maui's public bus system. The Maui Bus ($2) connects the Harbor Shops at Ma'alaea with Lahaina, Kahului and Kihei. Service depends on the route, but buses operate hourly from around 6am to 8pm.

Kealia Pond National Wildlife Refuge

A magnet for both birds and birdwatchers, **Kealia Pond National Wildlife Refuge** (Map p132; 808-875-1582; www.fws.gov/refuge/kealia_pond; Mokulele Hwy, Mile 6; 7:30am-4pm Mon-Fri) FREE harbors native waterbirds year-round and migratory birds, including ducks (October to April) and hawksbill (June and September), as well as Hawaiian sea turtles (June and September).. In the rainy winter months, Kealia Pond swells to 400 acres, making it one of the largest natural ponds in Hawaii. In summer it shrinks to half that size, creating the skirt of crystalline salt that gives Kealia ('salt-encrusted place') its name.

The visitor center (p149) occupies an abandoned catfish farm with footpaths atop the levees that separate the old fishponds, a layout that allows you to get very close to the birds and various species. This is also the best place to see wintering osprey, a majestic fish hawk that dive-bombs its prey in the fishponds.

You can view the pond from the coastal boardwalk (p149) on N Kihei Rd, as well as from the visitor center (p149) off Mokulele Hwy at the 6-mile marker. In both places you're almost certain to spot wading Hawaiian black-necked stilts, Hawaiian coots and black-crowned night herons – all native waterbirds that thrive in this sanctuary.

★Kealia Coastal Boardwalk WALKING

(Map p132; www.fws.gov/refuge/kealia_pond; Kealia Pond National Wildlife Refuge; ⏲6am-7pm) FREE This wonderful elevated boardwalk by Ma'alaea Bay seems to go on forever. It traverses over 2000ft of wetlands, making it a magnet for birders but also a great nature walk for anyone. Interpretive plaques and benches help along the way. In winter you may spot humpback whales. It's located 350yd north of the 2-mile marker on N Kihei Rd.

Information

Kealia Pond Visitor Center (Map p132; ☎808-875-1582; www.fws.gov/refuge/kealia_pond; Maui Veterans Hwy; ⏲11am-3pm Mon, 9am-3pm Tue-Fri) The main building has fascinating displays on native waterbirds and why we should protect them. Hawaii has more endangered animals than any other US state – the islands are home to 15,000 kinds of flora and fauna.

The helpful volunteer staff here can help in identifying different species and explain more about this unique sanctuary occupying 700 acres. Alternatively, pick up a comprehensive bird-spotting guide at the entrance.

Pu'unene

Sugar was the lifeblood of Pu'unene until the end of 2016. Fields of cane extended out from the Hawaiian Commercial & Sugar Company's rusty old mill, the last of its kind in Hawaii. This industrial hulk still looms large, and not so long ago it belched smoke as it boiled down the sugarcane, making the whole area smell of molasses. Hidden nearby are the remains of the plantation village, including an old schoolhouse and a long-abandoned church. This is a great place to grasp what island life would have been like back then – it's truly untouched by tourism.

Sights

Alexander & Baldwin Sugar Museum MUSEUM

(Map p132; ☎808-871-8058; www.sugarmuseum.com; 3957 Hansen Rd; adult/child 6-12yr/child under 6yr $7/2/free; ⏲9:30am-4:30pm, last entry 4pm) This homespun museum occupies the former residence of the sugar mill's superintendent. There's the usual display of industrial machinery, including a working model of a cane-crushing plant, but what lingers afterward is the human story. One exhibit traces how the sons of missionaries took control of Maui's fertile valleys and dug the amazing irrigation system that made large-scale plantations viable.

Compelling B&W photographs illuminate the labor and recreational aspects of plantation life. On display is an early-20th-century labor contract from the Japanese Emigration Company; it committed laborers to work the cane fields 10 hours a day, 26 days a month, for $15.

GREEN POWER

Windy Central Maui is a major-league player in alternative energy, with a percentage of Maui's electricity needs coming from the 50ft-high windmills located approximately 2000ft above Ma'alaea in the mountain area known as Kaheawa Pastures, where 34 of them line the ridge on the Lahaina Pali Trail. In addition, Maui has more than 1000 registered electric cars and roughly 100 charging ports. Solar power has also gained momentum on the island. A large-scale solar farm with 200,000 panels on the east side of Kuihelani Hwy is slated for construction in 2020 and is set to go online in 2022. The farm will produce clean energy for around 30,000 homes on the island. Currently, more than 30% of the electricity used in Maui County comes from renewable sources. Looking forward, officials hope to have a plan to harness geothermal power on Maui by 2040.

Shopping

★Old Pu'unene Bookstore BOOKS

(Map p132; ☎808-871-6563; www.mfol.org; ⏲9am-4pm Tue-Sat) This shack in the middle of a tiny village has been a used-book store since 1913. It's musty, unique and seriously good value. The selection is wide and it still sells most books for a quarter! Pick up secondhand DVDs and CDs here, too. Out front on the porch the books are free. Proceeds go to Maui public libraries.

It's behind Pu'unene School, near E Camp 5 Rd.

AT A GLANCE

POPULATION
Kihei: 22,200

MILES OF BEACHES IN KIHEI
6

BEST NEIGHBORHOOD JOINT
Nalu's South Shore Grill (p162)

BEST FESTIVAL
Maui Film Festival (p167)

BEST LAVA LANDSCAPE
La Perouse Bay (p173)

WHEN TO GO

Dec–Mar High season with whale-watching and holiday-season crowds; World Whale Day in February.

Jun–Aug Maui Film Festival in mid-June; summer vacation brings families.

Apr–May & Sep–Nov Shoulder seasons and a great time to avoid crowds.

La Perouse Bay (p173)
SUSANNE POMMER / SHUTTERSTOCK ©

Kihei & South Maui

Everyone stops for the sunset in South Maui – just look at the throngs crowding the beach wall at Kama'ole Beach Park II in the late afternoon. It's a scene repeated up and down the coast here daily. With an abundance of strip malls, condo complexes and upscale resorts, Kihei and Wailea look commercial and overbuilt at first glance. But dig deeper. You'll find a mixed plate of scenery and adventure, stretching from Kihei to Makena and beyond. You can snorkel reefs teeming with turtles, kayak to remote bays or paddle an outrigger canoe. And the beaches? Undeniably glorious. Add reliably sunny weather and a diverse dining scene, and South Maui is pretty darn irresistible.

INCLUDES

Kihei & South Maui Highlights

❶ **Keawakapu Beach** (p153) Watching the sun drop below the horizon from a golden crescent of sand.

❷ **Big Beach** (p171) Sunbathing on a remote stretch of gleaming sand tucked between wild forests and deep-blue waters in Makena State Park.

❸ **Monkeypod Kitchen** (p168) Savoring a mai tai and wood-fired pizza during the convivial happy hour in Wailea.

❹ **La Perouse Bay** (p154) Hiking the Hoapili Trail through an eerie yet beautiful field of black lava.

❺ **Makena** (p170) Snorkeling beside graceful green turtles at Turtle Beach, or paddling across Makena Bay in search of whales and marine life.

❻ **Kihei** (p162) Digging into a heaping plate of *loco moco* on the patio of Hawaiian-style Kihei Caffe, or sampling flagship beers and great food at Maui Brewing Co.

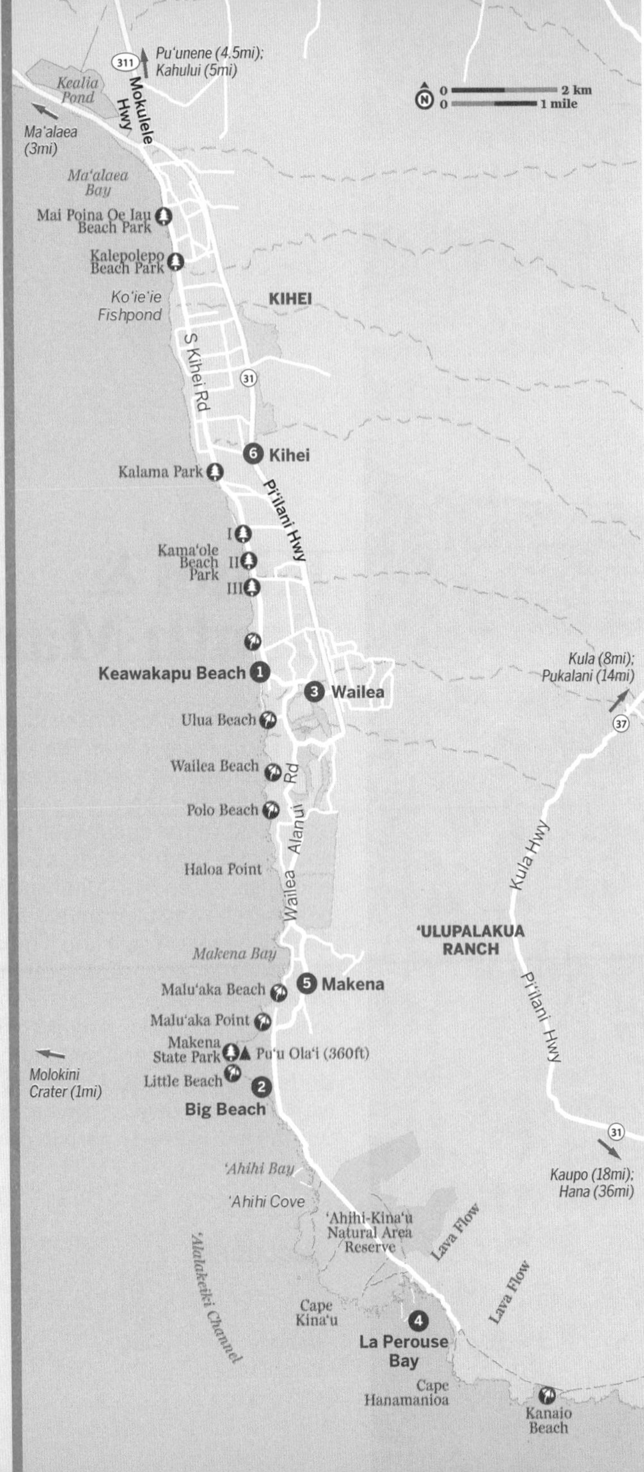

Kihei

Reasons to visit Kihei? The beaches, your budget and the weather. Yes, it's overrun with strip malls and traffic, but with 6 miles of easy-to-access beaches, loads of affordable accommodations and a variety of dining options, it offers everything you need for an enjoyable beach vacation. An energetic seaside town, Kihei also works well for short-trip vacationers seeking reliable sunshine – on average, Kihei is sunny 276 days per year. It's also home to the island's busiest bar scene.

To zip from one end of Kihei to the other, take the Pi'ilani Hwy (Hwy 31). It runs parallel to and bypasses the stop-start traffic of S Kihei Rd. Well-marked crossroads connect these two routes.

Beaches

The beaches improve dramatically as you travel south. At the northern end of Kihei, swimming is not advised, but kayaking is good in the morning and windsurfers set off in the afternoon.

Kama'ole Beach is having so much fun, it just keeps rolling along. And along. And along. Divided into three sections by rocky points, these popular strands are known locally as Kam I, Kam II and Kam III. All three are pretty, golden-sand beaches with full facilities (restrooms, showers, picnic tables, and grills) and lifeguards. There's a volleyball court at Kam I, and parking lots at Kam I and III.

Water conditions vary with the weather, but swimming is usually good. For the most part, these beaches have sandy bottoms with a fairly steep drop, which tends to create good conditions for bodysurfing, especially in winter.

For a list of facilities at each of the county beaches, visit www.mauicounty.gov.

Kalepolepo Beach Park BEACH

(Map p160; 808-879-4364; www.mauicounty.gov/Facilities; S Kihei Rd at Ka'ono'ulu St; P) This compact park beside the headquarters for the Humpback Whale National Marine Sanctuary (p158) is a nice spot for families with younger kids. A grassy lawn is fronted by the ancient Ko'ie'ie Fishpond (p158), whose stone walls create a shallow swimming pool with calm waters perfect for wading. There are also picnic tables, a grill and an outdoor shower.

Charley Young Beach BEACH

(Map p158; 808-879-4364; www.mauicounty.gov/Facilities; 2200 S Kihei Rd; P) On a side street, out of view of busy S Kihei Rd, this neighborhood beach is the least touristed strand in Kihei. It's a real jewel in the rough: broad and sandy, and backed by swaying coconut palms. You're apt to find fishers casting their lines, families playing volleyball and someone strumming a guitar. It also has some of the better bodysurfing waves in Kihei.

Kama'ole Beach Park I BEACH

(Map p158; 808-879-4364; www.mauicounty.gov/Facilities; 2400 S Kihei Rd; P) A pretty, golden-sand beach with full facilities and lifeguards, plus a volleyball court and a parking lot. Travelers with disabilities can access the ocean at Kam I using accessibility ramps and the sand beach chair. For details about the status of the sand beach chair (available 8:30am to 3:30pm), check the Kama'ole I listing at www.mauicounty.gov or call 808-270-6136.

Kama'ole Beach Park II BEACH

(Map p158; 808-879-4364; www.mauicounty.gov/Facilities; 2550 S Kihei Rd) This lovely beach has full facilities and lifeguards. A wooden accessibility ramp for visitors with disabilities leads from the park to the beach. Street parking only.

Kama'ole Beach Park III BEACH

(Map p158; 808-879-4364; www.mauicounty.gov/Facilities; 2800 S Kihei Rd; P) Covered in a blanket of golden sand, Kama'ole Beach Park III has full facilities and lifeguards, plus a playground and parking lot. Great spot for a beach day. The shaded picnic tables start filling up early on weekends. Also has accessibility parking, pathways and beach access for visitors with disabilities.

★ Keawakapu Beach BEACH

(Map p158; 808-879-4364; www.mauicounty.gov/Facilities; P) From break of day to twilight, this sparkling stretch of sand is a showstopper. Extending from south Kihei to Wailea's Mokapu Beach, Keawakapu is set back from the main road and less visible than Kihei's main roadside beaches just north. It's also less crowded, and is a great place to settle in and watch the sunset.

With its cushion-soft sand, Keawakapu is also a favorite for sunrise yoga and wake-up strolls. The ocean is a perfect spot for an end-of-day swim. Mornings are best for snorkeling: head to the rocky outcrops that form the northern and southern ends

HIKING IN KIHEI & SOUTH MAUI

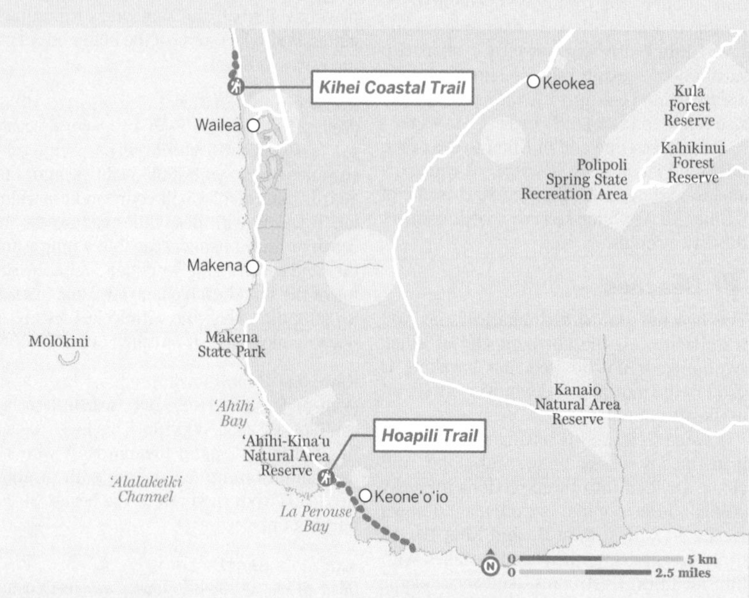

HOAPILI TRAIL

START LA PEROUSE BAY
END KANAIO BEACH
LENGTH ROUND TRIP 4 MILES; HALF-DAY
DIFFICULTY MODERATE

This section of the ancient King's Trail follows the coastline across jagged lava flows. It's a fascinating and diverse hike, but be prepared: wear hiking boots, bring plenty to drink, use sunscreen, start early and tell someone where you're going. It's a dry area with no water and little vegetation for shade, so it can get very hot.

At the **La Perouse Bay parking lot**, take a moment to scan the surf for spinner dolphins, which frequent the coast here. Walk south a short distance to the trailhead, marked by a large **Hoapili Trail sign** with a basic map and a list of safety tips plus guidelines about treating the historic sites and trail with cultural respect. Although some trail guides say the hike is 5.5 miles round trip, this sign confirms that the out-and-back distance to Kanaio Beach is 4 miles. Although four can feel like five on a hot and cloudless day here!

The **trail** (King's Hwy) begins at the edge of an inky black field of jagged *'a'a* lava. It tracks the coast, but a few short side trails lead to the ruins of the ancient Hawaiian community of **Keone'o'io**. Do not disturb the structures.

The trail then curves alongside the coast, passing through a cove before entering a kiawe forest hugging the sandy beach. You might encounter a few foraging goats. After the trail leaves the beach, at about 0.7 miles, you'll see an opening in a metal fence to your left, where the path heads into an expansive lava field. It's also possible to continue straight along the coast, following a spur trail for 0.75 miles down to the light beacon at the tip of Cape Hanamanioa.

Turn left through the **fence opening**, walking inland to the **Na Ala Hele sign**. From here, follow the King's Hwy as it climbs through rough lava. King Pi'ilani instigated the construction of the King's Trail more than

Trails never stray far from the coast in sunny South Maui, whether they're meandering over rocky bluffs or powering through old lava fields. All are gorgeous, but start early to beat the midday heat.

300 years ago to encourage commerce. The 200-mile highway once circled the entire island of Maui. This section was rebuilt by Governor Hoapili in the early 1800s. As the sun rises and you trudge across the rocky trail through the black lava, you might feel as if you're slowly roasting in an easy-bake oven. Walking on the loose rocks will also slowly wear you down, but views of the lava and ocean are superb. The trail continues through an older lava flow, returning to the coast at **Kanaio Beach**. Although the trail carries on, it becomes harder to follow and enters private property. Kanaio Beach is the recommended turn-around point.

If you don't include the lighthouse spur, the round-trip distance to Kanaio Beach is about 4 miles. For more details visit http://dlnr.hawaii.gov/recreation/nah, the state's trail and access website.

KIHEI COASTAL TRAIL

START KEAWAKAPU BEACH
END KAMA'OLE BEACH PARK III
LENGTH ROUND TRIP 1.2 MILES; ONE HOUR
DIFFICULTY EASY

This short trail meanders along coastal bluffs ideal for whale-watching and quiet meditation. You might even see an outrigger canoe glide past.

Begin a few steps south of the trailhead on the golden sands of **Keawakapu Beach** (p153), a beautiful place to stretch before your walk. Head north, walking between the rocky coast and the **Mana Kai Maui** (p161). A morning yoga class is held beside the beach here daily. Cross the parking lot to the trail, which tracks the lava-rock coast just west of the tidy lawn behind the **Kihei Surfside Resort** (p161). Follow the small trail signs north along the coast.

At the end of the lawn, continue north on the seaside path. The island of Kaho'olawe breaks the western horizon. Weathered signage beside the trail discusses the island's role as a navigational training spot for ancient Hawaiians, who were extremely skilled long-distance paddlers.

Walk north past the **Kihei boat ramp**, picking up the trail as it unfurls across a coastal bluff with expansive views of the sea. The path here is made of packed gray gravel outlined in white coral. Curiously, when the trail was being built, a storm washed hundreds of yards of bleached coral onto the shore here. The coral was not originally planned for the trail construction, but the volunteers building the trail consulted with a Hawaiian kahuna (priest) and were told ancient trails were often outlined in white coral so they could be followed at night. The Hawaiian gods were thanked for the gift of coral, which was then incorporated into the trail.

Along the bluff, look for the burrows of *'ua'u kani* (wedge-tailed shearwaters), ground-nesting seabirds that return to the same sites each spring. The birds lay a single egg and remain until November, when the fledglings are large enough to head out to sea. The trail ends beyond the grassy lawn at the southern end of **Kama'ole Beach Park III** (p153), a pleasant and shady spot to enjoy a picnic or simply gaze at the sea.

LAZY DAYS IN KIHEI & WAILEA

Dreaming of lounging all day in a tropical country club? Then make your way to south Kihei and Wailea, where relaxing is done in style – and usually framed by palm trees.

MORNING STROLLS

Early risers will be treated to watercolor hues and sweet tranquility on a sunrise stroll on the Wailea Beach Walk or the Kihei Coastal Trail. Empty kayaks sit on the beach, awaiting their morning paddlers. Outrigger-canoe clubs skim past shore on the gentle sea. Yoga enthusiasts stretch by the sand. And wildlife, on land and in the ocean, frolics in its last moments of peace before the day begins.

A DAY OF SAND AND SURF

Oh, the golden strands of South Maui. World-class snorkeling is just offshore and an army of paddleboards are ready to rent. Stylish groups of honeymooners, hipsters and rich retirees amp up the people-watching. And reading on the beach never looked so pretty.

ENJOYING THE AMENITIES

World-class spas, golf courses and tennis courts are only a shuttle ride away in Wailea. Chef-driven restaurants beckon from the resorts, as do infinity pools and splashy wonderlands. In south Kihei, sunsets at Kihei's Keawakapu Beach are free, unless you add in a 5 Palms cocktail. And you should.

1. Wailea Beach (p166)
2. Kama'ole Beach Park I (p153)
3. Keawakapu Beach (p153)

ELENA_SUVOROVA / SHUTTERSTOCK ©

3

JAMES WHEELER / SHUTTERSTOCK ©

South Kihei

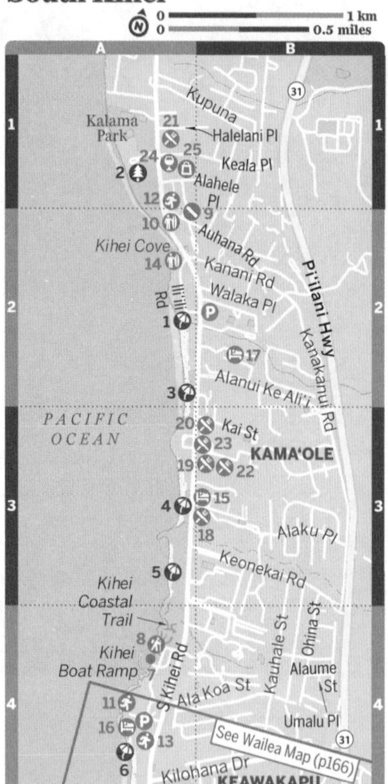

of the beach. During winter look for humpback whales, which come remarkably close to shore here.

Sights

Hawaiian Islands Humpback Whale National Marine Sanctuary Headquarters MUSEUM

(Map p160; ☎808-879-2818; http://hawaiihumpbackwhale.noaa.gov; 726 S Kihei Rd; ⊙10am-3pm Mon-Fri; P ♿) FREE The oceanfront deck at the marine sanctuary headquarters is an ideal spot for viewing the humpback whales that frequent the bay during winter. Free scopes are set up for viewing. Inside, displays and videos provide background, and there are informative brochures about whales and other endangered Hawaiian wildlife. Swing by at 11am on Tuesday or Thursday for the free '45-Ton Talks' about whales, and at 11am on Fridays for a green turtle talk.

Ko'ie'ie Fishpond HISTORIC SITE

(Map p160; S Kihei Rd at Ka'ono'ulu St; P ♿) In ancient Hawaii, coastal fishponds were built to provide a ready source of fish for royal families. The most intact fishpond remaining on Maui is the 3-acre Ko'ie'ie Fishpond. Constructed more than 400 years ago, it is on the National Register of Historic Places; it borders both Kalepolepo Beach Park and the Hawaiian Islands Humpback Whale National Marine Sanctuary headquarters. There are concerns that organized recreational activities are impacting this culturally significant and delicate site; best to enjoy it with respect.

David Malo's Church CHURCH

(Trinity Episcopal Church By-the-Sea; Map p160; ☎808-879-0161; www.trinitybts.org; 100 Kulanihako'i St; P) Philosopher David Malo, who built this church in 1852, was the first Hawaiian ordained to the Christian ministry. He was also co-author of Hawaii's first constitution and an early spokesperson for Hawaiian rights. While most of Malo's original church has been dismantled, a 3ft-high section of the wall still stands beside a palm grove. Pews are lined up inside the coral-block and river-stone walls. It's really quite beautiful.

Kalama Park PARK

(Map p158; ☎808-879-4364; www.mauicounty.gov/Facilities; 1900 S Kihei Rd; P ♿) Athletes, skateboarders and toddlers who need to roam will appreciate this expansive seaside park. Sports facilities include tennis and basketball courts, ball fields and a skateboard park. Also on site are a playground, picnic pavilions, restrooms and showers. Although there is a small beach, behind the whale statue, a runoff ditch carries wastewater here after heavy rains so best swim elsewhere.

Activities

South Maui's top activities are water-based.

Stand-up paddle surfing (SUP) looks easy, and it is a learnable sport, but currents off Maui can carry you down the coast very quickly. Best to start with a lesson before renting a board.

Maui Dreams Dive Co DIVING

(Map p158; ☎808-874-5332; www.mauidreamsdiveco.com; 1993 S Kihei Rd, Island Surf Bldg; shore dives $89-169, boat dives $139-169; ⊙7am-6pm) Maui Dreams is a first-rate, five-star PADI operation specializing in shore dives. With this family-run outfit, a dive trip is like going out with friends. Nondivers, ask

South Kihei

about the introductory dive ($99), and to zoom around underwater, check out the scooter dive ($99 to $129). Also rents snorkel gear.

Maui Dive Shop DIVING
(Map p160; ☎808-879-3388; www.mauidiveshop.com; 1455 S Kihei Rd; 2-tank dives $139-179, snorkel rentals per day $9; ⏰7am-7pm) This is a good spot to rent or buy water-sports gear, including boogie boards, snorkels and wetsuits. The company provides free transportation from South Maui resorts to tour departure points. Stop by for a free brochure with a map spotlighting good snorkeling spots. This location also rents Jeep Wranglers and Mustang convertibles.

Stand Up Paddle Surf School SURFING
(Map p132; ☎808-579-9231; www.standuppaddlesurfschool.com; 185 Paka Pl; 90min lesson $199; ⏰8am-2pm) This SUP school is owned by champion paddle-surfer Maria Souza, who was also the first woman surfer to tow into the monster waves at Jaws. Small classes and safety are priorities, and the paddling location is determined by weather and water conditions. Classes fill quickly, so call a few days – or a week – ahead. Multiday and yoga SUP classes are also available.

Maui Wave Riders – Kihei SURFING
(Map p158; ☎808-875-4761; www.mauiwaveriders.com; 2021 S Kihei Rd; surfing & SUP lessons from $70; ⏰surf lessons from 7:30am, SUP lessons 7:30am; 👪) Offers two-hour surfing and 90-minute SUP lessons. Also rents surfboards and paddleboards. Located in central Kihei, across the street from Kalama Park and a short walk from the Cove, a beginner-friendly surf spot.

The Cove SURFING
(Map p158; S Kihei Rd) At the south end of Kalama Park, the shallow waters off this tiny park are great for beginners, with small waves that break right and left. It can get crowded. You can rent surfboards and sign up for lessons at shops across the street.

Surf Shack WATER SPORTS
(Map p158; ☎808-875-0006; www.surfshackmaui.com; 2960 S Kihei Rd, Mana Kai Maui; ⏰8am-5pm) Spending the day at gorgeous Keawakapu Beach? Stop here to rent snorkel sets ($7 per day), kayaks (half-day $35 to $50), surfboards (half-day $20 to $25) and SUP boards (half-day $45). Beach chairs and coolers also available.

Maui Yoga Path YOGA
(Map p158; ☎808-283-9771; www.mauiyogapath.com; 2960 S Kihei Rd, Mana Kai Maui; class $25;

North Kihei

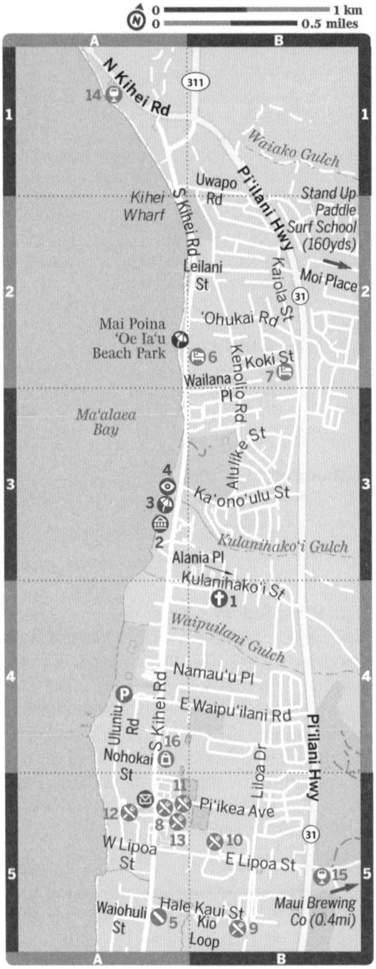

North Kihei

Sights

1 David Malo's Church B4
2 Hawaiian Islands Humpback Whale National Marine Sanctuary Headquarters A3
3 Kalepolepo Beach Park A3
4 Ko'ie'ie Fishpond A3

Activities, Courses & Tours

5 Maui Dive Shop A5

Sleeping

6 Nona Lani Cottages B2
7 Ocean Breeze Hideaway B2

Eating

8 Coconut's Fish Cafe A5
9 Eskimo Candy B5
10 Fabiani's Bakery & Pizza B5
11 Fork & Salad A5
Kihei Station Food Truck Park .... (see 11)
12 Nalu's South Shore Grill A5
Nutcharee's Authentic Thai Food .... (see 12)
13 Roasted Chiles A5
Tamura's Fine Wine & Liquors .... (see 10)

Drinking & Nightlife

14 Dina's Sandwitch A1
15 Sunsets Bar & Grill B5

Shopping

16 Yee's Orchard A4

beach yoga 7-8am, times vary for other classes) Take a morning yoga class beside stunning Keawakapu Beach. Open to all levels. Iyengar, vinyasa, yoga movement and private classes are also available.

South Maui Bicycles CYCLING

(Map p158; 808-874-0068; www.southmauibicycles.com; 1993 S Kihei Rd, Island Surf Bldg; per day $22-85, per week $99-350; 10am-6pm Mon-Sat) Rents top-of-the-line road bicycles, as well as basic around-town bikes and e-bikes. Bike lanes run along both the Pi'ilani Hwy and S Kihei Rd, but cyclists need to be cautious of inattentive drivers making sudden turns across lanes.

Tours

Blue Water Rafting RAFTING

(Map p158; 808-879-7238; www.bluewaterrafting.com; tours $41-115) In a hurry? Try the Molokini Express trip (adult/child $57/47) if you want to zip out to the crater, snorkel and be back within two hours.

An adventurous half-day trip heads southward on a motorized raft for snorkeling among sea turtles at remote coves along Maui's lava-rock coast, which is beyond La Perouse Bay. Trips depart from the Kihei boat ramp.

Festivals & Events

Kihei Fourth Fridays FAIR

(www.kiheifridays.com; 1279 S Kihei Rd, Azeka Mauka Shopping Center; 6-9pm 4th Fri of month;) Part of the **Friday Town Parties** (808-270-7710; www.mauifridays.com; Fri evenings;)

FREE series, this popular monthly festival draws locals with live music, food trucks, and arts and crafts.

World Whale Day CULTURAL
(www.mauiwhalefestival.org; 1900 S Kihei Rd, Kalama Park; mid-Feb;) Organized by the Pacific Whale Foundation, this family-friendly bash celebrates Maui's humpback whales with crafts, live music, food booths and environmental displays. Going for over 40 years, it's held at Kalama Park (p158) on a Saturday in mid-February.

Sleeping

Ocean Breeze Hideaway B&B $
(Map p132; 808-879-0657; www.hawaiibednbreakfast.com; 435 Kalalau Pl; r $149; P@) Alohas are warm at the Ocean Breeze, which has been thoughtfully run by owners Bob and Sande for 20 years – and they are a treasure trove of insider tips. Their low-key home, located in an easy-to-access residential neighborhood, has one comfortable guest room, with a king bed, refrigerator, A/C and private entrance.

★**Pineapple Inn Maui** INN $$
(808-298-4403; www.pineappleinnmaui.com; 3170 Akala Dr; r $209-219, cottage $295; P) One of South Maui's better deals, this inviting boutique property offers style and functionality with a personal touch, and it's less than a mile from the beach. The four rooms, which have ocean-view lanai (balcony) and private entrances, are as attractive as those at the exclusive resorts, but at a fraction of the cost. Rooms have kitchenettes, and the two-bedroom cottage comes with a full kitchen.

Kihei Kai Nani CONDO $$
(Map p158; 808-879-9088; www.kiheikainani.com; 2495 S Kihei Rd; 1 bedroom from $197; P) The welcoming staff is a highlight at this low-key property across the street from Kamaʻole Beach Park II (p153). Decor may be a little dated in some units, but the amenities at this low-rise condo complex rival more expensive properties. On-site are a large pool, a laundry room, shuffleboard, and barbecue grills and picnic tables – all fringed by colorful tropical landscaping.

★**Punahoa** CONDO $$
(Map p158; 808-879-2720; www.punahoabeach.com; 2142 Iliʻili Rd; studio $247, 1/2 bedroom $329/345, penthouse $324; P) Sip coffee, scan for whales, savor sunsets – it's hard to leave your lanai at Punahoa, a classy boutique condo where every unit has a clear ocean view. Tucked on a quiet side street, this 16-unit complex offers privacy and warm alohas. It's also next to a photogenic stretch of sand, Punahoa Beach, that's a favorite of turtles and surfers. Penthouse units have air-conditioning.

Cleaning fees from $125 per visit.

Nona Lani Cottages COTTAGE $$
(Map p132; 808-879-2497; www.nonalanicottages.com; 455 S Kihei Rd; cottages $309-340, r $235; P) Wooden cottages, cozy hammocks, picnic tables, swaying palms – this place looks like the tropical version of summer camp. Sporting recently refreshed interiors, the eight plantation-style cottages are compact but squeeze in a full kitchen, private lanai, living room with daybed and a bedroom with a queen bed, plus cable TV. Also offers four hotel-like rooms.

Kihei Surfside Resort CONDO $$
(Map p158; www.kiheisurfsideresort.com; 2936 S Kihei Rd; condo from $250; P) Tucked between the Kihei Coastal Trail (p155) and Keawakapu Beach (p153), with a fantastic view of the ocean, this six-story condo complex sports a bit of natty style – just look at that crisp, green lawn. Units are managed by a variety of management companies, and some individual owners. Photos, rates and contact information for each unit are on the Kihei Surfside website.

Mana Kai Maui CONDO $$$
(Map p158; 808-879-1561; www.manakaimaui.com; 2960 S Kihei Rd; r $290, 1/2 bedroom from $490/590; P) From her throne overlooking Keawakapu Beach, Mana Kai Maui has much to admire in her seaside kingdom. Guests can swim, snorkel and kayak in the ocean right outside the door. Sunset views from the beach – and rooms on the 7th and 8th floors – are some of the best in Kihei. The full-service restaurant here, 5 Palms (p164), is famous for its sunset happy hour.

Maui Coast Hotel HOTEL $$$
(Map p158; 808-874-6284; www.mauicoasthotel.com; 2259 S Kihei Rd; r/ste from $360/392; P@) One of just a handful of hotels in Kihei, the snazzy Maui Coast has a lot going for it – sharp, modern rooms and a fun poolside bar – but the daily resort fee of $25 is off-putting. The property is not on the beach, and it's more hotel than sprawling resort. The included local shuttle service is a nice touch.

Eating

Fork & Salad HEALTH FOOD $

(Map p160; ☎808-879-3675; www.forkandsaladmaui.com; 1279 S Kihei Rd, Azeka Mauka Shopping Center; mains $1-15; ⏰10:30am-9pm; 🌱) Local farms strut their stuff at this glossy salad emporium. Step up to the counter, choose a classic or chef-inspired salad – or build your own – and add a deliciously seasoned protein, from organic chicken to sustainable shrimp to seared ahi (yellowfin tuna). Ooh and ahh as staff toss it with Hawaiian-inspired dressings such as *liliko'i* (passion fruit) and mango. Sandwiches served too.

★ **Nalu's South Shore Grill** HAWAIIAN $

(Map p160; ☎808-891-8650; www.nalusmaui.com; 1280 S Kihei Rd, Azeka Makai Shopping Center; breakfast $10-14, lunch & dinner $9-17; ⏰8am-10pm; 🌱👪) This open-air eatery may sit in a strip mall, but the decor embraces all things Hawaiian, from the koa canoe hanging overhead to the enormous beach photos covering the walls. We also love the warm aloha spirit of the staff. Breakfasts are the showstoppers, from acai bowls to three-egg omelets to the vegetarian *loco moco*. The focus? Healthy, hearty and locally grown.

Tamura's Fine Wine & Liquors SEAFOOD $

(Map p160; ☎808-891-2420; www.tamurasfinewine.com; 91 E Lipoa St; fresh poke per lb $17.99; ⏰9:30am-8pm) What? Great *poke* (cubed, marinated raw fish) from a wine and liquor store? Yep, after browsing the aisles, which are well stocked with liquors, wines and beer, head to the tucked-away seafood counter for some of the island's best *poke*. Tamura's sells 11 different varieties.

808 Deli CAFE $

(Map p158; ☎808-879-1111; www.808deli.com; 2511 S Kihei Rd, Suite 102; breakfast $8-9, lunch $7-11; ⏰9am-5pm) With fresh breads, innovative spreads, gourmet hot dogs and 20 different sandwiches and paninis, this tiny sandwich shop across from Kam II is the place to grab a picnic lunch. For a spicy kick, try the roast beef with pepper jack and wasabi aioli.

Kihei Caffe CAFE $

(Map p158; ☎808-879-2230; www.kiheicaffe.com; 1945 S Kihei Rd, Kihei Kalama Village; mains $9-19; ⏰5am-3pm) Maybe it's the sneaky birds on the patio, or the quick-to-arrive entrees, or the hovering queue, but dining at this busy Kihei institution is not exactly relaxing. But that's part of the quirky charm. Order at the counter, fill your coffee cup at the thermos, snag a patio table and watch the breakfast burritos, veggie scrambles and *loco moco* (rice, fried egg and hamburger patty) flash by.

Da Kitchen Express HAWAIIAN $

(Map p158; ☎808-875-7782; www.dakitchen.com; 2439 S Kihei Rd, Rainbow Mall; mains $11-18; ⏰11am-9pm) Da Kitchen is da bomb. Come to this no-frills eatery for Hawaiian plate lunches done right. The local favorite is Da Lau Lau Plate (with steamed pork wrapped in taro leaves), but you won't go wrong with any choice, from charbroiled teriyaki chicken to the gravy-laden *loco moco*. We particularly liked the spicy *kalua* (pit-oven cooked) pork.

Cafe@LaPlage CAFE $

(Map p158; ☎808-875-7668; www.cafealaplage.com; 2395 S Kihei Rd, Dolphin Plaza; sandwiches $5-12; ⏰6:30am-5pm Mon-Sat, to 3pm Sun; 📶) They stack the sandwiches high at this small cafe and coffee shop. At breakfast, choose from five different bagel sandwiches or simply get your bagel slathered in cinnamon-honey butter. Lunchtime paninis include the Maui Melt, with turkey, bacon, pepper jack, avocados and jalapeños. Wi-fi is free.

Eskimo Candy SEAFOOD $

(Map p160; ☎808-891-8898; www.eskimocandy.com; 2665 Wai Wai Pl; mains $10-18; ⏰10:30am-7pm Mon-Fri; 👪) Wondering whether to order the seafood chowder? You should. This hearty treat primes the palate for the top-notch fresh seafood served in this busy fish market with a takeout counter. Raw-fish fanatics should home in on the *poke*, ahi wraps and fish tacos. The handful of tables fill quickly at lunchtime. Parents will appreciate the under-$9 kids' menu.

Kihei Station Food Truck Park FOOD TRUCK $

(Map p160; Pi'ikea Ave, near S Kihei Rd; mains $9-17; ⏰11am-6pm) If your group can't agree on a lunchtime restaurant, swing by this new food truck park behind the Azeka Mauka Center in north Kihei. A half-dozen or so food trucks serve up everything from burgers, BBQ, tacos and vegetarian dishes to coffee drinks, bubble tea and shave ice. The trucks surround a cluster of shaded outdoor tables.

Joy's Place SANDWICHES $

(Map p158; ☎808-879-9258; www.joysplacemauihawaii.com; 1993 S Kihei Rd; breakfast $8-10, sandwiches $8-10; ⏰7:30am-4pm Mon-Fri, 7:30am-2pm Sat, 8:30am-2pm Sun) You'll be greeted by staff when you enter this cozy and homespun cafe in the Island Surf Building. Listen to locals chitchat as you dig into healthy salads, wraps and sandwiches or carry your lunch across the street to Kalama Park.

Local Boys Shave Ice SWEETS $

(Map p158; ☎808-344-9779; www.localboysshaveice.com; 1941 S Kihei Rd, Kihei Kalama Village; small shave ice $5.50; ⊙10am-9pm) Load up on napkins at Local Boys, where they dish up hearty servings of shave ice drenched in a rainbow of sweet syrups. We like it tropical (banana, mango and 'shark's blood') with ice cream, Kaua'i cream and azuki beans. Cash only.

★ **Pa'ia Fish Market Southside** SEAFOOD $$

(Map p158; ☎808-874-8888; www.paiafishmarket.com; 1913 S Kihei Rd, Kihei Kalama Village; mains $10-25; ⊙11am-9:30pm) Word is out about this fantastic seafood joint, a spinoff from the popular Pa'ia Fish Market in the Upcountry. Across the street from Kalama Park, the open-air eatery serves *ono* (white-fleshed wahoo) and mahimahi burgers, fish and chips, and seafood pasta. Plate meals arrive with huge slabs of seasoned local fish and Cajun rice or home fries. It's pricey, but portions are big.

Expect a line at night.

★ **Café O'Lei** HAWAIIAN $$

(Map p158; ☎808-891-1368; www.cafeoleirestaurants.com; 2439 S Kihei Rd, Rainbow Mall; lunch $9-19, dinner $19-32; ⊙10:30am-3:30pm & 4:30-9:30pm) This strip-mall bistro looks ho-hum at first blush. But step inside: the sophisticated atmosphere, innovative Hawaii Regional Cuisine, honest prices and excellent service knock Café O'Lei into the fine-dining big league. For a tangy treat, order the blackened mahimahi with fresh papaya salsa. A sushi chef arrives at the sushi bar at 4:30pm (Tuesday to Saturday).

Famous martinis, too.

Fabiani's Bakery & Pizza ITALIAN $$

(Map p160; ☎808-874-0888; www.fabianis.com; 95 E Lipoa St; pastries $3-4, breakfast $5-14, lunch $10-17, dinner $14-24; ⊙7am-9pm) What puts the fab in Fabiani's? Definitely the prosciutto, mozzarella and arugula white pizza with truffle oil. Or maybe it's the linguini with sautéed clams. Or the chef-made pastries preening like celebrities as you walk in the door. Whatever your choice, you'll surely feel fabulous nibbling your meal inside this sparkling Italian eatery and pastry shop. There's also a rather nice bar.

Nutcharee's Authentic Thai Food THAI $$

(Map p160; ☎808-633-4840; www.nutcharees.com; 1280 S Kihei Rd, Azeka Makai Shopping Center; mains $14-21; ⊙11am-3pm & 5-9pm) Fans of Nutcharee Case's panang curry with fresh fish no longer have to drive to Hana to get their fix. She closed her beloved East Maui outpost a few years back and opened this restaurant soon after. Settle in for her acclaimed noodles and stir-fry dishes and a wide array of curries. Wine and beer available too.

Roasted Chiles MEXICAN $$

(Map p160; ☎808-868-4357; www.roastedchileshawaii.com; 1279 S Kihei Rd, Azeka Mauka Shopping Center; lunch $12-18, dinner $14-23; ⊙10am-9pm Mon-Sat) At most Mexican restaurants on Maui, the food is simply a buffer for the margaritas. But here? The margaritas are excellent, but so is the authentic Mexican cuisine, which is thoughtfully seasoned and pleasantly presented. Start with fresh guacamole or *ono* ceviche then take your pick of savory traditional dishes and numerous sauces, from the complex chocolate *mole* to the creamy green sauce.

Coconut's Fish Cafe SEAFOOD $$

(Map p160; ☎808-875-9979; www.coconutsfishcafe.com; 1279 S Kihei Rd, Azeka Mauka Shopping Center; mains $13-23; ⊙10am-9pm; 👪) For fresh, healthily prepared seafood in a family-friendly setting, try this chill spot in north Kihei. Order at the counter – we recommend the fish tacos – then settle in at one of the communal surfboard tables. All the fish is grilled and all ingredients are homemade (except the ketchup). Slightly overrated perhaps, but a solid choice nonetheless.

Cuatro LATIN AMERICAN $$$

(Map p158; ☎808-879-1110; www.cuatro808.com; 1881 S Kihei Rd, Kihei Town Center; mains $27-36; ⊙4-10pm) Come for the amazing spicy tuna nachos, stay for the Acapulco shrimp scampi, the Asian marinated grilled rib eye and the other impeccably flavored Latin American and Pacific Rim dishes. The place is small, so reservations are recommended. The nachos and other appetizers are 25% off during happy hour (4pm to 5pm). It's BYOB with a $10 corkage fee.

Sansei Seafood Restaurant & Sushi Bar JAPANESE $$$

(Map p158; ☎808-879-0004; www.sanseihawaii.com; 1881 S Kihei Rd, Kihei Town Center; appetizers $5-24, sushi $5-22, mains $24-65; ⊙5:30-10pm Sun-Wed, to 1am Thu-Sat) Maui is laid-back, but sometimes you have to plan ahead. Dinner at Sansei is one of those times – make a reservation or queue early for the sushi bar. The creative appetizer menu offers everything from a shrimp cake with ginger-lime chili butter to lobster-and-blue-crab ravioli. Fusion dishes include Japanese jerk chicken with garlic mashed potatoes and herb *beurre* fondue.

Self-Catering

Hawaiian Moons Natural Foods SUPERMARKET $

(Map p158; ☎808-875-4356; www.hawaiianmoons.com; 2411 S Kihei Rd, Kama'ole Beach Center; sandwiches $8-10; ⏰8am-9pm;) This natural foods market draws 'em in for its well-stocked hot and cold salad bars ($10-$11 per pound). The soups are so good you might see someone sipping straight from their bowl while checking out! Also sells fresh juices, organic coffee, smoothies, kombucha, acai bowls and sandwiches.

Foodland SUPERMARKET $

(Map p158; ☎808-879-9350; www.foodland.com; 1881 S Kihei Rd, Kihei Town Center; ⏰5am-1am) Handy supermarket known for its delicious *poke* bowls.

Drinking & Nightlife

Most bars in Kihei are across the street from the beach and have nightly entertainment. Kihei Kalama Village, aka the Bar-muda Triangle (or just the Triangle), is a lively place at night, packed with buzzy watering holes.

★5 Palms COCKTAIL BAR

(Map p158; ☎808-879-2607; www.5palmsrestaurant.com; 2960 S Kihei Rd, Mana Kai Maui; ⏰8am-11pm) For sunset cocktails beside the beach, this is the place. Arrive an hour before the sun goes down, because the patio bar, just steps from stunning Keawakapu Beach, fills quickly. During happy hour, selected sushi and an array of delicious appetizers are half price, with a one-drink minimum, while mai tais and margaritas are $8. Popular with tourists and locals alike.

Maui Brewing Co BREWERY

(☎808-213-3002; www.mauibrewingco.com; 605 Lipoa Pkwy, Maui Research & Technology Park; ⏰11am-11pm, tours 11:30am-4:30pm) Enormous windows draw your eyes toward West Maui at the glossy new restaurant and bar at Maui Brewing's Kihei production facility. Over 35 craft and seasonal beers are on offer, and the food menu shines with tasty farm-to-table pizzas and pub fare (mains $14-35). The adjacent taproom is open daily for pints, with beers flowing straight from holding tanks in the brewery.

Dog & Duck PUB

(Map p158; ☎808-875-9669; 1913 S Kihei Rd, Kihei Kalama Village; ⏰11am-2am Mon-Fri, from 8am Sat & Sun) This lively Irish pub with a welcoming vibe attracts a younger crowd. And yes, it has sports on TV, but it's not blaring from every corner. Decent pub grub goes along with the heady Guinness draft.

South Shore Tiki Lounge BAR

(Map p158; ☎808-874-6444; www.southshoretikilounge.com; 1913 S Kihei Rd, Kihei Kalama Village; ⏰11am-2am;) The drink maestros at this cozy tropical shack with a convivial lanai regularly win annual *MauiTime Weekly* awards for best bartenders. Live music daily from 4pm to 6pm. DJs and dancing nightly starting at 10pm.

What Ales You CRAFT BEER

(Map p158; ☎808-214-6581; www.whatalesyoumaui.com; 1913 S Kihei Rd, Kihei Kalama Village; ⏰11am-10pm Mon-Fri, from 8am Sat & Sun) In the Bar-muda Triangle, What Ales You serves 16 taps of cold craft beer, rotating daily. You'll also find wine and a short menu of appetizers, sandwiches and rice bowls.

Sunsets Bar & Grill BAR

(Map p160; ☎808-633-4220; www.sunsetsbarandgrill.com; 470 Lipoa Pkwy; ⏰10am-8pm) On a hill beside the Maui Nui Golf Course, this big-windowed watering hole is indeed a fine place to sip a beer while watching the sun go down. It's also rightfully renowned for its ahi *poke* nachos *pupu* (snacks), which fills a canoe-shaped bowl loaded with wontons, tortilla chips and *poke*.

Dina's Sandwitch PUB

(Map p132; ☎808-879-3262; 145 N Kihei Rd, Sugar Beach Resort; ⏰11am-10pm) The mai tais are handcrafted at this convivial, come-as-you-are locals' joint in north Kihei. For something decadent, try the Nutty Witches Tit – a scoop of mac-nut ice cream with Myers's Rum, vodka and banana liqueur. The walls are covered with $1 bills – thousands of dollars' worth according to Dina.

Shopping

Yee's Orchard FOOD

(Map p160; 1165 S Kihei Rd; ⏰11am-5pm Tue-Thu, Sat & Sun) For out-of-this-world mangoes from May through summer, pull over at this 60-year-old fruit stand just north of Longs Drugs. Also sells pineapples, bananas and fresh-cut papaya.

Kihei Kalama Village MARKET

(Map p158; ☎808-879-6610; www.kiheikalamavillage.com; 1941 S Kihei Rd; ⏲pavilion shops 10am-7pm) More than 40 shops, stalls and restaurants are clustered at this central shopping arcade. For fashionable women's island-wear, pop into **Mahina** (www.shop-mahina.com). Made-in-Hawaii jams, jellies and sauces are for sale in welcoming **Tutu's Pantry** (www.tutuspantry.com) – free samples are available.

Information

Kihei Police Station (☎808-244-6400; www.mauicounty.gov; 2201 Pi'ilani Hwy)

Longs Drugs (☎808-879-2033; www.cvs.com; 1215 S Kihei Rd; ⏲store 24hr, pharmacy 8am-9pm Mon-Fri, to 7pm Sat, 9am-6pm Sun) This convenience store, with a pharmacy, has one aisle loaded up with rubbah slippahs (flip-flops, yo).

Minit Medical Urgent Care (☎808-664-1454; www.minitmed.com; 1325 S Kihei Rd; ⏲8am-7pm Mon-Fri, to 6pm Sat, to 4pm Sun) This clinic accepts walk-in patients.

Post Office (Map p160; ☎808-879-1987; www.usps.com; 1254 S Kihei Rd; ⏲8:30am-4:30pm Mon-Fri, 9am-1pm Sat)

Getting There & Around

TO/FROM THE AIRPORT

Almost everyone rents a car at the airport (p309) in Kahului. Otherwise, expect to pay about $18 for shuttle service or $33 to $55 for a taxi, depending on your destination in Kihei. The airport is 10 miles from north Kihei and 16 miles from south Kihei.

A few rental car agencies can be found along N and S Kihei Rds. These are good options if you're looking for lower rates or a day-trip rental. **Kihei Rent A Car** (☎808-879-7257; www.kiheirentacar.com; 96 Kio Loop; per day/week from $35/175; ⏲7:30am-9pm) rents cars and 4WDs to those aged 21 and over, and includes free mileage. For the lowest rates, consider one of the older-model cars (which can be well worn!). The agency provides Kahului International Airport shuttle pickup and drop-off for rentals over five days.

Ride sharing with Uber or Lyft is available, and rates are about the same as a taxi, ranging from $25 to $38 per ride from the airport, depending on the Kihei destination.

BUS

The **Maui Bus** (☎808-871-4838; www.mauicounty.gov/bus; single ride $2, day pass $4, monthly pass $45) serves Kihei with two routes. Both operate hourly from around 6am to 8pm and cost $2.

Kihei Islander Connects Kihei with Wailea and Kahalui; stops include Kama'ole Beach Park III, Pi'ilani Village shopping center, and Uwapo Rd at S Kihei Rd.

Kihei Villager Primarily serves the northern half of Kihei, with eight stops along S Kihei Rd and at Pi'ilani Village shopping center and Ma'alaea.

Wailea

The golden-sand beaches in Wailea are the stuff of daydreams, famed for phenomenal swimming, snorkeling, sunbathing and consistently sunny skies.

With its tidy golf courses, protective privacy walls and discreet signage, Wailea itself looks like a members-only country club. South Maui's most elite haunt, it stands in sharp contrast to Kihei. Don't bother looking for gas stations or fast-food joints; this exclusive community is all about swank beachfront resorts and low-rise condo villas, with all the glitzy accessories.

If you're not staying here, say a loud *mahalo* (thank you) for Hawaii's beach-access laws that allow you to visit anyway, with dedicated public parking lots.

Beaches

Wailea's fabulous beaches begin at the southern end of Keawakapu Beach in Kihei and continue south toward Makena. All of the beaches that are backed by resorts have public access, with free parking, showers and restrooms. Posted signs mark the public access points. A small point separates Mokapu Beach and Ulua Beach, which share outdoor showers and restrooms.

Mokapu Beach BEACH

(☎808-879-4364; www.mauicounty.gov/Facilities; Haleali'i Place; P) The lovely Mokapu Beach is behind the Andaz Maui resort, on the northern side of a small point.

Ulua Beach BEACH

(☎808-879-4364; www.mauicounty.gov/Facilities; Haleali'i Pl; P) Snorkelers should head straight for Ulua, to the south of the point. The coral at the rocky outcrop on the right side of

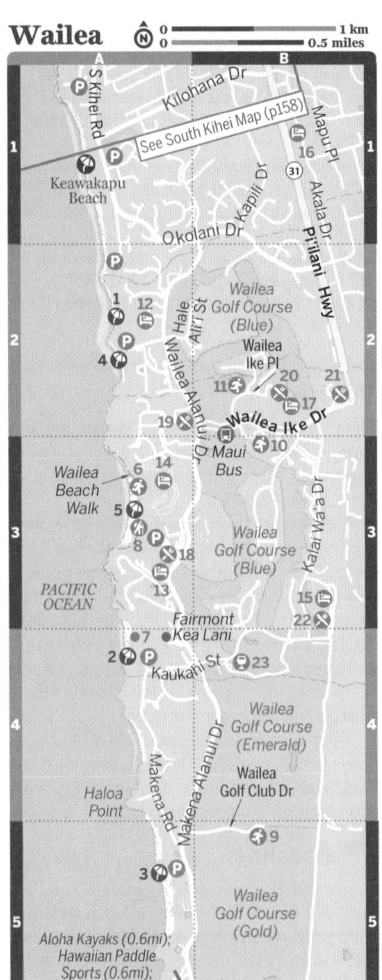

the beach offers Wailea's best easy-access snorkeling.

★**Wailea Beach** BEACH
(808-879-4364; www.mauicounty.gov/Facilities; off Wailea Alanui Dr; P) Sunbathe like a celebrity at this sparkling strand, which fronts the swish Grand Wailea and ever-posh Four Seasons resorts and offers a full menu of water activities. The beach slopes gradually, making it a good swimming spot. When it's calm, there's decent snorkeling around the rocky point on the southern end. Most afternoons there's a gentle shorebreak suitable for bodysurfing. Divers entering the water at Wailea Beach can follow an offshore reef that runs down to Polo Beach.

Polo Beach BEACH
(808-879-4364; www.mauicounty.gov/Facilities; Kaukahi St; P) In front of the Fairmont Kea Lani resort, Polo Beach is seldom crowded. When there's wave action, boogie boarders and bodysurfers usually find good shorebreaks here. When calm, the rocks to the north provide good snorkeling. At low tide, the lava outcropping at the southern end of the beach holds tide pools harboring spiny sea urchins and small fish.

Po'olenalena Beach BEACH
(Makena Alanui Dr; P) This long and lovely crescent-shaped beach, south of the resorts, is a favorite of local families on weekends. It's rarely crowded though, and the shallow, sandy bottom and calm waters make for excellent swimming. There's good snorkeling off both the southern and northern lava points. The parking lot is on Makena Alanui Dr, a half-mile south of its intersection with Makena Rd.

Activities

Wailea Golf Club GOLF
(808-875-7450; www.waileagolf.com; 100 Wailea Golf Club Dr; greens fee Gold & Emerald $149-250, Old Blue $125-200; varies, typically 7am-5pm) There are three championship courses in Wailea. The **Emerald course** is a tropical garden that consistently ranks at the top; the rugged **Gold course** takes advantage of volcanic landscapes; and the **Old Blue course** (808-879-2530; www.waileagolf.com; 100 Wailea Ike Dr) is marked by an open fairway and challenging greens.

Wailea Beach Walk WALKING
For the perfect sunset stroll, take the 1.3-mile shoreline path that connects Wailea's beaches and the resort hotels that front them. The undulating path winds above jagged lava points and back down to the sandy shore.

In winter this is a fantastic location for spotting humpback whales. On a good day you may be able to see more than a dozen of them frolicking offshore.

Wailea Tennis Club TENNIS
(808-879-1958; www.waileatennis.com; 131 Wailea Ike Pl; court fee per person $25, racket rental per day $10; 7am-6pm Mon-Fri, to 5pm Sat & Sun) Nicknamed 'Wimbledon West,' this award-winning complex has 11 Sportsmaster courts. Ninety-minute lessons are available

Wailea

Sights

1	Mokapu Beach	A2
2	Polo Beach	A4
3	Po'olenalena Beach	A5
4	Ulua Beach	A2
5	Wailea Beach	A3

Activities, Courses & Tours

6	Aqualani Beach & Ocean Recreation	A3
7	Hawaiian Sailing Canoe Adventures	A4
8	Wailea Beach Walk	A3
9	Wailea Golf Club	B5
10	Wailea Old Blue Clubhouse	B3
11	Wailea Tennis Club	B2

Sleeping

12	Andaz Maui	A2
13	Four Seasons Maui at Wailea	A3
14	Grand Wailea Resort Hotel & Spa	A3
15	Hotel Wailea	B3
16	Pineapple Inn Maui	B1
17	Residence Inn Maui Wailea	B2

Eating

18	Ferraro's	A3
19	Island Gourmet Kitchen	A2
	Ka'ana Kitchen	(see 12)
	Lineage	(see 19)
20	Matteo's Osteria	B2
21	Monkeypod Kitchen	B2
	Pita Paradise	(see 21)
22	Restaurant at Hotel Wailea	B3

Drinking & Nightlife

23	Mulligan's on the Blue	B4
	Pint & Cork	(see 19)
	Red Bar at Gannon's	(see 9)

Entertainment

	Four Seasons Maui at Wailea	(see 13)

Shopping

	Shops at Wailea	(see 19)

(clinic/private $40/152). Courts also open for pickleball – a tennis, badminton and ping-pong combo – for $15 per person.

Aqualani Beach & Ocean Recreation WATER SPORTS
(808-283-0384; www.aqualanibeach.com; 3850 Wailea Alanui Dr, Grand Wailea Resort; snorkel/boogie board per day $20/20, kayak/SUP per hour $55/55; 7am-5pm) On the beach behind the Grand Wailea, Aqualani rents all the gear you need for ocean fun. Paddle-free aqua gliders are also available for rent for $75 per hour with a land lesson included.

Tours

Hawaiian Sailing Canoe Adventures CANOEING
(808-281-9301; www.mauisailingcanoe.com; adult/child 4-14yr $179/129; tours 9am;) Learn about Native Hawaiian traditions and snorkel beside sea turtles on a 2½-hour trip aboard a Hawaiian-style outrigger canoe. Tours depart from Polo Beach.

Festivals & Events

Maui Film Festival FILM
(www.mauifilmfestival.com; mid-Jun) Hollywood celebs swoop in for this five-day extravaganza in mid-June. Join the stars under the stars at various Wailea locations, including the open-air 'Celestial Theater' on a nearby golf course and – in some years – the free 'Toes-in-the-Sand Cinema' on Wailea Beach.

Sleeping

★ **Four Seasons Maui at Wailea** RESORT $$$
(808-874-8000; www.fourseasons.com/maui; 3900 Wailea Alanui Dr; r/ste from $779/1599; P) From the plush lobby lounge with its framed ocean views to the accommodating staff and the inclusive pricing (no resort fee), the joy is in the details and the warm aloha spirit at this impressive getaway. All 383 rooms and suites are furnished with understated island elegance. Marble-floored bathrooms have lots of counter space and a choice of piped-in music.

Andaz Maui RESORT $$$
(808-573-1234; www.hyatt.com; 3550 Wailea Alanui Dr; r from $520; P) As you glide down the portico to the chic and airy lobby – home to a posh sandbox with lounge chairs and intricate sand art – it feels as if you're beginning a grand adventure. The impression continues in the uncluttered rooms: low beds, simple wooden furniture, plantation shutters. It's a beachfront base camp for your cushy tropical expedition. The terraced swimming pools are lovely.

Hotel Wailea HOTEL $$$
(808-874-0500; www.hotelwailea.com; 555 Kaukahi St; 1-bedroom ste from $529; P)

With its hilltop perch, lush grounds and striking stovepipe lobby, the Hotel Wailea just needs a frame for artistic completion. The 72 roomy suites gleam with elegant but inviting beach-modern style, from the coral and limestone walls to the bleached oak floors. Rooms at this adults-only hotel, the only Relais & Châteaux luxury property in Hawaii, come with kitchenettes, microwaves and mini-refrigerators.

Grand Wailea Resort Hotel & Spa RESORT **$$$**
(808-875-1234; www.grandwailea.com; 3850 Wailea Alanui Dr; r/ste from $699/1599; P ❄ @) For an exuberant, join-the-fun experience, this is the place. The elegant *joie de vivre* extends from the oceanside fountain to the million-dollar artwork to the guest rooms decked out in Italian marble. But it's not all highbrow. The resort, part of the Hilton's Waldorf Astoria line, boasts elaborate water-world wonders: an awesome series of nine interconnected pools with swim-through grottoes and towering waterslides.

Residence Inn Maui Wailea HOTEL **$$$**
(808-891-7460; www.marriott.com; 75 Wailea Ike Dr; ste from $474; P @) Rooms pop with bright accents – just look at those turquoise pillows – and hip modern style at this all-suites hotel up the hill from the Shops at Wailea. With kitchens, separate sitting areas and furnished balconies, rooms work well for extended-stay travelers seeking condo-style functionality. Amenities include a communal fire pit, outdoor grills and a spacious pool area.

Eating

Island Gourmet Kitchen DELI **$**
(808-874-5055; www.islandgourmethawaii.com; 3750 Wailea Alanui Dr, Shops at Wailea; breakfast mains $6-14, lunch & dinner mains $7-20; 6:30am-9pm) Tucked inside the Island Gourmet Market, this new deli is a great quick stop for pre-made and made-to-order takeout. Breakfast offerings, which are available all day, include omelets, pancakes, burritos and *huevos rancheros,* while the lunch and dinner options cover local favorites such as garlic shrimp and *kalua* pork plates, as well as pizza, sushi and fried chicken.

★ **Monkeypod Kitchen** PUB FOOD **$$**
(808-891-2322; www.monkeypodkitchen.com; 10 Wailea Gateway Pl, Wailea Gateway Center; lunch $16-30, dinner $16-50; 11am-11pm, happy hour 3-5:30pm & 9-11pm;) Happy hours are crowded but convivial at this ever-popular venture from chef Peter Merriman, where the staff, your fellow drinkers and the 36 craft beers and ciders on tap keep the alohas real. The gourmet pub grub comes with a delicious Hawaiian spin and typically incorporates organic and local ingredients, including Maui Cattle burgers and plenty of Upcountry veggies.

Lineage HAWAIIAN **$$**
(808-879-8800; www.lineagemaui.com; 3750 Wailea Alanui Dr, Shops at Wailea; small plates $7-15, mains $18-22; 5-11pm) The decor at this new venture from *Top Chef* favorite and restaurateur Sheldon Simeon may be modern and spare, but the hospitality is warm, old-school Hawaiian. Simeon stepped back from the kitchen in 2020, and new executive chef MiJin Kang Toride has created a menu that reflects her Korean heritage, with Chinese dishes as well. The Korean fried chicken comes sweet or spicy.

Matteo's Osteria ITALIAN **$$**
(808-891-8466; www.matteosmaui.com; 161 Wailea Ike Pl; dinner $18-44; bar only happy hour 3-5pm Mon-Fri, 4-5pm Sat & Sun, dinner 5-9:30pm) With more than 50 wines available by the glass, handmade pastas and pizza, and impeccable service, it's no surprise that Matteo's is a top pick in Wailea, even if it lacks ocean views. Savor a white pizza topped with cremini mushrooms, arugula, bresaola and truffle oil, or dig into wide-ribbon pappardelle with braised lamb, tomato ragù and caramelized vegetables. Fresh seafood mains available too.

Pita Paradise MEDITERRANEAN **$$**
(808-879-7177; www.pitaparadisehawaii.com; 34 Wailea Gateway Pl, Wailea Gateway Center; lunch $11-22, dinner $20-34; 11am-9:30pm) Although this Greek taverna sits in a strip mall with no ocean views, the inviting patio, the townscape mural and the tiny white lights – not to mention the succulent Mediterranean chicken pita – banish any locational regrets. Owner John Arabatzis catches his own fish, which are served in everything from pita sandwiches at lunch to grilled kabobs at dinner.

★ **Restaurant at Hotel Wailea** HAWAII REGIONAL **$$$**
(808-879-2224; www.hotelwailea.com/rhw; 555 Kaukahi St; mains $39-62; 5-9:30pm) Sunsets put on an astounding performance at this romantic hilltop hideaway, the only Relais & Châteaux restaurant in Hawaii. Helmed by

chef Zach Sato, a Maui native, the kitchen artfully presents a short but exquisite line-up of locally inspired seafood and meat dishes, all enhanced by fresh regional produce and a global array of flavors.

Ferraro's ITALIAN **$$$**
(808-874-8000; www.fourseasons.com/maui; 3900 Wailea Alanui Dr, Four Seasons Maui at Wailea; lunch $21-31, mains dinner $39-60; 11:30am-4pm & 5:30-9pm) No other place in Wailea comes close to this breezy restaurant for romantic seaside dining. Lunch features light options, such as an ahi wrap with avocado and Maui onions, and a seafood Cobb salad with lobster, prawns and seared ahi. Dinner gets more serious, showcasing a rustic Italian menu, plus meat and seafood dishes.

Ka'ana Kitchen HAWAIIAN **$$$**
(808-573-1234; www.hyatt.com; 3550 Wailea Alanui Dr, Andaz Maui; breakfast buffet $49, dinner $16-59; breakfast 6:30-11am, dinner 5:30-9pm) Ka'ana means 'to share,' and Maui's bounty is shared in high style at this chic spot at the Andaz. At breakfast, the buffet will keep you nibbling fruit, bread, cheese and cured fish and meats all morning. Locally sourced produce and seafood dishes fill the dinner menu, and they are prepared with global seasonings and cooking methods, keeping the selections creative.

Drinking & Nightlife

★ **Pint & Cork** BAR
(808-727-2038; www.thepintandcork.com; 3750 Wailea Alanui Dr, Shops at Wailea; noon-2am) This chic gastropub and wine bar would look right at home in Manhattan or Los Angeles, but the vibe is way more welcoming. And we hear it's a favorite with service-industry crowds looking for late-night noshes and libations. Big TVs overlook the 40ft soapstone bar, keeping sports fans happy. Opens early for games during football season, with a Bloody Mary bar.

Mulligan's on the Blue IRISH PUB
(808-874-1131; www.mulligansontheblue.com; 100 Kaukahi St; noon-10pm Tue-Sat, from 2pm Sun) Rising above the golf course, this open-air bar offers entertainment nightly, with anything from a seven-piece dance band to an eclectic dinner show to a lively magician to Celtic music. It's also a good place to quaff an ale while enjoying the distant ocean view, or catching a game on one of the 14 TVs. Opens early for big games.

REEF-SAFE SUNSCREEN: ZINC OR TITANIUM ONLY

Heading into the ocean to snorkel? Check your sunscreen bottle. Or better yet, check the label at the store before you buy it. Scientists have determined that many ingredients found in today's sunscreens are, along with other factors, killing coral reefs. What's safe? Zinc oxide and titanium dioxide sunscreens. As posted by the Department of Land & Natural Resources (DLNR) at 'Ahihi-Kina'u Natural Area Reserve, avoid sunscreens with this list of coral-destroying ingredients: oxybenzone, octinozate, avobenzone/avobenzine, homosalate, octisalate, octocrylene and ethylhexyl methoxycinnamate. For more information, check out the DLNR video at http://vimeo.com/180382413 or visit the Hawaii DLNR website http://dlnr.hawaii.gov.

You'll find reef-safe sunscreens at many surf shops across Maui.

Red Bar at Gannon's COCKTAIL BAR
(808-875-8080; www.gannonsrestaurant.com; 100 Wailea Golf Club Dr; 11am-9pm, happy hour 3-8:30pm) Everyone looks sexier when they're swathed in a sultry red glow. Come to this chic spot at happy hour for impressive food and drink specials, as well as attentive bartenders and stellar sunsets. The bar is located inside Gannon's, Bev Gannon's restaurant at the Gold and Emerald golf courses' clubhouse.

Entertainment

Four Seasons Maui at Wailea LIVE MUSIC
(808-874-8000; www.fourseasons.com/maui; 3900 Wailea Alanui Dr; 5-11pm) The lobby lounge has Hawaiian music nightly from 5pm to 11pm, with hula performances at sunset.

Shopping

Shops at Wailea MALL
(808-891-6770; www.theshopsatwailea.com; 3750 Wailea Alanui Dr; 9:30am-9pm;) This outdoor mall has dozens of restaurants, galleries and stores, with many shops flashing designer labels such as Louis Vuitton and Gucci, but there are solid island choices, too. Store hours may vary slightly from mall hours. Parking is free the first hour then $3 per half-hour. Also free for three additional hours with a $25 validated purchase.

Information

Urgent Care Wailea Makena (808-281-6580; www.urgentcarewaileamakena.com; 100 Wailea Ike Dr; 8am-8pm) Urgent care closest to Wailea's resorts. Next to Manoli's Pizza.

Getting There & Around

The **Maui Bus** (808-871-4838; www.mauicounty.gov) operates the Kihei Islander between Wailea and Kahului hourly until 8:27pm. The first bus picks up passengers on Wailea Ike Dr, just east of Shops at Wailea (p169), at 6:27am and runs north along S Kihei Rd, with a side trip to Pi'ilani Village shopping center, then continues to Queen Ka'ahumanu Center. For Lahaina, pick up the Kihei Villager at Pi'ilani Village, which travels to Ma'alaea. There, transfer to the Lahaina Islander. Fare is $2 per bus ride.

If you plan to do a lot of sightseeing, consider renting a car at the airport or at one of the Wailea resorts, which may have a rental-car desk and a small fleet on-site. Kihei Rent A Car (p165) in nearby Kihei is also an option.

Makena

Unfurling just south of well-manicured Wailea, Makena looks and feels a bit wild, like a territorial outpost that hasn't quite been tamed. It's also a perfect setting for aquatic adventurers who want to escape the crowds, offering primo snorkeling, kayaking and bodysurfing, plus pristine coral, reef sharks, dolphins and loads of sea turtles. And with the closure of the Makena Beach & Golf Resort, the vibe got even wilder – although heavy construction indicates that major changes are afoot.

The beaches are magnificent. The king of them all, Big Beach (Oneloa Beach), is an immense sweep of glistening sand and a prime sunset-viewing locale. The secluded cove at neighboring Little Beach is Maui's most popular nude beach – you *will* see bare buns. Together these beaches form **Makena State Park** (Maui District Office 808-984-8109; http://dlnr.hawaii.gov/dsp/parks/maui; Makena Rd; parking $5; parking gates 7am-7:45pm; P), but don't be misled by the term 'park,' as they remain in a natural state, with no facilities except for a couple of pit toilets and picnic tables. And those rumors about the nude Sunday-evening drum circle? Well...

PANIOLO ROOTS

Sitting beneath the slopes of Upcountry's 'Ulupalakua Ranch, Makena was once a *paniolo* village, home to Hawaiian cowboys who corralled cattle at the landing and loaded them onto barges bound for Honolulu slaughterhouses. To catch a glimpse of Makena's roots, stop at the **Keawala'i Congregational Church** (808-879-5557; www.keawalai.org; 5300 Makena Rd), just south of Makena Landing.

Beaches

Pack your beach gear and your picnic for the sandy beaches stretching along the Makena coast. These yellow strands are launchpads for kayaking, snorkeling and diving, but you won't find much commercial support in this remote landscape – just a few vans for the kayaking tours, plus a handful of food trucks and coconut stands.

Head to Big Beach (p171) at Makena State Park if you prefer to swim with lifeguards.

Makena Bay BAY

(Makena Landing Rd; P) Want to kayak along the coast? Then drop into this pretty bay. There's no better place on Maui for kayaking – as you might surmise from the collection of kayak-tour vans parked here every morning. When seas are calm, snorkeling is good along the rocks at the southern side of **Makena Landing**, the boat launch that's the center of the action. Makena Bay is also a good place for shore dives; divers should head to the north side of the bay.

Kayakers should paddle south along the lava coastline to Malu'aka Beach, where green sea turtles abound. Kayak-snorkel-tour operators meet just south of the landing for trips. South Pacific Kayaks (p172) will deliver pre-reserved kayaks here for rental at 6:45am (single/double $45/65). There are no kayak shops on-site.

Malu'aka Beach BEACH

(Makena Rd; P) Dubbed 'Turtle Beach,' this golden swath of sand behind the closed Makena Beach & Golf Resort is popular with snorkelers and kayakers hoping to glimpse the surprisingly graceful sea turtles, which feed along the coral and often swim within a few feet of snorkelers. Terrific coral is about 100yd out, and the best action is at the southern end of the beach. Come on a calm day – this one kicks up with a little wind, and when it's choppy you won't see anything.

Makena to La Perouse Bay

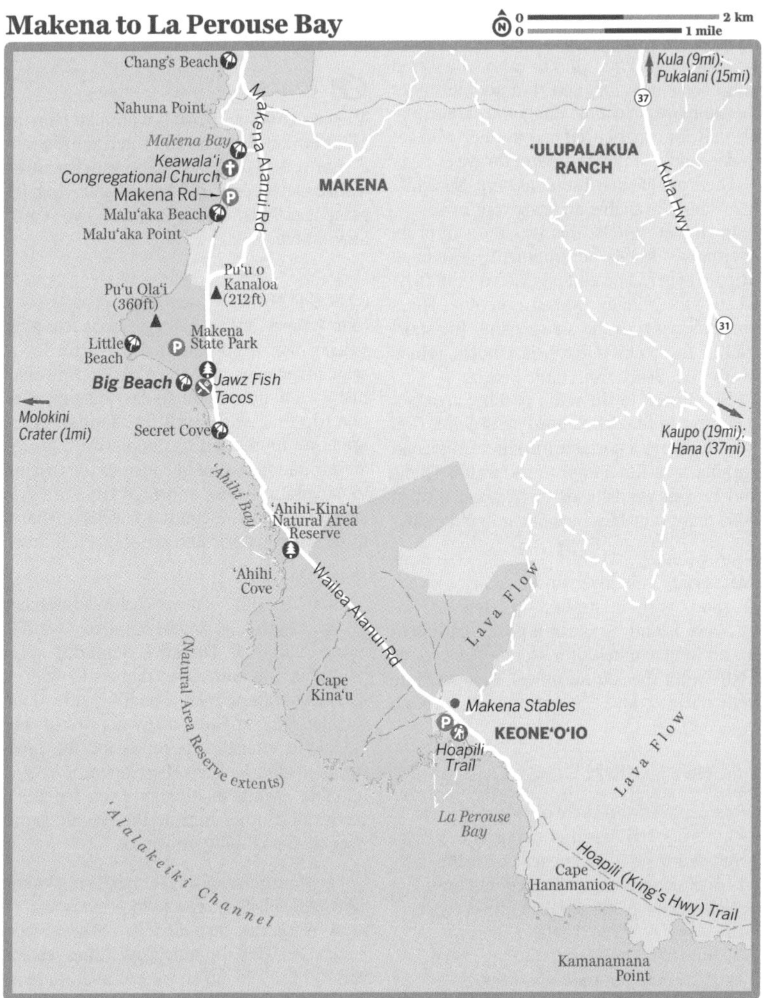

Little Beach BEACH

(Pu'u Ola'i Beach; Map p182; http://dlnr.hawaii.gov/dsp/parks/maui; Makena Rd; parking $5; parking gates 7am-7:45pm; P) Those folks with the coolers and umbrellas, walking north from the sandy entrance to Big Beach? They're heading to Little Beach, which is part of Makena State Park. Also known as Pu'u Ola'i Beach, this cozy strand is au naturel. Nudity is officially illegal, though enforcement is at the political whim of the day. The beach is hidden by a rocky outcrop that juts out from Pu'u Ola'i, the cinder hill marking Big Beach's northern end. Take the short but steep trail over the outcropping.

Little Beach fronts a sandy cove that usually has a gentle shorebreak ideal for bodysurfing and boogie boarding. When the surf's up, you'll find plenty of local surfers here as well. When the water's calm, snorkeling is good along the rocky point. For parking, use the northern lot at Big Beach.

★ **Big Beach** BEACH

(Oneloa Beach; www.dlnr.hawaii.gov/dsp/parks/maui; Makena Rd; parking $5; parking gates 7am-7:45pm; P) The crowning glory of Makena State Park, this untouched beach is arguably the finest on Maui. In Hawaiian it's called Oneloa, literally 'Long Sand.' And indeed the golden sands stretch for the better part of a mile and are as broad as they come. The waters are a beautiful turquoise. When they're calm, you'll find kids boogie boarding here, but at other times the shorebreaks can be dangerous and suitable only for experienced bodysurfers, who get tossed wildly in the transparent waves.

There are lifeguard stations here. No drinking water is available, so bring your own.

In the late 1960s, this was the site of an alternative-lifestyle encampment nicknamed 'Hippie Beach.' The tent city lasted until 1972, when police finally evicted everyone. For a sweeping view of the shore, climb the short trail to the rocky outcrop just north, which divides Big Beach from Little Beach.

The turnoff to the main parking area is a mile beyond the closed Makena Beach & Golf Resort. There's a portable toilet here. A second parking area lies 440yd to the south. Thefts and broken windshields are a possibility, so don't leave valuables in your car in either lot.

Secret Cove BEACH

(Makena Rd) This lovely, postcard-size swath of sand, with a straight-on view of Kaho'olawe island, is worth a peek – although it's no longer much of a secret. The cove is 440yd after the southernmost Makena State Park parking lot. The entrance is through an opening in a lava-rock wall just south of house No 6900.

SUNSET DRUM CIRCLE

The sunset drum circle on Sunday nights at Little Beach isn't much of a secret anymore. Just check out all the online footage – including a photo from ABC News – of Aerosmith's Steven Tyler banging a drum on the sand here. We hear he has a house nearby. The scene is pretty chill, but be warned: about 10% of the crowd is walking around naked and many of these folks are not shy about strutting their stuff. But most everyone is there for the same things: the surf, the sand and the sunset. And maybe some pot brownies. The fire dancing starts after the sun goes down. If you're feeling groovy, check it out. Get here an hour or two before sunset to snag a good spot on the narrow beach. And bring a headlamp. The trail back, which twists over a lava outcrop, is short but it's also steep and rocky. So far, state authorities have kept their distance, but they could shut it all down at any time. Walk this way...

Tours

Makena Landing (p170) is a popular starting point for kayak tours, and you can even take a **mermaid** (808-495-8919; www.hawaiimermaidadventures.com; 200 Nohea Kai Dr, Hyatt Regency Maui Resort & Spa; classes 7am;) lesson here.

Hawaiian Paddle Sports CANOEING

(808-442-6436; www.hawaiianpaddlesports.com; Makena Landing; outrigger canoe tour $159; tours 7am;) Snorkel in Turtle Town, scan for whales and learn about Hawaiian history and culture on an easy outrigger canoe trip that works well for families. There are never more than six paddlers in a group. Strong paddlers should consider the trip out to Molokini. Kayak and SUP trips are also available, and the company website shares interesting historic and eco-themed tidbits.

Aloha Kayaks KAYAKING

(808-270-3318; www.alohakayaksmaui.com; Makena Landing; adult/child 5-9yr from $85/60; tour 7:15am) For an eco-minded snorkel-kayak trip with an enthusiastic team of owner-operators, take a paddle with Aloha Kayaks. The mission of owners Griff and Peter? To educate guests about the environment and to keep their operations sustainable – while making sure you see green turtles and other marine life. Whale sightings are a possibility in winter.

South Pacific Kayaks & Outfitters KAYAKING

(808-875-4848; www.southpacifickayaks.com; kayak rental/tour from $45/74; kayak tours 7:15am;) This top-notch operation leads a variety of kayak-and-snorkel tours from Makena Landing (p170). Most tours tours leave at 7:15am daily, with a few also leaving at 10:30am Monday through Friday. Surfing and SUP lessons are also available, while windsurfing and kitesurfing lessons are offered at Kanaha Beach Park (p129) in Kahului.

Eating

Vendors with cold coconuts, pineapples and other fruit are sometimes found along Makena Alanui Dr near Big Beach.

Jawz Fish Tacos FOOD TRUCK $

(www.jawztacosmaui.com; Makena State Park; snacks $5-13; 10am-5:30pm) Get your beach snacks – tacos, burritos, shave ice – at this

OFF THE BEATEN TRACK

LA PEROUSE BAY

Earth and ocean merge at La Perouse Bay with a raw, desolate beauty that's almost eerie. Historians originally thought Maui's last volcano eruption occurred in 1790, but recent analysis indicates the lava flow occurred about 200 to 300 years earlier. Before the blast, the ancient Hawaiian village of Keone'o'io flourished here, and its remains – mainly house and heiau (temple) platforms – are scattered among the lava patches.

In 1786, renowned French explorer Jean François de Galaup La Pérouse became the first Westerner to land on Maui. As he sailed into the bay here, scores of Hawaiian canoes came out to greet him. A monument to the explorer is at the end of the road at La Perouse Bay.

From the volcanic shoreline, look for pods of spinner dolphins in the bay early in the day. Strong offshore winds and rough waters here rule out swimming, but the land is fascinating to explore.

Located just before the road ends, **Makena Stables** (808-879-0244; www.makenastables.com; 8299 Makena Rd; 90min trail rides $170-195; 8am-6pm) offers a morning horseback ride and a sunset tour. Both travel along the rocky lava coast and climb up into the ranchlands. Must be at least 13 years old to ride.

food truck at the back of the northernmost Big Beach parking lot.

Beyond Makena

Makena Rd turns adventurous after Makena State Park, continuing for three narrow miles through the lava flows of 'Ahihi-Kina'u Natural Area Reserve before dead-ending at La Perouse Bay.

Ahihi-Kina'u Natural Area Reserve NATURE RESERVE
(808-984-8100; http://dlnr.hawaii.gov; Makena Rd; 5:30am-7:30pm; P) Although scientists haven't been able to pinpoint the exact date, Maui's last lava flow probably spilled down to the sea here between 1480 and 1600 CE, shaping 'Ahihi Bay and Cape Kina'u. Today, the jagged lava coastline and the pristine waters fringing it have been recognized as a unique marine habitat and designated a reserve. Thanks in part to the prohibition on fishing here, the snorkeling is incredible but getting overcrowded. Consider coming for just the scenic drive. Obey all regulations and respect the fragile surroundings.

A few snorkelers head to the little roadside cove 175yd south of the first reserve sign. There is no parking here. Drive 350yd past the cove and look for a large parking lot on the right. A roadside path leads from the lot back to the cove, but note that the cove is not your best option. Instead, stop by the covered pavilion with the interpretive signage, which discusses the coral reefs here, and follow the coastal footpath south from the pavilion for five minutes to a black-sand beach with fantastic coral and clear water. Although this area, known informally as the Dumps, used to attract few visitors, the secret is out. Get here well before 9am to nab a decent parking spot – and maybe some solitude. The area now attracts up to 500 people per day.

To snorkel, enter the water from the left side of the beach, where access is easy and recommended by reserve officials. Look for the 'fish' signpost, which marks the entrance point. Snorkel in a northerly direction and you'll immediately be over coral gardens teeming with an amazing variety of fish. Huge rainbow parrotfish abound here, and it's not unusual to see turtles and the occasional reef shark.

A sign at the parking area reminds snorkelers to check their sunscreens before entering the water. Many suntan lotions contain ingredients that are fatal to reefs. Zinc oxide and titanium dioxide are safe.

Large sections of the 1238-acre reserve are closed to visitors, which allows the Department of Land & Natural Resources (www.dlnr.hawaii.gov) to protect the fragile environment from tourist wear and tear, and to develop a long-term protection plan. Visitation in the open areas is permitted between 5:30am and 7:30pm.

AT A GLANCE

POPULATION
Pa'ia: 2670

HEIGHT OF WAVES AT PE'AHI
30–80ft

BEST INDIE COFFEE SHOP
Grandma's Coffee House (p196)

BEST MALASADAS
Komoda Store & Bakery (p191)

BEST LOCAL MARKET
Mana Foods (p187)

WHEN TO GO

May–Jul Upcountry Ag & Farm Fair in late May or early June; Paniolo Parade in Makawao in July.

Sep–Oct Kula Fest in September; Halloween activities at Kula Farm in October.

Nov–Mar Big wave action at Pe'ahi in winter; holiday events in December.

Surfboards, Pa'ia (p177)

North Shore & Upcountry

Wild, lush and sometimes posh, this region of Maui holds extraordinary variety. In a half-hour drive you can ascend from the beaches of the North Shore (among them the world's windsurfing capital) through the jungle of the lower slopes, and emerge into open Upcountry hills, where cowboys still roam the range and farmers work Maui's garden belt. Communities change accordingly. The hip surfer town of Pa'ia gives way to Makawao's Old West architecture, which dissolves into a handful of stores in mud-on-boots Keokea, after which the road rolls on to eternity – and maybe, we've heard, to Oprah's house. The region begs for a lazy country drive, but the adventurous have plenty of activities too, including ziplining, paragliding and mountain biking.

INCLUDES

North Shore Highlights

1 Pa'ia (p177)
Sunbathing on the wide sandy strand at HA Baldwin Beach Park, and enjoying a bird's-eye view of expert windsurfers and kiteboarders riding the waves at Ho'okipa Beach Park & Overlook.

2 Makawao Forest Reserve (p190)
Exploring moody forest trails that wind through thick stands of pine and eucalyptus.

3 Hali'imaile General Store (p189)
Savoring cocktails made with locally sourced ingredients along with local Paniolo ribs or the catch of the day.

4 Hawaii Sea Spirits Organic Farm & Distillery (p193)
Learning how master distillers create fine spirits, then sampling the results of their labors.

5 Ali'i Kula Lavender (p194)
Following fragrant pathways through this lavender farm, then taking in the soaring views and trying lavender coffee on the pretty lanai (veranda).

6 Surfing Goat Dairy (p193)
Sampling all kinds of chèvre cheese, plus incredibly good goat-cheese chocolates, at this off-the-beaten-track farm.

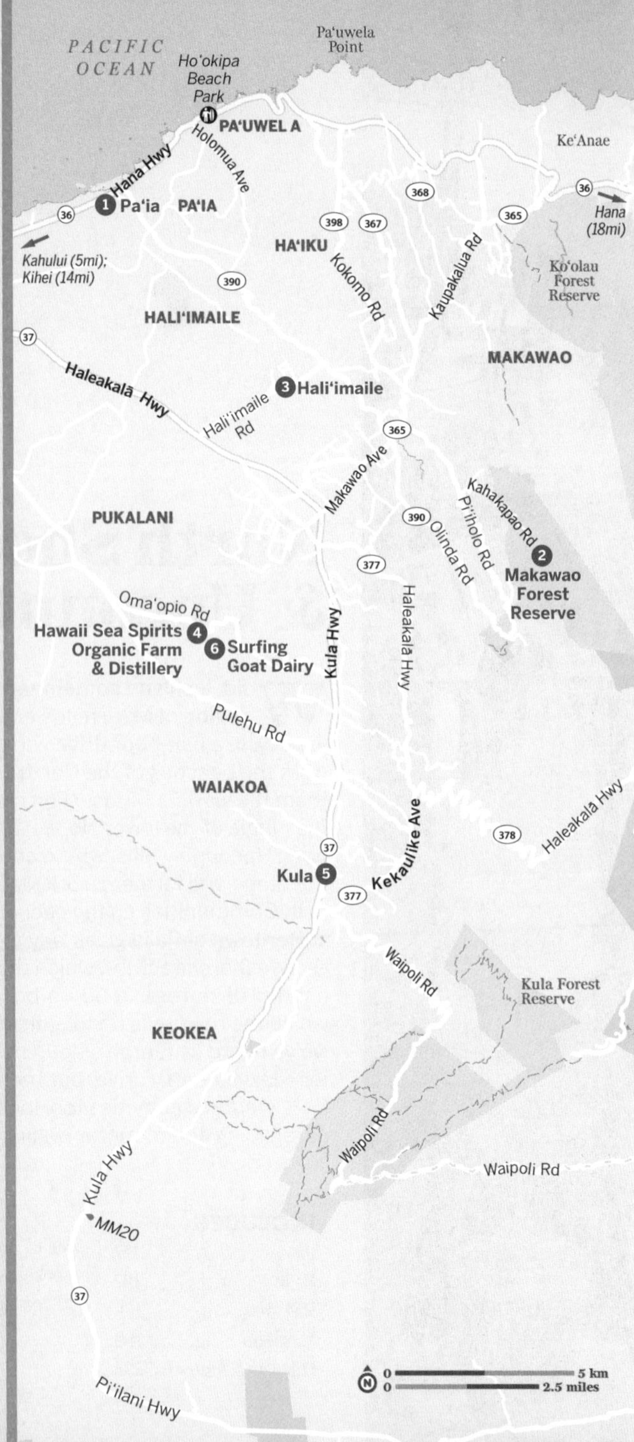

Pa'ia

An eclectic mix of surfers and soul-seekers clusters in Pa'ia, also known as Maui's hippest burg. Once a thriving plantation town of 10,000 residents, it declined during the 1950s when the local sugar mill closed. Then, like some other well-known sugar towns (eg Hanapepe on Kaua'i, and Honoka'a on Hawai'i, the Big Island), Pa'ia successfully reinvented itself. First came an influx of paradise-seeking hippies attracted by low rents. Next came windsurfers attracted by Ho'okipa Beach. Then came the tourists.

Today the town's aging, colourful wooden storefronts house a broad array of indie businesses facing a constant stream of traffic. It still feels like a dusty outpost at times, and that's all part of the allure.

Beaches

Ho'okipa Beach Park & Overlook BEACH

(Map p182; ☎808-572-8122; www.mauicounty.gov/facilities; Hana Hwy, Mile 9; ⏲7am-7pm; P) Ho'okipa is to daredevil windsurfers what Everest is to climbers. It reigns supreme as the world's premier windsurfing beach, with strong currents, dangerous shore breaks and razor-sharp coral offering the ultimate challenge. This is also one of Maui's prime surfing spots. While the action in the water is usually only suitable for pros, intermediate surfers can enjoy tamer days, and a lookout point on the eastern side of the park offers spectators a great bird's-eye view.

HA Baldwin Beach Park BEACH

(Map p182; ☎808-572-8122; www.co.maui.hi.us/facilities; Hana Hwy, Mile 6; ⏲7am-7pm; 👪) Bodyboarders and bodysurfers take to the waves at this palm-lined county park about a mile west of Pa'ia. The wide sandy beach is lovely for sunbathing but drops off quickly. When the swell is big, the shore dump here is too. Swimmers should beware of getting slammed. There are calmer waters at the eastern end, where a little cove is shaded by ironwood trees. There are picnic tables and a lifeguard.

Spreckelsville Beach BEACH

(Map p132; Kealakai Pl; 👪) Extending west from HA Baldwin Beach, this 2-mile stretch of sand is a good walking beach. Its nearshore reef makes it less than ideal for swimming, but it does provide protection for young kids. At the center of the beach you'll soon come to a section dubbed 'Baby Beach.'

Tavares Beach BEACH

(Map p182; Hana Hwy; P 👪) For a quiet 100yd stretch of sand, try this unmarked beach a short drive northeast from downtown, just beyond mile marker 7, although things liven up on weekend. There's a submerged lava shelf running parallel to the beach about 25ft from shore that's shallow enough for swimmers to scrape – it's easy to avoid if you look out for it. Parking at the shoreline access sign. No facilities.

Sights & Activities

Maui Dharma Center BUDDHIST SHRINE

(Map p185; ☎808-579-8076; www.mauidharmacenter.com; 81 Baldwin Ave; ⏲6:30am-6:30pm; P) Marked by its roadside stupa, this Tibetan Buddhist center offers meditation sessions, retreats and dharma talks. The stupa shrine was consecrated by the Dalai Lama in 2007.

Tours

Maui Cyclery CYCLING

(Go Cycling Maui; Map p185; ☎808-579-9009; www.gocyclingmaui.com; 99 Hana Hwy; 1-day rental from $30, tours from $150; ⏲8am-5pm Mon-Fri, to 4pm Sat, to noon Sun) The folks at Maui Cyclery make you feel welcome the moment you walk in the door. Credit goes to owner Donnie Arnoult, an experienced cyclist who runs one- to multiday cycling 'experiences' across the island. Open to all levels. Rentals are available, too.

Maui Photography Tours TOURS

(Map p185; ☎808-269-3998; www.danielsullivanphotography.com; 149 Hana Hwy; tours per hour $200) Tours with acclaimed photographer Daniel Sullivan, who has photographed vanishing civilizations around the world, take you to some of the most gorgeous spots on the island. You'll sharpen your skills while capturing some of Maui's most jaw-dropping scenery. Three- or seven-hour tours available. Located inside Sullivan's rug, photography and clothing shop, Indigo (p186).

Maui Easy Riders CYCLING

(☎808-344-9489; www.mauieasyriders.com; per person $135; ⏲8am-7pm) Offers a four-hour guided tour for groups of up to eight on comfy cruisers. Stops include Makawao and Pa'ia. The meeting point is at 19 Hana Hwy. Staff can arrange a sunrise viewing of Haleakalā followed by the bike ride (book way ahead). It also offers a self-guided bike tour ($110), group guided tours ($135) and private bike tours ($800).

HIKING IN THE NORTH SHORE & UPCOUNTRY

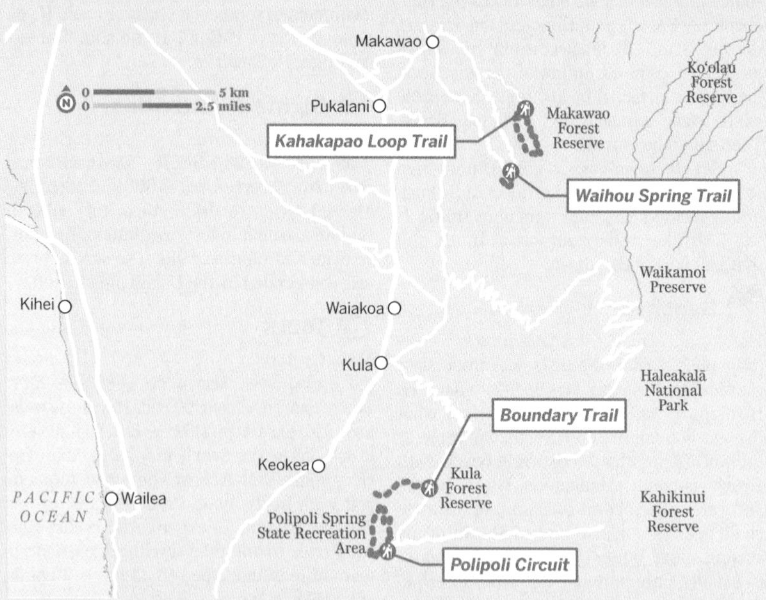

KAHAKAPAO LOOP TRAIL

START/END MAKAWAO FOREST RESERVE PARKING AREA
DISTANCE/DURATION 6.2 MILES ROUND TRIP; HALF DAY

Your companions on this walk through the woods? Dog walkers, mountain bikers, trail runners and friendly hikers, plus a thick, atmospheric forest. The trees in the reserve are mostly non-native, planted in the early 1900s to protect the watershed after native flora had been destroyed.

To reach Kahakapao Rd and the parking area, follow Pi'iholo Rd for 1.5 miles, turn left on Waiahiwi Rd and turn right after 0.4 miles. Continue to the reserve (open 6:30am to 8pm). After entering, cross four dips in the road, then enter the parking area 0.6 miles from the gate.

The trail runs through the Kahakapao Recreation Area within the 2093-acre Makawao Forest Reserve. From the parking area, walk to the information board at the back of the lot. A half-mile connector trail, leading to the loop, dives down into the forest just left of the sign. You'll pass a collection of skill courses and pump tracks for both beginner and expert cyclists. Bike-repair tools are attached to a pole by one of the tracks, along with an air pump.

The hard-packed trail is a mix of dirt and clay, often covered in leaves and broken by roots. It can get dangerously slick when wet. And it's often wet. A few single-track bike paths also cross the woods, connecting at various points along the main loop. Beyond the last pump track, the connector trail joins the main loop at another information kiosk.

The right side of the loop is called **Kahakapao Loop West**. Marked by red arrows, the trail runs 2.2 miles up the side of Haleakalā, twisting through a darkly wooded but lush ravine. One would hardly bat an eye if a hobbit or troll strolled past. The trees occasionally squeak from the wind, adding to the eeriness, especially if you're hiking solo. The trail passes a picnic table, then twists to the top of the loop. Here, pick

Trails twist through thick, sometimes eerie, groves of trees in the Upcountry, a green landscape that sweeps across the steep and often misty slopes of Haleakalā.

up **Kahakapao Loop East**, which drops through eucalyptus, ash and pine forests on its return to the start of the loop.

POLIPOLI CIRCUIT

START/END POLIPOLI SPRING STATE RECREATION AREA CAMPGROUND
DISTANCE/DURATION 5.3 MILES ROUND TRIP; HALF DAY

From the Polipoli campground parking area, the Redwood, Plum, Haleakalā Ridge and Polipoli Trails form a worthwhile 5.3-mile loop. The parking area sits at an elevation of 6200ft, so it's cooler here than on the coast. Temperatures can drop below freezing at night. Wear bright clothing, as hunters are active near the park.

To get to the Redwood Trail, follow paved Waipoli Rd to the Kula Forest Reserve. Once the pavement ends, it's another 4 miles to the campground and the trailhead. According to the sign, this unpaved stretch requires a 4WD vehicle. You'll really see why if the road is wet and muddy.

Proceeding counterclockwise, the 1.7-mile **Redwood Trail** leads from the right of the parking area. From there you'll descend into a towering redwood forest that feels more like California than Hawaii. You'll pass the **Tie Trail trailhead** and an old ranger's cabin before ending at a former Civilian Conservation Corps camp. The Redwood Trail is open to hikers and mountain bikers. The Plum and Boundary Trails meet here, too.

Follow the 1.7-mile **Plum Trail** as it ascends through stands of ash, redwood and sugi – all non-native. As its name suggests, plum trees also border the trail. From the Plum Trail, pick up the **Haleakalā Ridge Trail**. Stretching 1.6 miles, this scenic path climbs a rift on the southwest slope of the volcano. Look for pine and eucalyptus trees as well as cinders and native scrub.

Complete the loop back to the campground on the short but sweet **Polipoli Trail**, which ribbons beneath cypress trees and cedars, as well as the now-familiar pines.

WAIHOU SPRING TRAIL

START/END TOP OF OLINDA RD
DISTANCE/DURATION 2.2 MILES ROUND TRIP, AROUND ONE HOUR

For a quiet walk in deep woods, take this cool, tranquil and mostly easy trail, which begins 4.75 miles up Olinda Rd from central Makawao. A half-mile in you'll reach a short loop trail. A steep (and potentially muddy) offshoot from the loop descends to Waihou Spring, but for most the loop will be enough. See https://hawaiitrails.hawaii.gov/trails for a map.

BOUNDARY TRAIL

START/END ENTRANCE TO POLIPOLI SPRING STATE RECREATION AREA
DISTANCE/DURATION 3.8 MILES; 1½ TO TWO HOURS ROUND TRIP

This trail is the easiest way to experience the Polipoli Spring State Recreation Area without a 4WD. It begins about 200yd beyond the paved section of Waipoli Rd. Park before the cattle grate and walk to the trailhead. The hike is a steep, cool and atmospheric downhill walk, crossing gulches, woods of eucalyptus, pine and cedar, and native forest.

The smells and sounds of the forest are glorious, but in the afternoon the fog generally rolls in and visibility fades. Watch out for hunters and wear proper footwear, as the path narrows in sections and can be slippery when wet. The trail ends at the 1.5-mile marker, where you can return the way you came; alternatively, continue on 2.6 miles to connect with the Waiohuli Trail or 4 miles to the Redwood Trail. If you like a solitary hike, this one's for you.

CYCLING UPCOUNTRY TO NORTH SHORE

DOWNHILL FROM HALEAKALĀ TO PA'IA

START: HALEAKALĀ SUMMIT
END: PA'IA
DISTANCE/DURATION: 34 MILES ONE WAY; HALF DAY

Cycling from the summit of Haleakalā down to seaside Pa'ia has become an island rite of passage. The thrilling 34-mile journey, over a 10,000ft drop in elevation, offers tremendous views, a nail-biting ride and tremendous Upcountry sightseeing, including Makawao. It's also easy – the bikes are sturdy and have only one gear – although if you're inexperienced it's wise to keep your speed down. Bikers can reach 30mph on Haleakalā's roads, which can be perilous on the seriously steep corners: there have been accidents and even deaths.

If you're planning on descending the volcano only, fitness is not a concern. It's mostly free-wheeling with your ears popping and your jacket flapping in the wind. There's roughly one mile of actual pedaling to get to the bottom of the volcano.

Guided tours are no longer allowed to begin their trips inside the park. This prohibition does not apply to regular visitors (park entry with bike $15). If riding without a company, you will need to arrange a drop-off or pickup, unless you have legs of steel. Remember that many visitors leave soon after sunrise (one of the most popular activities in the park), so traffic is heaviest early in the morning.

After cycling up, or driving up in a drop-off vehicle, you will first pass the **Haleakalā Visitor Center** on your descent, where you can use the restrooms, check out the views, grab a park map and replenish your water. Next up is the **Kalahaku Overlook**, which is worth a stop for its lofty view of the crater. From here, the switchbacks really kick in. For more water, stop at the **Park Headquarters Visitor Center** before leaving the park.

Cycling from the summit of Haleakalā down to seaside Pa'ia has become an island rite of passage.

Guided bicycle tours begin just downhill from the park entrance at around 6500ft, riding 25 miles down the volcano. Different companies gather at separate pull-offs. Recommended outlets for a Haleakalā downhill ride include **Maui Easy Riders** (p177) and **Maui Sunriders** (p183), both of which offer self-guided tours with volcano drop-offs and guided tours with narrated extras; all equipment is included.

Haleakalā Hwy (also known as Crater Rd) is excellent quality, and has super-smooth asphalt, so there's no need to worry about potholes as you're zooming at speed. Downhill skateboarders love this stretch of road for that very reason. Switchbacks tighten as you ride down the green slopes, views of lavender fields on the volcano appear, and the fragrance of pine and eucalyptus fills the air as the landscape turns to thick forest in places.

From the straight stretch of pavement ahead, take your pick of pull-off spots for a photograph. The view of the Maui isthmus, tucked between two coasts and flanked by the West Maui Mountains, is simply stunning.

Turn right onto Hwy 377, passing **Kula Lodge & Restaurant** on your left (it's a good place to fuel up on farm-to-table food if you're hungry). At the Makawao/Olinda sign, turn right onto Kealaloa Rd. Continue to Hanamu Rd until it ends at Oskie Rice Arena. Turn left and twist down Olinda Rd until you reach the cowboy town of Makawao. Cross Makawao Ave. Continue on Baldwin Ave, which passes several galleries and indie shops with Western-style false-front architecture.

The scenery opens up as you drop down to the coast, with sugarcane fields, churches and schools lining the route. As you enter Pa'ia, it's time to start thinking about happy hour – try **Milagros Food Company** (p186), where you can relax on the terrace and chat about the epic cycle you've just had.

North Shore & Upcountry

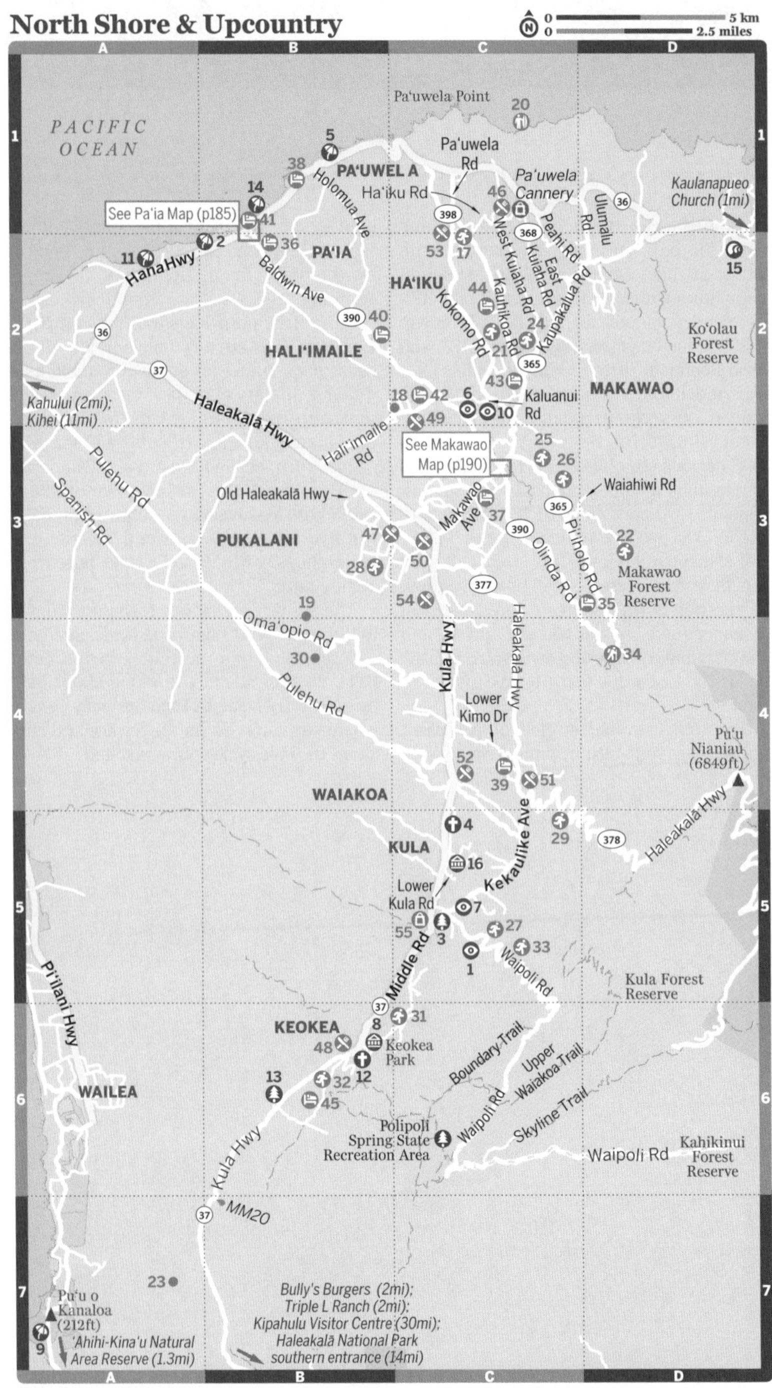

North Shore & Upcountry

Maui Sunriders CYCLING
(Map p185; 808-579-8970; www.mauisunriders.com; 71 Baldwin Ave; rentals per day from $40, tours per person $68; store 8:30am-4:30pm, tours 9am) Offers a daily Haleakalā downhill tour with a narrated van ride to the summit. After a beautiful ascent you'll be given a new Trek mountain bike, and off you'll go down the windy roads, starting at 6500ft. You don't have to return the bike until 4:30pm.

Sleeping

★ **Aloha Surf Hostel** HOSTEL $
(Map p182; 808-868-0117; www.alohasurfhostel.com; 221 Baldwin Ave; dm $46, s/d $119/136; reception 8am-10pm; P@) You can't miss this laid-back, beachy hostel: it's surrounded by a colorful fence made from surfboards. With sparkling-clean rooms, and only a 10-minute walk into town, it's the best budget stay in the area. Perks include free snorkel rental, communal garden and kitchen, TV lounge (with stacks of DVDs) and pool table, plus yummy pancake breakfasts.

Nalu Kai Lodge HOTEL $
(Map p185; 808-385-4344; www.nalukailodge.com; 18 Nalu Pl; r $125-185; P) Squeezed into a block near downtown, this throwback to 1960s Hawaii kitsch offers value studios

and rooms (sleeping up to three) without much privacy: bathrooms are closed off with a curtain. A bamboo fence conceals a small garden, a tiki bar and a fake waterfall. Rooms have mini-fridges and fans. Some have air-con. Two-night minimum.

★Inn at Mama's INN $$$

(Map p182; ☎808-579-9764; www.innatmamas.com; 799 Poho Pl; cottages $300-850, ste $425; P❄📶) Here the alohas are warm and the setting superb, with stylish cottages (studio, one bedroom and two bedroom) and luxurious suites with idyllic beachfront or garden settings, steps from one of Maui's best seafood restaurants.

★Pa'ia Inn BOUTIQUE HOTEL $$$

(Map p185; ☎808-579-6000; www.paiainn.com; 93 Hana Hwy; r from $329, ste from $479; P❄@📶) This classy boutique hotel offers the ultimate Pa'ia immersion. Step out the front and the town is on your doorstep; step out the back and you're on a path to the beach. With several stylish rooms in nine categories, you'll find something to your liking. Service is top notch. Guests have use of an intimate garden with sun loungers and beach views.

Makani Akau RENTAL HOUSE $$$

(Map p185; ☎808-575-9228; www.maui.cc/MakaniAkau-Maui.html; 55 Loio Pl; per night from $1000, cleaning fee $650; 📶) With sweeping views of Pa'ia Bay, this four-bedroom home is a contemporary classic. Bedrooms are well finished with teak touches, and folding glass doors bring all the surfing action into the living room. A 55ft pool fronts the sea. A huge kitchen, comfy leather couches and beautiful furniture complement the private setting.

Eating

★Tobi's Shave Ice DESSERTS, SEAFOOD $

(Map p185; ☎808-579-9745; 137 Hana Hwy; small shave ice $5, poke $13; ⏲10am-6pm) Come for the shave ice (flavors: tiger's blood, blue vanilla, sour grape and more), but stay for the *poke*. The raw-fish dish at this low-frills joint is the bomb. Top-notch choices include the seared ahi (yellowfin tuna) or fresh ahi ceviche. Plates come with two scoops of seaweed-dusted rice and salad. Cover it with hot sauce.

SEVEN-STORY SURFING

The North Shore harbors Maui's legendary big-wave surfing spot: **Jaws** (Pe'ahi; Map p182; Hahana Rd). In big swells, the wave reaches as high as a seven-story building. Local pros compare it to surfing a moving mountain, and it's a spectacular sight. Unfortunately for the public, there's no access to the viewpoint, which is on private land. Your best bet when it's on is to watch the news.

Choice Health Bar HEALTH FOOD $

(Map p185; ☎808-661-7711; https://choicehealthbar.com; 11 Baldwin Ave; mains $7-15; ⏲7:30am-8pm; ✍) Hip, modern counter-service spot for a healthy salad fix or wholesome breakfast or lunch. The superb-quality acai bowls, salads and grain bowls are vegan-friendly. Dishes like the green papaya and golden rice (with Thai vinaigrette, crushed almonds and green beans) or the wildflower tacos (with nasturtium-leaf taco shells) are awesomely creative.

Paia Bowls BREAKFAST $

(Map p185; ☎808-214-6504; www.paiabowls.com; 43 Hana Hwy; coffee $5.50, acai bowls from $12; ⏲11:30am-6pm) Craving a vitamin injection? Head to this small, palm-tree-shaded garden cafe off the main street that serves fine natural fruit bowls. Choose from three stacked acai creations (a fave is the surf bowl, with granola, banana, coconut and Hawaiian honey) and a range of 30 toppings, powders and seeds that you can add (from 75c each).

Pa'ia Bay Coffee CAFE $

(Map p185; ☎808-579-3111; www.paiabaycoffee.com; 115 Hana Hwy; items breakfast $3.50-12, lunch $12-14; ⏲7am-8pm; 📶) This tropical garden and coffee shop make an inviting sanctuary on a hot day. It's tucked into a busy side street (enter off Nalu Pl or via Ululani's Hawaiian Shave Ice on Hana Hwy). Grab bagels to go or settle in for yogurt with berries and granola, organic scrambled eggs with goat's cheese, or a smoked-salmon and avocado sandwich.

Kuau Store DELI $

(Map p182; ☎808-579-8844; www.facebook.com/kuaustoremaui; 701 Hana Hwy; sandwiches from $10; ⏲6:30am-7:30pm) Fuel up with coffee or a healthy juice before a drive on the Hana Hwy. Good sandwiches and salads are also available to go, plus items from lots of local independent producers, at this general store and deli. Look for the photogenic surfboard fence about 1 mile east of downtown Pa'ia.

Café des Amis CAFE $

(Map p185; ☎808-579-6323; www.cdamaui.com; 42 Baldwin Ave; crepes $6-13, curries from $14.50,

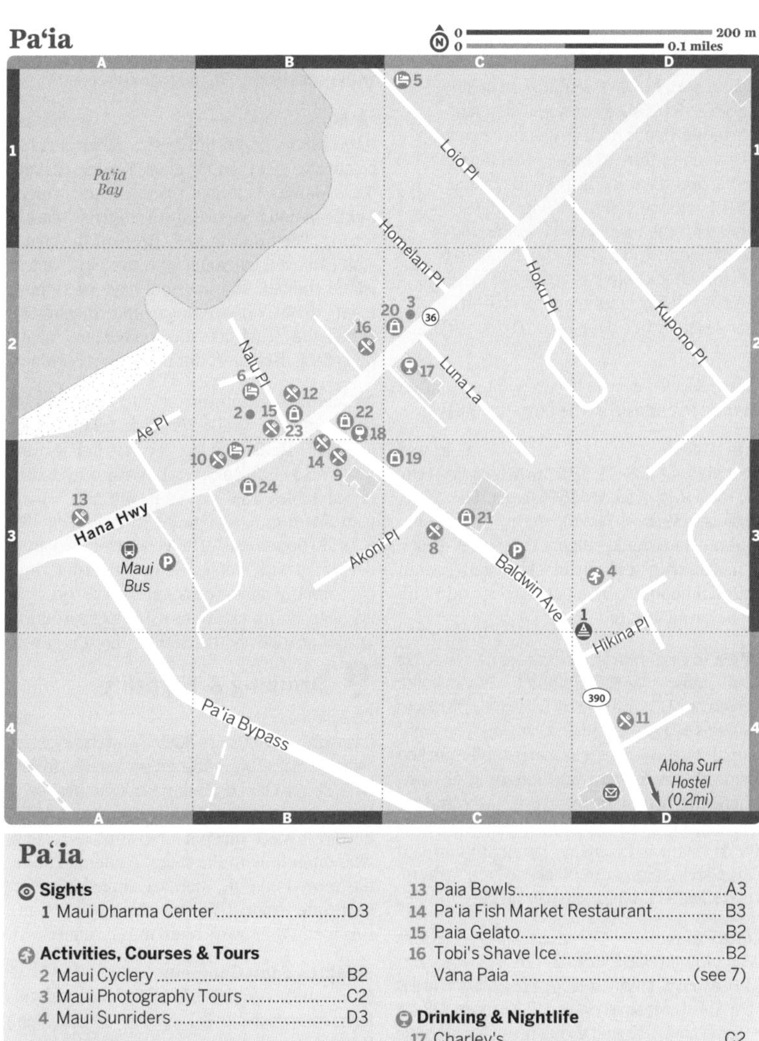

Pa'ia

Sights
1 Maui Dharma Center ... D3

Activities, Courses & Tours
2 Maui Cyclery ... B2
3 Maui Photography Tours ... C2
4 Maui Sunriders ... D3

Sleeping
5 Makani Akau ... C1
6 Nalu Kai Lodge ... B2
7 Pa'ia Inn ... B3

Eating
8 Café des Amis ... C3
9 Choice Health Bar ... B3
10 Flatbread Company ... B3
11 NyloS Restaurant ... D4
12 Pa'ia Bay Coffee ... B2
13 Paia Bowls ... A3
14 Pa'ia Fish Market Restaurant ... B3
15 Paia Gelato ... B2
16 Tobi's Shave Ice ... B2
Vana Paia ... (see 7)

Drinking & Nightlife
17 Charley's ... C2
18 Milagros Food Company ... B2

Shopping
19 Alice in Hulaland ... C3
20 Indigo ... C2
21 Mana Foods ... C3
22 Maui Crafts Guild ... B2
23 Sea La Vie & Sip Me ... B2
Simmer ... (see 15)
24 Wings Hawaii ... B3

salads $7-13; ⏲8:30am-9pm) Grab a seat in the shaded courtyard at this local-favorite eatery to dine on sweet or savory crepes, salads and a variety of curries. You'll also find vegetarian offerings, creative breakfasts and a tempting array of drinks, from fruit smoothies to fine

CROSSTOWN TRAFFIC

For a surfer town bursting with healthy bodies, Pa'ia sure has some clogged arteries. Roads, that is. If you're heading Upcountry from Kahului, avoid the main intersection at Baldwin Ave by taking the bypass. If you're staying awhile, head for the town lot first, as parking is a problem. And if you're heading on to Hana, check your gas gauge: Pa'ia has the last filling station on the highway, and Hana's has been known to run dry.

wines. Service can be leisurely. There's often evening live music in the fairy-lit courtyard.

Paia Gelato GELATO **$**
(Map p185; ☎808-579-9201; www.paiagelato.com; 99c Hana Hwy; 2 scoops $5.95, bagels from $6.95, sandwiches $9.95; ⊙7am-10pm) Dishes up 24 flavors of Maui-made gelato. The Sandy Beach is mixed with graham crackers and peanut butter. Smoothies, breakfast bagels and sandwiches available, too.

★**Pa'ia Fish Market Restaurant** SEAFOOD **$$**
(Map p185; ☎808-579-8030; www.paiafishmarket.com; 110 Hana Hwy, cnr Baldwin Ave; fish tacos $5, mains $10-22; ⊙11am-9:30pm;) The communal picnic tables are perpetually packed inside this consistent and longtime favorite, where the fish is always fresh, tasty and affordable. Ono fish and chips is a fave, but the whole menu is excellent. Try mahimahi and Cajun-style snapper or blackened ahi sashimi. The crowded tables turn over quickly.

Vana Paia BREAKFAST, JAPANESE **$$**
(Map p185; ☎808-579-6002; http://vanapaia.com; 93 Hana Hwy; breakfast items $12-22, lunch mains from $14, dinner small plates $10-22, mains $18-42; ⊙8am-2pm & 5-10pm) During brunch watch the chefs whip up your *huevos rancheros* (Mexican eggs), a Benedict, or avo on sourdough at this pleasant indoor-outdoor cafe tucked behind the Pa'ia Inn (p184). The menu also offers a short but appealing lunch list of salads and sandwiches, then goes full Japanese-Hawaiian in the evenings, with fresh sushi and seared local fish. Service can be leisurely.

Flatbread Company PIZZA **$$**
(Map p185; ☎808-579-8989; www.flatbreadcompany.com; 89 Hana Hwy; pizzas $13-24; ⊙11am-9:30pm) Wood-fired pizzas made with organic sauces, nitrate-free pepperoni, Maui pineapples – you'll never stop at a chain pizza house again. Fun combinations abound, from pure vegan to *kalua* (pit-oven-cooked) pork with goat cheese. Organic salads too.

★**Mama's Fish House** SEAFOOD **$$$**
(Map p182; ☎808-579-8488; www.mamasfishhouse.com; 799 Poho Pl; mains $48-85; ⊙11am-9pm) Mama's is a South Seas dream: superb food, top-notch service and a gorgeous seaside setting. The fish is literally fresh off the boat – staff can even tell you who caught it. Tropical island themed, the interiors have everything from driftwood to sugarcane machinery. When the beachside tiki torches are lit, it's one of the dreamiest dining settings on Maui.

★**NyloS Restaurant** AMERICAN **$$$**
(Map p185; ☎808-579-3354; https://nylosmaui.com; 115 Baldwin Ave; 3-course tasting menu $85; ⊙5:30-10:30pm Tue-Sat) With only half a dozen tables, this excellent, intimate American fine-dining restaurant in Pa'ia feels like a local supper club. The clean white room is decorated with vintage European posters, and chef Jeremy Solyn turns out cleverly presented gastronomic creations using local produce. Dishes change nightly. Reserve months ahead.

Drinking & Nightlife

Charley's BAR
(Map p185; ☎808-579-8085; www.charleysmaui.com; 142 Hana Hwy; ⊙8am-10pm Sun-Thu, to 2am Fri & Sat) Pa'ia's legendary saloon has been slingin' suds and pub grub since 1969. In its heyday it was a magnet for visiting rock stars, who often took to the stage. While that scene has moved on (OK, there's a slim chance that part-time resident Willie Nelson will pop in), this is still the town's main music venue.

Milagros Food Company BAR,
(Map p185; ☎808-579-8755; www.milagrosfoodcompany.com; 3 Baldwin Ave; ⊙11am-10pm) With sidewalk tables perched on Pa'ia's busiest corner, an island-style Tex-Mex menu (mains $12 to $24) and a variety of margaritas, this bar-restaurant is the perfect spot for a late-afternoon pit stop. Happy hour is from 3pm to 6pm, with $4 house beers and $5 house margaritas.

Shopping

★**Indigo** ARTS & CRAFTS
(Map p185; ☎808-579-9199; https://m.facebook.com/danielsullivangallery; 149 Hana Hwy; ⊙10am-6pm) Step into this inviting boutique for a shopping trip through Central and Southwest Asia. The gorgeous handcrafted rugs, furnish-

ings and traditional crafts were collected by the owners, Daniel Sullivan and Caramiya Davies-Reid. Sullivan also sells photographs taken during his travels, while Davies-Reid designs dresses and custom bathing suits.

★**Mana Foods** FOOD & DRINKS
(Map p185; ☎808-579-8078; www.manafoodsmaui.com; 49 Baldwin Ave; ⏰8am-8:30pm) Dreadlocked, Birkenstocked or just needing to stock up – everyone rubs shoulders at Mana, a friendly health-food store, bakery and deli. You'll find narrow aisles bursting with organic, rare goodies and coffee galore. Plus, there's a fantastic salad bar, and hot food to go.

Sea La Vie & Sip Me GIFTS & SOUVENIRS
(Map p185; ☎808-856-9154; www.sipmemaui.com; 106 Hana Hwy; ⏰coffee shop 9am-4pm, gift shop to 6pm) Top independent gift shop serving tasty brews from Sip Me coffee (from $2.45) and clever handcrafted gifts – like a surfboard incense stand and wooden cutlery.

★**Maui Crafts Guild** ARTS & CRAFTS
(Map p185; ☎808-579-9697; www.mauicraftsguild.com; 120 Hana Hwy; ⏰10am-6pm) Perched on the corner of the Hana Hwy and Baldwin Ave, this long-standing artists' co-op sells everything from pottery and jewelry to hand-painted silks and natural-fiber baskets at reasonable prices. All participating artists must be full-time Maui residents.

Simmer SPORTS & OUTDOORS
(Map p185; ☎808-579-8484; www.simmerhawaii.com; 99 Hana Hwy; ⏰10am-8pm) Started in the early '80s by Malte Simmer and his seamstress partner Cindy Allen, Simmer built durable windsurfing sails that would withstand Maui's fierce north-shore winds. The business has since morphed into a rockin' beachwear shop selling stylish men's and women's clothing and accessories.

Wings Hawaii CLOTHING, JEWELRY
(Map p185; ☎808-579-3110; www.wingshawaii.com; 69 Hana Hwy; ⏰9:30am-8pm) For truly unique clothing and jewelry – they call it beach boho chic – stop by this small shop that sells locally designed womenswear. The hip, minimalist artwork makes a change from the vibrant colored creations you see elsewhere.

Alice in Hulaland GIFTS & SOUVENIRS
(Map p185; ☎808-579-9922; www.aliceinhulaland.com; 19 Baldwin Ave; ⏰9am-8pm) Kitschy but fun souvenirs and Hawaiiana, plus T-shirts and ukuleles.

Information

Bank of Hawaii (☎808-579-9511; www.boh.com; 35 Baldwin Ave; ⏰8:30am-4pm Mon-Thu, to 6pm Fri)

Post Office (Map p185; ☎808-579-8866; www.usps.com; 120 Baldwin Ave; ⏰9am-4pm Mon-Fri, 10:30am-12:30pm Sat)

Getting There & Around

Pa'ia is 6.5 miles from Kahului airport. Maui Bus operates the Ha'iku Islander between the airport and Pa'ia ($2) every 90 minutes from 5:30am to 8:30pm. The **bus stop** (Map p185; www.mauicounty.gov/1310/Maui-Bus-Route-Maps; Hana Hwy) is located on the Hana Hwy beside the city parking lot on the right as you enter town, just beyond the Pa'ia Bypass Rd.

Ha'iku

Ha'iku is a lot like Pa'ia was before tourism took hold. Both have their roots in sugarcane – Maui's first 12 acres of the sweet stuff was planted in Ha'iku in 1869, and the village once had both a sugar mill and pineapple canneries. Thanks to its affordability and proximity to Ho'okipa Beach, it's also a haunt for pro surfers, who've helped rejuvenate the town.

Nestled in greenery, this is a low-key place to stay, with many excellent accommodations options and restaurants for its size.

Activities

Haleakalā Bike Co CYCLING
(Bike Maui; Map p182; ☎808-575-9575; www.bikemaui.com; Ha'iku Marketplace, 810 Ha'iku Rd; sunrise bike tour from $200) Want to watch the Haleakalā sunrise then bike down the volcano at your own pace? Book the Sunrise Special. After an early-morning van ride to the summit, followed by sunrise, you'll be dropped off just outside the park with bike, helmet, backpack, rain gear and map. From there it's 23 twisty miles down to Ha'iku. Be back by 4pm. Check-in 3am.

North Shore Zipline ADVENTURE SPORTS
(Map p182; ☎808-269-0671; www.nszipline.com; 2065 Kauhikoa Rd; zipline tour $119; ⏰tours 8am-3pm Mon-Sat) This canopy tour has seven ziplines connected by bridges and platforms. Participants jump from as high as 70ft and reach speeds of up to 40mph; the longest line is 900ft. Minimum age five; minimum weight 40lb, maximum 270lb. Allow two hours.

Kalakupua Playground PARK
(Fourth Marine Division Memorial Park; Map p182; 808-572-8122; www.mauicounty.gov; Kokomo Rd, Mile 2; 8am-7pm;) Known as 'Giggle Hill,' this jungle gym and playground – complete with turrets, boardwalks and slides – is great for kids. The 40-acre park here also has playing fields and covered picnic pavilions.

Sleeping

★ **Pilialoha** COTTAGE $
(Map p182; 808-572-1440; www.pilialoha.com; 2512 Kaupakalua Rd; d $175;) This sunny one-bed cottage sleeps two and feels like a second home. Ideal for exploring the Upcountry, the house blends countryside charm with modern conveniences. But it's the warm hospitality and attention to detail – from the picnic coolers to the coffee thermos – that really stand out. Other perks include free fresh fruits, juice and cereal on arrival. Three-night minimum.

Pililani RENTAL HOUSE $$$
(Map p182; 808-575-9228; www.maui.cc/Pili/Pililani-welcome.html; 110 Kane Rd; per night $1000-1500, cleaning fee $650;) Looking for your own Balinese resort? Connected by glass hallways, these three hardwood chalets on four manicured acres with swaying palms, stone pool deck, sauna and tennis courts certainly fit the bill. Seven-night minimum.

Eating

Baked on Maui BAKERY, CAFE $
(Map p182; 808-575-7836; Pa'uwela Cannery, 375 W Kuiaha; mains $7-16; 6:30am-5pm) Delicious homemade food, a full breakfast menu (nine omelet options, plus *shakshuka*, Benedicts, and biscuits and gravy), plus great salads, sandwiches and hand-pressed burgers for lunch, is on offer here. Makes this *the* local stop prior to tackling the Road to Hana.

★ **Veg Out** VEGETARIAN $
(Map p182; 808-575-5320; www.veg-out.com; 810 Kokomo Rd, Ha'iku Town Center; mains $8-11, 12in pizza $6-19; 10:30am-7:30pm Mon-Fri, 11:30am-7:30pm Sat & Sun;) Tucked inside a former warehouse, this rasta-casual vegetarian eatery serves up a dynamite burrito loaded with beans, hot tofu and jalapeños. Also right on the mark are the Middle Eastern plates (with baked falafels, hummus, saffron rice, salad and tahini) and the pesto-chèvre pizzas.

★ **Nuka** JAPANESE $$
(Map p182; 808-575-2939; www.nukamaui.com; 780 Ha'iku Rd; lunch $8-21, dinner small plates $5-25, mains $13-22, rolls $9-20; 4:30-10pm) One of Maui's best dining options marries a traditional Japanese restaurant with an elegant-casual dining room. Order classics such as sushi and tempura, alongside exotic rolls and *otsumami* (tapas), plus bowls (the Nuka bowl with ahi *katsu* is pretty special). Everything is presented with sophistication and without inflated prices. Wash it down with one of 10 types of sake.

Colleen's AMERICAN $$
(Map p182; 808-575-9211; www.colleensinhaiku.com; 810 Ha'iku Rd, Ha'iku Marketplace; mains breakfast $8-13, lunch $9-17, dinner $12-30; 6am-9:30pm) This boisterous bistro is the Ha'iku hangout for locals and visitors alike. Menu choices are straightforward – burgers, salads and build-your-own pizzas among them – but cooked to perfection, and supported by a wide range of craft beers. Excellent coffee and big breakfasts bring 'em in early.

Drinking & Nightlife

Maui Kombucha TEAHOUSE
(Map p182; 808-575-5233; www.mauikombucha.com; 810 Ha'iku Rd, Ha'iku Marketplace; kombucha from $4.75, coffee from $4.25, juice from $8, mains $7-13; 8am-5pm Sun-Fri, to 2pm Sat) Welcome to 'The Booch,' home of the alternative drink, kombucha. This hip hole-in-the-wall place overflows with fermented tea (with bubbles!) and a lively crowd. Also serves chai tea and cold-pressed coffee. Expect wraps, salads, pizza, burritos and lots of fun. Faces Kokomo Rd in Ha'iku Marketplace.

Wailuku Coffee Company COFFEE
(Map p182; 808-868-3229; http://wailukucoffeeco.com; 810 Kokomo Rd; 6am-5pm Mon-Fri, 7am-5pm Sat, 7am-3pm Sun) The second outpost of local coffee brand Wailuku Coffee Company is right here in Ha'iku. It serves excellent handcrafted drinks, 100% Kona coffee with a subtle flavor, plus homemade pastries, salads, sandwiches and eggs. This branch is smaller and not as atmospheric as the one in Wailuku, but the coffee is just as good.

Shopping

Da Kine SPORTS & OUTDOORS
(Map p182; Pa'uwela Cannery, W Kuiaha Rd) Founded in Hawaii, this top global adventure brand started in Ha'iku some 40 years ago. The bags are still some of the toughest-wearing gear you can buy – the suitcases come with a lifetime guarantee. Take a look around the first-ever store at the Pa'uwela Cannery.

Ha'iku Market FOOD & DRINKS
(Map p182; ☎808-575-9291; 810 Ha'iku Rd, Ha'iku Marketplace; ⏲6am-9pm) Has a large *poke* counter in addition to the usual groceries.

Pauwela Store FOOD & DRINKS
(Map p182; https://pauwelastoremaui.com; 375 W Kuiaha Rd; ⏲8am-10pm) Good general store selling organic local groceries from Maui farmers, plus sandwiches (try the yummy roasted goat's cheese vegetable wrap) and smoothies made in its kitchen.

Hali'imaile

Compared to years ago, the tiny pineapple town of Hali'imaile is practically hopping these days. Named for the sweet-scented maile plants – used in lei making – that covered the area before pineapples took over, the community is home to a microdistillery and a glass-blowing studio. Both are housed in Quonset huts across the road from the old general store (c 1918), which has been transformed into one of Maui's top restaurants.

Tours

Hali'imaile Distilling Company FOOD & DRINK
(Map p182; ☎808-633-3609; www.haliimailedistilling.com; 883 Hali'imaile Rd; $10; ⏲10am-4pm Mon-Fri) Sitting on the slopes of Haleakalā surrounded by pineapple fields, this microdistillery offers tasting tours with samples of its craft liquors, all infused with local ingredients. The flagship Pau Vodka is distilled from Maui Gold pineapples (taking 18 months to grow); the result is clean and pure with a hint of sweetness. Tours every 30 minutes.

Sleeping & Eating

Peace of Maui GUESTHOUSE $
(Map p182; ☎808-572-5045; www.peaceofmaui.com; 1290 Hali'imaile Rd; s/d with shared bath from $95/115, cottages per 2 people $250; @📶) This homey Upcountry sleep is in the middle of nowhere but within an hour's drive of nearly everywhere. Clean rooms are small, but comfortable, with refrigerator and TV. There's also a guest kitchen and common area. A two-bedroom, one-bath cottage offers a covered deck with mountain views and room for kids.

Kama Hele Cafe BREAKFAST $
(Map p182; ☎808-495-1591; 903 Hali'imaile Rd; coffee from $2.75, smoothies $5.50, mains from $9; ⏲9am-4pm Mon-Fri, to 3:30pm Sat & Sun) This blue food truck with a Hokusai-style wave emblazoned on the side is one of the best on Maui. Located near the Hali'imaile Distilling Company, it serves Maui-brewed coffee, delectable breakfast options – such as stuffed burritos with egg, cheese, sausage, fried potato and green chili – and lunch plates. Get the barbecue-pork sandwich on a pretzel bun with pineapple salsa. Yum.

★ **Hali'imaile General Store** HAWAIIAN $$$
(Map p182; ☎808-572-2666; www.bevgannonrestaurants.com; 900 Hali'imaile Rd; mains lunch $14-26, dinner $32-44; ⏲11am-2:30pm, 3-5:30pm & 5:30-9pm Mon-Fri, 5:30-9pm Sat & Sun; 🖉) The culinary sorceress behind this destination dining spot is chef Bev Gannon, one of the forces behind the Hawaii Regional Cuisine movement. In-the-know diners come to this inviting outpost. Try creations such as the mac-nut-crusted fresh catch, tandoori-rubbed salmon, or Paniolo ribs with Asian slaw.

Shopping

Makai Glass ARTS & CRAFTS
(Map p182; ☎808-269-8255; www.makaiglass.com; 903 Hali'imaile Rd; ⏲11am-5pm Mon-Fri, to 5pm Sat & Sun) Walk up to the 2nd-floor viewing area of this spacious gallery, inside a large Quonset hut, to watch glassblowers at work in the studio below. How they craft the glass into fantastic sculptures seems just short of magic. The *honu* (green sea turtles) are especially cool. It's a nice place to browse and hang out before the distillery tour (p189) next door.

Makawao

Dubbed Maka Wow on local T-shirts, this attractive town is a mélange of art haven and *paniolo* (Hawaiian cowboy) culture, with a twist of New Age hippie thrown in for good measure. A ranching town since the 1800s, its false-front buildings and hitching posts look transported from the Old West. The surrounding hills still contain cattle pastures and the weekend rodeo, but also expensive homes. Its popularity means the town has filled with attractive galleries and cafes. The main action is at the intersection of Baldwin and Makawao Aves, where you can enjoy some browsing, a meal and a bit of nightlife.

Sights

★ **Makawao History Museum** MUSEUM
(Map p190; ☎808-572-2482; 3643 Baldwin Ave; ⏲10am-5pm Mon-Sun) FREE Step into this tiny but informative museum for an

Makawao

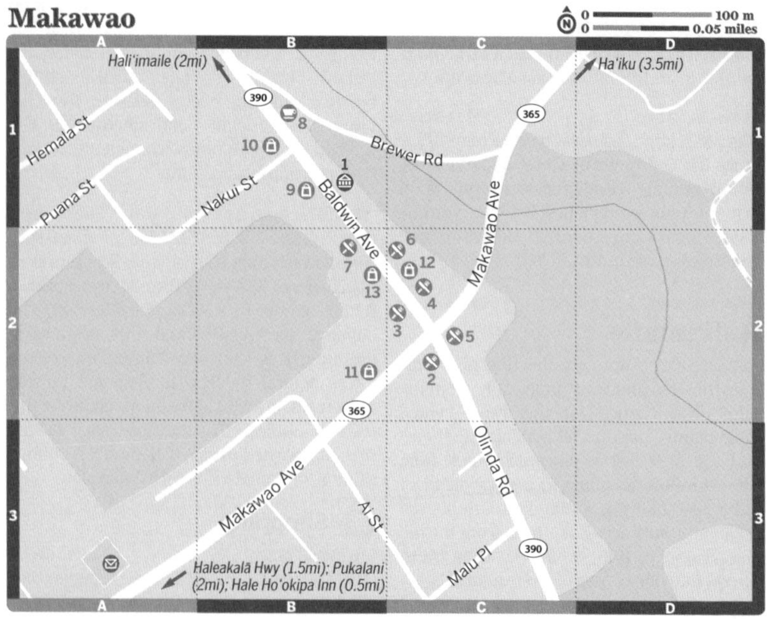

Makawao

Sights
1 Makawao History Museum B1

Eating
Casanova Deli .... (see 2)
2 Casanova Italian Restaurant C2
3 Komoda Store & Bakery C2
4 Makawao Garden Café C2
5 Polli's C2
6 Rodeo General Store C2
7 Satori B2

Drinking & Nightlife
8 Sip Me! B1

Shopping
9 Designing Wahine Emporium B1
10 Hot Island Glass B1
11 Maui Hands B2
12 Sherri Reeve Gallery C2
Viewpoints Gallery .... (see 10)
13 Wertheim Contemporary B2

overview of the town's cowboy. There are antique ranching tools on display, plus black-and-white photos of the town and its former inhabitants, and retro exhibits on local diets and culture throughout the years. Donations appreciated.

Sacred Garden of Maliko GARDENS
(Map p182; ☎808-573-7700; www.sacredgardenmaui.com; 460 Kaluanui Rd; ⏰9am-6pm; P) FREE This unique nonprofit is a self-described healing sanctuary offering a meditative moment on your trip. Your kids will love the rock-garden labyrinth walk beside Maliko Stream. Meanwhile, the exotic greenhouse is a peaceful place to relax in. You can buy plants, gifts and garden ornaments here.

Hui No'eau Visual Arts Center ARTS CENTER
(Map p182; ☎808-572-6560; www.huinoeau.com; 2841 Baldwin Ave; ⏰9am-4pm; P) FREE Occupying the former estate of sugar magnates Harry and Ethel Baldwin, Hui No'eau is a regal setting for a community arts center. In 1917 famed architect CW Dickey designed the main plantation house, which showcases the Hawaiian Regional architectural style he pioneered. Visit the galleries, which exhibit the work of island artists, and stroll the grounds, with stables converted into art studios.

Activities

Makawao Forest Reserve Trails MOUNTAIN BIKING, HIKING
(Map p182; ☎808-984-8100; Kahakapao Rd, Makawao Forest Reserve; ⏰6:30am-8pm) Mountain

bikers love zooming around this magical place, with eight tailor-made bike paths carved into a 2093-acre reserve. Walkers can enjoy the main 6.6-mile multiuse Kahakapao Loop Trail among towering trees, pungent forest smells and curious sounds of the forest. Trails are slick when wet.

Pi'iholo Ranch Stables HORSEBACK RIDING
(Map p182; ☎808-270-8750; www.piiholo.com; 325 Waiahiwi Rd; per person Cowboy for a Day $349, 2/3hr rides $239/349; ⊙Mon-Sat; 👪) Want to round up cattle like a *paniolo*? Then giddyap for the Cowboy for a Day experience. In a secluded glen, high up on the edge of a rainforest, this family-run cattle ranch also offers two- and three-hour group horseback rides for up to six people, with mountain, valley and pasture views galore.

Pi'iholo Ranch Zipline ADVENTURE SPORTS
(Map p182; ☎808-572-1717; www.piiholozipline.com; 799 Pi'iholo Rd; zip tours $145-165, canopy tours $145; ⊙tours 10am & 1pm, reservations 7am-7pm; 👪) This operation offers two options: a standard dual-line course of four/five lines, the latter with a 2800ft finale that hits 600ft in altitude, and a six-/seven-line canopy course. You can bring your own GoPro cam to mount on your helmet, but you'll need your own head straps. The Hike & Zip combo ($229) includes a waterfall hike on the Hana Hwy.

Festivals & Events

Maui Polo Club SPORTS
(www.mauipoloclub.com; adult/child under 12yr $10/free; ⊙1:30pm, gates 11am; 👪) A friendly tailgating party surrounds these Sunday matches held behind Oskie Rice Arena, 1 mile above town on Olinda Rd, early September through mid-November; and at the Manduke Baldwin Polo Arena, 1.7 miles up Haleakalā Hwy from Makawao Ave, from early April to late June.

Paniolo Parade PARADE
(⊙9-11am Jun or Jul) Held on the Saturday morning closest to July 4, this festive parade with horseback riders, floats, a marching band and classic cars goes right through the heart of Makawao.

Sleeping

Hale Ho'okipa Inn B&B $
(Map p182; ☎808-572-6698; www.maui-bed-and-breakfast.com; 32 Pakani Pl; r $150-190; 📶) A short walk from the town center, this arts-and-crafts-style house built in 1924 offers four guest rooms furnished with antiques. It's all very casual and homey, with country-style furnishings in the rooms and organic fruit from the yard on the breakfast table. Be sure to check out the enormous Norfolk pine tree in the backyard – it's 162ft high and 19ft around!

Aloha Cottage COTTAGE $$
(Map p182; ☎808-573-8555; www.alohacottage.com; 1875 Olinda Rd; cottages per night 7-14 nights from $259, 4-6 nights from $279; 📶) This gated love nest (suitable for two), an octagonal cottage with one large room, sits on a bluff way up steep Olinda Rd, about 10 minutes from Makawao. There's a full kitchen, a laundry, vaulted ceilings, a king-size bed, and a large lanai with hot tub. Cleaning fee $125.

★**Lumeria Maui** SPA HOTEL $$$
(Map p182; ☎808-579-8877; www.lumeriamaui.com; 1813 Baldwin Ave; r $339-479, ste from $529; 📶🏊) Set on tidy, garden-filled grounds on an Upcountry slope between Pa'ia and downtown Makawao, Lumeria is a gorgeous place to nourish mind and body. Farm-to-table breakfasts (included in rates) use the bounty from the on-site garden. Extras include massages and aromatherapy.

Eating

Komoda Store & Bakery BAKERY $
(Map p190; ☎808-572-7261; 3674 Baldwin Ave; ⊙7am-4pm Mon, Tue, Thu & Fri, to 2pm Sat) In operation for more than a century, this homespun bakery, legendary for its mouthwatering cream puffs, stick doughnuts and guava-filled *malasadas* (Portuguese fried doughnuts), is a Makawao landmark. Arrive early, as it often sells out by noon.

Satori SUSHI $
(Map p190; ☎808-214-6823; https://satorimaui.com; 3654 Baldwin Ave; hand rolls from $13; ⊙11am-5pm Tue-Sat; 🌶) Across from Rodeo General Store (p192), you'll find the most delicious farm-to-table sushi, served out of a gypsy-style food trailer. Sushi rolls include the 'Great Roll of China,' a veggie roll with bok choy, eggplant and homemade teriyaki sauce. Fish rolls are stuffed with marlin, ahi, shrimp or *kampachi*.

Casanova Deli DELI $
(Map p190; ☎808-572-0220; www.casanovamaui.com; 1188 Makawao Ave; mains $7-10; ⊙7:30am-5:30pm Mon-Sat) Makawao's hippest haunt brews heady espressos, and buzzes all day with folks enjoying buttery croissants, thick Italian sandwiches and hearty Greek

WORTH A TRIP

VIEWS & VERTIGO

For a steep, scenic drive with plenty of twists and turns, head into the hills above Makawao along Olinda Rd, which picks up in town where Baldwin Ave leaves off. Turn left onto Pi'iholo Rd near the top, and wind back down into town. The whole crazy loop takes about half an hour. Combine with the **Waihou Spring Trail** (Map p182; 2463 Olinda Rd; ⌚sunrise-sunset) for a cool midway break.

salads. Take it all out to the roadside deck for the town's best people-watching.

Rodeo General Store DELI $

(Map p190; ☎808-572-1868; 3661 Baldwin Ave; mains $7-9; ⌚6:30am-9pm) The deli counter at this busy general store sells a variety of to-go meals, from salads and sandwiches to Hawaiian *poke* and plate lunches. The *kalua* pork is tender and oh so tasty. It also sells beer, liquor and craft kombucha.

Makawao Garden Café CAFE $

(Map p190; ☎808-573-9065; http://makawaogardencafe.letseat.at; 3669 Baldwin Ave; sandwiches from $6.25; ⌚11am-3pm Mon-Sat) On a sunny day there's no better place for a light lunch than this outdoor cafe tucked into a courtyard at the northern end of Baldwin Ave. It's strictly sandwiches and salads. Everything's fresh, generous and made to order by the owner herself. Choose from fillings such as snow crab and avocado, and baby brie and bacon, or try the mahimahi salad.

Casanova Italian Restaurant ITALIAN $$

(Map p190; ☎808-572-0220; www.casanovamaui.com; 1188 Makawao Ave; mains lunch $12-24, dinner $14-46; ⌚11:30am-2pm & 5:30-9:30pm Mon, Tue & Thu-Sat, 5:30-9:30pm Wed & Sun) With classic antipasti Italian dishes, stone-baked kiawe-fired oven pizzas, and juicy Maui-raised steaks, it's hard to go wrong at this longtime Upcountry favorite. Casanova doubles as an entertainment venue, with happening live music or a nightclub on Wednesday, Friday and Saturday (10pm to 1am). Wednesday is Ladies' Night, when women get in free ($10 cover for men).

Polli's MEXICAN $$

(Map p190; ☎808-572-7808; www.pollismexicanrestaurant.com; 1202 Makawao Ave; mains $12-26, tacos from $5; ⌚11am-10pm) Parked on the corner of Baldwin and Makawao Aves, this atmospheric Tex-Mex restaurant is a longtime favorite. Have a cerveza at the small bar, or tackle sizzling fajitas in the nearby brown booths. Margaritas are $5 during happy hour (4pm to 5:30pm Monday to Friday).

Drinking

Sip Me! COFFEE

(Map p190; ☎808-573-2340; www.sipmemaui.com; 3617 Baldwin Ave; ⌚6am-5pm Mon-Sat, 7am-5pm Sun; 📶) Cute, inviting Sip Me! serves sustainable produce from local suppliers and global tea farms. It claims it's 93% organic. Inviting baked treats range from banana bread to artisan cookies, and there are gluten-free goodies. The 12oz coffee is a bargain at $1.50.

Shopping

★**Wertheim Contemporary** ART

(Map p190; ☎808-572-5973; www.wertheimcontemporary.com; 3660 Baldwin Ave; ⌚11am-6pm) Showcases the extraordinary art of Andreas Nottebohm, who etches flat sheets of aluminum to create an illusion of depth. You won't believe your eyes. Also shows works by local, national and globally known artists.

Maui Hands ART

(Map p190; ☎808-572-2008; www.mauihands.com; 1169 Makawao Ave; ⌚10am-6pm Mon-Sat, to 5pm Sun) A fascinating collection of high-quality Hawaii art, primarily from Maui, including photography, koa, ceramics, photographs, and a mix of traditional and contemporary paintings. Worth a stop.

Viewpoints Gallery ART

(Map p190; ☎808-572-5979; www.viewpointsgallerymaui.com; 3620 Baldwin Ave; ⌚10:30am-5pm) This classy gallery hosts the work of more than three dozen of the island's finest artists, and feels like a welcoming museum.

Hot Island Glass ART

(Map p190; ☎808-572-4527; www.hotislandglass.com; 3620 Baldwin Ave; ⌚9am-5pm) Watch artists in action at Maui's oldest handblown-glass studio from 10am to 4pm every day but Sunday. Everything from paperweights with ocean themes to high-art decorative pieces are available.

Designing Wahine Emporium GIFTS & SOUVENIRS

(Map p190; ☎808-573-0990; www.designingwahine.com; 3640 Baldwin Ave; ⌚10am-6pm Mon-Sat, 11am-5pm Sun) Decorative pillows, jewelry, children's clothing, quality gifts and much more fill this classic plantation cottage.

Sherri Reeve Gallery ART

(Map p190; ☎808-572-8931; www.sreeve.com; 3669 Baldwin Ave; ⏲9am-5pm Mon-Fri, 10am-4pm Sat & Sun) Floral watercolors in a jewel-toned palette on everything from T-shirts to full-size canvases. The artist is generally present.

Information

Post Office (Map p190; ☎808-572-0019; www.usps.com; 1075 Makawao Ave; ⏲9am-4:30pm Mon-Fri, to 11am Sat)

Getting Around

If you plan to spend the night and do any Upcountry exploring, your best bet is to rent a car. Alternatively, you can catch the Upcountry Islander bus every 90 minutes from 6am to 9pm. It stops across from the Makawao Public Library on Makawao Ave.

Minit Stop (☎808-573-9295; www.minitstop.com; 1100 Makawao Ave; ⏲5am-11pm) has gas and an ATM. It also serves legendary fried chicken: your budget lunch.

Pukalani & Around

True to its name, which means Heavenly Gate, Pukalani is the gateway to the lush Upcountry. Many just drive past Pukalani on the way to Kula and Haleakalā, unless they need food or gas (the last before the park). The big draw? The local produce, including seriously good goat's cheeses and a Saturday-morning Upcountry farmers market.

To reach the business part of town, get off Haleakalā Hwy (Hwy 37) at the Old Haleakalā Hwy exit, which becomes Pukalani's main street.

Activities

Pukalani Country Club GOLF

(Map p182; ☎808-572-1314; www.pukalanigolf.com; 360 Pukalani St; 18-hole greens fee $89, club rental $45; ⏲7am-dusk, clubhouse 8am-4pm Mon, to 8pm Tue-Fri, 7am-8pm Sat, to 4pm Sun) With its clubhouse in a mobile home, the Pukalani Golf Club doesn't present a pretty face, but the course is in excellent condition and one of the best deals on the island. Come after 2:30pm and golf nine holes the rest of the day for just $31. Small clubhouse cafe on-site.

Tours

★Hawaii Sea Spirits Organic Farm & Distillery DISTILLERY

(Map p182; ☎808-877-0009; www.hawaiiseaspirits.com; 4051 Oma'opio Rd; adult/child & youth under 21yr $15/free; ⏲tours 9:30am-4pm) From the sugarcane stalks to the bottling room to the end-of-tour tasting, the 45-minute guided tour at this vodka, gin and rum distillery tells an interesting story about the company's organic ethos. The flagship Ocean Vodka is made with deep-ocean mineral water sourced off the coast of Hawai'i (the Big Island).

★Surfing Goat Dairy FOOD & DRINK

(Map p182; ☎808-878-2870; www.surfinggoatdairy.com; 3651 Oma'opio Rd; ⏲store 9am-5pm Mon-Sat, to 2pm Sun; 🚼) 'Da' feta mo' betta' is the motto at this 42-acre farm, the source of all that luscious chèvre adorning the menus of Maui's top restaurants. There's a well-stocked store and free samples of cheese are provided on tours, or just come for the excellent cheese flights (six chèvres with crackers for $16).

Eating

★Upcountry Farmers Market MARKET $

(Map p182; www.upcountryfarmersmarket.com; 55 Kiopaa St; ⏲7-11am Sat) It's a rainbow of color at this happening farmers market: yellow apple-bananas, orange carrots, green broccoli, red strawberries. Plus star fruit, avocados, honey – if its edible and it grows on Maui, it's here. Local farmers – and a food truck or two – share fruit, vegetables and locally prepared fare in the parking lot just beyond Longs Drugs at the Kulamalu Shopping Center.

Farmacy Health Bar & Grill – Pukalani HEALTH FOOD $

(Map p182; ☎808-868-0443; www.facebook.com/Farmacyhealthbarpukalani; Pukalani Terrace Center, 55 Pukalani St, cnr Old Haleakalā Hwy; salads & sandwiches $12-14, acai bowls $7.50-17; ⏲8am-5:30pm) 🌿 Craving a healthy lunch? Pop into Farmacy for a juice, smoothie or acai bowl – all fruit loaded and fresh. A spin-off of the Farmacy (p142) in Wailuku, this place blends health and great taste with a bit of artistic flair. Plenty of good veggie-filled sandwiches, too.

Pukalani Superette SUPERMARKET $

(Map p182; ☎808-572-7616; www.pukalanisuperette.com; 15 Makawao Ave; prepared meals $3-12; ⏲5:30am-9pm Mon-Fri, 7am-8pm Sun) Pick up a picnic here on the way to Haleakalā's summit. It does reasonably priced sandwiches, salads and hot meals, such as *kalua* pork, chili chicken and Spam *musubi* (rice with a slice of fried Spam on top).

Foodland SUPERMARKET $

(Map p182; ☎808-572-0674; www.foodland.com; Pukalani Terrace Center, 55 Pukalani St, cnr Old

Haleakalā Hwy; ⏲5am-midnight) A convenient pit stop for people heading up and down Haleakalā.

Kojima's JAPANESE $$
(Map p182; ☎808-573-2859; www.kojimassushi.com; 81 Makawao Ave; sushi rolls $5.50-25; ⏲4-9pm Tue-Thu, 4-9:30pm Fri & Sat) The real deal. This cafe and sushi bar with a porch showcases the talents of Chef Kojima, who has been cooking traditional Japanese cuisine for more than three decades in Japan and the US. Try the long list of *maki* (sushi), including the rock 'n' roll: a crab-and-avocado roll topped with *unagi* (eel) glaze. BYO beer, wine and sake. No liquor.

Serpico's ITALIAN $$
(Map p182; ☎808-572-8498; www.serpicosmaui.com; 7 Aewa Pl, cnr Old Haleakalā Hwy; breakfast $8-12, mains $14-24, pizza $17-29; ⏲6am-10pm; 👪) In the center of Pukalani, this casual and slightly dingy Italian eatery makes decent pasta dishes and New York–style pizzas. Order up flavors such as 'the carnivore,' with bacon, sausage and pepperoni, or the classic 'old world' pizza, with fresh tomato, chopped garlic, basil, mozzarella and tomato sauce. Calzones are a bargain at $9.50.

Information

Bank of Hawaii (☎808-572-7242; www.boh.com; Pukalani Terrace Center, 55 Pukalani St, cnr Old Haleakalā Hwy; ⏲8:30am-4pm Mon-Thu, to 6pm Fri) The last bank and ATM before you reach Kula and Haleakalā National Park.

Kula

Think of this Upcountry heartland as one big garden and you won't be far off. So bountiful is Kula's volcanic soil that it produces most of the onions, lettuce and strawberries grown in Hawaii and almost all of the commercially grown exotic protea flowers. Sweet-scented lavender is finding its niche here, too. The magic is in the elevation. At 3000ft, Kula's cool nights and sunny days are ideal for growing all sorts of crops, making Kula synonymous with fresh veggies on any Maui menu.

Sights

Ali'i Kula Lavender GARDENS
(Map p182; ☎808-878-3004; www.aklmaui.com; 1100 Waipoli Rd; $3; ⏲9am-4pm) On a broad hillside with panoramic views of the West Maui Mountains and the Central Maui coast, this charming lavender farm is a scenic place to relax and is ideal for families. Follow fragrant pathways, visit a gift shop with lavender products, and enjoy a scone and a cup of lavender tea or coffee (surprisingly good) on a lanai with sweeping views.

Worcester Glassworks GALLERY
(Map p182; ☎808-878-4000; www.worcesterglassworks.com; 4626 Lower Kula Rd; ⏲noon-5pm Mon-Sat) This family-run studio and gallery has produced some amazing pieces over the years, particularly the sand-blasted glass in natural forms (eg seashells). Visitors can peruse the gallery, but at the time of research artists were taking a break from their solar-powered furnaces for a while. The adjacent store offers gorgeous pieces for sale. Call ahead to confirm it's open.

Kula Botanical Garden GARDENS
(Map p182; ☎808-878-1715; www.kulabotanicalgarden.com; 638 Kekaulike Ave; adult/child 6-10yr $10/3, under 6yr free; ⏲9am-4pm) 🍃 Walking paths wind through themed plantings, including native Hawaiian specimens and a 'taboo garden' of poisonous plants. Because a stream runs through it, the garden supports water-thirsty plants that you won't find in other Kula gardens. After rain the whole place is an explosion of color. There are more than 2500 plant species to view.

Harold W Rice Memorial Park PARK
(Map p182; ☎808-572-8122; www.mauicounty.gov/Facilities; 5700 Kula Hwy) On a hillside between the Kula Hwy and Lower Kula Rd, this grassy park is a nice place to enjoy a picnic while soaking up the sweeping views of the West Maui Mountains and coastline. A feral chicken or two might strut past.

Holy Ghost Church CHURCH
(Map p182; ☎808-878-1261; www.kulacatholiccommunity.org; 4300 Lower Kula Rd; ⏲8am-6pm) Waiakoa's hillside Holy Ghost Church was built in 1895 by Portuguese immigrants. The church features a beautifully ornate interior that looks like it came right out of the Old World, as indeed much of it did. The gilded altar was carved by renowned Austrian woodcarver Ferdinand Stuflesser and shipped in pieces around the Cape of Good Hope.

Activities

Proflyght Paragliding PARAGLIDING
(Map p182; ☎808-874-5433; www.paraglidemaui.com; 1598 Waipoli Rd; paraglide 1000/3000ft $145/265; ⏲office 7am-7pm, flights 2hr after sunrise) Strap into a tandem paraglider with a certified instructor and take a running

leap off the cliffs beneath Polipoli Spring State Recreation Area. This is thrilling stuff. Participants must be at least eight years old and under 230lb.

Skyline Eco-Adventures ADVENTURE SPORTS
(Map p182; ☎808-518-4189; www.zipline.com; 18303 Haleakalā Hwy; zipline tour adult/child under 18yr from $110/70; ⏰8:30am-2pm) Maui's first zipline has a prime location on the slopes of Haleakalā. The five lines are relatively short (100ft to 850ft) compared with the competition, although a unique 'pendulum zip' adds some spice. The highest jump is around 80ft and you'll zip from zero to 45mph in seconds.

Ultimate Frisbee Golf Park OUTDOORS
(Map p182; Waipoli Rd; ⏰sunrise-sunset) FREE Past Ali'i Kula lavender farm (p194) at the end of the first section of switchbacks on Waipoli Rd is a free 18-hole Frisbee-golf park hidden in the trees. Simply bring your own disc, park up on the left of the forest and start playing. Look for the metal-basket targets dotted around the area.

Tours

O'o Farm FOOD & DRINK
(Map p182; ☎808-667-4341; www.oofarm.com; 651 Waipoli Rd; tours $74; ⏰farm tour 10:30am-1:30pm Mon-Fri, coffee tour 8:30-11:30am Mon-Fri) Whether you're a gardener or a gourmet you're going to love a tour of this Upcountry farm, which supplies Pacifico restaurant and the Feast at Lele. Where else can you help harvest your meal, give the goodies to a gourmet chef and feast on the bounty? On the seed-to-cup coffee tours you'll learn about coffee cultivation. All tours by reservation only.

Festivals & Events

Holy Ghost Feast CULTURAL
(www.kulacatholiccommunity.org/feast.html; Holy Ghost Church, 4300 Lower Kula Rd; ⏰May or Jun; 👪) This festival, held at the Holy Ghost Church (p194) on Pentecost weekend (50 days after Easter), celebrates Kula's Portuguese heritage. It's a family event with games, craft vendors, a farmers market and a free Hawaiian-Portuguese lunch on Sunday.

Sleeping & Eating

Kula Lodge CABIN $$
(Map p182; ☎808-878-1535; www.kulalodge.com; 15200 Haleakalā Hwy; cabins $210-285; 📶) These five chintzy cabins are about 45 minutes from the summit of Haleakalā. All rustic units with brown wood and floral bedspreads come with lanai, coffee makers and extra blankets, but no TVs or kitchenettes. Four have open lofts, which are great for kids but offer no privacy. Wi-fi is available at the on-site restaurant.

Kula Sandalwoods Cafe & Cottages BREAKFAST $
(Map p182; ☎808-878-3523; www.kulasandalwoods.com; 15427 Haleakalā Hwy; meals from $9.75; ⏰8am-3pm Mon-Sat, to noon Sun; 📶) This retro diner offers a hearty breakfast – eggs Benedict, omelets, hotcakes and French toast – and is located on the doorstep of Haleakalā National Park. There are also six rustic cottages, offering sweeping views at a good price ($190 to $200 for one to two guests).

★ **Kula Lodge Restaurant** HAWAIIAN $$$
(Map p182; ☎808-878-1535; www.kulalodge.com; 15200 Haleakalā Hwy; mains breakfast $13-27, lunch $16-24, dinner $27-43; ⏰7am-9pm) Assisted by its staggering view, one of the best of any Maui restaurant, veteran chef Marc McDowell has the kitchen humming to a farm-to-table variety menu. Locally sourced salads are delicious. Outside, brick ovens provide build-your-own pizzas served under cabanas (11am to 8pm). A spectacular sunset here is the perfect ending to a day on the Haleakalā summit.

★ **Kula Bistro** ITALIAN $$$
(Map p182; ☎808-871-2960; www.kulabistro.com; 4566 Lower Kula Rd; pizza from $16, mains $35-48; ⏰7:30-10:30am & 11am-8pm Tue-Sun, 11am-8pm Mon) This superb bistro offers a retro dining room, sparkling service and delicious home cooking, including fabulous pizza, pasta and uber-fresh seafood dishes served with greens and rice or a potato-based side. Order a huge coconut-cream pie (enough for two) to finish. BYOB wine from Morihara Store (p196) across the street. No corkage fee.

La Provence CAFE $$$
(Map p182; ☎808-878-1313; 3158 Lower Kula Rd, Waiakoa; mains $22-35; ⏰9am-1.45pm Wed-Sun) One of Kula's best-kept secrets, this little courtyard restaurant in the middle of nowhere is a lovely spot for lunch (try the crepes). Mains include poulet cordon bleu, filet mignon with prawns, and rack of lamb with green-peppercorn sauce. Cash only.

Shopping

Kula Country Farms FOOD
(Map p182; ☎808-878-8381; https://kulacountryfarmsmaui.com; 6240 Kula Hwy; ⏰10am-4pm; 👪) If you're driving past this large produce stand in October with the kids, you will have

to pull over for the happenin' pumpkin patch. Resistance is futile – and the place does look fun. Otherwise, stop for the fresh fruit, vegetables and flowers from local farms, as well as a good selection of Maui-sourced jams, sauces and honeys, plus farm-themed gifts.

Morihara Store FOOD & DRINKS
(Map p182; ☎808-878-2502; 4581 Lower Kula Rd; ⊙6:30am-8pm Mon-Sat, 7:30am-8pm Sun) Grocery store for picnic supplies and BYOB booze for the Kula Bistro (p195) opposite.

Keokea

Blink-and-you'll-miss it Keokea is the last real town before Hana. The sum total of the town center consists of a coffee shop, an art gallery, a gas station, and two small stores: the Ching Store and the Fong Store. The latter are indicative of Hawaii's immigrant populations. Drawn by the rich soil, Hakka Chinese farmers migrated to this remote corner of Kula at the turn of the 20th century.

But the village isn't entirely off the world's radar – media powerhouse Oprah Winfrey has a home and property in the area. With a low-key vibe and a gorgeous backdrop of green fields and a deep blue sea, this is a pleasant place to hide out for days or hours.

Sights & Activities

Sun Yat-sen Park PARK
(Map p182; ☎808-572-8122; www.mauicounty.gov/Facilities; 13434 Kula Hwy, cnr Kula Hwy & Kamaole Rd; ⊙7am-7pm; P) For a time Sun Yat-sen, father of the Chinese nationalist movement, lived in Keokea. He's honored at Sun Yat-sen Park, found along the Kula Hwy (Hwy 37), 1.7 miles beyond Grandma's Coffee House (p196). The park has picnic tables and is a great place to soak up the broad vistas that stretch clear across to West Maui.

St John's Episcopal Church CHURCH
(Map p182; ☎808-878-1485; www.stjohnsmaui.org; 8992 Kula Hwy; ⊙services 7:30am & 9:30am Sun) Overlooking a gorgeous view of the coast, this local landmark (c 1907) still bears its name in Chinese characters. It hosts the annual Kula Fest in early fall.

Kwock Hing Society HISTORIC BUILDING
(Map p182; 178 Middle Rd) This colorful two-story period building (1907) was constructed to provide services to immigrant Chinese workers. Now on the National Register of Historic Places, it's one of two such halls surviving on Maui, and contains an interesting photo collection on the lives of Chinese immigrants. It's generally locked, but Richard Shim (☎808-264-1186) will let you in. Speak loudly.

Thompson Road SCENIC DRIVE
(Map p182; Thompson Rd) Just up from Grandma's Coffee House (p196), this narrow and steep country road swoops briefly through emerald-green pastures, flanked by a lava rock wall. Beyond the wall? More green and the deep blue coast. You'll be pulling over for photos, especially if clouds are adding a bit of sparkle to the light. It's magical – so drive slowly, and respect the neighbors.

Thompson Ranch HORSEBACK RIDING
(Map p182; ☎808-878-1910; www.thompsonranchmaui.com; cnr Middle & Polipoli Rds; morning/sunset/picnic rides $150/175/200; ⊙tour 10am; 👪) Join these folks for horseback rides across ranchland in the cool Upcountry bordering Polipoli Spring State Recreation Area. At elevations of 4000ft to 6000ft, it's a memorable ride for those who enjoy mountain scenery. Rides last about two hours. Children must be at least eight years old. Reserve ahead. Located 1 mile up Polipoli Rd, on the left.

Sleeping & Eating

Star Lookout COTTAGE $$
(Map p182; ☎907-250-2364; www.starlookout.com; 622 Thompson Rd; cottages $275; 📶) Starry skies, an outdoor hot tub and grounds so quiet you can hear the flowers bloom. Half a mile up a one-lane road from Keokea center, this two-bedroom cottage with a loft sleeps four comfortably, six in a pinch. There's also a full kitchen and wood-burning stove.

★**Grandma's Coffee House** CAFE $
(Map p182; ☎808-878-2140; www.grandmascoffee.com; 9232 Kula Hwy; coffee from $2.50, sandwiches $8-10, cakes from $5.75; ⊙7am-5pm Sun-Tue, to 8pm Wed-Sat) 🍃 Worthy of a Norman Rockwell painting, this charming island landmark with its creaking screen door and carved wooden tables grows its own coffee and dishes up tasty fresh salads, sandwiches and cakes (try the pineapple-banana dream cake). Take your goodies out on the lanai and eat right under the coffee trees.

Information

Kula Hospital (☎808-878-1221; www.mauihealthsystem.org; 100 Keokea Pl; ⊙emergency room 24hr)

OFF THE BEATEN TRACK

EXPLORING A CLOUD FOREST

This misty cloud forest on the western slope of Haleakalā takes you deep off the beaten path. Crisscrossed with lightly trodden trails, it offers cool, shady and refreshing hikes amid tall redwoods, where a profound stillness prevails.

Half the fun is just getting here. Access is via spectacular Waipoli Rd, off Hwy 377, not far from the latter's southern intersection with the Kula Hwy (Hwy 37). This narrow ribbon twists back and forth for miles, never seeming to end. Layers of clouds drift in and out, revealing panoramic vistas across green rolling hills to the islands of Lana'i and Kaho'olawe. In the morning, you might see paragliders floating overhead.

The road has some soft shoulders, but the first 6 miles are paved. It becomes dirt after entering the Kula Forest Reserve, and requires a 4WD, especially if mud prevails, although locals can be seen crawling slowly to the campground in 2WDs.

On the upper slopes of Haleakalā, the remote and heavily forested **Polipoli Spring State Recreation Area** (Map p182; ☎808-984-8109; http://dlnr.hawaii.gov/dsp/parks/maui; Waipoli Rd; ⏰6am-6pm; P) is the place for solitary hiking. Check the park website or call before you make the drive (4WD only), or hike in. Trails and facilities can be closed due to weather damage, with downed trees and flash floods affecting the trails. There's a cabin and camping facilities, but it sits at 6200ft, so it can get chilly at night. Bring wet-weather gear.

'Ulupalakua

The sprawling 18,000-acre 'Ulupalakua Ranch is home to thousands of cattle, as well as a small herd of Rocky Mountain elk, which dot the hillside pastures. The ranch is worked by *paniolo,* Hawaii cowboys who have been here for generations. Most people stop by to visit the bustling winery, which sits on 'Ulupalakua Ranch's land about 6 miles beyond Keokea.

Hwy 37 winds south through ranch country, offering good views of Kaho'olawe and the little island of Molokini. With a stop at the winery, the drive to 'Ulupalakua is a nice half-day excursion from Central Maui and Pa'ia. After the vineyard, it's another 25 dusty, bumpy miles to Kipahulu along Pi'ilani Hwy.

Activities

Triple L Ranch HORSEBACK RIDING

(☎808-280-7070; www.triplelranchmaui.com; 15900 Pi'ilani Hwy; 1/2hr $135/160, half/full day $285/375; ⏰9am-6:30pm) These personalized trail rides offer the opportunity to explore the volcanic Ka'naio region, from a 90-minute outing around the cattle ranch to half- and full-day excursions to the sea and back. For ages 12 and over. Reserve 24 hours ahead.

Tours

Maui Wine WINE

(Map p182; ☎808-878-6058; www.mauiwine.com; 14815 Pi'ilani Hwy; wines per glass from $7, per bottle $14-50; ⏰10am-5pm, tours 10:30am & 1:30pm) Formerly Tedeschi Vineyards, Maui's sole winery offers free tastings in its historic stone cottage and twice-daily 30-minute tours, also complimentary. It makes noteworthy products, from grape wines to novelty wines, using local fruit to great effect. Try the sweet Maui Splash, a light blend of pineapple and passion fruit, then stroll the historic grounds.

Festivals & Events

'Ulupalakua Holiday Tree Lighting CULTURAL

(☎808-878-6058; www.mauiwine.com; 14815 Pi'ilani Hwy; ⏰Dec;) On a Saturday in early December, 'Ulupalakua Ranch sponsors a fun holiday bash on the lawn of Maui Wine. Come by for children's games, live music, an outdoor movie and the lighting of a 25ft-tall decorated Monterey pine. There's wine tasting, too. It is free, but the winery requests that guests bring a canned good for Maui Food Bank.

Eating

'Ulupalakua Ranch Store DELI $

(Map p182; ☎808-878-2561; www.ulupalakuaranch.com; 14800 Pi'ilani Hwy; burgers $11-13; ⏰store 9:30am-5:30pm, grill 11am-4pm) Sidle up to the life-size wooden cowboys on the porch and say howdy. Then pop inside and check out the cowboy hats and souvenir T-shirts. If it's lunchtime, mosey over to the grill and treat yourself to an organic ranch-raised elk burger. The meats on the menu are Maui sourced. Eat on the lanai or in the relaxing garden out back.

AT A GLANCE

ENDANGERED NENE IN THE PARK
223

BEST HIKE
Keonehe'ehe'e (Sliding Sands) Trail (p202)

BEST WATERFALL
Makahiku Falls (p205)

BEST VIEW
Haleakalā Visitor Center (p210)

WHEN TO GO

Jan–Dec Summit temperatures can fluctuate rapidly, from below freezing to 50°F (10°C) to 60°F (15°C) year-round.

Jun–Aug Busy season, when families travel to Maui during their summer vacation.

Dec–Feb Park visitation numbers increase during holidays and across winter.

Pīpīwai Trail (p205)

Haleakalā National Park

To peer into the soul of Maui, climb to the dormant summit of Haleakalā volcano. Below the rim, mists caress a vast crater, which glows ethereally in the early light of sunrise. Lookouts provide breathtaking views of the moonscape below and the cinder cones marching across it.

The rest of this amazing park, which is divided into two distinct sections, is all about interacting with this mountain of solid lava and its rare life-forms, some of them found only here. You can hike down into the crater, follow lush trails on the slopes, or put your mountain bike through its paces. For the ultimate adventure, get a permit, bring a tent and camp beneath the stars. The experience will stick with you for a lifetime.

INCLUDES

Haleakalā National Park Highlights

1 Haleakalā Summit (p201) Watching the day break or the sun set above the clouds, or peering at the cosmos after sunset.

2 Pipiwai Trail (p205) Checking out gorgeous waterfalls and a magical bamboo forest.

3 Haleakalā Crater (p201) Hiking past cinder cones and other natural wonders on the Keonehe'ehe'e (Sliding Sands) Trail.

4 Hosmer Grove (p204) Scanning for native birds while ogling the towering – but non-native – trees.

5 Waterfalls (p205) Taking a photo of the cascading Ohe'o Gulch pools from the Kuloa Point Trail (p205).

6 Wild camping (p213) Spending the night in the depths of the crater or steps from the pounding sea at Kipahulu Campground.

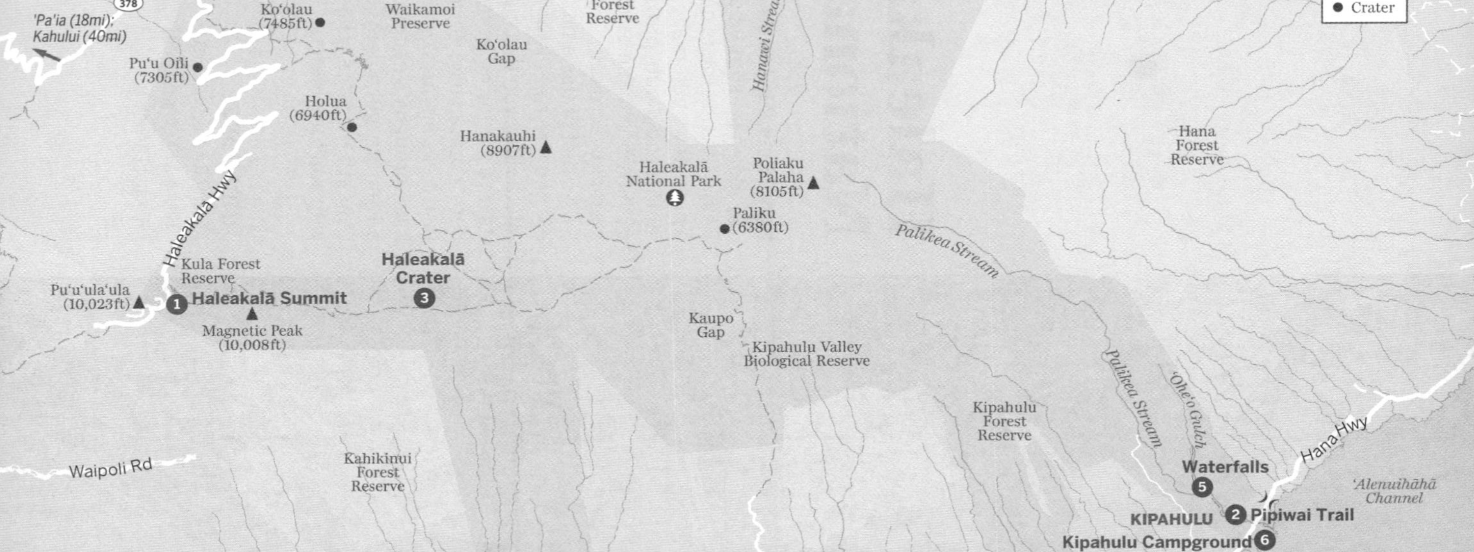

Information

Haleakalā National Park (808-572-4400; www.nps.gov/hale; 3-day pass car $30, motorcycle $25, individual on foot or bicycle $15; P) has two very different sections (not connected and must be visited separately): the ethereal Summit Area and the coastal Kipahulu Area. There is no direct access between them. Thus travelers typically visit the summit on one day and the Kipahulu Area on another (usually heading to or from Hana). One entrance ticket is good for both areas (it's valid for three days).

If you plan to watch the sunrise, remember to make a reservation at www.recreation.gov within 60 days of your visit, which covers your vehicle, or sign up for a commercial tour. You cannot enter the park between 3am and 7am without the reservation receipt and the photo ID of the reservation holder.

Summit Area

History

Ancient Hawaiians did not inhabit the summit, but they came up the mountain and built heiau (temples) at some of the cinder cones. The primary goddess of Haleakalā, Lilinoe (also known as the mist goddess), was worshipped here. Today, Native Hawaiians still connect spiritually on the summit, and also come to study star navigation.

In 1916 Haleakalā became part of Hawai'i National Park, along with its Big Island siblings, Mauna Loa and Kilauea. In 1961 Haleakalā National Park became an independent entity; in 1969 its boundaries were expanded down into the Kipahulu Valley. And in 1980 the park was designated an International Biosphere Reserve by Unesco.

There are around 50 federally listed (endangered and threatened) species in the perimeters of the park, the largest number in any US national park. This number includes plant species, birdlife, damselfly, one bat, a monk seal and sea turtles.

Sights

The summit is an unabashed showstopper. Often referred to as the world's largest dormant volcano, the floor of Haleakalā is a colossal 7.5 miles wide, 2.5 miles long and 3000ft deep – nearly as large as Manhattan. In its prime, Haleakalā reached a height of 12,000ft before water erosion carved out two large river valleys that eventually merged to form Haleakalā crater. Technically, as geologists like to point out, it's not a true 'crater,' but to sightseers that's just nitpicking. Valley or crater, complete with dramatic cinder cones, it's a phenomenal sight like no other in the US national-park system.

★ Pu'u'ula'ula (Red Hill) Overlook VIEWPOINT

(www.nps.gov/hale; Summit, Haleakalā Hwy; P) You may find yourself standing above the clouds while exploring Pu'u'ula'ula (10,023ft), Maui's highest point. The **summit building** provides a top-of-the-world panorama from its wraparound windows. On a clear day you can see Hawai'i (Big Island), Lana'i, Moloka'i and even O'ahu. When the light's right, the colors of the crater are nothing short of spectacular, with grays, greens, reds and browns.

Leleiwi Overlook VIEWPOINT

(www.nps.gov/hale; Haleakalā Hwy) For your first jaw-dropping look into the crater and its cinder cones, stop at Leleiwi Overlook (8840ft), midway between the Park Headquarters Visitor Center and the summit. You can literally watch the weather form at your feet, as ever-changing clouds float in and out. From the parking lot it's a five-minute walk (0.25 miles) across a gravel trail to the overlook.

Kalahaku Overlook VIEWPOINT

(www.nps.gov/hale; Haleakalā Hwy; P) Don't miss this one. Kalahaku Overlook (9324ft), 0.8 miles beyond Leleiwi Overlook, offers a bird's-eye view of the crater floor and the ant-size hikers on the trails snaking around the cinder cones below. At the observation deck, plaques provide information on each of the volcanic formations that punctuate the crater floor. From the deck you'll also get a perfect angle for viewing both the Ko'olau Gap and the Kaupo Gap on the rim of Haleakalā.

Haleakalā Summit Area VIEWPOINT

(www.nps.gov/hale; Haleakalā Hwy; P) Perched on the crater rim at 9745ft, the visitor center (p210) is the park's main viewing spot. Sun, shadow and clouds reflecting on the crater floor create a mesmerizing dance of light and color. The parking lot gets packed ahead of sunrise and sunset, and it stays pretty full in between. Leave the crowds behind by doing the 10-minute hike up Pa Ka'oao (White Hill), which begins at the eastern side of the visitor center and provides stunning views.

Hosmer Grove FOREST

(www.nps.gove/hale; P) A pleasant half-mile loop trail (20-minute walk) winds through

HIKING & CYCLING IN HALEAKALĀ NATIONAL PARK

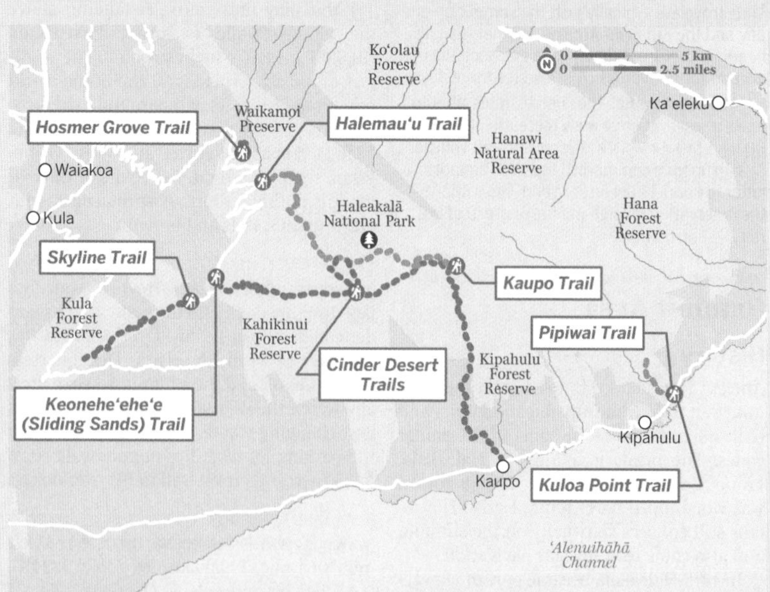

SUMMIT AREA

☆ Keonehe'ehe'e (Sliding Sands) Trail

START/END HALEAKALĀ VISITOR CENTER
DISTANCE/DURATION 17.8 MILES ROUND TRIP; TWO DAYS
DIFFICULTY STRENUOUS

The path descends into an unearthly world of stark lava sights and ever-changing clouds. The trailhead is at the entrance to the visitor center parking lot, beside Pa Ka'oao (White Hill). This hike is best done in two days, so secure a Paliku camping or cabin permit in advance.

The first thing you'll notice? The silence. The only sound is the crunching of volcanic cinders beneath your feet. If you're pressed for time, just descending 20 minutes will reward you with an into-the-crater experience and fabulous photo opportunities. The climb out, unfortunately, takes nearly twice as long.

The first 6 miles follow the southern wall, with great views. Vegetation is minimal, but you may see green kūpaoa plants and shimmering silverswords. At the first major overlook, after the long straightaway, you can see cinder cones dotting the bottom of the crater. The views only improve from here. Switchbacks drop from the overlook. A spur trail to Ka Lu'u o ka Ō'ō cinder cone, which arises to your left about 2 miles down, has been closed. Enjoy the view from where you are. Next up? A field of silverswords. After that a narrow path squeezes through a tall lava formation, framing the peaks ahead.

Four miles down, after an elevation drop of 2500ft, Keonehe'ehe'e Trail intersects with a spur that leads north into the cinder desert, where it connects with the Halemau'u Trail after 1.6 miles.

Continuing on Keonehe'ehe'e, head across the crater for 2 miles to Kapalaoa. Verdant ridges rise on your right, giving way to ropy *pahoehoe* (smooth-flowing lava). Kapalaoa is reached after roughly four hours.

From cinder cones to silverswords, the sights are otherworldly when hiking inside Haleakalā crater. Waterfalls and a bamboo forest keep views wild on the coast. And biking? Hold on tight!

From here to **Paliku** (p210), the descent is gentle and the vegetation gradually increases. Paliku (6380ft) is beneath a sheer cliff at the eastern end of the crater. In contrast to the crater's barren western end, this area receives heavy rainfall, with ohia forests climbing the slopes.

After an overnight in Paliku cabin or the adjacent campground, retrace your steps to the visitor center.

A shorter six-hour day-hike option is a 10.2-mile Keonehe'ehe'e (Sliding Sands) hike and Halemau'u Trail combo (only a small 45-minute uphill section on the whole route). For the combo trail, hike start at the Haleakalā Visitor Center and Keonehe'ehe'e (Sliding Sands) trailhead. Leave your car at the Halemau'u Trail and hitchhike up the mountain (there's a designated hitchhiking area near the Halemau'u trailhead for this very purpose).

☆ Halemau'u Trail

START/END 3.5 MILES ABOVE PARK HEADQUARTERS VISITOR CENTER
DISTANCE/DURATION 7.4 MILES ROUND TRIP; SEVEN TO EIGHT HOURS
DIFFICULTY MODERATE

With views of crater walls, lava tubes and cinder cones, the Halemau'u Trail down to the Holua campground and back is a memorable day hike. Just be sure to start early, before the afternoon clouds roll in and visibility vanishes. The first mile is fairly level and offers a fine view of the crater with Ko'olau Gap to the east.

Some choose to combine the trail with the Keonehe'ehe'e (Sliding Sands) Trail, adding an extra 4.5 miles but making it an even more enjoyable one-way hike that's nearly all downhill (except 45 minutes). The two trails combined (10.2 miles) take less time – around six hours – to complete because they are mostly downhill. Start at the Haleakalā Visitor Center (leave your car at the Halemau'u Trail and hitchhike up the mountain from the designated hitchhiking area near the Halemau'u trailhead).

The Halemau'u Trail on its own (if not combined with the Sliding Sands Trail) descends 1400ft along 2 miles of switchbacks to the crater floor and on to the Holua campground (6940ft). You'll see impressive views of the crater walls rising a few thousand feet to the west. Several lava tubes are visible from the trail, but since endangered species use them for shelter the Park Service has made them off-limits.

If you have the energy, push on just another mile to reach some colorful cinder cones, being sure to make a short detour onto the **Silversword Loop**, where you'll see the loop's namesake plants, also called *'ahinahina*, in various stages of growth. In summer their tall stalks should be ablaze with hundreds of maroon-and-yellow blossoms. But be careful: half of all *'ahinahina* today are trampled to death as seedlings, mostly by careless hikers who wander off trails and inadvertently crush the plants' shallow, laterally growing roots. The trail continues another 6.3 miles to the Paliku cabin.

The trailhead to Halemau'u is 3.5 miles above the Park Headquarters Visitor Center and about 6 miles below the Haleakalā Visitor Center. There's a fair chance you'll see nene (native geese) in the parking lot.

☆ Cinder Desert Trails

START/END HALEAKALĀ CRATER
DISTANCE/DURATION 1.5+ MILES ONE WAY (IN ADDITION TO CONNECTING TRAILS TO THE KEONEHE'EHE'E TRAIL OR HALEMAU'U TRAIL); ONE TO THREE HOURS
DIFFICULTY MODERATE

Two spur trails connect the Keonehe'ehe'e (Sliding Sands) Trail with the Halemau'u Trail between Paliku and Holua cabins. If you're camping you may have time to do them both, as the trails are not very long.

The spur trail furthest west takes in many of the crater's most kaleidoscopic cones, and the viewing angle changes with every step. If you prefer stark, black and barren, the other spur trail takes you through *'a'a* (rough, jagged lava) and *pahoehoe* (smooth-flowing lava) fields.

Both trails end up on the northern side of the cinder desert near Kawilinau, which is also known as the **Bottomless Pit**. There's not much to see, as you can't really get a good look down the narrow shaft. The real prize is the nearby short loop trail, where you can sit for a while in the saddle of prime vantage point Pele's Paint Pot Lookout.

☆ Kaupo Trail

START PALIKU CAMPGROUND
END KAUPO
DISTANCE/DURATION 8.6 MILES ONE WAY; ONE DAY
DIFFICULTY VERY STRENUOUS

The most extreme of Haleakalā's hikes is the unmaintained Kaupo Trail, which starts at the Paliku campground and descends to Kaupo on the southern coast. Be prepared for ankle-twisting conditions, blistered feet, intense tropical sun, torrential showers and a possibly hard-to-follow path. Your knees will take a pounding as you descend more than 6100ft over 8.6 miles.

The first 3.7 miles of the trail drop 2500ft in elevation before reaching the park boundary. It's a steep, rocky path through rough lava and brushland, with short switchbacks alternating with level stretches. From here you'll be rewarded with spectacular ocean views.

The last 4.9 miles pass through Kaupo Ranch property on a rough 4WD trail as it descends to the bottom of Kaupo Gap, exiting into a forest where feral pigs snuffle about. Here trail markings become vague, but once you reach the dirt road it's another 1.5 miles to the end at the eastern side of the Kaupo Store.

The 'village' of **Kaupo** is a long way from anywhere, with light traffic. Still, you'll probably manage a lift. If you have to walk the final stretch, it's 8 miles to the 'Ohe'o Gulch campground.

Because this is such a strenuous and remote trail, and it's easy to lose your way, it's not advisable to hike it alone. Get advice from rangers about current conditions before you set off. No camping is allowed on Kaupo Ranch property, so most hikers spend the night at the Paliku campground and then get an early start.

☆ Skyline Trail

START SCIENCE CITY
END POLIPOLI SPRING STATE RECREATION AREA
DISTANCE/DURATION 8.5 MILES ONE WAY; FOUR HOURS
DIFFICULTY MODERATE

This cinematic trail, which rides the precipitous spine of Haleakalā, begins just beyond the summit at a lofty elevation (9750ft) and leads down to the campground at Polipoli Spring State Recreation Area (6200ft). Get an early start to enjoy the views before clouds take over.

To get to the trailhead, go past Pu'u'ula'ula (Red Hill) Overlook and take the road to the left just before Science City. The road, which passes over a cattle grate, is signposted not for public use, but continue and you'll soon find a Na Ala Hele sign marking the trailhead.

The Skyline Trail starts in barren open terrain of volcanic cinder, a moon walk that passes more than a dozen cinder cones and craters. The first mile is rough lava rock. After three crunchy miles, it reaches the tree line (8500ft) and enters native mamane forest. In winter mamane is heavy with flowers that look like yellow sweet-pea blossoms. There's solitude on this walk. If the clouds treat you kindly, you'll have broad views all the way between the barren summit and the dense cloud forest. Eventually the trail meets the Polipoli access road, where you can either walk to the paved road in about 4 miles, or continue via the Haleakalā Ridge Trail and Polipoli Trail to the campground.

If you prefer treads to hiking boots, the Skyline Trail is also an exhilarating adventure on a mountain bike. Just look out for hikers!

☆ Hosmer Grove Trail

START/END HOSMER GROVE CAMPGROUND
DISTANCE/DURATION 0.5-MILE LOOP; 20 MINUTES
DIFFICULTY EASY

Anyone who is looking for a little greenery after hiking the crater will enjoy this shaded woodland walk, as will birders. The half-mile loop trail starts at Hosmer Grove campground, 0.75 miles south of the Park Headquarters Visitor Center, in a forest of lofty trees.

The exotics here were introduced in 1910 in an effort to develop a lumber industry in Hawaii. Species include fragrant incense cedar, Norway spruce, Douglas fir, eucalyptus and various pines. Although the trees adapted well enough to grow, they didn't grow fast enough at these elevations to make tree harvesting practical.

After the forest, the trail moves into native shrubland, with *'akala* (Hawaiian raspberry), mamane, *pilo, kilau* ferns and sandalwood. The *'ohelo,* a berry sacred to the volcano goddess Pele, and the *pukiawe,* which has red and white berries and evergreen leaves, are favored by nene. Two sets of birdwatching binoculars are set up for those wanting a closer look.

Listen for the calls of the native *'i'iwi* and *'apapane;* both are fairly common here. The *'i'iwi* has a very loud squeaking call, orange legs and a curved salmon-colored bill. The *'apapane,* a fast-moving bird with a black bill, black legs and a white undertail, feeds on the nectar of bright red ohia flowers, and its wings make a distinctive whirring sound. *'Amakihi,* Maui *'alauahio* and *'ākohekohe* birds can also be spotted here. A handy info board will help you identify them en route.

KIPAHULU AREA

☆ Pipiwai Trail

START/END KIPAHULU VISITOR CENTER
DISTANCE/DURATION 4 MILES ROUND TRIP; TWO HOURS
DIFFICULTY MODERATE

Ready for an adventure? This super-fun trail ascends alongside the 'Ohe'o stream bed, rewarding hikers with picture-perfect views of waterfalls and an otherworldly trip through a bamboo grove. The trail starts on the *mauka* (inland) side of the visitor center and leads up to Makahiku Falls (0.5 miles) and Waimoku Falls (2 miles). To see both falls, allow about two hours return. Can be muddy!

Along the path you'll pass large mango trees and patches of guava before coming to an overlook after about 10 minutes. **Makahiku Falls**, a long bridal-veil waterfall that drops into a deep gorge, is just off to the right. Thick green ferns cover the sides of 200ft basalt cliffs where the water cascades – a very rewarding scene for such a short walk.

Continuing along the main trail, you'll walk beneath old banyan trees, cross Palikea Stream (bug spray advisable here) and enter the wonderland of the **Bamboo Forest,** where thick groves of bamboo bang together musically in the wind. The upper section is muddy, but boardwalks cover most of the mud. Beyond the bamboo forest is **Waimoku Falls**, a thin, lacy 400ft waterfall dropping down a sheer rock face. When you come out of the first grove you'll see the waterfall in the distance. Forget swimming under Waimoku Falls – its pool is shallow and there's a danger of falling rocks.

Wear your grippy water shoes for this one.

☆ Kuloa Point Trail

START/END NEAR KIPAHULU VISITOR CENTER
DISTANCE/DURATION 0.5-MILE LOOP; 20 MINUTES
DIFFICULTY EASY

Even if you're tight on time, be sure to take this 20-minute stroll. The Kuloa Point Trail, a half-mile loop, runs from the Kipahulu Visitor Center down to the lower pools and back. A few minutes down you'll reach a broad grassy knoll with a gorgeous view of the Hana coast. On a clear day you can see Hawai'i (the Big Island) 30 miles away across 'Alenuihāhā Channel.

The large freshwater pools along the trail are terraced one atop the other and connected by gentle cascades. They may look calm, but flash floods have taken several lives here, so the Park Service does not recommend swimming in them.

Haleakalā Summit Area

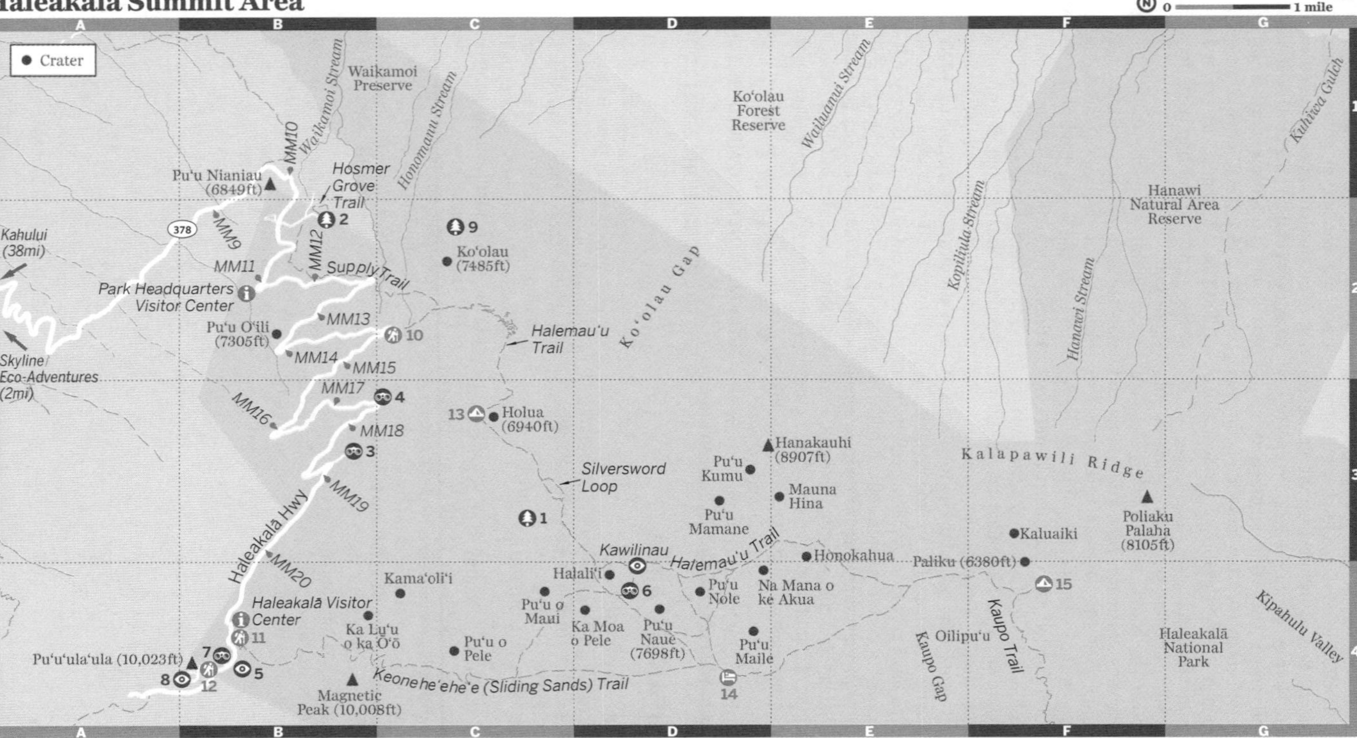

Haleakalā Summit Area

Hosmer Grove, which is home to non-native tree species – including pine, fir and eucalyptus – as well as native scrubland. The site is also popular with campers and picnickers. The whole area is sweetened with the scent of eucalyptus and alive with the red flashes and calls of native birds. Hosmer Grove sits on a side road just after the park's entrance booth.

Waikamoi Preserve NATURE RESERVE
(808-572-7849; www.nature.org; hiking tour 2nd Sat of month) FREE This windswept native cloud forest supports one of the rarest ecosystems on earth. Managed by the Nature Conservancy, the 8951-acre preserve provides the last stronghold for hundreds of species of native plant and forest bird. Open only by guided tour, the preserve is a place to look for the *'i'iwi* and the *'apapane* (both honeycreepers with bright red feathers).

Pele's Paint Pot Lookout VIEWPOINT
(Map p238; www.nps.gov/hale) Along the loop trail south of Kawilinau, and accessible via Halemau'u Trail and Keonehe'ehe'e (Sliding Sands) Trail, this is the crater's most brilliant vantage point.

Science City LANDMARK
(Haleakalā Observatories; www.ifa.hawaii.edu) As the sun rises, this collection of domed observatories shimmers just beyond the summit. Nicknamed Science City, this area is, unfortunately, off-limits to visitors, as it houses some very expensive equipment, including a telescope that can track objects the size of a basketball from 20,000 miles away. It's used for studying the sun and outer space.

Magnetic Peak MOUNTAIN
(www.nps.gov/hale) The iron-rich cinders in this flat-top hill, which lies immediately southeast of the summit building (in the direction of Hawai'i, the Big Island), pack enough magnetism to play havoc with your compass. Modest as it looks, it's also – at 10,008ft – the second-highest point on Maui.

Activities

Cycling

Cycling downhill from the summit to the sea, via Makawao and Pa'ia, is a popular pursuit. Several companies lead tours to the summit but, due to past problems, cannot begin the cycling part of the tour within the park. Cycling must begin outside park boundaries (starting at around 6000ft). If you want to explore the summit, tour vans will typically shuttle you to the top for a short visit then drive you down to a permissible starting point. From here, you will either pedal at your own pace or ride with a guide-led group, depending on the tour company. Many people combine a sunrise trip (p208) with a downhill ride, requiring a very early start.

Individual cyclists who are not part of a commercial tour are allowed to pedal from the summit without restriction. If you choose this option, you will need to arrange bike rental and transportation on your own. This is a cheaper option. Bike racks are typically provided with the rental for free or for a small fee. For rental equipment, see Island Biker (p134) in Kahului, or Maui Cyclery (p177) in Pa'ia.

Mountain Biking

The **Skyline Trail** (p204) is a wild ride from Science City Access Rd down to Polipoli Spring State Recreation Area. The trail may occasionally close due to weather damage. Check its status at https://hawaiitrails.hawaii.gov/trails or one of the local bike shops.

THE SUNRISE EXPERIENCE

Haleakalā' means 'House of the Sun.' So it's no surprise that, since the time of the first Hawaiians, people have been making pilgrimages up to Haleakalā to watch the sunrise. It is an experience that borders on the mystical. Mark Twain called it the 'sublimest spectacle' that he had ever seen.

In recent years the number of cars arriving at the summit has often exceeded the number of available parking spaces, leading to severe overcrowding. To escape the hordes, visitors have strayed into fragile endangered-species habitats or dangerous areas. Cars parking outside designated areas also threaten the fragile landscape and could block emergency vehicles. In January 2016 park officials said that cars exceeding parking spaces occurred 98% of the time, with an average of 600 people on the summit. In 2017, to manage crowds and protect the park, the park service began requiring reservations for those arriving between 3am and 7am. You can also catch the sunrise with a commercial tour group.

Plan to arrive at the summit an hour before the actual sunrise, which will guarantee you time to see the world awaken. Around that point, the night sky begins to lighten and turn purple-blue, and the stars fade away. Ethereal silhouettes of the mountain ridges appear. The gentlest colors show up in the fleeting moments just before dawn. The undersides of the clouds lighten first, accenting the night sky with pale silvery slivers and streaks of pink.

About 20 minutes before sunrise, the light intensifies on the horizon in bright oranges and reds. Turn around for a look at Science City (p207), whose domes turn a blazing pink. For the grand finale, the moment when the disk of the sun appears, all of Haleakalā takes on a fiery glow. It feels like you're watching the earth awaken.

Come prepared – it's going to be *c-o-l-d!* Temperatures hovering around freezing and a biting wind are the norm at dawn and there's often frosty ice on the top layer of cinders. If you don't have a winter jacket (ski wear) or a sleeping bag to wrap yourself in, bring a warm blanket from your hotel. However many layers of clothes you can muster, it won't be too many.

The best photo opportunities occur before the sun rises. Every morning is different, but once the sun is up, the silvery lines and the subtleties disappear.

One caveat: a rained-out sunrise is an anticlimactic event, but stick around. Skies may clear and you can enjoy a fantastic hike into the crater.

If you just can't get up that early, sunsets at Haleakalā are also exceptional, and favored by locals who want to avoid the sunrise crowds. The sunsets here have inspired poets throughout history, too.

Reservations

Reservations can only be made at www.recreation.gov; the cost is $1 per car (this fee is separate from the $30 entrance fee). You can make a reservation up to 60 days in advance, though a small number of last-minute tickets are also released online two days beforehand at 7am. To enter the park, the reservation holder must present the reservation receipt and photo ID.

Ranger Talks

Stop at the Park Headquarters Visitor Center (p210) to see what's happening. Free ranger talks on Haleakalā's unique natural history and Hawaiian culture are given at the Haleakalā Visitor Center and the Pu'u'ula'ula (Red Hill) Overlook; the schedule varies, but there are usually one or two each day.

Stargazing

On clear nights, stargazing is phenomenal on the mountain. You can see celestial objects up to the seventh magnitude, free of light interference, making Haleakalā one of the best places on the planet for a sky view.

The park no longer offers star talks. These are now run by private companies such as Maui Stargazing (p208). You can also pick up a free star map at the Park Headquarters Visitor Center (p210) and have your own cosmic experience.

Maui Stargazing OUTDOORS
(☎808-298-8254; www.mauistargazing.com; Haleakalā Summit Area; 60-90min tour adult/child under 16yr $170/158; ⏲office 8am-4pm, tours

3:30-8:30pm) Watch the sun drop below the horizon from the summit, then scan the skies to study the cosmos. Look for deep-sky objects through a 12in Dobsonian telescope – the largest portable telescope out there. When visible it's possible to see planets, nebulae, star clusters and the galaxies beyond. Tours meet at Kula Lodge (p195). Warm clothing provided, plus hot drinks and snacks.

Volunteering

★Volunteers on Vacation VOLUNTEERING
(☎808-249-8811, ext 1; www.volunteersonvacation.org) The Pacific Whale Foundation (p86) runs several free volunteer opportunities on Maui, lasting from two hours to about four hours, depending on the project. These projects include invasive-species removal at Haleakalā National Park, dune and trail maintenance along the coast, and pitching in at an organic farm.

Friends of Haleakalā National Park VOLUNTEERING
(☎808-876-1673, 808-669-8385; www.fhnp.org) This totally volunteer-led operation involves up to a dozen visitors who hike into the wild and stay for two nights in cabins owned by the National Park Service. Volunteers perform one of a number of tasks ranging from cabin maintenance to plant removal to nene-habitat improvement.

Sleeping

For one of the most unique overnight experiences in Hawaii, if not the entire US, consider camping in the crater or spending the night in one of its three rustic cabins. To spend the night at Haleakalā is to commune with nature. Bring Arctic-worthy camping gear.

Camping

All of the backcountry camping options are primitive. None have electricity or showers. You will find pit toilets and limited nonpotable water supplies that are shared with the crater cabins. Water needs to be filtered or chemically treated before drinking; conserve it, as water tanks occasionally run dry. Fires are allowed only in grills, and in times of drought are prohibited entirely. You must pack in all your food and supplies, and pack out all your trash. Also, be aware that during periods of drought you'll be required to carry in your own water.

Unlike at Hosmer Grove, permits are required for backcountry camping in the crater. They are free and issued at the Park Headquarters Visitor Center (p210) on a first-come, first-served basis between 8am and 3pm up to one day in advance. Photo identification and a 10-minute orientation video are required. Camping is limited to three nights in the crater each month, with no more than two consecutive nights at either campground. Because only 25 campers are allowed at each site, permits can go quickly when larger parties show up, a situation more likely to occur in summer.

Keep in mind that sleeping at an elevation of 7000ft is not like camping on the beach. You need to be well equipped – if you don't have a waterproof tent and a winter-rated sleeping bag, forget it.

Hosmer Grove Campground CAMPGROUND
(www.nps.gov/hale; 3 nights free) FREE Wake up to birdsong at Hosmer Grove, the only drive-up campground in the Summit Area section of the park. On the slopes of the volcano, surrounded by towering trees and adjacent to one of Maui's best birding trails, this campground at an elevation of 6800ft tends to be cloudy, but a covered picnic pavilion offers shelter if it rains.

Wilderness Cabins

Three rustic cabins dating from the 1930s lie along trails on the crater floor at Holua, Kapalaoa and Paliku. Each has a wood-burning stove with three long-burning logs per night, a propane burner, 12 bunks with sleeping pads (but no bedding), pit toilets, and a limited supply of water and firewood. There is no electricity. Hiking distances to the cabins from the crater rim range from 4 miles to just over 9 miles. There's a three-day-stay limit per month, with no more than two consecutive nights in any cabin. Each cabin is rented to only one group at a time.

The cabins can be reserved online up to six months ahead. Photo ID is required for the permittee, and all of those staying in the cabin must watch a 10-minute wilderness-orientation video.

Holua Cabin & Campground CAMPGROUND $
(☎808-572-4459, cabin reservations 877-444-6777; www.recreation.gov; Halemau'u Trail; cabins for 1-12 people $75, campsites free) Holua is the easiest of the three wilderness cabins to reach, located 3.7 miles down the Halemau'u Trail at an elevation of 6940ft. It has

RESPONSIBLE HIKING

To protect Haleakalā's fragile environment, keep to established trails and don't be tempted off them, even for well-trodden shortcuts through switchbacks. And for your own sake, come prepared. Remember that the climate changes radically as you cross the crater floor. In the 4 miles between Kapalaoa and Paliku cabins, rainfall varies from an annual average of 12in to 300in! Take warm clothing in layers, sunscreen, rain gear, a first-aid kit and lots of water. Hikers without proper clothing risk hypothermia. If camping, bring winter camping gear.

Here are recommended day hikes, depending on how much time you have available.

Six hours If you're planning a full-day outing, and you're in decent physical shape, the phenomenal 10.2-mile hike that starts down Keonehe'ehe'e (Sliding Sands) Trail and returns via Halemau'u Trail is the prize. It crosses the crater floor, taking in both a cinder desert and a cloud forest, showcasing the park's amazing diversity. Get an early start. As for getting back to your starting point, hitchhiking is allowed in the park and there's a designated place to hitch on Haleakalā Hwy opposite the Halemau'u trailhead. Alternatively, park your car at the Halemau'u Trail and hitch up to the Keonehe'ehe'e (Sliding Sands) Trail at the start of your hike, so you don't have to hitch after a long day. The advantage of this hike is that there is very little uphill walking: only 45 minutes of it on a section of the Halemau'u Trail. If walking other trails you descend and then have a slog back up the volcano.

Three hours For a half-day experience that offers a hearty serving of crater sights, follow Keonehe'ehe'e (Sliding Sands) Trail down to where it goes between two towering rock formations, before dropping steeply again. It takes one hour to get down. However, the way back is a 1500ft elevation rise, making the return a strenuous two-hour climb.

One hour Take to the forest on the Hosmer Grove Trail (p204) and see the green side of Haleakalā National Park.

pit toilets and nonpotable water, plus a log burner and three fire logs per booking. The cabin and the adjacent backcountry campground have unparalleled sunrise views. May be booked online.

Kapalaoa Cabin CABIN $
(Map p238; ☎808-572-4487, cabin reservations 877-444-6777; www.recreation.gov; cabins $75) This rustic cabin in Haleakalā Crater borders the Keonehe'ehe'e (Sliding Sands) Trail, and is located 5.6 miles from the trailhead. In the middle of the cinder desert, Kapalaoa enjoys the driest conditions of all the backcountry cabins. It sleeps up to 12 people, has pit toilets and nonpotable water, plus a log burner and three fire logs per booking.

Paliku Cabin & Campground CAMPGROUND $
(Map p238; ☎877-444-6777; www.nps.gov/hale; cabins for 1-12 people $75, campsites free) This wilderness cabin and backcountry campground are located a 9.3-mile hike into Haleakalā Crater, at an elevation of 6380ft. Those craving lush rainforest will find Paliku serene. The cabin sleeps up to 12 people, has pit toilets and nonpotable water, plus a log burner and three fire logs per booking.

ℹ Information

Park Headquarters Visitor Center (☎808-572-4459; www.nps.gov/hale; ⏰8am-3pm) Less than a mile beyond the entrance at 7000ft above sea level, this visitor center is the place to pick up brochures, a trail map and a map of the stars for stargazing. You can also buy a nature book, get camping permits, and find information about ranger talks and other activities offered during your visit.

Haleakalā Visitor Center (☎808-572-4400; www.nps.gov/hale; ⏰8am-3pm) Located near the summit at 9740ft, the visitor center has useful info about hikes and sights in the area. Thirty-minute volcano talks are held here daily at 10:30am. The center has displays on Haleakalā's volcanic origins and details on what you're seeing on the crater floor 3000ft below.

Nature talks are given, books on Hawaiian culture and the environment are for sale, and there are drinking fountains and restrooms.

DANGERS & ANNOYANCES

Driving This park can be a seriously dangerous place to drive, due to a combination of sheer drops with no guardrails, daily doses of thick mist, and strong wind. Exercise extra caution on winter afternoons, when a sudden rainstorm can add ice to the list.

Obey warning signs. They often mark a spot where a visitor has been hurt or killed by a fall, a flash flood or falling rocks.

Weather The weather can change suddenly from dry, hot conditions to cold, windswept rain. Although the general rule is sunny in the morning and cloudy in the afternoon, fog and clouds can blow in at any time, and the wind chill can quickly drop below freezing. Dress in layers and bring extra clothing.

Altitude At 10,000ft the air is relatively thin, so expect to tire more quickly, particularly if you're hiking. If exerting yourself you will need more water than usual: high altitude dehydrates us faster, and we're less likely to crave the water needed to hike. This also goes for cold temperatures, which may further reduce our cravings for water. The higher elevation also means that sunburn is more likely; always wear sunscreen in the park.

Visitors rarely experience **altitude sickness** at the summit. An exception is those who have been scuba diving in the past 24 hours: don't scuba dive the day before or after a Haleakalā visit. Plan your trip accordingly. Children, pregnant women and those in generally poor health are also susceptible. If you experience difficulty breathing, sudden headaches and dizziness, or more serious symptoms such as confusion and lack of motor coordination, descend immediately. Sometimes driving down the crater road just a few hundred feet will alleviate the problem. Panicking or hyperventilating only makes things worse.

Hunger and thirst Pack plenty of snacks, especially if you're going up for the sunrise. No food or drink are sold anywhere in the park. You don't want a growling stomach to send you back down the mountain before you've had a chance to see the sights.

ENTRANCE FEES & PASSES

Haleakalā National Park (p201) never closes, and the pay booth at the park entrance opens before dawn to welcome the sunrise crowd. The pay booth accepts credit cards, not cash. The fee covers both sections of the park. If you're planning several national-park trips in a year, or are going on to Hawai'i (the Big Island), consider buying an annual pass ($55), which covers all of Hawaii's national parks. The Interagency Annual Pass ($80) covers the entrance fee for all national parks and more than 2000 federally run recreation sites for one year; it will admit the pass holder and three adults.

MAPS

A current hiking-trail map can be downloaded from the park's official website (www.nps.gov/hale/upload/map-and-descriptions.pdf) or you can grab a physical copy at the visitor centers. Other planning materials and books can be purchased online from the park's partner: www.hawaiipacificparks.org.

SILVERSWORD COMEBACK

Goats ate them by the thousands. Souvenir collectors pulled them up by their roots. They were even used to decorate parade floats. It's a miracle that any of Haleakalā's famed *'ahinahina* (silverswords) are left at all.

It took a concerted effort to bring them back from the brink of extinction, but Haleakalā visitors can once again see this luminous chrome relative of the sunflower in numerous places around the park, including Kalahaku and Pu'u'ula'ula (Red Hill) overlooks and Silversword Loop.

The *'ahinahina* takes its name from its elegant silver spiked leaves, which glow with dew collected from the clouds. The plant grows above 6500ft and lives for up to 50 years before blooming for its first and last time. In its final year, it shoots up a flowering stalk that can reach as high as 9ft. During summer the stalk flowers gloriously with hundreds of maroon-and-yellow blossoms. When the flowers go to seed in late fall, the plant takes its last gasp and dies.

Today the *'ahinahina* faces new threats, including climate change and loss of its pollinators, ants. But at least its seemingly inhospitable but fragile natural environment has been protected. After years of effort, the National Park Service has finished fencing the entire park with a 32-mile-long fence to keep out feral goats and pigs. You can do your part by not walking on cinders close to the plant; this damages the shallow roots that radiate out several feet just inches below the surface.

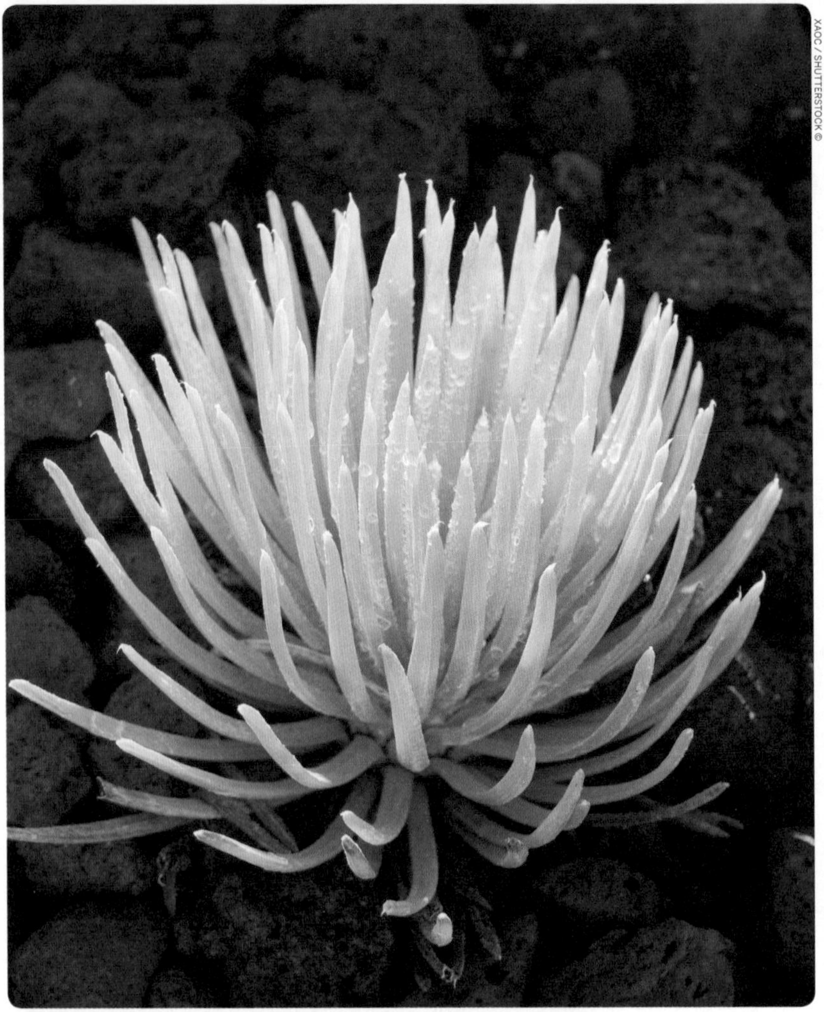

XAOC / SHUTTERSTOCK ©

RON DAHLQUIST / GETTY IMAGES ©

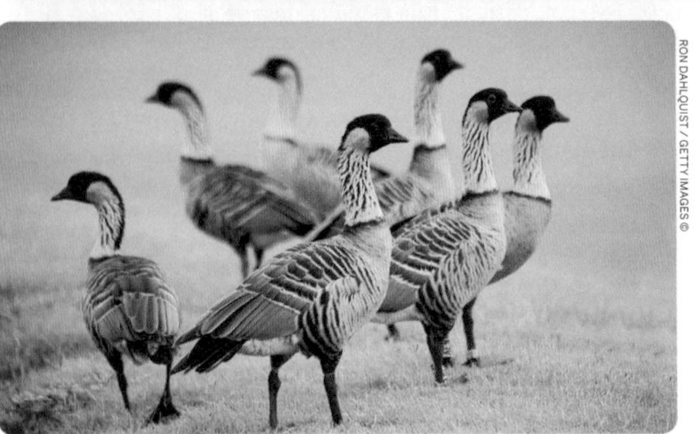

Top: Silversword plant
(p211)

Bottom: Nenes

NENE WATCH

The native nene, Hawaii's state bird, is a long-lost cousin of the Canada goose. By the 1950s hunting, habitat loss and predators had reduced its population to just 30. Thanks to captive breeding and release programs, it has been brought back from the verge of extinction and Haleakalā National Park's nene population is now more than 220.

Nene nest in shrubs and grassy areas from altitudes of 6000ft to 8000ft, surrounded by rugged lava flows with sparse vegetation. Their feet have gradually adapted by losing most of their webbing. The birds are extremely friendly and love to hang out where people do, anywhere from cabins on the crater floor to the Park Headquarters Visitor Center.

Their curiosity and fearlessness have contributed to their undoing. Nene don't fare well in an asphalt habitat and many have been run over by cars. Others have been tamed by too much human contact, so – no matter how much they beg for your peanut-butter sandwich – don't feed the nene. It only interferes with their successful return to the wild.

The nonprofit Friends of Haleakalā National Park runs an Adopt-a-Nene program (www.fhnp.org/nene.html). For $30 you get adoption papers, information about your nene, a certificate and a postcard. The money funds the protection of the nene habitat.

Getting There & Around

Getting to Haleakalā is half the fun. Snaking up the mountain, all of Maui opens up below you, with sugarcane and pineapple fields creating a patchwork of green on the valley floor. The highway ribbons back and forth, and in some places as many as four or five switchbacks are in view all at once.

Haleakalā Hwy (Hwy 378) twists and turns for 11 miles from Hwy 377 near Kula up to the park entrance, then another 10 miles to Haleakalā summit. It's a good and super-smooth paved road, but it's steep and winding, often with no barrier and a sheer drop on one side. You don't want to rush, especially when it's dark or foggy. Watch out for cattle wandering freely across the road.

The drive to the summit takes about 1½ hours from Pa'ia or Kahului, two hours from Kihei and a bit longer from Lahaina. If you need gas, fill up the night before, as there are no services on Haleakalā Hwy.

On your way back downhill, be sure to put your car in low gear to avoid burning out your brakes.

There is no public bus service to the park.

Kipahulu Area

Activities & Tours

Kipahulu 'Ohana CULTURAL

(Map p238; ☎808-248-8558; https://kipahulu.org/whatwedo/kapahufarm/hiketour; per person 2/3½hr hike $49/79; ⏲tours 10am & 2pm) Kipahulu was once a breadbasket, or more accurately a poi bowl, for the entire region. For fascinating insights into the area's past, join the ethnobotanical tour led by Kipahulu 'Ohana. Includes a sampling of Hawaiian foods and intriguing details about the native plants and ancient ruins along the way. Reservations required; $30 park fee not included. Two-person minimum.

Sleeping

Kipahulu Campground CAMPGROUND

(Map p238; ☎808-248-7375; www.nps.gov/hale) FREE This campground has an incredible setting on oceanside cliffs amid the stone ruins of an ancient Hawaiian village, but it's primitive. The simple facilities include pit toilets, picnic tables and grills. Drinking water is only available from the nearby visitor-center restrooms. Camping is first come, first served. Stays are limited to three nights in 30 days.

Information

Kipahulu Visitor Center (Map p238; ☎808-248-7375; www.nps.gov/hale; Hana Hwy; 3-day park pass car $30, motorcycle $25, person on foot or bicycle $15; ⏲park 24hr, visitor center 9:30am-5pm) Rangers offer cultural-history talks and demonstrations on the lives and activities of the early Hawaiians who lived in the area now within park boundaries. Daily talks take place at 4pm.

Getting There & Around

To explore the park in depth and on your own schedule, you'll need to rent a car. There is no public bus service to either district of the park. The summit is 40 miles from Kahului, just over an hour's drive. Kipahulu is 55 miles from Kahului via the Road to Hana. Expect the drive to take at least two hours. Guided tours also stop at both sections of the park.

AT A GLANCE

CURVES ON THE HANA HIGHWAY
620

BEST COASTAL WALK
Pi'ilani Trail (p219)

BEST SMOOTHIE
Huelo Lookout (p217)

BEST TROPICAL TREES
Ke'anae Arboretum (p223)

WHEN TO GO

Jan–Dec Start driving at dawn to beat the heaviest of the traffic.

Apr–May The road may be less busy between whale-watching season and summer vacation.

Sep–Oct Also sees fewer people, with kids in school and others waiting for winter holidays.

Three Bears Falls (p224)
MNSTUDIO / SHUTTERSTOCK ©

The Road to Hana

There's a sense of suspense you just can't shake while driving the Road to Hana, a serpentine road lined with tumbling waterfalls, lush slopes, rugged coasts and serious hairpin turns. Spanning the northeast shore of Maui, the legendary Hana Hwy ribbons tightly between jungle valleys and towering cliffs. Along the way, 54 one-lane bridges mark nearly as many waterfalls, some so sheer they kiss you with spray as you drive past. The drive is ravishingly gorgeous, but certainly not a breeze.

Roadside distractions include Eden-like swimming holes, sleepy seaside villages and hiking trails through cool forests. If you've never tried Maui banana bread, explored a spring-fed cave or gazed upon an ancient Hawaiian temple, set the alarm early.

INCLUDES

The Road to Hana Highlights

1. **Wai'anapanapa State Park** (p228) Exploring a stunning natural, rugged lava coast.
2. **Three Bears Falls** (p224) Photographing three lovely cascades.
3. **Pi'ilanihale Heiau & Kahanu Gardens** (p228) Admiring tropical plants and Polynesia's greatest temple.
4. **Ke'anae Peninsula** (p222) Strolling a seaside village evoking Old Hawaii.
5. **Rappel Maui** (p221) Traversing a roaring waterfall.
6. **Coconut Glen's** (p226) Slurping chili-chocolate ice cream.
7. **Waikamoi Nature Trail** (p224) Hiking into the jungle.
8. **Hana Lava Tube** (p228) Walking a pitch-black cave of ancient lava flows.
9. **Twin Falls** (p221) Enjoying a hike followed by a splash.

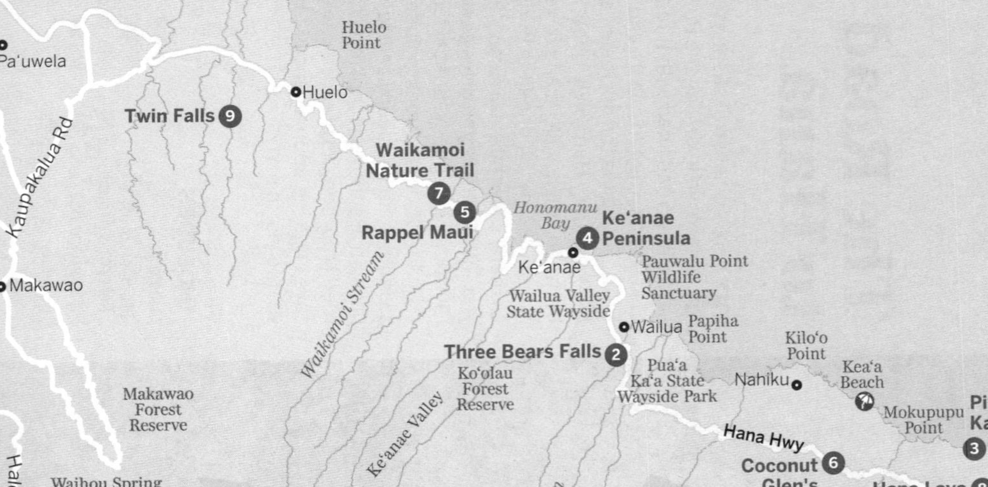

Getting There & Away

To drive the Road to Hana at your own pace, rent a car. The drive kicks off on the eastern fringe of Ha'iku, near Huelo, 20 miles east of Kahului International Airport (p309).

Several tour companies run Road to Hana trips, with buses and shuttles pulling over for key waterfalls and other roadside attractions. Valley Isle Excursions (p308), which includes breakfast and lunch on its Road to Hana tours, leaves Hana via the Pi'ilani Hwy (Back Road to Hana).

There is no public bus service to Hana or anywhere along the Road to Hana.

Read the Road to Hana Code of Conduct (most of which is common sense) before you set off. Don't cross private property, don't leave trash behind you, and don't park with your car protruding into the road or you will be subject to towing. Read the full code here: www.hawaiipublicradio.org/post/hana-highway-code-conduct#stream/0.

Huelo

With its abundant rain and fertile soil, Huelo once had a sizable plantation industry supporting more than 50,000 Hawaiians. Today it's a sleepy, scattered community of farms and enviable cliffside homes.

The double row of mailboxes and the green bus shelter that come up after a blind curve 0.5 miles past the 3-mile marker herald the start of the narrow road that leads into the village. The only sight, Kaulanapueo Church, is a half-mile down. There's no public beach access.

Sights

Kaulanapueo Church CHURCH

(Door of Faith Rd; P) Constructed in 1853 of coral blocks and surrounded by a manicured green lawn, this tidy church remains the heart of the village. It was built in early Hawaiian missionary style, with a spare interior and a tin roof topped by a green steeple. Swaying palm trees add a tropical backdrop. There are no formal opening hours, but the church may be unlocked during the day.

Sleeping & Eating

Tea House COTTAGE $

(800-215-6130; 370 Ho'olawa Rd; cottages $175; P) Welcome to the jungle – in an entirely pleasant way. Built from a recycled Zen temple, this rustic-romantic one-of-a-kind cottage is so secluded it's off the grid and uses its own solar power. Yet it has everything you'll need, including a kitchen with gas burners and an open-air shower in a redwood gazebo. Hosts Cameron and Megan bring warm alohas.

The grounds also contain a Tibetan-style stupa with a spectacular clifftop ocean view – the place is perfect for meditation or yoga. To get there follow Ulalama Loop, on the left after the 2-mile marker, to Ho'olawa Rd.

★ **Huelo Point Lookout** B&B $$$

(800-871-8645; www.maui-vacationrentals.com; 222 Door of Faith Rd; cottages $250-395; P@) Hidden well off the Hana Hwy, these four cottages, all linked by covered walkways, occupy an extremely private 2-acre complex with a verdant, park-like setting. A perennial honeymoon favorite, the well-stocked cottages have hot tubs and share a lovely pool; the Lookout House, in particular, has gorgeous coastal and Haleakalā volcano views. The thick mattresses are heavenly.

Huelo Lookout HEALTH FOOD $

(808-280-4791; 7600 Hana Hwy; smoothies $5-7; 8am-5:30pm) The fruit stand itself is tempting enough: drinking coconuts, pineapples, smoothies, acai bowls, banana bread and French crepes. But it doesn't stop there: take your goodies down the steps, where there's a shack selling waffles and sugarcane juice, and a table with a coastal panorama. Find it at mile 4.5.

KO'OLAU DITCH

Ko'olau Ditch (Hana Hwy) For more than a century the Ko'olau Ditch has been carrying up to 450 million gallons of water a day through 75 miles of flumes and tunnels from Maui's rainy interior to the dry central plains. You can get a close-up look by stopping at the small pull-off just before the bridge that comes up immediately after the 8-mile marker. Just 30ft above the road you'll see water flowing through a hand-hewn, stone-block section of the ditch before tunneling into the mountain.

HIKING AROUND THE HANA HIGHWAY

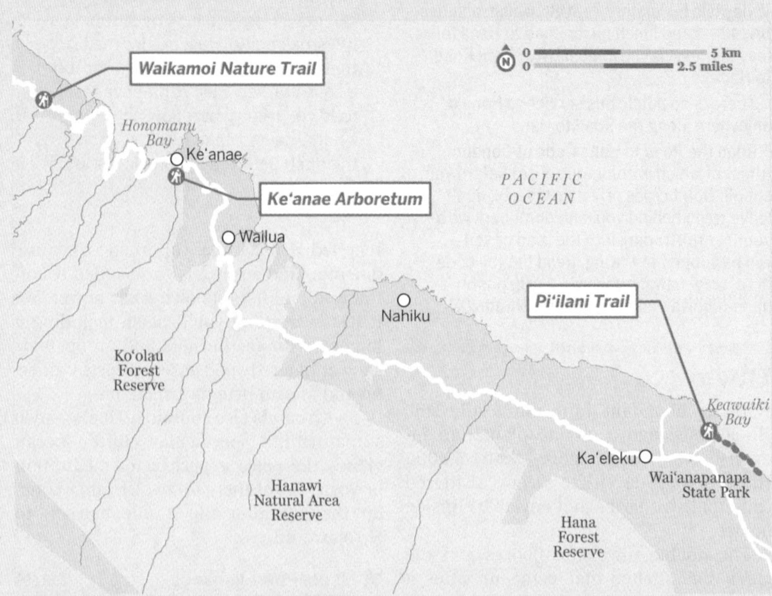

WAIKAMOI NATURE TRAIL

START/END WAIKAMOI NATURE TRAIL PARKING AREA
DURATION/DISTANCE 1.1 MILE, 30-MINUTE LOOP
DIFFICULTY EASY

Tree huggers, lace up your walking shoes. The majestic sights and spicy scents along this 1.1-mile loop through a leafy forest will introduce you to an array of tropical trees and ferns. On windy days you might hear trees 'squeaking' as they sway and stretch above you.

The signposted trailhead is 0.5 miles past the 9-mile marker. There's a dirt pull-off parking area wide enough for several cars with a map of the loop and the signposted lookout spots. Take a picture of it to refer to on the route. Wear shoes you don't mind getting dirty – this trail can get very muddy after it rains. There are two picnic tables on the hike (so bring snacks): one is beside the trailhead and the other is at the summit of the hike. It's 0.5 miles from the trailhead to the summit picnic area.

After a short climb from the parking area, walk past the trailhead picnic table and take the path to your right. You'll soon be welcomed by a stand of grand reddish *Eucalyptus robusta,* one of several types of towering eucalyptus tree that grow along the path.

In about five minutes you'll reach a ridge at the top of the loop. When there's not too much overgrown foliage you'll be treated to fine views of the winding Hana Hwy. After a few steps up the spur trail to your right, you'll enjoy great views of a huge green pincushion: a bamboo forest, facing you across the ravine.

As you climb the spur, watch your footing. Roots here are thick and slippery. You'll pass through a small bamboo grove before reaching a clearing with a covered picnic table at the top of the ridge. There's not much to see from the summit due to the thick foliage. Return to the main trail and follow the remainder of the loop back down. Look right for a short path to an overlook with a bench as you descend. From here it's an easy walk through the trees – which include a labeled Hawaiian koa – back

It's trails gone wild along the Road to Hana, where the daily dance of rain and sunshine makes maintenance a very tough job. Highlights? Jungle flora, lava coasts and island history.

to the parking area. Families should manage this loop fine (tell your kids to watch their footing on the vines); it's roughly a 650ft elevation gain.

PI'ILANI TRAIL

START PA'ILOA BEACH
END KAINALIMU BAY
DURATION/DISTANCE 3 MILES, 1½ TO TWO HOURS ROUND TRIP
DIFFICULTY MODERATE

This belter of a coastal trail offers a private, reflective walk on top of a raw lava field several feet above the sea, with windswept views of the Hana coast and the slopes of Haleakalā volcano. The route follows part of the ancient footpath known as the King's Trail that once circled the island. Some of the worn stepping stones along the path date from the time of the revered King Pi'ilani, who ruled Maui in the 16th century.

The trail packs a lot up front, so even if you just have time for the first half-mile, you won't regret it. Things to be aware of in spots include a loose lava-gravel path, often skirting sheer, potentially fatal drops into the sea – exercise caution and perhaps leave the kids behind before you set off. Bring water, as there's no shade, and good hiking shoes, as it gets rougher as you go along over volcanic rock. The trail parallels the coast the entire way, and is more well marked in some areas than in others; stick to the shoreline where the path is not as obvious and you can't get lost.

This hike begins at the black-sand shores of Pa'iloa Beach, then runs slightly north beside the ocean along lava sea cliffs, where you can search out caves, a burial ground, a natural sea arch and a blowhole on a precipice that roars to life whenever there's pounding surf (don't peer down into it: when it blows it might take you with it). Then return to the beach a little south, and watch for endangered Hawaiian monk seals basking on the shore. It looks tempting, but avoid swimming here when the seas are ferocious. There's a strong shore dump with an undertow.

Look for the ruins of the Ohala Heiau (a sacred ancient temple) as you head southeast, but don't disturb this lava-rock platform. After 0.75 miles you'll view basalt cliffs lined up all the way to Hana. There are plenty of dramatic scenes to behold, with a contrasting palette of brown ironwood and verdant foliage, bordered by deep cobalt-blue waters. Round stones mark the way across lava and a grassy clearing, fading briefly over a rugged sea cliff.

A dirt road comes in from the right as the trail arrives at Luahaloa, a ledge with a small fishing shack. Inland stands of ironwood heighten the beauty of the last mile of clifftop walking. Stepping stones hasten the approach to Kainalimu Bay ahead, as the trail dips down a shrubby ravine to a quiet, black-cobble beach that marks the end of the route.

Those who want to continue may do so on dirt roads leading another mile south to Hana. Most hikers choose to retrace their steps from here back to Wai'anapanapa State Park's parking lot. Alternatively, you can trek inland to the asphalt road, and walk or hitch back to your car.

KE'ANAE ARBORETUM

START/END 0.6 MILES AFTER MILE MARKER 16, ROAD TO HANA
DURATION/DISTANCE 0.9 MILES, 30 MINUTES ROUND TRIP
DIFFICULTY EASY

One for everyone, including non-hikers and families, this tropical botanical wonderland offers a super-easy, and calming, ramble through amazing exotic flora around a magnificent 6-acre timber, ornamental and food garden with plants from all over the tropics. The flat, paved 0.9-mile out-and-back trail is filled with the glorious smells, sights and sounds of the forest. It's a shaded spot following the gentle Pi'ina'au Stream under hanging vines, past a rainbow eucalyptus grove and bamboo plants. Signs point out nara and breadfruit, plus other wonders such as torch ginger and enormous taro leaves. Lots of flora is labeled by name and country of origin. Various tropical flowers and fruits appear here at different parts of the year. This plant lovers' arcadia is about half a mile after the 16-mile marker.

Ko'olau Forest Reserve & Around

This is where the Road to Hana starts to get wild! As the highway snakes along the edge of the Ko'olau Forest Reserve, the jungle takes over and one-lane bridges appear around every other bend. Ko'olau means 'windward,' and the upper slopes of these mountains squeeze a mighty 200in to 300in of rain from passing clouds annually, making for awesome waterfalls.

Kailua

After the 5-mile marker you'll pass through the village of Kailua. This little community of tin-roofed houses is largely home to employees of the East Maui Irrigation Company (EMI). EMI operates the extensive irrigation system carrying water from the rainforest to the thirsty sugarcane fields in Central Maui.

After leaving the village, just past the 6-mile marker, you'll be treated to a splash of color as you pass planted groves of **painted eucalyptus** with brilliant rainbow-colored bark. Roll down the windows and inhale the sweet scent of these majestic trees introduced from Australia.

> **HANA TRIPS TIPS**
>
> ➡ Hundreds of cars are making the journey each day. To beat the crowd, get a sunrise start.
>
> ➡ Fill up your tank in Pa'ia or Ha'iku; the next gas station isn't until Hana, and the station there sometimes runs dry.
>
> ➡ Bring snacks and plenty to drink.
>
> ➡ Wear a bathing suit under your clothes so you're ready for impromptu swims.
>
> ➡ Bring shoes that are good for hiking as well as scrambling over slick rocks.
>
> ➡ Pull over to let local drivers pass – they're moving at a different pace.
>
> ➡ The drive can feel a bit rushed at times. If you want to slow down, consider spending one or two nights in Hana – you can visit the attractions you missed on the way back the next day.
>
> ➡ Leave valuables at your hotel or carry them with you. Smash-and-grab thefts do occur.

Waikamoi Stream Area & Waterfalls

Sights

Garden of Eden Arboretum GARDENS

(☎808-572-9899; www.mauigardenofeden.com; 10600 Hana Hwy; adult/child 5-16yr/child under 5yr $15/5/free; ⏱8am-4pm; P) Why pay a steep $15 per person – not per carload, mind you – to visit an arboretum when the entire Road to Hana is a garden? Well, the garden does offer a tamer version of paradise. The winding paths are neatly maintained, the flowers are identified, and the hilltop picnic tables sport gorgeous views, including ones of Puohokamoa Falls and Keopuka Rock, which was featured in the opening shot of *Jurassic Park*. A good choice for those not up for slippery jungle trails.

Puohokamoa Falls WATERFALL

(Hana Hwy) Immediately after the 11-mile marker you'll pass Puohokamoa Falls. This waterfall no longer has public access, but you can get a glimpse of it from the bridge, or enter the Garden of Eden Arboretum (p220) for a photogenic bird's-eye view.

Kaumahina State Wayside Park STATE PARK

(http://dlnr.hawaii.gov/dsp/parks/maui; Hana Hwy; ⏱7am-7pm; P 🚻) Clean restrooms and a grassy lawn with picnic tables make this roadside park a family-friendly stop. The park comes up 350yd after the 12-mile marker. Take the short walk up the hill past the restrooms for an eye-popping view of coastal scenery. No drinking water. For the next several miles the scenery is absolutely stunning, opening up to a new vista at every turn. If it's been raining recently, you can see waterfalls galore crashing down the mountains.

Haipua'ena Falls WATERFALL

(Hana Hwy) For a secluded dip, Haipua'ena Falls, 0.5 miles past the 11-mile marker, provides a deep and serene pool. Since you can't see the pool from the road, few people know it's there. So it's not a bad choice if you forgot your bathing suit...

Waikamoi Falls WATERFALL

(Hana Hwy; P) There's only space for a few cars before the bridge at the 10-mile marker, but unless it's been raining recently don't worry about missing this one. The East Maui Irrigation Company diverts water from the stream, so the falls are usually a trickle. After the bridge, a green canopy of bamboo hangs over the road.

Tours

★Rappel Maui ADVENTURE SPORTS

(808-445-6407; www.rappelmaui.com; 10600 Hana Hwy; $219; tours 6:45am, 8am, 9:15am, 10:30am & 11:45am) 'Are you insane?' That's the general reaction to telling people you are rappelling (abseiling) down the face of a massive waterfall and into a large natural pool. The magic here is that after a few thrilling abseils this way-out sport seems easy by the end, even if you've had no previous experience. Van pick-up at Central Maui Park-n-Ride available. Lunch provided.

Eating

Peacocks Cafe Maui CAFE $

(10600 Hana Hwy; coffee $5, tacos $12, ice cream $7; 10am-4:30pm;) In a lovely setting, with purple benches and beautiful peacocks wandering around, this little food-truck cafe near the entrance to the Garden of Eden Arboretum (p220) (no entrance fee to visit the cafe) serves tasty tacos. Try Mexican, Thai or Hawaiian flavor with your choice of protein or veggie fillings. Wash your meal down with a fruit smoothie, juice or coffee.

If you've only time to do the first section of the Road to Hana, get a scoop of Coconut Glen's (p226) famous ice cream here. Wi-fi available – which is super handy in this cell-signal black spot.

Honomanu Bay

The striking, stream-fed Honomanu Bay comes into view at the 13-mile marker, where there's a roadside pull-off. This is the best stop on the first half of the Road to Hana. But you need to head down to the bay itself, via the inconspicuous road just after the 14-mile marker, to get the full effect.

DON'T MISS

TWIN FALLS

Twin Falls (Map p182; Hana Hwy; P) Just after the Hana Hwy's 2-mile marker, a wide parking area marks the start of the trail to Twin Falls. Local kids and tourists flock to the pool beneath the lower falls, about a 10-minute walk in. Billed as the 'first waterfall on the road to Hana,' Twin Falls can get a bit crowded, but if you're traveling with kids or you're up for a short, pleasant hike, this is a good choice. Two photogenic falls and a swimming hole are your rewards.

Sights

Honomanu Park PARK

(808-248-7022; www.mauicounty.gov/Facilities; P) Honomanu Bay's rocky black-sand beach is usually empty or being used by local surfers and fishers. Surfable waves form during big swells, but the rocky bottom and strong rips make it dangerous if you're not familiar with the spot; there's no lifeguard here. No restrooms. Pull off the highway near the 13-mile marker, taking the small road going toward the ocean.

Kalaloa Point VIEWPOINT

(Hana Hwy; P) For a fascinating view of the coast, stop at the pull-off on the ocean side of the highway, 0.6 miles past the 14-mile marker. From the point you can look clear across Honomanu Bay and watch ant-size cars snaking down the mountain cliffs on the other side.

Ke'anae

What awaits you at the halfway point on the drive to Hana? Dramatic landscapes and the friendliest seaside village on the route. And we haven't even mentioned the delicious banana bread.

Starting way up at the Ko'olau Gap in the rim of Haleakalā Crater and stretching clear down to the coast, Ke'anae Valley radiates green, thanks to 150in of rainfall each year. At the foot of the valley lies Ke'anae Peninsula, created by a late eruption of Haleakalā that sent lava gushing all the way down Ke'anae Valley and into the ocean. Unlike

Road to Hana: Twin Falls to Ke'anae

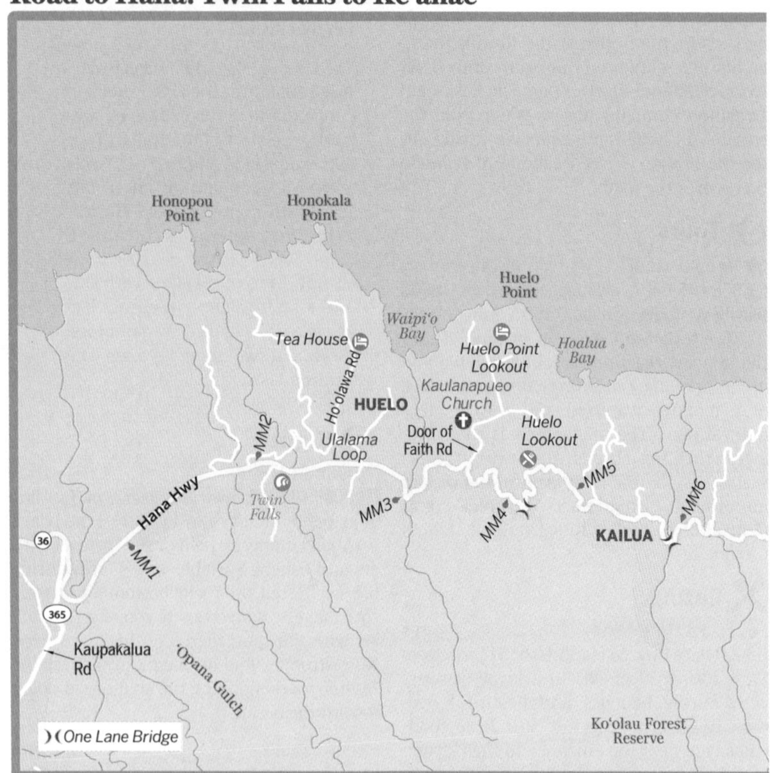

its rugged surroundings, the volcanic peninsula is perfectly flat, like a leaf floating on the water.

Sights come up in quick succession. After you pass the YMCA Camp 0.5 miles past the 16-mile marker, the arboretum pops up on the right and the road to Ke'anae Peninsula heads off to the left around the next bend.

Sights

★Ke'anae Peninsula VILLAGE
(Ke'anae Rd; P) This rare slice of 'Old Hawaii,' home to an 1860s church and a wild lava coast, is reached by taking Ke'anae Rd on the *makai* (seaward) side of the highway just beyond Ke'anae Arboretum (p223). Families have tended stream-fed taro patches here for generations.

Ke'anae Congregational Church CHURCH
(Lanakila 'Ihi'ihi o Iehova Ona Kaua; 325 Ke'anae Rd) Surrounded by palm trees, and marking the heart of the village, is this church built in 1860. Enter over the steps of the adjacent cottage. The church is made of lava rocks and coral mortar. It's a welcoming place with open doors and a guest book. Note the cameo portraits in the adjacent cemetery.

Ching's Pond NATURAL FEATURE
(3670 Hana Hwy) The stream that feeds Ke'anae Peninsula pauses to create a couple of swimming holes just below the bridge, 0.9 miles after the 16-mile marker. If you pull off immediately before the bridge you'll find a deep, crystal-clear pool beneath. You will likely see many people swimming here, but there are 'No Trespassing' signs and 'Residents only, no visitors' signs around the falls. It's best to observe the pool but not take a dip.

Ke'anae Peninsula Lookout VIEWPOINT
(Ke'anae Rd; P) For a superb bird's-eye view of the lowland peninsula and village, including the patchwork taro fed by Ke'anae

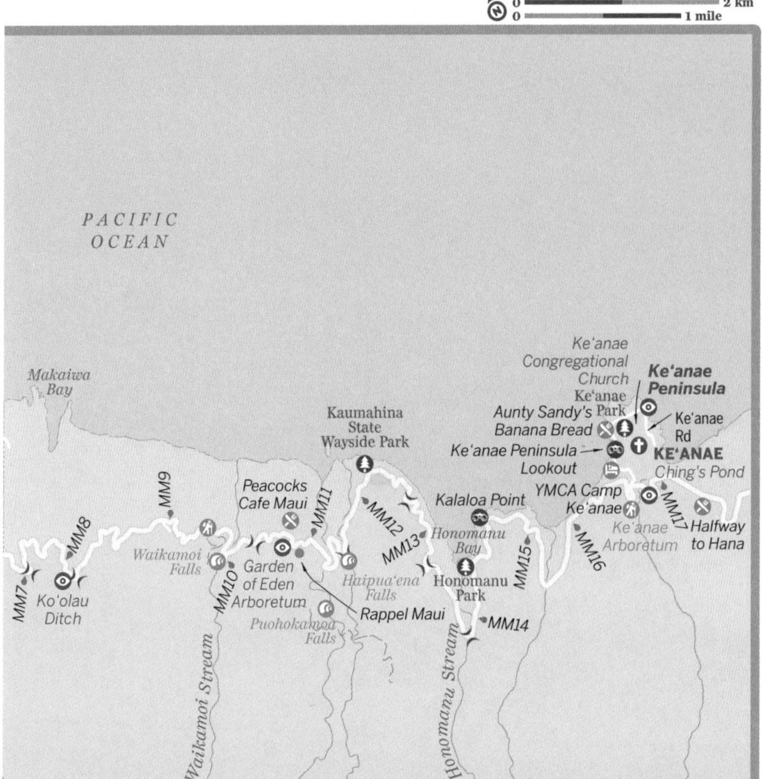

Stream, stop at the paved pull-off just past the 17-mile marker on the *makai* side of the road. There's no signpost, but it's easy to find if you look for the yellow tsunami speaker. If it's been raining lately, look to the far left to spot a series of cascading waterfalls.

Ke'anae Park PARK

(www.mauicounty.gov/Facilities; Ke'anae Rd; 7am-7pm; P) Ke'anae Park is a large green space opposite the scenic coastline of jagged black lava and hypnotic white-capped waves. Forget swimming, as the water is rough and there's no beach. There are restrooms here.

Ke'anae Arboretum HIKING

(https://hawaiitrails.org; 13385 Hana Hwy) FREE Hikers and nonhikers alike will enjoy this pleasant paved stroll through amazing tropical flora. The scented scenic trail here follows the Pi'ina'au Stream past magnificent trees and plants, from taro leaves and bamboo trees to hanging vines and colorful flowers, much of it labeled by name and country of origin. It's a lovely atmospheric side trip on the Road to Hana.

Pull over 0.6 miles after the 16-mile marker for the Ke'anae Arboretum. Park opposite the entrance gate and follow the paved trail. It turns to dirt and finally grows over after you hit a fence.

Sleeping & Eating

YMCA Camp Ke'anae CABIN $

(808-248-8355; www.ymcacampkeanae.org; 13375 Hana Hwy; campsites per adult/child/child under 6yr $30/15/free, cabins per adult/child/child under 6yr $35/20/free, cottages $285, ste $205-375) This bluff-top YMCA with gorgeous coastal views has many options, from tent camping and hostel-style cabin dorms (no linen) to a four-person suite (linen provided) and an oceanview cottage (linen provided). However, it books up with groups, so drop-in availability is rare. Make a reservation. Cottages and suites

Road to Hana: Wailua to Wai'anapanapa State Park

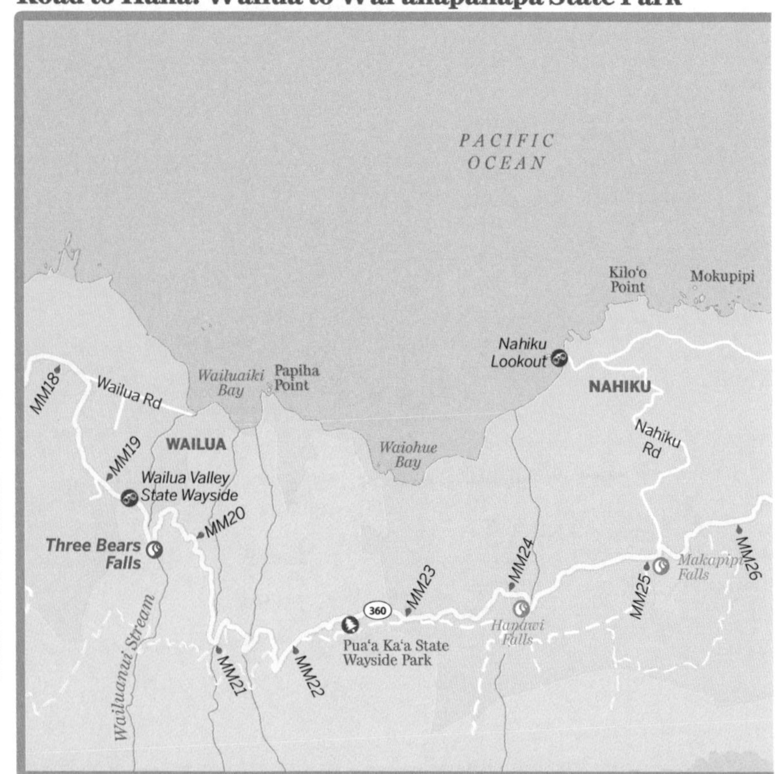

have a cleaning fee of $75 to $100, plus a two-night minimum stay.

★**Aunty Sandy's Banana Bread** HEALTH FOOD $

(☎808-248-7448; 210 Ke'anae Rd; banana bread $6, snacks $4-6, sandwiches from $6.50; ⌚8:30am-2:30pm) 'Da best' banana bread on the entire Road to Hana is baked fresh every morning by Aunty Sandy and her crew, and it's so good you'll find as many locals as tourists pulling up here. You can also get fresh fruit, hot dogs, *kalua* (pit-oven-cooked) pork sandwiches, drinks and shave ice. Located in the village before Ke'anae Park.

Halfway to Hana FAST FOOD $

(www.halfwaytohanamaui.com; 13710 Hana Hwy; shave ice $5.50, banana bread $6, lunch mains from $6.50; ⌚8am-4:30pm) This aptly named old-timer has been slinging burgers, hot dogs and ice cream to midway road trippers for 30 years. The only ATM on the highway is here, as well as some portable restrooms. Also sells shave ice, and the sandwiches and burgers will see you through to the other side.

Ke'anae to Nahiku

Waterfalls are a highlight on the twisting stretch of the highway between Ke'anae and Nahiku. Feeling hungry? Nahiku is a good place to pull over for a late lunch or afternoon snack.

Sights

★**Three Bears Falls** WATERFALL

(Upper Waikani Falls; Hana Hwy) Got your camera? This beauty takes its name from the triple cascade that flows down a steep rock face on the inland side of the road, 0.5 miles past the 19-mile marker. Catch it after a rainstorm and the cascades come

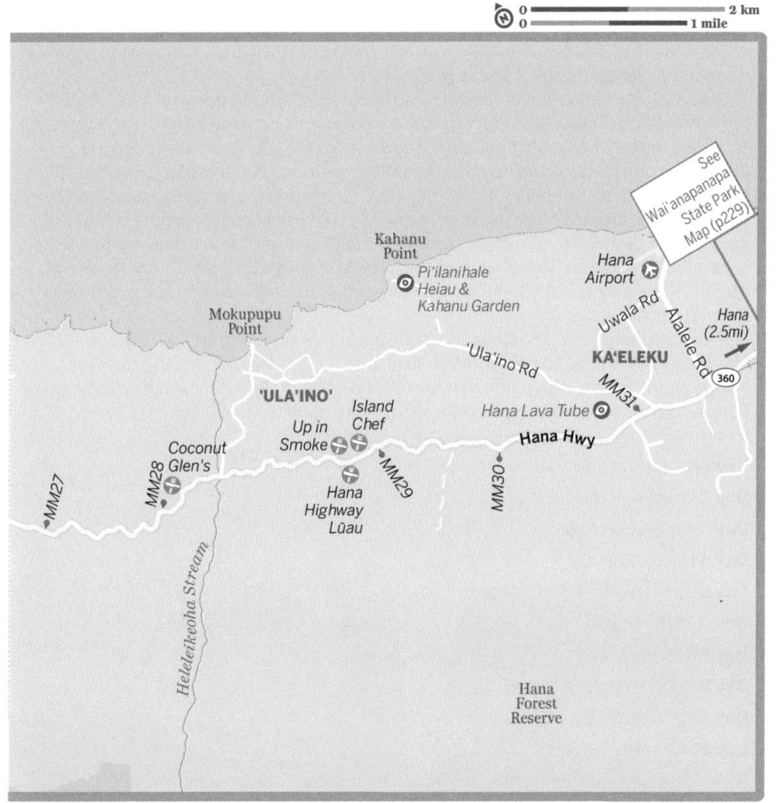

together and roar as one mighty waterfall. There's limited parking up the hill to the left after the falls.

Wailua Valley State Wayside VIEWPOINT
(http://dlnr.hawaii.gov/dsp/parks/maui; Hana Hwy; P) Near the 19-mile marker, Wailua Valley State Wayside lookout comes up on the right. The overlook provides a broad view into verdant Ke'anae Valley, which appears to be 100 shades of green. You can see a couple of waterfalls (when they're running), and Ko'olau Gap, the break in the rim of Haleakalā crater, on a clear day. Turn toward the sea for an outstanding view of Wailua Peninsula as well – don't miss this.

Pua'a Ka'a State Wayside Park PARK
(http://dlnr.hawaii.gov/dsp/parks/maui; Hana Hwy; 6am-6pm; P) The highway cuts right through this delightful 5-acre rainforest park whose name, Pua'a Ka'a, means Rolling Pig. Some unlucky passersby will see just the restrooms on the ocean side of the road and miss the rest. But you brought your beach towel, didn't you? Cross the highway from the parking area and head inland to find a pair of delicious waterfalls cascading into pools. The park is 0.5 miles after the 22-mile marker.

Hanawi Falls WATERFALL
(Map p238; Hana Hwy) A waterfall with a split personality, Hanawi Falls sometimes flows gently into a quiet pool and sometimes gushes wildly across a broad rock face. No matter the mood, it always invites popping out the camera and snapping a pic. The falls are 175yd after the 24-mile marker. There are small pull-offs before and after the bridge.

Makapipi Falls WATERFALL
(Map p238; Hana Hwy) This powerful cascade makes its sheer plunge right beneath your feet as you stand on the ocean side of the Makapipi Bridge, 175yd after the 25-mile

OFF THE BEATEN TRACK

THE KING'S TRAIL

Attention, adventurers: this one is hard to beat.

Over 300 years ago, King Pi'ilani (of heiau fame) led the construction of a path around the entire island of Maui in an effort to improve commerce between its far-flung regions. Today the King's Trail, or what's left of it, offers the opportunity to see the island in a unique and unforgettable way: by walking around it. Around 200 miles long, the trail skirts the coastline the entire way, providing access to remote areas where traditional Hawaiian life is still practiced. It can be covered (if you're fit enough) in approximately 10 days. But be careful – this is not for the faint of heart. The trail has not been maintained in its entirety. There are places where it disappears, or where the highway has been built upon it. There may be cars, steep cliffs and crazy dogs to contend with. And you'll need to bring lots of water, gallons of it.

If you only have time for a taste, try a section such as the Lahaina Pali Trail from Ma'alaea(p148) to Papalaua Beach, the Hoapili Trail (p158) from La Perouse Bay to Kanaio, or the Pi'ilani Trail (p225) between Wai'anapanapa State Park and Hana Beach Park, where the ancient trail once began. A complete itinerary is a variation of this if walking between 15 and 20 miles per day:

Day 1 Ha'iku–Waihe'e

Day 2 Waihe'e–Kahakuloa

Day 3 Kahakuloa–Napili

Day 4 Napili–Oluwalu

Day 5 Oluwalu–Kihei

Day 6 Kihei–Kanaio

Day 7 Kanaio–Kaupo

Day 8 Kaupo–Hana

Day 9 Hana–Ke'Anae

Day 10 Ke'Anae–Ha'iku

For more information and route planning, contact Daniel Sullivan at Indigo (p186) in Pa'ia. He's not only walked the entire trail but created an extraordinary photographic record, which he includes in his book *The Maui Coast: Legacy of the King's Highway* (www.danielsullivan.photoshelter.com).

marker. Most waterfall views look up at the cascades, but this one offers a rare chance to experience a waterfall from the top. You don't see anything from your car so if you didn't know about it, you'd never imagine this waterfall was here. And sometimes it isn't, as it flows intermittently.

Nahiku

The rural village of Nahiku is down near the coast, and cut by Nahiku Rd. Apart from an attractive lookout point, there's not much to tempt visitors. However, just before the 29-mile marker you'll find the Nahiku Marketplace, the jungle's best attempt at a food court. Outlets range in cuisine and style from a tent to a tin roof, and the smells of smoked-barbecue goodness linger, tempting drivers to stop. It's also your best chance to fuel up before Hana, but be aware that vendors have very flexible opening hours.

Sights

Nahiku Lookout VIEWPOINT

(Nahiku Rd) If you're looking for a visual feast, turn left just past the 25-mile marker. After winding down to the sea over 2.5 miles, you'll find a great coastline view with waves crashing against the shore. Park and stretch your legs with a short walk down to this fine picnic spot.

Eating & Drinking

★**Coconut Glen's** ICE CREAM $

(Map p238; ☎808-248-4876; www.coconutglens.com; Hana Hwy, Mile 27.5; scoop of ice cream $7;

10:30am-5pm;) From his inviting roadside food truck Coconut Glen (aka Glen Simkins) is trying to 'change the world one scoop at a time.' Pull over for his rather good 100%-vegan ice cream, in six flavors – among them pineapple and banana, lemongrass and ginger, and original coconut. It's so tasty you won't notice it's made from coconut milk, not cream. Cash only.

★Hana Pizza Company PIZZA $
(Map p238; Nahiku Marketplace, Hana Hwy, Mile 29; pizzas $12; 11am-3pm) This sophisticated street-side stall is a welcome break for road-trippers on their way to Hana. Hardworking pizza chefs cook fresh, 10in island-style pizzas in an outside stone oven (pies ready in 10 minutes). There are five well-baked varieties, including huli huli pork and chicken, Hawaiian, pepperoni, and straight-up cheese.

★Hana Huli Huli BBQ BARBECUE $
(Map p238; Nahiku Marketplace, Hana Hwy, Mile 29; chicken/pork rib plate $12/13) The smell in the air tempts you in before you've even parked your car. The flavorsome chicken and pork ribs are cage-grilled over an open fire and turned rotisserie style. Meat is served with rice or vegetables. Eat it all up in a pleasant canopy-covered, wooden-decked area with fairy lights.

Up in Smoke HAWAII REGIONAL $
(Map p238; Nahiku Marketplace, Hana Hwy, Mile 29; mains $3.50-9; 10am-3pm Sun-Wed) This bustling barbecue stand at the Nahiku Marketplace is *the* place to try kiawe-smoked breadfruit, plus *kalua* (pit-oven-cooked) pig tacos. Your kids will enjoy the giant hot dogs, too. It's located at mile marker 29.

Island Chef SEAFOOD $
(Map p238; Nahiku Marketplace, Hana Hwy, Mile 29; mains $12-20; 11am-3pm) The coconut shrimp served at this food truck is so good that it brings people out of Hana. Other plates include mediocre beef and rice. Tuck in under a shaded tin canopy on plastic chairs.

Hana Highway Lūau HAWAIIAN $
(Map p238; Nahiku Marketplace, Hana Hwy, Mile 29; dishes $12-20; 11am-3pm) For traditional Hawaiian fare on the Road to Hana, try this satisfying little roadside vendor at Nahiku Marketplace. Order healthy poke bowls (with Hana-caught fish, drizzled with mayo-sriracha and soy-ginger marinade), and papaya shrimp salad. Meanwhile, the luau (feast) plates are exactly that – a tasting plate of Hawaiian eats. (Note that most folks find them an acquired taste.)

You'll be served up lau lau – pork and sweet potato wrapped in a taro leaf – with lomi salad, poi, cut pineapple and greens. For breakfast the dragon-fruit acai bowl is a decent option that comes with local ingredients galore – Kaua'i granola, Hana banana, Maui pineapple, Greek yogurt, strawberry, blueberry, coconut flakes and honey.

Nahiku Cafe CAFE
(Map p238; Nahiku Marketplace, Hana Hwy, Mile 29; 10am-5pm) For those in need of a pick-me-up on the Hana Hwy, you can't go wrong with Nahiku Cafe, serving a decent cup of Maui joe, plus coconut (or mac nut) lattes and espresso milkshakes. Grab a slice of the yummy pineapple-and-coconut banana bread for later.

'Ula'ino Road

'Ula'ino Rd begins at the Hana Hwy, just south of the 31-mile marker. Cottage rentals, restaurants and food stands become more prevalent along the Hana Hwy between Ula'ino Rd and the town of Hana.

LOST TEMPLE

Every once in a while visitor stats make no sense at all, and here's a fine example: Pi'ilanihale Heiau & Kahanu Garden (p228) is easily the most important site on the Road to Hana, yet hundreds of visitors pass by every day without stopping. The reason is threefold. By the time they reach the outskirts of Hana, many visitors have run out of time: this site closes mid-afternoon. Or they hear 'garden' and think 'I've seen enough!' Since the heiau (ancient Hawaiian temple) is part of the garden, it's often lost in the mix, rather than being seen as a destination unto itself. And finally, low visitation has meant a limited tour schedule and scant marketing. In the end, though, all of this is good news for you, because you could well have this extraordinary place to yourself.

★ **Pi'ilanihale Heiau & Kahanu Garden** HISTORIC SITE

(Map p238; ☎808-248-8912; www.ntbg.org; 650 'Ula'ino Rd; adult/child under 13yr $10/free, guided tour $25/free; ⏰9am-3pm Mon-Fri, to 2pm Sat, tours by appointment 11am Mon-Fri; P 🚻) Probably the most significant stop on the entire Road to Hana, this site combines a 294-acre ethnobotanical garden with the magnificent Pi'ilanihale Heiau, the largest temple in all of Polynesia. A must-do tour provides fascinating details of the extraordinary relationship between the ancient Hawaiians and their environment. This is perhaps the best opportunity in Hawaii to really understand what traditional Hawaiian culture was like prior to contact with the West. Amazingly, very few people visit.

★ **Hana Lava Tube** CAVE

(Ka'eleku Caverns; Map p238; ☎808-248-7308; www.mauicave.com; 305 'Ula'ino Rd; self-guided tour adult/child under 5yr $12.50/free; ⏰10:30am-4pm; P 🚻) Who's afraid of the dark? Test yourself at the end of this underground walk by switching off your flashlight. Eerie! One of the odder sights on the Road to Hana, this mammoth cave was formed by ancient lava flows some 960 years ago. It once served as a slaughterhouse – 17,000lb of cow bones had to be removed before it was opened to visitors. It's the 18th largest lava tube in the world and the largest by far on Maui.

Wai'anapanapa State Park

Swim in a cave, sun on a black-sand beach, explore ancient Hawaiian sites, use the public restrooms – this is one extraordinary park. A sunny coastal trail and a friendly seaside campground make it a tempting place to dig in for a while. Honokalani Rd, which leads into **Wai'anapanapa State Park** (Map p238; ☎808-248-4843; http://dlnr.hawaii.gov/dsp/parks/maui; P 🚻), is just after the 32-mile marker.

The road ends overlooking the park's centerpiece, the jet-black sands at Pa'iloa Bay. Go early and you'll have it all to yourself. Most sites are within a short walk of the parking areas.

ISLAND INSIGHTS

On certain nights of the year the waters in the lava-tube caves at Wai'anapanapa State Park (p228) take on a red hue. Legend says it's the blood of a princess and her lover who were killed in a fit of rage by the princess's jealous husband after he found them hiding together here. Less romantic types attribute the phenomenon to swarms of tiny bright-red shrimp called *'opaeula*, which occasionally emerge from subterranean cracks in the lava.

Beaches

★ **Pa'iloa Beach** BEACH

(Honokalani Beach; Map p238; ☎808-984-8109; http://dlnr.hawaii.gov/dsp/parks/maui; Wai'anapanapa State Park; P) The small beach here is a stunner – hands down the prettiest black-sand beach on Maui. Walk on down, sunbathe, enjoy. But if you jump in, be very cautious. It has a vicious shore dump and undertow, with a bottom that drops quickly and water conditions that are challenging even for strong swimmers. Powerful rips are the norm (Pa'iloa means 'always splashing'). Drownings occur here.

Sights

Lava Caves CAVE

(Map p238; ☎808-984-8109; http://dlnr.hawaii.gov/dsp/parks/maui; Wai'anapanapa State Park; P) A 10-minute loop path north of the beach parking lot leads to a pair of freshwater lava-tube caves. Their garden-like exteriors are draped with ferns, while their interiors harbor deep spring-fed pools with resident fish. Wai'anapanapa means 'glistening waters' and the pools' crystal-clear mineral waters reputedly rejuvenate the skin. They will certainly invigorate – these sunless pools are refreshingly brisk!

Blowhole NATURAL FEATURE

(Map p238; Wai'anapanapa State Park) When the sea is ferocious, on the early part of the Pi'ilani Trail (p225) and just north of Pa'iloa Beach (p228) you'll find this dramatic blowhole (it's signposted). Connected to a submerged cave, it violently spews water out of the precipice up to around 15ft during its mightiest roars – you'd best be standing back when it does. However, it's not an everyday event; keep an eye on local swell charts or surf reports if you're hoping to see it in action.

Wai'anapanapa State Park

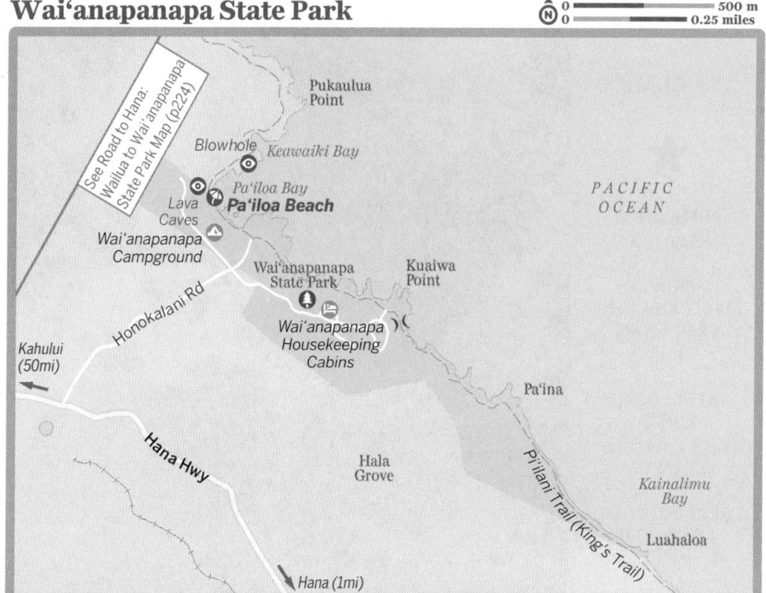

Sleeping

Wai'anapanapa Campground CAMPGROUND **$**
(Map p229; ☎808-984-8109; https://camping.ehawaii.gov/camping; Wai'anapanapa State Park; campsites for up to 6 people $18) Fall asleep to the lullaby of the surf at this central campground, located on a shady lawn near the beach in Wai'anapanapa State Park. It's a great spot, but since this is the rainy side of the island, it can get wet at any time. State camping permit required. Restrooms and outdoor showers. Reservations can be made online.

Wai'anapanapa Housekeeping CABIIN **$**
(Map p229; ☎808-984-8109; https://camping.ehawaii.gov/camping; Wai'anapanapa State Park, 9 Honokalani Rd; cabins for up to 6 people $90; P) Each simple and comfortable wood-decked cabin sleeps six and comes with electricity, running water, a refrigerator, electric hotplates and a microwave. No linens. They're located within walking distance of the parking area, facing the sea. Cabins are in demand; book months in advance (online booking available). Two-night minimum.

Information

Division of State Parks (☎808-984-8109; http://dlnr.hawaii.gov/dsp/hiking/maui; 54 S High St, Room 101, Wailuku; ⏲8am-3:30pm Mon-Fri)

AT A GLANCE

POPULATION
Hana: 1235

OPENING OF HASEGAWA GENERAL STORE
1910

BEST LOCAL LUNCH
Hana Farms Grill (p243)

BEST OUTDOOR ADVENTURE
Skyview Soaring (p239)

BEST HISTORIC SITE
Charles Lindbergh's Grave (p246)

WHEN TO GO

Jan–Dec To avoid the heaviest crowds, start the Road to Hana at dawn, or take your time and spend the night in Hana.

Apr–May Slightly lighter crowds in the spring; East Maui Taro Festival in April.

Sep–Oct Crowds also drop in the fall.

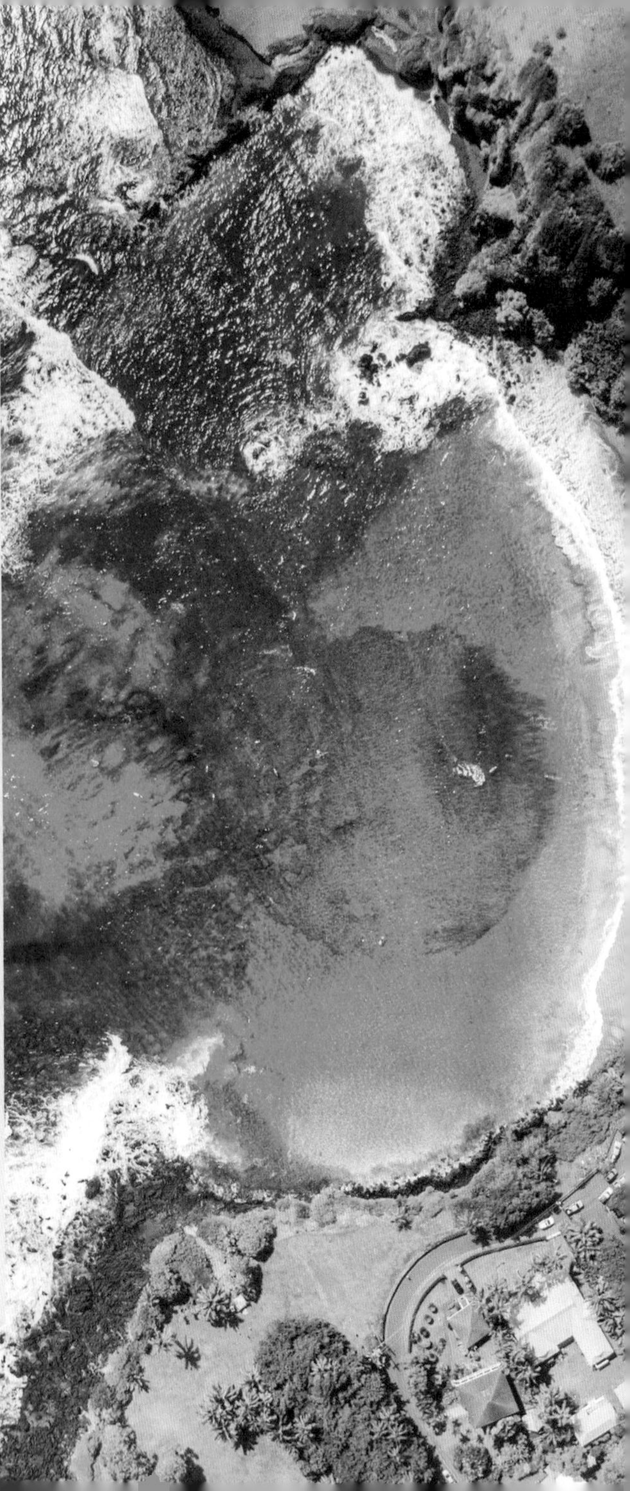

Hamoa Beach (p233)
JUERGEN_WALLSTABE/SHUTTERSTOCK

Hana & East Maui

Rugged and remote, East Maui is the go-to spot for Mauians looking to get away from it all in a place that's hardly changed in ages. Overgrown jungles, lonely churches and narrow roads to the coast – it's wild yet welcoming. In slow-moving Hana you'll learn to talk story – l-o-n-g story – with people who take a personal approach to everything. You'll want more than a few hours here. Continuing clockwise you'll reach Haleakalā National Park, followed by sleepy Kipahulu, which makes Hana look urban. Then it's a wild drive on the Pi'ilani Hwy to Kaupo, where the main street has one building. Finally, you'll disappear into miles of spectacular open country on the back side of Haleakalā.

INCLUDES

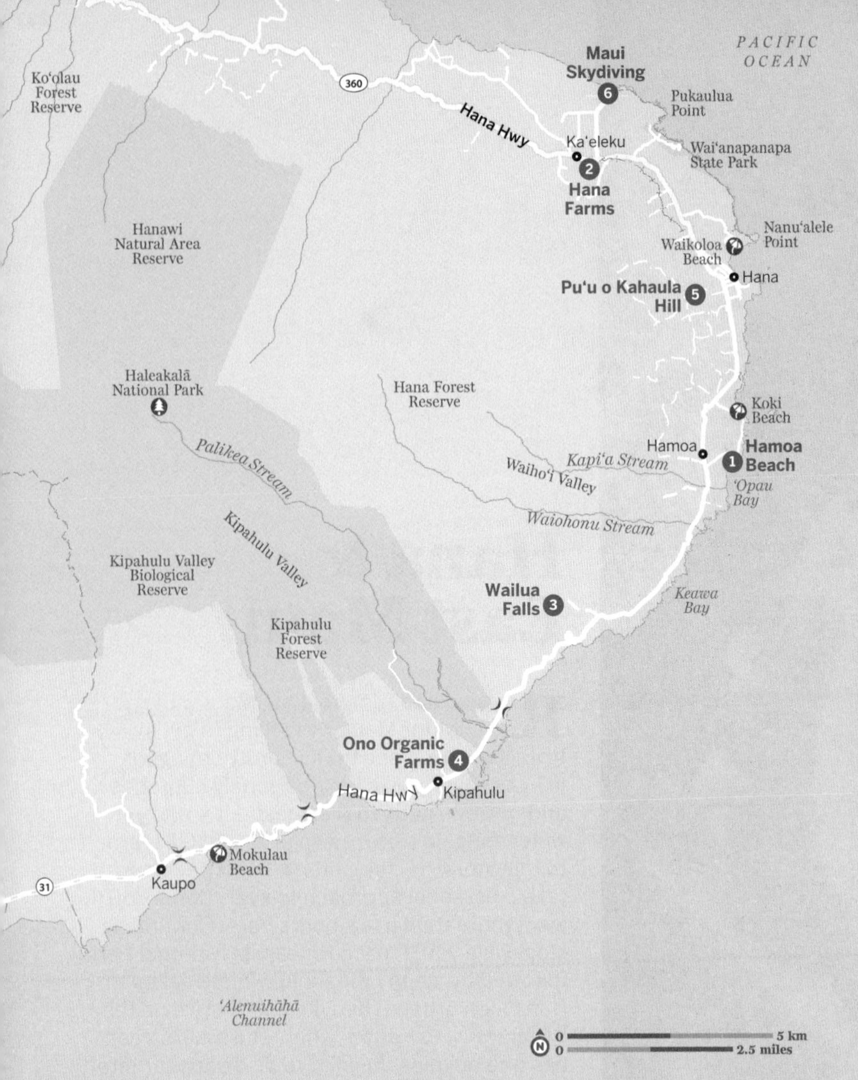

Hana & East Maui Highlights

1. **Hamoa Beach** (p233) Sunning and surfing on picture-perfect tropical shores.
2. **Hana Farms** (p243) Joining locals for seafood plates and slow-cooked-pork sandwiches.
3. **Wailua Falls** (p246) Ogling the most dramatic cascade on a drive full of drama.
4. **Ono Organic Farms** (p246) Tasting exotic fruit on a tour of an oh-so-local farm.
5. **Pu'u o Kahaula Hill** (p239) Hiking to a hilltop with sweeping views of Hana.
6. **Maui Skydiving** (p239) Free falling from 10,000ft during an adrenaline-fueled jump.

Hana

Heavenly Hana. Is it paradise at the end of the rainbow or something a little bit different? Due to its history and its isolated location at the end of Hawaii's most famous drive, Hana has a legendary aura. But many travelers are disappointed when they arrive to find a sleepy hamlet, population 1235. But that's because Hana takes more time to understand.

Surprisingly, Hana doesn't try to capitalize on the influx of day-trippers that arrives each afternoon. This is one of the most Hawaiian communities in the state, with a timeless rural character, and it's also home to many transplants willing to trade certain luxuries for a slow, thoughtful and personal way of life in a beautiful natural setting. Though 'Old Hawaii' is a cliché, it's hard not to think of Hana in such terms. Slow down, spend a night or two and enjoy the pace. There aren't many places like this left.

History

According to Hawaiian folklore, the god Maui discovered the region of Hana and, although it's now impossible to imagine, Hana was the epicenter of Maui. This village produced many of ancient Hawaii's most influential *ali'i* (chiefs). Hana's great 16th-century chief Pi'ilani marched from here to conquer rivals and become the first leader of a unified Maui.

The landscape changed in 1849 when ex-whaler George Wilfong bought 60 acres to plant sugarcane. Hana became a booming plantation town. In the 1940s Hana could no longer compete with larger sugar operations in Central Maui and the mill went bust.

Enter San Francisco businessman Paul Fagan, who purchased 14,000 acres in Hana in 1943. Starting with 300 Herefords, Fagan converted the cane fields to ranch land. He later opened a six-room hotel as a resort for well-to-do friends and brought his baseball team, the San Francisco Seals, to Hana for spring training. Visiting sports journalists gave the town the moniker 'Heavenly Hana.'

Hana Ranch and the legendary Hana-Maui hotel were the backbone of the local economy for decades thereafter. In recent years the hotel has been sold and transformed into Travaasa Hana resort. In 2014 the ranch section of Hana Ranch's landholdings was brought under the Maui Cattle Company label. It also has 7 acres of land growing fruits, including papayas, bananas, breadfruit and citrus fruits.

AGRICULTURAL ZONING

Understanding local zoning regulations is key to understanding Hana. In order to preserve the town from development, many properties are zoned agricultural. As a result, it's extremely difficult to build a commercial property, so almost all restaurants, and some other businesses, inhabit temporary structures – sometimes eye-catchingly so. You might find them in thatched huts or tents, or under great blue tarps. Ice-cream vendors may be in trucks that serve as semi-mobile kitchens or simply in stands.

For visitors the upshot is this: don't be afraid to eat under a blue tarp. Hana has some rather good chefs, and these structures are part of the town's charm.

Beaches

Hana Bay Beach Park is in downtown Hana. Hamoa Beach and Koki Beach sit alongside photogenic Haneo'o Rd, which loops for 1.5 miles off the Hana Hwy just south of town.

Hana Bay Beach Park BEACH

(Map p242; 808-248-7022; www.co.maui.hi.us/Facilities; 150 Keawa Pl; P) Croquet by the beach? Why not? Welcome to Hana's version of the town plaza, a bayside park where children splash in the surf, picnickers enjoy the view from the rocky black-sand beach and musicians strum their ukuleles. And others play croquet. When water conditions are very calm, snorkeling and diving are good out past the pier. Currents can be strong, and snorkelers shouldn't venture beyond the headland. Surfers head to Waikoloa Beach at the northern end of the bay.

Koki Beach BEACH

(Map p238; Haneo'o Rd; P) This picturesque tan beach sits at the base of red cliffs with views toward tiny 'Alau Island. Bodysurfing is excellent here, as it's shallow for quite a distance, but a rip current has been known to sweep people out to sea. Shell picking is good at the tide pools along the edge.

★ **Hamoa Beach** BEACH

(Map p238; Haneo'o Rd; P) Author James Michener once called it the only beach in the North Pacific that looked as if it belonged in the South Pacific. When the surf's up, surfers and bodyboarders flock here, though beware of rips and currents.

ROAD TRIP: PI'ILANI HIGHWAY

The spectacular, untamed Pi'ilani Hwy (Hwy 31), also known as the Back Road to Hana, travels 25 scenic miles between Kipahulu and 'Ulupalakua. It skirts the southern flank of Haleakalā, encompassing lush jungle, snaking bends and numerous gulches. Then, on the dry side of the island, the road breaks into wide-open scenery, with everything from the crashing sea to the volcano above. And hardly anyone is on it.

The Back Road to Hana is rough with potholes and narrow in a few spots early on, and there's a series of unpaved sections; part of the road, however, has a smooth blacktop surface. It's easily driveable in a 2WD, but the authorities recommend a 4WD. Don't follow any vehicle too closely: someone ahead of you may need to stop and back up.

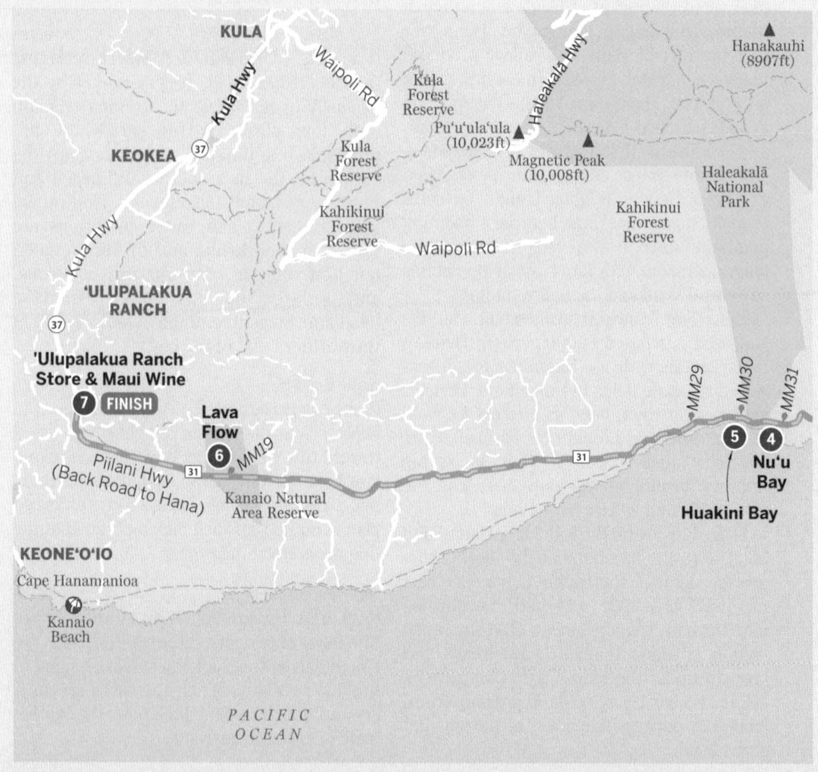

Start: Kipahulu

End: Maui Wine, 'Ulupalakua

Length: 25 miles; two hours

Inquire about current conditions at the national park's Kipahulu Visitor Center (p213).

❶ Kalepa Bridge

Leaving Kipahulu, you'll drive beneath intimidating, sheer cliffs. The Pi'ilani Hwy officially starts at the Kalepa Bridge, near mile marker 38.5. The most hair-raising bend comes a short distance later; just drive slowly and honk your horn. It's a tight, one-way turn between a cliff and the sea – with no railings.

The Drive > The road remains tight and twisty and the pavement soon gives way to short dirt stretches. The open side of Haleakalā crater becomes visible and a mile later you'll enter Kaupo.

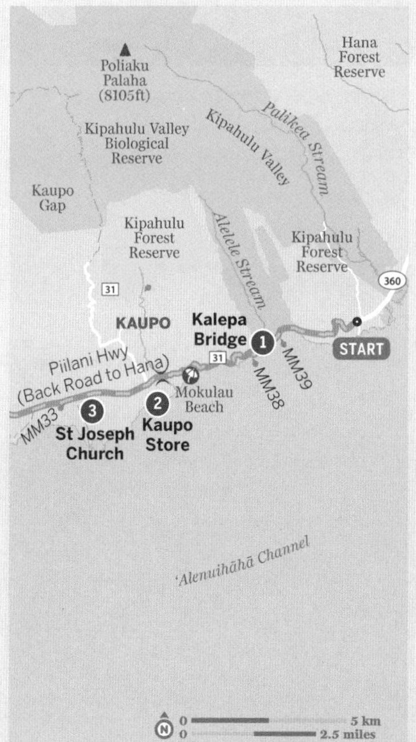

❷ Kaupo

This scattered community is the stomping ground of *paniolo* (Hawaiian cowboys). Kaupo is home to several ancient heiau (temples) and two 19th-century churches. Kaupo Store (p247) is just beyond mile marker 35.

❸ St Joseph Church

A mile later St Joseph Church ((1862; p247) appears on the left. With its mountain backdrop, this is Kaupo's prettiest site. You might see enormous waterfalls through Kaupo Gap, the great gash in the side of Haleakalā. Photogenic views open up at mile marker 33.

❹ Nu'u Bay

Past Kaupo village, you enter the dry side of the island. Near the 31-mile marker, a short 4WD road runs down to Nu'u Bay, favored by locals for fishing. Watch out for riptides.

The Drive > Just east of the 30-mile marker you'll see gateposts that mark the path to Huakini Bay.

❺ Huakini Bay

Park near the highway and walk down the rutted dirt drive a couple of minutes. This rock-strewn beach is whipped by violent surf. After the 29-mile marker, look for a natural lava sea arch that's visible from the road.

The Drive > As you approach 'Ulupalakua, eight windmills mark the return of modern times. Pull over for signage about the windmills and the people who lived here between 1500 and 1800.

❻ Lava Flow

At the 19-mile marker the road crosses a vast **lava flow** (Kanaio Natural Area Reserve; Pi'ilani Hwy, Mile 19) dating from between 1480 and 1600, Haleakalā's last-gasp eruption.

Just offshore is Kaho'olawe.

❼ 'Ulupalakua Ranch Store & Maui Wine

For lunch, it's 4 miles to **'Ulupalakua Ranch Store** (p197), serving juicy, organic, ranch-raised burgers (try the elk patty!). Opposite is **Maui Wine** (p197), where you can toast the end of one spectacular drive.

LAZY DAYS IN HANA & EAST MAUI

How laid-back is Hana? We've heard that some honeymooners have left after just one night because it's simply too quiet and slow paced. Still interested? Then gear up – or gear down – for beach days, fresh lunches, big views and leisurely walks.

ENJOYING THE BEACH

Sunbathing. Shell collecting. Picnics. Maybe a game of croquet. Hana's beach scene tends to be more low-key than others on the island, although you will see surfers and bodyboarders. The ocean can be a bit rough for everyday visitors, but confident swimmers and seafarers can snorkel and kayak when it's calm.

LINGERING OVER LUNCH

Beyond meals at Travaasa Hana resort, lunch options are communal, with folks queuing at roadside food trucks. Their kitchens aren't big, so people talk story at picnic tables while they wait. It's a great place to pick up well-priced local produce, and tips from fellow travelers.

VIEW FROM PU'U O KAHAULA HILL

The grass covering Pu'u o Kahaula Hill, also known as Lyon's Hill, glows green after it rains. A short climb ends at a commanding summit platform with a towering cross and tiki torches. Prepare for thoughts on nature and beauty and as you gaze over Hana town and the coast.

1. Hamoa Beach (p233)
2. Pu'u o Kahaula Hill (p239)
3. Food truck fare, Hana (p233)

DEJETLEY / SHUTTERSTOCK ©

NAOMI RAHIM / GETTY IMAGES ©

East Maui

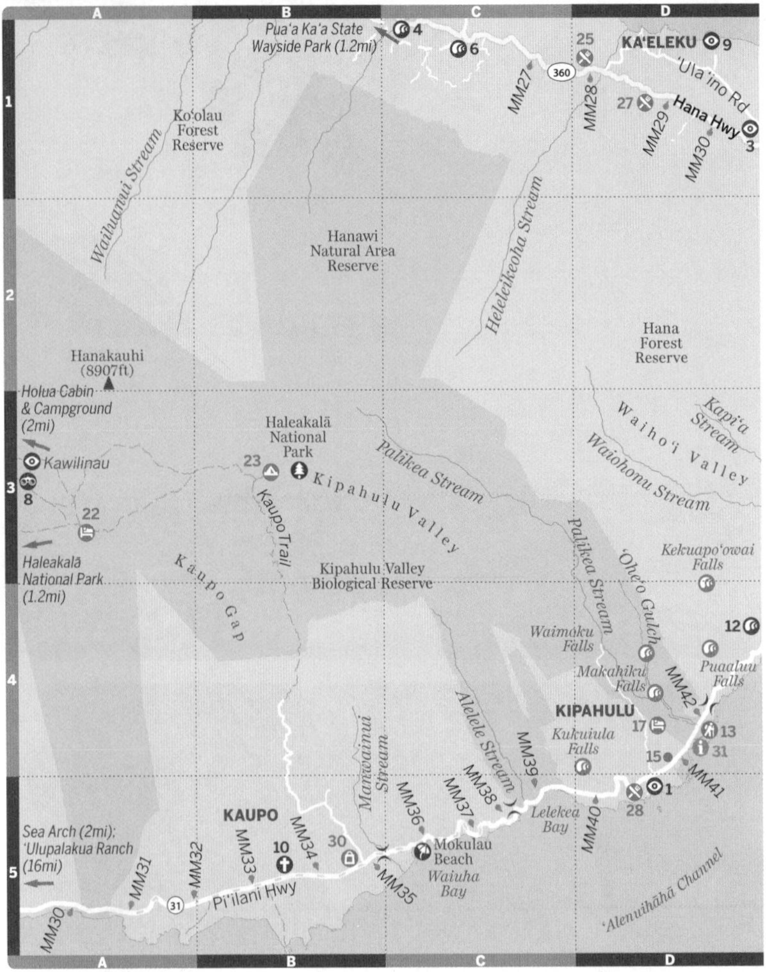

Sights

Hasegawa General Store HISTORIC SITE

(Map p242; ☎808-248-8231; 5165 Hana Hwy; ⏰7am-7pm Mon-Sat, 8am-6pm Sun; P) This tin-roofed store is jam-packed with a little bit of everything, from hardware to produce to tourist brochures. The Hasegawa family has operated a general store in Hana since 1910, and this icon is frequented by locals, and travelers stopping for snacks and the ATM.

Wananalua Congregational Church CHURCH

(Map p242; ☎808-248-8040; 10 Hauoli Rd, cnr Hana Hwy & Hauoli Rd) On the National Register of Historic Places, this church – built in the 1840s – has such hefty walls that it resembles an ancient Norman cathedral. The crumbling mausoleums in the cemetery, watched over by the draping arms of a massive banyan tree, are a poignant sight. The church and the courthouse are the only surviving structures from the 1800s in Hana.

Hana Cultural Center MUSEUM

(Map p242; ☎808-248-8622; www.hanaculturalcenter.org; 4974 Uakea Rd; donation $3; ⏰10am-3pm Wed & Thu; P) This down-home museum displays some interesting local artifacts. The best is an entire three-bench courthouse

(c 1871). Although it looks like a museum piece, this tiny court is still used one day a month when a judge shows up to hear minor cases, sparing Hana residents the need to drive all the way to Wailuku to contest a traffic ticket. Original paintings of Teddy Roosevelt and Admiral Dewey are a blast from the past.

Opening hours can be irregular.

Hana Community Center LANDMARK
(Map p242; ☎808-248-7022; www.co.maui.hi.us/Facilities; 5091 Uakea Rd; P 🚻) Anchors the town park, which has a baseball field, tennis courts and a playground, all behind Travaasa Hana resort. There are also public restrooms.

Activities

Travaasa Hana resort organizes many activities for its guests, including outrigger-canoe trips and stand-up paddleboarding. Its horseback-riding tours are open to nonguests. Alternatively, have Hana imprinted in your mind forever by skydiving over the coast.

★Skyview Soaring GLIDING
(Map p238; ☎808-344-9663; www.skyviewsoaring.com; Hana Airport, 700 Alalele Pl; 30min/1hr $160/300; ⌚by reservation) Haleakalā has excellent soaring conditions, and a sailplane is a rewarding and safe way to see the mountain. After he cuts the engine, experienced pilot Hans Pieters will fly over the crater (weather permitting), and will let you fly too, before gliding silently back to Hana Airport.

Pu'u o Kahaula Hill HIKING
(Lyon's Hill; Map p242; Hana Hwy) This paved walkway up Pu'u o Kahaula Hill, behind Travaasa Hana resort's parking lot (use the gate in the left corner), makes for a fine 30-minute walk (roughly 1.5 miles round trip). It leads to Hana's most dominant landmark, a tasteful memorial to former Hana Ranch owner Paul Fagan. It's like a mountaintop heiau (stone temple), with a huge cross. Hana is laid out below.

Maui Skydiving SKYDIVING
(Map p238; ☎808-379-7455; www.mauiskydiving.info; Hana Airport, 700 Alalele Pl; tandem jumps from $299) To get an adrenaline-fueled prospect of the stunning Hana coastline, jump out of a plane with Maui Skydiving. Jumps include a free fall for around 20 seconds from 10,000ft before the instructor pulls the chute and you both drift to ground level. It's a view you'll never forget. Special-deal standby jumps go for $250 per person.

Spa at Travaasa Hana SPA
(Map p242; ☎888-820-1043; www.travaasa.com; Travaasa Hana, 5031 Hana Hwy; 1hr lomilomi massage $175; ⌚9am-7pm) If the long drive to Hana has tightened you up, this posh spa can work out the kinks with *lomilomi* (traditional Hawaiian massage). Other treatments include Thai, Swedish and *pohaku wela* (hot stone) massage. While the place is nicely laid out, with a plunge pool, steam rooms and a lava-rock whirlpool, the treatment rooms are a bit clinical.

East Maui

Sights
- Blowhole .... (see 11)
- 1 Charles Lindbergh's Grave D5
- 2 Hamoa Beach E3
- 3 Hana Lava Tube D1
- 4 Hanawi Falls C1
- 5 Koki Beach F3
- Lava Caves .... (see 11)
- 6 Makapipi Falls C1
- 7 Pa'iloa Beach E1
- 8 Pele's Paint Pot Lookout A3
- 9 Pi'ilanihale Heiau & Kahanu Garden D1
- 10 St Joseph Church B5
- 11 Wai'anapanapa State Park E1
- 12 Wailua Falls D4

Activities, Courses & Tours
- Kipahulu 'Ohana .... (see 13)
- 13 Kuloa Point Trail D4
- 14 Maui Skydiving E1
- 15 Ono Organic Farms D4
- Pipiwai Trail .... (see 13)
- 16 Skyview Soaring E1

Sleeping
- 17 Anya's House D4
- 18 Ekena E1
- Garden Room .... (see 18)
- 19 Guest Houses at Malanai E3
- 20 Hamoa Bay House & Bungalow E3
- 21 Hana's Tradewind Cottages E1
- 22 Kapalaoa Cabin A3
- Kipahulu Campground .... (see 13)
- 23 Paliku Cabin & Campground B3
- Wai'anapanapa Campground .... (see 11)
- 24 Wai'anapanapa Housekeeping Cabins E1

Eating
- 25 Coconut Glen's D1
- Hana Farms Grill .... (see 29)
- 26 Hana Fresh Market E2
- Hana Highway Lūau .... (see 27)
- Hana Huli Huli BBQ .... (see 27)
- Hana Pizza Company .... (see 27)
- 27 Island Chef D1
- 28 Laulima Farm D5
- Up in Smoke .... (see 27)

Drinking & Nightlife
- Nahiku Cafe .... (see 27)

Shopping
- 29 Hana Farms E1
- 30 Kaupo Store B5

Information
- 31 Kipahulu Visitor Center D4

Luana Spa SPA
(Map p242; 808-248-8855; www.luanaspa.com; 5050 Uakea Rd; 30min/1hr massage $45/80, scrub/facial from $100/85; 9am-6pm) From a papaya-pineapple scrub to a nourishing noni wrap, treatments here embrace local ingredients and traditions. Luana offers treatments in a secluded yurt on Ka'uiki Hill, opposite Hana Ball Park. Spa treatments can be combined with an overnight stay in the yurt (p241).

Hana Ball Park TENNIS
(Map p242; 808-248-7022; www.co.maui.hi.us/Facilities; cnr Uakea Rd & Hauoli Rd; 7am-7pm;) Offers very nice public tennis courts and a playground for kids. Plus restrooms.

Tours

Travaasa Hana Stables HORSEBACK RIDING
(Map p242; 808-270-5276, reservations 808-359-2401; www.travaasa.com; Travaasa Hana, 5031 Hana Hwy; 1hr ride $74; tours 9am & 10:30am) Enjoy a gentle trail ride through pastures and along Hana's black-lava coastline. Riders must be at least nine years old. Rides depart from stables just south of Travaasa Hana resort. Open to nonguests; book at the front desk.

Festivals & Events

★ **East Maui Taro Festival** CULTURAL
(www.tarofestival.org; Apr) Maui's most Hawaiian town throws its most Hawaiian party. If it's native, it's here – a taro-pancake breakfast, poi making, hula dancing and a big jam-fest of Hawaiian music. Held on the last weekend in April, it's Hana at its finest. Book accommodations well ahead. Events take place around town, including on Hana Ball Park.

Hana Canoe Regatta SPORTS
(http://hawaiiancanoeclub.org/programs/regatta; Hana Bay Beach Park; Apr) Outrigger canoes race out to sea in April, marking the start of canoe season.

Hana Surfing Classic SPORTS
(www.mauisurfohana.org; Koki Beach; Sep) Annual amateur surfing contest, with a kids' heat; held in mid-September.

Sleeping

Rental cottages are the way to go if you're seeking somewhere unique with privacy and gorgeous views. Most are tucked here and there on lonely roads in the mountains or near the coast. For resort-style luxury and on-site dining, Travaasa Hana is your best bet. For camping, head north to Wai'anapanapa Campground (p229) or south to the Kipahulu (p213) section of Haleakalā National Park.

Hana's Tradewind Cottages COTTAGE $
(Map p238; ☎808-248-8980; http://tradewindscottage.net; 135 Alalele Pl; cottages $195, extra person $25; 📶) Tucked on the lush grounds of a tropical-flower farm, this cottage is private and offers great value. The cozy two-bedroom Tradewind Cottage has space to accommodate a small family (one room with two single beds and one room with a double bed), and there's a hot tub on the lanai (porch). Two-night minimum stay; $50 cleaning fee.

Garden Room B&B $
(Map p238; ☎808-248-8071; www.anyashouse.com/gardenroom.html; 255 Kalo Rd; r $169; 📶) This quiet and comfortable room with kitchenette, in a private wing of a house 10 minutes from Hana, overlooks a garden on 4 acres. The amiable owner caters to one-night stays. Continental breakfast.

Hale Ka'uiki YURT $
(Map p242; ☎808-248-8855; www.luanaspa.com; 5050 Uakea Rd; d $150, per night for 2 or more nights $135; 📶) Available for rent if you book a treatment, this back-to-nature yurt at Luana Spa (p240) fuses outdoor living with indoor comforts, including a well-equipped kitchenette. The yurt is perched on a secluded hill overlooking Hana Bay. Shower outdoors in a bamboo enclosure and enjoy spectacular stargazing over the bay – this is pure Hana.

★**Hamoa Bay House & Bungalow** COTTAGE $$
(Map p238; ☎808-248-7884; www.hamoabay.com; bungalows 1 bedroom $285, houses 2 bedroom $325-395; 📶) 'Tropical Asian fusion' describes these two beautifully designed and very private cottages (with one and two bedrooms) nestled in greenery near Hamoa Beach. Slate floors, soaking tubs, Balinese touches and fine woodwork create warm, comfortable spaces spiced with exotic romance and set in peaceful gardens. Ideal for those seeking a spiritual retreat; you may never leave the lanai.

★**Ekena** RENTAL HOUSE $$
(Map p238; ☎808-248-7047; www.ekenamaui.com; 290 Kalo Rd; 1/2 bedroom $295/495; 📶) An impressive winding road leads uphill to this two-story pole house with vaulted ceilings, wraparound decks and 360-degree views of sea, forest and mountain. Cable TV, washer-dryer and barbecue are provided. There's a three-night minimum.

★**Anya's House** CABIN $$
(Map p238; ☎808-248-8071; www.anyashouse.com; Kipahulu; 2 people $250, extra person $40, cleaning fee $75) You're really off the grid now – and in an ohia-post cabin with spring-fed water, solar panels and great views across verdant hills to the sea. The one-bedroom cabin has a large living area and a fully stocked kitchen, and sleeps four (with couch). Two-night minimum.

Hana Kai-Maui CONDO $$
(Map p242; ☎808-248-8426, reservations 800-346-2772; www.hanakaimaui.com; 4865 Uakea Rd; r $235-475, service fee per night $20; 📶) Hana's only condo complex, comprising one ocean*front* building and an ocean*view* building behind it, is just a stone's throw from black-pebble Waikoloa Beach. Standard rooms have different owners and varying decor; unit 1 has corner glass aimed straight down the beach. Two-night minimum stay. Stylish unit 105 works well for solo travelers.

Bamboo Inn HOTEL $$
(Map p242; ☎808-248-7718; www.bambooinn.com; 4869 Uakea Rd; ste $225-305; 📶) The quiet Bamboo Inn, which overlooks black-pebble

KAIHALULU (RED SAND) BEACH

You may hear rumors about this clothing-optional red-sand beach, which is tucked in a hidden cove beneath a sheer red cliff, all protected by a volcanic dyke that was created by an ancient fissure. The beach is a 10-minute hike from the Hana Community Center.

While unique, the beach and its access trail are located on private property. The steep trail is also narrow, crumbly and dangerous; there have been numerous injuries to hikers who have fallen here, with a few requiring an airlift out for medical care. Also, on the way to and from the beach, the trail runs near an old Japanese cemetery. There is evidence of disrespectful wear and tear to the site by careless hikers as they pass the cemetery grounds.

Hana

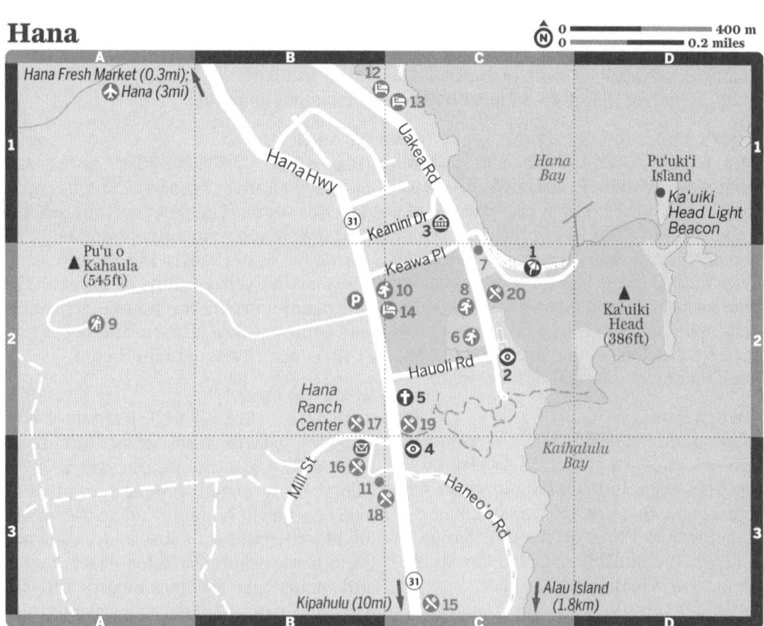

Hana

Sights
1 Hana Bay Beach Park C2
2 Hana Community Center C2
3 Hana Cultural Center C1
4 Hasegawa General Store C3
5 Wananalua Congregational Church C2

Activities, Courses & Tours
6 Hana Ball Park C2
7 Hana-Maui Kayak & Snorkel C2
8 Luana Spa C2
9 Pu'u o Kahaula Hill A2
10 Spa at Travaasa Hana C2
11 Travaasa Hana Stables B3

Sleeping
12 Bamboo Inn B1
Hale Ka'uiki .... (see 8)
13 Hana Kai-Maui C1
14 Travaasa Hana C2

Eating
15 Braddah Hutt's BBQ C3
16 Hana Ranch Restaurant B3
17 Hana Ranch Store B2
18 Ono Farmers Market C3
Shaka Pops .... (see 18)
19 Surfin' Burro C2
20 Thai Food by Pranee C2

Drinking & Nightlife
Preserve .... (see 10)

Shopping
Hana Coast Gallery .... (see 10)

Waikoloa Beach, offers three quality suites, all with nice seaward lanai offering great sunrises and interesting views of the Waikoloa Peninsula. Two-person Jacuzzi tubs are the place to end the day. A central location makes for a very convenient stay. Outdoor BBQ, too.

Guest Houses at Malanai B&B $$
(Map p238; ☎808-248-8706; www.hanaguesthouses.com; 6780 Hana Hwy; cottages $295-325; wi-fi) Two charming country cottages (with one and two bedrooms) sit on 2 acres right off the highway. The slightly smaller Hale Ulu Lulu cottage was built in the early 1900s is one of the few remaining original plantation houses in Hana. Amenities include kitchens, gas barbecues, and washer-dryers.

Travaasa Hana RESORT $$$
(Map p242; ☎888-820-1043, 808-359-2401; www.travaasa.com; 5031 Hana Hwy; d from $525; wi-fi, pool) The historic resort (formerly Hotel Hana-Maui and Honua Spa) has left its roots behind in an effort to create a contemporary high-end experience – with prices to match. The country-club atmosphere is not what

Hana is about, but staff members keep the alohas real. The big, breezy cottages and gorgeous grounds are the stuff of honeymoons.

Eating

You won't find a traditional restaurant scene in Hana and East Maui. What you will find? Food trucks. And they serve the best food around, typically at lunch. Unless you catch an early-evening meal, it's self-catering or hotel restaurants at dinnertime.

★ Thai Food by Pranee THAI $
(Map p242; 5050 Uakea Rd; meals $10-15; ⊙10:30am-4pm) Hana's ever-popular Thai lunch is served from an oversize food truck surrounded by picnic tables. Step up to the counter for a large and tasty meal, including fiery curries with mahi-mahi and fresh stir-fried dishes. The crispy *'opakapaka* (pink snapper) with green-mango salad is out of this world. Get here early for the best selection. Located opposite Hana Ball Park.

★ Shaka Pops ICE CREAM $
(Map p242; www.shakapopsmaui.com; ice pops $4.75; ⊙11am-4pm Sun-Fri) A friendly *shaka* wave greets travelers passing this happy mobile tricycle, where frozen treats-on-a-stick come in fresh, tropical flavors from Liliko'i Cheesecake to Pineapple Ginger. Locally made, the pops use seasonal produce and are definitely worth a lick. Look for the cart by Hana Gas.

Surfin' Burro MEXICAN $
(Map p242; ☎808-269-9775; Hana Hwy; mains $4-10; ⊙8am-7pm Wed-Mon) Tacos? In Hana? Yep, and they're darn good too. Also serves quesadillas, breakfast burritos and fresh-made salsa. Look for the orange food truck parked between the Hotel Travaasa and Hasegawa General Store. Vegan dishes available.

Braddah Hutt's BBQ BARBECUE $
(Map p242; ☎808-264-5582; 5305 Hana Hwy; meals $10-16; ⊙10am-2pm Mon-Fri) This place is like a barbecue at your neighbor's house. Here, diners sit on folding chairs under a canvas awning. Favorites include the barbecue chicken and the fish tacos. Expect a crowd at noon.

Ono Farmers Market MARKET $
(Map p242; ☎808-248-7779; www.onofarms.com; Hana Hwy; ⊙10am-6pm) This fruit stand is the place to pick up Kipahulu-grown coffee, jams and the most incredible array of fruit, from papaya to rambutan. Look for it in the parking lot just south of the gas station.

BACK ROAD TO HANA RESTRICTIONS

You may find that hotel staff, park rangers and even some locals strongly discourage tourists from driving the staggeringly beautiful but notorious bottom loop of highway south of Hana, named the Pi'ilani Hwy and also known as the Back Road to Hana. Their reasoning is threefold. One, the potholed road isn't in the best condition, and having hundreds of tourists on it each day will only exacerbate its disrepair. Two, locals can no longer easily use the top section of road due to the streams of visitors driving it each day; locals use the Back Road to commute to West Maui, so encouraging tourists to use it will create unwanted traffic. Three, while the road is easily navigable by competent drivers, there are occasional sheer drops with no barriers – tourists with little driving experience have been known to abandon their cars at these points instead of negotiating the turns, causing big problems for other drivers, who have very little room to maneuver and are often forced to turn back.

Aside from the above, unpaved roads do cause more damage to rental cars, so many of Maui's car-rental companies have banned renters from driving the Back Road to Hana altogether. Check your contract before you set off: there could be hefty fees if you break down on this incredible, but often narrow, stretch of road.

Hana Fresh Market HEALTH FOOD $
(Map p238; ☎808-248-7515; www.hanahealth.org; 4590 Hana Hwy; coffee $3, mains $10-13; ⊙11am-3pm Mon-Fri) Located between mile markers 34 and 35, this 7-acre farm has a roadside stand in front of Hana Health selling organic produce grown on-site, plus healthy takeout plates featuring locally caught fish. Coffee, smoothies and yogurt bowls are also on offer.

Hana Ranch Store SUPERMARKET $
(Map p242; ☎808-248-8261; 1 Mill St; ⊙6am-7:30pm) The place to stock up on groceries and liquor. Also has an ATM. Off Hana Hwy.

★ Hana Farms Grill GRILL $$
(Map p238; ☎808-248-7553; www.hanafarmsonline.com; 2910 Hana Hwy; mains $14-18; ⊙11am-3pm Sat-Thu, 5-8pm Fri) Behind the Hana Farms

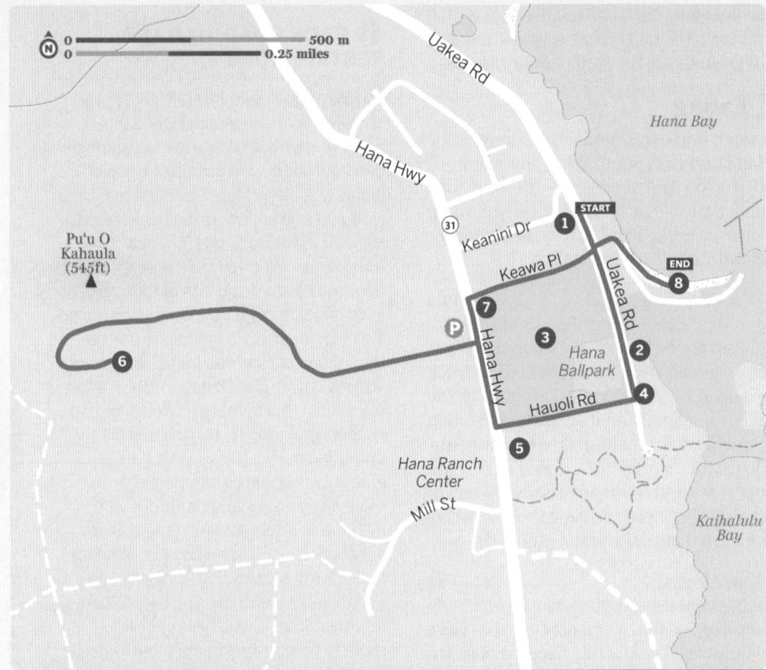

Walking Tour
Hana Walk

START HANA CULTURAL CENTER
END HANA BAY BEACH PARK
LENGTH 2.5 MILES ROUND TRIP; ONE HOUR

Artifacts at the 1 **Hana Cultural Center** (p238) spotlight the customs of 1800s Hawaii. Step into the tiny 1871 courthouse (still in use as a court once a month) to learn about the tsunami that hit northern Maui and Hana in 1946, killing 14 people and destroying 77 homes. The adjacent Kauhale Village replicates the compound of an ancient Hawaiian chieftain.

From here, follow Uakea Rd south, crossing Kiawe Pl. A sign reading 'Thai Food' on your left marks the driveway to excellent food truck 2 **Thai Food by Pranee** (p243), serving fresh-fish curries. On your right, the back lawn of 3 **Travaasa Hana resort** (p242) unfurls in well-manicured glory, merging seamlessly with the town's ball park. 4 **Hana Community Center** (p239) is ahead on the left. At the end of the block, turn right onto Hauoli Rd, which divides Travaasa Hana. Watch out for golf carts scooting around.

The simple but striking 5 **Wananalua Congregational Church** (p238), built in the 1840s, anchors the corner of Hauoli Rd and the Hana Hwy. Cross the highway and walk toward the stone wall surrounding Travaasa Hana's parking lot. Open the gate to follow the half-mile trail to the top of 6 **Pu'u o Kahaula Hill** (p239), surmounted by a large cross. In the right mix of sun and rain clouds, the pastures here glow a rich green. At the top, stone benches and tiki torches surround the cross, a simple but powerful memorial to former Hana Ranch owner Paul Fagan. From here you can enjoy the view of Hana and Hana Bay.

Return the way you came and cross the Hana Hwy. A sidewalk to the left leads through a small garden before you arrive at 7 **Hana Coast Gallery** (p245), home to Hawaii-made art. From here, walk carefully along the shoulder of Kiawe Pl down to 8 **Hana Bay Beach Park** (p233). Savor the view of the tranquil sea.

stand, this little gem is *the* local choice for a lunch stop. It serves fresh seafood plates – with *liliko'i* (passion fruit) butter, turmeric-lemongrass rice, and two sides – plus slow-cooked pork-shoulder sandwiches, tacos, and juicy, grass-fed Maui beef burgers.

Hana Ranch Restaurant AMERICAN **$$**
(Map p242; ☎808-270-5280; https://hanaranchrestaurant.com; Hana Ranch Center, Mill St; mains $17-32; ⏰11am-8:30pm) The wall of ukuleles is perfect for an Instagram photo at this revamped restaurant, one of a handful of dinner options in Hana. Enjoy the ocean view from inside or from the patio. Serves American and Hawaiian fare, from market-fresh *poke* and Hawaiian barbecue-pork ribs to fish tacos and rib-eye steak. Located off the Hana Hwy.

Drinking & Nightlife

If you're looking for nightlife, don't come to Hana: this sleepy town is quiet in the evenings – very quiet. You can head over to Hana Ranch (p245) for drinks, but it closes early compared to bars in big cities.

Preserve BAR
(Map p242; ☎808-248-8211; www.travaasa.com; Travaasa Hana, 5031 Hana Hwy; ⏰restaurant 7:30am-2pm & 5-9pm, bar till later) When it comes to Hana nightlife, this is the only game in town. Maui beers, cocktails and farm-to-table bar fare are on offer. Local musicians perform Wednesday and Thursday nights from 6:30pm to 8.30pm, sometimes accompanied by hula dancers.

Shopping

Hana Coast Gallery ARTS & CRAFTS
(Map p242; ☎808-248-8636; www.hanacoast.com; 5031 Hana Hwy; ⏰9am-5pm) Even if you're not shopping, visit this excellent gallery at the northern side of Travaasa Hana resort to browse the museum's well-curated wooden bowls, paintings and Hawaiian featherwork from about 40 Hawaii artists.

Hana Farms FOOD
(Map p238; www.hanafarmsonline.com; 2910 Hana Hwy; ⏰8am-6:30pm Sun-Thu, to 8pm Fri & Sat) This small 7-acre farm grows a large variety of tropical fruits, flowers and spices. Its well-done roadside stand offers banana bread, exotic fruit preserves, tropical hot sauces, island candies, coffee and spices. It's a great place to find a unique and tasty gift. There's a farm restaurant (p243) next door.

Information

Hana Ranch Center (Mill Rd) is the commercial center of town.

Bank of Hawaii (☎808-248-8015; www.boh.com; Hana Ranch Center, Mill St; ⏰3-4:30pm Mon-Thu, 3-6pm Fri) No ATM.

Hana Health (☎808-248-8294; www.hanahealth.org; 4590 Hana Hwy; ⏰clinic 7am-5pm Mon-Fri, 8am-noon Sat, emergency care 24hr) At the northern side of town.

Post Office (Map p242; ☎808-248-8258; www.usps.com; Hana Ranch Center, 1 Mill St; ⏰11am-4pm Mon-Fri)

Getting There & Around

Enterprise (☎808-871-1511; www.enterprise.com; Travaasa Hana, 5031 Hana Hwy; ⏰booking office in Kahului 7am-5pm Mon-Fri, 8am-noon Sat & Sun) Travaasa Hana resort has an outlet of this car-rental agency, with a very small fleet of cars. Book ahead.

Hana Airport (Map p238; ☎808-248-4861; http://airports.hawaii.gov/hnm; 700 Alalele Pl) There are daily flights from Kahului to this small airport (and return) with Mokulele Airlines (www.mokuleleairlines.com), cutting a two-hour drive to a 20-minute flight.

Hana Gas (5170 Hana Hwy; ⏰7am-8pm Mon-Sat, to 6pm Sun)

Haneo'o Road Loop

Author James Michener was so taken by Hamoa Beach along this 1.5-mile scenic loop drive that he compared it to the South Pacific. To see what tickled him, travel south from Hana on the Hana Hwy and turn left onto Haneo'o Rd just before the 50-mile marker.

At the base of a red cinder hill, the chocolate-brown sands of Koki Beach (p233) attract local surfers. The offshore isle topped by a few coconut palms is **'Alau Island**, a seabird sanctuary. Incidentally, those trees were planted by Hana residents to provide themselves with drinking coconuts while fishing from the island.

A little further on is Hamoa Beach (p233). The waves here are popular with surfers and boogie boarders. Watch out for riptides and currents if you decide to take a dip. Dr Beach named Hamoa one of the top 10 beaches in the US in 2015.

Hana to Kipahulu

The lush drive south from Hana to Kipahulu brims with raw natural beauty. Along its twists and turns are one-lane bridges and drivers trying to take in all the sights. It's a slow-moving 10 miles, so allow yourself a half hour just to reach Kipahulu.

En route you'll pass 'Ohe'o Gulch, your entry point to the Kipahulu section of Haleakalā National Park. This is the undisputed highlight of the drive, offering fantastic falls, cool pools, and incredible tropical paths to hike. The area can experience flash floods, so the Park Service does not recommend swimming in the pools. Note: the volcano summit cannot be accessed from here by car; this requires driving to a different entrance 2½ hours away.

The tiny community of Kipahulu, which hides estates and organic farms behind its lush facade, hugs the Hana Hwy 1 mile south of the park.

★Wailua Falls WATERFALL

(Map p238; Hana Hwy) Before you reach Kipahulu you'll see orchids growing out of the rocks, and jungles of breadfruit and coconut trees. Around 0.3 miles after the 45-mile marker, you'll come upon the spectacular Wailua Falls, which plunge a mighty 100ft just beyond the road. There are usually plenty of people lined up snapping photos.

Kipahulu

Less than a mile south of 'Ohe'o Gulch and the national park lies the little village of Kipahulu. It's hard to imagine, but this sedate community was once a bustling sugar--plantation town. After the mill closed in 1922, most people found jobs elsewhere. Today, mixed among modest homes, organic farms and back-to-the-landers living off the grid, there's a scattering of exclusive estates, including the former home of aviator Charles Lindbergh.

VOLUNTEER ON AN ORGANIC FARM

There are so many organic farms that need volunteer labor in Hawaii that World Wide Opportunities on Organic Farms (WWOOF), a global organization that puts volunteers and organic farms together, runs a special Hawaii operation. In East Maui, sponsors include Hana Farms (p245) and Ono Organic Farms (p246). Unpaid terms are typically three to six months, but people with particularly valuable skills will be considered for shorter placements. One thing's for sure: volunteers will eat extremely well during their stay. For a full list of opportunities, see www.wwoofhawaii.org.

Sights

Charles Lindbergh's Grave CEMETERY

(Map p238; ☎808-269-2736; www.palapalahoomau.org; Palapala Ho'omau Congregational Church; P) Charles Lindbergh, the first man to fly nonstop across the Atlantic Ocean, moved to Kipahulu in 1968. After being diagnosed with terminal cancer, he decided to forgo treatment lived out his final days here. Following his death in 1974, Lindbergh was buried in the graveyard of Palapala Ho'omau Congregational Church. The church is also noted for its window painting of a Polynesian Christ.

Lindbergh's grave is a simple granite slab laid upon lava stones in the yard behind the church. The epitaph is a quote from the Bible: 'If I take the wings of the morning, and dwell in the uttermost parts of the sea.' Walk seaward and you'll find a viewpoint aimed at those uttermost parts.

To find the church, turn left 350yd south of the Hana Hwy's 41-mile marker and follow the road a short distance. The church is at the end of a long driveway on the left.

There's a pretty park in the grounds to relax in, with beautiful views onto the rugged coastline.

Tours

★Ono Organic Farms FOOD & DRINK

(Map p238; ☎808-248-7779; www.onofarms.com; Hana Hwy; tours adult/child under 10yr $45/free; ⏲tours 1:30pm Tue) This fascinating 90-minute tour of a wildly exotic business begins with a delicious tasting of tropical fruit. The variety is amazing: ever tried Suriname cherries, rambutan, red bananas, santol or jaboticaba? The tour then heads into the fields of the 300-acre farm, of which 70 acres are planted.

The farm is on the inland side of the road just south of the national park; look for 'Ono' on the mailbox. You can also sample the goods at Ono Farmers Market (p243) in Hana.

Eating

There are no full-service restaurants in town, just a handful of fruit and farm stands with very fresh and very local produce.

CHARLES LINDBERGH: THE LONE EAGLE

In 1927 the first man flew solo and nonstop across the Atlantic Ocean, piloting the *Spirit of St Louis* from Long Island to Paris in 33½ hours. Six others had died in the attempt. That pioneering aviator was 25-year-old Charles Lindbergh, who was born in Michigan and would die in Maui.

Lindbergh shot to fame after his transatlantic flight, but in 1932 tragedy struck: his young son, Charles Jr, was kidnapped and murdered. In the wake of unrelenting press coverage, Lindbergh and his American wife, Anne, secretly fled to Europe, where they lived until they returned to the US in 1939.

As he was an advocate of noninterventionism and he disagreed with the interference of the British in Germany's affairs, Lindbergh has been accused of being a Nazi sympathizer, but he seemed to revise his views on WWII after the Japanese attacked Pearl Harbor. Lindbergh helped the US military by providing reports on the growing capabilities of German aircraft.

After the war Lindbergh frequently traveled to Europe, where he built many secret lives, fathering seven children with three women in Germany and Switzerland. One woman was a Bavarian hatmaker; the second was her sister, a painter who lived in Grimisuat; and the third was his private secretary, who lived in Baden-Baden. He thus had four families at once. None of the children knew that their half-siblings existed until well after Lindbergh's death. He told his mistresses never to tell a soul who he was, and he used a pseudonym with his children – perhaps to protect them after the trauma of his son's murder, and to protect himself. He maintained his secrecy even until days before his death when he wrote to all his mistresses, and some of his children have continued to keep their stories private.

In his later life Lindbergh turned his efforts to the environment, fearing for the future of the natural world. He joined efforts to protect endangered species and he helped safeguard his beloved East Maui region by working to have the Kipahulu Valley added to Haleakalā National Park in 1969.

Lindbergh was diagnosed with cancer in the final years of his life, and he chose to live out his remaining time in Maui's tiny community of Kipahulu, where he retreated from the world almost entirely. Visitors can view his grave (p246) on the serene grounds of the Palapala Ho'omau Congregational Church.

The famous *Spirit of St Louis* now hangs in the National Air & Space Museum in Washington, DC, the state where Lindbergh spent much of his childhood. It's a fitting monument to a very transatlantic life.

Laulima Farm MARKET $

(Map p238; www.laulimafarm.com; 40755 Hana Hwy; coffee from $4, fruit sampler from $12; ⏲9am-5pm) Pull over for coffee (hand roasted), veggies and fruit, fresh off the adjoining 13-acre farm. Get the fruit sampler – it's delicious. Enjoy your treats under bamboo-shaded seating. Located between mile markers 40 and 41.

Kaupo & Around

Sights

St Joseph Church CHURCH

(Map p238; https://friendsofstjoseph-kaupo.org; 33622 Pi'ilani Hwy) Established by Catholic missionaries in the 19th century, St Joseph Church celebrated its 150th anniversary in 2012. The church offers a noon Mass on the fifth Sunday of the month in months with five Sundays. Confirm dates on the website. Visitors are welcome to respectfully stroll the church grounds and historic cemetery. Located between mile markers 33 and 34.

Shopping

Kaupo Store FOOD & DRINKS

(Map p238; ☎808-248-8054; 34793 Pi'ilani Hwy; ⏲hours vary) Selling snacks and drinks, this cash-only store is off the grid. Don't rely on its being open when you drive past, as it's often closed. If it's open, however, it's worth popping inside just to see the shelves, which are filled with vintage displays, including a camera collection dating to 1911.

AT A GLANCE

POPULATION
Lana'i City: 3100

SWITCHBACKS ON THE KALAUPAPA TRAIL
26

BEST LAVA LANDSCAPE
Keahiakawelo (p259)

BEST DIVING
Cathedrals (p258)

BEST HAWAIIAN FOOD
Kualapu'u Cookhouse (p270)

WHEN TO GO

Nov–Mar Cool nights in lofty Lana'i City; east Moloka'i gets rainy; beaches balmy and warm.

Apr–Aug Winter rains taper off in April; breezy tropical comfort May through August.

Sep–Oct Lana'i City and central Moloka'i in the sunny 70s (above 21°C); coasts in the low 80s (above 26°C).

Keahiakawelo (Garden of the Gods; p259)
ALEKSEI POTOV / SHUTTERSTOCK ©

Lana'i & Moloka'i

Among Hawaii's six main islands, the two with the smallest populations and the least number of visitors could not be more different. Lana'i was never home to many people – its most active time in history was fairly recently, when it earned its moniker 'the pineapple island' after much of it was given over to cultivation of the spiky fruit. Today, under the ownership of billionaire tech mogul Larry Ellison, it offers a very low-key island escape from islands that are already an escape. Moloka'i is much more varied. It has a strong cultural past, with many ancient Hawaiian sites and a very deeply felt reverence for its heritage. It has rugged natural beauty but remains off the radar for most travelers.

INCLUDES

Lana'i & Moloka'i Highlights

1. **Hulopo'e Beach** (p257) Snorkeling the protected reef at the island's best beach.
2. **Lana'i City** (p251) Browsing the shops and sampling the simple cafes around Dole Park.
3. **Munro Trail** (p252) Hiking through Lana'i's small but lush heart, above Lana'i City.
4. **Halawa Valley** (p253) Hearing echoes of Hawaii's past while hiking in this pristine and deeply spiritual setting of waterfalls.
5. **Twenty Mile Beach** (p268) Discovering underwater delights, or just lazing the day away.
6. **Kalaupapa National Historical Park** (p271) Learn how people live in this former leper colony.
7. **Kaunakakai** (p262) Wandering Moloka'i's unrefined and charming historic main town.

LANA'I

Although Lana'i is the most central of the Hawaii islands – on a clear day you can see five islands from here – it's also the least 'Hawaiian.' Now-closed pineapple plantations are its main historic legacy, and the locals are a mix of people descended from immigrant field workers from around the world, mostly the Philippines.

Its signature (imported) Norfolk and Cook Island pines give the island a feel that could just as well come from a remote corner of the South Pacific. And therein lies the charm of Lana'i, a small island (at its widest point only 18 miles across) that's an off-the-beaten-path destination. Hidden beaches, archaeological sites, oddball geology and a sense of isolation let you get away from it all, without going far.

Of course, looming over Lana'i is billionaire Larry Ellison, who owns 98% of the island, and makes efforts to transform the island in fits and starts.

Getting There & Away

AIR

Lana'i Airport (LNY; Map p254; 808-565-7942; http://hawaii.gov/lny) is about 3.5 miles southwest of Lana'i City. Southern Airways, operated by Mokulele (p309, runs two daily direct flights from Maui's Kahului International Airport (p309) to Lana'i.

BOAT

Expeditions Maui–Lana'i Ferry (800-695-2624; www.go-lanai.com; Manele Harbor; adult/child 1 way $30/20) links Lahaina Harbor (Maui) with Manele Bay Harbor (p257) on Lana'i (one hour) several times daily. A channel usually provides a relatively calm crossing between the islands, with the most tranquil waters early in the morning. In winter you may spot whales, and dolphins are a common sight year-round. Car-rental agencies, hotel shuttles and activity operators will meet the ferry if you call ahead. Most people do a day trip to Lana'i from Maui.

CAR

The island's only gas station, Lana'i City Service (p257), sells (pricey) fuel.

Most vehicle rentals on Lana'i are expensive 4WDs, but they're necessary for any real exploration. Outfits on the island are not equipped to offer insurance with their vehicles, so unless you have a comprehensive policy that covers around $30,000 for the car, it's unlikely that local companies will rent to you. Also, vehicles are scarce: you will need to book weeks, if not months, ahead to secure one. Meanwhile, there are numerous restrictions on where you can drive your 4WD; confirm these in advance to avoid hefty fines. All drivers should be aware that there are 7000 wild deer roaming around Lana'i, often darting across the road and causing accidents. Also, speed limits are significantly lower than in other parts of Hawaii, ranging from 15mph to 20mph in Lana'i City to a maximum of 45mph on highways. With low crime rates, the police have plenty of time to issue speeding tickets.

Small firms on the island offering car rental:

ABB Executive Rentals (808-649-0644; per day $145-180) Offers 4WDs and a 2WD car and will arrange pickup and drop-off.

Lana'i Cheap Jeeps (808-489-2296; Hula Hut, 416 8th St; per day $175) Rents 4WD Jeeps and Subarus.

Getting Around

Outside Lana'i City there are only three paved roads: Keomuku Rd (Hwy 44), which extends northeast to Shipwreck Beach; Kaumalapa'u Hwy (Hwy 440), which extends west past the airport to Kaumalapa'u Harbor; and Manele Rd (also Hwy 440), which flows south to Manele and Hulopo'e Bays. To really see the island you'll need to rent a 4WD weeks ahead of your visit (your own car insurance is required). Lana'i's dirt roads vary from good to impassable, largely depending on the weather. Rain can turn them into scarlet-hued bogs. The Lana'i Guide app is a useful resource with an interactive map (including dirt roads and walking trails) and info on tourist sights. Download it onto your phone or view it via www.lanaiguideapp.org.

Lana'i City

Lana'i City's main square, **Dole Park**, is surrounded by tin-roofed houses and shops, with not a chain store in sight. The architecture is little changed since the plantation days of the 1920s, although the gardening is much improved thanks to the

A DAY TRIP TO LANA'I

Take the early-morning ferry (p251) from Lahaina on Maui; keep an eye out for schools of dolphins as the boat approaches Manele Bay. Catch the shuttle into Lana'i City and pour your own coffee for breakfast at Blue Ginger Café (p255) before strolling the town's shops and superb Culture & Heritage Center (p254). In the afternoon, snorkel at Hulopo'e Beach (p257) or snuba (p258) at Manele Bay before heading back to Maui on the sunset ferry.

HIKING IN LANA'I & MOLOKA'I

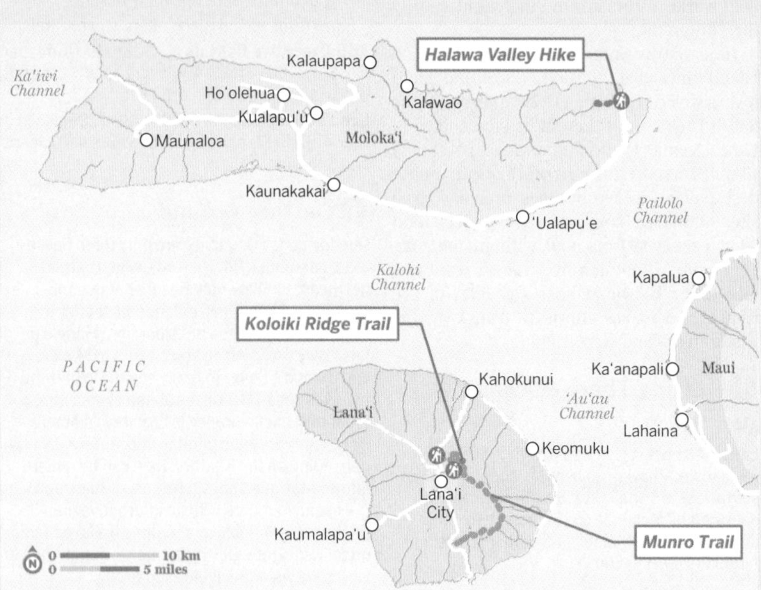

MUNRO TRAIL, LANA'I

START/END LANA'I CEMETERY /MANELE RD
LENGTH 12 MILES ONE WAY; FIVE TO SEVEN HOURS
DIFFICULTY MODERATE TO DIFFICULT

This exhilarating 12-mile adventure through verdant forest with soaring valley views can be hiked or mountain biked but not driven in its entirety. For the best views, and to avoid getting caught at dusk, get an early start. Those hiking should be prepared for steep grades and allow a whole day. Watch out for sheer drops, especially when mist, fog and clouds limit visibility.

To start, head north on Hwy 44 from Lana'i City. About a mile past the Lodge at Koele resort, turn right onto the paved road that ends in half a mile at the island's cemetery. The Munro Trail starts left of the cemetery on a 4WD path that runs for a couple of miles before reaching the Koloiki Ridge Trail (p253) intersection on the left. This offshoot footpath is a nice 0.5-mile up-and-back walk to Koloiki Ridge overlook, with staggering views of the Naio Gulch and Moloka'i and Maui in the distance. If continuing straight on the Munro Trail you'll eventually reach a gate (which 4WD vehicles cannot pass). The footpath is usually completely deserted, offering a wonderful opportunity to soak up the sights and sounds of nature. You'll likely encounter wild deer, and perhaps an exotic frog or two, who like this cool and often damp terrain. The trail itself is lined with eucalyptus groves as it climbs the ridge. The path is studded with *'ohi'a lehua,* ironwood, eucalyptus and Norfolk Island pine trees.

The trail looks down on deep ravines cutting across the east flank of the mountain and passes Lana'ihale (3370ft), Lana'i's highest point. You'll discover various lookout points along the trail. On a clear day you can see all the inhabited Hawaii islands except for distant Kaua'i and Ni'ihau along the route. Stay on the main trail, which descends 6 miles to the central plateau. Keep the hills to your left and turn right at the big fork in the road. The

In Lana'i, the Munro Trail swoops past non-native trees, ravines and lookouts, while the Koloiki Ridge Trail ends with a panoramic view of the island. It's all about waterfalls and history in the Halawa Valley on Moloka'i.

trail ends back on Manele Rd (Hwy 440) between Lana'i City and Manele Bay.

You can follow the trail with the help of the Lana'i Guide app, which will keep you on track the whole way, following your GPS location (visit www.lanaiguideapp.org for info). Bring a sunhat and lots of water, as there are no services on the route.

KOLOIKI RIDGE TRAIL, LANA'I

START/END LODGE AT KOELE OR MUNRO TRAILHEAD
LENGTH 5 MILES ROUND TRIP; TWO TO THREE HOURS
DIFFICULTY MODERATE

This cool 5-mile hike leads up to one of the most scenic parts of Lana'i: the jaw-dropping vista from Koloiki Ridge. It offers sweeping views of the Naio Gulch and remote Maunalei valley (translated as 'mountain garland'), where taro was once grown and water was harvested for the Dole pineapple plantation.

Trail access is possible from the trailhead of the Munro Trail (p252) near Lana'i Cemetery (you can join up with the Koloiki Ridge path around 2 miles along on the left), or you can start at the rear of the Lodge at Koele resort (p255). A path leads to the resort's golf clubhouse, and from there walkers can follow the shaded, signposted path past Norfolk Island pines until they reach a hilltop bench with a plaque bearing Rudyard Kipling's poem 'If'.

Follow the trail down through a thicket of guava trees to an abandoned dirt service road and you'll intersect with the Munro Trail; after a few minutes you'll pass Kukui Gulch, named for the *kukui* (candlenut trees) that grow there. Continue along the trail until you reach a thicket of tall sisal plants, where you should keep your eyes peeled for mouflon sheep and axis deer. About 50yd after that, bear right to reach Koloiki Ridge, where you'll be rewarded with gorgeous panoramic views of much of the island.

Download the Lana'i Guide app (www.lanaiguideapp.org) for map info. Bring lots of water, as there are no services on the route.

HALAWA VALLEY HIKE, MOLOKA'I

START/END HALAWA VALLEY BEACH PARK
LENGTH 4 MILES ROUND TRIP; TWO TO FOUR HOURS
DIFFICULTY MODERATE

The hike and spectacle of the twin 250ft **Mo'oula and Hipuapua Falls** (p269), which cascade down the back of the lush Halawa Valley, are a highlight of many Moloka'i visits. The falls are reached via a 2-mile trail lined with river crossings and historical sites. Visiting the falls requires a hike with a local guide ($60 per person, usually departing at 9am daily); book online weeks ahead of your trip.

There are numerous cultural sites along the path, and you'll pass through lush tropical foliage during the walk. Look for the bright-orange blossoms of African tulip trees and the brilliant green of beach heliotrope trees. Pungent fallen noni fruit, recognizable by its bumpy, greenish-yellow exterior, scatters the path in fall and can attract fruit flies. Those who dare can taste as many as they wish. Continue on to see the ruins of an ancient burial ground that may date to 650 CE, plus the remains of a seven-tier stone temple.

Walks with commentary can take two to five hours, depending on the ability of the people in your group. Expect muddy conditions and wear stout shoes so that you can navigate rivers and over river boulders. The crescendo of the hike is reaching the dreamy falls, clasped by a rich green valley that appears forgotten by time. Most people take a bracing plunge into the pools at the bottom of the falls and swim up to the cascade.

Be sure to bring sturdy hiking shoes or sandals, a swimsuit, plenty of water, a snack, sunscreen, mosquito repellent, and a poncho or other protection from the rain.

Lana'i

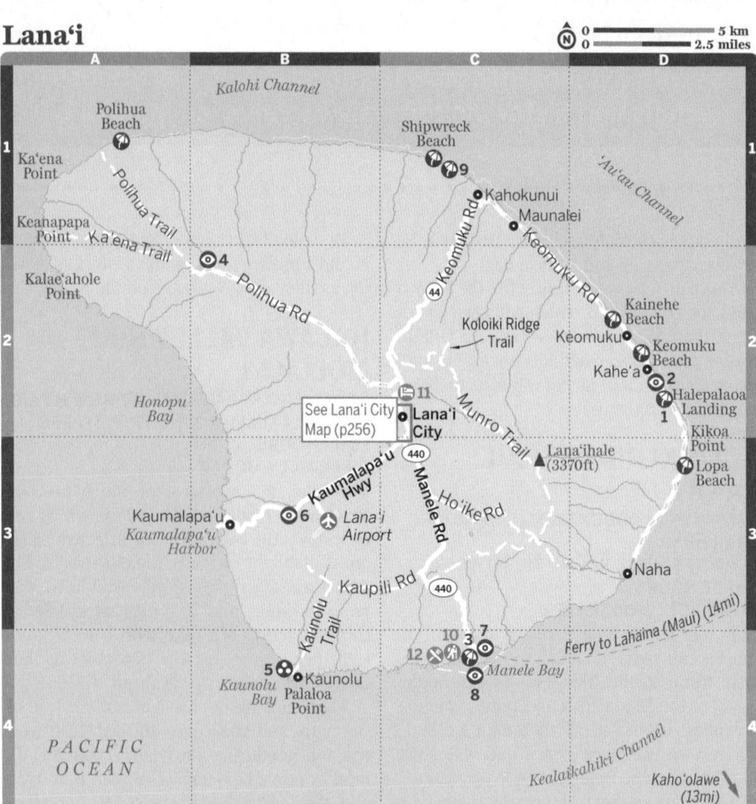

efforts of Larry Ellison's island-management company, Pulama Lana'i. (*Pulama* means to care for or cherish.)

Wander between the small but delightfully varied collection of eateries and shops, all with a low-key feel.

Sights

★Lana'i Culture & Heritage Center MUSEUM

(Map p256; www.lanaichc.org; 730 Lanai Ave; ⏲8:30am-3:30pm Mon-Fri) FREE This engaging small museum is the best place to start before exploring the rest of Lana'i. It has displays with cultural artifacts covering the island's mysterious history, plus photos and a timeline showing how it became the world's pineapple supplier. The lives of the plantation workers are shown in detail: they were expected to plant up to 10,000 pineapple plants per day.

Activities

Lana'i Surf School & Surf Safari SURFING

(☎808-649-0739; www.surfinglanai.com; 3hr surf lessons per person from $200, rental per 24hr boogie board/kayak $25/80, surfboard delivered $100, per hr SUP $50) Lana'i native Nick Palumbo offers half-day surfing and stand-up paddleboarding (SUP) lessons (two-person minimum) at secluded spots. Boogie-board and kayak rental also available.

Tours

Expeditions Maui-Lana'i Ferry (p251) runs a 4WD tour (from $187 per person; two people minimum) taking in the most popular sights.

Festivals & Events

Pineapple Festival CULTURAL

(www.lanaipineapplefestival.com; Dole Park; ⏲early Jul) Lana'i's main bash, the Pineapple Festival, is held on or near July 4 and celebrates

Lana'i

Sights

Activities, Courses & Tours

Sleeping

Eating

Shopping

the island's pineapple past with games and live music at Dole Park. (Note: any pineapple you see is imported!)

Sleeping

Dreams Come True GUESTHOUSE **$**

(Map p256; ☎808-565-6961; www.dreamscometruelanai.com; 1168 Lana'i Ave; r from $161; @) This spiffy plantation-style house, a two-minute walk from Dole Park, was one of the first built in Lana'i City (1925). It has a long porch and a large, pleasant garden. The rooms have hardwood floors and are furnished with a mixture of comfy antique and modern pieces. There are numerous amenities, including laundry, a communal kitchen and private marble baths.

★**Hotel Lana'i** HOTEL **$$$**

(Map p256; ☎808-565-7211; www.hotellanai.com; 828 Lana'i Ave; r from $250, cottages $650;) From 1923 to 1990 the Hotel Lana'i was the only hotel on the island, and it seems that little has changed over the decades, in Lana'i City at least. The tropical plantation-inspired rooms have hardwood floors, marble showers and splashes of color.

Lodge at Koele RESORT **$$$**

(Map p254; ☎800-505-2624; www.fourseasons.com/koele; 1 Keomuku Hwy;) The quieter of the island's two Four Seasons resorts, this 100-room property is meant to evoke an English country estate. Inside the soaring central building, however, there are just enough local touches to remind you that you're in Hawaii. It's been undergoing renovation since 2015. Check the website for pricing once it reopens (scheduled for 2019 but ongoing).

Eating & Drinking

Blue Ginger Café CAFE **$**

(Map p256; ☎808-565-6363; www.bluegingercafelanai.com; 409 7th St; mains $7.50-20; 6am-8pm Thu-Mon, to 2pm Tue & Wed) Don't worry: the care goes into the food, not the decor, at this bare-bones diner, where you can serve yourself a coffee, grab a newspaper and settle in at a table inside or out. Muffins arrive warm from the bakery, and the daily specials are indeed pretty special – try a mahi-mahi burger, a mixed plate or grilled pork chops.

Cafe 565 DINER **$**

(Map p256; ☎808-565-6622; 408 8th St; mains $6.50-13; 10am-8pm Mon-Fri, to 3pm Sat;) This classic yellow plantation house with simple interior design on Dole Park serves burgers and local *grinds* (food). Choose blackened *ono* (white-fleshed wahoo), chicken *katsu* (deep-fried fillets), *loco moco* (rice, fried egg and a hamburger patty topped with gravy) or a 12in sub sandwich, or make your own calzone. Look out for occasional Filipino specials. The patio is a popular local hangout.

★**Pele's Other Garden** ITALIAN **$$**

(Map p256; ☎808-565-9628; 811 Houston St; pizza from $11, mains $10-25; kitchen 11am-2pm & 5-8pm Mon-Fri, 5-8pm Sat) This restored plantation house decorated with number plates has tables indoors and outside. Owners Barb and Mark cook creative takes on Italian cuisine and serve up classic spaghetti and meatballs, crispy thin-crust pizza and some first-rate pesto. Salads are made with organic local greens; desserts are large.

★**Lana'i City Bar & Grille** FUSION **$$**

(Map p256; ☎808-565-7211; www.hotellanai.com; Hotel Lana'i, 828 Lana'i Ave; mains $20-42; kitchen 5-9pm Wed-Sun) The charming restaurant

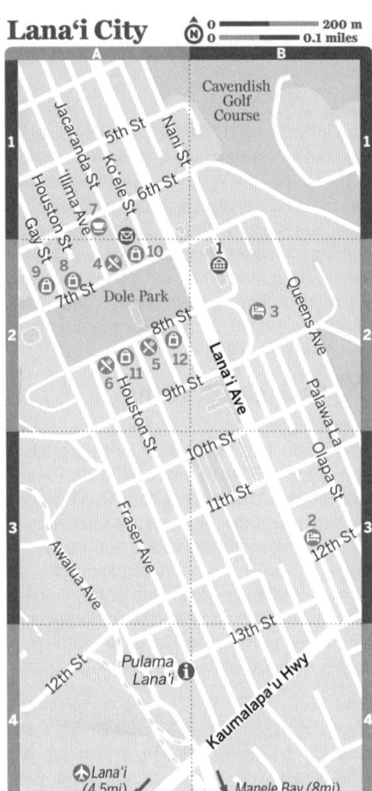

Lana'i City

Sights

1 Lana'i Culture & Heritage Center....... B2

Sleeping

2 Dreams Come True.......... B3
3 Hotel Lana'i.......... B2

Eating

4 Blue Ginger Café.......... A2
5 Cafe 565.......... A2
Lana'i City Bar & Grille.......... (see 3)
6 Pele's Other Garden.......... A2

Drinking & Nightlife

7 Coffee Works.......... A1

Shopping

8 Lana'i Art Center.......... A2
9 Local Gentry.......... A2
10 Mike Carroll Gallery.......... A2
11 Pine Isle Market.......... A2
12 Richard's Market.......... A2

within the Hotel Lana'i (p255) is the best midrange option in town. It has a country-chic feel and a menu combining fresh seafood with various meats, with options ranging from local venison loin and grilled Angus burgers to excellent snapper ceviche and sweet-spicy-glazed mahi-mahi in lobster broth.

Coffee Works COFFEE
(Map p256; ☎808-565-6962; www.coffeeworkshawaii.com; 604 'Ilima Ave; espresso from $3.05; ⌚7am-3pm Mon, to 4pm Tue-Fri, 8am-noon Sat) Sweet local coffee shop set in an old plantation house with a lovely porch. It serves espresso-based Hawaiian blends with tropical flavors, plus cold brew, acai bowls, smoothies, bagels and chili-hot-dog rice bowls.

Shopping

★**Mike Carroll Gallery** ART
(Map p256; ☎808-565-7122; www.mikecarrollgallery.com; 443 7th St, cnr Ko'ele St; prints from $25; ⌚10am-5:30pm Mon-Sat, 9am-2pm Sun) Art-lovers enjoy Mike Carroll Gallery, where you can find the eponymous owner either creating new work or busy displaying the work of another artist. It's also a good source for local books, plus Asian antiques.

Lana'i Art Center ART
(Map p256; ☎808-565-7503; www.lanaiart.org; 339 7th St; ⌚10am-4pm Mon-Sat) Staffed by local artist volunteers. You can choose from works in many mediums or learn how to create your own from the artists themselves. A great place to get *very* local recommendations.

Local Gentry CLOTHING
(Map p256; ☎808-565-9130; www.facebook.com/thelocalgentrylanai; 363 7th St; ⌚10am-6pm Mon-Fri, to 5pm Sat, to 2pm Sun) Lovers of laid-back island style love the Local Gentry, a clothing store with color and flair. Get swimwear and sunscreen here, too.

Richard's Market SUPERMARKET
(Map p256; ☎808-565-3781; 434 8th St; ⌚6am-10pm) Richard's Market (owned by Larry Ellison) is as close to Whole Foods as you're going to get on Lana'i, with prices to match. It has a reasonable wine selection, a salad bar, a *poke* (cubed raw fish mixed with shōyu, sesame oil, salt, chili pepper, 'inamona or other condiments) counter and fresh local fruits. There are prepared foods and sandwiches, plus outdoor tables where you can sip a coffee drink.

Pine Isle Market FOOD & DRINKS
(Map p256; ☎808-565-6488; 356 8th St; ⌚8am-7pm Mon-Sat, to 5pm Sun) Basic grocery store selling snacks, drinks and household items.

Information

First Hawaiian Bank (☎808-565-6969; www.fhb.com/en; 644 Lana'i Ave; ⌚8:30am-4pm Mon-Thu, to 6pm Fri, ATM 24hr)

Lana'i Community Hospital (☎808-565-8450; 628 7th St; ⌚24hr) Offers emergency medical services.

Post Office (Map p256; ☎808-565-6517; 620 Jacaranda St; ⌚9am-3pm Mon-Fri, 9:30-11:30am Sat)

Rainbow Pharmacy (☎808-565-9332; https://rainbowpharmacy.com; 431 7th St; ⌚9am-5:30pm Mon-Fri, to 1pm Sat) Anything you need that is not in stock can be sourced in a day.

Getting There & Away

Lana'i City Service (☎808-565-7227; 1036 Lana'i Ave; ⌚6:30am-10pm) The island's one (pricey) gas station. Also sells good fresh sub sandwiches (from $10.49).

Hulopo'e & Manele Bays

Lana'i's finest beach (and one of the best in Hawaii) is the golden crescent of sand at Hulopo'e Bay. Enjoy snorkeling in a marine preserve, walking to a fabled archaeological site or just relaxing in the shade of palms. Nearby, Manele Harbor provides a protected anchorage for sailboats, other small craft and the Maui ferry. It's just a 10-minute walk from Hulopo'e Beach.

Manele and Hulopo'e Bays are part of a marine-life-conservation district that prohibits the removal of coral and restricts fishing activities, all of which makes for great snorkeling and diving. Spinner dolphins enjoy the place as much as humans. During winter *kona* (leeward) storms, currents and swells enliven the calm and imperil swimmers.

Beaches

★**Hulopo'e Beach** BEACH
(Map p254; 👪) The island's main beach is kept looking beautiful, with manicured lawns and clean restrooms, thanks to Pulama Lana'i's legion of groundskeepers. Everybody loves this free public beach, and it's one of Hawaii's finest – locals take the kids for a swim, tourists visit on day trips from Maui and many lose track of time here. It's located off Manele Rd (Hwy 440).

Sights & Activities

★**Pu'u Pehe** NATURAL FEATURE
(Sweetheart Rock; Map p254) FREE From Hulopo'e Beach (p257) a path (of around 0.75 miles) leads south to the end of **Manele Point**, which separates Hulopo'e and Manele Bays. The point is a volcanic cinder cone that's sharply eroded on its seaward edge. The lava here is a rich rust red with swirls of gray and black, and its texture is bubbly and brittle – so brittle that huge chunks of the point have broken off and fallen onto the coastal shelf below.

Manele-Kapakuea Heritage Trail ARCHAEOLOGICAL SITE
(Map p254; Manele Rd/Hwy 440) FREE East of Manele Habor is a 0.6-mile trail that leads to the 8m-wide, 2m-high Ka Hana Lawa'a (Fishermen's Temple), stacked with boulders. Fishermen would make offerings here by leaving their first catch of the day.

Also here is the partial wreck of the *Naia*, a 40ft-long passenger boat operated by the Hawaiian Pineapple Company to ferry workers between Maui and Lana'i. It was wrecked in the 1940s, but in the '60s its engine was found in the harbor and brought to shore.

Manele Harbor HARBOR
(Map p254) This harbor, off Hwy 440, is where the ferry from Maui docks. There are bathrooms and a few sheltered picnic tables here, plus a convenience store (p259). During the early 20th century cattle were herded to Manele Bay for shipment to Honolulu.

CAT SANCTUARY

Easily Lana'i's most peculiar attraction, the **Lana'i Cat Sanctuary** (Map p254; ☎808-215-9066; http://lanaicatsanctuary.org; 1 Kaupili Rd; ⌚10am-3pm) is a volunteer-run, 3-acre feline wonderland housing 620 cats that have been 'rescued' from the wild. Locals say that cats destroy the local bird populations, so they're housed here. Located on a former pineapple field, the sanctuary has many activities for its inhabitants. Guests are welcome to watch or pet the creatures and will discover a range of kitty personalities. Donations encouraged. It's off Hwy 440.

LARRY ELLISON'S LANA'I

Decades of sleepy seclusion for Lana'i were interrupted in 2012 when one of the richest men in America, Larry Ellison – the wealthy co-founder of huge software developer Oracle – bought out the island's longtime owner Castle & Cooke, which once ran the ubiquitous pineapple plantations under the Dole name.

It's the biggest change to the island since Castle & Cooke stopped farming and built the Four Seasons resorts in the early 1990s. For his estimated $600-million purchase price, Ellison got 98% of Lana'i (the rest is private homes or government land). Given that the island has struggled economically since the glory days of pineapples, Ellison's wide-ranging plans have generated intense interest.

However, owning an island doesn't mean that you're exempt from government regulations. Regulatory hurdles and local political opposition have delayed projects. Still, under Pulama Lana'i, the Ellison-owned company that manages the island, the changes have been many. An outline:

- Community projects include renovating the cinema, restoring historic buildings and reopening the local swimming pool.
- Initially, large construction projects, such as the Four Seasons Resort Lana'i, put a strain on the island's residents. During 2016 both Four Seasons resorts were closed; the resulting dramatic downturn in visitors caused several long-running businesses to close. Business is now flowing back to the island.
- One of the the Four Seasons resorts, the Lodge at Koele, was still undergoing a $75-million renovation at the time of research, with its initial reopening date of late 2019 having been revised to 2020 or later.
- One of Ellison's ventures includes a hydroponic farm with a tech-driven greenhouse system to grow more local produce, allowing the island to curb its need for expensive imported goods.
- At the end of 2019 Ellison took new proposals to the state. He hopes to start a $340-million project that involves turning 200 acres of agricultural land near the airport into urban land, creating more housing, a university campus, a tennis school and film studios. If these plans are completed it's estimated that the island's population could increase by 50% by 2030.

For some residents, life on Lana'i feels a bit like a soap opera as plans and schemes are floated; others are excited by the positive changes to facilities. Achieving economic self-sufficiency on Lana'i may be the biggest challenge of Ellison's life.

★**Cathedrals** DIVING
(Map p254) Diving in the bay is excellent. Coral is abundant near the cliffs, where the bottom quickly slopes to about 40ft. Beyond the bay's western edge, near Pu'u Pehe (p257), is Cathedrals, the island's most spectacular dive site, featuring arches and grottos around a 100ft-long lava tube.

Kapiha'a Village Interpretive Trail HIKING
(Map p254) FREE This ancient trail makes delivers superb coastal views. En route you'll see a *kulana kauhale* (village) that was home to Lana'i's early inhabitants, who thrived through fishing these bountiful shores. The gentle stroll begins on the coast just beneath the Four Seasons Resort Lana'i.

Tours

Trilogy Lana'i Ocean Sports WATER SPORTS
(☎808-874-5649; www.sailtrilogy.com; tours from $220) Runs trips from Maui to Lana'i on a catamaran, then you'll disembark at Hulopo'e Beach for swimming, snorkeling, volleyball sessions or hikes, and have a plantation barbecue lunch. Optional snuba upgrades allow divers to descend 10ft by getting their air via a hose to the surface. It's possible to see octopuses, sea turtles, manta rays and dolphins in these waters.

Sleeping

Hulopo'e Beach Camping CAMPGROUND $
(Map p254; ☎808-215-1107; http://lanai96763.com; site permit for up to 4 guests $80; check-in 7am-8:30 pm) This well-maintained campsite

is one of the best in Hawaii but comes at a steep price. That said, it's still the cheapest option on Lana'i. Eight pitches sit on a grassy expanse behind gorgeous Hulopo'e Beach (p257). The site has drinking water, outdoor showers and two clean restrooms, and barbecue grills. Maximum three-night stay. Advance bookings essential.

★**Four Seasons Resort Lana'i** RESORT $$$
(Map p254; 808-565-2000; www.fourseasons.com/lanai; 1 Manele Bay Rd; r from $1000;) The premier destination on Lana'i, this resort reopened in 2016 after a lavish redesign that saw rooms and public spaces thoroughly revamped to reflect a minimalist tropical aesthetic. New pools have naturalistic features and the gardens invite meandering. The 213 rooms and suites feature every luxury. Views of Manele Bay's azure waters and beach are sublime.

Eating

Views at Manele Golf AMERICAN $$
(Map p254; 808-565-2000; www.fourseasons.com/manelebay; Four Seasons Resort Lana'i, 1 Challenge Dr; mains $20-29; 11am-3pm) The coastal panorama from the private cliffside tables here is the best view from any of the island's restaurants, and it's surprisingly little known. The menu has a broad array of familiar dishes such as salads, sandwiches and burgers; all are prepared with color and flair.

★**Nobu** JAPANESE $$$
(Map p254; 808-565-2832; www.noburestaurants.com/lanai; Four Seasons Resort Lana'i, 1 Manele Bay Rd; sashimi per piece from $6, meals $50-200; dinner 6-9:30pm, bar 4:30-10:30pm) Created by chef Nobuyuki Matsuhisa, worldwide chain Nobu is known for ultra-fresh and creative sushi and other Japanese dishes. Newly redesigned, the dining and bar area at this Four Seasons branch is on a broad, minimalist-yet-elegant terrace with superb views, and menu items feature Hawaiian elements.

The bar serves creative cocktails, including a fabulous sidecar.

One Forty AMERICAN $$$
(Map p254; 808-565-2000; www.fourseasons.com/lanai; Four Seasons Resort Lana'i, 1 Manele Bay Rd; dinner mains $45-80; 6:30-11am & 6-9pm) Overlooking the ocean, this restaurant offers top-end steaks and fresh local seafood. Eat as the sun goes down against flickering tiki torches and the beautiful bay beneath. Don't miss the massive breakfast buffet ($48 per person) and à la carte options (from $12) until 11am. It's primarily enjoyed by resort guests, but outside guests are welcome.

Shopping

Convenience Store FOOD & DRINKS
(Map p254; Manele Harbor; 7am-7pm Mon-Sat, to 4pm Sun) This much-needed small store on the harbor has all the basics, plus fast foods (from $6) – breakfast burritos, Spam *musubi* (a block of rice with a slice of fried Spam on top) and other dishes that you can heat in the microwave. You can buy your cold drinks and snacks for the beach or the ferry ride here.

Keomuku Road

The best drive on Lana'i, Keomuku Rd (Hwy 44) heads north from Lana'i City into cool upland hills, where fog drifts above grassy pastures. Along the way, impromptu overlooks offer views of the undeveloped southeast shore of Moloka'i and its tiny islet Mokuho'oniki, in marked contrast to Maui's sawtooth high-rises in Ka'anapali off to your right.

The 8-mile road gently slopes down to the coast in a series of switchbacks, through a mostly barren landscape punctuated by eccentrically shaped rocks. The paved road ends near the coast and you're then in 4WD country. To the left, a dirt road leads to Shipwreck Beach, while turning right onto Keomuku Rd takes the adventurous to Keomuku Beach or all the way to Naha.

Keep your eyes open: sightings of wild mouflon sheep on the inland hills are not uncommon.

GARDEN OF THE GODS

Inside the Kanepu'u Preserve is **Keahiakawelo** (Map p254; Polihua Rd) a dramatic place, also known as Garden of the Gods. It was formed by the eruption of a volcano, the lava bombs that spewed out of a crater and thousands of years of erosion. Weirdly shaped volcanic rocks are strewn about on red dust in a seemingly martian landscape. The multihued rocks and earth, with a palette from amber to rust to sienna, are stunning. The site is only accessible via 4WD.

WORTH A TRIP

KAUNOLŪ

Perched around the highest sea cliffs on Lana'i (at 1080ft above sea level) is **Kaunolū** (Map p254), a vast archaeological site home to the island's largest collection of ruins. It's easy to get goosebumps wandering the structures of this ancient Hawaiian village, complete with houses, shrines, petroglyphs and ceremonial sites. In the 1790s King Kamehameha used it as a vacation spot between battles. He enjoyed fishing for *kawakawa* (bonito) here and famously took leaps into the ocean from a 60ft platform. More recently, it has been the site of cliff-diving championships.

A highlight is the Halulu Heiau (Temple of Halulu), where those who broke *kapu* (ancient Hawaiian law) could opt for self-imprisonment and potentially be absolved of their wrongdoing. The structure of the temple still remains intact up to a few meters high.

At Kaunolū, you can also walk right to the edge of the vertigo-inducing **Kahekili's Leap** (Lele Kawa a Kahekili; Map p254) and look down to the ocean 63ft below. Kings and warriors would leap from here to prove their righteousness hundreds of years ago. Also, people accused of crimes or offenses against the gods could atone by jumping from this platform. If they were innocent, they would survive the fall.

The well-marked Keālia Kapu-Kaunolū Heritage Trail, with information boards throughout, runs 0.5 miles around the archaeological sites and structures, such as a fishermen's shrine and a canoe longhouse. You'll likely have the whole place to yourself, as the road down here is rough.

To reach little-visited Kaunolū from Lana'i City, follow the Kaumalapa'u Hwy (Hwy 440) 0.6 miles past the airport, and turn left onto a partial gravel-and-dirt road that runs south through abandoned pineapple fields for 2.2 miles. A carved stone marks the turn onto a much rougher but still 4WD-accessible road down to the sea. A further 2.5 miles from the stone, you'll see the sign for the heritage trail. Another 0.3 miles brings you to a parking area amid the ruins.

Sights

Shipwreck Beach BEACH
(Map p254) You can stroll along this blustery shore for 7 miles looking for flotsam and shipwrecks, and taking in the views of Moloka'i and Maui. This area is the island's windiest and currents are strong, so it's a hazardous area for navigation: a dozen ships have met their end here. Ironically, the enormous steel-and-concrete WWII-era navy fuel ship visible from shore was docked here deliberately, not shipwrecked, but it adds a perfect note of drama to the scene.

Pōāiwa Petroglyph Trail HISTORIC SITE
(Map p254) Near Shipwreck Beach, a 0.5-mile trail leads directly inland to the Pōāiwa petroglyphs – a cluster of more than 20 fragile carvings on dense basalt-lava boulders marked by a sign reading 'Cultural/Historical Site Boundary'. Some locals say that the simple figures here date back more than a century. An interpretive board shows you all the carvings to search out in the area.

Keomuku to Naha

Keomuku Rd from Kahokunui to Naha is just the journey for those looking for real adventure on Lana'i. Overhanging kiawe trees shade long stretches of the 12-mile dirt road, which varies from smooth to deeply cratered (and impossibly soupy after storms). This is where your 4WD will justify its daily fee, as you explore the remnants of failed dreams and discover magical beaches. If the road is passable, driving the entire length should take about an hour, but plan for more. The reef-protected shore is close to the road but usually not quite visible.

Sights

★**Halepalaoa Beach** BEACH
(Map p254) Running southeast from the pier at Halepalaoa Landing is the reef-protected and shaded Halepalaoa Beach. It's tricky to get to and only accessible with a 4WD, but you'll have it to yourself. In winter the number of whales breaching offshore may outnumber the humans basking on the sand.

Halepalaoa Landing HISTORIC SITE
(Map p254) Just under 2 miles southeast along the road from Keomuku you'll reach Halepalaoa Landing, from which the sugar company planned to ship out its product. But little was accomplished during its short life (1899–1901), other than to shorten the lives of scores of Japanese workers, who are buried in a small cemetery with a sign reading 'Japanese Memorial Shrine.'

Keomuku HISTORIC SITE
The center of a short-lived sugarcane plantation, Keomuku is 6 miles southeast of Maunalei. The highlight is the beautifully reconstructed **Ka Lanakila o Ka Malamalama Church**, originally built in 1903. Look for the ruins of a steam locomotive, old buildings, and an old boat towards the water. The site is only accessible via 4WD.

Naha HISTORIC SITE
Four miles south of Halepalaoa you'll come to Naha, which is both the end of the road and the site of ancient fishponds just offshore. This is a dramatic and desolate setting where the wind whistles in your ears and the modern world seems very far away.

MOLOKA'I

A local T-shirt design proclaiming that 'Moloka'i time is when I want to show up' sums up this idiosyncratic island perfectly: feisty and independent, while not taking life too seriously. Visiting the 'Friendly Isle' means slowing waaay down and taking your sense of rhythm from the locals.

Moloka'i is often said to be the 'most Hawaiian' of the islands, and in terms of bloodlines this is true – more than 50% of residents are at least part Native Hawaiian. But whether the island fits your idea of 'most Hawaiian' depends on your definition. If your idea of Hawaii includes great tourist facilities, forget it.

But if you're after a place that best celebrates the islands' geography and indigenous culture, then Moloka'i is for you. Ancient Hawaiian sites in the island's beautiful tropical east are carefully protected and restored, and island-wide consensus eschews development of the often sacred west.

Getting There & Around

The Maui ferry no longer runs.

Renting a car is essential if you intend to explore the island or if you're renting a house or condo and will need to shop. All of Moloka'i's highways and primary routes are good, paved roads. The free tourist map, widely available on the island, is useful. James A Bier's *Map of Moloka'i & Lana'i* (from $5) has an excellent index.

AIR

Moloka'i Airport (MKK, Ho'olehua; Map p262; ☎808-567-9660; http://hawaii.gov/mkk; 3980 Airport Loop, Ho'olehua) Small: you claim your baggage on a long bench. Single-engine planes are the norm; sit right behind the cockpit area for spectacular views forward. Because of weight limits for individual bags (around 45lb/20kg), pack a small duffel bag in case you have to redistribute your belongings.

Makani Kai Air (☎808-834-1111; http://makanikaiair.com) Offers scheduled and charter flights to Kalaupapa (entry with permit or tour only), plus Honolulu (its fares on this route are often the cheapest).

Mokulele Airlines (☎866-260-7070; www.mokuleleairlines.com) Has frequent services to Honolulu and Maui; flights from Moloka'i don't require security checks.

Ohana (☎800-367-5320; www.hawaiianairlines.com) The commuter carrier of Hawaiian Airlines serves Honolulu, Lana'i and Maui from Moloka'i.

A taxi from the airport costs $28 to $32 to Kaunakakai, depending on where in town you need to go. **Hele Mai Taxi** (☎808-336-0967; www.molokaitaxi.com; Mon-Sat) services the island. Many accommodations can arrange transfers.

BUS

MEO Bus (☎808-553-3216; www.meoinc.org; bus trips free; Mon-Fri), a government economic-development service, runs a free shuttle bus around Moloka'i from roughly 6am to 4pm. From a stop by Misaki's market in Kaunakakai routes go east past the Hotel Moloka'i (p265) to Puko'o at mile marker 16, west to Maunaloa via the airport and to Kualapu'u. The buses run roughly every two hours, but it's essential that you confirm all details in advance and with the driver if you're hoping to make a round-trip. Stops are not marked.

CAR

Keep in mind that most rental cars are technically not allowed on unpaved roads. If you intend to explore remote parts of the island, such as the Kamakou Preserve, you'll at least need a vehicle with high clearance, probably a 4WD, and even then some rental agencies prohibit travel on unpaved roads. Book well in advance, especially if you're planning a weekend visit.

There are two gas stations in Kaunakakai. Expect sticker shock at the pump.

Alamo Rental Car (www.alamo.com; Bldg 2, Moloka'i Airport, 3980 Airport Loop, Ho'olehua;

Moloka'i

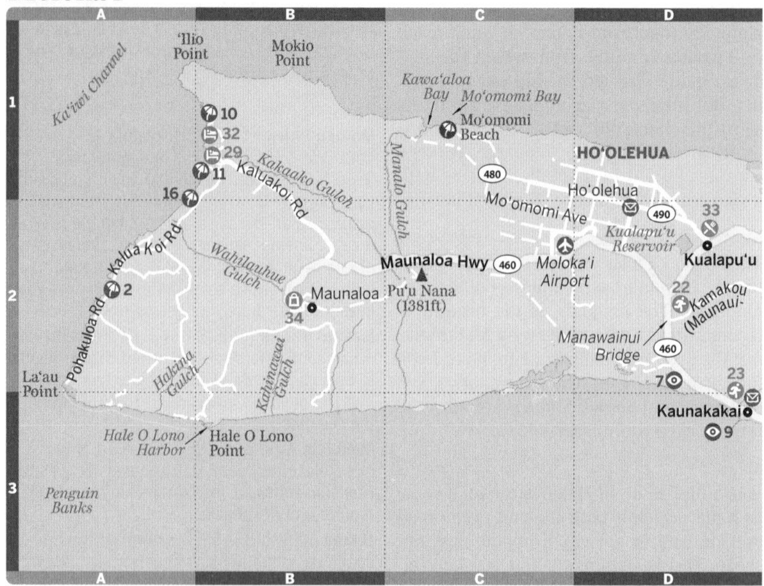

⏲6am-8pm) has a desk at the airport. The main office is just across the small parking area. It's the only choice for international visitors without US car insurance (as insurance is offered at the desk). Alamo's contract includes no off-roading.

Local outfits often have the lowest rates. **Mobettah Car Rentals** (☎808-308-9566; www.mobettahcarrentals.com; per day/week $48/300) offers cheap weekly rates and arranges pickup and drop-off at the airport; renters must have their own car insurance and provide details of this when picking up the car. **Molokai Car Rental** (☎808-336-0670; www.molokaicars.com; 109 Ala Malama Ave; per day car/bike from $45/10; ⏲9am-3pm Mon-Fri, to noon Sat) is a small local firm with a limited selection of cars and vans; cars are left for customer pickup at the airport. Renters must also have their own car insurance and provide details of this when picking up the car.

Driving Times from Kaunakakai

Average driving times and distances from Kaunakakai:

Destination	Miles	Time
Halawa Valley	27	1¼hr
Moloka'i Airport	6.5	10min
Kalaupapa Trailhead	10	20min
Maunaloa	17	30min
Papohaku Beach	21.5	45min
Puko'o	16	20min
Twenty Mile Beach	20	40min

BICYCLE

Moloka'i is a good place for cycling. The Kaunakakai bike shop Moloka'i Bicycle (p263) is a treasure.

Kaunakakai

View a photo of Moloka'i's biggest town from 50 years ago and the main drag won't look much different. Worn wood-fronted buildings with tin roofs that roar in the rain seem like refugees from a Clint Eastwood Western. But there's no artifice to Kaunakakai: it's the real deal. All of the island's commercial activities are here, and you'll visit often – if nothing else, for its shops and services.

Walking around the town can occupy a couple of hours if you take the time to get into the rhythm of things and do a little exploring. While there are stop signs, there are no stoplights. Try to visit on Saturday morning, when the street market draws crowds.

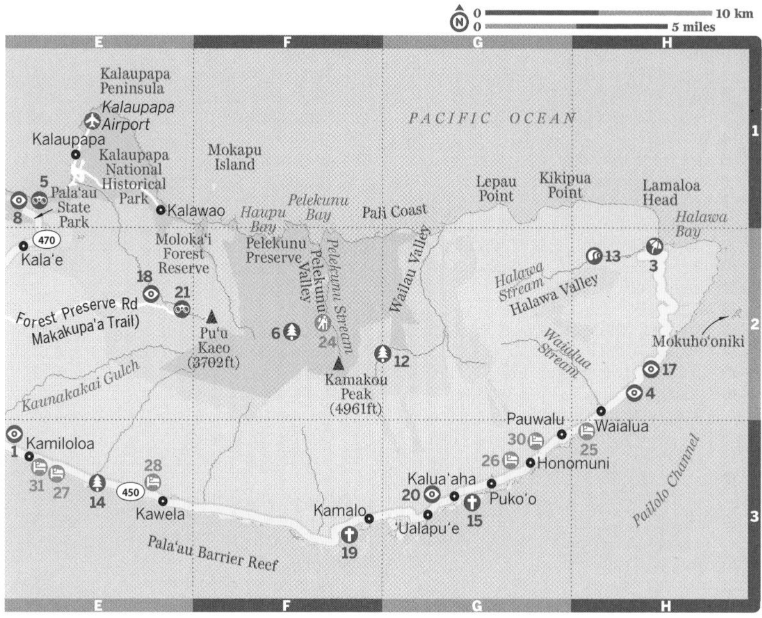

Sights

Kapua'iwa Coconut Grove HISTORIC SITE
(Map p262; 30 Maunaloa Hwy) Moloka'i was the favorite island playground of Kamehameha V. He had the royal 10-acre Kapua'iwa Coconut Grove planted near his sacred bathing pools in the 1860s. Standing tall about a mile west of downtown, the grove makes a wonderful place to enjoy the sunset. Be careful where you walk (or park): coconuts frequently plunge silently to the ground. At research time the facilities were under refurbishment and the park was closed to the public.

Kaunakakai Wharf PORT
(Map p262; Kaunakakai Pl) Come here to witness Moloka'i's busy commercial lifeline. OK, it's not that busy... a freight barge occasionally chugs in, skippers unload their catch of the day, and a local boat club practices for a canoe race. A roped-off area with a floating dock provides a place for kids to swim. Some of Moloka'i's fishing and ocean-based tours leave from here.

One Ali'i Beach Park PARK
(Map p262; Maunaloa Hwy) Three miles east of town, this park is split into two areas. One side has a coconut-palm-lined shore, a playing field, a children's playground, a run-down picnic pavilion and bathrooms, and although not especially attractive, it's very popular with local families for huge weekend barbecues. The other side is a greener and more attractive picnic area. The water is shallow and murky.

Activities

★**Moloka'i Bicycle** CYCLING
(Map p262; ☎808-553-5740; www.mauimolokaibicycle.com; 80 Mohala St; bike rental per day/week from $25/75; ⏲3-6pm Wed, 9am-2pm Sat & by appointment) Owner Phillip Kikukawa has a great depth of knowledge about cycling across the island. He'll do pickups and drop-offs outside opening hours. Repairs, parts and sales are available, and there's a wide selection of bikes to rent, including mountain bikes. Prices include helmet, lock, pump and maps.

Beach Break Moloka'i OUTDOORS
(Map p262; ☎808-567-6091; Holomua Junction, cnr Hwys 460 & 470; ⏲10am-4pm Mon-Sat) Offers a wide range of surf gear, SUP and surfboard rentals (from $20), and snorkeling sets (from $10 per day); you can also rent beach gear, including chairs, coolers and umbrellas. Pick up local fashion, yoga mats, cultural books and ukuleles, and grab various gifts to take home. The owners provide tourist information, too.

Moloka'i

Sights

1 Baseball Field ... E3
2 Dixie Maru Beach ... A2
3 Halawa Beach Park ... H2
4 Kahinapohaku Fishpond ... H2
5 Kalaupapa Overlook ... E1
6 Kamakou Preserve ... F2
7 Kapua'iwa Coconut Grove ... D2
8 Kauleonanahoa ... E1
9 Kaunakakai Wharf ... D3
10 Kawakiu Beach ... B1
11 Kepuhi Beach ... B1
12 Moloka'i Forest Reserve ... G2
13 Mo'oula & Hipuapua Falls ... H2
14 One Ali'i Beach Park ... E3
15 Our Lady of Seven Sorrows ... G3
16 Papohaku Beach ... A1
Pelekunu Valley Overlook ... (see 6)
Pu'u o Kaiaka ... (see 11)
17 Rock Point ... H2
18 Sandalwood Pit ... E2
Softball Field ... (see 1)
19 St Joseph's Church ... F3
Twenty Mile Beach ... (see 4)
20 'Ualapu'e Fishpond ... G3
21 Waikolu Lookout ... E2

Activities, Courses & Tours

22 Beach Break Moloka'i ... D2
23 Moloka'i Bicycle ... D2
24 Pepe'opae Trail ... F2
Third Hole ... (see 16)

Sleeping

25 Dunbar Beachfront Cottages ... H3
26 Hale Leilani ... G3
27 Hotel Moloka'i ... E3
28 Ka Hale Mala ... E3
29 Ke Nani Kai ... B1
30 Moloka'i Hilltop Cottage ... G3
31 Moloka'i Shores ... E3
Pala'au State Park Campground ... (see 8)
32 Paniolo Hale ... B1

Eating

A Taste of Moloka'i ... (see 23)
Hiro's Ohana Grill ... (see 27)
Kamo'i Snack-N-Go ... (see 23)
Kualapu'u Cookhouse ... (see 33)
Mana'e Goods & Grindz ... (see 26)
Ono Fish N' Shrimp ... (see 23)
33 'Ono Skoopz ... D2

Drinking & Nightlife

Coffees of Hawaii ... (see 33)

Shopping

Big Wind Kite Factory & Plantation Gallery ... (see 34)
Kualapu'u Market ... (see 33)
34 Maunaloa General Store ... B2

Information

Department of Parks & Recreation ... (see 1)

Tours

★ Moloka'i Outdoors OUTDOORS
(877-553-4477, 808-633-8700; www.molokai-outdoors.com; SUP or kayak tour adult/child from $90/47, 7-8hr island tour $166/87) Moloka'i Outdoors can custom design adventures and arrange activities. It's known for paddling and SUP experiences, plus day tours across the island. Offers kayak and SUP rentals (from $67 per day). It can arrange whale-watching and scuba diving, mule rides and hiking to Kalaupapa Peninsula, and transport and pickups across the island.

★ Walter Naki BOAT TOUR
(Molokai Action Adventures; 808-558-8184, 808-213-5655; 4hr tours from $150) Walter Naki, who is also known for his cultural tours and treks, offers deep-sea fishing, whale-watching and highly recommended north-shore boat tours that include the Pali Coast. Prices negotiable; minimum of four people.

Moloka'i Fish & Dive OUTDOORS
(Map p266; 808-553-5926; www.molokaifishanddive.com; 53 Ala Malama Ave; snorkeling trips from $79 per person, shore dives from $145, discovery dive incl equipment $210; 6am-7pm) This is really the Big Kahuna of activities on the island. It operates whale-watching trips, plus snorkeling and diving trips to the island's pristine southern reef and more than 40 diving spots. It also arranges fishing trips and rents out gear and has a range of beach accessories.

Moloka'i Ocean Tours BOATING
(808-553-3290; www.molokaioceantours.com; tours per person from $75; 10am-4pm Mon-Fri, 9am-noon Sat) Local boat company offering whale-watching, snorkeling, snuba, troll fishing, sunset cruises and other cruises.

Festivals & Events

Ka Moloka'i Makahiki CULTURAL
(late Jan) The ancient makahiki festival, held after the year's main harvest was

complete, is still celebrated on Moloka'i. It features traditional ceremonies, an Olympics-esque competition of ancient Hawaiian sports, as well as crafts and activities.

Moloka'i Ka Hula Piko CULTURAL
(www.kahulapiko.com; May or Jun) FREE As Moloka'i is known as the birthplace of hula, its three-day hula festival has some profound roots. It opens with a solemn ceremony at 3am at Pu'u Nana (the site of Hawaii's first hula school), followed by a festival including performance, food and crafts.

Moloka'i Hoe SPORTS
(www.molokaihoe.com; Oct) Beginning more than 65 years ago, the Moloka'i Hoe canoe race is one of the longest-running annual team sporting events in Hawaii. Around 1000 participants from across the globe descend on Moloka'i to paddle tough currents over 41 miles from Hale O Lono Harbor in the west to Waikiki, O'ahu. The journey takes around five hours.

Sleeping

Ka Hale Mala B&B $
(Map p262; 808-553-9009; https://bnbmolokai.com; Kamakana Pl; apt from $90;) At the end of a cul-de-sac off Kamehameha V Hwy, 5 miles east of Kaunakakai, guests can enjoy a 900-sq-ft one-bedroom apartment with an exposed-beam ceiling. The two-story house is charmingly dated, and secluded within a lush garden. The owners add to the bounty with organic vegetables and healthy breakfasts.

Moloka'i Shores CONDO $
(Map p262; 877-367-1912, 808-545-3510; www.castleresorts.com; Kamehameha V Hwy; 1/2-bed condos from $119/235;) This 1970s development has around 100 one- and two-bedroom units ranging from atrocious to charming, depending on the whims of the individual owners; choose your unit carefully. All have full kitchen, cable TV, lanai and ceiling fans.

★ **Hotel Moloka'i** HOTEL $$
(Map p262; 808-553-5347; www.hotelmolokai.com; 1300 Kamehameha V Hwy; r $160-250;) Moloka'i's only hotel, with an enormous vintage canoe dangling from the ceiling in the lobby, has a Hawaiian feel. Rooms are well finished with native design touches, and have kitchenettes; some rooms have balconies. The grounds are compact, with a small pool and hammocks along the reef-protected silty shore. Some units are privately owned and rented on Airbnb.

Eating

★ **Maka's Korner** CAFE $
(Map p266; 808-553-8058; 35 Mohala St; meals $5-10; 7am-9pm Mon-Fri, 8am-2pm Sat & Sun) A dead-simple corner location belies the fine yet basic fare here. Moloka'i's best burgers come with excellent fries, although many patrons are simply addicted to the grilled mahi-mahi sandwich (go nuts and order it dressed with two shrimp tempura). Pancakes are served throughout the day. Sit at the tiny counter or at a picnic table outside.

Ono Fish N' Shrimp SEAFOOD $
(Map p262; 808-553-8187; 53 Ala Malama Ave; lunches $10-14; 10:30am-2pm Mon-Fri) For some of the best seafood plates (or should that be takeout boxes?) in town, this white food truck offers up seared mahi-mahi, fish and chips, steak and shrimp combos, plus fish tacos and shrimp plates. The preparations are creative and the fish is über-fresh.

Kamo'i Snack-N-Go DESSERTS $
(Map p262; Moloka'i Professional Bldg, 28 Kamoi St; ice-cream scoops $2; 10am-9pm Mon-Fri, 9am-9pm Sat, 11am-9pm Sun;) This candy store is loaded with sweets and, more importantly, delicious Honolulu-made Dave's Hawaiian Ice Cream. The banana fudge is truly a treat. *Ube* (purple yam) is subtle and the ice cream is a beautiful purple color. Other choices include Hawaiian mud pie, toasted macadamia nut, and *liliko'i* (passion fruit). Ask to try before you buy.

Moloka'i Burger BURGERS $
(Map p266; 808-553-3533; 20 Kamehameha V Hwy; mains $6.50-18; 7am-9pm Mon-Sat;) Moloka'i's only drive-through restaurant is a slick operation. The burgers come in many forms but are all thick and juicy. There are also sandwiches, fried chicken, and Hawaiian plates such as *loco moco*, salmon and teriyaki chicken. The dining room is pleasant enough, with a sophisticated tiled floor, while the front terrace is peacefully shady. Soft-serve ice cream is a treat.

Kanemitsu Bakery BAKERY $
(Map p266; 808-553-5855; 79 Ala Malama Ave; loaf of bread $5; 7am-5pm Wed-Mon) A simple bakery selling rather good fresh-baked goods, Kanemitsu is known for its Moloka'i sweet bread and crackers (the macadamia-nut ones are extraordinary). The best stuff is usually gone by 1pm. There's a restaurant onsite serving full breakfasts (eggs, pancakes,

Kaunakakai

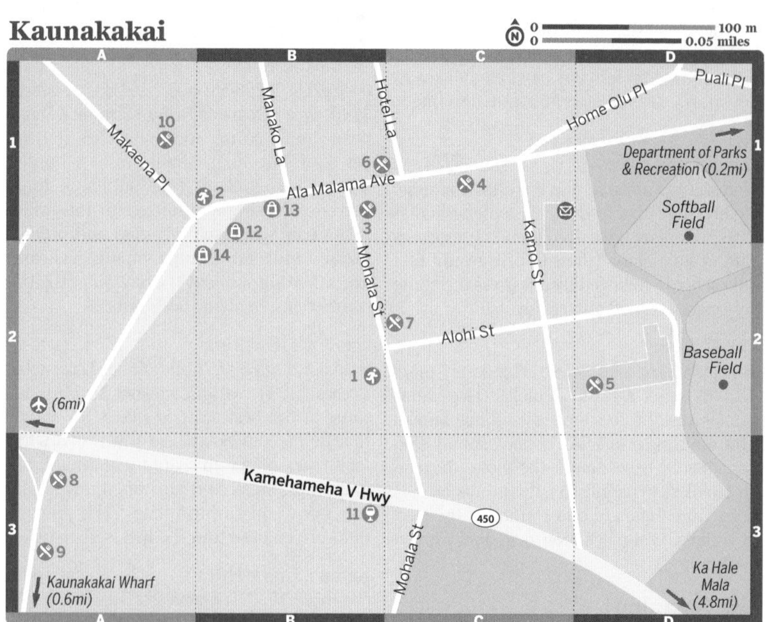

hashes) and lunches (sandwiches, hamburgers and noodles) that's open until 1pm.

A Taste of Moloka'i POKE $
(Map p262; ☎808-658-1726; cnr Ala Malama Ave & Mohala St; poke/acai bowls from $9.50/8.50; ⏰10am-4:30pm Mon-Fri, 8:30am-2pm Sat) For a heaped bowl of the best *poke* in town, head to this humble food truck. It serves fresh fish dowsed in *shōyu,* spicy or masago sauce. In the mornings, try the yummy acai bowls, heaped with your choice of blueberry, pineapple, mango and more.

Friendly Market Center SUPERMARKET $
(Map p266; ☎808-553-5595; 90 Ala Malama Ave; ⏰8am-8pm Mon-Fri, to 6:30pm Sat) The best selection of any supermarket on the island. In the afternoon fresh seafood from the wharf often appears.

Moloka'i Pizza Cafe PIZZA $
(Map p266; ☎808-553-3288; 15 Kaunakakai Pl; meals $5.50-32; ⏰11am-10pm Sun-Thu, to 11pm Fri & Sat; ❄) Have a seat in a retro booth in the starkly lit dining area at this pizza joint, or order takeout from the counter (and play Pac-Man while you wait). It serves reasonable fresh-dough pizzas (with neither thick nor thin bases), plus salads, burgers, pasta and sub sandwiches.

★ **Hiro's Ohana Grill** HAWAIIAN $$
(Map p262; ☎808-660-3400; www.hirosohanagrill.com; Hotel Moloka'i, 1300 Kamehameha V Hwy; mains $22-36; ⏰11am-9pm Mon-Fri, 7am-10am & 11am-9pm Sat & Sun) Casual fine-dining restaurant in an awesome sunset-watching setting opposite the ocean. All the delicious plates are spot on. Choose *poke* and crab-stuffed mushrooms, panko-crusted calamari or the

fresh catch of the day. The shrimp with linguini in a spiced Szechuan sauce is locally renowned. Live Hawaiian music with ukulele musicians and singers happens nightly.

Drinking & Nightlife

Paddler's Inn PUB

(Map p266; ☎808-553-3300; www.paddlersrestaurant.com; 10 Mohala St; ⏲8am-1am Mon-Sat; 📶) The island's only real pub has a dive feel, with a large terrace that makes up in cheer for what it lacks in charm. The long menu is served between 10am and 9pm. Items include deep-fried pub grub, burgers, steaks and pastas. There are regular live performances by local musicians. Happy hour, with discounted selected drinks, runs 2pm to 5pm daily.

Shopping

★ **Kalele Bookstore & Divine Expressions** BOOKS

(Map p266; ☎808-553-5112; http://molokaispirit.com; 64 Ala Malama Ave; ⏲10am-5pm Mon-Fri, 9am-2pm Sat; 📶) A community treasure. Besides books, get free maps or enjoy a coffee and meet some locals out back on the shady terrace. Owner Teri Waros is a fount of info on all things Moloka'i. Make this one of your first stops.

Saturday Morning Market MARKET

(Map p266; Ala Malama Ave; ⏲8am-2pm Sat) This weekly market at the western end of Ala Malama Ave is the place to browse local crafts, try new fruits, stock up on organic produce and pick up some flowers. You'll find most of Moloka'i here before noon.

Moloka'i Art from the Heart ART

(Map p266; ☎808-553-8018; http://molokaigallery.com; 64 Ala Malama Ave; ⏲10am-5pm Mon-Fri, 9am-2:30pm Sat) Run by local artists, this small shop is packed with arts and crafts. Works in all mediums can be found here; quality ranges from the earnest to the superb. The T-shirts with local sayings are the real finds in the souvenir department.

ℹ Information

Bank of Hawaii (☎808-553-3273; www.boh.com; 20b Ala Malama Ave; ⏲8:30am-1pm & 2-4pm Mon-Thu, to 6pm Fri, ATM 24hr)

Moloka'i General Hospital (☎808-553-5331; www.molokaigeneralhospital.org; 280 Home Olu Pl; ⏲24hr) Emergency services.

Post Office (Map p262; 120 Ala Malama Ave; ⏲9am-3:30pm Mon-Fri, to 11am Sat) Most visitors prefer the fun-filled Ho'olehua post office (Map p262; ☎808-567-6144; Pu'u Peelua Ave; coconut posting from $14.20; ⏲8:30am-4pm Mon-Fri), which posts coconuts to your friends and relatives (p269).

ℹ Getting There & Around

Kaunakakai is a walking town.

Rawlin's Chevron (☎808-553-3214; cnr Maunaloa Hwy & Ala Malama Ave; ⏲office 6:30am-8:30pm Mon-Thu, to 9pm Fri & Sat, to 6pm Sun) Has credit-card-operated pumps that are available 24 hours. The bathrooms are surprisingly clean.

East Moloka'i

The oft-quoted road sign 'Slow down, this is Moloka'i' really applies as you head east. Whether you're on the island for a day or a week, the 27-mile drive on Hwy 450 (aka Kamehameha V Hwy) from Kaunakakai to the Halawa Valley is simply a must.

Unlike the arid west, this is tropical Moloka'i, with palm trees arching over the road, and banana, papaya, guava and passion fruits hanging from the lush foliage, ripe for the picking. As you drive you'll catch glimpses of ancient fishponds, the neighboring islands of Lana'i and Maui, stoic old wooden churches, beaches and much more.

Each curve yields a new vista. The final climb up and over into the remote Halawa Valley is simply breathtaking.

Kawela to Kalua'aha

★ **St Joseph's Church** CHURCH

(Map p262; http://damienchurchmolokai.org; Hwy 450/Kamehameha V Hwy) Only two of the four Moloka'i churches that missionary saint Father Damien (who selflessly comforted leprosy patients for 16 years) built outside the Kalaupapa Peninsula are still standing. One of them is this quaint white-wood building; the other is **Our Lady of Seven Sorrows** (Map p262; http://damienchurchmolokai.org; 8300 Hwy 450/Kamehameha V Hwy, Kalua'aha; ⏲doors usually open, service 7am Sun) further east. This simple one-room church, dating from 1876, has a steeple, a bell, five rows of pews and some of the original wavy-glass panes. It's just past mile marker 10. The door is usually open.

Puko'o to Rock Point

Puko'o was once the seat of local government (complete with courthouse, jail, wharf and post office), but the center of island life shifted to Kaunakakai when the plantation folks built that more centrally located town. Nowadays, Puko'o is a small, sleepy, slow-paced place.

Beaches

Twenty Mile Beach BEACH
(Murphy's Beach; Map p262; Hwy 450/Kamehameha V Hwy) This spot is well protected by a reef, and the curve of fine sand fronts a large lagoon that's great for snorkeling. Near shore there are rocks and the water can be very shallow, but work your way out and you'll be rewarded with schools of fish, living sponges, octopuses and much more.

Rock Point NATURAL FEATURE
(Map p262; Hwy 450/Kamehameha V Hwy) The pointy clutch of rocks sticking out as the road swings left before the 21-mile marker is, appropriately enough, called Rock Point. This popular **surf spot** is the site of local competitions and is the place to go if you're looking for east-end swells.

Sleeping & Eating

The market attached to Mana'e Goods & Grindz (p268) is small but well stocked.

Moloka'i Hilltop Cottage COTTAGE $
(Map p262; ☎808-357-0139; 9415 Hwy 450/Kamehameha V Hwy; cottages from $160) Instead of sleeping down near the water, stay here and put your head in the clouds. The wraparound lanai (veranda) is almost as big as the living space, and you can savor views of the neighboring islands by day or the millions of stars by night. There's one nicely furnished bedroom, a full kitchen and laundry facilities. Two-night minimum.

Dunbar Beachfront Cottages COTTAGE $$
(Map p262; ☎808-558-8153; www.molokai-beachfront-cottages.com; 9962 Hwy 450/Kamehameha V Hwy; cottages from $210;) The layout and furnishings are tidy and functional at these two vacation cottages just east of mile marker 18. Each cottage sleeps four and comes with fully equipped kitchen, TV, ceiling fans, laundry, lanai and barbecue grill. Both have good views. Three-night minimum; cleaning fee $90.

★ **Hale Leilani** RENTAL HOUSE $$$
(Map p262; ☎808-264-8442; www.greatrentalsonmaui.com; cottages from $475;) Perched partway up a hill near mile marker 16 on Hwy 450 (near Mana'e Goods & Grindz), this four- to six-bedroom contemporary home with tropical bedspreads has 3800 sq feet of living space and sweeping views to Maui and beyond. The large kitchen will inspire you to cook even on holiday. The adjoining cottage is good for a couple. Four-night minimum.

★ **Mana'e Goods & Grindz** HAWAIIAN $
(Map p262; ☎808-558-8186; 8615 Hwy 450/Kamehameha V Hwy; meals $5-13; kitchen 8am-3pm Thu-Tue, store 6:30am-5.30pm Mon-Fri, 8am to 4:30pm Sat & Sun;) Even if it wasn't your only option, you'd still want to stop here. The plate lunches are something of a local legend: tender yet crispy chicken *katsu*, specials such as pork stew, and standards such as excellent teriyaki burgers and fresh fish sandwiches served on perfectly grilled buns.

Halawa Valley

With stunningly gorgeous scenery, the Halawa Valley enjoys end-of-the-road isolation, which residents guard jealously with gates

FISHPONDS

Starting just east of Kaunakakai and continuing past mile marker 20 along Hwy 450 are dozens of *loko i'a* (fishponds), huge circular walls of rocks that are part of one of the world's most advanced forms of aquaculture. Monumental in size, backbreaking in creation, the fishponds operate on a simple principle: little fish swim in, big fish can't swim out. Some of the ponds are obscured and overgrown by mangroves, but others have been restored by locals anxious to preserve this link to their past.

Kahinapohaku Fishpond (Map p262; Hwy 450/Kamehameha V Hwy), about half a mile past mile marker 19, is in excellent shape, tended by *konohiki* (caretakers) who live simply on site. You can see ancient fishing techniques in use today. Another good example is **'Ualapu'e Fishpond** (Map p262; Hwy 450/Kamehameha V Hwy), at mile marker 13, half a mile beyond the Wavecrest Resort condo development. A National Historic Landmark, it has been restored and restocked with mullet and milkfish, two species that were raised here in ancient times.

DON'T MISS

POST-A-NUT

Why settle for a mundane postcard when it comes to taunting folks in the cold climes you've left behind? Instead, send a coconut. Gary Lam, the world-class postmaster of the Ho'olehua post office (p267), has baskets of them available for free. Choose from the oodles of markers and write the address right on the husk. Add a cartoon or two. Imagine the joy when a loved one waits in a long line for a parcel and is handed a coconut! Depending on the size of your nut, postage costs $14.20 to $25 and takes three to six days to reach any place in the US; other countries cost more and take longer – and you may run into quarantine issues.

If Lam, who takes the time to apply a panoply of colored stamps to each coconut, were in charge of the postal service, its current financial woes would likely vanish. Should you want your nut made especially ornate, Teri Waros of Kalele Bookstore (p267) does custom paint jobs.

and 'No trespassing' signs. It was an important settlement in precontact Moloka'i, with a population of more than 1000 and a complex irrigation system watering more than 700 taro patches. Remains of a burial ground that may date to 650 CE and a seven-tiered stone temple are scattered over the pathway to the Mo'oula and Hipuapua Falls. Three heiau (ancient stone temple) sites are believed to have been in this area, and two of these are thought to have been *luakini* (where human and animal sacrifices were made). You'll probably still feel the charge down here.

As late as the mid-19th century the fertile valley still had a population of about 500 and produced most of Moloka'i's taro. However, taro production came to an abrupt end in 1946 when a massive tsunami swept up the Halawa Valley, wiping out the farms and much of the community. A second tsunami hit the valley in 1957. Only a few families now remain.

Sights

★Halawa Beach Park BEACH

(Map p262; 14777 Hwy 450/Kamehameha V Hwy) Where the road ends at the east of the island you'll find gorgeous Halawa Beach, clasped by verdant tropical hills. It was a surfing spot for Moloka'i chiefs, although these days you probably won't see a soul. The beach has double coves separated by a rocky outcrop, with the north side a bit more protected than the south. The hike to Mo'oula & Hipuapua Falls (p269) also starts from here (although hikers are required to book a guide to complete it).

★Mo'oula & Hipuapua Falls WATERFALL

(Map p262; ☎808-542-1855; http://halawavalleymolokai.com; hikes per person $60; ⊗hikes usually begin 9am) Cascading down the back of the lush Halawa Valley are the mesmerizing twin 250ft Mo'oula and Hipuapua Falls, hidden in a rich valley and reached by a two-hour hike. When you get there you can swim in a large pool and up to the surging falls. The trail (p253) crosses private property, so visiting the falls requires a booking with a local guide – visit the website for availability.

Central Moloka'i

Central Moloka'i is really two places. In the west are the dry and gently rolling Ho'olehua Plains, which stretch from the remote and rare sand dunes of Mo'omomi Beach to the former plantation town and current coffee-growing center of Kualapu'u. To the east, the terrain rises sharply to the misty, ancient forests of Kamakou. Enjoy one of the island's great adventures here by going on a hike that takes you back in evolutionary time.

Moloka'i's second most popular drive (after the Halawa Valley drive in the east) runs from Kualapu'u up Hwy 470 to Pala'au State Park, site of the Kalaupapa Overlook (p270), where you'll find one of the island's most captivating views.

Kamakou Area

The best reason to rent a 4WD vehicle on Moloka'i is to enjoy the views from the Waikolu Lookout before you discover the verdant mysteries of the Nature Conservancy's Kamakou Preserve, where you'll find the island's highest peaks. Exploring this secret side of Moloka'i is pure adventure. Besides gazing down into two deep valleys on the island's stunning and impenetrable north coast, you'll explore a near-pristine rainforest that is home to more than 200 native plant species and some of Hawaii's rarest birds. Although you can't quite reach the island's highest point, Kamakou Peak (4961ft), you'll still get your head in the clouds.

Sights

★Kamakou Preserve PARK

(Map p262) Hiking back through three million years of evolution on the **Pepe'opae Trail** (Map p262) is Kamakou's star attraction. Crossed by a boardwalk, this undisturbed Hawaiian montane bog is a miniature primeval forest of stunted trees, dwarf plants and lichens that make it feel as though it's the dawn of time. From the trail's end at **Pelekunu Valley Overlook** (Map p262), you'll be rewarded with a fantastic view of majestic cliffs, and, if it's not too cloudy, you'll see the ocean beyond.

Moloka'i Forest Reserve PARK

(Map p262) The 10-mile 4WD drive up to **Waikolu Lookout** (Map p262; Moloka'i Forest Reserve) takes about 45 minutes (follow the dirt path near the Homelani Cemetery sign on Rte 460/ Maunaloa Hwy. Road conditions can be muddy. You pass through open land with trees and scrub; little is developed and signs are few. A mile before the lookout you'll find the 19th-century **Sandalwood Pit** (Lua Na Moku 'Iliahi; Map p262), a grassy depression on the left.

Kualapu'u

Kualapu'u is the name of both a 1017ft hill and a nearby village. At the base of the hill lies the world's largest rubber-lined reservoir, its 1.4 billion gallons of water piped in from the rainforests of eastern Moloka'i. It is the only source of water for the Ho'olehua Plains and the dry West End of the island.

In the 1930s the headquarters of the Del Monte pineapple plantation were located here and a company town grew. Pineapples ruled for nearly 50 years, until Del Monte pulled out of Moloka'i in 1982.

While farm equipment rusted in overgrown pineapple fields, small-scale farming developed: watermelons, dryland taro, macadamia nuts, sweet potatoes, seed corn, string beans and onions. The soil is so rich here that some feel that Moloka'i has the potential to be Hawaii's breadbasket, although the realization of this dream has been elusive.

Eating & Drinking

'Ono Skoopz BREAKFAST $

(Map p262; ☎808-312-7350; www.facebook.com/ono.skoopz.9; Farrington Ave; acai bowls from $5; ⏰9:30am-2pm) Offering a healthy start to the day is this simple food truck near the Kualapu'u Cookhouse (p270), serving hearty bowls of acai with banana, blueberry, strawberry, granola, almond and agave.

★Kualapu'u Cookhouse HAWAIIAN $$

(Kamuela Cookhouse; Map p262; ☎808-567-9655; 102 Farrington Ave; mains $6-33; ⏰7am-8pm Tue-Sat, 9am-2pm Sun, 7am-2pm Mon) This kitsch roadhouse serves the best meals on the island. Portions are generous – breakfasts feature huge omelets – and plate-lunch options include excellent pork *tonkatsu* (breaded and fried cutlets). For dinner, try the tasty sautéed *ono* with *liliko'i*–white wine butter. Beer and wine can be purchased at the grocery across the street. Cash only.

Coffees of Hawaii CAFE

(Map p262; ☎808-567-9490; www.coffeesofhawaii.com; 1630 Farrington Ave, cnr Hwys 470 & 490; ⏰7am-4pm Mon-Sat, to 2pm Sun; 📶) Coffees of Hawaii grows and roasts its own coffee on small plots around its attractive setting. You can enjoy a cup of the local coffee and a snack here.

Shopping

Kualapu'u Market FOOD & DRINKS

(Map p262; ☎808-567-6243; 311 Farrington Rd; ⏰8:30am-6pm Mon-Sat) This local grocery store sells food and drinks, plus alcohol that you can enjoy with your meal at the Kualapu'u Cookhouse next door.

Pala'au State Park

Sights

★Kalaupapa Overlook VIEWPOINT

(Map p262; Pala'au State Park) This spot offers a scenic overview of the Kalaupapa Peninsula, formerly an isolation zone for sufferers of Hansen's disease (leprosy), from the edge of a 1600ft cliff. It's easy to see the lay of the land from up here, and you'll get a good feel for just how far you'll travel if you descend the nearby 1664ft-elevation Kalaupapa Trail, the only way into the village by land.

Kauleonanahoa CULTURAL SITE

(Map p262) Kauleonanahoa (the penis of Nanahoa) is Hawaii's premier phallic stone, standing proud in a little clearing inside an ironwood grove about a five-minute walk from the parking area near Kalaupapa Overlook. The legend goes that Nanahoa hit his wife Kawahuna in a jealous rage and, when they were both turned to stone, he came out looking like a dick, literally. (The stone has been modified through the years to emphasize its appearance.)

Sleeping

Pala'au State Park Campground CAMPGROUND $
(Map p262; ☎808-567-6923; https://login.ehawaii.gov; Pala'au State Park; campsites per night resident/nonresident $12/18) Camping is allowed in a peaceful grassy field a quarter of a mile before the Pala'au overlook. There's a nice picnic pavilion and a portable toilet (and good bathrooms near the main parking area). It rains a lot here, and outside of the summer dry season your tent will likely be drenched by evening showers. Permits (bookable online) required.

Kalaupapa National Historical Park

The spectacularly beautiful Kalaupapa Peninsula is the most remote part of Hawaii's most isolated island. The only way to reach this lush green peninsula, edged with long, white-sand beaches, is on a twisting trail down the steep *pali* (sea cliffs) – the world's highest – or by plane. This remoteness is the reason that it was where Hansen's disease patients were forced into isolation.

From the colony's inception until separation ended in 1969, 8000 patients were forced to come to Kalaupapa. Less than a dozen residents remain. They have chosen to stay in the only home they have ever known and have resisted efforts to move them away. The peninsula has been designated a national historical park and is managed by the Hawaii State Department of Health and the **National Park Service** (☎808-567-6802; www.nps.gov/kala).

Since visitor numbers are limited each day, you must have a booking with a local guide, such as Kalaupapa Rare Adventures.

History

In 1835 doctors in Hawaii diagnosed the state's first case of leprosy, one of many diseases introduced by foreigners. Alarmed by its spread, Kamehameha V signed a law that banished people with Hansen's disease to Kalaupapa Peninsula, beginning in 1866.

Hawaiians call leprosy *i mai ho'oka'awale*, which means 'separating sickness,' a reference to how the disease tore families apart. Once the afflicted arrived on Kalaupapa Peninsula, there was no way out, not even in a casket. Early conditions were unspeakably horrible and life spans short.

Father Damien (Joseph de Veuster), a Belgian priest, arrived at Kalaupapa in 1873. A talented carpenter, he built 300 simple houses, nursed the sick and buried the dead. Damien's work inspired others, including Mother Marianne Cope, who stayed 30 years and came to be known as the mother of the hospice movement. Damien died of leprosy in 1889 at the age of 49. In 2009 he was canonized by Pope Benedict and became Hawaii's (and America's) first Catholic saint.

Tours

★**Kalaupapa Rare Adventures** TOURS
(Molokai Mule Ride; ☎808-567-6088; www.muleride.com; Hwy 470/Kalae Hwy; mule ride $210, hike $79; ⊙8am-3pm Mon-Sat) A mule ride is the only way down the *pali* into Kalaupapa apart from hiking (which the outfit also offers), but be prepared: this is not an easy ride. You'll be sore afterward even if you're an experienced rider – and it's a safe bet that you've never experienced a ride like this one. Make reservations well ahead.

Getting There & Away

Makani Kai Air (☎877-255-8532, 808-834-1111; www.makanikaiair.com; round-trip tour package from Moloka'i/Honolulu $249/315; ⊙office 6am-6pm) Runs regular flights to Kalaupapa from Ho'olehua on Moloka'i and from Honolulu that are timed to allow for day trips. Anyone who wants to visit Kalaupapa but is not sponsored by a Kalaupapa resident should sign up for a tour with Kalaupapa Rare Adventures, which will provide them with a permit to enter the settlement (contact kramolokai@gmail.com or phone ☎808-567-6088).

West End

Home to some of the finest beaches on the island, the seemingly deserted West End occupies a surprisingly significant place in Hawaii's history and culture. Pu'u Nana is the site of Hawaii's first hula school and the Maunaloa Range was once a center of sorcery.

In recent decades much of the land has been controlled by the Moloka'i Ranch, which ran into trouble after residents saw its plans as overdevelopment. Its fortunes have affected the entire island. The ranch closed and offered for sale for $260 million in 2018. It is yet to secure a buyer.

Hale O Lono Harbor in the southwest is the launching site for long-distance outrigger-canoe races, and the island's pristine and longest sandy beach, Papohaku, dominates the west coast.

Given the economic woes of Moloka'i Ranch, the atmosphere out west is a bit bleak, while the Kaluakoi resort area is beset by financial troubles. Still, you can escape all the earthly turmoil on one of the area's many paradise beaches.

Kaluakoi Resort Area

Beaches

★Kepuhi Beach BEACH
(Map p262; near Ke Nani Kai) Kepuhi is a rocky, white-sand dream, but swimming here can be a nightmare. There's a tough shore break, and strong currents, even on calm days. During winter the sand-filled waves provide a brutal exfoliation. A five-minute hike to the top of **Pu'u o Kaiaka** (Map p262), a 110ft-high promontory at the southern end, is rewarded with a nice view of Papohaku Beach.

★Kawakiu Beach BEACH
(Map p262) Kaluakoi's northernmost beach is also the best. Those with a sense of adventure can search out this secluded crescent of white sand and bright-turquoise waters. It's partially sheltered from the winds and when seas are calm, Kawakiu is safe for swimming. To get there, continue to the end of Kakaako Rd, pull over and park. Walk to the beach on a pathway (around 1.2 miles one way).

Sleeping

Ke Nani Kai CONDO $
(Map p262; 858-679-2016, 800-490-9042; www.kenanikai.com; 50 Kepuhi Pl; 1/2-bedroom units from $140/150;) This tidy operation sets an example for the area. The 100-plus units are large and well maintained (though the decor may vary depending on the owner). The pool is big. The ocean isn't right outside, so the premium for 'ocean view' units is debatable.

Paniolo Hale CONDO $
(Map p262; www.paniolohale.org; Lio Pl; studios from $100, 1/2-bedroom units from $150/180;) Large trees shade this plantation-style complex, giving it a hidden, secluded air. Each of the 77 units has a long, screened-in lanai overlooking the grounds; as always with condos, shop around to get one recently renovated. It's a short walk to the gorgeous Make Horse Beach. Additional cleaning fees usually apply.

Maunaloa

★Big Wind Kite Factory & Plantation Gallery ARTS & CRAFTS
(Map p262; 808-552-2364; www.bigwindkites.com; 120 Maunaloa Hwy; 8:30am-5pm Mon-Sat, 10am-2pm Sun) Big Wind custom makes kites for high fliers of all ages. It has hundreds ready to go in stock or you can choose a design and watch production begin. Lessons are available; enquire within. There's a range of other goods to browse as well, including an excellent selection of Hawaii-themed books, artwork, clothing and crafts.

Maunaloa General Store MARKET
(Map p262; 808-552-2346; Maunaloa Hwy; 10am-5pm Mon-Fri, 9am-2pm Sat, 9am-noon Sun) The Maunaloa General Store provides the village with basics. It has a limited selection of (pricey) groceries and alcohol.

West End Beaches

★Papohaku Beach BEACH
(Map p262; campsites residents/nonresidents $12/18) The light-hued sands of Papohaku Beach run for an astounding 2.5 miles. Come here for the solitude – the sand is soft and you can often stroll from one end to the other without seeing another soul. Offshore, **Third Hole** (Map p262) is one of the island's most challenging surf breaks. Do not swim here: there's a tangle of undertow and unpredictable currents. And there's no easy shade. You can bring an umbrella, but the often strong winds may send it O'ahu bound.

Dixie Maru Beach BEACH
(Kapukahehu Beach; Map p262) At the southern end of Pohakuloa Rd there's a parking lot with access to a narrow, round inlet that the ancient Hawaiians knew as Kapukahehu. It is now called Dixie Maru, after a ship that went down in the area long ago. It's the most protected cove on the west shore, and the most popular swimming and snorkeling area.

Understand Maui

History

Maui's early history mirrors the rest of Hawaii's, with warring chiefs, periods of peace, missionaries, whalers and sugarcane. More recently, tourism has become a driving economic force across Maui and much of the state as a whole.

How does Maui stand apart today? In the 21st century the Valley Isle has been a leader in eco-activism, establishing parks and reserves, banning plastic bags and leading the charge against genetically modified foods.

The Great Canoe Voyages

The earliest Polynesian settlers of Hawaii came ashore around 500 CE. Archaeologists disagree on exactly where these explorers came from, but artifacts indicate that the first to arrive were from the Marquesas Islands. The next wave of settlers were from Tahiti and arrived around 1000 CE. Unlike the Marquesans, who sparsely settled the tiny islands at the northwest end of the Hawaiian Islands, the Tahitians arrived in great numbers and settled each of the major islands in the Hawaiian chain. Though no one knows what set them on course for Hawaii, when they arrived in their mighty double-hulled canoes they were prepared to colonize a new land, bringing with them pigs, dogs, taro roots and other crop plants.

The Tahitian discovery of Hawaii may have been an accident, but subsequent journeys were not. The Tahitians were highly skilled seafarers, using only the wind, the stars and wave patterns to guide them. Yet, incredibly, they memorized their route over 2400 miles of open Pacific and repeated the journeys between Hawaii and Tahiti for centuries.

And what a story they must have brought back with them, because vast waves of Tahitians followed to pursue a new life in Hawaii. Such was the number of Tahitian migrations that Hawaii's population probably reached a peak of 250,000 by 1450. The voyages back and forth continued until around 1500, when all contact between Tahiti and Hawaii appears to have stopped.

TIMELINE

900,000 years ago

The volcanoes that formed Maui rise from the sea; the build-up continues until 400,000 BCE.

300–600 CE

Polynesian colonists, traveling thousands of miles across open seas in double-hulled canoes, arrive in Hawaii. They most likely came from the Marquesas Islands.

1000–1300

Sailing from Tahiti, a second wave of Polynesians arrives. Their tools are made of stone, shells and bone. They bring taro, sugarcane, coconuts, chickens and pigs.

Royal Power Struggles

From the early days of Polynesian settlement, Maui was divided into separate kingdoms, with rival chiefs occasionally rising up to battle for control of this and other islands in the archipelago.

In the 16th century Pi'ilani, the king of the Hana region, marched north to conquer Lele (now Lahaina) and Wailuku, uniting Maui for the first time under a single royal rule. He called for the continued construction of footpaths begun by ancient Hawaiians. His son, Kiha-a-Pi'ilani, began building the Pi'ilani Hwy, which would connect trails to form the King's Hwy, a road that eventually looped 138 miles around Maui and connected all 12 regions, know as *moku*.

During the 1780s Maui's King Kahekili became the most powerful chief in all Hawaii, bringing both O'ahu and Moloka'i under Maui's rule.

In 1790, while Kahekili was in O'ahu, Kamehameha the Great of Hawai'i launched a bold naval attack on Maui. Using foreign-acquired cannons and two foreign seamen, Isaac Davis and John Young, Kamehameha defeated Maui's warriors. The battle at 'Iao Valley was so fierce and bloody that the waters of 'Iao Stream ran red for days.

An attack on his own homeland of Hawai'i by a Big Island rival forced Kamehameha to withdraw from Maui, but the battle continued over the years. When the aging Kahekili died in 1794, his kingdom was divided among two quarreling heirs, leaving a rift that Kamehameha quickly exploited.

In 1795 Kamehameha invaded Maui again, now with a force of 6000 canoes. This time he conquered the entire island and brought it under his permanent rule. Later that year Kamehameha went on to conquer O'ahu and unite all of the Hawaiian Islands – except Kaua'i – under his reign.

In 1802 Kamehameha established Lahaina as his court, where he built a royal residence made of brick, the first Western-style building in Hawaii. The king of Kaua'i agreed to cede to Kamehameha's rule in 1810, allowing Kamehameha to become the first *mo'i* (king) of the Kingdom of

The community website www.hawaiihistory.org offers an interactive timeline of Hawaii's history plus essays delving into every aspect of ancient Hawaiian culture, with evocative images and links.

EARLY LAND DIVISIONS

Before contact with Europeans, rulers on Maui divided the island into 12 districts, each known as a *moku*. Eight of these districts dropped to the sea from Pōhaku Pālaha, a rock on the northeast rim of Haleakalā. The 12 *moku* were further divided into subregions known as *ahupua'a*. These wedge-shaped regions were separated by ridge lines and other natural formations. Each *ahupua'a* contained the resources necessary for the survival of the communities living within the wedge.

1500

The migration voyages between the South Pacific and Hawaii come to an end.

1778

Briton Captain James Cook becomes the first known Westerner to sight Maui.

1786

French explorer La Pérouse becomes the first Westerner to land on Maui.

1790

Kamehameha the Great invades Maui, decimating island warriors in a bloody battle at 'Iao Valley.

Hawaii. Lahaina remained the kingdom's capital until 1845, when Kamehameha III moved the capital to Honolulu on O'ahu.

European Explorers

On January 18, 1778, an event occurred on the islands that would change the life of Hawaiians in ways inconceivable at the time. On that day British explorer Captain James Cook sighted Hawaii while en route to the Pacific Northwest, in search of a possible 'northwest passage' between the Pacific and Atlantic Oceans.

Cook's appearance was not only the first Western contact but it also marked the end of Hawaii's 300 years of complete isolation following the cessation of the Tahitian voyages. Cook anchored on the Big Island, across the channel from Maui, and stayed long enough to refresh his food supplies before continuing his journey north.

Cook sighted Maui but never set foot on the island. The first Westerner to land on Maui was French explorer Jean-François de Galaup, comte de La Pérouse, who sailed into Keone'o'io Bay (now called La Perouse Bay) on Maui's southern shore in 1786, traded with the Hawaiians and left after two days of peaceful contact.

In *Blue Latitudes: Boldly Going Where Captain Cook Has Gone Before* (2002), Tony Horwitz examines the controversial legacy of Captain Cook's South Sea voyages, interweaving amusing real-life adventure tales with bittersweet oral history.

Here Come the Westerners

After Captain Cook's ships returned to England, news of his discovery quickly spread throughout Europe and America, opening the floodgates to an invasion of foreign explorers, traders, missionaries and fortune hunters.

By the 1820s Hawaii had become a critical link in the strengthening trade route between China and the US, with British, American, French and Russian traders all using Hawaii as a mid-Pacific stop for provisioning their ships.

A PLACE OF REFUGE

In ancient Hawai'i, a very strict code – called the *kapu* (taboo) system – governed daily life. If a commoner dared to eat *moi*, a type of fish reserved for *ali'i* (royalty or chiefs), for example, it was a violation of *kapu*. Penalties for such transgressions could be harsh, even including death. Furthermore, in a society based on mutual respect, slights to honor – whether of one's chief or extended family – could not be abided.

Although ancient Hawai'i could be a fiercely uncompromising place, it offered forgiveness for errors. Anyone who had broken *kapu* or been defeated in battle could avoid the death penalty by fleeing to a *pu'uhonua* (place of refuge). At the heiau (stone temple), a kahuna (priest) would perform purification rituals, lasting from a few hours up to several days. Absolved of their transgressions, *kapu* breakers were free to return home in safety.

1810

Kamehameha the Great (aka Kamehameha I) moves to Maui, declaring Lahaina the royal seat of the Hawaiian kingdom.

1819

Kamehameha the Great dies and the Hawaiian religious system is cast aside..

RICHIE CHAN / SHUTTERSTOCK ©

➡ Statue of Kamehameha I

1820

Christian missionaries arrive, filling the gap left by the abandonment of Hawaii's traditional religion.

Missionary Activities

By a twist of fate, the first missionaries to Maui arrived at a fortuitous time, when Hawaiian society was in great upheaval after the death of Kamehameha the Great in 1819. The missionaries were able to make inroads with Hawaiian leaders, and it made their efforts to save the souls of the 'heathen' Hawaiians much easier. The *ali'i* (royalty), in particular, were keen on the reading lessons the missionaries offered in the Hawaiian language, which had never before had a written form. Indeed, by the middle of the 1850s, Hawaii had a higher literacy rate than the USA.

Lahaina became a center of activity for missionaries and their various projects. In 1831 Lahainaluna Seminary (now Lahainaluna High School), in the hills above Lahaina, became the first secondary school to be established west of the Rocky Mountains, while Lahaina's newspaper, *Ka Lama Hawaii* (The Hawaiian Luminary), was likewise a first west of the Rockies.

But the New England missionaries also helped to destroy traditional Hawaiian culture. They prohibited hula dancing because of its lewd and suggestive movements and denounced the traditional Hawaiian chants and songs as they paid homage to the Hawaiian gods. In the late 19th century, missionary teachers even managed to prohibit the speaking of the Hawaiian language in schools as another means of turning Hawaiians away from their 'hedonistic' cultural roots – a major turnaround from the early missionary days, when all students were taught in Hawaiian.

Missionary-Era Sites

Baldwin House

Hale Pa'i

Bailey House museum

David Malo's Church

Native Hawaiian Sites

Pi'ilanihale Heiau

Haleki'i-Pihana Heiau State Monument

Brick Palace

Hauola Stone

Hoapili Trail (King's Hwy Trail)

Hana Cultural Center

Whalers

The first whaling ship to stop in Maui was the *Balena,* which anchored at Lahaina in 1819. The crew was mostly New England Yankees with a sprinkling of Gay Head Indians and former slaves. As more ships arrived, men of all nationalities roamed Lahaina's streets, most in their teens or twenties and ripe for adventure. Lahaina became a bustling port of call with shopkeepers catering to the whalers; saloons, brothels and hotels boomed.

A convenient way station for whalers of both the Arctic and Japanese whaling grounds, by the 1840s Hawaii was the whaling center of the Pacific. In Lahaina the whalers could transfer their catch to trade ships bound for America, allowing them to stay longer in the Pacific and resulting in higher profits. At the peak of the whaling era, more than 500 whaling ships were pulling into Lahaina each year.

Whaling brought big money to Maui and the dollars spread beyond its main port. Many Maui farmers got their start supplying the whaling ships with potatoes. Hawaiians themselves made good whalers, and sea

1826

Missionaries formulate a 12-letter alphabet (plus glottal stop) for the Hawaiian language and set up the first printing press. It is said that Queen Ka'ahumanu learned to read in five days.

1830

To control destructive herds of feral cattle, Spanish-Mexican cowboys (dubbed *paniolo*) are recruited. They introduce Hawaiians to the guitar and ukulele.

1831

Lahainaluna Seminary, the first secondary school west of the Rocky Mountains, is built in Lahaina.

1848

Under the influence of Westerners, the first system of private land ownership is introduced in the islands.

captains gladly paid a $200 bond to the Hawaiian government for each Hawaiian sailor allowed to join their crew. Kamehameha IV even set up his own fleet of whaling ships that sailed under the Hawaiian flag.

Part political statement, part historical treatise, *To Steal a Kingdom: Probing Hawaiian History* (1995) by Michael Dougherty takes a hard look at the legacy of Western colonialism and the lasting impacts of missionary culture on the islands.

Whaling in the Pacific peaked in the mid-19th century and quickly began to burn itself out. In a few short years, all but the most distant whaling grounds were being depleted and whalers were forced to go further afield to make their kills.

The last straw for the Pacific whaling industry came in 1871, when an early storm in the Arctic caught more than 30 ships by surprise, trapping them in ice floes above the Bering Strait. Although more than 1000 seamen were rescued, half of them Hawaiian, the fleet itself was lost.

Sugarcane

Maui's role in sugar production began in 1839, when Kamehameha III issued small parcels of land to individual growers who were then required to have their crop processed at the king's mill in Wailuku. Half of every crop went to the king. Of the remaining half, one fifth was taken as a tax to support the government and the remainder went to the grower.

In the heyday of sugar, there were as many as 10 plantations on Maui, cultivating thousands of acres of land throughout the island. One of the most prominent mills, the Pioneer Mill in Lahaina, was founded in 1863 by American entrepreneurs. In 1876 the Hamakua Ditch began transporting water from the rainy mountains to irrigate the dry plains, allowing the plantations to spread. In the 1880s a train began transporting freshly cut sugarcane to Pioneer Mill.

Immigration for Labor

As sugar production increased, sugar barons were worried about the shortage of field laborers, who were mostly Hawaiian. There had been a severe decline in the Native Hawaiian population due to introduced diseases, such as typhoid, influenza and smallpox, for which the Hawaiians had no immunity. To expand their operations, plantation owners began

A BLOODY CONFRONTATION

In January 1790 the American ship *Eleanora* arrived on Maui, eager to trade Western goods for food supplies and sandalwood. Late one night a party of Hawaiian men stole the ship's skiff. In retaliation, Captain Simon Metcalf lured a large group of Hawaiians to his ship under the pretense of trading with them. Instead he ordered his men to fire every shipboard cannon and gun at the Hawaiians, murdering over 100 men, women and children. This tragic event, one of the first contacts between Westerners and Maui islanders, is remembered as the Olowalu Massacre.

1868

Thousands of Japanese laborers arrive on Maui to work newly planted sugarcane fields.

1873

A Belgian Catholic priest, Father Damien Joseph de Veuster, arrives at Moloka'i's leprosy colony. He stays for 16 years, dying of leprosy (now called Hansen's disease) himself in 1889.

1893

While attempting to restore Native Hawaiian rights, Queen Lili'uokalani is overthrown by American businessmen.

1898

Hawaii is annexed by the USA and becomes a US territory.

to look overseas for a cheap labor supply. First they recruited laborers from China, then recruiters went to Japan in 1868, and in the 1870s they brought in Portuguese workers from Madeira and the Azores islands.

Labor contracts typically lasted two to three years, with wages as low as $1 per week. Workers lived in ethnically divided 'camps' set up by the plantations that included modest housing, a company store, a social hall and other recreational amenities. At the end of their contracts, some workers returned to their homelands, but most remained on the islands, integrating into the multicultural mainstream. Alexander & Baldwin, a company created by the sons of missionaries, opened a sugar plantation on Maui in 1870. The plantation's immigrant past is explored in the on-site museum (p149).

After Hawaii's 1898 annexation, US laws, including racially biased prohibitions against Chinese immigration, were enforced in Hawaii. Because of these new restrictions, plantation owners turned their recruiting efforts to Puerto Rico and Korea. Filipinos were the last group of immigrants brought to Hawaii to work in the fields and mills, between 1906 and 1946.

The Great Land Grab

Throughout the period of the monarchy, the ruling sovereigns of Hawaii fought off continual efforts on the part of European and American settlers to gain control of the kingdom.

In 1848, under pressure from foreigners who wanted to own land, a sweeping land-reform act known as the Great Māhele was instituted. This act allowed, for the first time, the ownership of land, which had previously been held exclusively by monarchs and chiefs. The chiefs had not owned the land in the Western sense but were caretakers of both the land and the commoners who lived and worked on it, giving their monarchs a portion of the harvest in return for the right to stay.

The reforms of the Great Māhele had far-reaching implications. For foreigners, who had money to buy land, it meant greater economic and political power. For Hawaiians, who had little or no money, it meant a loss of land-based self-sufficiency and enforced entry into the low-wage labor market, primarily run by Westerners.

When King David Kalakaua came to power in 1874, American businessmen had gained substantial control over the economy and were bent on gaining control over the political scene as well. King Kalakaua was an impassioned Hawaiian revivalist, known as the 'Merrie Monarch.' He brought back the hula, reversing decades of missionary repression against the 'heathen dance,' and he composed 'Hawaii Ponoi,' which is now the state song. The king also tried to ensure a degree of self-rule for Native Hawaiians, who had become a minority in their own land.

For more than a century beginning in 1866, Moloka'i's Kalaupapa Peninsula was a place of involuntary exile for those afflicted with leprosy (now called Hansen's disease). In *The Colony: The Harrowing True Story of the Exiles of Molokai* (2006), John Tayman tells the survivors' stories with dignity, compassion and unflinching honesty.

1901

The Pioneer Inn, Maui's first hotel, is built on the waterfront in Lahaina.

1912

Duke Kahanamoku wins gold and silver medals in freestyle swimming at the Stockholm Olympics; he goes on to become the ambassador of surfing around the world.

1916

Hawai'i National Park is established. It initially encompasses Haleakalā on Maui and Kilauea and Mauna Loa on the Big Island; these later become Haleakalā National Park and Hawai'i Volcanoes National Park, respectively.

1927

Convict road gangs complete the construction of the Hana Hwy.

Overthrow of the Monarch

When King Kalakaua died in 1891, his sister ascended the throne. Queen Lili'uokalani was a staunch supporter of her brother's efforts to maintain Hawaiian independence.

In January 1893 Queen Lili'uokalani was preparing to proclaim a new constitution to restore royal powers when a group of armed US businessmen occupied the Supreme Court and declared the monarchy to be overthrown. They announced a provisional government, led by Sanford B Dole, son of a pioneer missionary family.

After the monarchy's overthrow, the new government leaders pushed hard for annexation by the US, believing that it would bring greater stability to the islands, and more profits to Caucasian-run businesses. Although US law required that any entity petitioning for annexation must have the backing of the majority of its citizens through a public vote, no such vote was held in Hawaii.

Nonetheless, on July 7, 1898, President William McKinley signed a joint congressional resolution approving annexation. Some historians feel that Hawaii would not have been annexed if it had not been for the outbreak of the Spanish–American War in April 1898, which sent thousands of US troops to the Philippines, making Hawaii a crucial Pacific staging point.

WWII

On December 7, 1941, when Japanese warplanes appeared above the Pearl Harbor area, most residents thought that they were mock aircraft being used in US Army and Navy practice maneuvers. Even the loud anti-aircraft gunfire didn't raise much concern. Of course, it *was* the real thing, and by the day's end hundreds of ships and airplanes had been destroyed, more than 1000 Americans had been killed and the war in the Pacific had begun.

The impact on Hawaii was dramatic. The army took control of the islands, martial law was declared and civil rights were suspended. Unlike on the mainland, Japanese Americans in Hawaii were not sent to internment camps because they made up most of the labor force in the cane fields in Hawaii's sugar-dependent economy. Thousands of Japanese Americans, many from Hawaii, eventually fought for the US. Many were decorated for their bravery.

The War Department stationed the 4th Marine Division on Maui, where thousands of marines conducted training exercises for combat in the Pacific theater. The marines also had recreation time, with dances, movies, boxing matches and plenty of beer-drinking filling their post-training hours. The marines are memorialized at the 4th Marine Division Memorial Park (p188), the site of their camp and training ground in Ha'iku.

American author Mark Twain, who spent time on Maui in the 1860s, began a long tradition of Westerners writing about the state's exoticism in his book *Letters from the Sandwich Isles* (published in 1939).

1941

Japanese warplanes attack Pearl Harbor; Hawaii becomes a war zone under martial law.

1946

On April 1 the most destructive tsunami in Hawaiian history (generated by an earthquake in Alaska) kills 159 people across the islands and causes $10.5 million in property damage.

1959

On August 21, Hawaii becomes the 50th state of the USA.

1961

Elvis Presley stars in *Blue Hawaii*, the first of his three Hawaii movies. Along with *Girls! Girls! Girls!* and *Paradise, Hawaiian Style*, these set the mood for Hawaii's post-statehood tourism boom.

Statehood

Throughout the 20th century, numerous Hawaiian statehood bills were introduced in Congress, only to be shot down. One reason for this lack of support was racial prejudice against Hawaii's multi-ethnic population. US congressmen from a still-segregated South were vocal in their belief that making Hawaii a state would open the doors to Asian immigration and the so-called Yellow Peril threat that was perceived as being so rampant at the time. Others believed that Hawaii's labor unions were hotbeds of communism.

However, the fame of the 442nd Regimental Combat Team in WWII went a long way toward reducing anti-Japanese sentiment. In March 1959 Congress voted again, this time admitting Hawaii into the Union. On August 21, President Eisenhower signed the admission bill that officially deemed Hawaii the 50th state.

The Lahaina Historic Trail passes 65 sights – with interpretive markers – relevant to the story of Lahaina over the last 500 years. Pick up a trail brochure ($2.50) at the Lahaina Visitor Center or follow the map online at www.lahainarestoration.org.

Hollywood Backdrop

At the time of statehood in 1959, Maui's population was a mere 35,000. In 1961 Maui retained such a backwater appearance that director Mervyn LeRoy filmed his classic *The Devil at 4 O'Clock* in Lahaina, where the dirt roads and untouristed waterfront doubled for the sleepy South Pacific isle depicted in his adventure movie. Spencer Tracy and Frank Sinatra not only shot many of their scenes at Lahaina's Pioneer Inn but stayed there, too. More recently, Adam Sandler and Jennifer Aniston filmed scenes from *Just Go With It* at the Grand Wailea resort.

FROM SUGARCANE TO CITRUS TREES

The sugar mill operated by Hawaiian Commercial & Sugar in Pu'unene in Central Maui shut down in 2016. Owned by Alexander & Baldwin (A&B), a company with roots stretching back to the island's earliest missionaries, the mill had come under intense criticism in recent years for its sugarcane burns. Many residents were concerned that the resulting smoke was linked to lung disease. But the reason for the closure? Past and projected operating losses. The sugarcane plantation, which opened in 1870 and eventually covered 36,000 acres, was the last in Hawaii. In 2018 the Maui Pono farming company and agricultural park purchased 41,000 acres of the plantation's land, and about a year later the company began planting red potatoes on 40 acres there. The potatoes were the first nonsugar crop grown on the plantation's land in 150 years. They are also the first batch of a slew of non-GMO (genetically modified) crops scheduled for planting. Citrus fruit, avocados, coffee and macadamia nuts are among the proposed future harvests.

1968

Hawaii Five-O begins its 12-year run, becoming one of American TV's longest-running crime dramas.

1976

Native Hawaiian activists illegally occupy the island of Kaho'olawe.

KAREN KASMAUSKI / GETTY IMAGES ©

➡ Kaho'olawe

1978

The 1978 Constitutional Convention establishes the Office of Hawaiian Affairs (OHA), which holds the Hawaiian Home Lands in trust to ensure that they are used for the benefit of Native Hawaiians.

Tourism & Development

Statehood had an immediate economic impact on Hawaii, most notably in boosting the tourism industry. Coupled with the advent of jet airplanes, which could transport thousands of people per week to the islands, tourism exploded, creating a hotel-building boom previously unmatched in the US. Tourism became the largest industry on Maui.

In 1962 sugar giant Amfac transformed 600 acres of Ka'anapali canefields on Maui into Hawaii's first resort destination outside Waikiki. Things really took off in 1974 with the first nonstop flight between the mainland USA and Kahului, and Maui soon blossomed into the darling of Hawaii's tourism industry.

In her book *The Wave* (2010), Susan Casey chronicles Laird Hamilton's big-wave riding off the coast of Maui.

The growth spurt hasn't always been pretty. In the mid-1970s developers pounced on the beachside village of Kihei with such intensity that it became a rallying call for antidevelopment forces throughout Hawaii. Recent years have been spent catching up with Kihei's rampant growth, mitigating traffic and creating plans intent on sparing the rest of Maui from willy-nilly building sprees.

Hawaiian Renaissance & Sovereignty Movement

By the 1970s Hawaii's rapid growth meant new residents (mostly mainland transplants) and tourists were crowding island beaches and roads. Runaway construction was rapidly transforming resorts almost beyond recognition, and the relentless peddling of 'aloha' got some islanders wondering what it meant to be Hawaiian. Some Native Hawaiians turned to *kapuna* (elders) and the past to recover their heritage, and by doing so became more politically assertive.

In 1976 a group of activists illegally occupied Kaho'olawe, an island in Maui County dubbed 'Target Island.' The government had taken the island during WWII and used it for bombing practice until 1990. During another protest occupation attempt in 1977, two members of the Protect Kaho'olawe 'Ohana (PKO) – George Helm and Kimo Mitchell – disappeared at sea, instantly becoming martyrs. Saving Kaho'olawe became a rallying cry and it radicalized a nascent Native Hawaiian–rights movement.

When the state held its landmark Constitutional Convention in 1978 it passed a number of amendments of special importance to Native Hawaiians. For example, it made Hawaiian the official state language (along with English) and mandated that Hawaiian culture be taught in public schools. At the grassroots level, the islands were experiencing a renaissance of Hawaiian culture, with a surge in residents – of all ethnicities –

1990

After much litigation and more than a decade of grassroots Hawaiian activism, the US Navy is forced to stop bombing Kaho'olawe. Control over that island isn't officially returned to the state until 2003.

1993

President Bill Clinton signs the 'Apology Bill,' acknowledging the US government's role in the kingdom's illegal takeover 100 years before.

2002

Partly as a response to Democratic Party corruption scandals, mainland-born Linda Lingle is elected Hawaii's first Republican governor in 40 years.

2008

Born and raised in O'ahu, Barack Obama is elected US president with more than 70% of the vote.

joining hula *halau* (schools), learning to play Hawaiian instruments and rediscovering traditional crafts such as feather-lei making.

In 2011 then-governor Neil Abercrombie signed into law a bill recognizing Native Hawaiians as the state's only indigenous people and establishing a commission to create and maintain a list of qualifying Native Hawaiians. For those who qualified, this was the first step toward eventual self-governance.

Climate Change & Eco-Awareness

Mauians know intimately the consequences of global warming. Extended periods of drought have become commonplace. Some years the droughts end with record-setting bursts of torrential rain that wash down the slopes, flooding low-lying communities and muddying coral reefs. Heavy rains in the fall of 2016 caused severe flooding in parts of Central Maui, with heavy damage to 'Iao Valley State Monument and Kepaniwai Park. Both parks were temporarily closed for repairs and reconstruction. Destructive brushfires made headlines in 2018 and 2019.

Most Mauians take climate change seriously, and even big-wave surfer Laird Hamilton recognizes climate change as a source of the 100ft surf he rides off Maui's North Shore.

Maui has a long history of protecting the environment. It was the first island in Hawaii to ban single-use plastic bags, and, in a move to decrease their carbon emissions, Mauians supported the erection of windmills on the island.

Maui citizens voted in 2014 to temporarily ban the planting of genetically modified organisms (GMOs) until environmental and health impacts could be analyzed. The ban was not implemented due to legal challenges from large-scale GMO producers. In 2016 a federal judge ruled that Maui County could not enact any bans affecting state agricultural matters, which include genetically modified crops.

A bit of good environmental news? The National Oceanic and Atmospheric Administration (NOAA) announced that nine out of 14 recognized populations of humpback whales could be removed from the endangered-species list. Humpback whales, as a species, were placed on the list in 1970, so 40 years of protective efforts appear to have paid off. Despite the delisting, a moratorium on whaling will stay in effect.

History Museums

Alexander & Baldwin Sugar Museum

Lahaina Heritage Museum

Wo Hing Museum

2011

Maui becomes the first Hawaiian island to ban single-use plastic bags. Violaters are fined $500.

2016

Hawaiian Commercial & Sugar closes its sugar mill in Central Maui, the last still operating in Hawaii.

2017

Haleakalā National Park begins requiring reservations for anyone arriving between 3am and 7am to watch the sunrise.

2018–19

The Central-South Maui brushfire scorches more than 9000 acres, forcing road closures and evacuations.

DEBORAH KOLB / SHUTTERSTOCK ©

The People of Maui

All Mauians are bonded by a sense of *aloha 'aina* – a love of the land. Add to this strong family ties and a culture that embraces generosity and hospitality, and you've got a style of community now rarely seen on the hard-charging US mainland. There's also an appreciation for chitchatting, known as 'talking story' – a refreshingly 'retro' mode of communication still in fashion here.

Island Identity

Nobody sweats the small stuff on Maui. It's all good. No worries. No problem. And if somebody is noticeably wound up? They're from the mainland, guaranteed. Folks on Maui tend to have sunny dispositions, and they're more laid-back than their mainland cousins, dressing more casually and spending more time outside. On weekends everybody can

Above Hawaiian fire dance

be found hanging on the beach in T-shirts and bikinis, and wearing those ubiquitous flip-flops known in Hawaii as 'rubbah slippahs.'

Located 2500 miles from the nearest continent, the Hawaiian Islands are practically another country. On Maui, most streets have Hawaiian names, mixed-race people are the norm, and school kids participate in hula contests. You'll find no daylight-saving time and no significant changes of season. The geographical distance puts local, rather than national, news on the front page.

People on Maui never walk by anybody they know without partaking in a little 'talk story,' stopping to ask how someone is doing (and meaning it) and to share a little conversation. Islanders prefer to avoid heated arguments and generally don't jump into a controversial topic just to argue a point. Politically, most residents are middle-of-the-road Democrats and tend to vote along party, racial, ethnic, seniority and local/nonlocal lines.

To locals, it is best to avoid embarrassing confrontations and to 'save face' by keeping quiet. At community meetings or activist rallies, the most vocal, liberal and passionate will probably be mainland transplants. Of course, as more and more mainlanders settle in Hawaii, the traditional stereotypes are fading.

Mauians tend to be self-assured without being cocky. Though Honolulu residents may think other Hawaiian Islands are 'da boonies,' they generally give a different nod to Maui. In the greater scheme of Hawaiian places, Maui is considered the more sophisticated sister, with a more polished scene than the Big Island or Kaua'i.

Lifestyle

Take a Sunday-afternoon drive along the West Maui coast and you'll see the same scene repeated at the different beach parks: overflowing picnic tables, smoking grills and multi-generational groups enjoying the sun and surf. On Maui, the *'ohana* (family) is central to the lifestyle. *'Ohana* includes all relatives, as well as close family friends. Growing up, 'auntie' and 'uncle' are used to refer to those who are dear to you, whether by blood or by friendship. Weekends are typically set aside for family outings, and it's not uncommon for as many as 50 people to gather for a family picnic.

People are generally early risers, often taking a run along the beach or hitting the waves before heading to the office. Most work a 40-hour week – overtime and the workaholic routine common elsewhere in the US are the exceptions here.

In many ways, contemporary culture in Maui resembles contemporary culture in the rest of the US. Mauians listen to the same pop music and watch the same TV shows. The island has rock bands and classical musicians, junk food and nouvelle cuisine. The wonderful thing about Maui, however, is that the mainland influences largely stand beside, rather than engulf, the culture of the island.

Not only is traditional Hawaiian culture an integral part of the social fabric, but so are the customs of the ethnically diverse immigrants who have settled here. Maui is more than a meeting point for East and West: it's a place where the cultures merge, typically in a manner that brings out the best of both worlds.

Recent decades have seen a refreshing cultural renaissance in all things Hawaiian. Hawaiian-language classes are thriving, local artists and craftspeople are returning to traditional mediums and themes, and hula classes are concentrating more on the nuances behind hand movements and facial expressions than on the stereotypical hip-shaking.

Visitors will still encounter packaged Hawaiiana that seems almost a parody of island culture, from plastic lei to theme-park luau. But the

KOZUP PHOTOGRAPHY / SHUTTERSTOCK ©

Old Lahaina Luau (p95)

growing interest in traditional Hawaiian culture is having a positive impact on the tourist industry, and authentic performances by hula students and Hawaiian musicians are now the norm. Resorts are adding cultural talks and outrigger-canoe tours. Outdoor outfitters are adding educational elements to their trips, often discussing history and sharing tips that guests can use to protect the land and sea.

Folks on Maui are quite accepting of other people, which helps to explain the harmonious hodgepodge of races and cultures here. Sexual orientation is generally not an issue and gay men and lesbians tend to be accepted without prejudice. In 2013 Hawaii became the 15th state to legalize marriage between same-sex couples.

Most locals strive for the conventional 'American dream': kids, home ownership, stable work and ample free time. Generally, those with less standard lifestyles (eg B&B owners, artists, singles and world travelers) are mainland transplants, and for working-class people it generally takes two incomes to make ends meet.

The median price of a single-family home on Maui was $695,000 in 2017. That's steep when you consider that the median annual household income was $72,762 between 2013 and 2017. Even worse, the median price of a single-family home jumped to a historic and eye-popping high of $837,500 in the fall of 2019.

According to one recent report, the cost of living in Hawaii is the highest of any state, with the price of groceries and other services, like utilities, much higher than on the mainland. Financially, it can be a tough go in paradise. Yet most agree that nothing compares to living on Maui and would leave only if absolutely necessary.

MITHUN PANDIT / SHUTTERSTOCK ©

Surfers (p52)

Multicultural Maui

Maui is one of the most ethnically diverse places in the US. Need proof? Just look at its signature dish: the plate lunch. This platter, with its meat, macaroni salad and two scoops of rice, merges the culinary habits of Native Hawaiians with those of a global array of immigrants – Portuguese, Japanese, Korean, Filipino – to create one heaping plate of deliciousness. An obvious metaphor never tasted so good.

But the diversity is both eclectic and narrow at once. That's because Hawaii's unique blend of races, ethnicities and cultures is quite isolated from the rest of the world. On one hand, Hawaii is far removed from any middle-American city. On the other, it lacks major exposure to certain

WHO'S WHO

Haole White person, Caucasian. Often further defined as 'mainland haole' or 'local haole.'

Hapa Person of mixed ancestry, most commonly referring to *hapa haole* who are part white and part Asian.

Hawaiian Person of Native Hawaiian ancestry. It's a faux pas to call a non-native Hawaii resident 'Hawaiian.'

Kama'aina Person who is a resident of Hawaii, literally defined as 'child of the land.'

Local Person who grew up in Hawaii. Locals who move away retain their local 'cred,' at least in part, but longtime transplants never become local. To call a transplant 'almost local' is a compliment.

Neighbor Islander Person who lives on any Hawaiian Island other than O'ahu.

Transplant Person who moves to the islands as an adult.

races and ethnicities, particularly blacks and Mexican Hispanics, that are prevalent in the US mainland population.

Any discussion regarding multiculturalism must address whether we are talking about locals (insiders) or nonlocals (outsiders). Among locals, social interaction has hinged on old plantation stereotypes and hierarchies since statehood. During plantation days, whites were the wealthy plantation owners and, for years afterward, minorities would joke about their being the 'bosses' or about their privileges due to race. As the Japanese rose to power economically and politically, they tended to capitalize on their 'minority' status, emphasizing their insider standing as former plantation laborers. But the traditional distinctions and alliances are fading as the plantation generation dies away.

Of course, any tension among local groups is quite benign compared with racial strife on the US mainland. Locals seem slightly perplexed at the emphasis on 'political correctness.' Just consider the nickname for overdeveloped Kihei in South Maui. It's been dubbed 'Haole-wood' by the locals. Haole? It's the Hawaiian term for Caucasian. Among themselves, locals good-naturedly joke about island stereotypes: talkative Portuguese, stingy Chinese, goody-goody Japanese and know-it-all haole.

When nonlocals enter the picture, the balance shifts. Generally, locals feel a bond with other locals. While tourists and transplants are welcomed, they must earn the trust and respect of the locals. It is unacceptable for an outsider to assume an air of superiority and to try to 'fix' local ways. Such people will inevitably fall into the category of 'loudmouth haole.'

That said, prejudice against haole is minimal. If you're called a haole, don't worry: it's generally not an insult or threat (if it is, you'll know). Essentially, locals are warm and gracious to those who appreciate island ways.

Shaka Sign

Islanders greet each other with the *shaka* sign, made by folding down the three middle fingers to the palm and extending the thumb and little finger. The hand is then shaken back and forth in greeting. On Maui, it's as common as waving.

Island Etiquette

Dial it down a notch when you get to Maui. Big-city aggression and type-A maneuvering won't get you far. As the bumper sticker here says, 'Practice Aloha.'

When driving on narrow roads like the Road to Hana and the Kahekili Hwy, the driver who reaches a one-way bridge first has the right of way, if the bridge is otherwise empty. If you're facing a steady stream of cars, yield to the entire queue.

Remember the simple protocol when visiting sacred places: don't place rocks at the site as a gesture of thanks; better to use words instead. It is also considered disrespectful to stack rocks or build rock towers. Finally, don't remove rocks from national parks. Obey all signage at historic sights. Similarly, respect any 'Kapu – No Trespassing' signs that you may encounter.

When surfing there's a pecking order, and tourists are at the bottom. The person furthest outside has the right of way. When somebody is up and riding, don't take off on the wave in front of them. Wait your turn, be generous and surf with a smile.

Hawaiian Arts & Crafts

Stop, look and listen. The sensory experience of the Hawaiian Islands is manifold, reflecting the creativity of its diverse inhabitants. Native Hawaiian song and dance are powerful, reflecting deep *aloha 'aina* (respect for the land). Significant contributions to Hawaii's creative milieu came with subsequent ethnic groups, from the Portuguese ukulele to plantation-era immigrants' collective invention of pidgin English.

Hula

In ancient Hawai'i, hula was performed sometimes as a solemn ritual, in which *oli* (chants) and *mele* (songs) were offerings to the gods or celebrated the accomplishments of *ali'i* (chiefs). At other times hula was lighthearted entertainment, in which chief and *maka'ainana* (commoners) danced together, such as during the annual *makahiki* harvest festival.

Above Hula dancer, Old Lahaina Luau (p95)

Traditionally, dancers trained rigorously in *halau* (schools) under a *kumu* (teacher), so their hand gestures, facial expressions and synchronized movements were precise. In a culture without written language, chants were important, giving meaning to the dances and preserving Hawaii's oral history, which ran the gamut from creation stories to royal genealogies. Songs often contained *kaona* (hidden meanings), which could be spiritual, but also slyly amorous or sexual.

There are many hula troupes active on Maui. Some practice in public places, such as in school grounds and at parks, where visitors are welcome to watch. Although many of the *halau* rely on tuition fees, others receive sponsorship from hotels or shopping centers and give weekly public performances in return. One place presenting authentic hula is the Old Lahaina Luau (p95) in Lahaina. If you're in Maui in early November, don't miss the Hula O Nā Keiki (p110) competition in Ka'anapali.

Island Music

Hawaiian music is rooted in ancient chants. Foreign missionaries and sugar-plantation workers introduced new melodies and instruments, which were incorporated and adapted to create a unique local musical style. *Leo ki'eki'e* (falsetto, or 'high voice') vocals, sometimes just referred to as soprano for women, employs a signature *ha'i* (vocal break, or split-note) style, with a singer moving abruptly from one register to another. Contemporary Hawaiian musical instruments include the steel guitar, slack key guitar and ukulele.

But if you tune your rental-car radio to today's island radio stations, you'll hear everything from US mainland hip-hop beats, country-and-western tunes and Asian pop hits to reggae-inspired 'Jawaiian' grooves. A few Hawaii-born singer-songwriters, most famously Jack Johnson, have achieved international stardom. To discover new hit-makers, check out this year's winners of the Na Hoku Hanohano Awards (www.nahokuhanohano.org), Hawaii's version of the Grammies.

For a top-notch slack key guitar performance, settle in at Napili Kai Beach Resort (p116) on Wednesday nights for the Masters of Hawaiian Music Slack Key Show hosted by George Kahumoku Jr. In the Upcountry, head to long-time favorite Charley's (p186) in Pa'ia for live shows, from rock to blues. You'll find live music nightly along Front St in Lahaina and at most beach resorts. For a list of weekly performances, pick up the independent weekly *Maui Time,* published on Thursday.

Gifted ukulele player Eddie Kamae is also a talented and prolific filmmaker. Among his documentaries, look for *Keepers of the Flame* (1988), which profiles three revered Hawaiian cultural experts: Mary Kawena Pukui, 'Iolani Luahine and Edith Kanaka'ole.

Ukulele

Heard all across the islands is the ukulele, derived from the *braguinha,* a Portuguese stringed instrument introduced to Hawaii in 1879. Ukulele means 'jumping flea' in Hawaiian, referring to the way players' deft fingers swiftly move around the strings. The ukulele is enjoying a revival as a young generation of virtuosos emerges, including Nick Acosta, who plays with just one hand, and genre-bending rockers led by Jake Shimabukuro, whose album *Peace Love Ukulele* (2011) reached number one on Billboard's world music chart.

Both the ukulele and the steel guitar contributed to the lighthearted *hapa haole* (Hawaiian music with predominantly English lyrics) popularized in the islands after the 1930s, of which 'My Little Grass Shack' and 'Lovely Hula Hands' are classic examples. For better or for worse, *hapa haole* songs became instantly recognizable as 'Hawaiian' thanks to Hollywood movies and the classic *Hawaii Calls* radio show, which broadcast worldwide from the banyan-tree courtyard of Waikiki's Moana hotel from 1935 until 1975.

Cowboy Heritage

Spanish and Mexican cowboys introduced the guitar to Hawaiians in the 1830s. Fifty years later, O'ahu-born high-school student Joseph Kekuku started experimenting with playing a guitar flat on his lap while sliding a pocket knife or comb across the strings. His invention, the Hawaiian steel guitar *(kika kila),* lifts the strings off the fretboard using a movable steel slide, creating a signature smooth sound.

In the early 20th century, Kekuku and others introduced the islands' steel guitar sounds to the world. The steel guitar later inspired the creation of resonator guitars such as the Dobro, now integral to bluegrass, blues and other genres, and country-and-western music's lap and pedal steel guitars. Today Hawaii's most influential steel guitarists include Henry Kaleialoha Allen, Alan Akaka, Bobby Ingano and Greg Sardinha.

Slack Key Guitar

Since the mid-20th century, the Hawaiian steel guitar has usually been played with slack key *(ki ho'alu)* tunings, in which the thumb plays the bass and rhythm chords, while the fingers play the melody and improvisations, in a picked style. Traditionally, slack key tunings were closely guarded secrets among *'ohana* (extended family and friends).

The legendary guitarist Gabby Pahinui launched the modern slack key guitar era with his first recording of 'Hi'ilawe' in 1946. In the 1960s, Gabby and his band the Sons of Hawaii embraced the traditional Hawaiian sound. Along with other influential slack key guitarists such as Sonny Chillingworth, they spurred a renaissance in Hawaiian music that continues to this day. The list of contemporary slack key masters is long and ever growing, including Keola Beamer, Ledward Ka'apana, Martin and Cyril Pahinui, Ozzie Kotani and George Kuo.

Traditional Crafts

In the 1970s, the Hawaiian renaissance sparked interest in artisan crafts. The most beloved traditional craft is lei-making, stringing garlands of flowers, leaves, berries, nuts or shells. More lasting souvenirs include wood carvings, woven baskets and hats, and Hawaiian quilts. All of these have become so popular with tourists that cheap imitation imports from across the Pacific have flooded into Hawaii, so shop carefully and always buy local.

Traditional crafts take the spotlight during the annual Celebration of the Arts (p121) festival, held in April at the Ritz-Carlton Kapalua. Artisans from across the islands sell their crafts and provide demonstrations for lei-making, weaving and jewelry design. Whalers Village (p113) offers free lei-making classes on Tuesday, Thursday and Friday at 10:30am.

You'll find a mix of traditional and modern crafts at the Saturday-morning Maui Swap Meet (p138) on the grounds of Maui College in Kahului. The Maui Crafts Guild (p187) is a collective of basket weavers, ceramists, jewelers, photographers and other artists, all residents of Maui. The guild has a store in downtown Pa'ia.

Fabric Arts

Lauhala weaving and *kapa* (cloth made by pounding the bark of the paper mulberry tree) making are two ancient Hawaiian crafts practiced only by a small number of experts today.

Traditionally *lauhala* was stripped and woven to serve as floor mats, canoe sails and protective capes. Weaving the *lau* (leaves) of the *hala* (pandanus) tree requires skill, but preparing the leaves, which have razor-sharp spines, is messy work that takes real dedication. Today the most common *lauhala* items are hats, placemats and baskets. Most are mass-produced, but you can find handmade pieces at specialty stores.

VERONIKA HANZLIKOVA / SHUTTERSTOCK ©

Woven baskets

Making *kapa* (called *tapa* elsewhere in Polynesia) is no less laborious. First, seashells are used to scrape away the rough outer bark of the *wauke* (paper mulberry) tree. Strips of softer inner bark are cut (traditionally with shark's teeth) and pounded with mallets until thin and pliable; they are soaked in water between beating to let them ferment and further soften.

Once soft enough, the bark strips are layered atop one another and pounded together in a process called felting. Large sheets of finished *kapa* are colorfully dyed with plant materials and hand-stamped or hand-painted with geometric patterns before being scented with flowers or oils.

In ancient times, *kapa* was fashioned into everyday clothing and used as blankets for everything from swaddling newborns to burying the dead. Today authentic handmade Hawaiian *kapa* cloth is rarely seen outside of museums, fine-art galleries and private collections.

Honolulu magazine's list of 50 must-read Hawaii books (www.honolulumagazine.com/Honolulu-Magazine/May-2018/50-Hawaii-Books-You-Should-Read-in-Your-Lifetime) is smart and comprehensive, including ancient history, culture, biography, memoir and fiction.

Hawaiian Quilting

The **Maui Quilt Shop** (www.mauiquiltshop.com; 1280 S Kihei Rd) in Kihei offers a two-hour introductory class in Hawaiian quilt making. The store sells everything you need to make your own tropical blanket. During the fall **Kula Fest** (☎808-878-1485; http://stjohnsmaui.org/kulafestival; 8992 Kula Hwy, St John's Episcopal Church, Keokea; ⏰late Sep), colorful quilts from the Maui Quilt Guild are on display – and you might find one or two for sale in the silent auction.

Island Writings

Until the late 1970s, Hawaii's literature was dominated by visiting Western writers who observed the 'exotic' Hawaiian Islands from the outside. In the late 1800s, world travelers Mark Twain and Isabella Bird described the islands in their letters-based travelogues. Popular modern novels set in Hawaii include James Michener's historical saga *Hawaii* (1959) and Paul Theroux's caustically humorous *Hotel Honolulu* (2001). Nonlocal writers who settled in Hawaii sometimes embraced island themes as did Maui-based, Pulitzer Prize–winning poet WS Merwin in his collection *The Folding Cliffs* (1998).

Meanwhile, locally born contemporary writers have created an authentic literature of Hawaii that evokes island life from the inside. Leading this movement has been Bamboo Ridge Press (www.bambooridge.com), which since 1978 has published new local fiction and poetry in an annual journal, launching the careers of many successful writers in Hawaii. The University of Hawai'i Press (www.uhpress.hawaii.edu) and Bishop Museum Press (www.bishopmuseum.org) have also made space for local voices.

The largest bookstore in Maui is the glossy Barnes & Noble (p139) in Kahului. It's well stocked, but die-hard book-lovers may have more fun at the Old Pu'unene Bookstore (p149) in Central Maui. This used-book shack is crammed with musty tomes and sits behind a schoolhouse in a one-time sugar-plantation village.

Pidgin to Da Max, by Douglas Simonson (aka Peppo), Pat Sasaki and Ken Sakata, is a laugh-out-loud, illustrated dictionary in print since 1981 because it's still spot-on, revealing and hilarious.

Hawaii on Screen

Ever since Hollywood introduced the South Seas genre to moviegoers in the 1930s, Hawaii has symbolized island paradise in the popular imagination. Whether the mood is silly or serious, whether Hawaii is the actual setting or a stand-in for another tropical locale, the familiar tropes rarely change. Honeymoons, desert-island castaways or surfer dudes, perhaps. The islands' history of colonization is rarely addressed.

Hollywood arrived in Hawaii in 1913, more than a decade after Thomas Edison first journeyed here to make movies that you can still watch today at Lahaina's Wo Hing Museum (p82). By 1939 dozens of Hollywood movies had been shot in Hawaii, including the musical comedy *Waikiki Wedding* (1937), in which Bing Crosby crooned the Oscar-winning song 'Sweet Leilani.' Later favorites include the WWII–themed drama *From Here to Eternity* (1953), the musical *South Pacific* (1958) and Elvis Presley's goofy postwar *Blue Hawaii* (1961).

Today, Hawaii actively supports a lucrative film industry by maintaining state-of-the-art production facilities and providing tax incentives. Hundreds of feature films have been shot in the state, including box-office hits *Raiders of the Lost Ark* (1981), *Jurassic Park* (1993), *Pearl Harbor* (2001), *50 First Dates* (2004), *Pirates of the Caribbean: On Stranger Tides* (2011), *The Hunger Games: Catching Fire* (2013) and *Jurassic World* (2015).

Hawaii has hosted dozens of TV series since 1968, when the original *Hawaii Five-O*, an edgy cop drama unsentimentally depicting Honolulu's gritty side, debuted. In 2010 *Hawaii Five-O* was rebooted as a prime-time drama, filmed on O'ahu. That island also served as the location for the hit series *Lost*, which, like *Gilligan's Island* (the pilot of which was filmed on Kaua'i), is about a group of island castaways trying to get home.

For a complete filmography and a list of hundreds of TV episodes filmed here, including what's currently being shot around the islands, check the Hawaii Film Office website (http://filmoffice.hawaii.gov).

Hawaiian Folktales, Proverbs & Poetry

- *The Legends and Myths of Hawai'i*, by King David Kalakaua
- *Folktales of Hawai'i*, compiled by Mary Kawena Pukui and illustrated by Sig Zane
- *Hawaiian Mythology*, by Martha Beckwith
- *'Olelo No'eau*, illustrated by Dietrich Varez
- *Obake Files*, by Glen Grant

ALVIS UPITIS / GETTY IMAGES ©

Lei

Greetings. Love. Honor. Respect. Peace. Celebration. Spirituality. Good luck. Farewell. A Hawaiian lei – a handcrafted garland of fresh tropical flowers – can signify all of these meanings and many more. Lei-making may be Hawaii's most sensuous and transitory art form. Fragrant and ephemeral, lei embody the beauty of nature and the embrace of *'ohana* (extended family and friends) and the community, freely given and freely shared.

The Art of the Lei

In choosing their materials, lei makers express emotions and tell stories, since flowers and other natural artifacts often embody Hawaiian places and myths. Traditional lei makers use feathers, nuts, shells, seeds, seaweed, vines, leaves and fruit, in addition to fragrant flowers. The most common methods of making lei are by knotting, braiding, winding, stringing or sewing raw materials together.

LEI: DOS & DON'TS

➡ Do not wear a lei hanging down like binoculars around your neck. Instead, drape a closed (circular) lei over your shoulders, making sure equal lengths are hanging over your front and back.

➡ When presenting a lei, bow your head slightly and raise the lei above your heart. Do not drape it with your own hands over the head of the recipient because this isn't respectful; let them do it themselves.

➡ Never refuse a lei, and do not take one off in the presence of the giver.

➡ Resist the temptation to wear a lei intended for someone else. That's bad luck.

➡ Closed lei are considered unlucky for pregnant woman, so give an open (untied) lei or *haku* (head) lei instead.

➡ When you stop wearing your lei, don't trash it. Remove the string and return the lei's natural elements to the earth (eg scatter flowers in the ocean, bury seeds or nuts).

Worn daily, lei were integral to ancient Hawaiian society. They were important elements of sacred hula dances and given as special gifts to loved ones, as healing medicine to the sick and as offerings to the gods, all practices that continue today. So powerful a symbol were they that on ancient Hawai'i's battlefields, a lei could bring peace to warring armies.

Today, locals wear lei for special events, such as weddings, birthdays, anniversaries and graduations. It's no longer common to make one's own lei, unless you belong to a hula *halau* (school). For ceremonial hula, performers are often required to make their own lei, gathering raw materials by hand, never taking more than necessary and always thanking the tree and the gods.

You can find lei across the island. Keep your eyes out for eye-catching Ni'ihau shell lei.

Modern Celebrations

For visitors to Hawaii, the tradition of giving and receiving lei dates back to 19th-century steamships that brought the first tourists to the islands. Later, disembarking cruise-ship passengers were greeted by vendors who would toss garlands around the necks of *malihini* (newcomers).

In 1927 the poet Don Blanding and Honolulu journalist Grace Tower Warren called for making May 1 a holiday to honor lei. Every year, Lei Day is still celebrated across the islands with Hawaiian music, hula dancing, parades, and lei-making workshops and contests.

The tradition of giving a kiss with a lei began during WWII, allegedly when a hula dancer at a USO club was dared by her friends to give a military serviceman a peck on the cheek when offering him a flower lei.

On the 'Garden Island,' leathery, anise-scented *mokihana* berries are often woven with strands of glossy, green maile vines. Mokihana trees thrive on the rain-soaked western slopes of Mt Wai'ale'ale.

Landscapes & Wildlife

You don't have to be a geologist, botanist or marine biologist to appreciate the Valley Isle's myriad natural charms, although you might find yourself picking up an interest in a new field of study after a morning snorkel or a hike atop Haleakalā. Trust us, it won't take long to feel the *aloha 'aina* (love for the land), too.

The Land

Maui is the second-largest Hawaiian island, with a land area of 728 sq miles. Set atop a 'hot spot' on the Pacific Plate, Maui rose from the ocean floor as two separate volcanoes. Lava flows and soil erosion eventually built up a valley-like isthmus between the volcanic masses, linking them in their present form. This flat region provided a good setting for sugarcane fields and is home to Maui's largest urban center, the twin towns of Kahului and Wailuku.

Above Green sea turtle

The eastern side of Maui, the larger and younger of the two volcanic masses, is dominated by lofty Haleakalā (10,023ft). This dormant volcano, whose crater-like floor is dotted with cinder cones, last erupted between 1480 and 1600. The second, more ancient volcano formed the craggy West Maui Mountains, which top out at Pu'u Kukui (5788ft). Both mountains are high enough to trap moisture-laden clouds carried by the northeast trade winds, bringing abundant rain to their windward eastern sides. Consequently, the lushest jungles and gushiest waterfalls are found along the Hana Hwy, which runs along Haleakalā's eastern slopes, while the driest, sunniest beaches are on the western coasts.

Flora & Fauna

All living things that reached Maui were carried across the sea on wing, wind or wave – seeds clinging to a bird's feather, or insects in a piece of driftwood. Scientists estimate that successful species arrived once every 70,000 years – and they included no amphibians and only two mammals: a bat and a seal.

However, the flora and fauna that made it to Maui occupied an unusually rich and diverse land. In a prime example of 'adaptive radiation,' the 250 flowering plants that arrived evolved into some 1800 native species. Lacking predators, new species dropped defensive protections – thorns, poisons and strong odors disappeared, which explains why they fare so poorly against modern invaders. So many plant and animal species have been lost that the state has been dubbed 'the extinction capital of the world.'

The Polynesians brought pigs, chickens, coconuts and about two dozen other species, not to mention people. The pace of change exploded after Western contact in the late 18th century. Cattle and goats were introduced and set wild, with devastating consequences. Even today, sitting on a Kihei beach looking out at Kaho'olawe in the late afternoon, you'll notice a red tinge from the dust whipping off the island, a consequence of defoliation by wild goats released there a century ago.

But there is progress. On Kaho'olawe the goats are gone and native reforestation has begun; Haleakalā National Park (p201) has made great strides in reintroducing and protecting native species; and the first public garden totally dedicated to endemic Hawaiian species, Maui Nui Botanical Gardens (p129), sits on the site of a former exotic zoo.

If you see a wild animal in distress, report it to the state **Division of Conservation & Resource Enforcement** (DOCARE; ☎808-643-3567).

Best Places to Honor the Sun

- *Haleakalā Crater for sunrise*
- *Wai'anapanapa State Park for sunrise*
- *Big Beach (Oneloa Beach) for sunset*
- *Papawai Point for sunset*
- *Fleetwood's on Front St for sunset*

Animals

Most of Maui's wildlife attractions are found in the water or on the wing. Hawaii has no native land mammals.

Marine Life

Of the almost 700 fish species in Hawaiian waters, nearly one-third are found nowhere else in the world. Maui's nearshore waters are a true rainbow of color: turquoise parrotfish, bright-yellow tangs and polka-dotted puffer fish, to name a few.

Honu (green sea turtles) abound in Maui's waters. To the delight of snorkelers and divers, *honu* can often be seen feeding in shallow coves and bays. Adults can grow to more than 3ft – an awesome sight when one swims past you. Much less common is the hawksbill sea turtle, which occasionally nests on Maui's western shores.

The sheltered waters between Maui, Lana'i and Moloka'i are the wintering destination for thousands of North Pacific humpback whales. The majestic creatures are the fifth largest of the great whales, reaching lengths of 45ft and weighing up to 45 tons. Humpbacks are coast-huggers and are visible from the beach in winter along Maui's west and southwest coasts.

Maui is also home to a number of dolphins. The spinner dolphin (named for its acrobatic leaps) comes into calm bays during the day to rest.

With luck you might see the Hawaiian monk seal, which lives primarily in the remote northwestern Hawaiian Islands but occasionally hauls out on Maui beaches. It was nearly wiped out by hunting in the 1800s, but conservation efforts have edged the species back from the brink of extinction – barely, with a total population of about 1400 in 2018.

Don't touch, approach or disturb marine mammals; most are protected, making it illegal to do so. Watch dolphins, whales, seals and sea turtles from a respectful distance.

Birds

Many of Hawaii's birds have evolved from a single species, in a spectacular display of adaptive radiation. For example, all 54 species of Hawaiian honeycreepers likely evolved from a single finch ancestor. Left vulnerable to introduced predatory species and infectious avian diseases, half of Hawaii's native bird species are already extinct, and more than 30 of those remaining are still under threat. According to a recent article in *Audubon,* one in three endangered bird species in the US is a Hawaiian bird.

The threatened nene, Hawaii's state bird, is a long-lost cousin of the Canada goose. Nene nest in high cliffs on the slopes of Haleakalā and their feet have adapted to the rugged volcanic environment by losing most of their webbing. Nene have black heads, light-yellow cheeks, a white underbelly and dark-gray feathers.

At least three birds native to Maui – the *kiwikiu* (Maui parrotbill), *'akohekohe* (crested honeycreeper) and *'alauahio* (Maui creeper) – are found nowhere else in the world. The Maui parrotbill and *'akohekohe* are federally listed endangered species. The Maui parrotbill exists solely in the Kipahulu section of Haleakalā National Park and in a small section of high-elevation forest on the northeast slope of Haleakalā volcano. The cinnamon-colored *po'ouli* (black-faced honeycreeper) was last seen in 2004 and may already be extinct. Alas, it's unlikely you'll see any of those birds. But other native forest birds, including the *'apapane* (a vivid red honeycreeper), can be sighted in Hosmer Grove in Haleakalā National Park.

MAUI'S TOP PROTECTED AREAS

'Ahihi-Kina'u Natural Area Reserve (p173) A pristine bay, lava flows and ancient sites; good for hiking and snorkeling.

Haleakalā National Park: Summit Area (p201) Large, dormant volcano; good for hiking, camping and horseback riding.

Haleakalā National Park: Kipahulu Area (p201) Towering waterfalls, cascading pools and ancient sites; good for hiking, swimming and camping.

'Iao Valley State Monument (p144) The park features streams, cliffs and swimming holes; good for hiking and photography.

Kealia Pond National Wildlife Refuge (p148) Bird sanctuary; good for bird-watching.

Molokini Crater (p51) A submerged volcanic crater; ideal for snorkeling and diving.

Pi'ilanihale Heiau & Kahanu Garden (p228) A national botanic garden and ancient site; good for walking.

Polipoli Spring State Recreation Area (p197) With cloud forest and uncrowded trails; good for hiking, camping and mountain biking.

Wai'anapanapa State Park (p228) Lava tubes and a trail over rugged sea cliffs to Hana; good for hiking and camping.

Ae'o (Hawaiian black-necked stilt)

Maui's two waterbird preserves, Kanaha Pond Bird Sanctuary (p129) and Kealia Pond National Wildlife Refuge (p148), are nesting sites for the *ae'o* (Hawaiian black-necked stilt), a wading bird with a white underbelly and long orange legs.

For more information about honeycreepers and the *kiwikiu* (there are fewer than 300 left), visit the **Maui Forest Bird Recovery Project** (www.mauiforestbirds.org) website. This group specializes in recovering endangered honeycreepers. Also check the group's website for details about speakers and Maui Brewing Pint Nights, a fundraiser held twice per year at the brewery's Kahana location (p115). Through the group, you can also sponsor a tree to be planted on Maui, which will aid in habitat recovery for the birds.

Plants

Maui seems suitable for just about anything with roots. On a mile-for-mile basis, Hawaii has the highest concentration of climatic and ecological zones on earth. They vary from lowland deserts along the coast to lush tropical rainforests in the mountains, and the diversity within a small region can be amazing. In the Upcountry there are so many microclimate zones that hillside farms can grow tropical fruit trees just a few sloping acres from where temperate roses thrive. Another mile up, don't even bother looking for tropical fruit trees as you're now in the zone for cool-weather crops.

Many native species, such as Maui's endangered silversword, have adapted to very narrow geographic ecosystems: the silversword plant grows at the summit of Haleakalā.

Flowering Plants & Ferns

For travelers, the flower most closely identified with Hawaii is the hibiscus, whose generous blossoms are worn by women tucked behind their ears.

RAPID OHIA DEATH

A dangerous fungus – it has a 100% mortality rate – is killing hundreds of thousands of native ohia trees on the Big island and has recently been detected on Kaua'i. The ohia is a key part of the forest ecosystem across the Hawaiian islands as it provides a habit for endangered species. It also has cultural significance. To prevent the disease from spreading to Haleakalā National Park, officials are asking all visitors who arrive from the Big Island to clean and remove dirt and debris from their shoes, and to spray their shoes, clothing and equipment with a 70% alcohol spray. The ohia is found only in the state of Hawaii.

Thousands of varieties of hibiscus bushes grow in Hawaii; on most, the flowers bloom early in the day and drop before sunset.

Two native plants at the beach are *pohuehue*, a beach morning glory with pink flowers that's found just above the wrack line; and beach *naupaka*, a shrub with oval leaves and a small, white five-petal flower that looks as if it's been torn in half.

Throughout the Upcountry you'll find gardens filled with protea, a flashy flower originally from South Africa. Named after the Greek god Proteus (who could change shape at will), blossoms range from small pincushiony heads to tall stalk-like flowers with petals that look like feathers.

There are about 200 varieties of Hawaiian fern and fern ally (such as mosses) found in rainforests and colonizing lava flows.

Trees & Shrubs

The most revered of the native Hawaiian forest trees is the koa, found at higher elevations on Maui. Growing up to 100ft, this rich hardwood is traditionally used to make canoes, surfboards and even ukuleles.

Brought by early Polynesian settlers, the *kukui* tree has chestnut-like oily nuts that the Hawaiians used for candles, hence its common name, candlenut tree. It's recognizable in the forest by its light silver-tinged foliage.

Two coastal trees that were well utilized in old Hawaii are the *hala,* also called pandanus or screwpine, whose spiny leaves were used for thatching and weaving, and the *niu* (coconut palm), which loves coral sands and yields about 75 coconuts a year.

The kiawe, a non-native tree, thrives in dry coastal areas. A member of the mesquite family, the kiawe is useful for making charcoal but is a nuisance for beachgoers as its sharp thorns easily pierce soft sandals. Also plentiful along the beach are stands of ironwood, a conifer with drooping needles, which act as natural windbreaks and prevent beach erosion.

National, State & County Parks

Haleakalā National Park (p201) accounts for nearly 10% of Maui's land area. The park not only offers superb hiking and other recreational activities but also protects Hawaiian cultural sites and the habitat of several endangered species. Maui's numerous state and county parks also play an important role in preserving undeveloped forest areas and much of Maui's coastline. The parks are well used by Maui residents – from surfers to pig hunters – as well as by tourists.

The state's **Department of Land and Natural Resources** (DLNR; ☎808-984-8109; http://dlnr.hawaii.gov; camping Hawaii residents/nonresidents $12/18, cabins Hawaii residents/nonresidents $60/90) has useful online information about hiking, aquatic safety, forestry and wildlife. The DLNR oversees the **Division of State Parks** (☎808-984-8109; www.hawaiistateparks.org; 54 S High St, Room 101, Wailuku; ⏰8am-3:30pm Mon-Fri), which issues camping permits on Maui, and **Nā Ala Hele** (https://hawaiitrails.hawaii.gov/trails), which coordinates public access to hiking trails.

Survival Guide

DIRECTORY A–Z . . . 302

TRANSPORTATION . 309

Directory A–Z

Climate

Kaunakakai

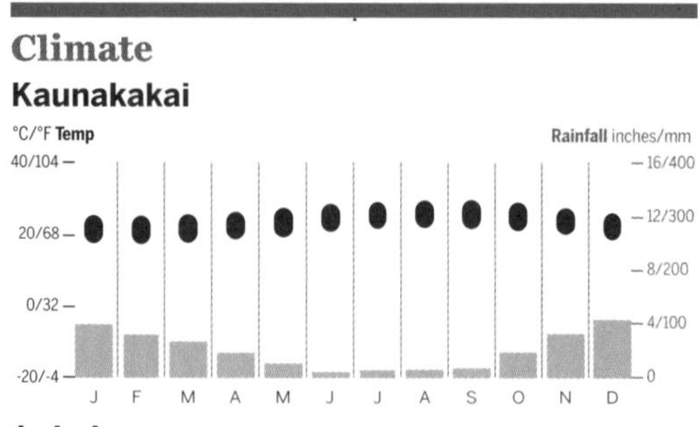

Lahaina

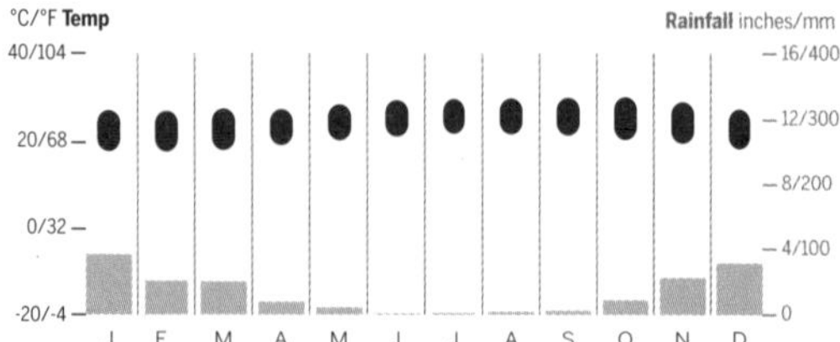

Lana'i City

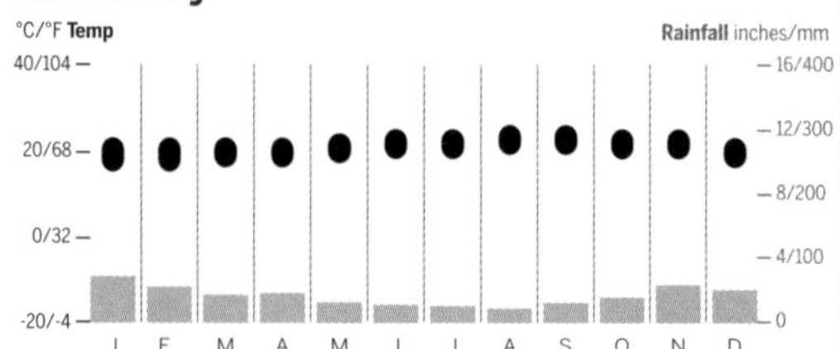

Accessible Travel

Maui has decent infrastructure for travelers with disabilities, and most public places comply with Americans with Disabilities Act (ADA) regulations. Many of the major resort hotels have elevators, TTD-capable phones and wheelchair-accessible rooms, while major car-rental companies will install hand controls and provide accessible transportation to the vehicle pickup site with advance notification. A disability parking placard issued by other states or countries for parking in designated accessible parking spaces is valid in Hawaii. Most public buses are wheelchair accessible.

Travelers with visual impairments are allowed to bring guide or service dogs into Hawaii without quarantine, provided they meet the Department of Agriculture's requirements, which include your dog's having a current rabies vaccination and a standard health certificate issued fewer than 30 days prior to arrival. As of January 2019 it is illegal to knowingly represent that your pet is a service animal. Contact the **Animal Quarantine Station** (☎808-483-7151; http://hdoa.hawaii.gov) for more details.

Resources

Download Lonely Planet's free Accessible Travel guide from https://shop.lonelyplanet.com/categories/accessible-travel.

Customs Regulations

➡ Currently each international visitor (21 years of age or older) is allowed to bring 1L of liquor and 200 cigarettes into the USA. You may also bring in up to $100 worth of gift merchandise without incurring any duty. For more complete, up-to-date information, visit the US Customs and Border

Protection (www.cbp.gov) website.

➡ Hawaii is a rabies-free state and there are strict regulations regarding the importation of pets, so don't plan on bringing your furry friend on a short vacation.

➡ Many fresh fruits and plants cannot be brought into Hawaii. For complete details, visit the Hawaii Department of Agriculture (http://hawaii.gov/hdoa) website.

Agricultural Checks

All luggage and carry-on bags leaving Hawaii for the US mainland are checked by an agricultural inspector using an x-ray machine. You cannot take out fresh flowers of jade vine and Mauna Loa, citrus or citrus-related flowers, leaves or plant parts, even in lei, though most other fresh flowers and foliage are permitted. You can take home pineapples and coconuts, but most other fresh fruits and vegetables are banned. Other things not allowed to enter mainland states include plants in soil, berries including fresh coffee berries (roasted beans are OK), cactus and sugarcane.

However, seeds, fruits and plants that have been certified and labeled for export aren't a problem. For more information, contact the **Plant Protection & Quarantine Office** (☎844-820-2234; www.aphis.usda.gov) and check the full list online.

Emergency & Important Numbers

Emergency	☎911
Country code	☎1
Area code	☎808
International access code	☎011

Electricity

Type A
120V/60Hz

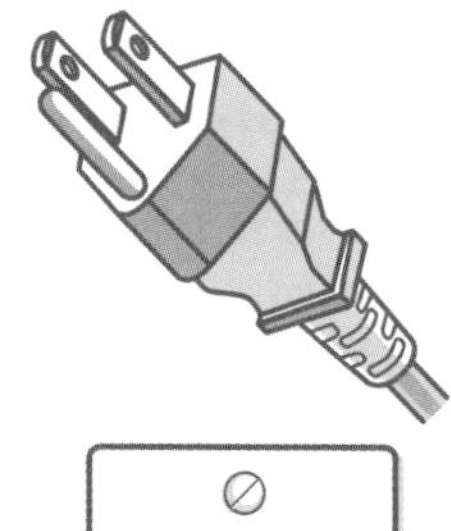

Type B
120V/60Hz

Entry & Exit Formalities

➡ Be warned that all visa information is highly subject to change. US entry requirements keep evolving as national security regulations change. All travelers should double-check current visa and passport requirements *before* coming to the US.

➡ For information about the USA's entry requirements for travelers, access the Visa section of the US State Department (www.travel.state.gov) website and also the Travel section of the US Customs and Border Protection (www.cbp.gov) website. The Department of Homeland Security's registration program (DHS; www.dhs.gov), called the Office of Biometric Identity Management, includes every port of entry and covers nearly every foreign visitor to the USA. Most visitors must register into the US-Visit program and have a digital photo and electronic (inkless) fingerprints taken. For more information, see the Department of Homeland Security website.

➡ Depending on your home country, you may not need a visa. The Visa Waiver Program (VWP) allows citizens of certain countries to enter the USA for stays of 90 days or less without first obtaining a US visa. There are 39 countries currently participating, including Australia, France, Germany, Ireland, Italy, Japan, the Netherlands, New Zealand, Norway, Singapore, Sweden, Switzerland and the UK. For a full list of countries and details, log onto the State Department's website.

➡ Under the VWP you may need to supply evidence of a return ticket or onward travel to enter Hawaii. Border agents can refuse you entry to the state if they suspect that you intend to remain.

➡ All VWP travelers must register online at least 72 hours before arrival with the **Electronic System for Travel Authorization** (ESTA; https://esta.cbp.dhs.gov), which currently costs $14. Once approved, registration is valid for two years (or until your passport expires).

LEEWARD & WINDWARD

Maui's high central mountains trap the trade winds that blow from the northeast, capturing moisture-laden clouds and bringing abundant rainfall to the windward side of Maui. The jungly Road to Hana lies smack in the midst of windward Maui and simply gushes with waterfalls.

The same mountains keep clouds and hence rain from reaching the southwest side of the island. So it's in places such as Kihei and Makena that you'll find the driest, sunniest conditions. It's no coincidence that the great majority of Maui's resorts are found on its dry leeward side.

- With the exception of Canadians and visitors who qualify for the VWP, foreign visitors to the USA need a visa. To apply, you need a passport that's valid for at least six months longer than your intended stay. The process is not free, involves a personal interview and can take several weeks.
- Visa applicants may be required to 'demonstrate binding obligations' that will ensure their return home. Because of this requirement, those planning to travel through other countries before arriving in the USA are better off applying for their US visa in their home country rather than on the road.
- The validity period for a US visitor visa depends on your home country. The actual length of time you'll be allowed to stay in the USA is determined by US officials at the port of entry.

Passports

- A machine-readable passport (MRP) is required for all foreign citizens to enter the USA.
- Your passport must be valid for six months beyond your expected dates of stay in the US.
- As of April 1, 2016, you must have an e-passport to enter into the Visa Waiver Program. E-passports contain an electronic chip that is scanned upon arrival to identify the traveler.

Visas

Generally not required for stays of up to 90 days for citizens of Visa Waiver Program countries.

GLBTIQ Travelers

Maui is a popular destination for gay and lesbian travelers. The state has strong legislation to protect minorities and a constitutional guarantee of privacy that extends to sexual behavior between consenting adults. In 2013 Hawaii became the 15th state to legalize same-sex marriage. That said, people tend to be private so you won't see many public open displays of affection.

There isn't a big, boisterous 'out' scene. Kihei is the most open town on Maui, low-key as it is. Websites including www.gogayhawaii.com list LGBTIQ-friendly cafes, bars and events. Also check www.mauipride.org for a list of events, including monthly hikes. Maui Pride events are the first weekend in October.

Health

Before You Go

HEALTH INSURANCE

International visitors should buy travel insurance for emergencies before they visit Maui. US citizens should check their health-insurance policies to see if they are covered for treatment on Maui.

RECOMMENDED VACCINATIONS

No vaccinations are required for a trip to Maui, but it's always worth packing a basic first-aid kit and some iodine or peroxide if you're planning on swimming near coral.

MEDICAL CHECKLIST

There are plenty of drugstores and pharmacies on Maui where travelers can pick up household medical items.

- Health insurance is a must.
- Iodine is a handy extra for your first-aid kit if you're going in the water.
- SPF 30+ sunblock is advisable for Maui. You can also check the UV rating for your trip at http://uv.willyweather.com.

In Maui

AVAILABILITY & COST OF HEALTH CARE

Health care is readily available on Maui. Clinics such as Doctors on Call Maui (www.doctorsoncallmaui.com) and Minit Medical (www.minitmed.com) are open 365 days a year. However, consultations on the island are expensive, ranging from $150 to $200 before tax.

STAPHYLOCOCCUS (MRSA)

It's possible to contract *staphylococcus aureus* (MRSA) in Hawaii, and some types of antibiotic-resistant staph infection can be fatal. Staph infections are caused

BOOK YOUR STAY ONLINE

For more accommodation reviews by Lonely Planet authors, check out http://lonelyplanet.com/hotels/. You'll find independent reviews, as well as recommendations on the best places to stay. Best of all, you can book online.

by bacteria that enter the body through an open wound. To prevent infection, practice good hygiene, apply antibiotic ointment to any open cuts or sores and keep them out of recreational water; if they're on your feet don't go barefoot, even on the sand. If a wound becomes painful, looks red, inflamed or swollen, leaks pus or causes a rash or blisters, seek medical help immediately.

TAP WATER

Maui's tap water is safe to drink and meets all standards set out by the federal and state governments. The taste of the water differs in parts of the county, depending on the mineral content in the water. Even though the water is completely safe to drink, travelers who are not used to a particular mineral content may find it unsettles their stomach. Bottled water is easy to pick up at supermarkets, but consider refilling a reusable water bottle to reduce plastic waste.

PRACTICALITIES

Newspapers Maui's main daily newspaper is the *Maui News* (www.mauinews.com). *Lahaina News* (www.lahainanews.com) is a weekly newspaper focusing on West Maui.

Radio For Hawaiian music and personalities tune into KPOA 93.5FM (www.kpoa.com). Hawaii Public Radio KKUA 90.7FM (www.npr.com) features island programs and music.

TV All major US TV networks and cable channels are available.

Smoking Tobacco smoking is prohibited in enclosed public places, including restaurants, retail settings and hotel lobbies as well as in indoor and outdoor recreational settings such as nightclubs and sports arenas. Smoking is also banned in state parks and beaches, except in those areas that have been specifically designated for smoking. Since 2016 the prohibition now includes e-cigarettes. The sale of cigarettes and e-cigarettes to anyone under the age of 21 is also illegal. In Maui County, smoking is also prohibited at county parks and recreational facilities. This county ban currently does not include e-cigarettes.

Insurance

Purchasing travel insurance to cover theft, loss and medical problems is highly recommended. Some insurance policies do not cover 'risky' activities such as scuba diving, trekking and motorcycling, so read the fine print. Make sure your policy at least covers hospital stays and an emergency flight home.

Certain insurers require policyholders to get preauthorization before receiving medical treatment – contact the call center. Keep your medical receipts and documentation for claims reimbursement later.

Paying for your airline ticket or rental car with a credit card may provide limited travel accident insurance. If you already have private US health insurance or a homeowners or renters policy, find out what those policies cover and only get supplemental insurance. If you have prepaid a large portion of your vacation, trip-cancellation insurance may be a worthwhile expense.

Worldwide travel insurance is available at www.lonelyplanet.com/bookings. You can buy, extend and claim online anytime – even if you're already on the road.

Internet Access

Most towns have cafes offering free internet access if you purchase something. Access is also available at libraries with a $10 nonresident library card, lasting three months. Most Maui hotels and many condos and B&Bs have wi-fi. Some of the larger hotels offer business centers with computers and internet access for guests; fees vary. You can find free wi-fi at the Queen Ka'ahumanu Center in Kahului and at most McDonald's restaurants. When wi-fi is available in an establishment, it's marked with a symbol. If you bring a laptop from outside the USA, make sure you bring along a universal AC and plug adapter.

Legal Matters

Legal rights Anyone arrested in Hawaii has the right to have the representation of a lawyer from the time of their arrest to their trial, and if a person cannot afford a lawyer the state must provide one for free. You're presumed innocent unless or until you're found guilty in court.

Alcohol laws The legal drinking age is 21. It's illegal to have open containers of alcohol in motor vehicles, and drinking in public parks or on beaches is also illegal. Drunk driving is a serious crime and can incur stiff fines, jail time and other penalties. In Hawaii, anyone caught driving with a blood-alcohol level of 0.08% or greater is guilty of driving 'under the influence' and will have their driver's license taken away on the spot.

Maps

The maps in this guide are sufficient for most exploring. You can also find a driving

EATING PRICE RANGES

The following price ranges refer to a standard main dish on Maui. Prices don't include tax.

$ less than $15

$$ $15–$25

$$$ more than $25

map of the island's main roads on the state tourism website (www.gohawaii.com).

Money

ATMs are common. Credit cards are widely accepted; they're often required for car and hotel reservations. The US dollar is the only currency used on Maui.

ATMs

Major banks such as the Bank of Hawaii (www.boh.com) and First Hawaiian Bank (www.fhb.com) have ATM networks throughout Maui that give cash advances on major credit cards and allow cash withdrawals with affiliated ATM cards. In addition to bank locations, you'll find ATMs at most grocery stores, mall-style shopping centers and convenience stores.

Changing Money

If you're carrying foreign currency, it can be exchanged for US dollars at larger banks around Maui.

Credit Cards

Major credit cards are widely accepted on Maui, including at car-rental agencies and at most hotels, restaurants, gas stations, grocery stores and tour operators. Some B&Bs and condos (including some handled through rental agencies) may refuse them. You may not be able to use them at some food trucks.

Tipping

Taxis Tip 15% of the metered fare, rounded up to the next dollar.

Restaurants Good waiters are tipped 15% to 20%, while very dissatisfied customers make their ire known by leaving 10%. There has to be real cause for not tipping at all.

Hotels and airports Give $2 per bag.

Valets At least $2 when your car is returned.

Travelers Cheques

Traveler's checks are becoming obsolete. Foreign visitors carrying traveler's checks will find things easier if the checks are in US dollars. Many top-end restaurants, hotels and shops accept US-dollar traveler's checks and treat them just like cash.

Out-of-state personal checks are not readily accepted on Maui.

Opening Hours

Opening hours may vary slightly throughout the year. High-season opening hours are provided in listings; hours generally decrease in shoulder and low seasons.

Banks 8:30am–4pm Monday to Friday; some to 6pm Friday and 9am–noon or 1pm Saturday

Bars and clubs noon–midnight daily; some to 2am Thursday to Saturday

Businesses 8:30am–4:30pm Monday to Friday

Post offices 8:30am–4:30pm Monday to Friday; some also 9am–noon Saturday

Shops 9am–5pm Monday to Saturday, some also noon–5pm Sunday; major shopping areas and malls keep extended hours

Post

You can get detailed 24-hour postal information by dialing toll-free 800-275-8777 or visiting www.usps.com. First-class mail between Maui and the US mainland usually takes three to four days and costs 55¢ for letters up to 1oz and 35¢ for standard-size postcards. International Global Forever stamps, for postcards and letters, are $1.15.

Public Holidays

When a public holiday falls on the weekend, it's often celebrated on the nearest Friday or Monday instead. These long weekends can be busy, as people from other Hawaiian Islands often take advantage of the break to visit Maui. If your visit coincides with a holiday, be sure to book your hotel and car well in advance.

New Year's Day January 1

Martin Luther King Jr Day Third Monday of January

Presidents Day Third Monday of February

Good Friday March or April

Prince Kuhio Day March 26

Memorial Day Last Monday of May

King Kamehameha Day June 11

Independence Day July 4

Statehood Day Third Friday of August

Labor Day First Monday of September

Election Day Second Tuesday of November in even-numbered years

Veterans Day November 11

Thanksgiving Fourth Thursday of November

Christmas Day December 25

Safe Travel

Hazards & Trespassing

Flash floods, rockfalls, tsunamis, earthquakes, volcanic eruptions, shark attacks, jellyfish stings and, yes, even possibly getting knocked out by a falling coconut – the potential dangers of traveling in

Hawaii might seem alarming at first. But as the old saying goes, statistically you're more likely to get hurt crossing the street at home. The key pieces of advice? Pay attention to your surroundings and watch for changing conditions.

When exploring, remember to mind your manners and watch your step. Hawaii has strict laws about trespassing on both private land and government land not intended for public use. As a visitor to the islands, it's important to respect all '*Kapu*' or 'No trespassing' signs. Always seek explicit permission from the landowner or local officials before venturing onto private or public land that is closed to the public, regardless of whether it is fenced or signposted as such. Doing so not only respects the *kuleana* (rights) of local residents and the sacredness of the land but also helps ensure your own safety.

Rental Cars

Break-ins Maui is notorious for smash-and-grabs. They can happen within seconds, whether in a secluded parking area at a trailhead or in a crowded beach parking lot. Don't leave valuables in the car. If you must, pack things well out of sight before you arrive at your destination; thieves wait and watch to see what you put in the trunk.

Availability If you see a good rate online before your trip, book the car. Unexpected shortages and rate spikes are not uncommon.

Tsunamis

Tidal waves, or tsunamis as they're called in the Pacific, are rare, but when they do hit they can be deadly. Maui has a warning system, aired through yellow speakers mounted on telephone poles around the island. Emergency Alert Systems are tested on the first working day of each month at 11:45am for about two minutes. If you should hear one at any other time and you're in a low-lying coastal area, immediately head for higher ground.

Telephone

Pay phones are a dying breed, but you may find them at larger public parks and local community centers. To make long-distance calls consider buying a prepaid phone card at a convenience store or pharmacy.

Always dial 1 before toll-free numbers (☎800, 888 and 877). Some toll-free numbers may only work within the state or from the US mainland, while others work from Canada, too. But you'll only know by making the call.

Cell Phones

International travelers need GSM multiband phones. Buy prepaid SIM cards locally.

COVERAGE

Cell-phone coverage is good on most of Maui but spotty in remote areas such as the Road to Hana. Verizon has an extensive cellular network on Maui, and AT&T and Sprint also have decent coverage.

EQUIPMENT

International travelers, take note: most US cell-phone systems are incompatible with the GSM 900/1800 standard used throughout Europe and Asia, and will need a multiband phone. Check with your cellular service provider before departure about using your phone on Maui.

Long Distance & International Calls

Calls to Hawaii If you're calling Maui from abroad, the international country code for the US is 1. All calls to Hawaii are then followed by the area code (808) and the seven-digit local number.

International calls from Maui To make international calls direct from Maui to any country other than Canada, dial 011 + country code + area code + number. To make calls direct to Canada, dial 1 + area code + number.

Operator assistance For international operator assistance, dial 0. The operator can provide specific rate information and tell you which time periods are the cheapest for calling.

Calls within Hawaii If you're calling from one place on Maui to any other place on Maui you do not need to dial the 808 area code. However, you must dial 1 + 808 when making a call from one Hawaiian island to another.

Time

Hawaii-Aleutian Standard Time (HAST) is GMT minus 10 hours. Hawaii does not observe daylight-saving time. It has about 11 hours of daylight in midwinter and almost 13½ hours in midsummer.

RESOURCES

Hawaii Visitors and Convention Bureau (www.gohawaii.com/islands/maui) Official tourism site; comprehensive events calendar and multilingual planning guides.

The Maui News (www.mauinews.com) Latest headlines.

Maui Time (http://mauitime.com) Weekly newspaper with in-depth local news features and entertainment listings.

Lonely Planet (www.lonelyplanet.com/usa/hawaii/maui) Destination information, hotel bookings, traveler forum and more.

SHARK ATTACKS: DO YOU NEED TO WORRY?

Bringing up shark attacks in a travel context seems rather, well, rude. Our apologies. But attacks off the coast of Maui have garnered headlines in recent years. In the first fatal attack in Hawaii since 2015, a swimmer was mauled off the coast of Ka'anapali in 2019. In 2016, however, there were seven shark attacks in Maui waters and 10 statewide. In Maui, no attack was fatal and only two resulted in serious injuries, while five across the state resulted in no injury at all. The norm for Hawaii is roughly three or four attacks per year.

When and why do they happen? No one is 100% sure. Some scientists think that there may be an increase in incidents in the fall, when female tiger sharks are most likely to be pregnant and perhaps more aggressive. But not all of the recent incidents were at the end of the year. A spike in attacks between 2012 and 2013 provoked a Department of Land and Natural Resources study to examine tiger-shark behavior off the Maui coast. The study found that islands in Maui County (Maui, Moloka'i, Lana'i and Kaho'olawe) have more preferred tiger-shark habitats than all the other major Hawaiian Islands combined.

Do you need to be concerned? Not particularly. Although there were two fatal attacks in 2013, the last previous shark-attack fatality in Hawaii was in 2004. According to the International Shark Attack File, your odds of being bitten are about one in 11.5 million. To be extra cautious, though, try not to swim or snorkel in murky water (which is more likely to appear later in the day) and try to swim where there are lots of people.

Tourist Information

Maui County's tourist organizations have visitor information on their websites and will mail out material to those not online. There's an **information desk** (Map p132; %808-872-3893; www.gohawaii.com/maui; Kahului Airport; h5am-10pm) at Kahului airport.

Local Tourist Offices

Lahaina Visitor Center (Map p84; ☎808-667-9175; www.visitlahaina.com; 648 Wharf St, Old Lahaina Courthouse; ⏰9am-5pm) This excellent tourist office is located on the 1st floor of the **Old Lahaina Courthouse** (Map p84; visitor center ☎808-667-9193; http://lahainarestoration.org/old-lahaina-courthouse; 648 Wharf St, Banyan Tree Park; ⏰9am-5pm) FREE. You can get gifts, books, info and a walking-tour map ($2.50).

Tours

A number of tour-bus companies operate half-day and full-day sightseeing tours on Maui, covering the most visited island destinations. Popular routes include day-long jaunts to Hana, and Haleakalā trips that take in the major Upcountry sights.

There are also specialized adventure tours such as whale-watching cruises, snorkeling trips to Lana'i and helicopter tours.

Polynesian Adventure Tours (☎888-206-4531; www.polyad.com; tours adult/child 3-11yr from $145/97) Part of Gray Line Hawaii, Polynesian is one of the major Hawaiian tour companies. It offers tours to Haleakalā National Park (sunrise tours from $159), the Road to Hana (from $160.90), and combined tours of Maui, Lahaina and the 'Iao Valley and Haleakalā (from $145).

Roberts Hawaii (☎800-831-5541; www.robertshawaii.com; Hana tours adult/child 4-11yr $179/104) In operation for more than 75 years, Roberts Hawaii runs tours to Hana, the 'Iao Valley and Lahaina, and Haleakalā National Park.

Valley Isle Excursions (☎808-871-5224; www.tourmaui.com; tours adult/child 0-12yr from $156/135; ⏰office 5am-9pm) It costs a bit more, but Valley Isle has hands down the best Road to Hana tour (from $160 per person if booked online). Vans take just 12 passengers, and guides offer more local flavor and less canned commentary. Includes continental breakfast and, in Hana, a Hawaiian barbecue-chicken lunch.

Volunteering

Opportunities for volunteering abound on Maui. Some require extended time commitments, but many ask for just a few hours. The Pacific Whale Foundation and the Hawaii Tourism Authority organize short-term projects on Maui through their joint **Volunteers on Vacation** (☎808-249-8811, ext 1; www.volunteersonvacation.org) program.

Work

Finding serious 'professional' employment is difficult on Maui since the island has a tight labor market. But casual work, such as waiting on tables at restaurants and working on checkout counters in shops, has a lot of openings, especially in Lahaina. Folks with language, scuba and culinary skills might investigate better-paying employment with resorts.

Transportation

GETTING THERE & AWAY

Air

Maui has a large number of nonstop flights to/from cities on the mainland, including Los Angeles, San Diego, San Francisco, Seattle and Denver, as well as Vancouver in Canada. Otherwise it's common to connect through Honolulu.

Kahului International Airport (OGG; Map p132; ☎808-872-3830; www.airports.hawaii.gov/ogg; 1 Kahului Airport Rd) All transpacific flights to Maui arrive in Kahului, the island's main airport. There's a staffed **Visitor Information Desk** in the baggage-claim area that's open 7:45am to 10pm daily. There are racks of local travel brochures beside the desk.

Kapalua Airport (JHM; Map p104; ☎808-665-6108; www.airports.hawaii.gov/jhm; 4050 Honoapi'ilani Hwy) Off Hwy 30, south of Kapalua in West Maui, this regional airport has flights with **Mokulele Airlines** (☎866-260-7070; www.mokuleleairlines.com) to Moloka'i and Honolulu.

To & From the Airport

Kahului International Airport Most people rent a car when they arrive. Bus service is limited. Roberts Hawaii, with a booking counter in baggage claim, offers frequent service to most tourist points. Book ahead for the shuttle vans of Hawaii Executive Transportation and Speedi Shuttle. The latter carries surfboards.

Kapalua Airport Taxis to West Maui resorts cost $20 or less.

Sea

The **Expeditions Ferry** (Map p84; ☎808-661-3756; www.go-lanai.com; Lahaina Harbor; adult/child one way $30/20) is worth it just for the ride. It links Lahaina Harbor with Manele Bay Harbor on Lana'i (one hour) several times daily. In winter there's a fair chance of seeing humpback whales; spinner dolphins are a common sight all year, especially on morning sails.

The Moloka'i ferry no longer runs.

GETTING AROUND

To reach both cities and off-the-beaten-path sights, you'll need your own car. Bus service is limited to major roads linking the main towns such as Lahaina, Kihei and Kahului. Much of the island is not suitable for bicycle.

Air

Mokulele Airlines offers daily flights from Kahului to tiny **Hana Airport** (Map p238; ☎808-248-4861; http://airports.hawaii.gov/hnm; 700

CLIMATE CHANGE & TRAVEL

Every form of transport that relies on carbon-based fuel generates CO_2, the main cause of human-induced climate change. Modern travel is dependent on airplanes, which might use less fuel per kilometre per person than most cars but travel much greater distances. The altitude at which aircraft emit gases (including CO_2) and particles also contributes to their climate change impact. Many websites offer 'carbon calculators' that allow people to estimate the carbon emissions generated by their journey and, for those who wish to do so, to offset the impact of the greenhouse gases emitted with contributions to portfolios of climate-friendly initiatives throughout the world. Lonely Planet offsets the carbon footprint of all staff and author travel.

Alalele Pl), cutting a two-hour drive to a 20-minute flight.

Bicycle

Cyclists on Maui face a number of challenges: narrow roads, an abundance of hills and mountains, and the same persistent winds that so delight windsurfers. Maui's stunning scenery certainly will entice hard-core cyclists, but casual riders hoping to use a bike as a primary source of transportation around the island may well find such conditions daunting.

Getting around by bicycle within a small area can be a reasonable option for the average rider, however. For example, the tourist enclave of Kihei is largely level and now has cycle lanes on its two main drags, S Kihei Rd and the Pi'ilani Hwy. Elsewhere, bike lanes are still sparse.

It's easy to rent a bike in most tourist areas of Maui. Rental rates range from $15 to $100 per day, depending on the style and quality of the bike.

Bringing your own bike to Hawaii costs from $75 to $150 on flights from the mainland. The bicycle can usually be checked at the airline counter, the same as any baggage, but you'll need to prepare the bike by doing some disassembly. Check with the airlines for details.

In general, bicycles are required to follow the same state laws and rules of the road as cars. State law requires all cyclists under the age of 16 to wear a helmet.

Bus

Maui Bus (☎808-871-4838; www.mauicounty.gov/bus; single ride $2, day pass $4, monthly pass $45) offers an extensive public bus system between the main towns, but not to out-of-the-way places, such as Haleakalā National Park or Hana. Buses come with front-load bike racks.

The main routes run every hour daily, roughly 7am to 9:30pm. Kahului is a hub.

Routes The handiest routes for visitors:

- ➡ Ha'iku Islander (Kahului–Ha'iku)
- ➡ Ka'anapali Islander (Lahaina–Ka'anapali)
- ➡ Kihei Islander (Kahului–Wailea)
- ➡ Kihei Villager (Ma'alaea–Kihei)
- ➡ Lahaina Islander (Kahului–Lahaina)
- ➡ Lahaina Villager (Wharf Cinema Center–Lahaina Gateway)
- ➡ West Maui Islander (Lahaina–Kapalua)
- ➡ Wailuku Loop (Kahului–Wailuku)

The Upcountry Islander and Haiku Islander routes stop at Kahului Airport.

Costs Fares are $2 per ride, regardless of distance. There are no transfers; you have to pay the fare each time you board a bus. A day pass costs only $4.

Carry-on All buses allow you to carry on only what fits under your seat or on your lap, so forget the surfboard.

Resort shuttle Many of the Ka'anapali and Wailea resorts operate shuttles for guests that serve the resort areas.

Ka'anapali trolley Open to the public, this free shuttle loops past the Ka'anapali resorts, Whalers Village and the golf courses every 20 to 30 minutes between 10am and 10pm.

DRIVING TIMES

Average driving times and distances from Kahului are as follows. Allow more time during weekday morning and afternoon rush hours, and any time the surf is up on the North Shore.

DESTINATION	MILES	DURATION
Haleakalā Summit	36	1½hr
Hana	51	2hr
Ka'anapali	26	1hr
Kapalua	32	1hr
Kihei	12	25min
La Perouse Bay	21	50min
Lahaina	23	45min
Makawao	14	30min
'Ohe'o Gulch	61	2¾hr
Pa'ia	7	15min
Wailuku	3	15min

Car & Motorcycle

All the major car-rental firms have offices at Kahului International Airport. Most of these rental companies also have branches in Ka'anapali and will pick you up at the nearby Kapalua Airport. For a green option, consider **Bio-Beetle** (☎808-873-6121; https://maui carrentals.us; 55 Amala Pl; per day/week from $40/240) in Kahului. Also check out **Kihei Rent A Car** (☎808-879-7257; www.kiheirentacar.com; 96 Kio Loop; per day/week from $35/175; ⏰7:30am-9pm).

Be sure to check for any road restrictions on your rental contract. Some agencies, for instance, may prohibit driving on the Kahekili Hwy between Honokohau and Waihe'e and in the Kaupo district of the Pi'ilani Hwy.

Driver's License

➡ US citizens with a driver's license from another state can legally drive in Hawaii if they are at least 18 years old.

➡ International visitors can legally drive in Hawaii with a valid driver's license issued by their home country (minimum age 18).

➡ Car-rental companies will generally accept foreign driver's licenses written in English with an accompanying photo. Otherwise, be prepared to present an International Driving Permit (IDP), obtainable in your home country, along with your foreign driver's license.

Fuel

You will find gas stations in all major cities and towns in Maui. There is nowhere to fuel up on the Road to Hana, but there is one gas station in Hana itself. Gas up ahead of time, though, in case it's closed. There are no gas stations on the Pi'ilani Hwy in East Maui or the Kahekili Hwy in West Maui.

Insurance

➡ Required by law, liability insurance covers any people or property that you might hit. For damage to the rental vehicle, a collision damage waiver (CDW), also called a loss damage waiver (LDW), costs about $32 per day.

➡ If you decline CDW, you will be held liable for any damages up to the full value of the car.

➡ Even with CDW, you may be required to pay the first $100 to $500 for repairs; some agencies will also charge you for the rental cost of the car during the time it takes to be repaired.

➡ If you have vehicle insurance at home, it might cover damages to car rentals; ask your insurance agent before your trip.

➡ Some credit cards offer reimbursement coverage for collision damages if you rent the car with that card; check on this in advance.

➡ Most credit-card coverage isn't valid for rentals over 15 days or for 'exotic' models (eg performance cars, 4WD jeeps).

Rental

➡ Most rental companies require that you be at least 25 years old, possess a valid driver's license and have a major credit card, not a debit or check card.

➡ However, a few major companies will rent to drivers between the ages of 21 and 24, typically for an underage surcharge of around $27 to $29 per day; call ahead to check.

➡ Without a credit card, many agencies simply won't rent you a vehicle, while others require prepayment by cash, traveler's checks or debit card with an additional refundable deposit of $500 per week, proof of return airfare and more.

➡ When you pick up your vehicle, most agencies will request the name and phone number of the place where you're staying. Some agencies are reluctant to rent to visitors who list a campground as their address; a few specifically add 'No Camping Permitted' to car-rental contracts.

Safety Laws

➡ Texting on a handheld device (eg cell phone) while driving is illegal. This includes when you are stopped at a red light or stop sign. Talking on a cell phone is only allowed for adult drivers (age 18 and over) who use a hands-free device.

➡ Driving under the influence (DUI) of alcohol or drugs is a serious criminal offense. It's illegal to carry open containers of alcohol (even if they're empty) inside a car. Unless the containers are still sealed and have never been opened, store them in the trunk instead.

➡ The use of seat belts is required for the driver and all passengers, even those riding in the back seat.

➡ Child safety seats are mandatory for children aged three and younger. Those aged four to seven must ride in a booster or child safety seat.

Taxi

Taxis operate in the main towns and tourist areas. Uber and Lyft are also available.

Behind the Scenes

SEND US YOUR FEEDBACK

We love to hear from travelers – your comments keep us on our toes and help make our books better. Our well-traveled team reads every word on what you loved or loathed about this book. Although we cannot reply individually to your submissions, we always guarantee that your feedback goes straight to the appropriate authors, in time for the next edition. Each person who sends us information is thanked in the next edition – the most useful submissions are rewarded with a selection of digital PDF chapters.

Visit **lonelyplanet.com/contact** to submit your updates and suggestions or to ask for help. Our award-winning website also features inspirational travel stories, news and discussions.

Note: We may edit, reproduce and incorporate your comments in Lonely Planet products such as guidebooks, websites and digital products, so let us know if you don't want your comments reproduced or your name acknowledged. For a copy of our privacy policy visit lonelyplanet.com/legal.

WRITER THANKS

Amy Balfour

Mahalo to Libby Fulton and Errol Buntuyan for your continued local expertise, and Bob and Sande for your great Kihei tips over the years. Much gratitude for your hospitality and readiness for imbibing, er, I mean adventuring in Wailea. Craig Lowell and Jessica Bermudez, Julie Gosch, Julee Messerich and Kennon Savage – thank you for your Maui recommendations and connections. A big thank you to my co-writer Jade Bremner and to senior product editor Vicky Smith for entrusting me with this awesome assignment.

Jade Bremner

Many thanks to local expert Daniel Sullivan for his tips on walking the ancient King's Pathway, and Abner Nakihei for hooking me up with a surfboard and sharing surf-spot knowledge. Thanks to Hana Farms for making its addictive banana coconut curry hot sauce and to Harriet Sinclair for holding the fort, plus thanks to everyone working hard behind the scenes.

ACKNOWLEDGEMENTS

Climate map data adapted from Peel MC, Finlayson BL & McMahon TA (2007) 'Updated World Map of the Köppen-Geiger Climate Classification', *Hydrology and Earth System Sciences*, 11, 1633–44.

Cover photograph: Maui coastline, Fotosearch/Getty Images ©

THIS BOOK

This 5th edition of Lonely Planet's *Maui* guidebook was researched and written by Amy Balfour and Jade Bremner. The previous two editions were written by Amy, Glenda Bendure, Jade, Ned Friary and Ryan Ver Berkmoes.

This guidebook was produced by the following:

Senior Product Editors Vicky Smith, Sandie Kestell

Regional Senior Cartographer Corey Hutchison

Cartographer Julie Dodkins

Product Editor Ronan Abayawickrema

Book Designer Fergal Condon

Assisting Editors Janet Austin, Sarah Bailey, James Bainbridge, Anne Mulvaney

Cover Researcher Brendan Dempsey-Spencer

Thanks to Sasha Drew, Karen Henderson, Genna Patterson, Fergus O'Shea, Kirsten Rawlings, Claire Rourke, Gabrielle Stefanos

Index

Map Pages **000**
Photo Pages **000**

Map Pages **000**
Photo Pages **000**

K

L

M

N

O

P

Map Pages **000**
Photo Pages **000**